SEVENTH EDITION

INTRODUCTION TO PERSONALITY
Toward an Integration

WALTER MISCHEL
Columbia University

YUICHI SHODA
University of Washington

RONALD E. SMITH
University of Washington

WILEY

JOHN WILEY & SONS, INC.

Acquisitions Editor   *Tim Vertovec*
Assistant Editor   *Lili DeGrasse*
Marketing Manager   *Kate Stewart*
Production Editor   *Sandra Dumas*
Designer/Design Director   *Madelyn Lesure*
Photo Editor   *Sara Wight*
Photo Researcher   *Elyse Reider*
Production Management Services   *Progressive Publishing Alternatives*

Cover: Pablo Picasso, *J'aime Eva*. Photo provided courtesy Columbus Museum of Art, Columbus Ohio, ©2003 Estate of Pablo Picasso/Artists Rights Society (ARS), New York.

This book was typeset in 10/12 New Caledonia by Progressive Information Technologies and printed and bound by R. R. Donnelley (Willard). The cover was printed by Lehigh Press.

The paper in this book was manufactured by a mill whose forest management programs include sustained yield harvesting of its timberlands. Sustained yield harvesting principles ensure that the number of trees cut each year does not exceed the amount of new growth.

This book is printed on acid-free paper.

Library of Congress Cataloging-in-Publication Data

Mischel, Walter.
   Introduction to personality / Walter Mischel. — 7th ed.
    p. cm.
   Includes bibliographical references and indexes.
   ISBN 0-471-27249-3
    I. Personality. I. Title.

BF698.M555 2003
155.2 — dc21

2003053487

Mischel, Walter; Shoda, Yuichi; Smith, Ronald, E.
Introduction to Personality: Toward An Integration, Seventh Edition

ISBN 0-471-27249-3
ISBN 0-471-45153-3 (WIE)

Printed in the United States of America.

10 9 8 7 6 5 4 3 2

PREFACE AND TEXT ORGANIZATION

This extensive revision by a new team of authors contains more than 50 percent fresh material. The book has been updated and reorganized to reflect the growth and transformation of personality psychology in recent years while also remaining true to and respectful of the field's rich history of theories and methods for understanding personality. We present personality as a growing, vibrant field that speaks directly to how students live their lives and how they think about themselves. We have rewritten the text to make it readily accessible to students, and to make mastery of the material more enjoyable as well as informative and stimulating.

First, a few words about the reasons for the substantive changes and for the new subtitle: *Toward an Integration*. Instructors familiar with earlier versions of this text, published in its first edition more than thirty years ago, may wonder what prompted these major changes in a well-established text. Personality psychology was founded as the area within psychology devoted to understanding how factors studied at different levels of psychological analysis combine and interact distinctively within the individual. The aim was to study the person—and personality—as a coherent and unique whole. The hope was for personality psychology to be the hub where all the levels of analysis become integrated within the functioning person.

For many years the field of personality—and particularly its texts, including earlier editions of this one—became divided into alternative approaches that competed against each other. The implication was that if a given approach at a particular level proved to be "right" and useful, the other approaches and levels were bound to be somehow "wrong" or less important. The questions usually asked were: "Which one is best? Which one is right?" In time, however, it has become increasingly clear that the different theoretical approaches ask different questions and address different phenomena at different levels of analysis. Consequently they usually deal only with selected aspects of personality versus the construct in its entirety. Historically, this was understandable, given the limits to what any one researcher or theorist can know and study, especially as the knowledge base in the area grew at an accelerated pace. But this approach also undermined the original ambitious mission of personality psychology to become the locus of integration.

The good news is that personality psychology is moving into a new stage (e.g., Duke, 1986; Carver, 1996; Cervone & Mischel, 2002; Morf, 2003). One gets a sense of this movement toward integration just from some of the titles of the articles, for example: *Rethinking and reclaiming the interdisciplinary role of personality psychology: The science of human nature should be the center of the social sciences and humanities.* (Baumeister & Tice, 1996). Fortunately, the explosion of research findings at different levels of analysis has been so great that the pieces of the puzzle are starting to fit together. The insights from different levels complement each other increasingly well and help to build a more integrated and cumulative view of the person as a whole.

This seventh edition of **Introduction to Personality** reflects these new developments in the field, as indicated in its subtitle. At the same time, we continue to provide

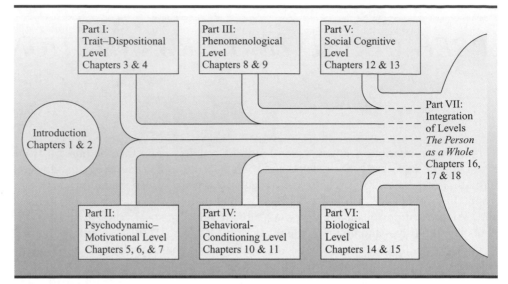

Organization of the text.

coverage of the essential features and contributions from this rich heritage. To do so, this edition first covers in a balanced manner the key ideas and pioneering work that shaped the field for many decades in the last century. But the focus is on distilling how they still speak to and inform each other, and how they add to the current state of the science.

A variety of features are used to help the student to see the interplay among the insights obtained at the six major levels of analysis pursued in personality psychology, namely the trait-dispositional, psychodynamic-motivational, phenomenological, biological, behavioral-conditioning, and social-cognitive levels. Throughout the book, we show how the discoveries made at each level enrich the understanding of the whole. We also show how each level has practical applications for benefiting personal adjustment, self-understanding, and effective coping. In a feature new to this edition, we highlight the "personal side of the science" by inviting students to ask specific questions about how this level applies to themselves. Consistent with the theme of integration, *part preludes* orient the reader to each major section of the text that follows by placing it in a broader conceptual framework. Review sections conclude each part with a segue into the next part to enhance the integration.

After providing a solid background in the six levels of analysis, and pointing out their interconnections, the final part of this text—*Integration of Levels: The Person as a Whole*—is the most notable innovation, found in no other current personality text. It consists of three completely fresh, integrative chapters that focus on the contemporary scene. These chapters demonstrate the complementary relations among all the levels for gaining a rich sense of the personality as a whole. They examine the person engaged in goal pursuit and self-regulation, functioning and adapting proactively within his or her context and culture. The organization of the entire text is depicted in the graphic above, showing the six levels and their flow into the integration presented in the last three chapters which illustrate how each contributes to the total picture of the person.

Much of the text was rewritten while retaining only its best, time-tested features. The extensive rewriting not only reflects the growth and transformation of personality psychology in recent years but also our goal to make the book more readily accessible to today's students and to make mastery of the material more enjoyable as well as informative and stimulating.

Based on previous teaching experience—cumulatively the authors have spent more than 60 years teaching the undergraduate course in personality—new features are added to facilitate mastery of the material. One important pedagogical addition consists of *focus questions*, which occur in the margin of the book adjacent to important concepts and facts. The focus questions are designed to facilitate active processing of content by the reader and to function as study guides and retrieval cues. Their inclusion was based on educational research in controlled studies that showed that questions like ours significantly enhanced retention of facts and concepts. With our own students over the years, this approach has proven so successful (increasing test scores appreciably in groups of randomly selected groups of students who used such questions compared with others who were not provided with them) that we have made it an integral learning tool in this text. In addition, to highlight important points more effectively, we have replaced the essay-style summaries of earlier editions with bullet point summaries at the end of each chapter.

We found the preparation of this edition a wonderful adventure in which we learned much about our own field. We hope that both instructors and students will share our excitement about the current state and future of personality psychology, and our appreciation for the richness of its heritage. Your comments on earlier editions have helped shape this text, and we trust that we have heard and been responsive to your suggestions.

Walter Mischel
Columbia University

Yuichi Shoda
University of Washington

Ronald E. Smith
University of Washington

May, 2003

ACKNOWLEDGEMENTS

The authors owe a great debt to more people than can be acknowledged here. Walter Mischel had the extraordinary benefit of studying and working directly with historical pioneers who helped build the field, and who influenced him profoundly. These notably included his mentors George Kelly and Jules Rotter at Ohio State University, and Gordon Allport, Henry Murray, and David C. McClelland, who were his senior colleagues at Harvard University, and he remains grateful to them all. In the preparation of this edition, Ozlem Ayduk, Rodolfo Mendoza-Denton, and Ethan Kross all played significant roles, commenting on many early drafts and contributing to them. A special debt is owed to Amy Blum who generously helped to prepare the manuscript, commenting and working diligently and constructively on it from its earliest versions into its final production.

Yuichi Shoda owes his beginning in psychology to the confluence of idealistic subculture at UC Santa Cruz in the early 1980s that encouraged asking big questions and such social and personality psychologists as Elliot Aronson, Tom Pettigrew, Brewster

Smith, and in particular, David Harrington. Through the years at Stanford and Columbia as a graduate student, he was fortunate to absorb by osmosis, the philosophies and approaches to science of such mentors and colleagues as Larry Aber, Ozlem Ayduk, Al Bandura, Geraldine Downey, Carol Dweck, Tory Higgins, Dave Krantz, Bob Krauss, Rudy Mendoza-Denton, Phil Peake, Ewart Thomas, Jack Wright, and above all, Dan Cervone, whose infectious love of good ideas and dedication to our field drew Yuichi to it and sustained him throughout. The University of Washington is now his intellectual home, and he gratefully acknowledges his colleagues and students, particularly Ron Smith, for their inspiration and support. Most important of all, however, he has had the privilege of pursuing a shared vision of personality as a dynamic, multifaceted yet coherent whole, with his mentor and friend, Walter Mischel, for over two decades. This textbook is an expression of this vision.

Ronald Smith would like to acknowledge the contributions made to his training by the clinical and personality faculty at Southern Illinois University, including Janet Rafferty and Donald Shoemaker, who were former students of Rotter and Kelly, respectively. Other important mentors at SIU were Loren Chapman, Peter Lewinsohn, Edward Lichtenstein, and Nathan Azrin. For the past 30 years, the University of Washington has offered a wonderful intellectual and collegial environment for the study of personality. Special thanks are due to Irwin and Barbara Sarason for being such an important part of this environment. Finally, he thanks the countless undergraduate and graduate students in his personality courses for stimulating his thinking about the field and how to present it as an instructor.

The editorial and production staff, and particularly Tim Vertovec, Lili DeGrasse, and Kimberly Martin, worked hard and intensively to make the project go well, and were a pleasure to deal with from start to finish: we thank them for going all the way. Last, but by no means least, we are indebted to the effort, care, and time of the many instructors and colleagues who helped in the review process, and thank them sincerely:

Bob Bornstein, Gettysburg College
Kelly A. Brennan, SUNY Brockport
Eva G. Clarke, Old Dominion University
Jean M. Edwards, Wright State University
Howard Ehrlichman, Queens College of CUNY
Jeannine Feldman, San Diego State University
Steve Funk, Northern Arizona University
David A. Haaga, American University
Heather Haas, Colby College
Christopher Layne, University of Toledo
Mark Lenzenweger, Harvard University
Rich Lewine, University of Louisville
Herbert Mirels, Ohio State University
Joseph A. Reilly, Drexel University
Carolin J. Showers, University of Oklahoma

Tables 1 and 2 present a suggested list of chapter assignments for a quarter system, or a semester system:

TABLE 1   Suggested schedule for a quarter system

Week 1	**INTRODUCTION** CHAPTER 1 *Orientation to Personality* CHAPTER 2 *Data, Methods, and Tools*
Week 2	**PART I THE TRAIT-DISPOSITIONAL LEVEL** CHAPTER 3 *Types and Traits* CHAPTER 4 *The Expressions of Dispositions*
Week 3	**PART II THE PSYCHODYNAMIC-MOTIVATIONAL LEVEL** CHAPTER 5 *Psychodynamic Theories: Freud's Conceptions* CHAPTER 6 *Post-Freudian Psychodynamics and Motives*
Week 4	CHAPTER 7 *Psychodynamic Processes* Exam 1
Week 5	**PART III THE PHENOMENOLOGICAL LEVEL** CHAPTER 8 *Phenomenological Conceptions* CHAPTER 9 *The Internal View*
Week 6	**PART IV THE BEHAVIORAL-CONDITIONING LEVEL** CHAPTER 10 *Behavioral Conceptions* CHAPTER 11 *Analyzing and Modifying Behavior*
Week 7	**PART V THE SOCIAL COGNITIVE LEVEL** CHAPTER 12 *Social Cognitive Conceptions* CHAPTER 13 *Social Cognitive Processes*
Week 8	Exam 2 **PART VI THE BIOLOGICAL LEVEL** CHAPTER 14 *Heredity and Personality*
Week 9	CHAPTER 15 *Evolution, Brain, and Personality* **PART VII INTEGRATION OF LEVELS: The Person as a Whole** CHAPTER 16 *Personality in the Pursuit of Goals*
Week 10	CHAPTER 17 *Self-Regulation: From Goal Pursuit to Goal Attainment* CHAPTER 18 *Personality in Its Context and Culture*
Week 11	Final Exam

TABLE 2   Suggested schedule for a semester course

Week 1	**INTRODUCTION** CHAPTER 1 *Orientation to Personality*
Week 2	CHAPTER 2 *Data, Methods, and Tools* **Part I: THE TRAIT-DISPOSITIONAL LEVEL** CHAPTER 3 *Types and Traits*
Week 3	CHAPTER 4 *The Expressions of Dispositions* **Part II: THE PSYCHODYNAMIC-MOTIVATIONAL LEVEL** CHAPTER 5 *Psychodynamic Theories: Freud's Conceptions*
Week 4	CHAPTER 6 *Post-Freudian Psychodynamics and Motives* CHAPTER 7 *Psychodynamic Processes*
Week 5	Review and integration of Parts I and II Exam 1
Week 6	**Part III: THE PHENOMENOLOGICAL LEVEL** CHAPTER 8 *Phenomenological Conceptions* CHAPTER 9 *The Internal View*
Week 7	**Part IV: THE BEHAVIORAL-CONDITIONING LEVEL** CHAPTER 10 *Behavioral Conceptions* CHAPTER 11 *Analyzing and Modifying Behavior*
Week 8	Review and integration of Parts III and IV Exam 2
Week 9	**Part V: THE SOCIAL COGNITIVE LEVEL** CHAPTER 12 *Social Cognitive Conceptions* CHAPTER 13 *Social Cognitive Processes*
Week 10	**Part VI: THE BIOLOGICAL LEVEL** CHAPTER 14 *Heredity and Personality* CHAPTER 15 *Evolution, Brain, and Personality*
Week 11	Review and integration of Parts V and VI Exam 3
Week 12	**Part VII: INTEGRATION OF LEVELS: The Person as a Whole** CHAPTER 16 *Personality in the Pursuit of Goals* CHAPTER 17 *Self-Regulation: From Goal Pursuit to Goal Attainment*
Week 13	CHAPTER 18 *Personality in Its Context and Culture* Review and integration, Parts I to VII
Week 14	Final Exam

BRIEF CONTENTS

CONTENTS

CHAPTER 4

THE EXPRESSIONS OF DISPOSITIONS **69**

PART III

THE PHENOMENOLOGICAL LEVEL **169**

CHAPTER 8 *PHENOMENOLOGICAL CONCEPTIONS* **171**

CHAPTER 9   *THE INTERNAL VIEW*   **194**

PART V

THE SOCIAL COGNITIVE LEVEL **269**

CHAPTER 12   *SOCIAL COGNITIVE CONCEPTIONS* **271**

PART VII

INTEGRATION OF LEVELS: THE PERSON AS A WHOLE **367**

CHAPTER 16   *PERSONALITY IN THE PURSUIT OF GOALS* **371**

CHAPTER 17   *SELF-REGULATION: FROM GOAL PURSUIT TO
                    GOAL ATTAINMENT* **392**

1

ORIENTATION TO PERSONALITY

▶ WHAT IS PERSONALITY PSYCHOLOGY?

Personality is a psychological concept that has many meanings, reflecting the richness and complexity of the phenomena to which the term refers. Here is an example of one aspect of the concept.

Stable, Coherent Individual Differences

Charles and Jane both are first year college students taking an introductory course in economics. Their instructor returns the midterm examination in class, and both receive a D grade. Right after class, Charles goes up to the instructor and seems distressed and upset: He sweats as he talks, his hands tremble slightly, he speaks slowly and softly, almost whispering. His face is flushed and he appears to be on the edge of tears. He apologizes for his "poor performance," accusing himself bitterly: "I really have no good excuse—it was so stupid of me—I just don't know how I could have done such a sloppy job." He spends most of the rest of the day alone in his dormitory, cuts his classes, and writes a long entry in his diary.

Jane, on the other hand, rushes out of the lecture room at the end of class and quickly starts to joke loudly with her friend about the economics course. She makes fun of the course, comments acidly about the instructor's lecture, and seems to pay little attention to her grade as she strides briskly to her next class. In that class, Jane participates more actively than usual and, surprising her teacher, makes a few excellent comments. This example illustrates a well-known fact: Different people respond differently to similar events. One goal of personality psychology is to find and describe those *individual differences* between people that are psychologically meaningful and stable.

Though the concept of personality has to do with how an individual differs from others, it implies more. What if, on the next day, it was Jane, not Charles, who became very upset when they learned they didn't do well in another class? Does that suggest their behaviors on either day (or both days) aren't characteristic of their personality? If you answered yes, that suggests another key component of personality. That is, personality refers to qualities of individuals that are relatively *stable*. If a person's behavior changes from time to time, then it may not be indicative of personality.

Let's further suppose that you learned a little more about what happened the second day: The course in which they received a poor grade on the second day was English Composition. Not only did they receive a poor grade, they also learned that their classmates thought poorly of the essays they wrote and shared with their classmates. Now, does this additional information help make sense of their behaviors? If you answered yes, think about why.

One possibility is that with the new information about what happened on the second day, one can begin to see why their behaviors changed from the first day to the second day. One can begin to form a mental picture of the kind of person who doesn't seem upset by a bad grade in Economics but is devastated by a poor grade in English and/or her peer's unenthusiastic response to her essay. Similarly, one may form an impression of a person who is very upset by a poor grade in Economics but is unaffected by a bad grade in English composition or his peer's reactions. The information about the circumstances has transformed the change from one that is puzzling to one that makes sense. The change is potentially meaningful, because even though on the surface Charles and Jane's behaviors changed, there is coherence in the way they changed. That is, *coherence* in the pattern of change in an individual's behavior may be another key component of personality.

Describing, Predicting, Understanding

The term "personality" usually implies *continuity* or *consistency* in the individual. Personality psychologists therefore ask questions like: How consistent are the observed differences between people? How would Charles and Jane respond to a D in physical education? How would each respond if they were fired from their part-time jobs? What do the differences in the reactions of the two students to their grade suggest about their other characteristics? For example, how do they also differ in their academic goals and in their past achievements and failures?

If the answers to such questions are yes, then the observed differences may be meaningful indicators of individual differences in the personality of these two students. Identifying consistent, stable individual differences is an important goal for personality psychologists—and for everyday life—because it makes it possible both to describe people and to try to predict their future behavior, and so to get to know what we can expect from them.

In addition to mapping out the differences between people in terms of their characteristic ways of behaving—that is, thinking, feeling, and acting—personality psychologists try to understand what it is that underlies these differences. They ask: Why did Jane and Charles react so differently to the same event? What within each person leads to his or her distinctive ways of behaving? What must we know about each person to understand—and perhaps sometimes even predict—what he or she will think and feel and do under particular conditions? Personality psychologists ask

1.1 Which two aspects of individuality give rise to the concept of personality?

1.2 How do situational factors (circumstances) contribute to perceived personality coherence?

1.3 Describe three goals of personality psychologists.

questions of this sort as they pursue the goal of trying to explain and understand the observed psychological differences between people.

Defining Personality

What *is* personality? The term *personality* has many definitions, but no single meaning is accepted universally. In popular usage, personality is often equated with social skill and effectiveness. In this usage, personality is the ability to elicit positive reactions from other people in one's typical dealings with them. For example, we may speak of someone as having "a lot of personality" or a "popular personality," and advertisements for self-help courses promise to give those who enroll "more personality."

Less superficially, personality may be taken to be an individual's most striking or dominant characteristic. In this sense, a person may be said to have a "shy personality" or a "neurotic personality," meaning that his or her dominant attribute appears to be shyness.

In personality psychology, the concept goes much beyond these meanings. The definition begins with the assumption that there are stable individual differences. It is further assumed that these differences reflect an underlying *organization*. In one classic and still influential working definition, the idea of organization is central to the definition. Personality psychology is:

> . . . the dynamic organization within the individual of those psychophysical systems that determine his characteristic behavior and thought (Allport, 1961, p. 28).

As the science matures, there is a growing consensus about the findings and concepts that have stood the test of time. Consequently, a unifying conception of personality and, more modestly, at least a broadly acceptable definition, is becoming possible. A good candidate for such a definition was offered by Pervin (1996, p. 414):

> Personality is the complex organization of cognitions, affects, and behaviors that gives direction and pattern (coherence) to the person's life. Like the body, personality consists of both structures and processes and reflects both nature (genes) and nurture (experience). In addition, personality includes the effects of the past, including memories of the past, as well as constructions of the present and future.

Consistent with that definition, David Funder (2001, p. 198) defines the mission of personality psychology as needing to "account for the individual's characteristic patterns of thoughts, emotion, and behavior together with the psychological mechanisms—hidden or not—behind those patterns."

As discussed above, individual differences are always a core part of the definition of this field, but they are not the whole of it. Thus the term personality psychology does not need to be limited to the study of differences between individuals in their consistent attributes. Rather, "personality psychology must also . . . study how people's [thoughts and actions] . . . interact with—and shape reciprocally—the conditions of their lives" (Mischel, 1980, p. 17).

This expanded view recognizes that human tendencies are a crucial part of personality. But it also recognizes the need to study the basic processes of adaptation through which people interact with the conditions of their lives. Personality thus includes in the person's unique patterns of coping with, and transforming, the psychological environment. This view of personality focuses not only on *personal tendencies* but also on *psychological processes* (such as learning, motivation, and thinking) that interact with *biological-genetic processes* to influence the individual's distinctive patterns of adaptation throughout the life span.

In summary, to capture the richness of human behavior, the personality construct has to encompass the following aspects:

1.4 Cite five aspects of the construct of personality as currently conceived.

- Personality shows continuity, stability, and coherence.
- Personality is expressed in many ways—from overt behavior through thoughts and feelings.
- Personality is organized. In fact, when it is fragmented or disorganized it is a sign of disturbance.
- Personality is a determinant that influences how the individual relates to the social world.
- Personality is a psychological concept but it also is assumed to link with the physical, biological characteristics of the person.

▶ THEORY AND LEVELS OF ANALYSIS IN PERSONALITY PSYCHOLOGY

Early "Big Picture" Theory

Personality psychology is a relatively young science but it has been practiced from the time that people began asking questions about human nature: Who should I fear? Who can I trust? Who do I select for a mate? Who am I?

In Western societies, since the time of the ancient Greeks, philosophers have long pondered questions about human nature and attempted classification schemes for making sense of the varieties of individual differences in important attributes and their causes. As early as 400 B.C., Hippocrates philosophized about the basic human temperaments (e.g., choleric, depressive), and their associated traits, guided by the biology of his time. For example, he thought physical qualities like yellow bile, or too much blood, might underlie the differences in temperament. He began a tradition—trait and type psychology—whose modern versions date to the start of the last century. It is a tradition that is still very much alive and well, although completely transformed in current scientific practice, drawing extensively both on modern measurement methods and on the biology of today.

Aristotle postulated the brain to be the seat of the rational mind, or the "conscious and intellectual soul that is peculiar to man" (Singer, 1941, p. 43). This view has become a foundation of the Western view of human mind. For example, in his dualistic view of the human being as consisting of mind and body, Descartes viewed the mind as what gives us the capacities for thought and consciousness, which sets us apart from the physical world of matter. The mind "decides" and the body carries out the decision.

In the early 1900s, Sigmund Freud, living and working in Vienna as a physician, upset the rational view of human nature that characterized his time with a powerful and comprehensive theory of personality. Freud's theory made reason secondary and instead made primary the unconscious and its often unacceptable, irrational motives and desires, thereby forever changing the view of human nature. The tradition he began also continues to influence contemporary personality psychology, but again in ways that are much changed, both by the work of his many followers and by developments in other areas of the science that made it possible to reinterpret much of his work and to revise it as needed.

From Grand Theories to Levels of Analysis

In the first half of the twentieth century, personality psychology was inspired by grand theories of personality that were being developed by several "big picture" innovators such as Sigmund Freud: Each proposed distinctive conceptions of the nature of personality, and tried to present a comprehensive view of all of personality in all of its diverse aspects. Like Freud, many of these theorists were working in Western Europe as therapists treating psychologically disturbed and distressed individuals. As practicing therapists, they used the cases of their patients as the basis for broader generalizations on the nature of personality. Consequently their ideas helped to shape clinical psychology and psychiatry as well as personality psychology. One hazard here was that because their work was based on their experience with emotionally disturbed patients, they may have focused more on the disturbed aspects of personality than on its healthier versions in less troubled people.

Broad theories like Freud's provide an orientation and perspective that stimulates different types of research within the field and different types of real-life applications, such as clinical practice with people experiencing psychological problems. Most notably, they lead to different lines of research and to different forms of therapy or intervention designed to modify or enhance personality constructively. They also lead to different approaches to assess personality and to think about persons, including oneself, and thus matter a great deal to the image one develops of personality and individuality, and indeed of oneself as a person. As such they are valuable.

1.5 What kinds of scientific contributions have been made by broad theories of personality? What are their scientific shortcomings?

In spite of the growth of personality psychology as a field of scientific research, however, most of the grand theories of personality, like Freud's, did not lend themselves to precise scientific testing that allowed them to be either supported or disconfirmed clearly on the basis of empirical studies (Meehl, 1990, 1997). Reasons for this range from the difficulty of specifying the theoretical premises in testable terms, to various types of experimental and statistical limitations in conducting and evaluating the test results. But even beyond these limitations, grand theories often function more like general guidelines or orientations for studying personality and interpreting the results from a particular perspective or framework. Thus it is difficult to firmly reject or support a given theory on the basis of empirical studies. As one pundit put it, many big theories in all areas of science generally are never really disconfirmed: They just die of loneliness as they gradually are replaced by approaches that seem more fruitful and lead to more informative new research that raises new questions and suggests new—always tentative—answers.

In the second half of the last century, after World War II, American personality psychology grew into a substantial field in its own right. It was influenced by European psychology but also developed in its own directions within the larger science of psychology. The influences in the United States came from traditions that sprang up in university psychology departments that were devoted to turning psychology away from philosophy and into science. Researchers working both with normal and disturbed populations developed and applied increasingly sophisticated scientific methods to address many central issues in personality psychology. In time, it became possible to examine important questions about personality with research evidence that accumulated at a rapid rate and pointed to exciting new directions as the science evolved.

From the 1960s to about the 1980s, the field of personality psychology was full of seemingly insoluble controversies among apparently irreconcilable broad theoretical approaches. The result was much debate and new research that helped to clarify important questions but that also created much divisiveness among alternative view-points. In contrast, in the current scene there are numerous encouraging signs of integration and constructive syntheses of the insights coming from theorists and researchers that are working at different **levels of analysis,** addressing different aspects of personality. It is increasingly seen that each level has its legitimacy and usefulness, and each requires distinctive methods and concepts. But the findings from different levels do not necessarily conflict. On the contrary, they usually add to the understanding and clarification of the whole. Each level of analysis yields many solid answers—as well as raising new questions—and each contributes to building a cumulative and coherent view of personality psychology.

▶ LEVELS OF ANALYSIS: ORGANIZATION OF THIS BOOK

1.6 At which six levels of analysis is personality being studied? What kinds of questions can we ask about ourselves and others at each level?

In this book you will learn some of the major theoretical approaches to personality that have guided thinking and research, and see how research and theory-building is done, at each level of analysis. We will survey some of the main concepts developed to describe and understand the important psychological differences among people, and we will consider the concepts and findings that are central to diverse views of human nature.

To capture the essentials, this text is organized into the six major levels of personality study from a century of work in psychology as a science and profession. Each part of the text presents the main concepts, methods, and findings associated with that level of analysis, and each focuses attention on distinctive aspects of personality. Each level adds to the appreciation of the richness and complexity of personality. Each level also led to discoveries that have important practical and personal applications that we will examine. In combination, the six levels provide an overview of the many complex and diverse aspects of human personality. The final part of the text shows how the levels interconnect and become integrated to give a more coherent view of the person as a whole. The organization of the text highlights how each level adds to the whole, and suggests their evolving integration. This organization can be seen at a glance in Figure 1.1.

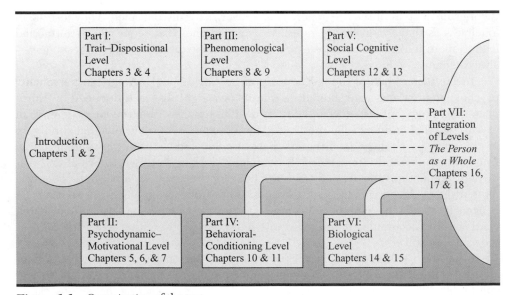

Figure 1.1 Organization of the text.

After an Introduction section that gives an overview of the data, methods, and tools of the science, Part I presents contributions from the Trait-Dispositional Level; Part II focuses on those coming from the Psychodynamic-Motivational Level; followed by Part III, the Phenomenological Level; Part IV, the Behavioral-Conditioning Level; Part V, the Social Cognitive Level; and Part VI, the Biological Level. Below we will look at an overview of each of the levels. As Figure 1.1 suggests, the contributions from each level are cumulative and come together in the final Part VII, Integration of Levels: The Person as a Whole, which explicitly shows their interconnections. Each level asks distinctive questions although both the questions and the levels overlap.

Almost everyone becomes interested in the science of personality because they want to understand people, and particularly themselves and those they care about, as fully as possible. In this sense, the science of personality also has a distinctly personal side: the questions that researchers ask at each level in formal scientific terms also have personal relevance. Often they are asked more informally by most people. Therefore, to make those connections explicit, the key questions pursued at each level of analysis are summarized in In Focus 1.1, and phrased in personal ways that invite you to ask them about yourself.

IN FOCUS 1.1

THE PERSONAL SIDE OF THE SCIENCE

Some Key Questions at Different Levels of Analysis Phrased as Questions That Can Be Asked About Oneself:

- **Trait-Dispositional Level:** What am I like as a person? How am I different from other people "on the whole"? In what general ways are people different from each other? Does what I usually do and think and feel depend mostly on myself or on the situation in which I find myself? When and how is my behavior influenced by the situation? How does my personality influence the situations I choose to be in? How does my personality influence the effects that different kinds of situations have on me?

- **Psychodynamic-Motivational Level:** Does what I do sometimes puzzle me? How and why? What are the real motives that drive or underlie my behavior? How can I explain irrational fears and anxieties? How do I try to protect myself psychologically against getting hurt? How much of what I do is unconscious or done without awareness? What might be some unconscious influences on my behavior? Do I have motives that make me uncomfortable? If yes, what do I try to do about that?

- **Phenomenological Level:** Who am I really? Who do I want to become? How do I see myself? How do I see my parents? What do I feel about myself when I don't meet my parents' expectations? How

is my real self different from the self I would ideally like to be? What is my ideal self? How am I different from my mother but similar to my father? How can I think my way out of my childhood?

- **Behavioral-Conditioning Level:** How is what a person *does* linked to what happens to him or her when he does it? How are important behavior patterns, including emotions and fears, learned? How does what I do and feel depend on my earlier experiences? How can my behavior and feelings be modified by new learning experiences? Do aspects of my personality depend on the contexts in which I am? How am I different when with a good friend at school and when with my family at home for the holidays? Why?

- **Social Cognitive Level:** What is the role in personality of what people know, think, and feel? How does what I know, think, and feel about myself and the social world influence what I do and can become? What can I do to change how I think and feel? Will that change my personality and behavior? How much of who and what I am and do is "automatic"? How much is open to "willpower" and self-regulation? How do willpower and self-regulation work? How can I enhance my control over my life?

- **Biological Level:** What in my personality comes from my parents and the genes I inherited from them? How is my personality a reflection of my life experiences? How does my personality reflect my basic biological predispositions? Can my experiences change my biology; for instance, does my brain change when I'm depressed? How do the same experiences affect people with different genetic predispositions? Why is my personality so different (or similar) to my siblings? How does my biology influence my pursuit of life goals? How does evolutionary theory help me understand dating and social behavior today?

Now let's consider each level to get an overview.

The Trait-Dispositional Level

The trait-dispositional level seeks to identify the types of stable psychological qualities and behavioral dispositions that characterize different individuals and types consistently. In everyday life, people may ask themselves questions like those listed for this level in In Focus 1.1: "What am I like as a person? How am I different from other people 'on the whole'? In what general ways are people different from each other?" Using the natural language of trait terms, people often ask and answer such questions easily, not just about themselves but about other people: He or she seems friendly, assertive, aggressive, submissive, conscientious, and so on. Examples of such traits used in current research include broad characteristics such as agreeableness, conscientiousness, and open mindedness. At this level, one also studies the diverse but stable expressions over time and across situations of these types and traits to see how consistent they are.

1.7 Describe the focus of the trait-dispositional level of analysis.

This level of analysis has become one of the most vigorous and widely researched in recent years. This progress has been supported by the development of some straightforward, well-established self-report methods that are being used by researchers throughout the world. Consequently, the usefulness of trait level analyses is being extensively investigated and has led to findings showing the stability of personality over time. Work at this level is also yielding a broad taxonomy for classifying individuals with regard to major traits, providing a map on which people, groups, and even cultures can be compared.

Work at this level of analysis especially in recent years also has been getting answers to questions such as: Does what we do and think and feel characteristically depend mostly on the individual or on the situation? How do the two—the person and the situation—interact?

The Psychodynamic-Motivational Level

The psychodynamic-motivational level probes the motivations, conflicts, and defenses, often without one's awareness, that can help explain complex consistencies and inconsistencies in personality. Questions you might ask yourself when thinking about this level of analysis, as In Focus 1.1 suggests, include: "Does what I do sometimes puzzle me? How and why? What are the real motives that drive or underlie my behavior? How can I explain irrational fears and anxieties? How do I try to protect myself psychologically against getting hurt?"

1.8 Which aspects of personality are addressed at the psychodynamic-motivational level of analysis?

Work at this level is relevant for understanding many puzzles of personality, for example, when people turn out to be more complex and unpredictable than expected and seem to change as one knows them better. Here is an example:

Roberto was confusing his girlfriend. She felt she was getting more smoke than light—the longer she knew him, the less she felt she really understood him, and she was beginning to lose her trust. Before they moved in together, she thought she knew him—warm, friendly, fun and easy to be with. Later she began to see the sadness, the inside rage, the fears and the unpredictability. After a while, he stayed in bed most of the day. When asked what's going on he'd say, "I'm fine," denying any anxiety or depression, and he seemed to mean it. He was reassuring, yet she remained quite unconvinced.

Roberto's girlfriend intuitively understood that what Roberto said and seemed to honestly believe was not necessarily the whole story and that there were other reasons that he could not acknowledge even to himself. The kind of insight needed to understand Roberto's behavioral and emotional inconsistencies is at the heart of the psychodynamic motivational level of analysis.

Much of the work at this level has been done in clinical situations, beginning with Sigmund Freud a century ago. He worked, for example, on the case of Hans, a four-year-old child who had developed an irrational fear of going outdoors because horses might be there and he had become terrified of them although he had never been hurt by one. Freud created a theory that used the concept of the unconscious and the child's unacceptable sexual and aggressive wishes to explain how a fear like that could have developed.

An important key here was the discovery that certain impulses, such as a young child's aggressive impulses toward his father, are treated by socializing agents as taboo and punished, making the child anxious. Because the impulses still persist but create painful anxieties, the child may unconsciously redirect them at other objects, for example, by becoming afraid of horses that remind him of his father who might punish him.

The Phenomenological Level

Each person sees the world subjectively in his or her own personal ways. To understand this privately experienced side of personality, we must examine the nature of subjective experience; we have to try to see how people perceive their world. Workers at this level of analysis are genuinely interested in hearing and exploring fully the answers people give to questions (from In Focus 1.1) like these: "Who am I really? Who do I want to become? How do I see myself? How do I see my parents? What do I feel about myself when I don't meet my parents' expectations?

1.9 What is the major focus of the phenomenological level of analysis?

Here is a sample of self-reported personal feelings taken from a self-description by a college student about to take a final examination:

. . . When I think about the exam, I really feel sick . . . so much depends on it. I know I'm not prepared, at least not as much as I should be, but I keep hoping that I can sort of snow my way through it. . . . I keep trying to remember some of the things he said in class, but my mind keeps wandering. God, my folks—What will they think if I don't pass and can't graduate? Will they have a fit! Boy! I can see their faces. Worse yet, I can hear their voices: "And with all the money we spent on your education." Mom's going to be hurt. She'll let me know I let her down. She'll be a martyr . . . Oh hell! What about Anne [girlfriend]? She's counting on my graduating. We had plans. What will she think? . . . I've got to pass. I've just got to . . . What's going to happen to me? . . . The whole damn world is coming apart (extracted from Fischer, 1970, pp. 121–122).

Work at this level begins by listening closely and trying to understand the individual's experience as he or she perceives it. The focus is on subjective experience, feelings, the personal view of the world and the self. The focus also is on people's positive strivings and their tendencies toward growth and self-actualization.

These concerns require studying the internal or mental processes through which individuals interpret experience. A distinguished psychologist, Ulric Neisser, for example, put it this way (1967, p. 3): "Whether beautiful or ugly or just conveniently at hand, the world of experience is produced by [the person] who experiences it." That statement, of course, does not imply that there is no "real" world out there, but just that it is *the experienced world* that is basic for understanding phenomena like personality and the important differences between people. Ideally, researchers at this level would like to look at the world through the eyes of the persons they are studying, to stand in that person's shoes, to know emotionally as well as intellectually what it might be like to *be* that person.

Although for many years this level of analysis was treated with suspicion by the rest of the field, more recently there has been an explosion of solid research on the self and close relationships. This work is restoring the self as an important concept in current personality psychology. It is addressing the processes through which the self develops, and telling us much about the links between the self and personality adjustment, mental health, and positive functioning.

The Behavioral-Conditioning Level

1.10 ▶ What questions about personality are addressed at the behavioral-conditioning level?

As In Focus 1.1 indicates, work at this level of analysis has asked questions like: "How are important behavior patterns, including emotions and fears, learned? How does what I do and feel depend on my earlier experiences? How can my behavior and feelings be modified by new learning experiences?"

Consider this dilemma:

> *Jake was upset because he could not accept the management job he had been so eager to get when he learned that it was on the 80th floor: just the thought of riding up in the elevator terrified him—but he had never been afraid of elevators in the past.*

If this description makes you think here come more examples for the psychodynamic-motivational level like Freud's case of little Hans, you are right. Work at the behavioral-conditioning level also tries to provide accounts of irrational behaviors that puzzle the people who are tortured by them, similar to many of the same basic personality phenomena that Freud discovered. But they get there through a different route and reach different conclusions that lead to important revisions in some of the earlier ideas for dealing with such problems.

The behavioral-conditioning level analyzes specific patterns of behavior that characterize individuals and the situations or conditions that seem to regulate their occurrence and strength. It studies the determinants of learning and applies learning principles to modify problematic patterns of behavior, including emotional reactions like fears. Behavioral analyses focus on an important behavior—such as the stutter of a person suffering from public speaking anxieties, or the inability to stay concentrated on one's studying before exams. Then they analyze the situations or conditions that seem to control that behavior, that is, the conditions in which the stutter or the studying becomes worse or improves. Finding the conditions under which the problem improves becomes the basis for designing treatments to modify the behavior to help reduce or eliminate the problem. Behavioral analyses have helped us understand the conditions through which behaviors relevant to personality—from stutters through poor self-concepts, and troublesome behavior in interpersonal relationships—are learned and can be modified.

The results have been applied to help people overcome a variety of serious personal difficulties, ranging from common but debilitating fears, to weight problems, to learning deficits and handicaps, to increasing personal assertiveness and self-esteem. Originally this level of analysis dealt mostly with learning and conditioning based on animal work. In new direction, behavioral levels of analysis have a second life because advances in brain imaging, for example, and in other areas of cognitive science—the modern study of mental processes—make it possible to analyze mental functions previously considered too mysterious for behavioral study with the objective methods of science.

The Social Cognitive Level

Personality research at this level focuses on the role of personal theories and beliefs, expectations, motivations, and emotions as determinants of individual differences in social behavior. The focus here includes the person's social knowledge of the world, and the goal is to understand how people make sense of other people and themselves and cope as they negotiate their interpersonal lives. Questions that you might ask about yourself at this level of analysis (In Focus 1.1) are: "How does what I know, think, and feel about myself and the social world influence what I do and can become? What can I do to change how I think and feel?"

This level examines individual differences in how social knowledge is used in dealing with the world, in the construction of the self, in self-regulation, and in self-control. The specific focus is on the individual's characteristic ways of thinking and processing information, both cognitively and emotionally, as determinants of his or her distinctive and meaningful patterns of experience and social behavior. For example:

> Yolanda and Virginia, now college students, both lost their young mothers last year from breast cancer. Both women know that their total family histories put them at high risk for having a genetic predisposition for this type of cancer early in life. At the college health service the specialist they see points out the risks of their situation in great detail. He urges that they adhere strictly to monthly breast self-examination as an important part of their health-maintenance program.
>
> When Yolanda tries self-examination, she remembers the risks the doctor described and she imagines them vividly. Her thoughts flow from anticipating finding the lump, to thinking "I'm going to die," to a flood of panic feelings. She thinks "what will be will be" and stops trying to self-examine. When Virginia begins, she also remembers the physician's words but she imagines that if there is a lump she will find it early, it can be removed, and she can be successfully treated. She thinks: Above all I will have at least some control over my fate.

An important challenge at this level is to understand such internal mental and emotional processes and their links to the characteristic behavior patterns that may enduringly distinguish different individuals and types of people. The goal is not only to "get inside the head" but to understand the stable mental-emotional processes and structures that generate the diverse individual differences that are observed. Most attention in recent years is given to studying the basic psychological processes through which individuals construct, interpret, and understand their social-personal world. Questions here include: How do individuals come to deal with their worlds in the stable cognitive, emotional, and behavior patterns that characterize them? What is the "self" and how do self-concepts and perceptions about the self influence what the person thinks, feels, and becomes?

1.11 How does the social cognitive level of analysis differ from the behavioral-conditioning approach?

The Biological Level

1.12 What kinds of biological factors are known to underlie individual differences in personality?

An important goal of personality study at the biological level is to try to specify the role of genetic determinants and of the social environment in shaping who and what we become. The focus in much of this work in the past has been to answer the age-old question: How much of personality reflects nature, and how much nurture—and above all, how do these two sources of influence interact in shaping our characteristics? When you learn what is now known at this level of analysis, you will be able to answer questions like: "To what extent does my personality come from my parents and the genes I inherited from them? To what extent is my personality a reflection of my life experiences? To what extent does my personality reflect my basic biological predispositions?"

This level of analysis also addresses the fact that humans are biological beings who evolved in adaptive ways that endowed the species with biological characteristics, constraints, and possibilities. These influence human nature and the way we fight, mate, socialize, and create. The goal at this level of analysis is to examine how aspects of personality may have evolved in response to the evolutionary pressures and history that shaped our species over time. Here is an example of the kinds of problems it studies and the questions this level asks:

> *Consider two identical twin baby girls who were separated at birth and grew up in very different worlds. Jane was raised on a rural Iowa farm, an only child, with hard-working but unloving parents. Nahid's life unfolded in the capital of Iran, nurtured by loving parents in a large middle-class family. The identical twins started life with the same DNA and therefore with virtually identical brains. Suppose the twins were reunited at age 30 and tested extensively, how similar will their personalities turn out to be?*

Levels of Analysis Applied to Understand Unexpected Aggression: The Texas Tower Killer

The different levels of analysis discussed throughout this text can complement each other constructively. Taken together, they increase the total understanding of personality as a whole. To illustrate, we next look at the types of questions that each level asks when confronted by the real-life puzzles of personality. In this example, you can see that the phenomena addressed by all levels interact concurrently within a personality.

The example here is the case of Charles Whitman, a University of Texas college student. Late one hot summer night, Charles Whitman killed his wife and mother. The next morning he went to a tower on the University of Texas campus and opened fire on the crowded campus below with a high-powered hunting rifle. In 90 horrifying minutes, he killed 14 people, wounded another 24, and even managed to hit an airplane before he was killed by police. After the Whitman incident, the first question asked was a familiar one: What caused this mild-mannered young man to explode into violence?

The night before the killing, Whitman wrote the following letter, reflecting his internal subjective experiences at the time:

> *I don't really understand myself these days. I am supposed to be an average, reasonable, and intelligent young man. However, lately (I can't recall when it started) I have been the victim of many unusual and irrational thoughts. These thoughts constantly recur, and it requires a tremendous mental effort to concentrate on useful and progressive tasks. In March when my parents made a physical break I noticed a great deal of stress. I consulted a Dr. Cochrum at the University Health Center and asked him to recommend someone that I could consult with about some psychiatric disorders I felt I had. I talked with a doctor*

Charles Whitman: The Texas Tower Killer

once for about two hours and tried to convey to him my fears that I felt overcome by over-
whelming violent impulses. After one session I never saw the doctor again, and since then
I have been fighting my mental turmoil alone, and seemingly to no avail. After my death
I wish that an autopsy would be performed on me to see if there is any visible physical dis-
order. I have had some tremendous headaches in the past and have consumed two large
bottles of Excedrin in the past three months.

Applied to the Whitman case, at the **trait-dispositional level** of analysis, psychologists will test the person on measures like those described in the next chapter.
The main questions will be: Would Whitman be likely to have a distinctive trait profile
on such tests that shows, for example, high levels of angry hostility, impulsiveness, and
neuroticism, with poor impulse control and little ability to handle stress? If he was not
characterized by such a profile before the incident, did Whitman undergo personality
change, at least as defined at the trait level? Or were there any subtle indications in
his behavioral tendencies that might have allowed one to predict his actions? The profile resulting from such tests would provide a rich description of his characteristics.
Many of these might not have been evident from his previous behaviors, but might
now help one to make sense of his violent outburst and the character traits with which
it was consistent.

At the **psychodynamic-motivational level,** to understand Whitman's violence
one might first focus on the "unusual and irrational thoughts" to which he referred and
to his "overwhelming violent impulses." Using the methods of psychodynamic theory
(Chapters 5, 6, 7), one seeks to understand the unconscious conflicts and struggles that
underlie them. According to psychoanalytic theory, for example, human aggression is
an outgrowth of the continuous conflict between strong and often unconscious
impulses and the defenses developed by the ego to keep them in check. Might

1.13 How do the six
levels of analysis address
different potential causes
of Charles Whitman's
killing spree?

Whitman's defenses against his own anger and hostility have become so rigid and extreme that he could not express his aggressive impulses even in indirect or disguised forms? A question asked at the psychodynamic level then is: Will the unreleased pressures build up to an explosion point? Work at this level assumes that the provocation that triggers unexpected destructive outburst is usually trivial. Instead, it searches to try to infer underlying conflicts and unconscious dynamics that might account for the unexpected and seemingly inexplicable change in his typical behavior.

At the **phenomenological level,** the focus would shift to trying to illuminate Whitman's own views of what he did and why, and of what he believed was happening to him, beginning with the letter he wrote, and extending in various other directions. The concern would be to understand how his perceptions and interpretations of what was happening to him misguided him to the actions that then erupted explosively. In the effort to unscramble his confusions and misperceptions, attention would be focused on his disturbed sense of self and his panic in trying to deal with the internal conflicts, loss of control, and feelings of fragmentation, despair, and helplessness that he was experiencing. In these efforts, work at this level and work at the psychodynamic level would become complementary, with researchers at both levels converging on some of the same questions albeit with somewhat different concepts and methods.

At the **behavioral-conditioning level,** the focus is on the ways in which the person's behavior reflects and is shaped by his or her learning history and present life conditions. Applied to Charles Whitman, at this level, one would seek the answer in Whitman's previous learning experiences and the culture he grew up in. A question at this level would be whether there was a history of fascination and rewarding experiences with guns, as well as exposure to role models that displayed violent behaviors. One may also ask whether there was an influence by the culture or subculture and the rewards it offered for aggression in diverse forms. Perhaps the environment in which he developed had primed him to solve his problems in a violent manner, particularly when he was overwhelmed by the recent life stresses that he described in his letter.

At the **social cognitive level,** how people perceive and interpret events, and the internal states and mental-emotional processes that these perceptions activate, determine how they behave. To understand what Whitman did requires understanding these mental and emotional processes that were activated in him at the time of his outburst, the specific situations he was exposed to, and his characteristic cognitive and affective dynamics that generated his extraordinary aggression. Perhaps his aggression was prompted by perceptions that he had been terribly wronged in ways that allowed him to justify his actions at least to himself. By blaming a person or group for real or imagined wrongs, people can create an image of a hated enemy fully deserving of whatever aggression is directed toward them. But why did Whitman do something so extreme that most people would not do under similar circumstances, and with equally good reasons? What was going on in Whitman's mind that was so different and that could plausibly account for the extremeness of his aggression? What kinds of skills, self-regulatory controls, and values did he lack that could allow such behavior? What were the beliefs and expectations that led him to his actions? These are the kinds of questions that drive work at this level of analysis. While there is no way to answer such questions in hindsight, the challenge is to be able to do so—at least sometimes—in advance. In pursuing the answers, work at this level and at several of the other levels converges and each again complements the others.

At the **biological level,** to understand Whitman, one would begin by considering the possible links between the brain and aggression that might underlie his ferocious outburst. To understand the Whitman case at this level, a postmortem examination was conducted to follow up on his reference to intense headaches. It revealed a highly malignant tumor in an area of the brain hypothesized to be involved in aggressive behavior. Some experts therefore suggested that Whitman's damaged brain might have predisposed him to violent behavior. On the other hand, although many efforts have been made to locate and study areas of the brain involved in aggressive behavior, even with modern methods these relations are still poorly understood, and emerging evidence suggests that the relationship between brain areas and behavior is not simple. Although certain areas of the brain may have coordinating functions in aggression, we also know that these regions are closely regulated by other areas of the brain that process information coming in from the environment. Certain kinds of brain damage or disorders can produce violent and unpredictable behavior in humans, too. In the majority of individuals who behave aggressively, however, there is no evidence of brain damage, although the aggression is being triggered by a variety of brain mechanisms.

Nevertheless, biological and genetic factors do appear to play a more general role in aggressive behavior (Baron & Richardson, 1994; Loehlin, 1992). Identical twins, who are genetic carbon copies of each other, are more similar in their aggressive and dominant behavior patterns than are fraternal twins who differ genetically from one another (Plomin & Rende, 1991). This is the case even if the identical twins are raised in different homes with presumably different social environments (Bouchard and others, 1990). But, behavior geneticists also remind us that genetic factors never operate in isolation; they always interact with environmental factors. In recent years, new discoveries about the brain, and new methods of studying its activities, have encouraged great interest and much research at this level. If Whitman were tested today, biological level measures (such as brain scans) would allow much fuller analyses of the links between his thoughts, actions, and brain processes. Most important, as you will see later in this text (Chapter 17), recent advances in the study of brain mechanisms are giving us an increasingly clear picture of the neural mechanisms in the brain that can go wrong when people have violent outbursts of aggression (Davidson, Putnam, & Larson, 2000). Recent work at this level, discussed in the final part of the text, also makes it clear that the biological and the psychological aspects of personality are in a continuous reciprocal influence process, each affecting the other. Consequently, contributions from the different levels of analysis again continuously enrich each other.

Integration of Levels: The Person as a Whole

In sum, the different levels all add their distinctive insights to understanding the total person "as a whole" and they inform each other and interact. In this text we will focus first on each level separately so that each can be studied in depth, and then consider their interconnections and integration in the final Part's three chapters. When taken together, the work done at these different levels addresses every conceivable cause for any behavior or mental event central for personality. At times, to be sure, work at the different levels can also produce critical findings that contradict each other and generate real conflicts, and that has happened often in the field's history, and will continue in the future as it does in every science. But those are some of the most exciting moments in science and often set the stage for dramatic progress. In fact, in recent years, personality psychologists working at different levels seem to be crossing more freely over what used to be rigid boundaries. As one reviewer of ongoing work within diverse research orientations put it:

1.14 What kinds of theoretical integrations are occurring as personality psychologists seek a unified understanding of the person?

Their research programs frequently inform one another. The complementary findings are beginning to portray a coherent (albeit incomplete) picture of personality structure and functioning. Personality psychologists have found common ground (Cervone, 1991, p. 371).

A more comprehensive view of the person is emerging that seeks to incorporate many of the insights and findings from each of the diverse levels within one broader, unifying framework (e.g., Baumeister & Tice, 1996; Carver, 1996; Cervone & Mischel, 2002; Mischel & Shoda, 1998). If this trend continues, it promises to be an exciting time for the field. It indicates that personality psychology is becoming a more cumulative science in which knowledge and insights add to each other, allowing each generation of researchers to revise earlier conclusions and to build progressively on each other's work. If so, major contributions provided by each stream of work will ultimately become more integrated, retaining those elements that stand the test of time and research as the science matures.

There also are indications that boundaries are being crossed productively between personality psychology and related fields, both at more molar, social-cultural levels of analysis (e.g., Nisbett, 1997) and at more molecular levels, particularly in cognitive neuroscience and in behavioral genetics (Plomin, DeFries, McClearn, & Rutter, 1997; Rothbart, Posner, & Gerardi, 1997). It has long been the hope of personality psychology that it could some day provide an integrated view of the person (e.g., Allport, 1937) that at least begins to capture the complexity and depth of its subject matter: optimists in the field are beginning to think that day might not be too far off (Cervone & Mischel, 2002, Chapter 1).

Practical Applications: Coping and Personal Adaptation

1.15 In what sense is personality an applied science?

To speak to why most people really want to study personality, we also will look at how the discoveries made already can allow a better understanding of oneself as a person and as at least a partial architect of one's own future. Personality theories are often *applied* to help improve the psychological qualities of one's lives. Even people whose problems are not severe enough to seek help from professionals still search for ways to live their lives more fully and satisfyingly. But what constitutes a fuller, more satisfying life? Given the diversity and complexity of human strengths and problems, it seems evident that simple notions of psychological adequacy in terms of "good adjustment" or "sound personality" are naive. More adequate definitions of "adaptation" and "abnormality," of "mental health" and "deviance," hinge on the personality theory that is used as a guide. The work discussed through the text offers distinctive notions about the nature of psychological adequacy and deviance. On closer examination, it will be seen that even these conceptions from different levels of analysis in fact have clear common themes. But each also adds to the strategies that can be chosen to try to change troublesome behaviors and to encourage better alternatives.

Many personality psychologists are searching for useful techniques to deal with the implications of personality for human problems, such as depression, anxiety, and poor health, and to foster more advantageous patterns of coping and growth. In addition to having enormous practical and social importance, attempts to understand and change behaviors provide one of the sharpest testing grounds for ideas about personality. These efforts include different forms of psychotherapy, drugs, and physical treatments, various special learning programs, and changes in the psychological environment to permit people to develop to their full potential. Research on these topics informs us about the usefulness and implications of different ideas about personality change in normal well-functioning people as well as in those who are distressed. The concepts, methods, and findings relevant to personality assessment, change, and growth will be discussed at many points as they apply to each of the major approaches and the levels of analysis that they guide.

SUMMARY

WHAT IS PERSONALITY?
- The term "personality" implies stable and coherent individual differences that can be described or predicted.
- In personality psychology, "personality" refers to the person's unique patterns of coping with and transforming the psychological environment.
- Personality psychologists study how personality dispositions and psychological and biological-genetic processes influence people's distinctive patterns of behavior.

THEORY AND LEVELS OF ANALYSIS
- In the first half of the last century, grand theories of personality (e.g., those of Freud) developed, introducing many lines of research and therapeutic practices.
- Work in personality psychology can now be grouped into six different major levels of analysis.

LEVELS OF ANALYSIS
- These six levels provide an overview of the many complex and diverse aspects of human personality.
- The trait-dispositional level tries to identify consistencies in the basic expressions of personality, conceptualized as stable personality characteristics.
- The psychodynamic-motivational level probes the motivations, conflicts, and defenses—often unconscious—that may underlie diverse aspects of personality.
- The phenomenological level focuses on the inner experiences of the person and his or her way of seeing and interpreting the world.
- The behavioral-conditioning level analyzes specific patterns of behavior that characterize individuals and identifies the conditions that regulate their occurrence.
- The social cognitive level focuses on the distinctive patterns of thoughts, expectations-beliefs, goals-values, emotional reactions, and self-regulatory efforts that characterize the person.
- The biological level explores the biological bases of personality, including the role of heredity, the brain, and evolution.
- The example of Charles Whitman shows how each level of analysis contributes to a fuller understanding of individual personality and behavior.

TOWARD AN INTEGRATIVE SCIENCE
- Work at each level provides basic concepts and strategies for seeking information about people and for constructively changing maladaptive behavior patterns.
- An increasingly comprehensive view of the person seems to be emerging that incorporates many of the insights and findings from each level of analysis.
- Boundaries are also being crossed between personality psychology and other related fields.

PRACTICAL APPLICATIONS

- The findings of personality psychologists address diverse human problems, such as depression, anxiety, impulse control, and poor health.

KEY TERMS

behavioral-conditioning
   level   14
biological level   14
levels of analysis   6

phenomenological
   level   14
psychodynamic-
   motivational level   13

social cognitive level   14
trait-dispositional level   13

DATA, METHODS, AND TOOLS

▶ WHY A SCIENCE OF PERSONALITY? BEYOND HINDSIGHT UNDERSTANDING

Much of our lives are spent trying to understand, after the fact, our own and others' behavior. In the words of the Danish philosopher Sören Kierkegaard, "Life is lived forwards, but understood backwards." And, as the saying goes, hindsight is 20/20. But that is also the problem with hindsight understanding. Past events can be explained in many ways, and there is no sure way to determine which, if any, of the alternative explanations is the right one.

Akira Kurosawa's classic film *Rashomon* tells the tale of the rape of a woman and the murder of a man, seen entirely in flashbacks from the perspectives of four narrators. Each story makes perfect sense when taken by itself, but together, they do not add up and the contradictions become evident. The characters are the same in all four versions of the story, as are many of the details. But much is different, as well. The film

2.1 Describe and compare two basic approaches to understanding behavior and its causes. What are the advantages of a scientific approach to understanding?

never tells what really happened, leaving the viewer with a feeling of ambiguity and an appreciation of how what we see depends on who we are. In real life, we don't have the moviegoer's advantage of viewing the same event through different people's eyes. Rather, like the characters in the film, we see only through our own eyes, and are convinced we see the truth, without realizing how different other accounts of the same event can be when seen through different eyes.

It is not that after-the-fact understanding is useless. Often, there may be no alternative and hindsight can help one at least try to make sense of events that otherwise cannot be understood. But that is very different from the essence of scientific inquiry. A science begins by creating a language to describe phenomena in a way that allows a single common understanding to emerge, in order to avoid multiple alternative accounts that vary with each observer. The goal is not just to find a common understanding, but to be able to use it to make accurate predictions and to test if they really are accurate, remaining ready to disconfirm and modify them if they are unsupported. Therefore, researchers try to arrange conditions under which they can test hypotheses about the various causal factors that might influence the occurrence of the behavior or event of interest. If one understands the causes of a given behavior, then it may be possible to predict when it will occur again, and when it will not, with reasonable accuracy. In time, this knowledge also makes it possible to build a theory to understand what is the process or mechanism that underlies the behavior being studied. That is why, at least in the view of most personality researchers, we need a science of personality. And that in turn requires attention to the methods and tools needed to pursue that goal.

Personality psychologists are committed to studying persons by means of scientific methods, but they are equally eager to avoid oversimplifying their subject matter and reducing the complexities of personality into a stereotypically "scientific" collection of formulae and variables. They recognize that "the most distinguishing feature of persons is that they construct meaning by reflecting on themselves, their past, and the future" (Cervone & Mischel, 2002, p. 5).

In that spirit, it makes sense to begin the study of persons by asking individuals how they see and understand themselves, and what they are like in their own eyes—while also recognizing that this personal "internal" vantage point will necessarily be limited and incomplete. So, as a first step in this text, we begin by considering a case study of Gary W. As you proceed through the text, you will learn about Gary's personality and the information made available about him, which is based on his clinical files but was modified sufficiently in order to protect confidentiality and to illustrate points in the text. Because researchers pay much attention to case material at some levels but not at others, information about Gary is more complete in some parts of the text and more limited in others.

In Focus 2.1 presents some of what Gary said when "asked to describe yourself as a person"—an exercise that you the reader may also want to try on yourself. He was asked to describe himself on his first visit to the university campus clinic in the psychology department of a large university.

The impressions Gary gives us about himself, while interesting, are of uncertain value: We know neither their accuracy nor their meaning. Then how can we find out more? To convert personality speculations about people into ideas that can be studied scientifically, we must be able to put them into *testable* terms using good measures. There is a wide range of these available to personality researchers, as considered next.

IN FOCUS 2.1

GARY W., THE TEXT'S CASE—GARY'S SELF-DESCRIPTION

I'm twenty-five years old, and a college graduate. I'm in business school working toward an MBA.

. . . I'm an introspective sort of person—not very outgoing. Not particularly good in social situations. Though I'm not a good leader and I wouldn't be a good politician, I'm shrewd enough that I'll be a good businessman. Right now I'm being considered for an important job that means a lot to me and I'm sweating it. I know the powers at the office have their doubts about me but I'm sure I could make it—I'm positive. I can think ahead and no one will take advantage of me. I know how to work toward a goal and stick with whatever I start to the end—bitter or not.

The only thing that really gets me is speaking in a large group. Talking in front of a lot of people. I don't know what it is, but sometimes I get so nervous and confused I literally can't talk! I feel my heart is going to thump itself to death. I guess I'm afraid that they're all criticizing me. Like they're almost hoping I'll get caught with my pants down. Maybe I shouldn't care so much what other people think of me—but it does get to me, and it hurts—and I wind up sweating buckets and with my foot in my mouth.

I'm pretty good with women, but I've never found one that I want to spend the rest of my life with. Meanwhile I'm enjoying life. I hope someday to find a woman who is both attractive and level-headed. Someone who is warm and good but not dominating and who'll be faithful but still lead a life of her own. Not depend on me for every little thing.

My childhood was fairly typical middle-class, uptight. I have an older brother. We used to fight with each other a lot, you know, the way kids do. Now we're not so competitive. We've grown up and made peace with each other—maybe it's just an armistice, but I think it may be a real peace—if peace ever really exists. I guess it was his accident that was the turning point. He got pretty smashed up in a car crash and I guess I thought, "There but for the grace of God. . . ." I count a lot on being physically up to par.

Dad wasn't around much when we were growing up. He was having business troubles and worried a lot. He and Mother seemed to get along in a low-key sort of way. But I guess there must have been some friction because they're splitting now—getting divorced. I guess it doesn't matter now—I mean my brother and I have been on our own for some time. Still, I feel sorry for my Dad—his life looks like a waste and he is a wreck.

My strengths are my persistence and my stamina and guts—you need them in this world. Shrewdness. My weaknesses are my feeling that when it comes to the crunch you can't really trust anybody or anything. You never know who's going to put you down or what accident of fate lies around the corner. You try and try—and in the end it's probably all in the cards. Well, I guess that's about it. I mean, is there anything else you want to know?

▶ THE RANGE OF PERSONALITY-RELEVANT MEASURES

Imagine going to a hospital for a comprehensive checkup. You may see a radiologist who would take X-rays and perform CAT scans. You may see an endocrinologist who analyzes the levels of various hormones in your blood. You may see a neurologist who performs a variety of diagnostic tests to study the functioning of your nervous system and taps your reflexes. You may see an immunologist who examines your immune system, and you may see a cardiologist who specializes in determining how well your heart is working. All these experts will offer a snapshot of a given aspect of your body. Yet they all reflect one thing, your body, which is a *system* of many, many interdependent components. The different levels of analyses of personality psychology work in a similar way. Each will provide data about one aspect of your total functioning personality, and an ultimate challenge is putting them all together for an understanding of how the personality as a system operates.

Psychologists approaching personality at different levels of analysis obtain information about people from many sources and through diverse strategies. The result is a collection of diverse observations about many aspects of persons. A central goal of

2.2 How do levels of analysis contribute to the diversity of personality measures available to personality psychologists?

personality psychology is to figure out how these diverse aspects about an individual relate to each other and help us to understand what is going on in the individual as a whole. But before we get there (which we will, in Chapter 16), we need to first see just what kinds of data are available; and the range is huge. This chapter is an introduction to the sources and types of data that are made available from each level, and to the concepts and tools used to make sense of those data.

Interviews

2.3 Describe some strengths and weaknesses of interviews.

A valuable source of information is the **interview**—a verbal exchange between the participant and the examiner, favored particularly by workers at the psychodynamic-motivational level and those at the phenomenological level. Some interviews are tightly structured and formal: the examiner follows a fixed, prescribed format. For example, in research to survey people's sexual activities, the interviewer might follow a standard series of questions, starting with questions about the person's earliest experiences and going on to potential problems in current relationships.

The interview is the oldest method for studying personality, and it remains the most favored for psychodynamic research and assessment (Watkins, Campbell, Nieberding, & Hallmark 1995). Its usefulness as an assessment tool depends on many considerations, including how the interview is guided and structured, and how the interviewee's responses are recorded, coded, and interpreted. Each of these steps requires attention to the same issues that apply to other methods that rely on the clinician's judgment, as was just discussed for projective techniques. In recent years, unobtrusive video and sound recording has made the interview a method that is more open to manageable scoring, coding, and data analysis. These procedures often can be made even more flexible by computerized programs. The interview therefore is being used with renewed interest in efforts to systematically improve psychodynamic assessment (Horowitz and associates, 1989; Perry & Cooper, 1989).

Interviews, while popular, tend to be expensive and time consuming to conduct, as well as to code or score, because it is not easy to have all interviews with different people conducted the same standard way so that they can be compared easily. Therefore many researchers seek short cuts by using various tests, often in the form of ratings and self-reports. These short cuts were used particularly early in the field's development as discussed in In Focus 2.2.

Tests and Self-Reports

2.4 Differentiate between performance and self-report tests.

A **test** is any standardized measure of behavior, including verbal behavior, as in self-reports. Some tests involve **performance measures.** For example, researchers interested in seeing how personality measures in childhood predict academic performance in later life might use measures like the SAT as an outcome assessment. Likewise, those interested in anxiety might use a measure in which the ability to repeat long strings of numbers under difficult, stressful conditions is measured. On this measure, the examiner verbalizes long lists of numbers and the respondent has to repeat them backwards, knowing that a poor score will be taken as an index of low intelligence.

Some tests are in the form of **self-reports**—a term that refers to any statements people make about themselves. Respondents are asked to react to sets of questions or items with one of a limited number of prescribed choices (e.g., "yes," "no," "strongly

EARLY PERSONALITY MEASUREMENT

Interest in self-description or self-report as a method of personality assessment was stimulated by an inventory devised during World War I (Watson, 1959). This was Woodworth's *Personal Data Sheet*, later known as the *Psychoneurotic Inventory*. It was aimed at detecting soldiers who would be likely to break down under wartime stress. Because it was impractical to give individual psychiatric interviews to recruits, Woodworth listed the kinds of symptoms psychiatrists would probably ask about in interviews. He then condensed them into a paper-and-pencil questionnaire of more than 100 items. Examples are: "Do you wet your bed at night?" and "Do you daydream frequently?" The respondent must answer "yes" or "no" to each question. Soldiers who gave many affirmative responses were followed up with individual interviews. This

method was valuable as a simplified and economic alternative to interviewing everyone individually. Often questionnaires are still employed as substitutes for interviews.

The Woodworth questionnaire was not used widely, but it was a forerunner of the many other self-report devices that flourished in the 1920s and 1930s, and new versions of similar measures are still used currently. These self-reports compared people usually with respect to a single summary score. This total score served as an index, for example, of their "overall level of adjustment," just as single scores or mental quotients were developed to describe the level of "general intelligence." In addition to efforts to assess adjustment, attempts to measure individuals on various personality dimensions soon became extremely popular.

agree," "frequently," "don't know"), not unlike multiple choices on tests in academic courses. Examples are shown in Figures 2.1 and 2.2.

Self-reports offer quick ways of getting information the person is willing and able to reveal. For example, Table 2.1 shows a self-report measure of anxiety with multiple items. The responses are scored and added to estimate the person's overall self-reported level of anxiety.

Projective Measures

Projective tests were developed more than 60 years ago and continue to be popular in clinical use. With these methods, assessors present the person with ambiguous stimuli and ask them ambiguous questions that have no right or wrong answers. For example, they ask "What could this remind you of?" [while showing an inkblot], or ask you to tell an imaginative story in response to a highly ambiguous scene shown on a card. Measures like these are of theoretical importance to much of the work at the psychodynamic-motivational level and therefore are described more fully in Part II, especially in Chapter 7.

2.5 What are projective tests? With what level of analysis are they most often associated?

Naturalistic Observation and Behavior Sampling

Just as astronomers cannot manipulate the actions of heavenly bodies, psychologists often cannot—or should not—manipulate certain aspects of human behavior. For example, one could not or would not create home environments in which children become delinquent or marital conflicts are provoked. Although such phenomena cannot be manipulated, often they can be observed closely and systematically. Ethical considerations often prevent psychologists from trying to create

2.6 Describe and compare naturalistic observation and remote behavior sampling methods.

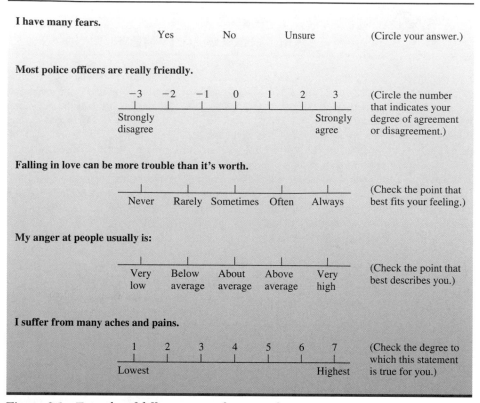

Figure 2.1 Examples of different types of structured test items.

Figure 2.2 Examples of adjective scales. Rate yourself for the degree to which these terms describe you. (Check the point that describes you best on each scale.)

Source: Adapted as illustrations, selected from 40 adjective items used by McCrae & Costa to identify personality dimensions from ratings and questionnaires. McCrae, R. R., & Costa, P. T., Jr. Updating Norman's "adequacy taxonomy": Intelligence and personality in dimensions in natural language and in questionnaires. *Journal of Personality and Social Psychology, 49,* 710–721. © 1985 by the American Psychological Association. Reprinted with permission.

TABLE 2.1 Items Similar to Those on Anxiety Scales

Item	Responses Indicative of Anxiety
I cannot keep my mind focused on anything.	True
I am a worrier.	True
I am often afraid.	True
I feel safe most of the time.	False
I don't fret a lot.	False
I sleep well before exams.	False
Often I think I am nervous.	True

Note: The participant must respond "true" or "false."

powerful, lifelike experimental treatments in the laboratories (see Consent Form, Figure 2.5).

Even when some variables can be manipulated in experiments, the investigator often prefers to observe behavior as it naturally occurs, without any scientific interference. Some of the most informative work using this method, called *naturalistic observation*, comes from students of animal behavior, who unobtrusively observe the moment-by-moment lives of such animals as chimpanzees in their natural environment. Such methods have been adapted to study families interacting in their own homes (Patterson, 1990).

Gerald Patterson and coworkers at the Oregon Social Learning Center developed a behavioral coding system having 29 categories with very specific definitions. Both parents' and children's behavior could be coded, including specific types of aversive behaviors (e.g., yell, negativism, hit, whine, refused to comply). In one large project, trained observers came to the families' homes at dinnertime, when problem

Concealed video cameras and one-way mirrors allow unobtrusive observation by researchers who remain unseen by participants.

interactions most often occur. Every interaction of the child with another family member was coded, so that it was possible to study the entire sequence of interactions. The data indicated that in distressed families, the problem children's aversive behaviors continued in "chains" over longer periods of time, with an escalating pattern of hostile interchanges with family members. When the parents in the problem families reacted with punishment, it tended to prolong the escalation of aggression as the child reacted with defiance or resumed aversive behaviors shortly afterwards. These behaviors translated into poor social skills, noncompliance at school, poor school achievement, rejection by peers, and, in many cases, antisocial behavior as an adolescent (Patterson & Fisher, 2002).

In a somewhat similar fashion, but usually on a smaller scale, unseen observers may study children from behind a one-way mirror in such settings as a playroom or a preschool class (Mischel, Shoda, & Rodriguez, 1989). Of course, observation is a commonplace method in everyday life; through observation we form impressions and learn about events and people. The distinguishing feature of observation as a scientific tool is that it is conducted as precisely, objectively, and systematically as possible.

In clinical applications, direct observation may give both client and assessor an opportunity to assess life problems and to select treatment objectives. Direct observation of behavior samples also may be used to assess the relative efficacy of various treatment procedures.

Remote Behavior Sampling: Daily Life Experiences

It is not practical or possible for behavioral assessors to follow people around from situation to situation on a daily basis. In addition, assessors are frequently interested in unobservable events, such as emotional reactions and thinking patterns, that may shed considerable light on personality functioning. Through remote behavior sampling, researchers and clinicians can collect samples of behavior from respondents as they live their daily lives. A tiny computerized device carried by respondents pages them at randomly determined times of the day. When the "beeper" sounds, respondents record their current thoughts, feelings, or behaviors, depending on what the researcher or therapist is assessing (Csikszentmihalyi, 1990; Singer, 1988; Stone, Shiffman, & DeVries, 2000). Respondents may also report on the kind of situation they are in so that situation–behavior interactions can be examined. The data can either be stored in the computer or transmitted directly to the assessor.

Remote sampling procedures can be used over weeks or even months to collect a large behavior sample across many situations. This approach to personality assessment has great promise, for it enables researchers and clinicians to detect patterns of personal functioning that might not be revealed by other methods (Stone et al., 2000).

2.7 Describe methods that are used in remote behavior sampling research.

In recent years, many personality researchers have moved outside the lab to study people's daily experiences by obtaining the person's self-reported reactions to daily experiences that cannot be observed directly (Tennen, Suls, & Affleck, 1991). For example, researchers use daily mood measures on which participants indicate the degree to which they experienced various emotions (such as enjoyment/fun, pleased; depressed/blue) in each reporting period (Larsen & Kasimatis, 1991). Such reports can be linked to other aspects of experience, such as minor illnesses and psychological well-being (e.g., Emmons, 1991). Likewise, daily reports of everyday reactions to various stressors and hassles, such as interpersonal conflicts at home, can be related to other

TABLE 2.2   Illustrative Methods for Sampling Daily Life Experiences

Method	Examples	Source
Preprogrammed time samples	Digital watch alarm signals time for respondents to record their tasks, behavior, and perceptions at the moment	Cantor, Norem, Langston, Zirkel, Fleeson, & Cook-Flannagan, 1991
Systematic diaries	Self-reports of reactions to daily stressors (e.g., overload at work, family demands, arguments)	Bolger & Schilling, 1991
Sampling emotions, symptoms, and other internal states	Self-ratings of emotional states (e.g., pessimistic, optimistic, full–hungry), occurrence and duration of symptoms (e.g., backache, headache), reported personal strivings and well-being	Larsen & Kasimatis, 1991; Emmons, 1991; Diener et al., 1995; David et al., 1997

measures of personality (Bolger & Schilling, 1991; David, Green, Martin, & Suls, 1997). Experience samples also are used to study reactions to common life problems such as adjusting to college life in terms of such personal tasks as getting good grades and making friends (e.g., Cantor and associates, 1991). Examples of different behavior sampling methods are shown in Table 2.2.

Physiological Functioning and Brain Imaging

Personality researchers have long searched for practical methods to assess emotional reactions. One of the classic measures of physiological functioning is the **polygraph,** an apparatus that records the activities of the autonomic nervous system. Measures of bodily changes in response to stimulation also provide important information, especially when the stimuli are stressful or arousing. The polygraph apparatus contains a series of devices that translate indices of body changes into a visual record by deflecting a pen across a moving paper chart. A popular component of polygraphic measurement is the **electrocardiogram (EKG).** As the heart beats, its muscular contractions produce patterns of electrical activity that may be detected by electrodes placed near the heart on the body surface. Another component is the changes in blood volume that may be recorded by means of a **plethysmograph.** Other useful measures include changes in the electrical activity of the skin due to sweating (recorded by a galvanometer and called the **galvanic skin response** or **GSR**), changes in blood pressure, and changes in muscular activity (Cacioppo, Berntson, & Crites, 1996; Geen, 1997).

Intense emotional arousal is generally accompanied by high levels of "activation" in the brain (Malmo, 1959; Birbaumer & Ohman, 1993). The degree of activation in the cerebral cortex may be inferred from "brain waves" recorded by the **electroencephalograph (EEG),** as illustrated in the records shown in Figure 2.3. As the EEG patterns in this figure indicate, the frequency, amplitude, and other characteristics of brain waves vary according to the participant's arousal state, from deep sleep to great excitement.

The biological level of analysis has achieved increasing influence in the study of personality, thanks to technical advances in the measurement of physiological reactions, genetic functions, and brain processes, as you will see in later chapters. For example, new brain imaging procedures make it possible to examine relations between neural

2.8 What types of physiological measures are used to measure biological aspects of personality?

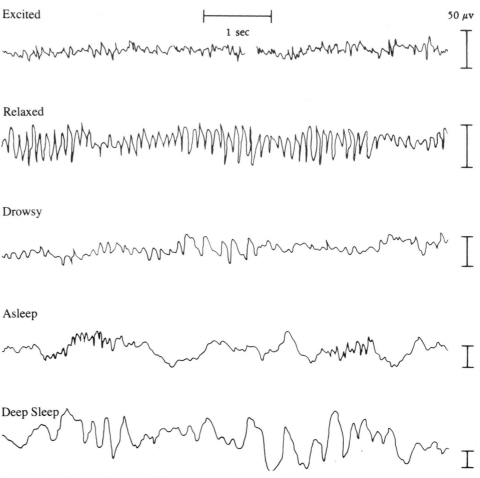

Figure 2.3 Various human EEG patterns under several arousal states.
Source: Jasper, H. (1941). In Penfield & Erickson (Eds.), *Epilepsy and cerebral localization.* Courtesy of Charles C. Thomas, Publisher, Springfield, IL and of Wilder Penfield Archive.

functions and behaviors. **Positron emission tomography (PET) scans** measure the amount of glucose (the brain's main fuel) being used in various parts of the brain and provide an index of activity as the brain performs a particular function.

Functional magnetic resonance imaging or fMRI measures the magnetic fields created by the functioning nerve cells in the brain and with the aid of computers depicts these activities as images. These pictures virtually "light up" the amount of activity in different areas as the person performs mental tasks and experiences different kinds of perceptions, images, thoughts, and emotions. They thus allow a much more precise and detailed analysis of the links between activity in the brain and the mental states we experience while responding to different types of stimuli and generating different thoughts and emotions. These can range, for example, from thoughts and images about what we fear and dread to those directed at that we crave the most. The result is a virtual revolution for work that uses the biological level of neural activity to address questions of core interest for personality psychology.

Advances in brain imaging offer a new way to study mental activity.

▶ CONCEPTUAL AND METHODOLOGICAL TOOLS

Constructs and Operational Definitions

To conduct scientific research (or even to carry on intelligent discourse), it is necessary to clearly identify and specify the phenomena that one wants to understand. The vocabulary of psychology is filled with terms like aggression, extraversion, intelligence, stress, learning, and motivation. All of these are simply words or concepts—scientists prefer the term **constructs**—that refer to classes of behaviors, thoughts, emotions, and situations. Every personality term that we will discuss in this book is a construct (including the term *personality*). These words represent nonmaterial ideas—concepts and not things—and they may have different meanings for different people. For example, the term *dependency* refers to a particular class of behaviors, but the specific types of behavior that are labeled "dependent" may differ from one person to another. Unless two people have a common definition of what dependent means, they can't be sure they're communicating effectively when they talk about "dependent" people. "What do you mean by that?" is a question psychologists must answer very precisely if they are to study a psychological phenomenon.

Operationalization translates these constructs into something observable and measurable. It refers to the specific procedures used to produce or measure it in a particular study. Sometimes, a construct is operationalized in terms of a condition to which someone is exposed. For example, the construct hunger could be operationally defined as "the number of hours that a person is deprived of food." At other times, a construct is operationalized in terms of some behavior of the participant. Thus, we could also define hunger in terms of people's ratings of how hungry they feel or in terms of how much effort they will make to obtain food. Regardless of the method used to operationalize a construct, it cannot be studied scientifically unless it can be tied to something observable.

2.9 What are psychological constructs? Why do they require operationalization?

An Example: Defining the Construct of Aggression

To illustrate these points, let us consider the construct of aggression. If we ask the question, "What is aggression?" we are trying to specify the meaning of the construct itself. That's no easy matter, for the term is used in many different ways in our daily discourse, and with different connotations. Thus, an athlete may be praised for being an "aggressive competitor," whereas an "aggressive schoolyard bully" may evoke disapproval.

2.10 How have psychologists defined aggression at a conceptual level?

Over the years, researchers have offered various construct definitions. One early one was "the delivery of noxious stimuli to another organism" (Buss, 1961). Other psychologists agreed that when we aggress, we deliver aversive stimulation of some kind to the target of the aggression, but they found the definition too broad. For example, if a person accidentally bumps into you, it may be aversive, but is it aggression? If a doctor gives a child a painful vaccination, she's delivering noxious stimulation, but is it an act of aggression? Over time, these concerns were addressed with more elaborate definitions. Today, a definition adopted by most psychologists who study aggression is the following: **aggression** is "any form of behavior directed toward the goal of harming or injuring another living being who is motivated to avoid such treatment" (Baron & Richardson, 1994, p. 7). Notice that this definition has a number of facets:

1. Aggression is behavior, not an emotion. The behaviors may take many forms, including physical and verbal acts. It may even involve not doing something, as when a person deprives another of something needed and thus harms that individual.

2. Aggression is motivated behavior, with the intent being to hurt another. Thus, unintentional acts that harm another would not be considered aggression.

3. The target of the behavior is a living being, not an inanimate object. However, if the purposeful destruction of an inanimate object, such as a prized vase, harms another person, the act would be considered aggression.

4. The recipient must be motivated to avoid the treatment. Thus, an assisted suicide would not be classified as an aggressive act if the deceased person wanted to die, even though it may legally be classified as manslaughter.

Given a working definition of the construct, we must find a way to operationally define it in terms of observable events if we are to study it scientifically. A variety of operational definitions, some quite ingenious, have been used to measure individual differences in aggression. Here are a few of the ways that aggression has been operationally defined and measured in various studies:

2.11 What kinds of measures have been used to provide operational definitions of aggression?

*   Archival records, such as school suspensions, rates of violent behavior, or arrests for such acts.

*   Verbal reports of aggressive behavior, obtained in interviews and on questionnaires.

*   Scores on personality measures designed to measure aggressiveness.

*   Ratings and reports from others on a person's aggressive behavior.

*   Observations of aggressive behavior in natural and laboratory settings.

*   Unnecessary honking of one's automobile horn at other motorists.

*   Administration of electric shock or aversive noise to another person in a laboratory setting.

- Written or spoken insults during laboratory interactions with another person.
- Negative evaluations of another person who has provoked study participants.

► ESTABLISHING RELATIONSHIPS AMONG OBSERVATIONS

Once observations are made, the next step is to determine the relationships among them. First, how objective is the measure: do the measured results fluctuate across different occasions? Do multiple observers agree with each other? Are self-reports and observers' ratings consistent with direct observations of relevant behaviors? Second, how does the measure relate to measures of other constructs: is social anxiety related to loneliness? Do extraverts have happier lives than introverts? What personality factors distinguish happily married couples from those headed for divorce? Do firstborn versus later-born children differ in personality? Is the amount of television violence a child is exposed to related to antisocial aggression later in life? These and countless other psychological questions ask about *associations* between naturally occurring events or variables.

Correlation: What Goes with What?

Data that psychologists who study personality collect, regardless of their source, are conceptualized as variables. A **variable** is an attribute, quality, or characteristic that can be given two or more values. For example, a person's height is a variable, and a psychological characteristic such as attitude toward premarital sex can be quantified using a seven-point scale in which 0 is neutral, +3 is extremely positive, and −3 is extremely negative (Figure 2.1). Often, two or more variables seem to be associated—seem to "go together"—in such a way that when we know something about one variable, we can usually make a good guess about the other variables. For example, people who are taller generally tend to weigh more; when we know how tall someone is, we can roughly predict the person's weight. This "going together," "co-relationship" or joint relationship between variables, is what psychologists mean by the term **correlation.**

The degree of relationship or correlation may be expressed quantitatively by a number called a **correlation coefficient.** Correlation coefficients can range from −1.00 through .00 to +1.00. A coefficient of +1.00 means that there is a perfect positive relation between X and Y—that is, the person having the highest score on X also has the highest score on Y, the person having the second highest score on X has the second highest score on Y, and so on. A correlation of −1.00 signifies a perfect negative relation so that the higher a person's score is on X, the lower the score on Y. A correlation of .00 means that there is no relation at all between X and Y. The correlation coefficient thus indicates both the direction (positive or negative) and the strength of the statistical relation between the two measures.

Suppose we want to know how scores on a psychological test of anxiety are related to students' performance. We can obtain a score on each of the two measures for each student in our sample and graph these data in a scatter plot like those shown in Figure 2.4. Each point in the scatter plot represents the intersection of an individual participant's scores on the two variables of interest, which we'll call variable X (anxiety) and variable Y (average performance level).

The scatter plots in Figure 2.4 illustrate three kinds of correlational results: positive, in which high scores on anxiety are related to high performance averages; negative, in which high scores on anxiety are related to low performance averages; and a zero correlation, in which there is no relation between the two variables and the data points are

2.12 What is meant by correlation?

2.13 What is a correlation coefficient? In what two ways do correlation coefficients differ?

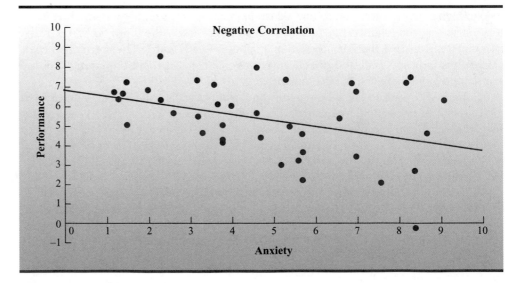

Figure 2.4 Examples of positive correlation, no correlation, and negative correlation between anxiety levels and performance levels.

scattered about in a random pattern. Correlations can be any value between $+1.00$ and -1.00. As mentioned above, a correlation of 0 (i.e., no relationship whatsoever) indicates the weakest relationship. The closer to $+1.00$ or -1.00 the correlation, the more strongly the two variables are related. Thus, a correlation of $-.59$ indicates a stronger association between X and Y than does a correlation of $+.37$. In case you're wondering about the previous examples, moderate negative correlations (typically around $-.30$) exist between anxiety and student performance. As a basis for comparison, a correlation of about $+.50$ exists between height and weight in the general population.

Interpreting Correlations

One useful feature of the correlation coefficient is that by squaring the coefficient, we arrive at an estimate of what percentage of the variation in one of the variables is accounted for by differences in the other. For example, squaring the correlation of $-.30$ between anxiety and grade point average tells us that 9 percent of the total group variation in grades can be accounted for (linked to) differences in anxiety $(-.30 \times -.30 = .09)$. This means that there can be 10 other variables, each accounting for 9 percent of the total variance in grades, that are totally unrelated to anxiety and with each other (i.e., each can have a $+.30$ or $-.30$ correlation with grades, while the correlations among them and with anxiety are 0.0). Together, these 11 variables would account for 99 percent of the variance.

2.14 If we square a correlation coefficient, what does the product tell us?

Correlations that are even close to perfect are very rare in psychology, showing that although many psychological variables are, indeed, associated with each other, the association usually is not very strong. Correlations of about .30 to .50, either positive or negative, are fairly common in psychology. Such correlations may allow predictions that significantly exceed chance guesses, but they are still far from perfect. Statistical computations are used to evaluate the **statistical significance** of particular correlation coefficients reflecting how far a given association exceeds that which would be expected by chance.

Correlations are useful, but they do not indicate cause and effect. If variable X and Y are correlated with each other, there are actually three possibilities:

2.15 What kinds of causal interpretations can be made on the basis of a statistically significant correlation coefficient?

1. Variable *X* causes Variable *Y*.
2. Variable *Y* actually causes Variable *X*.
3. A third factor (Variable *Z*) causes both *X* and *Y*, so that there's no direct causal relation between *X* and *Y*.

Consider the positive correlation between people's shoe sizes and height. Does it mean larger shoes cause people to grow taller (the first possibility above), or does it mean that greater height causes larger shoes (the second possibility), or does it mean that a third factor was responsible for both (e.g., genes and nutrition that influence physical growth determined height and foot size, the latter of which is in turn reflected in shoe size)? The correlation would only alert you to the many things that might make the two tend to occur together.

Although correlations among measures do not allow us to establish causality, they are useful in prediction. If two measures are highly related, either positively or negatively, knowledge of the score on one measure allows us to predict (within certain limits) the score on the other. Thus, admissions officers use college entrance examination scores to predict probable college grades and success because these measures are positively correlated. Insurance premiums are likewise established on the basis of correlations among certain risk factors and medical/accident outcomes. In a sense, your insurance company is betting that you will not demolish your car, become seriously ill, or die before you are statistically "supposed to" based on the information about you, such as your driving record and whether or not you smoke. Because insurers' predictions are based on sound correlational data, the odds are solidly in their favor.

▶ RELIABILITY AND VALIDITY OF OBSERVATIONS AND MEASURES

In order to be scientifically useful, the observations and measures we use to operationally define the constructs we wish to study must have certain characteristics. First, they must be consistent, or reliable, in a number of ways. Secondly, they must be valid indicators of the constructs we are interested in. Much scientific activity is devoted to developing reliable and valid measures, because without good measurement tools, scientific activity cannot proceed.

Reliability: Are the Measurements Consistent?

2.16 What is meant by reliability of measurement?

A number of techniques are available for estimating the consistency or "reliability" of personality measures. When the same test is given to the same group of people on two occasions, a retest correlation or "coefficient of stability" is obtained. This measure provides an index of **temporal reliability.** Generally, for measures of constructs that are expected to remain stable, temporal reliability of a measure should be high.

Other reliability estimates are more concerned with the consistency with which different parts or alternate forms of a test measure behavior. The correlation between parts of a single form is called **internal consistency.** A special type of internal consistency is measured by the correlation between scores on alternate forms of a test administered to the same set of people. For example, a test of anxiety may be given before an intervening procedure, such as psychotherapy, and an "alternate form" of the same measure, using items that are not identical to the form used earlier is given after the intervention. By using two different forms, researchers can avoid the contaminating effects of administering the same form twice.

If subjective judgment enters into scoring decisions, a special kind of reliability check is needed. This check is called **interscorer agreement** or consistency. It is the degree to which different scorers or judges arrive at the same statements about the same test data. For example, if three judges try to infer personality traits from a person's interview behavior and dream reports, it would be necessary to establish the degree to which the three assessors reach the same conclusions. As noted before, interscorer agreement is easiest to achieve when scoring is objective, as on highly structured tests (for example, when all answers are given as either "yes" or "no").

Validity: What Is Being Measured?

2.17 What is meant by validity of measurement? Distinguish between content and criterion validity.

A woman's self-report on a 10-item questionnaire provides her *stated* reactions to the items under the specific testing conditions. Thus if a person reports that she is "very friendly," that is just what she *says* about herself on the test. To know more than that, one needs validity research to establish the meaning and implications of the test answers.

Content Validity. **Content validity** is the demonstration that the items on a test adequately represent a defined broader *class* of behavior. For example, judges would have to agree that the different items on a "friendliness" questionnaire all in fact seem to deal with the class or topic of friendliness. In practice, content validity often is assumed rather than demonstrated. Even if the content validity of the items is shown acceptably, it cannot be assumed that the answers provide an index of the individual's "true" trait position. We do not know whether or not the person who says she is friendly, for example, is really friendly. A self-description is a self-description, and a description by another person is another person's description, and the relationships between such data and other events or measures have to be determined.

Criterion Validity. To go beyond description of the sampled behavior, one has to determine the relationship between it and the score on other measures that serve as referents or standards, thus providing **criterion validity.** For example, psychiatrists' ratings about progress in therapy, teachers' ratings of school performance, the person's behavior on another test, or self-reported progress on another occasion, may be selected as criteria. Criterion validity may be established by a correlation among concurrently available data (such as current test score and present psychiatric diagnosis). This is called **concurrent validity.** Criterion validity also can be predictive if it comes from correlations between a measure and data collected at a later time, for example, pretherapy diagnosis and adjustment ratings after a year of psychotherapy. The term for that is **predictive validity.** Correlations may be looked for between data that seem to have a strong surface similarity in content, such as a child's arithmetic performance on an IQ test and his future success in an arithmetic course. Or they may be sought between measures whose contents appear quite dissimilar, such as a patient's drawings and a psychiatric diagnosis.

Tests based on criterion validity may be used for various practical purposes, depending on their specific validation procedures. Obviously a test may have criterion validity with regard to criteria measured roughly at the same time and still be unable to predict future behavior. Likewise, a test may have predictive validity without concurrent validity if, for example, it can predict suicide five years before a patient kills himself but relates to no other measure at the time of administration.

Construct Validity: Elaborating the Meaning of the Construct. Personality psychologists guided by trait theory usually want to infer and describe a person's dispositions from his or her test responses. **Construct validity** is the effort to elaborate the inferred traits determining test behavior (Campbell, 1960; West & Finch, 1997). Basically, it tries to answer the question: What does this test measure? The concept of "construct validity" was introduced for problems in which:

> . . . no existing measure as a definitive criterion of the quality with which he is concerned. Here the traits or qualities underlying test performance are of central importance (American Psychological Association, 1966, pp. 13–14).

2.18 What is construct validity? How is it established?

Traditionally, construct validity involves the following steps. The investigator begins with a hunch about a dimension on which individuals can be compared, for example, "submissiveness." The researchers might regard submissiveness as a "tendency to yield to the will and suggestions of others" (Sarason, 1966, p. 127). To study this tendency, they devise a measure of submissiveness. They have no one definite criterion, however, but instead the validity of the measure is indicated by the degree to which it predicts behaviors hypothesized to reflect the construct it measures (e.g., submissiveness). If the prediction turns out to be accurate, our confidence in the construct validity of the measure is increased. But what if the predicted behavior was not observed? Perhaps the measure does not reflect the construct. Or, perhaps the hypothesis is wrong. To resolve this dilemma, construct validity research will turn to test other hypotheses about behaviors believed to reflect submissiveness. If many of these behaviors are successfully predicted by the measure of submissiveness, our confidence in the measure is increased, and our confidence is decreased in the first hypothesis that failed to receive support. Construct validity therefore follows an ever-evolving spiral of increased precision in both the measures and the hypotheses about the construct (West & Finch, 1997).

▶ THE EXPERIMENTAL APPROACH

2.19 What is the advantage of experimental research over correlational research?

So far, we have looked at examples of research strategies that examine the relationships between naturally existing differences among people in various personal qualities as well as behavior. But how would one know if changes in one variable would cause changes in another? To answer such questions, psychologists employ an experimental method in which the experimenter varies one or more factors and then measures how another variable has been affected. The logic behind this approach is that if two or more groups of equivalent participants are treated identically in all respects but the variable that is intentionally varied, and if the behavior of the groups differs, then that difference in behavior is likely to have been caused by the factor that was varied.

Independent and Dependent Variables. In psychological experiments, the researcher is interested in relations between conditions that are manipulated and behaviors that are measured. The condition that is controlled or manipulated by the experimenter is called the **independent variable;** the resulting behavior that is measured is called the **dependent variable.** To look at it another way, the independent variable is the cause, or the stimulus, and the dependent variable is the effect, or the response. Both the independent and dependent variables reflect underlying constructs that have to be operationally defined.

2.20 Differentiate experimental and control groups.

Experimental and Control Groups. Suppose that we want to test the hypothesis that frustration increases aggression. Frustration and aggression are both constructs that can be applied to a variety of circumstances and behaviors. To test the hypothesis experimentally, we need to operationally define both frustration and aggression. To operationally define frustration, we do the following: Participants are given a set of 15 items with strings of 7 random letters and told that the letters can be rearranged into words. Any person who can unscramble them within 10 minutes will win a monetary prize. However, half of the participants are given letter sets that are impossible to solve, which we assume will be frustrating to the participants. This group is termed the **experimental group.** To be sure that the frustration has an effect on subsequent aggression, a second group is given a set of easily solvable scrambled words. This group that is not subjected to the frustration is the **control group.**

After the participants are exposed to the frustrating or nonfrustrating condition, they participate in a second, supposedly unrelated, experiment where they are asked to assist the experimenter in a study of the effects of punishment on learning. They are seated before a box with 10 buttons that deliver increasingly intense levels of electric shock. Whenever the learner (seated in an adjoining room) makes a mistake, the participant selects the shock level and presses the button. In reality, the learner is not being shocked, but the participant does not know that. The average intensity of shocks administered by each participant is the operational definition of that person's aggression.

2.21 Why do experimenters employ (a) random assignment to conditions and (b) double-blind designs?

To make the experimental and control groups as similar as possible in all respects other than exposure to the frustration, we assign participants to the experimental and control groups on a random basis. To guarantee random assignment, we can assign each person a number and then either draw numbers out of a hat or use a table of randomly ordered numbers devised by statisticians for this purpose. Random assignment is intended to minimize group differences on other factors (such as intelligence or social class) that might affect the dependent variable.

Double-Blind Designs.   Many studies have shown that if experimenters expect to obtain certain results, they are more likely to get them (Rosenthal & Rubin, 1978). In some of these studies, experimenters showed participants a standard set of facial photographs and obtained ratings of how successful the persons in the photos had been. Some of the experimenters were told that the people in the photos had been very successful and that most past participants had rated them as being successful. Other experimenters were told just the opposite. Actually, the people in the photos had been rated by earlier participants as being neither successful nor unsuccessful. Experimenters who expected "successful" ratings tended to get more of them, and those who expected low success ratings tended to receive such ratings, even though they apparently did nothing intentional to influence their participants.

Because of potential problems involving experimenter expectancy effects, experiments are usually set up so that an experimenter collecting data from participants is unaware of the experimental condition to which the participants have been assigned. When both the participant and the experimenter are blind to the independent variable manipulation, the design is referred to as a **double-blind experiment.**

Some types of behavior can be studied only in their natural settings where little or no control is possible; others can be studied under highly controlled laboratory conditions. The decision to study behavior in a natural setting as opposed to a laboratory involves some important trade-offs. On the one hand, identifying the true causes of behavior in a real-world setting poses problems because there is no way to rule out other possible causes by controlling them. On the other hand, when people are observed in their native habitat, the researcher can be more confident that the results can be applied to other similar real-life settings. In case studies and in observational research carried out in natural settings, it is also possible to observe the full complexity of person–environment relations. This very complexity, however, can make it difficult to identify the causal factors with complete confidence.

Because of the advantages and disadvantages of the various personality research methods, many personality psychologists stress the desirability of using all of the methods, moving from the real world to the laboratory and back again. When consistent results are found in both settings, we can have increased confidence in our observations. In many instances in personality research, the movement is from observations made in natural settings to the laboratory, where greater control of variables is possible.

▶ ETHICS IN PERSONALITY RESEARCH

Some of the studies we have reviewed in this chapter have involved exposing participants to frustrating conditions or using deception. Although the large majority of personality research does not involve such manipulations, some studies do. Sometimes, in order to study important problems, personality researchers walk an ethical tightrope, balancing the importance of the knowledge to be gained and the benefits that may result from its application against the use of deception or the exposure of participants to stressful conditions. When personality data are collected from people who can potentially be identified, invasion of privacy issues also arise.

The desire to protect the privacy and welfare of human participants has resulted in a set of explicit ethical guidelines. For example, according to the research guidelines of the American Psychological Association (APA), participants cannot be placed in either

2.22 What measures are taken by personality researchers to protect the privacy and well-being of participants in their studies?

physical or psychological jeopardy without their informed consent. A typical consent form is shown in Figure 2.5. As the form indicates, participants must be told about the procedures to be followed and warned about any risks that might be involved. If deception is necessary in order to carry out the research, then participants must be completely debriefed after the experiment and the entire procedure must be explained to them. Special measures must be taken to protect the confidentiality of data, and participants must be told that they are free to withdraw from a study at any time without penalty.

When children, seriously disturbed mental patients, or others who are not able to give true consent are involved, consent must be obtained from their parents or guardians. Strict guidelines also apply to research in prisons. Inmates cannot be forced to participate in research, nor can they be penalized for refusing to do so. In research dealing with rehabilitation programs, inmates must be permitted to share in decisions

---

CONSENT FORM

FOR PARTICIPATION IN AN EXPERIMENT IN _____

PSYCHOLOGY IN THE LABORATORY OF _____

1. In this experiment, you will be asked to
2. The benefit we hope to achieve from this work
3. The risks involved (if any)

CONSENT AGREEMENT

I have read the above statement and am consenting to
participate in the experiment of my own volition. I
understand that I am free to discontinue my
participation at any time without suffering
disadvantage. I understand that if I am dissatisfied
with any aspect of this program at any time, I may report
grievances anonymously to _____

Signed: _____
Date: _____

Figure 2.5 A typical consent form for participation in a psychological study. Ethical standards require that participation in research comes only after volunteers understand the task and freely consent.

concerning program goals. Researchers who violate the code of research ethics face serious legal and professional consequences.

The ethical and moral issues in psychology are not simple ones. They are quite similar to those that confront medical researchers. In some instances, the only way to discover important knowledge about behavior or to develop new techniques to enhance human welfare is to deceive participants or to expose them to potentially stressful situations. To help researchers balance the potential benefits against the risks involved and to ensure that the welfare of participants is protected, academic and research institutions have created scientific panels that review every research proposal. If a proposed study is considered ethically questionable, or if the rights, welfare, and personal privacy of participants are not sufficiently protected, the methods must be modified or the research cannot be conducted.

SUMMARY

STUDYING PERSONS: SOURCES OF INFORMATION

- Psychologists want to understand personality to predict future behavior and understand present and past behavior.
- Case studies are a method used to evaluate the individual intensively. They can be conducted at each level of analysis and over many occasions. The case of "Gary W." will be used as a case example throughout the text.
- Psychologists utilize various types of personality tests or structured interviews to assess personality in a quantifiable way.
- Naturalistic observation is especially useful when aspects of behavior cannot—or should not—be manipulated.
- Direct behavior measurement samples behavior in diverse situations. It includes both verbal and nonverbal behavior, as well as physiological measurements of emotional reactions.
- Through remote behavior sampling and daily diary studies, researchers can collect samples of behavior from respondents as they live their daily lives.
- To measure changes in the autonomic nervous system, researchers often utilize data from the EKG, plethysmograph, galvanic skin responses (GSR), and EEG.
- PET scans help to examine neural activity in the brain.

CONCEPTUAL AND METHODOLOGICAL TOOLS

- Constructs are concepts that refer to classes of behaviors and situations.
- Operationalization refers to the specific procedures used to produce or measure constructs in a particular study.

ESTABLISHING AND QUANTIFYING THE RELATIONSHIPS AMONG OBSERVATIONS

- The correlational approach utilizes statistical analysis to measure whether two phenomena or *variables* are related to one another.
- The degree to which two variables are related is mathematically represented by the correlation coefficient.

RELIABILITY AND VALIDITY

- Reliability is found when the results of a measure can be repeated both within the confines of the study and with different investigators.
- Validity refers to how well an assessment device actually measures what it claims to measure. It includes content validity, construct validity, and criterion validity, both concurrent and predictive.

THE EXPERIMENTAL APPROACH

- The experimental approach tries to demonstrate causal relations by manipulating one variable—the independent variable—and measuring the effects on a second variable—the dependent variable.
- In order to minimize experimenter expectancy effects, experiments may be set up to be double-blind.

ETHICS IN PERSONALITY RESEARCH

- To help researchers take into account the privacy and welfare of their participants, the American Psychological Association (APA) has set up guidelines to ensure that participants cannot be placed in either physical or psychological jeopardy without their informed consent.

KEY TERMS

aggression 30
concurrent validity 35
construct 29
construct validity 35
content validity 34
control group 36
correlation 31
correlation coefficient 31
criterion validity 35
dependent variable 36
double-blind
  experiment 37
electrocardiogram
  (EKG) 27

electroencephalograph
  (EEG) 27
experimental group 36
functional magnetic
  resonance imaging
  (fMRI) 28
galvanic skin response
  (GSR) 27
independent
  variable 36
internal consistency 34
interscorer
  agreement 34
interview 22

operationalization 29
performance
  measures 22
plethysmograph 27
polygraph 27
positron emission
  tomography (PET)
  scans 28
predictive validity 35
self-reports 22
statistical significance 33
temporal reliability 34
test 22
variable 31

PART

I

THE TRAIT-DISPOSITIONAL LEVEL

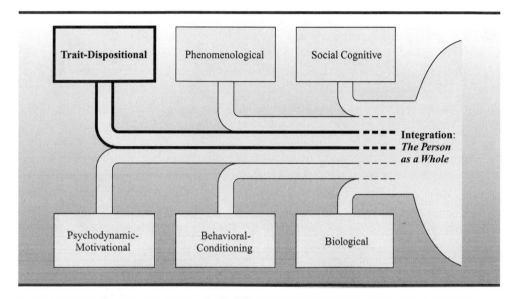

▶ PRELUDE TO PART I: THE TRAIT-DISPOSITIONAL LEVEL

"My roommate is a really closed-in person who just doesn't like to relate. Regardless of how nice I try to be to her the most I get is courtesy—and she seems like that with everybody—a loner. She's a total contrast from the fun-lover I was so lucky to have last year."

Individuals differ consistently from each other in their personality characteristics. These differences are readily perceived and with much agreement among observers, including in the self-perceptions of the people who are being characterized. Workers at this level of analysis search for these differences, and attempt to find those that are most important, consistent and perhaps even universal.

Two questions drive work at the trait-dispositional level:

- What are the basic psychological traits that characterize people?
- How can the consistent differences between people in these traits be best captured and described?

Theory and research at this level to answer these questions provides one of the most productive and enduring traditions for the study of personality. The answers have contributed greatly to the measurement, description, classification, and analysis of personality since the start of the field. Most work at this level of analysis has been driven by the assumption that the important qualities that characterize a person consist of a finite number of broad traits. Traits are defined as "dimensions of individual differences in tendencies to show consistent patterns of thoughts, feelings, and actions" (McCrae et al., 1998). It is assumed that these traits will be expressed consistently in behavior across many different situations and with much stability over time. It also is assumed that traits are quantifiable—some people are more sociable than others, and some are more modest than others, for example. Guided by these assumptions, the focus and goal has been to develop methods to quantify people's social–personal traits. The methods are used to create taxonomies for classifying and capturing the fundamental traits of personality so that people can be compared on the amounts of the different traits that they possess.

From the start of the field, work at this level has provided both concepts and methods for describing and comparing human individual differences on a vast array of attributes and qualities, and many of the highlights are discussed in Chapter 3. It provides an overview of major work in the early phases of this tradition. The chapter then turns to the current developments and advances that now provide measures for comparing people on the main traits that have emerged from a century of active research. In the last few decades of the twentieth century, work at this level of analysis has experienced a great resurgence and made significant advances.

Chapter 4 examines how dispositions are expressed in behavior. It shows that people are characterized not only by broad traits. People also display patterns of behaviors that are connected to particular types of situations in distinctive ways. For example, the phrase "Monica is warm and friendly when starting a relationship but she begins to withdraw when people get really close to her" may accurately capture that this person shows a distinctive "*if* . . . *then* . . ." pattern in her behavior: she is warm at the outset but cools as a relationship becomes close. Such patterns can also provide clues to characteristic underlying motivations and goals that may enrich the understanding of the individual's personality. This part of the text examines the various types of consistency that characterize personality, the attempts to measure them, and the theories that have been developed to try to account for them, at the trait-dispositional level of analysis.

The Personal Side of the Science

Some questions at the trait-dispositional level you might ask about yourself:

▶ What am I like as a person?

▶ How am I different from other people "on the whole"? In what general ways are people different from each other?

▶ Does what I usually do and think and feel depend mostly on myself or on the situation in which I find myself?

▶ When and how is my behavior influenced by the situation?

▶ How does my personality influence the situations I choose to be in?

▶ How does my personality influence the effects that different kinds of situations have on me?

3

TYPES AND TRAITS

"My father is a really great guy. He's absolutely dependable; I can always count on him."

"Nancy's very quiet and withdrawn. She never says hello to anybody."

Descriptions like those above are examples of everyday trait psychology. We see analyses at the trait level whenever people describe and group the differences among themselves into slots or categories. We all tend to classify each other readily on many dimensions: sex, race, religion, occupation, friendliness, and competitiveness are a few examples. Good–bad, strong–weak, friend–enemy, winner–loser — the ways of sorting and classifying human qualities seem virtually infinite.

Most sciences classify and name things in their early efforts to find order. You see this, for example, in the classification system of biology, in which all life is sorted into genera and species. This effort to categorize also occurs in psychology, where, as the oldest and most enduring approach to individuality, it is known as the **trait approach.** Many psychologists working at this level of analysis try to label, measure, and classify people, often but not always using the trait terms of everyday language (for example, friendly, aggressive, honest) in order to describe and compare their psychological attributes and to make sense of them (John, 1990).

3.1 What are the general goals of the trait-dispositional approach to personality?

▶ TYPES AND TRAITS

3.2 Differentiate between traits and types.

Traditionally, analyses at this level have been guided by the assumption that behavior is primarily determined by stable generalized **traits**—basic qualities of the person that express themselves in many contexts. Many investigators have searched vigorously for these traits, trying to find the person's position on one or more trait dimensions (for example, intelligence, introversion, anxiety) by comparing the individual with others under similar uniform conditions. Guided by the belief that positions on these dimensions tend to be stable across situations and over time, the focus in the study of individuality at this level becomes the search to identify the person's basic stable and consistent traits or characteristics.

Types

Some categorizations sort individuals into discrete categories or *types* (Eysenck, 1991; Matthews, 1984). In the ancient theory of temperaments, for example, the Greek physician Hippocrates assigned persons to one of four types of temperament: *choleric* (irritable), *melancholic* (depressed), *sanguine* (optimistic), and *phlegmatic* (calm, listless). In accord with the biology of his time (about 400 B.C.), Hippocrates attributed each temperament to a predominance of one of the bodily humors: yellow bile, black bile, blood, and phlegm. A choleric temperament was caused by an excess of yellow bile; a depressive temperament reflected the predominance of black bile; the sanguine person had too much blood; and phlegmatic people suffered from an excess of phlegm.

Other typologies have searched for constitutional types, seeking associations between physique and indices of temperament. Such groupings in terms of body build have considerable popular appeal, as seen in the many stereotypes linking the body to the psyche: Fat people are "jolly" and "lazy," thin people are "morose" and "sensitive," and so on.

One of the important typologies used repeatedly by personality theorists has grouped all people into **introverts** or **extraverts.** According to this typology, the introvert withdraws into herself, especially when encountering stressful emotional conflict, prefers to be alone, tends to avoid others, and is shy. The extravert, in contrast, reacts to stress by trying to lose himself among people and social activity. He is drawn to an occupation that allows him to deal directly with many people, such as sales, and is apt to be conventional, sociable, and outgoing.

The very simplicity and breadth that makes such typologies appealing also reduces their value. Because each person's behaviors and psychological qualities are complex and variable, it is difficult to assign an individual to a single slot. Nevertheless, important typologies continue to be explored and are useful for many purposes. For example, the Type A pattern is particularly interesting because some of its ingredients, particularly chronic levels of hostility and anger, seem to have value in predicting a variety of dangerous health outcomes, most notably a proneness to premature coronary disease (see In Focus 3.1).

Traits: Individual Differences on Dimensions

3.3 What is meant by the scalability of a trait? How does this differ from a type conception?

Traits Defined. While typologies assume discontinuous categories (like male or female), traits are continuous dimensions like "friendliness" (see Figure 3.1). On such dimensions, differences among individuals may be arranged quantitatively in terms of the degree of the quality the person has (like degrees of "conscientiousness"). Psycho-

AN EXAMPLE: TYPE A PERSONALITY

In collaborative research, psychologists and physicians have looked at the psychological variables in men at higher risk of coronary heart disease early in life. A coronary-prone behavior pattern was identified (Friedman & Roseman, 1974; Glass, 1977) and designated as *Type A*. This behavior pattern is characterized by:

1. ***Competitive Achievement Striving.*** Type As are likely to be involved in multiple activities, have numerous community and social commitments, and participate in competitive athletics. In laboratory studies, they are persistent and behave as though they believe that with sufficient effort they can overcome a variety of obstacles or frustrations.

2. ***Exaggerated Sense of Time Urgency.*** Type As show great impatience and irritation at delay (for example, in a traffic jam, on a waiting line, when someone is late for a meeting).

3. ***Aggressiveness and Hostility.*** Type As may not be generally more aggressive than other people, but they become more aggressive under circumstances which threaten their sense of task mastery, for example, when under criticism or high time pressure.

Individuals who manifest these behaviors to a great degree are called Type As. Those who show the opposite patterns of relaxation, serenity, and lack of time urgency are designated as Type B. The two types differ in many ways, including in their family environments (Woodall & Matthews, 1989).

A number of studies have suggested that Type A people may have at least twice the likelihood of coronary heart disease as Type B people. They also smoke more and have higher levels of cholesterol in their blood. Type A people also tend to describe themselves as more impulsive, self-confident, and higher in achievement and aggression. Both Type A men and women fail to report physical symptoms and fatigue (Carver *et al.*, 1976; Weidner & Matthews, 1978). This tendency to ignore symptoms may result in a Type A individual failing to rest or to seek medical care in the early phases of heart disease and may be one reason why these people push themselves into greater risk of premature death from coronary heart disease. Identifying individuals at high risk for heart disease and teaching them to pay more attention to physical symptoms may be an important part of programs aimed at reducing the toll of heart disease.

There may be a less strong relationship between the total pattern of Type A behavior and coronary disease than was suggested initially, especially among high-risk people (Matthews, 1984). Rather than looking at the relationship between the Type A pattern as a whole and coronary disease, it may be more useful to isolate such specific components of the pattern as anger and hostility. These components were found to be related to coronary disease even in the more recent studies (Miller and colleagues, 1996). In sum, it now seems that specific behaviors, rather than the more global typology, are linked to a higher risk of coronary disease.

logical measurements usually suggest a continuous dimension of individual differences in the degree of the measured quality: most people show intermediate amounts, and only a few are at each extreme, as Figure 3.1 shows. For example, on the introversion–extraversion typology, individuals differ in the extent to which they show either quality but usually do not belong totally to one category or the other. It is therefore better to think of a psychological continuum of individual differences for most qualities or traits.

Traits are assumed to be quantifiable and scalable:

> *"By [scalability] we mean that a trait is a certain quality or attribute, and different individuals have different degrees of it. . . . If individuals differ in a trait by having higher or lower degrees of it, we can represent the trait by means of a single straight line. . . . Individual trait positions may be represented by points on the line" (Guilford, 1959, pp. 64–65). In its simplest meaning, the term "trait" refers to consistent differences between the behavior or characteristics of two or more people. Thus, a **trait** may be simply defined as ". . . any distinguishable, relatively enduring way in which one individual varies from another" (Guilford, 1959, p. 6).*

3.4 Describe the characteristics of the Type A personality. What is its significance for physical health?

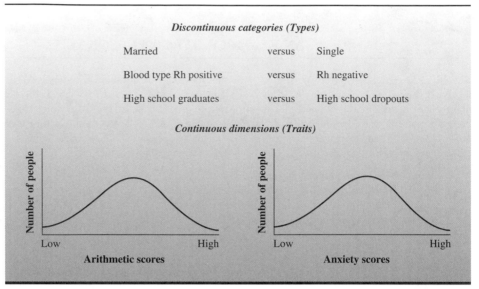

Figure 3.1 Examples of discontinuous categories (types) and continuous dimensions (traits).

The search for traits begins with the commonsense observation that individuals often differ greatly and consistently in their responses to the same psychological situation or stimulus. That is, when different people are confronted with the same event—the same social encounter, the same test question, the same frightening experience—each individual tends to react in a somewhat different way. The basic idea that no two people react identically to the same stimulus is shown schematically in Figure 3.2. Moreover, in everyday life most of us are impressed with the distinctive *consistency* of one individual's responses over a wide variety of stimulus situations: We expect an "aggressive" person to differ consistently from others in his or her responses to many stimuli.

3.5 What everyday observations stimulate the search for traits?

Describing and Explaining. In addition to using trait labels to describe individual differences, some theorists also see traits as explanations: In their view, the trait is the property within the person that accounts for his or her unique but relatively stable reactions to stimuli. Thus, the trait becomes a construct to explain behavior—a hypothesized reason for enduring individual differences. Before looking at formal trait theories,

3.6 Describe the descriptive and explanatory uses of traits.

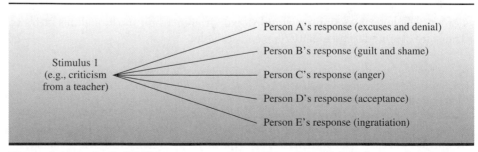

Figure 3.2 Individual differences in response to the same stimulus. The trait approach emphasizes consistent differences among people in their response to the same stimulus.

however, we should consider how traits are used informally by people in daily life. Indeed we are all trait theorists in the sense that we generate ideas about our own dispositions and the characteristics of other people.

Trait Attributions

When people describe each other in daily life, they spontaneously use trait terms. We all characterize each other (and ourselves) with such terms as aggressive, dependent, fearful, introverted, anxious, submissive—the list is almost endless. We see a person behaving in a particular way—for example, sitting at a desk for an hour yawning, and we attribute a trait, "unmotivated" or "lazy" or "bored" or "dull."

These simple trait attributions are often adequate to "explain" events for many everyday purposes in commonsense psychology (Heider, 1958; Kelley, 1973; Ross & Nisbett, 1991). In these commonsense explanations, traits are invoked not just as descriptions of what people do but also as the causes of their behavior. Thus in everyday practice, traits may be used first simply as adjectives describing behavior ("He behaves in a lazy way"), but the description is soon generalized from the behavior to the person ("He *is* lazy") and then abstracted to "He has a lazy disposition" or "He is unmotivated." These descriptions pose no problems as long as their basis is recalled—he is seen as behaving in a lazy way and no more. A hazard in trait attribution is that we easily forget that nothing is explained if the state *we* have attributed to the person from his behavior ("He has a trait of laziness") is now invoked as the *cause* of the behavior from which it was inferred. We then quickly emerge with the tautology, "He behaves in a lazy way because he has a lazy disposition," or because he is "unmotivated." The utility of trait terms therefore depends on their ability to make predictions about people's behaviors in a new situation based on their behaviors observed in the past in a different situation.

The trait approach to formal personality study begins with the commonsense conviction that personality can be described with trait terms. But it extends and refines those descriptions by arriving at them quantitatively and systematically. Efforts to explain individual differences by formal trait theories face some of the same problems that arise when traits are offered as causes by the layman. However, numerous safeguards have been developed to try to control some of these difficulties, as discussed in later sections.

Gordon Allport

One of the most outstanding trait psychologists was Gordon Allport, whose 1937 book *Personality: A Psychological Interpretation* launched the psychology of personality as a field and discipline. In this classic work and many later contributions, he made a convincing case that a distinctive field was needed, devoted to understanding the person as a coherent, consistent whole individual. His view of personality was broad and integrative, and he was sensitive and attentive to all its diverse aspects. Reacting against the tendency of researchers to study isolated part processes, such as learning and memory, in ways that failed to take account of individual differences, he wanted the field to pursue two goals. One was to understand the differences between people in personality; the other was to see how the different characteristics and processes (like learning, memory, and biological processes) that exist within an individual interact and function together in an integrated way. His vision underlies much of what is still the definition and main mission of personality psychology today, as discussed in the introduction of

3.7 In Allport's theory, what are the characteristics of traits, and how are they linked to basic psychological processes?

Gordon Allport (1897–1967)

this text. In particular, Allport's conception of traits continues to guide much of the work at the trait-dispositional level of analysis. In Allport's theory, traits have a very real existence: They are the ultimate realities of psychological organization. Allport favored a biophysical conception that

> *does not hold that every trait-name necessarily implies a trait; but rather that behind all confusion of terms, behind the disagreement of judges, and apart from errors and failures of empirical observation, there are none the less* bona fide *mental structures in each personality that account for the consistency of its behavior (1937, p. 289).*

According to Allport, traits are determining tendencies or predispositions to respond. In other words, a trait is

> *a generalized and focalized neuropsychic system (peculiar to the individual) with the capacity to render many stimuli functionally equivalent, and to initiate and guide consistent (equivalent) forms of adaptive and expressive behavior (1937, p. 295).*

Allport implied that traits are relatively general and enduring: they unite many responses to diverse stimuli, producing fairly broad consistencies in behavior. This relationship is seen in Figure 3.3.

Allport was convinced that some people have dispositions that influence most aspects of their behavior. He called these highly generalized dispositions **cardinal traits.** For example, if a person's whole life seems to be organized around goal achievement and the attainment of excellence, then achievement might be his or her cardinal trait. Less pervasive but still quite generalized dispositions are **central traits,** and

3.8 Differentiate between Allport's notions of cardinal and central traits. What is their relation to secondary dispositions?

Stimuli		Responses
1. Meeting a stranger		1. outgoing, pleasant
2. Working with peers	Trait: friendliness	2. helpful, encouraging
3. Visiting family		3. warm, interested
4. Dating a girlfriend		4. attentive, thoughtful

Figure 3.3 An example of a trait as the unifier of stimuli and responses.

Allport thought that many people are broadly influenced by central traits. Finally, more specific, narrow traits are called **secondary dispositions** or "attitudes."

Allport believed that one's pattern of dispositions or "personality structure" determines one's behavior. This emphasis on structure rather than environment or stimulus conditions is seen in his colorful phrase, "The same fire that melts the butter hardens the egg" (1937, p. 102). Allport was a pioneering spokesman for the importance of individual differences: No two people are completely alike, and hence no two people respond identically to the same event. Each person's behavior is determined by a particular **trait structure.**

Allport thought that traits never occur in any two people in exactly the same way: They operate in *unique* ways in each person. This conviction was consistent with his emphasis on the individuality and uniqueness of each personality. To the extent that any trait is unique within a person rather than common among many people, it cannot be studied by making comparisons among people. Consequently, Allport urged the thorough study of individuals through intensive and long-term case studies. He also believed, however, that because of shared experiences and common cultural influences, most persons tend to develop some *roughly* common kinds of traits: they can be compared on these common dispositions.

Many of Allport's theories were most relevant to the in-depth study of lives and experience rather than to the quantitative study of groups. He contributed to trait theory, but he was critical of many of the statistical methods and quantitative research strategies favored by other trait theorists. Nevertheless, his influence has been most important for the study of common "global" traits, for which he is still considered a model (Funder, 1991).

Raymond B. Cattell

Raymond B. Cattell (1950, 1965) is another important trait theorist. For Cattell, the trait is also the basic unit of study; it is a "mental structure," inferred from behavior, and a fundamental construct that accounts for behavioral regularity or consistency. Like Allport, Cattell distinguished between **common traits,** which are possessed by all people, and **unique traits,** which occur only in a particular person and cannot be found in another in exactly the same form.

Cattell also distinguished **surface traits** from **source traits** (see Table 3.1 for selected examples). Surface traits are clusters of overt or manifest trait elements (responses) that seem to go together. Source traits are the underlying variables that are the causal entities determining the surface manifestations. In research, trait elements (in the form of test responses or scores) are analyzed statistically until collections of

TABLE 3.1 Surface Traits and Source Traits Studied by Cattell

Examples of Surface Traits (Cattell, 1950)	Integrity, altruism—dishonesty, undependability Disciplined thoughtfulness—foolishness Thrift, tidiness, obstinacy—lability, curiosity, intuition
Examples of Source Traits (Cattell, 1965)	Ego strength—emotionality and neuroticism Dominance—submissiveness

Note: These are selected and abbreviated examples from much longer lists.

3.9 Describe Cattell's approach to identifying the structure of personality traits. What three types of data were used to discover source traits?

elements that correlate positively in all possible combinations are discovered. This procedure, according to Cattell, yields surface traits.

For Cattell, source traits can be found only by means of the mathematical technique of factor analysis (discussed below in this chapter). Using this technique, the investigator tries to estimate the factors or dimensions that appear to underlie surface variations in behavior. According to Cattell, the basic aim in research and assessment should be identification of source traits. In this view, these traits are divided between those that reflect environmental conditions (**environmental-mold traits**) and those that reflect constitutional factors (**constitutional traits**). Moreover, source traits may either be *general* (those affecting behavior in many different situations) or *specific*. Specific source traits are particularized sources of personality reaction that operate in one situation only, and Cattell pays little attention to them.

Cattell uses three kinds of data to discover general source traits: *life records,* in which everyday behavior situations are observed and rated; *self-ratings;* and *objective tests,* in which the person is observed in situations that are specifically designed to elicit

Raymond B. Cattell (1905–1998)

responses from which behavior in other situations can be predicted. The data from all three sources are subjected to factor analysis. In his own work, Cattell shows a preference for factor analysis of life-record data based on many behavior ratings for large samples of persons. Some 14 or 15 source traits have been reported from such investigations, but only six have been found repeatedly (Vernon, 1964).

In Cattell's system, traits may also be grouped into classes on the basis of how they are expressed. Those that are relevant to the individual's being "set into action" with respect to some goal are called **dynamic traits.** Those concerned with effectiveness in gaining the goal are **ability traits.** Traits concerned with energy or emotional reactivity are named **temperament traits.** Cattell has speculated extensively about the relationships between various traits and the development of personality (1965).

Hans J. Eysenck

The extensive researches of Hans Eysenck have complemented the work of the American trait theorists in many important ways. Eysenck (1961, 1991) has extended the search for personality dimensions to the area of abnormal behavior, studying such traits as *neuroticism–emotional stability.* He also has investigated *introversion–extraversion* as a dimensional trait (although Carl Jung originally proposed "introvert" and "extravert" as personality *types*). Eysenck and his associates have pursued an elaborate and sophisticated statistical methodology in their investigations of these personality dimensions. In addition to providing a set of descriptive dimensions, Eysenck and his colleagues have studied the associations between people's positions on these dimensions and their scores on a variety of other personality and intellectual measures, and developed an influential model of personality designed to account for the roots of these traits in ways that connect to the biological level of analysis, and will be considered in those sections of the text.

3.10 According to Eysenck, which two trait dimensions can be used to describe individual differences in personality?

Hans J. Eysenck (1916–1997)

Eysenck emphasized that his dimension of introversion–extraversion is based entirely on research and "must stand and fall by empirical confirmation" (Eysenck & Rachman, 1965, p. 19). In his words:

> *The typical extravert is sociable, likes parties, has many friends, needs to have people to talk to, and does not like reading or studying by himself. He craves excitement, takes chances, often sticks his neck out, acts on the spur of the moment, and is generally an impulsive individual. He is fond of practical jokes, always has a ready answer, and generally likes change; he is carefree, easygoing, optimistic, and 'likes to laugh and be merry.' He prefers to keep moving and doing things, tends to be aggressive and loses his temper quickly; altogether his feelings are not kept under tight control, and he is not always a reliable person.*

> *The typical introvert is a quiet, retiring sort of person, introspective, fond of books rather than people; he is reserved and distant except to intimate friends. He tends to plan ahead, 'looks before he leaps,' and mistrusts the impulse of the moment. He does not like excitement, takes matters of everyday life with proper seriousness, and likes a well-ordered mode of life. He keeps his feelings under close control, seldom behaves in an aggressive manner, and does not lose his temper easily. He is reliable, somewhat pessimistic and places great value on ethical standards.*

Eysenck and his colleagues recognized that these descriptions may sound almost like caricatures because they portray "perfect" extraverts and introverts, while in fact most people are mixtures who fall in the middle rather than at the extremes of the dimensions (see Figure 3.4). As Figure 3.4 shows, Eysenck suggested that the second

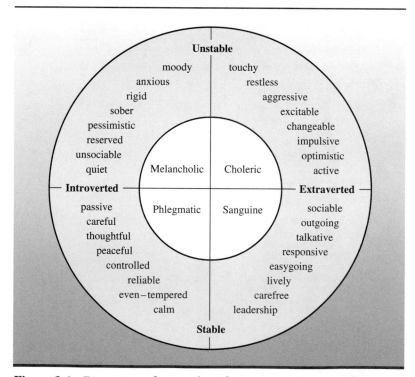

Figure 3.4 Dimensions of personality. The inner ring shows the "four temperaments" of Hippocrates; the outer ring shows the results of modern factor analytic studies of the intercorrelations between traits by Eysenck and others (Eysenck & Rachman, 1965).

**TABLE 3.2 Sexual Activities Reported by Introverted (I) and
Extraverted (E) Students[a]**

		Males		Females	
Activity		I	E	I	E
Masturbation at present		86	72	47	39
Petting: at seventeen		16	40	15	24
at nineteen		3	56	30	47
at present		57	78	62	76
Coitus (intercourse): at seventeen		5	21	4	8
at nineteen		15	45	12	29
at present		47	77	42	71
Median frequency of coitus per month (sexually active students only)		3.0	5.5	3.1	7.5
Coitus partners in the last twelve months (unmarried students only)	One	75	46	72	60
	Two or more	18	30	25	23
	Four or more	7	25	4	17

[a] The numbers are the frequencies of endorsements by each group.

Source: Based on data from Giese, H. & Schmidt, S. (1968). *Studenten sexualitat.* Hamburg: Rowohlt; cited in Eysenck, H. J. (1973). Personality and the law of effect. In D. E. Berlyne & K. B. Madsen (Eds.), *Pleasure, reward, preference,* New York: Academic Press.

major dimension of personality is **emotional stability** or **neuroticism.** This dimension describes at one end people who tend to be moody, touchy, anxious, restless, and so on. At the other extreme are people who are characterized by such terms as stable, calm, carefree, even-tempered, and reliable. As Eysenck stressed, the ultimate value of these dimensions will depend on the research support they receive.

To clarify the meaning of both dimensions, Eysenck and his associates have studied the relations between people's positions on them and their scores on many other measures. An example of the results found is summarized in Table 3.2, which shows self-reported differences in the sexual activities of extraverts and introverts (reported in Eysenck, 1973). As expected, the extraverts generally reported earlier, more frequent, and more varied sexual experiences. While the groups differed on the average, there was still considerable overlap, making it difficult to predict any particular individual's behavior from her introversion–extraversion score alone. But the results of many studies of this type provide an increasingly comprehensive picture of Eysenck's dimensions. In addition, Eysenck's ideas are notable in stimulating a search for the biological foundations of dispositions.

▶ COMMON FEATURES OF TRAIT THEORIES

Now consider the principal common characteristics of trait approaches.

Inferring Traits from Behavioral Signs

In the search for dispositions, one always *infers* traits from behavior—for example, from what people say about themselves on a questionnaire. The person's responses or behaviors are taken as *indicators* of underlying traits. The trait approach to personality is a "sign" approach in the sense that there is no interest in the test behavior itself. That is, test responses are of value not in their own right but only as *signs* of the traits that underlie them; test behavior is always used as a sign of nontest behavior (Loevinger, 1957). Thus, the interest is not in answers on an inventory or IBM score sheet for their

3.11 From what kinds of observations are traits inferred?

own sake, but only in these responses to a test as cues or signs of dispositions. It is therefore essential to demonstrate the relation between test behaviors and the traits they supposedly represent.

Traits are inferred from questionnaires, ratings, and other reports about the person's dispositions. Usually, these self-reports are taken as direct signs of the relevant dispositions. For example, the more often you rate yourself as aggressive, the more you are assumed to have an aggressive disposition. So the relationship between what is sampled and the inferred trait is *direct* and *additive:* the more frequently a behavioral tendency is reported or described, the greater the amount of the underlying disposition.

Generality and Stability of Traits

3.12 What is the importance of behavioral consistency in trait theories?

Trait theorists often have disagreed about the specific content and structure of the basic traits needed to describe personality, but their general conceptions have much similarity and they remain popular (Funder, 1991). They all use the trait to account for consistencies in an individual's behavior and to explain why persons respond differently to the same stimulus. Most view traits as dispositions that determine such behaviors. Each differentiates between relatively superficial traits (e.g., Cattell's surface traits) and more basic, underlying traits (e.g., Cattell's source traits). Each recognizes that traits vary in breadth or generality. Allport puts the strongest emphasis on the relative generality of common traits across many situations. Each theorist also admits trait fluctuations, or changes in a person's position with respect to a disposition. At the same time, each is committed to a search for relatively broad, stable traits.

Traits and States Distinguished

3.13 How does an anger state differ from an anger trait?

It is one thing to be irascible, quite another thing to be angry, just as an anxious temper *is different from* feeling anxiety. *Not all men who are sometimes anxious are of an anxious temperament, nor are those who have an anxious temperament always feeling anxious. In the same way there is a difference between intoxication and habitual drunkenness* . . .

Cicero (45 B.C.)

This ancient wisdom (quoted in Chaplin, John, & Goldberg, 1988) is used by modern trait theorists to illustrate a distinction that is often made, both intuitively and by trait psychologists, between *traits* and *states* (Chaplin, John, & Goldberg, 1988; Eysenck, 1983). Both traits and states are terms that refer to the perceived attributes of people. Both refer to categories that have fuzzy boundaries, and both are based on prototypes or ideal exemplars (e.g., Cantor & Mischel, 1979). The difference between them is that prototypic traits are seen as enduring, stable qualities of the person over long time periods and as internally caused. In contrast, prototypic states refer to qualities that are only brief in duration and attributable to external causes, such as the momentary situation (Chaplin, John, & Goldberg, 1988). Examples of terms that people tend to classify as traits are gentle, domineering, and timid, while terms like infatuated, uninterested, and displeased tend to be seen as states.

Search for Basic Traits

Guided by the assumption that stable dispositions exist, trait psychologists try to identify the individual's position on one or more dimensions (such as neuroticism, extraversion). They do this by comparing people tested under standardized conditions. They believe that positions on these dimensions are relatively stable across testing situations and over long time periods. Their main emphasis in the study of personality is the development of instruments that can accurately tap the person's underlying traits. Less attention has been paid to the effects of environmental conditions on traits and behavior. The search for traits, and for useful ways to measure them, in modern personality psychology has a long history, and it began in response to urgent practical considerations at the time of the first world war, as was discussed in Chapter 2.

Quantification

A main feature of the trait approach has been its methodology, and you saw many examples in Chapter 2 of self-report questionnaires and ratings by self and others. This methodology is "psychometric" in the sense that it attempts to measure individual differences and to quantify them. Psychometricians study persons and groups on trait dimensions by comparing their scores on tests. To do this, they sample many people, compare large groups under uniform testing conditions, and devise statistical techniques to infer basic traits. Their methods over the years have become increasingly sophisticated and effective for meeting a wide range of measurement goals (e.g., Jackson & Paunonen, 1980; John, 1990).

Aggregating Across Situations to Increase Reliability

Although they acknowledge that the situation is important, many psychologists working at the trait level are convinced that past research has underestimated the personal constancies in behavior. They point out that if we want to test how well a disposition (trait) can be used to predict behavior, we have to sample adequately not only the disposition but also the behavior that we want to predict (Ajzen & Fishbein, 1977; Block, 1977; Epstein, 1979, 1983). Yet in the past, researchers often attempted to predict single acts (for example, physical aggression when insulted) from a dispositional measure (e.g., self-rated aggression on a personality scale). Generally, such attempts did not succeed. But while measures of traits may not be able to predict such single acts, they may do much better if one uses a *"multiple act criterion"*: a pooled combination of many behaviors that are relevant to the trait, and a pooled combination of many raters (e.g., McCrae & Costa, 1985, 1987).

The methods and results of this line of research are illustrated in a study in which undergraduate women were given the "dominance scale" from two personality inventories (Jaccard, 1974). The women also were asked whether or not they had performed a set of 40 dominance-related behaviors. For example, did they initiate a discussion in class, argue with a teacher, ask a male out on a date. The dominance scales from the personality inventories did not predict the individual behaviors well. But the researcher found that when the 40 behavioral items were summed into one pooled measure, they related substantially to the personality scores. Namely, women high on the dominance scales also tended to report performing more dominant behaviors, and the reverse was also true. Thus a longer, aggregated, and therefore more reliable behavioral measure revealed associations to other measures (the self-reports on the personality tests) that would not otherwise have been seen. Similar results were found when the behaviors were measured directly by observation (e.g., Weigel & Newman, 1976).

In the same direction, it has been shown that reliability will increase when the number of items in a test sample is increased and combined. Making this point, Epstein (1979) demonstrated that temporal stability (of, for example, self-reported

3.14 How did the Jaccard and Epstein studies illustrate the importance of aggregating behaviors to improve correlations between trait measures and behavior?

emotions and experiences recorded daily, and observer judgments) becomes much larger when it is based on averages over many days than when it is based on only single items on single days. His demonstrations also indicate that even when one cannot predict what an individual will do in a specific situation, it is often possible to predict the person's overall standing relative to other people when the behaviors are aggregated (combined) across many situations (Epstein, 1983).

▶ TAXONOMY OF HUMAN ATTRIBUTES

A widely shared goal is to find a universal taxonomy or classification system for sorting the vast array of human attributes into a relatively small set of fundamental dimensions or categories on which most individual differences can be described. From this perspective, researchers attempt to identify "the most important individual differences in mankind" (Goldberg, 1973, p. 1).

Psycholexical Approach

3.15 Describe the assumptions underlying the psycholexical approach to identifying the major traits that underlie personality.

Researchers in this approach assume that the most significant individual differences—those that are most important in daily human relationships—enter into the natural language of the culture as single-word trait terms. They use a variety of methods to identify basic trait terms in the language and to categorize them into smaller groupings. This is an enormous classification task, given that English includes thousands of trait terms (over 18,000 in one count of the dictionary). The researchers hope that an extensive, well-organized vocabulary for describing human attributes in trait terms will lead to better theories of personality and better methods of personality assessment. This research strategy is called the **psycholexical approach.** Its basic data are the words in the natural language that describe human qualities. In these studies, many people are asked to rate how well each of many trait terms describes or fits a particular person they know well. In some studies, this is a peer; in some studies, participants rate how well the words describe them. In each study, the results are then analyzed to see which sets of trait terms tend to cluster or "go together" when individuals are described. Using statistical procedures called factor analysis, the researchers try to specify a small number of factors or dimensions that seem to capture the common element among adjectives that are closely associated (e.g., Goldberg, 1990).

This approach is illustrated in a comprehensive taxonomy of the **domain of interpersonal behavior** (Wiggins, 1979, 1980) that yielded the dimensions shown in Figure 3.5. Note that each dimension is bipolar, that is, has two opposite ends or poles. The dimensions are structured in a circular pattern like a pie. Each pole is made up of a set of adjectives so that *Ambitious (Dominant),* for example, is defined with such terms as persevering, persistent, industrious. The opposite pole, *Lazy (Submissive),* includes such terms as unproductive, unthorough, unindustrious. Wiggins reports that these dimensions fit well the results of earlier descriptions of the interpersonal domain (Leary, 1957). They seem to be reasonably robust and useful when different samples of people are rated on them and continue to be revised and refined (Wiggins, Phillips, & Trapnell, 1989).

The "Big Five" Trait Dimensions

For many years in the long search for a "universal taxonomy" of traits, researchers disagreed actively as to which personality dimensions they should use to describe personality. Some proposed as many as 16; others, as few as two or three (Vernon, 1964).

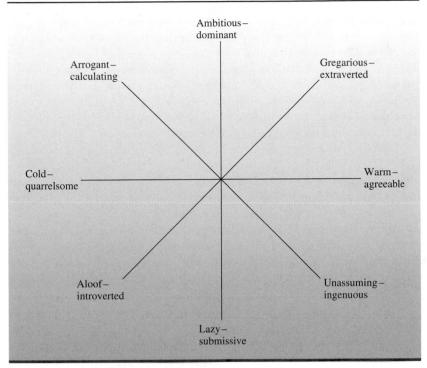

Figure 3.5 Wiggins' (1980) taxonomy of the interpersonal domain.
Source: Wiggins, J. S. A psychological taxonomy of trait-descriptive terms: The interpersonal domain. *Journal of Personality and Social Psychology, 37,* 399, fig. 2. © 1979 by the American Psychological Association. Reprinted with permission.

More recently, however, consensus has grown among many researchers to focus on five dimensions of personality (Goldberg, 1991; John, 1990; McCrae & Costa, 1985, 1987, 1999) that emerge from ratings using English-language trait adjectives. These dimensions are found by using the method of factor analysis, and we consider that method next and then turn to its findings.

Factor Analysis to Find Dimensions: The NEO-PI-R

Trait terms number in the thousands, as a look at the dictionary makes clear. But they have to be simplified and organized to become manageable units for describing people systematically. Consider, for example, the mass of data yielded by responses to a self-report measure with 550 items answered by 100 persons. To extract order from such a stack of facts, investigators searching for underlying traits try to group responses into more basic clusters. For this purpose, many trait psychologists turn to **factor analysis.** This is a mathematical procedure that helps to sort test responses into relatively homogeneous clusters of items that are highly correlated. Working in the psycholexical approach, a number of researchers have reached reasonable agreement about the five types of dimensions or factors on which English trait terms may be clustered, often called the "Big Five Structure" (e.g., Goldberg, 1991; John, 1990).

These dimensions emerged from mathematical analyses of the responses with the method of factor analysis. Factor analysis is a very useful tool for reducing a large set of correlated measures to fewer unrelated or independent dimensions. As such, it can be a powerful aid to psychological research by clarifying which response patterns go together. Suppose, for example, that 50 students have answered 10 personality questionnaires, each of which contains 100 questions. A factor analysis of this mass of information can show which parts of the test performances go together. It essentially finds and connects the items that tend to "go together" (covary) with each of the other items in the total set. The analogy would be a procedure that allows you to go to a stack of several hundred unsorted books in the library and that finds and groups together those that are alike on certain dimensions (e.g., size, color, length, language, content areas) but different in other respects. Factor analysis, however, does not necessarily reveal the basic traits of persons any more than it reveals the nature of the knowledge in the library sample you are sorting. The results depend on what is put into the procedures, such as the test items and the people selected by the researcher, and on the details of his or her procedures and decisions.

As has long been recognized (Overall, 1964), factor analysis cannot establish which characteristics of persons or things being measured are "real" or "primary." The factors obtained are simply names given to the correlations found among the particular measures. In other words, factor analysis yields a greatly simplified patterning of the data put into it. However, it cannot go beyond the limitations of the original tests or measures. And what comes out of the analysis depends on many decisions by the investigator (e.g., in the type of factor analysis he or she conducts). Consequently, while the factor analytic search for hypothesized underlying traits may yield mathematically pure factors, their psychological meaningfulness and relevance for the person's actual behavior has to be demonstrated.

3.16 How was factor analysis used to identify the Big Five traits that are thought by some theorists to describe personality? Describe the five factors using the acronym OCEAN to capture their first letters.

The factor analytic approach to describing trait dimensions is illustrated in a series of pioneering factor analytic studies (Norman, 1961, 1963; Tupes & Christal, 1958, 1961). These studies investigated the factors obtained for diverse samples of people rated by their peers on rating scales. The scales themselves came from a condensed version of the thousands of trait names originally identified by Allport and Odbert's search many years earlier for trait names in the dictionary. After much research, 20 scales were selected and many judges were asked to rate other people on them. The results were carefully factor analyzed. The same set of five relatively independent factors appeared consistently across several studies and continues to form the basis of what has become the **Big Five Structure** (e.g., John, 1990; Goldberg, 1992). It consists of five factors measured with a personality inventory now called the **NEO-PI-R** (Costa & McCrae, 1997), as shown in Table 3.3.

The Big Five Factors include: Neuroticism (N), for example, worrying and insecurity; Extraversion (E) or surgency (positive emotionality), as reflected by terms like friendly, talkative; **Openness to experience (O); Agreeableness (A);** and **Conscientiousness (C).** See Table 3.3 for descriptions of each factor. In the NEO-PI-R, each factor is also more finely described in terms of a number of different facets through which the particular super trait may be expressed, illustrated in Table 3.4.

The Big Five resemble the dimensions initially proposed by Norman (1963) and found repeatedly in research, although sometimes given slightly different names. Each dimension includes a collection of bipolar rating scales, such as "calm–worrying" and "timid–bold," that refer to types of feelings or behaviors. For each dimension, Table 3.3 gives examples of the adjectives describing the two ends of some of the rating scales used.

To illustrate the type of research that underlies the development of the Big Five, in one study, 187 college students rated how well each of 1,710 trait terms described him or her (Goldberg, 1991). Statistical analysis showed that these terms clustered into five major factors or dimensions much like the Big Five (McCrae & Costa, 1987). Thus, when people are described with trait terms like those shown in Table 3.3, a reliable clustering occurs consisting of five large descriptive categories or "super traits." This Big Five Structure seems to characterize major dimensions of personality in natural

TABLE 3.3   The Big Five Factors and Illustrative Components

Factor (Trait Dimension)	Adjective Items[a]
I. **Neuroticism (N)** (negative emotions, e.g., anxiety, depression)	Calm — worrying Unemotional — emotional Secure — insecure Not envious — jealous
II. **Extraversion (E)** (versus introversion)	Quiet — talkative Aloof — friendly Inhibited — spontaneous Timid — bold
III. **Openness to Experience** (versus closed-minded)	Conventional — original Unadventurous — daring Conforming — independent Unartistic — artistic
IV. **Agreeableness (A)** (versus antagonism)	Irritable — good-natured Uncooperative — helpful Suspicious — trusting Critical — lenient
V. **Conscientiousness (C)** (versus undirectedness)	Careless — careful Helpless — self-reliant Lax — scrupulous Weak-willed — goal-directed

[a] Illustrative adjectives describing the two ends of the scales that comprise the dimension.

Source: Adapted from McCrae, R. R., & Costa, P. T., Jr. (1987). Validation of the five-factor model of personality across instruments and observers. *Journal of Personality and Social Psychology, 52,* 81–90. Essentially similar results were found in John, O. P. (1990). The big-five factor taxonomy: Dimensions of personality in the natural language and questionnaires. In L. A. Pervin (Ed.), *Handbook of personality: Theory and research* (pp. 66–100). New York: Guilford Press; and in Normak, W. T. (1963). Toward an adequate taxonomy of personality attributes: Replicated factor structure in peer nomination personality ratings. *Journal of Abnormal and Social Psychology, 66,* 574–583.

English-language words. A number of personality trait questionnaires and personality ratings using these types of trait terms provide descriptions of persons that seem to fit the Big Five reasonably (Costa & McCrae, 1992a; Costa, McCrae, & Dye, 1991).

Considerable stability has been demonstrated on trait ratings and questionnaires related to the Big Five (e.g., McCrae & Costa, 1990) even for long time spans. Stability tends to be particularly high during the adult years (Costa & McCrae, 1997; McCrae & Costa, 1999). It is notable that in spite of the many changes that often occur in life structures during adulthood over long time periods — including the changes produced

3.17   How stable are the Big Five dimensions over time?

TABLE 3.4   Illustrative Facet Scales for the Big Five Factor

Neuroticism: anxiety, angry hostility, depression, impulsiveness, vulnerability

Extraversion: warmth, gregariousness, assertiveness, activity, excitement-seeking positive emotions

Openness to Experience: fantasy, aesthetics, feelings, actions, ideas, values

Agreeableness: trust, straightforwardness, altruism, compliance, modesty, tender-mindedness

Conscientiousness: competence, order, dutifulness, achievement, striving, self-discipline, deliberation

Source: Reproduced by special permission of the Publisher, Psychological Assessment Resources, Inc., 16204 North Florida Avenue, Lutz, Florida 33549, from *The NEO Personality Inventory-Revised,* by Paul Costa, and Robert McCrae, Copyright 1978, 1985, 1989, 1992 by PAR, Inc. Further reproduction is prohibited without permission of PAR, Inc.

TABLE 3.5   Stability of NEO-PI Scales (Ages 25–56)

NEO-PI Scale	Men	Women
N (Neuroticism)	.78	.85
E (Extraversion)	.84	.75
O (Open-minded)	.87	.84
A (Agreeable)	.64	.60
C (Conscientiousness)	.83	.84

Note: Retest interval is 6 years for N, E, and O scales, 3 years for short forms of A and C scales.

Source: Adapted from *Personality in Adulthood* (p. 88), by R. R. McCrae and P. T. Costa Jr., 1990, New York: Guilford.

by marriage, children, divorce, residential and occupational moves, and health issues—the status of most individuals on the Big Five dimensions tends to show high stability (see Table 3.5)

Supportive Evidence for the Five-Factor Model

3.18 Cite four lines of evidence for the generality of the Five Factor Model.

An explosion of research has provided extensive empirical documentation for the robustness of the Five Factor Model, or Big Five. The kinds of evidence that has accumulated is impressive (e.g., McCrae & Costa, 1997, 1999; McCrae, et al., 1998), and too large to summarize beyond the general conclusions to which it leads:

- The Big Five Factor Structure has often been replicated in research by diverse investigators using a variety of English-speaking samples.
- Especially the N, E, and A factors listed in Table 3.3 have been found to replicate well even when the languages, cultures, and item formats used differ. Replicability has been reported for diverse languages and language families that span Sino-Tibetan, Uraic, Hamito-Semitic, and Malayon-Polynesian.
- Overall, the results are impressive and broadly generalizable across diverse cultures (McCrae et al., 1998), although unsurprisingly some of the factors may take different forms in different samples and cultures.
- The factor structure of individuals as described by this model tends to be relatively stable in adults over long periods of time.

In sum, the total evidence is impressive for the broad robustness and potential universality of this taxonomy as a comprehensive descriptive system for describing people in trait terms at a broad, highly abstract "super trait" level. The value of having such a robust and comprehensive trait "map" for describing and comparing people is considerable and it is widely recognized (e,g., MacDonald, 1998).

The Big Five dimensions offer a useful replicable taxonomy of trait terms, potentially not only in the English language but across diverse languages (Costa & McCrae, 1997; DeRaad, Perugini, Hrebickova, & Szarota, 1998; McCrae et al., 1998). Its focus on language as the route for identifying what humans care about with regard to personality makes good sense. It is based on the idea that the languages people develop contain clusters of trait terms that go together and that reflect what they care about when they describe and evaluate other people and themselves (Saucier & Goldberg, 1996). Factor analysis has been used effectively to identify these clusters, and they provide a robust view of personality qualities that matter to people importantly in everyday life.

At the same time, the limitations of the model also are being expressed (e.g., McAdams, 1992). The deepest concern is the one stated by Block (1995, 2001; Pervin, 2003). While himself a major contributor to the trait-dispositional level of personality, Block calls attention to the fact that labeling a person's position (e.g., low on "conscientiousness") with regard to the Big Five, or on any other descriptive taxonomy, does not itself provide an understanding of the personality processes that underlie and account for the labeled phenomena, and that need to be clarified.

Stability of Traits over Time

Are a person's qualities stable? Do early characteristics predict later qualities? When parents say "Fred was always so friendly, even as a little baby," are their comments justified? Can we predict the six-year-old's behavior from responses in the first year of life? Is there much continuity in the qualities and behaviors of the child throughout childhood? Research has made it clear that although behavior depends on context, and the same person may be quite different in very different contexts, there also is significant trait stability over time, particularly after the first few years of life.

3.19 At what point does temporal stability begin to emerge, and which behaviors show stability?

Many important connections have been found over time in the life course. For example, lower sensitivity to touch on the skin in the newborn predicted more mature communications and coping at age two and one-half and at age seven and one-half. High touch sensitivity and high respiration rates at birth were related to low interest, low participation, lower assertiveness, and less communicativeness in later years (Bell, Weller, & Waldrop, 1971; Halverson, 1971a, 1971b). But these links between newborn and later behaviors were exceptions, and the associations that were found generally were not strong. So there are some connections between a newborn's qualities and characteristics later in life, but in the individual case, one could not predict confidently from responses at birth to later characteristics:

> To use an analogy, newborn behavior is more like a preface to a book than a table of its contents yet to be unfolded. Further, the preface is itself merely a rough draft undergoing rapid revision. There are some clues to the nature of the book in the preface, but these are in code form and taking them as literally prophetic is likely to lead to disappointment (Bell et al., 1971, p. 132).

As one progresses beyond the "preface of the book" to the first few chapters (to the early years of life), continuities in development do become increasingly evident (Block & Block, 1980; McCrae & Costa, 1996; Mischel et al., 1989). Children who are seen as more active, assertive, aggressive, competitive, outgoing, and so on at age three years are also more likely to be described as having more of those qualities later in development, for example. In sum, the specific links between qualities of the child, say in the fourth year and in the eighth year, may be complex and indirect. But a thorough analysis of the patterns indicates that significant threads of continuity do emerge over time (Caspi, 1987, 1998). Thus childhood characteristics may be connected coherently to later behavior and attributes to some degree (Arend, Gove, & Sroufe, 1979; Block, 1971; Mischel et al., 1989). Experiences in the early pages of the book affect what happens in the later pages, although these early experiences do not prevent the possibility of genuine changes later. The amount of stability or change over time varies for different types of characteristics and different types of experiences at different points in development (Caspi, 1998; Caspi & Bem, 1990).

To illustrate with one concrete example, studies of lives over many years indicate that "ill-tempered boys become ill-tempered men" (Caspi & Bem, 1990, p. 568). These continuities in development reflect the fact that stable qualities of the individual, whether adaptive (such as the ability and willingness to delay gratification), or aversive and maladaptive (such as inappropriate displays of temper), can have profound "chain effects" that quickly accelerate. Beginning early in life, they can trigger long sequences of interconnected events that impact on the person's subsequent opportunities and options, often greatly limiting them. As Caspi and Bem note, a child's ill temper rapidly produces trouble in school, which in turn makes school a negative experience, which provokes the school authorities and can lead to expulsion, which permanently limits occupational opportunities and constrains the future. The unhappy network of consequences is illustrated in Figure 3.6.

The network of outcomes associated with early ill-temperedness is broader than just school and career. For example, Bem and Caspi reported that almost half of the men (46 percent) with a history of ill-tempered behavior as children were divorced by age forty while only 22 percent of the other men studied were divorced at that age.

3.20 What is the temporal stability of results derived from self-descriptions and ratings?

Taken collectively, studies of individual differences on trait dimensions after early childhood have produced many networks of meaningful correlations. These associations tend to be large and enduring when people rate themselves or others with broad trait terms (e.g., Block, 1971; Caspi & Bem, 1990; Costa & McCrae, 1988; E. L. Kelly, 1955). Such ratings suggest significant continuity and stability in how people are perceived over the years as well as in how they perceive themselves. For example, long-term stability was shown using rating methods in some early landmark studies that closely followed children into adulthood (Block, 1971), as summarized in Table 3.6. It is also high on many personality trait inventories, and ranges on average from median correlations of .34 to .77 (Costa & McCrae, 1997).

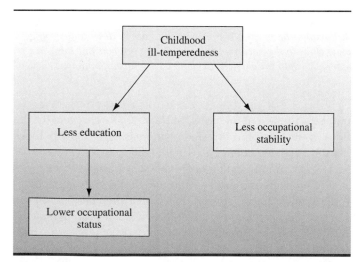

Figure 3.6   Some long-term outcomes associated with childhood ill-temperedness. Statistically significant correlations are shown. Data are for 45 men from middle-class origins.

Source: Figure and data adapted from "Moving against the world: Life-course patterns of explosive children," by A. Caspi, G. H. Elder, Jr. and D. J. Bem (1987). *Developmental Psychology, 23,* pp. 308–313.

TABLE 3.6   Examples of Significant Stability over Time in Ratings of Personality

	Correlations From		Item Rated
	Junior to Senior H. S.	Senior H. S. to Adulthood	
Males	.57	.59	Tends toward undercontrol of needs and impulses; unable to delay gratification
	.58	.53	Is genuinely dependable and responsible person
	.50	.42	Is self-defeating
Females	.50	.46	Basically submissive
	.48	.49	Tends to be rebellious, nonconforming
	.39	.43	Emphasizing being with others, gregarious

Source: Based on Block J. (1971). *Lives through time*. Berkeley, CA: Bancroft.

When ongoing behavior in specific situations is sampled objectively by different, independent measures, however, the association generally tends to be much more modest. Thus while people often show consistency on questionnaires and ratings, these data may not very accurately predict their actual behavior, as has been noted even by advocates of trait level analysis (Funder, 2001). Therefore, one has to be cautious about generalizing from a person's personality test behavior, including the robust and well-established measures of the Big Five, to his or her behavior outside the test.

Links Between Perceiver and Perceived: Valid Ratings

One enduring concern about the factors that have emerged from trait ratings was that they may reflect the social stereotypes and concepts of the judges rather than the trait organization of the rated persons. Mulaik (1964), for example, conducted three separate factor analytic studies, using many trait-rating scales, to determine the degree to which the method reveals the subject's personality factors as opposed to the rater's conceptual factors. The judges in one study rated real persons on the scales, including family members, close acquaintances, and themselves. In a second study, they rated stereotypes like "suburban housewife," "mental patient," and "Air Force general." The raters in the third study rated the "meaning" of 20 trait words. There was much similarity between the factors found for ratings of real persons and those found for ratings of stereotypes and words. Results like these led many investigators to conclude that personality factors that emerge from ratings may reflect the raters' conceptual categories rather than the traits of the subjects being judged (Mischel, 1968; Peterson, 1968).

It is quite possible that raters' stereotypes and preconceptions enter into these ratings, and it is also the case that different investigators may arrive at somewhat different views of trait organization. Nevertheless, a few basic trait dimensions have been found over and over again, as the evidence for the Big Five makes clear. And, most importantly, the characterizations of people on these dimensions, based on ratings by peers, reasonably agree with the self-ratings of the rated individuals themselves

3.21 What evidence exists that trait ratings may be influenced by stereotypes and preconceptions? Cite research evidence that trait ratings can nonetheless predict independent behavior ratings reflecting the same traits.

(e.g., McCrae & Costa, 1987). Thus, even if stereotypes and oversimplifications enter into these judgments, as they probably do, they are made reliably, shared widely, and seem significantly linked to qualities of the rated persons (Funder & Colvin, 1997).

In sum, there has been extensive debate about the limitations and usefulness of trait ratings (e.g., Block, 1995; Block, Weiss, & Thorne, 1979; Pervin, 1994; Romer & Revelle, 1984; Shweder, 1975). Nevertheless, it is clear that the descriptions of people obtained from different raters in different contexts often agree with each other. This basic conclusion was reached more than four decades ago and still stands. To illustrate, in one classic study, agreement was found between peer judgments on dimensions of aggressive and dependent behavior and separate behavior ratings of actual aggressive and dependent behavior (Winder & Wiggins, 1964). Participants were first classified into high, intermediate, and low groups on aggression and dependency on the basis of their peer reputations. Separate behavior ratings made later indicated that the three groups differed from each other significantly in the amount of aggression and dependency they displayed in an experimental situation. Similarly, college students were preselected as extremely high or low in aggressiveness (on the basis of ratings by their peers). They tended to be rated in similar ways by independent judges who observed their interaction (Gormly & Edelberg, 1974). Thus, there are linkages between a rater's trait constructs and the behavior of people he or she rates (e.g., Funder & Colvin, 1997; Jackson & Paunonen, 1980; McCrae & Costa, 1987; Mischel, 1984).

Personality Judgments to Predict Behavior

Do trait judgments reflect the constructs of perceivers rather than the behavior of the perceived? What are the links between the perceiver's judgments of what people "are like" and the behaviors that those people actually display? Some theorists argue that personality structure exists "all in the head" of the perceiver (Shweder, 1975). Others believe it is "all in the person" perceived (Epstein, 1977; Funder & Colvin, 1997). Still others favor the view that it depends both on the beliefs of observers and on the characteristics of the observed (e.g., Cantor & Mischel, 1979; Magnusson & Endler, 1977; Mischel, 1984). They believe that ratings may be influenced by the rater's expectations but have roots in the behavior of the perceived.

For many years, most researchers studied either the judgments of the perceiver or the behavior of the perceived; they rarely considered the fit between the two. One study tried to relate observers' overall judgments of children's aggressiveness (and other traits) to the children's independently coded actual behavior (Mischel, 1984; Wright & Mischel, 1987). Specifically, their trait-related acts were recorded during repeated observation periods on 15 separate occasions distributed across three camp situations during a summer. Examples of behaviors coded as aggressive are: "I'm gonna punch your face" or "Let's go beat up . . ." or lifting a dog by his collar and choking him.

The question was: Do raters' judgments of the child's overall aggression relate to the actual frequency of the child's aggressive acts as coded by other independent observers? The results clearly answered the question: Yes. Thus, children who are rated by independent observers as more aggressive, actually tend to be aggressive more frequently. For instance, they yell and provoke more. These differences, however, were seen primarily only in certain situations, namely in those stressful situations that greatly taxed or strained the competencies of the children. In sum, personality judgments seem to have links to the judged person's actual behavior, although that behavior may be visible only in certain types of situations in which the relevant individual differences emerge.

In sum, the findings discussed so far indicate that trait ratings involve judgments that are widely shared about characteristics of people that often are stable over time and that are expressed in behavior in different types of situations. Given that these judgments are widely made in everyday life and can have important consequences, it also becomes interesting to ask how such judgments of what someone (or something) "is like" are made, and that question is addressed in In Focus 3.2.

IN FOCUS 3.2

PROTOTYPES: "TYPICAL" PEOPLE

Psychologists concerned with the classification of human attributes also try to identify how we judge the **prototypicality** or "typicality" of different members of a category, whether it is a trait category, such as one of the Big Five, or an everyday, "natural" category, such as the category "birds." To demonstrate the idea of typicality to yourself, think of the most typical, representative, or "birdlike" bird. You probably will think of a bird that is something like a robin or sparrow—not a chicken or an ostrich. The point is simply that some members of a category (in this case, birds) are better or more typical examples of a category: Some reds are "redder" than others, some chairs are more chair-like than others. This point has been elegantly documented for everyday categories of natural objects like furniture (Rosch, Mervis, Gray, Johnson, & Boyce-Braem, 1976). Thus natural categories may be organized around *prototypical* examples (the best examples of the concept), with less prototypical or less good members forming a continuum away from the central one (Rosch, 1975; Tversky, 1977).

The important point here is that trait categories, like other categories, often are not well-defined, distinct, nonoverlapping categories in which each member of a category has all its defining features. (While many birds sing, not all do, and some nonbirds surely do.) Well-defined, nonoverlapping categories are built into artificial, logical systems, but they are rare in the real world. If we turn from the abstract world of logic and formal, artificial systems to common, everyday categories—to furniture, birds, and clothing—the categories become "fuzzy." As the philosopher Wittgenstein (1953) first pointed out, the members of common, everyday categories do not all share all of a set of single, essential features critical for category membership. If you closely examine a set of natural objects all labeled by one general term (like "birds") you will not find a single set of features that all members of the category share: Rather, a *pattern* of overlapping similarities—a *family resemblance* structure—seems to emerge.

"Typicality" and "family resemblance" and "fuzziness" also may characterize everyday judgments about categories of people (Cantor & Mischel, 1979; Cantor, Mischel, & Schwartz, 1982; Chaplin, John, & Goldberg, 1988; John, 1990). When making these judgments while forming our everyday impressions of people, we seem able to agree about who is a more or less typical or even "ideal" kind of personality, just as we agree that a robin is a more birdlike bird than a chicken. For instance, such qualities as "sociable" and "outgoing" are the characteristics of a "typical extravert."

The study of prototypicality rules and family resemblance principles in judgments of people helps in understanding how consistency and coherence are perceived in spite of variations in behavior (Kunda, 1999; Mischel, 1984). To illustrate, someone who really knows Rembrandt's work, who has seen dozens of his paintings, can easily identify whether a previously unseen painting is a real Rembrandt, an imitation, or a fake. The art expert seems able to extract a central distinctive gist from a wide range of variations. The same processes that permit such judgments must underlie how we identify personality coherence in the face of behavioral variability, and agree that someone is or is not a "real" introvert, or an anxious neurotic, or a sincere, friendly person. One attractive feature of this prototypicality approach to traits is that it seems highly compatible with attempts to quantify interpersonal behavior into dimensions of the sort discussed throughout this chapter (John, Hampson, & Goldberg, 1991).

Interaction of Traits and Situations

3.22 How can the study of interactions between traits and situations contribute to an understanding of personal individuality?

It has become increasingly recognized that a comprehensive approach to the study of traits must deal seriously with how the qualities of the person and the situation influence each other—that is, their "interaction" (Higgins, 1990; Magnusson, 1990; Mischel & Shoda, 1998). The behavioral expressions of a person's traits depend on his or her psychological situation at the moment. For example, rather than exhibit aggression widely, an individual may be highly aggressive but only under some set of relatively narrow circumstances, such as when psychological demands are very high (Shoda, Mischel & Wright, 1994; Wright & Mischel, 1987). Moreover, this aggressiveness may be expressed in some ways (such as verbally) but not in others (for example, physically). The implications of these specific interactions for contemporary personality theory will become evident when we consider the topic of interaction and the nature of consistency in the next chapter.

Are Traits Explanations or Summaries?

An enduring and difficult question at the trait level of analysis concerns the causal status of traits. The question is, do traits when defined and studied in the ways described in this chapter really serve to explain individual differences or do they simply provide useful ways to measure and describe those observed differences? The question is particularly important because the use of traits like "sociability" to explain individual differences in the behaviors that define sociability (warmth, friendliness) is readily criticized as circular. Sensitive to this concern, not all theorists working at this level of analysis view traits as causes.

3.23 How did Buss and Craik suggest a descriptive rather than causal interpretation of personality traits?

Buss and Craik (1983) are a notable case in point. They moved away from the traditional trait view of dispositions as underlying internal causes (or explanations) of cross-situational consistencies in behavior. Instead, they see dispositions like the Big Five as summary statements of **act trends** or behavioral trends, not explanations. In this view, dispositions are natural categories made up of various acts. The acts within a category differ in the degree to which they are prototypical or ideal members. Most importantly, this view of dispositions emphasizes that dispositions do not provide explanations of behavior; instead, they are summary statements of behavioral trends that must themselves be explained (Buss & Craik, 1983; Wiggins, 1980).

This revised view of dispositions reflects attempts to take account of the explanatory limitations of classical global trait theories like Allport's (1937), which have been widely criticized for several decades (Mischel, 1968; Ross & Nisbett, 1991; Wiggins, 1980). It is a revision, however, that is by no means completely shared: some voices still call for a return to the earlier approach to traits as global entities that provide adequate explanations (Funder, 1991).

In thinking about the meaning and uses of traits, keep in mind that even if traits like the Big Five don't explain why people behave as they do, they can be of great value for many goals. They are providing a common map for comparing individuals, groups, and even cultures on meaningful dimensions or factors of trait terms. Such terms are used by people in daily life to characterize and evaluate themselves and other persons. They provide a language and taxonomy for personality assessment that has long been needed for quantifying and comparing people in their broad characteristics. And they raise fascinating questions about the possible bases of these traits, their functions, and the ways they are expressed in the life course.

SUMMARY

TYPES AND TRAITS

- Personality types refer to discrete categories of people that have similar features of characteristics (physically, psychologically, or behaviorally).
- Carl Jung divided people into two types: introverts (withdrawn, shy) and extroverts (sociable, outgoing).
- Traits are basic, stable qualities of the person. Unlike types, traits are continuous dimensions on which individual differences may be arranged.
- Trait theorists conceptualize traits as underlying properties, qualities, or processes that exist in persons.
- Trait constructs have been used to account for observed behavioral consistencies within persons and for the behavioral differences among them.

GORDON ALLPORT

- For Allport, traits are the ultimate realities of psychological organization.
- In Allport's theory, traits are the general and enduring mental structures that account for consistency in behavior.
- They range in generality from highly generalized cardinal traits to secondary traits or more specific "attitudes."
- For Allport, "personality structure" is the individual's stable pattern of dispositions or traits.
- Allport urged the intensive study of the individual.

R. B. CATTELL

- Cattell distinguished between surface traits and source traits.
- Through factor analysis, Cattell tried to estimate the basic dimensions or factors underlying surface variations in behavior.
- Cattell differentiated between environmental-mold traits, which reflect environmental conditions, and constitutional traits, which reflect constitutional factors.

HANS J. EYSENCK

- Eysenck used empirical analyses to explore dimensional traits.
- He found that introverts are more reserved, quiet, and introspective than extraverts who are more sociable, active, and carefree.

COMMON FEATURES OF TRAIT LEVEL ANALYSES

- Trait theorists assume traits to be general underlying dispositions that account for consistencies in behavior.
- Some view traits as causes and explanations for behaviors; others interpret them as summaries of behavioral tendencies.
- Some traits are considered to be relatively superficial and specific; others are more basic and widely generalized.
- Traits are seen as enduring, stable qualities of the person over long time periods, while states refer to qualities that are brief in duration and attributable to external causes.
- This level of analysis tries to identify and measure the individual's position on one or more dispositional dimensions.

- Psychometric strategy is used to sample, quantify, and compare the responses of large groups of people to discover basic traits.
- To test the stability of a given trait, psychologists sample the individual's behavior over the course of multiple situations.

TAXONOMY OF HUMAN ATTRIBUTES

- The psycholexical approach to personality categorizes natural-language trait terms in order to describe and understand basic human qualities.
- The "Big Five" identified five primary dimensions of personality through factor analysis: neuroticism, extraversion, openness to new experience, agreeableness, and conscientiousness.
- Each of the five dimensions (or factors) includes specific personality characteristics represented as adjectives on a bipolar scale (for example, quiet–talkative, suspicious–trusting).
- The NEO-PI-R is a widely used personality inventory designed to rate individuals on these Big Five factors.
- Trait research focuses on correlations among trait ratings obtained from self-reports, paper-and-pencil inventories, and questionnaires. The results often show significant stability in traits over time and between independent raters.
- There is increasing recognition that the qualities of the person interact with those of the situation(s) in which he or she functions.

KEY TERMS

ability traits   51
act trends   66
agreeableness (A)   58
big five structure   58
cardinal traits   48
central traits   48
common traits   49
conscientiousness (C)   58
constitutional traits   50
domain of interpersonal
  behavior   56
dynamic traits   51

emotional stability   53
environmental-mold
  traits   50
extraversion (E)
  (extraverts)   44
factor analysis   57
introverts
  (introversion)   44
NEO-PI-R   58
neuroticism (N)   53
openness to
  experience (O)   58

prototypicality   65
psycholexical
  approach   56
secondary
  dispositions   49
source traits   49
surface traits   49
temperament traits   51
trait   44
trait approach   43
trait structure   49
unique traits   49

THE EXPRESSIONS OF DISPOSITIONS

Carmen and Dolores are both moderately high on measures of extraversion and their total scores on that scale are similar. But those who know the two well also see a distinctive difference between their patterns of typical behavior. Carmen is more outgoing in big groups and you count on her to be the center of attention and the life of the party at campus events. When with just a few people having dinner, however, she tends to be more on the quiet side. She also seems to have many casual acquaintances but few intimate friends that she really relates to. Dolores, in contrast, is at her warmest in one-on-one relations—she is the close friend you are sure to have fun with when in a small group or just going out together for the evening.

Do differences like these tell us something about the nature of traits and dispositions? This chapter examines that question, and the answers have yielded some surprises. In Chapter 3 we saw that people differ reliably and stably from each other in their personality. Some people may be distinctly more benevolent, benign, congenial, cordial, generous, good-humored, gracious, likable, sociable, and welcoming than others. Observers tend to agree with each other about peoples' personal qualities. And these qualities are stable over time, sometimes over many decades. Is there also a distinctive *pattern* in the behaviors individuals engage in, and the thoughts and feelings they express characteristically? What are these patterns and what do they mean? In what ways are one person's behaviors distinct from others? This chapter explores the question of the regularities and distinctiveness that exist in the observable patterns of thoughts, feelings, and behaviors that characterize different individuals and types.

▶ TRAITS, SITUATIONS, AND THE PERSONALITY PARADOX

Individual Differences in Behavior Tendencies

Some people may be more likely to behave in a friendly manner; some tend to behave more aggressively than others; some often show disagreeable behavior—the list of individual differences in behavior tendencies is long. And for every type of behavior, one also can think of a corresponding personal quality that makes a person display that behavior more often, or more strongly, than other people. Think of adjectives that describe a type of behavior: helpful, kind, agreeable, conscientious, or aggressive. For every adjective like that there is a noun that refers to a personal quality: helpfulness, kindness, agreeableness, conscientiousness, and aggressiveness. In fact, for any given type of behavior, one can hypothesize a corresponding personal quality that leads people to enact it. The grammatical convention in English makes it easy to name these qualities: just attach -*ness* at the end of the adjective.

The Intuitive Assumption of Consistency

4.1 What was the surprising result of research on the consistency of behavior across situations? What did behavioral specificity suggest about personality dispositions?

As you saw in Chapter 3, people differ reliably in their personality characteristics, and many if not all of such characteristics do take the form of xxx-ness, where xxx refers to a type of behavior. It seems obvious that people differ reliably in their tendency to display any given type of behavior. So, if you see a person behave in a very friendly manner, it's reasonable to assume she has a friendly personality, and expect that next time you see her, she will behave in a friendly way also. That is, to the extent that people differ reliably in their tendency to display a behavior, we expect them to behave in a similar way in a variety of situations. Of course our behaviors do vary from one situation another; everyone is more somber when her softball team has suffered a season-ending loss in a close game, compared to winning a championship. But the person who is particularly excited after her team's success may be the one who manages to find something to laugh about in a crushing loss. In short if in one situation, a person displays more of behavior X than other people, then we expect him, in other situations as well, to display more of that behavior than other people. So imagine the surprise when in the 1960s and 1970s researchers examined people's behaviors and found that this is not necessarily the case. So although intuitive, it seems obvious that individuals do differ consistently in the kinds of behavioral tendencies that they exhibit in many different situations, the puzzle was that the results in study after study failed to support this assumption when researchers tried to predict actual social behavior from trait measures. This discrepancy between intuition and data became a challenge to the field that deeply influenced its future course.

The 1968 Challenge

Personality psychologists for many years had searched for evidence to document the breadth and power of global personality traits. In the late 1960s, a number of them began to note that these efforts consistently yielded disappointing results (Mischel, 1968;

Peterson, 1968; Vernon, 1964). Mischel (1968) in particular reviewed research that showed that what people do varies to a surprising degree with the particular situation and context. For example, the person who seems conscientious about work may show a very different pattern with family.

Thus, serious questions were raised about the use of broad trait scores for predicting what a given person will do in different kinds of situations and for explaining the seeming inconsistency or variability that was observed across those situations. It was routine for research articles to end with an apology that the tests used did not predict what people would actually do in particular situations. And generally these disappointing results were seen as due to poor methods, bad judges, and unreliable tests, not to any possible problems with the guiding assumptions about the nature of trait consistency.

Over the course of many years, a massive literature had developed on the low consistency of the individual's behaviors when measured in different situations. That implies that Jane, for example, might be highly conscientious in one type of situation but not necessarily in another type of situation. Reviews of this literature, beginning in the 1920s (e.g., Hartshorne & May, 1928; Newcomb, 1929), and reexamined later (e.g., Mischel, 1968; Mischel & Peake, 1982; Pervin, 1994; Shoda, 1990), repeatedly added to the bewilderment, noting that consistency across different types of situations (e.g., from home to school to work) was surprisingly low. Low consistency was found regularly in the behavioral referents for such traits as rigidity, social conformity, dependency, and aggression; for attitudes to authority; and for virtually any other personality dimension (Mischel, 1968; Peterson, 1968; Vernon, 1964). This raised a disturbing question: Might personality dispositions be less global—and more *situation-specific*—than had been assumed? If so, where was the consistency of personality that we all believe intuitively must be there?

The Paradox Defined

The Mischel (1968) book, *Personality and Assessment,* raised this question most forcefully and caused a crisis for the field by asking: "What if the problem is not just with bad methods and poor data but also with wrong assumptions?" The defiant part of this monograph was the proposal that the findings it reviewed might reflect not just imperfect methods and measurement noise, but also the state of nature. This created a challenge that upset the field of personality for many years and generated what Bem and Allen (1974) called the **personality paradox:** Namely, the data from research indicated lack of consistency. Nevertheless, human intuition, and a long tradition of Western thought dating to the ancient Greeks, and including much modern personality research and practice, led to the conviction that the opposite was true. Which one was right, the research or the intuition? A long debate resulted, as discussed in In Focus 4.1.

4.2 How did the "personality paradox" create conflict in the field of personality while promoting the position of situationism?

▶ INCORPORATING SITUATIONS INTO TRAITS

If we accept that people's behaviors vary widely across situations, how do we reconcile that with our intuitive conviction that each individual is characterized by stable and distinctive qualities? What remains consistent through the changing stream of thoughts, feelings, and behaviors? How might one capture what is constant? The finding of large variations in people's behaviors across situations challenged the ultimate goal of personality psychology, which is to identify the coherence and stability that underlie individuals' thoughts, feelings, and behaviors.

THE PERSON *VERSUS* SITUATION DEBATE

This debate consisted of a prolonged and heated controversy about personality dispositions, consistency, and the role of the situation that consumed much of the agenda of personality psychology in the 1970s and early 1980s.

Situationism. At the height of the debate, many social psychologists amassed evidence for the power of the situation as the main determinant of behavior. Some also argued that often the situation is so powerful that individual differences and personality don't make much difference. The emphasis on the power of situational variables, and the belief that personality was less important than the situation, was named **situationism.** This view also proposed that people tend to make erroneous explanations of the causes of behavior. The error is that they systematically neglect the role of the situation and instead invoke personality dispositions as favorite—but incorrect—explanations of social behavior (e.g., Nisbett & Ross, 1980). Called the **fundamental attribution error,** the tendency to focus on dispositions in causal explanations soon was seen as a mistake committed by laypersons in everyday life, as well as by the psychologists who study them (Ross, 1977).

Evidence of systematic judgmental errors in personality assessment and inferences, of course, had been noted often in the past. Before, however, the limitations of judgments about personality had been dismissed as merely due to unreliable, imperfect methods, open to correction by improving the quality of measurement. Now instead, they were read as reflecting human nature (e.g., Nisbett & Ross, 1980). In its most extreme form, some critics argued that personality was mostly a fictitious construction in the mind of the perceiver (e.g., Shweder, 1975).

Revival of the Traditional Paradigm. At the opposite pole, many personality psychologists renewed even more intensely their efforts to retain the traditional paradigm for the study of traits. In the early 1980s, a resurgence of the factor analytic approach occurred in the study of traits. It was founded on an agreement among many researchers to reach a consensus concerning the set of major traits or basic dispositions needed for a comprehensive taxonomy of personality using factor analyses based on traits ratings, in the form of the "Big Five" (e.g., McCrae & Costa, 1999). Many similar factor analytic studies and taxonomies had been done in earlier years, and their strengths and limitations had been duly noted (e.g., Fiske, 1994; Mischel, 1968; Peterson, 1968). The difference now was that they agreed about what those factors were and proposed that the Big Five at least approximated the basic structure of personality. It turned out that this consensus actually was a useful way to revitalize enthusiasm for the study of traits, by showing the power and breadth of the broad trait level of analysis, as you saw in the last chapter.

The Role of the Situation. To understand this debate and the passions it stirred requires a quick look at the history of personality psychology. Since the inception of the field a century ago, the trait level of analysis was mostly devoted to studying the person apart from the situation. In contrast, the field of social psychology was devoted to understanding the general effects and power of situations regardless of individual differences. In that framing, in social psychology the person became the **error variance**—the noise—that had to be removed. In contrast, in personality psychology it was believed that one had to remove the effects of situations—and treat them as noise or error—in order to glimpse the true situation-free personality that remained consistent.

Given the way that the mission of personality and social psychology as disciplines was defined then, many personality psychologists heard a strong argument for the importance of the situation as trying to undermine personality as a field and as a construct. In contrast, most social psychologists hailed it as supporting the importance and power of the situation and the relative insignificance of individual differences in personality. The mistaken belief that to the degree that the person was important, the situation was not, and vice versa, led to the unfortunate **person versus situation debate.** Its resolution is discussed throughout the remainder of this chapter.

4.3 What is the fundamental attribution error? How was it used to promote situationism among social psychologists?

Within the patterns of intraindividual variation, however, there may be a distinctive temporal order, a stable pattern over time that is unique to each individual. On the surface, the thoughts, feelings, and behaviors of an individual may vary considerably, and on the surface, this may appear to go against the central tenet of the construct of personality—that personality is relatively invariant or consistent over time and across situations. But when we look beneath the surface, and focus on how the variation occurs and on what external and internal situations it depends, there may be a regular pattern that is distinctive for each individual, and that goes beyond the surface level variation.

If . . . Then . . . Situation–Behavior Signatures

While still relatively small, the number of investigators focusing on, and finding, such **stable intraindividual patterning** is increasing (e.g., Eizenman, Nesselrode, Featherman, & Rowe, 1997; Fleeson, 2001; Rhodewalt & Morf, 1998; Zelenski & Larsen, 2000). For example, Larsen and Kasimatis (1990) found that some individuals' affective experiences clearly follow a seven-day weekly cycle, while others do not show such a pattern. Similarly, Brown and Moskowitz (1998) showed that some individuals have discernible daily cycles in their interpersonal behaviors such as dominance–submissiveness, and agreeableness–quarrelsomeness, whereas others do not. Rusting and Larsen (1998) found that an "evening-worse" pattern was associated with neuroticism, depression, and anxiety as well as a cognitive style indicative of hopelessness. Cote & Moskowitz (1998) found that in individuals who score high on agreeableness, the pleasant emotions they feel in a given interpersonal interaction and the agreeableness of their behavior were more strongly related.

Sometimes, however, regularities in the stream of behaviors contain even more information. Behaviors do not occur in a vacuum; they occur in specific situations. When the situation changes, so do the behaviors, but the relationship between the situations and behaviors may be stable, and may express an individual's distinctive underlying personality system. For instance, suppose two professors on the whole display the same average amount of sociability. However, the first one is extremely sociable and warm with students but unfriendly and cold with colleagues. In contrast, the second professor shows the opposite pattern, and is unfriendly and disinterested with students but very sociable with colleagues. Research indicates that many people are reliably characterized by such patterns. Such profiles seem to constitute a sort of **signature of personality** that does reflect some of the essence of personality coherence and promises to provide a route to glimpse the underlying system that generates them (Mischel & Shoda, 1995; Shoda, Mischel, & Wright, 1994).

To give another example, in situation A, people rarely initiate personal interactions while in situation B, they commonly do so. Suppose also that Mark tends to become irritated when he thinks he is being ignored (likely to happen in situation A), whereas April is happier when she is left alone and even becomes irritated when people tell her personal stories about themselves (which happens often in situation B). Then Mark will become irritated in situation A, but not in situation B, and April will show the opposite *if . . . then . . .* **pattern,** annoyed if B, but not if A. These feelings further activate other thoughts and feelings in each situation in a characteristic pattern for each individual. If so, then even if both people have similar overall levels of irritability, they will generate distinctive, predictable *if . . . then . . .* patterns.

The point is that an individual's personality may be seen not only in the overall average frequency of particular types of behavior shown but also in when and where that behavior occurs. The *if . . . then . . .* patterns of situation–behavior relationships that unfold—if they are stable—can then provide a key to the personality. That is an expression of personality coherence that is eliminated when the situation is removed by aggregating the behavior across different situations or by ignoring the situation altogether.

4.4 What are behavioral signatures? How does this "*if . . . then . . .*" concept preserve the coherence and consistency of personality?

Evidence for Signatures Indicative of Personality Types

Researchers have tested this proposition and found clear support for it (Shoda, Mischel, & Wright, 1989, 1993a, b, 1994). In these studies, children were systematically observed for more than 150 hours per child in a residential summer camp setting over the course of six weeks (e.g., Shoda et al., 1993a, 1994). As predicted, children tended to display stable, distinctive patterns of *if . . . then . . .* relationships. To illustrate (Fig. 4.1), some children were consistently more verbally aggressive than others when warned by an adult, but were much less aggressive than most when their peers approached them positively. In contrast, another group of children with a similar overall average level of aggression was distinguished by a striking and opposite *if . . . then . . .* pattern: they were more aggressive than any other children when peers approached them positively, but were exceptionally unaggressive when warned by an adult (Shoda et al., 1994). A child who regularly becomes aggressive when peers try to play with him is quite different from one who expresses aggression mostly to adults

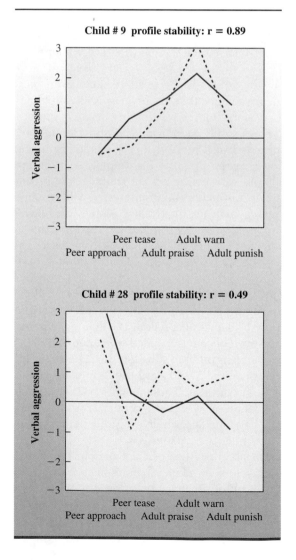

Figure 4.1 Individual *if . . . then . . .* situation-behavior signatures for two children. Their aggressive behavior was observed in five different situations many times. Half of the observations are shown as dotted lines; half as solid lines. Profile stability is the correlation between the two sets of observations.

Source: Shoda, Y., Mischel, W., & Wright, J. C. Intra-individual stability in the organization and patterning of behavior: Incorporating psychological situations into the idiographic analysis of personality. *Journal of Personality and Social Psychology, 67,* 674–687, fig. 1. © 1994 by the American Psychological Association. Adapted with permission.

who try to control him, even if both are equal in their overall aggressive behavior. In short, stable *if . . . then . . .* personality signatures, not just stable levels of average overall behavior, were found to characterize individuals, and their patterns seem to be meaningful reflections of the personality system.

To summarize, individuals differ stably in their distinctive *if . . . then . . .* strategies and behavior patterns. Consequently, they will behave in their characteristic ways within a given type of situation, but they will *vary* their behavior predictably when the "if" changes, thus producing behavioral variability across situations. Then, by aggregating behavior across situations in their search for broad behavioral dispositions, researchers risk eliminating the distinctive individuality and stability that they are trying to find! Like their handwritten counterpart, behavioral signatures can be seen as an expression of individuality that identifies the person. To illustrate this more concretely, Gary W's behavioral signatures are summarized next.

Gary W's Behavioral Signatures

Gary's behavior depends on the psychological situation as well as on the type of behavior involved. For example, while he may respond pessimistically and with defensive withdrawal in many interpersonal situations, when tasks call for quantitative skills he is self-confident and optimistic. And while on average, Gary is not a "generally aggressive person," he does have disruptive outbursts of anger, especially when he feels ignored or rejected. It is notable that, *if* Gary feels provoked or threatened in an intimate relationship with a woman, *then* he becomes vulnerable to outbursts of rage. On the other hand, *if* he feels secure, *then* he can be extremely caring. Such *if . . . then . . .* relationships provide a window for seeing Gary's unique but stable patterns, the "signature" of his personality. In short, this perspective emphasizes that both the person and the situation need to be considered when trying to predict and understand individuals and the important ways they differ from each other.

Consider the differences between Gary W (dotted line) and Charles W, his older brother (solid line). Figure 4.2 illustrates their self-reported (in daily diaries) emotional states (from extremely stressed, upset, and negative affect at the top of the scale to extremely pleased and positive at the bottom). As the figure shows, Gary and Charles are similar in becoming very upset in situation 1. This is when they feel "provoked or threatened" in close personal relations with women. They differ, however, in the other events that upset them most. In situation 2, public speaking (for example, in seminar presentations), Gary becomes distressed; Charles enjoys those occasions and looks forward to them. Likewise, while Gary becomes extremely unhappy and "mad" when he gets negative feedback about his work (situation 4), Charles readily dismisses complaints from unhappy patients or colleagues as "part of the grumbling you have to expect. . . . There are always people you can't please." Interestingly, the pattern reverses when the brothers must deal with quantitative work problems (situation 3), for example, when writing research reports in their technical specialties. Gary finds those tasks a "real high—a challenge"; Charles experiences them as anxiety-provoking, fearing that his inadequate grasp of the quantitative method he uses in his medical research will be revealed.

Behavioral Signatures of Different Personality Types

Are behavioral signatures meaningful, and can they help us generalize and predict behaviors in a different context? Can they also be used to predict future behaviors in new situations? One way to address these questions is by identifying patterns of *if . . . then . . .*

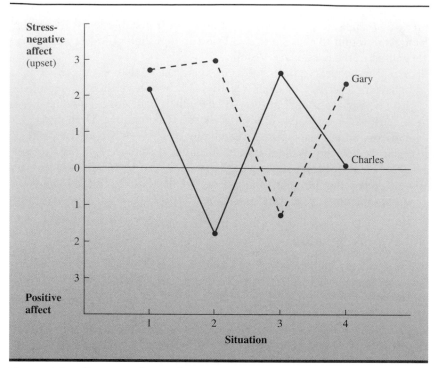

Figure 4.2 Illustrative *if . . . then . . .* signatures. Self-reported stress and emotion, for Gary and Charles, in four situations (sampled repeatedly in daily diaries for 3 months)

relations that characterize not just one person, but a group of people or a type. Once one knows that an individual has a certain type of *if . . . then . . .* signature, it would become possible to make predictions about her behavior based on what is already known about that type. That approach is being applied to important personality types, and we next look at two examples.

4.5 Summarize the behavioral signature of the narcissistic personality type.

The Narcissistic Signature. Narcissists are people whom most of us have met, and when we do, we rarely forget them; although when we get to know them, we often find them extremely difficult to deal with and wish we had never met them. Think of the vain would-love-to-be a movie star type, deeply in love with himself, and ever-eager to prove how wonderful he is—almost desperately trying to convince himself as well as the world that he is really the greatest. The most striking feature of the "signature" of narcissists (Morf & Rhodewalt, 2001a,b) is the narcissist's chronic vigilance for situational opportunities in which their grandiose self-concepts can be affirmed and bolstered (Morf, Ansara, and Shia, 2001; Morf, Weir, & Davidov, 2000; Rhodewalt & Eddings, 2002). Thus they are characterized by the pattern of *if* opportunities to promote self, *then* much effort toward providing evidence for self's superiority. Simultaneously, narcissists have cynical and unempathic views of others and seem insensitive to other's concerns and situational constraints. Thus, if in situations that call for modesty, as when others out-perform them, they nevertheless may derogate their competitors, belittling their achievements—even when the long-term costs are self-defeating and relationship-destructive. Furthermore, they provide post hoc interpretations of

Narcissists have grandiose self-concepts.

experiences that ingeniously amplify the positive feedback to them while discounting the negative (documented in Morf & Rhodewalt, 2001a,b)—in short, they walk around the world trying to convince themselves that everybody really loves them—although they also seem to have a hard time believing they are really lovable.

The Signature of Rejection Sensitivity. It is widely assumed that dependency in adults is linked to a broad disposition of passivity–submissiveness, but fine-grain analyses of the actual behavior indicate that within some situations, dependency is in fact related to high levels of activity and assertiveness. Specifically, while dependent individuals who are focused on getting along with a peer will self-denigrate, they will self-promote when concerned mostly with pleasing an authority figure (Bornstein, Riggs, Hill, & Calabrese, 1996).

In particular, there has been much research on individuals who have intense anxieties about interpersonal rejection, called rejection sensitivity or RS (Downey & Feldman, 1996). Their rejection sensitivity is seen *if* in an intimate relationship they encounter what could be construed as uncaring behavior (e.g., partner is attentive to someone else), *then* becoming overly worried that "she doesn't love me." These thoughts in turn tend to trigger expectations of rejection, abandonment, feelings of anger and resentment, and anxiety and rage at the prospect of abandonment. Coercive and controlling behaviors then become activated, but typically are blamed on the partner's behavior. However, they are not overall more likely than others to express anger, disapproval, and coercive behaviors in certain types of intimate situations. For example, high RS women tend to be especially solicitous, putting the other person's needs first in their relationships (e.g., Purdie & Downey, 2000).

Distinctive situation–behavior signatures like these are interesting to many personality psychologists because they give clues for understanding the person's underlying

4.6 How is the trait of rejection sensitivity expressed as a personality signature?

The high RS person easily feels rejected when the partner withdraws attention.

personality. For example, in the narcissist signature described on page 76, narcissists treat interpersonal situations as challenges for eagerly showing off how good they are by out-doing and out-performing other people while trying to take center stage in the process. Their signatures hint at some of these underlying qualities. In contrast, rejection sensitive people view the same situations in order to anxiously scan them. They want to see how likely they are to be personally rejected and hurt, and are ready to magnify the slightest possible criticism and to overreact to it.

Two Types of Consistency

4.7 Differentiate between Type 1 and Type 2 consistency.

Taken collectively, the results in the search for consistency in the behavioral expressions of personality suggest that there are two different aspects of consistency. Both need to be considered in the study of individual differences and personality dispositions at the trait level of analysis, and each has its distinctive uses, advantages, and limitations.

- **Type 1: Average overall levels of behavior tendencies.** The first or "classic" form of consistency is in the overall average differences in the levels of typical behavior of different kinds (such as aggressiveness, sociability) that characterize the individual. The trait level of analysis captures these by aggregating indices of what the individual is like and does across many different types of situations, as when people are described with regard to their status on broad factors.
- **Type 2: *If . . . then . . .* (situation–behavior) signatures.** These consistencies are seen in patterns of stable links between types of situations and types of characteristic behavior, as illustrated in the signatures of the narcissistic and rejection sensitive types of persons.

Uses of the Two Types of Consistency

Is it more useful to try to infer broad traits or situation-specific signatures? The answer always depends on the particular purpose. Inferences about global traits may have limited value for the practical prediction of a person's specific future behavior in specific situations, or for the design of specific psychological treatment programs to help facilitate constructive change. But broad traits have many other uses. Indeed, they have value for everyday inferences about what other people seem like on the whole, as when you get first impressions about a stranger, or form a quick opinion about a new acquaintance (e.g., McAdams, 1999). With people we know well and who are important to us, however, we also want to know "what makes them tick." Therefore, we try to understand their goals, motivations, and feelings in order to make sense of the *if . . . then . . .* patterns—the personality signatures that characterize them as we get to know them better (Chen-Idson & Mischel, 2001).

The first type of consistency—average overall behavior tendencies on broad dimensions—can be enhanced by the method of aggregation introduced in the last chapter. In this method, behavior on a dimension is simply averaged across many different situations to estimate the person's overall true level of the characteristic. Bolstered by this method, the case can be made that global dispositions as traditionally conceptualized are "alive and well" if one routinely aggregated multiple observations and measures across different situations. That serves to eliminate the role of the situation by averaging it out. This strategy now acknowledges that specific behaviors across different types of situations could not be predicted by such a model (e.g., Epstein, 1979), and continues to treat the situation as a source of noise by removing it as before. On the positive side, by aggregating the individual's behavior across many different kinds of situations, it is in fact possible to increase greatly the strength of the overall average differences that will be found between individuals "on the whole" for diverse traits (e.g., Epstein, 1983).

Inferences about broad traits also have practical value for gross initial screening decisions (as in personnel selection), studying average differences between groups of individuals in personality research (Block & Block, 1980), or the layman's everyday perception of persons (e.g., Funder & Colvin, 1997; Schneider, 1973; Wright & Mischel, 1988). And as was seen in the last chapter, when measures are combined or aggregated over a variety of situations, one can demonstrate stable differences among individuals in their relative overall standing on many dimensions of social behavior.

In sum, overall average differences between individuals can be obtained easily, particularly with rating measures, and used to discriminate among them for many purposes (Funder & Colvin, 1997; Kenrick & Funder, 1988). For other goals, however, more specific levels of analysis that consider *if . . . then . . .* , situation–behavior signatures and that take the situation into account may be more useful. Knowing how your friend behaved before can help you predict how he or she probably will act again in similar situations. The impact of any situation or stimulus depends on the person who experiences it, and different people differ greatly in how they cope with most stimulus conditions. It is a truism that one person's favorite "stimulus" may be the stuff of another's nightmares and that in the same "stimulus situation" one individual may react with aggression, another with love, a third with indifference. Different people act differently with some consistency in particular classes of situations, but the particular classes of conditions tend to be narrower than traditional trait theories have assumed (e.g., Cantor, 1990; Cantor & Kihlstrom, 1987; Mischel, 1990). For purposes of important individual decision-making, one may need highly individualized assessments of what the specific situations mean to the person.

The significant consistency that exists is at least in part reflected in stable patterns of behavior *within* similar types of psychological situations (Mischel & Peake, 1982; Mischel & Shoda, 1995). As the similarity between situations decreases, so does the cross-situational consistency of the person's behavior (Krahe, 1990; Shoda, 1990; Shoda, Mischel, & Wright, 1994). Then it becomes difficult to predict from what individuals did

4.8 What are the practical advantages of the two methods of studying consistency? What is required in order to obtain Type 1 consistency?

4.9 In what situations are behavior signatures a more useful way to approach personality consistency? Under which circumstances will it be difficult to predict behavior using Type 2 consistency?

in one type of situation to what they will do in a very different type of situation. On the other hand, within particular types of situations, individuals do show characteristic stable patterns. These patterns are expressed as stable *if . . . then . . .* relationships, such that when the situation (the "if") remains stable (e.g., if "teased by peers about his glasses and appearance"), then so does the behavior (e.g., he becomes physically aggressive). So for the people we know well, we have a sense not only of what they are like in general (in trait terms) but also of what they are likely to do in particular types of situations (e.g., at the holiday dinner, in an argument about money, on a date).

To apply these abstract points more concretely, think again about Gary. It is certainly possible to form some generalizations about his seemingly major qualities, strengths, and problems. Such generalizations help us to differentiate Gary from other people, and to compare him with them. Suppose that we learned, for example, from trait tests that Gary tended to be low on extraversion, relatively high on neuroticism and anxiety, high on conscientiousness, and intermediate on both sociability and open-mindedness scales. Such characterizations may help one to gain a quick overall impression of Gary. But in order to predict what Gary will do in specific situations, or to make decisions about him (as in therapy or vocational counseling), it would be necessary to conduct a much more individually oriented study that considers the specific qualities of Gary as they relate to the specific situations of interest in his life.

Just when does Gary become more—or less—neurotic and anxious? Under what conditions does he *not* avoid close relations with people? When is he likely to be more and less sociable in ways that are distinctive and predictable? The analysis and prediction of specific behavior requires that we ask questions like these to link behavior to conditions, and to capture their distinctive pattern and meaning, in addition to painting personality portraits with more general characterizations that also have their many valuable uses.

▶ INTERACTIONISM IN PERSONALITY PSYCHOLOGY

Interactionism in personality is the idea that the individual's experience and action cannot be understood as the result of separate personal and situational factors. Rather, it is a product of dynamic interactions between aspects of personality and situations (Magnusson, 1999; Magnusson & Endler, 1977; Mischel, 1973). Interactionism focuses on how the expressions of the stable personality system are visible in the person's unique *patterns* of *if . . . then . . .* , situation–behavior relationships.

The Meaning of Person × Situation Interaction

4.10 What is meant by a person × situation interaction? What does it add to a knowledge of a person's traits?

In the interactionist view, knowledge of individual differences often tells us more if it is combined with information about the conditions and situational variables that influence the behavior of interest. Conversely, the effects of conditions depend on the individuals in them. Thus, the interaction of individual differences and particular conditions, and not just the individual or the context separately, is important (Bem & Funder, 1978; Magnusson, 1990; Shoda, Mischel, & Wright, 1994; Wright & Mischel, 1987). *If . . . then . . .* , behavioral signatures of individuals, and those of groups of individuals such as the "narcissists," illustrate the basic principles of interactionism.

An Example: Uncertainty Orientation. An example of **person × situation interaction** involving an individual difference dimension comes from research on **uncertainty orientation.** This personality dimension is defined at one end by individuals who are relatively comfortable dealing with uncertainty and strive to resolve it, and on the other end by those who are more uncomfortable with uncertainty and likely to avoid situations that increase their subjective sense of uncertainty (Sorrentino & Roney, 1986, 2000). Now consider this question: Would experiencing a situation in which one didn't have control over the outcome make people approach, rather than avoid, new information? Would students do better on a test if they are told that the test is diagnostic of an important ability? The answers to these questions depend on an individual's uncertainty orientation. For those who are high in uncertainty orientation (i.e., those who are comfortable with uncertainty and seek to master it), the answer is yes to both questions. But for those who are uncomfortable with uncertainty, the answer is very different (Huber, Sorrentino, Davidson, & Epplier, 1992). For example, they do better on a test if they are told it is not diagnostic of important abilities (Sorrentino & Roney, 1986). Further, when individuals low in uncertainty orientation experience uncontrollability, they avoid new information, especially if they are also mildly depressed (Walker & Sorrentino, 2000). So it all depends on the interaction between the type of person with the type of situation: the situation that suits one person may distress another.

Note that differences in personality are expressed here not in the overall average behavior tendencies but rather in the different effects of situations, be it the experience of uncontrollability or the perceived meaning of a test. A similar insight was captured in an example Gordon Allport (1937) used. He asked: What is the difference between butter and raw eggs? They differ in the *effect* of cooking heat: as heat increases one softens and melts, but the other one hardens. The question of which is harder *in general* is meaningless unless one specifies the temperature. It results in one answer if the food is in the refrigerator, but another if the food is in the frying pan. Depending on the situations in which participants in a study find themselves, one would make opposite predictions for their behavior. And that, put most simply, is the basic **principle of interactionism.**

4.11 How does research on uncertainty orientation illustrate the value of an interactionist approach?

Definition of Triple Typology.   In a thoughtful analysis of the importance of interactions for personality psychology and for understanding personality dispositions, Daryl Bem (1983) summarized a mission of personality psychology, or any science for that matter, with great simplicity. Whether or not one is studying molecules, plants, or people, there are millions of specific instances of them. A goal of science is to produce a way to categorize them into a manageably small number of *meaningful* categories. Because objects can be categorized in many arbitrary ways, "meaningful" of course is the key concept. In what sense should it be meaningful?

Bem's answer to that question was that a meaningful way to categorize people, behaviors, and situations was one that allows accurate statements in the form: *"this type of person will do these types of behaviors in these types of situations."* This is a **triple typology** in the sense that it classifies together three categories: types of people, types of behavior, and types of situations. A meaningful system of categorizing people, behaviors, and situations is one that allows the personality psychologist to spell out precise *if . . . then . . .* regularities in describing types of people. For example, "narcissists" is a more meaningful way of categorizing people than "people who shop at supermarkets." For narcissists, we can say, *"if* they encounter situations that can be seen as an opportunity to bolster their grandiose self-concept, *then* they will seek to demonstrate their superiority." It would be much more difficult to generate *if . . . then . . .* statements about the social and interpersonal behaviors of "people who shop at supermarkets" that apply to most members of that category.

4.12 What is the basic question posed in Daryl Bem's triple typology? How is it illustrated in the case of narcissism?

Note that the *if . . . then . . .* statement describing narcissists already contains references to types of behaviors and types of situations. That is, "seeking to demonstrate their superiority" is a type of behavior, and "situations that can be seen as an opportunity to bolster their grandiose self-concept" is a type of situation. There are meaningful categories of behaviors and situations precisely because they allow a simple description of narcissists in one *if . . . then . . .* statement. The practical challenge of course is to find meaningful categories of people, behaviors, and situations.

4.13 Describe the approach taken to produce a triple typology of hostility. What psychological processes were found to underlie the tendency to keep anger in or let it out?

In one promising direction, modern computer technology is beginning to provide hope that a triple typology is in fact attainable. For example, Van Mechelen and his colleagues have devised a computer algorithm that simultaneously tries out many different ways to categorize people, behaviors, and situations. It searches for the best system of typologies that allow the fewest number of *if . . . then . . .* statements to describe the data with the least amount of errors (Van Mechelen & Kiers, 1999; Vansteelandt & Van Mechelen, 1998). To see how this works, read In Focus 4.2.

IN FOCUS 4.2

A TRIPLE TYPOLOGY FOR HOSTILITY

To test their methodology, the researchers asked study participants to describe what specific responses they would exhibit when faced with a specific type of situation. They chose these situations carefully to get a wide spectrum of potentially frustrating situations in order to obtain a variety of response patterns. Some of the situations they used were: you are in a restaurant and have been waiting a long time to be served (low frustration); you are trying to study and there is incessant noise (moderate frustration); your instructor unfairly accuses you of cheating on an examination (high frustration). The responses provided were also intended to reflect a wide variety of potential hostile responses, such as turning away; wanting to strike something or someone; hands tremble; heart beats faster; cursing; becoming tense; feeling irritated; or becoming enraged (taken from S-R Inventory of Hostility, Endler and Hunt, 1968).

When the data were analyzed by a computer program designed by Van Mechelen and colleagues, the result was a grouping of people, behaviors, and situations. In this classification, each group of people was succinctly and accurately characterized by a set of *if . . . then . . .* statements describing how this group of people tends to display these types of behaviors in these types of situations. For example, people of type 3 were likely to respond to a situation that is highly frustrating by becoming tense, having their heart beat faster, sweating, and having their hands tremble. People of type 2 would respond to the same type of situations by wanting to strike something, cursing, and becoming tense or irritated. In a situation that is not very frustrating, such as when you accidentally

bang your shins against a park bench, neither type 2 nor type 3 people would respond in a hostile manner. However, a person of type 7 would likely have an increased heart rate, grimace, become tense, and curse (Vansteelandt & Van Mechelen, 1998). Because these person types directly reflect *if . . . then . . .* behavioral signatures, this sort of typology can be used to predict the probability of a certain type of individual producing certain types of behavior when faced with a certain type of situation.

After Van Mechelen and his colleagues formulated these typologies, they were able to examine some of the psychological processes that linked the type of person to the type of situation–response patterns they produced. They designed a questionnaire that asked about the participant's interpretation of situations, expectations about the consequences of different types of behavior, and whether they kept their anger in or let it out. These questions were designed to engage thoughts and feelings that were related to hostile and aggressive behavior. For example, participants were asked to agree or disagree with the following statements: "When other people get me in trouble, I rapidly think that they do it on purpose" (interpretation); "I think that, in general, the expression of anger is not appreciated by others" (expectation); "I easily suppress feelings of frustration" (anger-in); "When I feel frustrated, I show it easily" (anger-out) (Vansteelandt & Van Mechelen, 1998). They also asked the participants to fill out a questionnaire designed to measure the participant's ability to tolerate frustration (Van Der Ploeg, Defares, & Spielberger, 1982). The researchers then looked at how the person types related to the presence or absence of each of the types of thoughts and feelings measured.

Their findings showed the feasibility of forming meaningful categories of people, behaviors, and situations simultaneously. They also indicated that the resultant typology provided glimpses into the internal psychological processes that underlie the observed *if . . . then . . .* behavior sig-natures characteristic of various types. The different types were clearly different in the patterns they used for responding to different types of frustrating situations from very mild to the highly frustrating. The types also differed in the ways in which they typically expressed hostility, all the way from no hostile responses to cursing and readiness to strike out physically in different types of situations.

Interaction as a Rule in Science

Although the concept of interactionism has been controversial in personality psychology, the fact that organisms and environment interact to determine behavior and development is a general conclusion in most sciences dealing with living organisms. In biology, evidence of organism–environment interaction is commonplace. As Lewontin (2000) points out, genetic and environmental influences are intertwined, making development "contingent on the sequence of environments in which it occurs" (p. 20). In the example of plant growth, Lewontin notes that cloned samples of seven different individuals of a given plant species that were grown at different elevations showed little cross-environment consistency in the rank-ordering of their size of mature plants, because a particular plant that flourishes at one altitude may readily have below-average growth in another context. Consequently, one has to represent plant growth not in terms of the average growth tendencies of an individual organism but in graphs that take into account the environment in which the organism develops. To understand plant growth and predict the size of a given plant relative to others, one has to take into account the particular environmental conditions that are present—in other words, one has to identify and understand the *if . . . then . . .* contingencies.

Other examples abound in the biological sciences, including an analysis of the "plasticity" (modifiability) of neural systems (Edelman, 1992; Kolb & Whishaw, 1998) and the ways in which cultural and biological factors interact in human evolution (Durham, 1991). Ehrlich (2000) focusing on the interplay of genetic endowment and environmental experience obtained similar findings for the importance of interaction. He concluded that the psychologist's typical strategy of partitioning the determinants of behavioral characteristics into separate genetic versus environmental causes was no more sensible than asking which areas of a rectangle are mostly due to length and which mostly due to width. Yet curiously the implications of interactionism for understanding the multiple cognitive, behavioral, and physiological mechanisms through which personality functions have been extremely difficult to accept in traditional trait level analyses of personality (as discussed in Cervone & Mischel, 2001, Chapter 1).

4.14 How general is interactionism throughout the sciences? Give some examples.

Resolution of the Personality Paradox

If stable *if . . . then . . .* , situation–behavior patterns are meaningful reflections of the personality, they also should be linked to the person's self-perceptions about his or her own consistency. The relationship between the stability of the person–situation profile that characterizes an individual in a particular domain of behavior and the self-perception of consistency has been closely examined. The results directly speak to Bem's classic "personality paradox" which, as you saw earlier, has motivated much of

4.15 Are self-perceptions of behavioral consistency related to actual consistency? Consistency of what?

the research agenda in studies at the trait level. As Bem pointed out in the 1970s, while our intuitions convince us that people have broad behavioral dispositions that we believe are seen in extensive consistency in their behaviors across situations, the research results on cross-situational consistency in behavior persistently contradict our intuitions (Bem & Allen, 1974). Recall that to resolve this dilemma, and prove our intuitions are better than our research, Bem and Allen noted that traditional methodologies assume that all traits belong to all persons. But if a given trait is in fact irrelevant for some people, their inconsistency with regard to it will obscure the consistency of the subset of people for whom the trait is relevant. Therefore, Bem and Allen reasoned that a solution to the consistency problem requires first selecting only those persons who perceive themselves as consistent in the given disposition. We then should expect to find high cross-situational consistency in their behavior in that domain, but not in the behavior of those who see themselves as inconsistent with regard to it, or to whom it is irrelevant.

Initially, Bem and Allen (1974) obtained some encouraging support for this prediction. A few years later, in a more comprehensive test in a large field study at a college in the midwest of the United States, researchers observed behavior relevant to "college conscientiousness" and friendliness as it occurred over multiple situations and occasions (Mischel & Peake, 1982). Each of the 63 participating college students were observed repeatedly in various situations on campus relevant to their conscientiousness in the college setting. The specific behaviors and contexts selected as relevant were supplied by undergraduates themselves in pretesting at the college. Conscientiousness was sampled in various situations such as in the classroom, in the dormitory, in the library, and the assessments occurred over repeated occasions in the course of the semester.

These data were used to examine the links between the students' self-perceptions of consistency and their actual behavior (Mischel & Shoda, 1995). As the first set of two columns of Figure 4.3 shows, those who perceived themselves as consistent (the first light column) did not show greater overall cross-situational consistency than those who did not. In contrast, the second set of columns clearly supports the hypothesis of coherence in terms of pattern stability: For individuals who perceived themselves as consistent, the average *if . . . then . . .* , situation–behavior signature stability correlation was near .5, whereas it was trivial for those who saw themselves as inconsistent.

In short, the self-perception of consistency seems to be predictable from the stability in the situation–behavior signatures. That, in turn, indicates that the intuition of consistency is neither paradoxical nor illusory: it is linked to behavioral consistency, but not the sort for which the field was searching for so many years.

Summary: Expressions of Consistency in Traits–Dispositions

4.16 How does the concept of behavioral signatures help resolve the personality paradox? What does this resolution suggest about how we might view the coherence of personality?

This chapter started with the basic personality paradox as the problem to untangle. To recapitulate, the construct of personality rests on the assumption that individuals are characterized by distinctive qualities that are relatively invariant across situations and over a span of time. This assumption seems also intuitively true. The paradox was that in a century of personality research, evidence showed that individual differences in social behaviors tend to be surprisingly variable across different situations. Research that sought regularities in the patterns of variability has begun to provide a resolution of this paradox. Namely, the variability across situations seen as the person's behavior unfolds across different situations is not simply random fluctuations. Rather, it in part is a stable and meaningful characteristic of an individual that may provide a window into the underlying system that produced them. This type of behavioral signature of person-

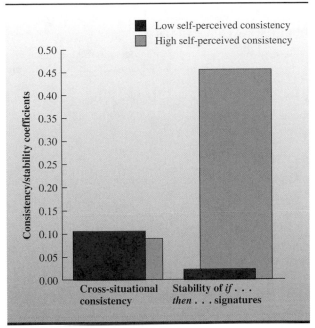

Figure 4.3 Cross-situational consistency and the stability of *if . . . then . . .* signatures for people high versus low in self-perceived consistency in conscientiousness. Self-perceived consistency is predicted by stability of the *if . . . then* signatures.

Source: Based on data from Mischel, W., & Shoda, Y. (1995). A cognitive-affective system theory of personality: Reconceptualizing situations, dispositions, dynamics, and invariance in personality structure. *Psychological Review, 102,* 246–268.

ality is lost if one treats the situation as error or noise and eliminates it by simply averaging behavior over diverse situations.

The intuition of consistency in the behavior of the people we know and in ourselves, then, is neither paradoxical nor illusory. It just turns out to be based on a different type of behavioral consistency than the one for which psychologists searched for so many years. Such variability seems to be an essential expression of the enduring underlying personality system itself and its organization. The person–situation debate is resolved not just by recognizing that the person and the situation both are important— a fact that has long been acknowledged. Rather, it dissolves if one thinks of personality in ways that make the predictable variability of behavior across situations an essential aspect of its behavioral expression in the form of meaningful and stable interactions between types of persons and types of situations. Furthermore, to the degree that people are characterized by stable and distinctive patterns of variations in their behavior across situations, their level of cross-situational consistency cannot be very high (Shoda, 1990) and there is no reason to expect it to be. It likewise follows that the "situation," then, is not necessarily a source of error to be removed in the search for personality. Rather, it is a locus in which personality is expressed and within which it can be more fully understood. The challenging question then becomes: what is the nature of that underlying system and organization that accounts for the two types of behavioral consistency that have been found to characterize people stably? That is the question we will continue to pursue in the rest of this text.

SUMMARY

TRAITS, SITUATIONS, AND THE PERSONALITY PARADOX

- Despite intuition and a long tradition of Western thought, researchers found it difficult to show that individuals display highly consistent types of behavior across a variety of different situations.

- In the person–situation debate, it seemed that psychologists had two choices: Either they could view situation information as "noise" that obscures the true, consistent personality, or they could recognize the power of situations.

INCORPORATING SITUATIONS INTO TRAITS

- Alternatively, they could take into account situational features when interpreting individual behavior patterns.

- Personality may be seen both in the overall average frequency of behaviors and in the link between the type of behavior and the type of situation in which it occurs.

- The *if . . . then . . .* , situation–behavior signatures that have been studied show significant stability. Two types of personality consistency emerge, a) the average of overall behavioral tendencies and b) distinctive *if . . . then . . .* , situation–behavior signatures.

- Measures of traits are often not able to predict single acts, but they may predict a pooled combination of behaviors across different situations.

- Knowledge of an individual's specific *if . . . then . . .* signature may help predict what that individual will do in similar types of situations.

INTERACTIONISM IN PERSONALITY

- *Interactionism* is the idea that the individual's behaviors are the product of dynamic interactions between personality and the psychological environment.

- Some personality psychologists try to categorize people, situations, and behaviors into triple typologies.

- Biological sciences treat the dynamic interaction between organisms and their environments as a given.

- The intuition of consistency is neither paradoxical nor illusory: Personality coherence is seen in the individual's meaningful, stable situation–behavior signatures.

KEY TERMS

error variance   72
fundamental attribution
    error   72
if . . . then . . . pattern
    (signature)   73
interactionism   80
person versus situation
    debate   72

person × situation
    interaction   80
personality
    paradox   71
principle of
    interactionism   81
signature of
    personality   73

situationism   72
stable intraindividual
    patterning   73
triple typology   81
uncertainty
    orientation   80

PART I

THE TRAIT-DISPOSITIONAL LEVEL

▶ OVERVIEW: FOCUS, CONCEPTS, METHODS

As we conclude Part One and the presentation of work at the trait-dispositional level of analysis, we pause to put it in perspective and consider the essence of its contributions. So much has been done within trait-dispositional approaches that it becomes easy to lose the essential characteristics, which are summarized in Table A. The summary reminds you that the main aim of the trait approach was to provide methods to infer and quantify people's social–personal traits. In classic trait theories of personality, these traits were assumed to be stable and broadly consistent dispositions that underlie a wide range of behaviors across a number of related situations. As summarized in Table A, traits are inferred from questionnaires, ratings, and other reports about the subject's dispositions. Usually, the person's self-reports are taken as direct signs of the relevant dispositions. For example, the more often you rate yourself as aggressive, the more you are assumed to have an aggressive disposition. The focus of research is on measurement to develop quantitative ways of finding and describing important stable individual differences. Traditionally, the trait approach has recognized that behavior varies with changes in the situation, but it has focused on individual differences in the overall response tendency averaged across many situations. Individual differences on any given dimension are more visible in some situations than in others, and not all dimensions are relevant for all individuals. Some psychologists within this perspective now view traits as "act trends"— summaries of behavior—rather than as explanations or determinants of behavior.

Increasingly, some theorists and researchers also try to take systematic account of the situation as it interacts with the individual's qualities and are incorporating the situation into the conception and assessment of personality dispositions. This alternative

TABLE A Dispositions Expressed as Overall Behavioral Tendencies

Basic units:	Inferred trait dispositions
Causes of behavior:	Generalized (consistent, stable) dispositions
Behavioral manifestations of personality:	Direct indicators of traits
Favored data:	Test responses (e.g., on questionnaires); trait ratings, including self-ratings
Observed responses used as:	Direct signs (indicators) of dispositions
Research focus:	Measurement (test construction), description of individual differences and their patterning; taxonomy of traits
Approach to personality change:	Not much concerned with change: Search for consistent, stable characteristics
Role of situation:	Acknowledged but of secondary interest

TABLE B   Dispositions Expressed as *If . . . then . . .* Behavioral Signatures

Basic units:	*If . . . then . . .* behavioral signatures of personality
Causes of behavior:	Underlying personality processes/dynamics
Behavioral manifestations of personality:	Patterns of behavioral signatures; inconsistencies across different kinds of situations
Favored data:	Behavior sampling, situation-specific diaries, field studies of behavior in context as it unfolds naturally, *if . . . then . . .* self-reports, Person X Situation interactions
Observed responses used as:	Indicators of underlying personality processes (e.g., motives, goals)
Research focus:	Identifying stable personality signatures and understanding their meaning
Approach to personality change:	By understanding the meaning of the personality signatures and modifying them if desired (discussed in Part VII)
Role of situation:	Essential; needs to be incorporated into the conception and measurement of dispositions and personality

approach, summarized in Table B, includes the overall level of a given type of behavior in the study of individual differences. It focuses, however, on the situation-specific expression of traits in the form of stable *if . . . then . . .* , situation–behavior signatures of personality. These signatures are seen as a second type of behavioral consistency that needs to be captured in a comprehensive assessment of dispositions. They provide clues to the motives, goals, and other aspects of the personality system that may underlie them. As Table B indicates, that requires sampling behavior in relation to the situations in which it occurs, and leads to alternative methods for measuring and thinking about personality and its expressions.

▶ ENDURING CONTRIBUTIONS OF THE TRAIT-DISPOSITIONAL LEVEL

Research and theory at this level of analysis represents one of the longest and richest research traditions in the study of personality. For a century, it has made essential contributions to the quantification and objective measurement of personality, for evaluating test results, and for measuring treatment effects. From the start of the field, it has provided both concepts and methods for describing and comparing human individual differences with regard to a vast array of attributes. Its yield has been great, identifying and quantifying the consistencies that characterize different individuals and types of people on trait dimensions. It now provides reliable taxonomies for describing people, identifying their stable positions on a map of trait factors. The Big Five provides such a map that is currently state-of-the-art, and there is considerable, although by no means complete, consensus that it usefully captures much or most of the trait domain. It is useful for many goals, enabling descriptions of the broad trait differences that characterize individuals and groups, and it has greatly stimulated research in the area. It helps psychologists to capture the general gist of what individuals or groups and even cultures "are like on the whole" and to obtain a broad impression that compresses much information.

Nevertheless, work at this level has limitations that even its advocates recognize. Basically, it is not that the work is wrong or technically flawed. The limitation, rather, is that it is only one piece—an extremely important piece—needed for putting together a conception of the whole of personality and all its diverse aspects, and therefore it is incomplete. It offers a first part or stage for an account of personality. Oliver John (1990), a major leader in research on the Big Five, also has been one of its most perceptive critics. He sees that the categories are at such a broad level of abstraction that "they are to personality what the categories 'plant' and 'animal' are to the world of biological objects—extremely useful for some initial rough distinctions, but of less value for predicting specific behaviors of a particular object" (John, 1990, p. 93). An ideal taxonomy, in John's view, needs to be built on causal and dynamic psychological principles and needs to be cast at different levels of abstraction from the broad to the more specific. The rest of this text discusses each of those other levels, and as noted in the Introduction, illustrates their integration in the final part.

The challenge for the trait level will be to connect its work to that coming from the other levels (e.g., Mischel & Shoda, 1998; John, 2001). That also will make it possible to link the individual's position on trait maps to the underlying psychological processes needed to help us understand more about the "why" of personality, that is, to what the mechanisms are that underlie and generate their observed consistencies. Even when we know that someone generally "is a sociable person," for example, the psychologist still needs to explain and understand *why* the person is that way and why and how the psychological and behavioral expressions of his or her sociability take the particular forms that they do.

Work at this level of analysis also has shown that the consistency that characterizes people is seen in their stable *if . . . then . . .* patterns, as well as in their overall average levels of different types of behaviors. Thus, within particular types of situations, individuals do show characteristic stable patterns, and these are reflections and expressions of their underlying personalities. Capturing these signatures, clarifying the underlying processes that generate them, and linking them to work at other levels of analysis will be an important piece of the agenda for the future. These signatures, as well as the overall average levels of behavior that characterize the person at the super trait level, will together provide useful windows for studying the underlying organization and nature of personality. In the history of personality psychology, a major step toward understanding such signatures was pioneered in the work described in the next part of the text, Part II: The Psychodynamic-Motivational Level.

II

THE PSYCHODYNAMIC-MOTIVATIONAL LEVEL

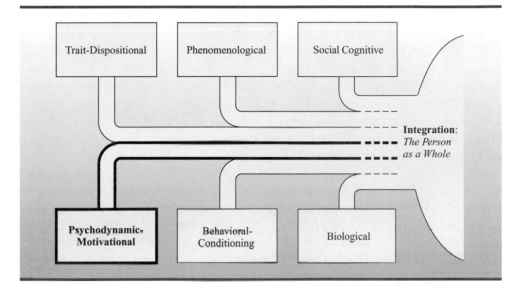

▶ PRELUDE TO PART II: THE PSYCHODYNAMIC-MOTIVATIONAL LEVEL

The trait-dispositional level identified the consistencies and the variability in people's behavior, as you saw in Part I. A next question is: what accounts for and underlies these consistencies? And what accounts for the puzzling inconsistencies and changes in behavior that sometimes develop with distressing emotional consequences? These questions were first addressed in depth by Sigmund Freud, who was working with emotionally disturbed patients in Vienna at about the same time that the trait level of analysis began to develop in the United States.

A hundred years ago in Vienna, a young woman sought help from her physician, Dr. Freud, because she suddenly could no longer see. In a careful examination, Freud found nothing physically wrong with her visual system, and there had been no accident or plausible incident to make her lose her sight. Another patient, while waiting for her appointment, could not resist once again scrubbing her already immaculate hands; that morning she had already washed them dozens of times. In other respects she seemed normal, rational, and was functioning well except for these new symptoms. Sigmund Freud had to find a way to make sense of such problems and those of many of his other patients who needed help because their symptoms made no sense to them either and seemed to be in conflict with other aspects of their personalities. Work at the psychodynamic-motivational level of analysis was begun to meet these challenges.

Freud's approach to the question and his methods for answering it began with a hypothesis that he had formed early in his work with mental patients. Their behavior, he thought, simply could not be understood by looking only at the consistencies in what they did. The answers, he proposed, must be found by understanding their *inconsistencies*. For many years, he struggled to understand the ways in which those inconsistencies might reveal internal contradictions and motives of which the individual seemed to be unaware. If the causes were outside people's awareness, then the real meaning of their behavior could not be seen in what they said at the "surface level" of their self-descriptions.

The more deeply he delved, the more he became convinced that human behavior often is not rational and reflects unconscious motives, conflicts, and processes that are considered taboo by society and therefore condemned and avoided. To make sense of this, the theories that Freud and his followers proposed at first upset the world greatly, as revolutions often do. In time, however, his work set much of the agenda for personality psychology, and it is still relevant today, although often in extensively revised forms. Freud's theories were extremely broad. He tried to explain virtually everything about the human mind and its expressions in ways that he hoped would be universally true for all people across all cultures. His work has been debated and attacked, often with good reason, mostly for not being testable scientifically and for failing to be validated in many of the tests that have been attempted. Yet his contributions changed the view of human nature and gave the world new insights into the self-defensive and often self-defeating characteristics of the human personality. Freud addressed not just the development of abnormal problems but the ways in which essentially normal individuals may function to protect themselves from their own conflicts and anxieties beginning in early childhood.

Chapter 5 presents Freud's basic concepts. Chapter 6 highlights the work he directly influenced at this level for many years, including in the study of motives such as competence and achievement that go much beyond those that Freud emphasized. Chapter 7 examines basic mechanisms and processes central to these ideas, and the implications for personality assessment, change, and treatment.

The Personal Side of the Science

Some questions at the psychodynamic-motivational level you might ask about yourself:

▶ Does what I do sometimes puzzle me?

▶ How and why?

▶ What are the real motives that drive or underlie my behavior?

▶ How can I explain irrational fears and anxieties?

▶ How do I try to protect myself psychologically against getting hurt?

▶ How much of what I do is unconscious or done without awareness?

▶ What might be some unconscious influences on my behavior?

▶ Do I have motives that make me uncomfortable?

▶ If yes, what do I try to do about that?

PSYCHODYNAMIC THEORIES: FREUD'S CONCEPTIONS

Although his contribution to the conception of personality and of the human mind began a century ago, Freud's impact on society, as well as on the social sciences and humanities, still is almost universally hailed as profound; its significance is frequently compared with that of Darwin. Freud's monumental contributions set the stage for the psychodynamic level of analysis that focuses on the unconscious motivations and conflicts underlying much of our behavior. He revolutionized conceptions of the human psyche, provided strikingly powerful metaphors for the mind and human condition, opened the topic of childhood sexuality, and pioneered twentieth-century psychiatry with his approach to the treatment of psychological problems.

Sigmund Freud (1856–1939) started his career in medicine with research on cocaine. In 1884, the properties of this new drug intrigued him, partly because it helped him to get some relief from his own episodes of depression. When he became aware of cocaine's dangers, he soon gave it up, both for personal use and as a research problem. Studying for six months with the neurologist Jean Charcot in Paris in 1885, he became interested in the use of hypnosis to help patients deal with various nonorganic symptoms of "nervous disorders," particularly "hysteria."

Freud's breakthroughs began from his clinical observations of patients he was seeing in his private practice when he returned to Vienna. Imagine scenes like this one in his consulting room on a pleasant residential street in the Vienna of 1905. Freud is presented with a young girl who feels compelled to rinse out her wash basin over and over, dozens of times after each time she washes herself. Her habit becomes so intense and upsetting that her whole life revolves around it. Why? A young boy becomes terrified of horses although he himself was never hurt by one. Why? It was puzzles like these that intrigued the Viennese physician Sigmund Freud who invented psychoanalysis, reshaped the field of psychology, and influenced many later developments in all the social sciences and in Western concepts of human nature.

5.1 How did Freud's views conflict with the prevailing beliefs of his time?

From these puzzles, Freud created a theory and a treatment method that changed our view of personality, health, and the mind itself. Working as a physician treating disturbed people in Vienna at the turn of the century, he formulated a theory that upset many cherished assumptions about human nature and startled the neo-Victorian world. Before Freud, people's behavior was believed to be under their conscious and rational control. Freud turned that conception upside down. Rather than seeing consciousness as the core of the mind, Freud compared personality to an iceberg: only the tip shows itself overtly, the rest lies below. Rather than viewing the person as a supremely rational being, he saw people as driven by impulses and striving to satisfy deep and lasting sexual

Sigmund Freud (1856–1939)

and aggressive urgings. Rather than relying on people's reports about themselves as accurate self-representations, he interpreted what they said and did as highly indirect, disguised, symbolic representations of unconscious underlying forces.

In the course of more than 40 years of active writing and clinical research, Freud developed a theory of personality, a method of treatment for personality disturbances, and a wealth of clinical observations based on his therapeutic experiences as well as on his analyses of himself. Freud based both his theory and his psychoanalytic treatment on his extensive clinical observations of disturbed persons. He first noted certain **sensory anesthesias,** which are losses of sensory ability, as in blindness, deafness, or loss of feeling in a body part. He also found patients with motor paralyses that seemed to have no neurological origin. He proposed that these symptoms expressed a way of defending against unacceptable unconscious wishes. For example, a soldier who cannot admit his fear of facing battle develops a motor paralysis without a neurological basis. Or a young bride, unable to admit her hostility to her husband, becomes confined to her chair, although she shows no physical disease. All these examples illustrate **hysteria.** The fundamental feature of hysteria, according to Freud, is the presence of massive repression and the development of a symptom pattern that indirectly or symbolically expresses the repressed needs and wishes. On the basis of careful clinical observations, Freud gradually developed his theory of personality, continuously changing his ideas in the light of his growing clinical experiences and insights.

5.2 How did the study of hysteria influence Freud's views?

▶ BASIC ASSUMPTIONS: UNCONSCIOUS MENTAL DETERMINISM

Two key assumptions underlie much of Freud's conception:

- First, his unique innovation was to propose that behavior is never accidental: it is psychologically determined by mental motivational causes. This is called the principle of **motivational determinism.**
- Second, these causes are outside of the person's complete consciousness or awareness.

5.3 What two major assumptions underlie Freud's ideas?

The Unconscious

Freud the scientist wanted to try to explain the irrational behavior he witnessed in his patients. They seemed compelled to do things that they could not explain or sometimes even remember. Most puzzling, he could not attribute their symptoms to organic causes such as brain injuries or physical diseases: physically they were intact. They were consciously trying to stop their symptoms, desperate to relieve them, but they simply could not control them. Freud's insight was to propose that some unconscious irrational force was behind the symptom psychologically. The battles between the conscious will and the unconscious became the war of mental life in his theory.

Around the year 1900, Freud first divided mental processes into conscious, preconscious, and unconscious (Freud, 1905). We are instantly aware of our **conscious** thoughts. The immediately available level of consciousness refers to what is in one's attention at a given moment. The many events that we can bring into attention more or less easily, from the background music on the radio to memories of things experienced years ago, are **preconscious.** Thus even though we are not aware of preconscious thoughts at a given moment, we can bring them into awareness voluntarily and fairly easily. In contrast, outside this range of the potentially available lies the **unconscious.**

5.4 Define and give an example of each of Freud's three levels of consciousness.

This third zone is not responsive to our deliberate efforts at recall, and it is the layer that was Freud's core concern. Because their content is threatening, unconscious mental activities are kept beyond awareness by a mechanism of repression that works actively to keep them away from our awareness, so that we simply are unable to raise them into consciousness.

The Roads to the Unconscious

Freud was eager to find methods for his work that would make his ideas more than abstract claims or beliefs. It was through these methods that his conception achieved its richness and ultimately made its enormous impact. If the unconscious mind was so important for understanding psychological causes, then the challenge was how to get to it.

5.5 Why do dreams occupy a position of importance in psychoanalytic theory? How are they related to neurotic symptoms?

Dreams.   Freud probed the unconscious most deeply through his explorations of dreams. He saw his 1899 book, *The Interpretation of Dreams*, like the adventures of a Columbus of the mind, a voyage into the darkest regions. The dream, Freud proposed, was the dreamer's unconscious effort to fulfill a wish that could not be expressed more directly. The analyst's task was to discover the hidden secrets underneath the surface content of the dream. To uncover those buried meanings, the analyst must overcome the dreamer's own resistance to facing himself or herself honestly, no matter how frightening or ugly the discoveries might prove to be.

In his voyage into the unconscious, Freud proceeded by scrutinizing his own dreams to try to face the motivations deep within his own personality. Unflattering self-revelation often resulted. For example, Freud is troubled by fears about plagiarizing, and he dreams about himself being treated as a thief stealing overcoats in lecture halls (Roazen, 1974, p. 99). Through self-analysis, Freud constructed his theory of the unconscious and the devious self-deceptions with which people try to disguise their own wishes from themselves.

In *The Interpretation of Dreams,* Freud built the case that in the dream we can find the hidden fulfillment of a desire that the person is trying to avoid experiencing consciously. Interestingly, this insight into the wish-fulfilling nature of dreams also led to the view that dreams, rather than disturbing sleep, actually function as the "guardians" of sleep. More than 50 years later, experiments discovered that in fact people need their dreams and become deeply troubled if their sleep is deprived of the phases in which dreaming naturally occurs (Roazen, 1974).

From his pioneering theory of dreams, Freud moved on to analyze the meaning of the disturbed behaviors and the anxieties his patients displayed and to develop a systematic theory about how to treat them. The main sources of anxiety, according to Freud, were the person's own unconscious sexual desires and aggressive impulses. He saw both sexual and aggressive urgings as basic human impulses or instincts, part of our heritage. He believed that sexuality does not begin with puberty but is visible early in childhood. It shows itself also in the young girl's affection for her father and the boy's infantile desires for his mother. Emotional attitudes, moreover, arise in these early relationships.

In the face of the objections and prudishness of the Victorian Age, he insisted that the route to self-acceptance was the honest recognition of one's instinctual sexuality and aggressiveness. Avoiding self-deception was the key. Making the unconscious impulses conscious was the road to health. The symptoms, Freud believed, were simply the indirect and sometimes symbolic expression of the unacceptable impulses that the person was unable to face consciously because of the anxiety they created.

Free Association.   Much of Freud's thinking was built on the analysis of dreams, but that was not the only method he favored. His second road to the unconscious, sometimes called the "royal road," became the therapeutic method of **free association.** In this method, the patient, reclining on a couch, is encouraged to simply say anything and everything that comes to mind, no matter what it is or how irrational it might seem, without censoring it. In Focus 5.1 discusses how free association is encouraged. In this way, the unconscious begins to become conscious. Although "resistance" to this process occurs often, it is gradually "worked through" until the unacceptable wishes can be faced. Then the patient is freed from having to manifest them indirectly through such symptoms as hysterical paralysis or other neurotic expressions.

IN FOCUS 5.1

ENCOURAGING FREE ASSOCIATION

Free association and the analysis of dreams are the methods of personality study that come most directly from Freud's work. Both methods are used in the context of the patient–therapist meetings during psychoanalysis.

In free association, you are instructed to give your thoughts complete freedom and to report daydreams, feelings, and images, no matter how incoherent, illogical, or meaningless they might seem. This technique may be employed either with a little prompting or by offering brief phrases ("my mother . . ."; "I often . . .") as a stimulus to encourage associations.

Freud believed that dreams were similar to the patient's free associations. He thought the dream was an expression of the most primitive workings of the mind. Dreams were interpreted as fulfilling a wish or discharging tension by inducing an image of the desired goal. Freud felt that through the interpretation of dreams he was penetrating into the unconscious.

The following passages illustrate some typical instructions and responses in the process of encouraging free association during psychoanalytic interviews. The patient complains that she does not have any thoughts at the moment.

Therapist: It may seem that way to you at first, but there are always some thoughts there. Just as your

heart is always beating, there's always some thought or other going through your mind.

Patient: Your mentioning the word "heart" reminds me that the doctor told my mother the other day she had a weak heart.

In a later interview the same woman became silent again and could not continue.

Therapist: Just say what comes to you.

Patient: Oh, odds and ends that aren't very important.

Therapist: Say them anyway.

Patient: I don't see how they could have much bearing. I was wondering what sort of books those are over there. But that hasn't anything to do with what I'm here for.

Therapist: One never can tell, and actually you're in no position to judge what has bearing and what hasn't. Let me decide that. You just report what comes into your mind regardless of whether you think it's important or not (Colby, 1951, p. 153).

▶ PSYCHIC STRUCTURE: ANATOMY OF THE MIND

To understand how we deal with unconscious wishes, Freud (1933) also developed an "anatomy" of the mind that occupied him in the early part of the 1920s. This led to the structural view of personality consisting of three "institutions" or mental "agencies": the id, ego, and superego. These institutions form in the course of early experience, with the superego, the last to emerge, crystallizing some time after the sixth year.

TABLE 5.1   The Freudian Conception of Mental Structure

Structure	Consciousness	Contents and Function
Id	Unconscious	Basic impulses (sex and aggression); seeks immediate gratification regardless of consequences; impervious to reason and logic; immediate, irrational, impulsive
Ego	Predominantly conscious	Executive mediating between id impulses and superego inhibitions; tests reality; seeks safety and survival; rational, logical, taking account of space and time
Superego	Both conscious and unconscious	Ideals and morals; strives for perfection; incorporated (internalized) from parents; observes, dictates, criticizes, and prohibits; imposes limitations on satisfactions; becomes the conscience of the individual

These three agencies are closely linked to the three layers of consciousness. The id is in the unconscious layer, characterized by mental processes outside one's awareness; the ego is predominantly conscious; and the superego includes a mix of conscious and unconscious processes. Although the three parts interact intimately, each has its own characteristics, which are summarized in Table 5.1 and discussed next.

The Id: At the Core

5.6   Describe the id and the process that governs its operation.

The **id** is the mental agency that contains everything inherited, especially the instincts. It is the basis of personality, the energy source for the whole system, and the foundation from which the ego and superego later develop. The id, according to Freud, is the innermost core of personality, and it is closely linked to biological processes.

The id's instincts, Freud thought, have their source biologically within the excitation states of the body. They act like drives, pressing for discharge (release). They are motivated, in the sense that their *aim* is to seek reduction, that is, to lower the state of excitation. Thus the tension that the build-up of the unexpressed drive creates has to be released, much like the build-up of steam in an overheating boiler has to be let out or the system explodes. Instinctual drives are biological and inborn, but the objects involved in attempts to reduce the drives depend on the individual's particular early experiences.

The Pleasure Principle.   Increases in energy from internal or external stimulation produce tension and discomfort that the id cannot tolerate. The id seeks immediate tension reduction, regardless of the consequences. This tendency toward immediate tension reduction Freud called the **pleasure principle.** The id obeys it, seeking immediate satisfaction of instinctual wishes and impulses, regardless of reason or logic or consequences.

Sexual and Aggressive Instincts.   Freud (1940) classified these impulses or instincts into the categories of life, or sexual instincts, and death, or aggressive instincts. The psychological representations of these instincts are wishes, and they often are irrational and unconscious.

Primary Process Thinking.   To discharge tension, the id forms an internal image or hallucination of the desired object. The hungry infant, for example, may conjure up an internal representation of the mother's breast. The resulting image is considered a wish fulfillment, similar to the attempted wish fulfillment that Freud believed characterized normal dreams and the hallucinations of psychotics. **Primary process thinking** was Freud's term for such direct, irrational, reality-ignoring attempts to satisfy needs. Because mental images by themselves cannot reduce tension, the ego develops.

The Ego: Tester of Reality

The **ego** is a direct outgrowth of the id. Freud described its origin this way:

> *Under the influence of the real external world around us, one portion of the id has under-gone a special development. From what was originally a cortical layer, equipped with the organs for receiving stimuli and with arrangements for acting as a protective shield against stimuli, a special organization has arisen which henceforward acts as an intermediary between the id and the external world. To this region of our mind we have given the name of* ego *(Freud, 1933, p. 2).*

5.7   How does the ego derive from the id, and what are its functions and operating principles?

The ego is in direct contact with the external world. It is governed by considerations of safety, and its task is preservation of the organism. The ego wages its battle for survival against both the external world and the internal instinctual demands of the id. In this task, it has to continuously differentiate between the mental representations of wish-fulfilling images and the actual outer world of reality. In its search for food or sexual release, for example, it must find the appropriate tension-reducing objects in the environment so that tension reduction can actually occur. That is, it must go from image to object, and get satisfaction for id impulses while simultaneously preserving itself.

The Reality Principle.   The ego's function is governed by the **reality principle,** which requires it to test reality and to delay discharge of tension until the appropriate object and environmental conditions are found. The ego operates by means of a "secondary process" that involves realistic, logical thinking and planning through the use of the higher or cognitive mental processes. That is, while the id seeks immediate tension reduction by such primary process means as wish-fulfilling imagery and direct gratification of sexual and aggressive impulses, the ego, like an executive, mediates between the id and the world, testing reality and making decisions about various courses of available action. For example, it delays impulses for immediate sexual gratification until the environmental conditions are appropriate.

Freud believed the ego was the only hope for the world, the part of the mind that would allow humans to emerge from the irrationality and primitivism of being driven wildly by their biological impulses. The ego was the way toward a life of reason: "Where id was," Freud wrote, "there shall ego be," and psychoanalysis was the road for that transformation from the person's domination by impulsivity to rationality and insightfulness.

The Superego: High Court in Pursuit of Perfection

Freud's third mental structure was the **superego.** He wrote:

> *The long period of childhood, during which the growing human being lives in dependence on his parents, leaves behind it as a precipitate the formation in his ego of a special agency in which this parental influence is prolonged. It has received the name of* superego. *In so far as this superego is differentiated from the ego or is opposed to it, it constitutes a third power which the ego must take into account (Freud, 1933, p. 2).*

5.8   How does the superego develop, and what are its functions?

Thus, the superego is the agency that internalizes the influence of the parents. It represents the morals and standards of society that have become part of the internal world of the individual in the course of the development of personality. The superego is the conscience, the judge of right and wrong, of good and bad, in accord with the internalized standards of the parents and thus, indirectly, of society. It represents the ideal. Whereas the id seeks pleasure and the ego tests reality, the superego seeks perfection. The superego, for Freud, involved the internalization of parental control in the form of self-control. For example, the individual with a well-developed superego resists "bad" or "evil" temptations, such as stealing when hungry or killing when angry, even when there are no external constraints (in the form of police or other people) to stop him.

In the theory, the superego develops around age five out of the human infant's long period of helplessness and extreme dependency on caregivers. The young child desperately fears the possible loss of this early love; the threat of parents withdrawing protection and gratification is terrifying. At first this fear is rooted in the objective anxiety of losing love and satisfaction due to the child's own actions (being "bad"). In time, an active *identification* occurs as the child incorporates the parental images and commands into itself psychologically. As the parental wishes become incorporated through this process, the conscience becomes an internal voice rather than an external control.

Once fully developed, the superego can become a compelling and even irrational force of its own, just as demanding as the id. Examples of this force are seen in severe depressions characterized by extreme self-hatred and self-destructiveness. The tyranny of the superego is thus added to the demands of the id. It is the burden of the ego to continuously try to compromise among these competing forces while testing the waters of "reality."

▶ CONFLICT, ANXIETY, AND PSYCHODYNAMICS

5.9 What three ego activities are involved in psychodynamic processes?

Psychodynamics are the processes through which personality works. In Freud's view, they concern three continuous tasks of the ego: (1) the control of unacceptable impulses from the id; (2) the avoidance of pain produced by internal conflict in the efforts to control and master those unacceptable impulses; and (3) the attainment of a harmonious integration among the diverse components of personality in conflict. Much of Freud's own energy was directed at understanding the **transformation of motives:** the basic impulses persist and press for discharge, but the objects at which they are directed and the manner in which they are expressed are transformed (1917).

Conflict

5.10 Describe the basic conflicts that characterize personality dynamics.

According to Freud (1915), the three parts of the psychic structure—id, ego, and superego—are always in dynamic conflict. The term *dynamics* refers to this continuous interaction and clash between id impulses seeking release and inhibitions or restraining forces against them—an interplay between driving forces and forces that inhibit them. These forces and counterforces propel personality.

The id's drive for immediate satisfaction of impulses reflects human nature: people are motivated to avoid pain and achieve immediate tension reduction. This drive for immediate satisfaction of instinctual demands leads to a clash between the individual and the environment. Conflict develops to the degree that the environment and its representatives in the form of other persons, notably the parents in childhood, and later the superego, punish or block immediate impulse expression.

Persons in time come to incorporate into their superegos the values by which they are raised, largely by internalizing parental characteristics and morals. In Freud's view, perpetual warfare and conflict exist between humans and environment. Insofar as societal values become internalized as part of the person, this warfare is waged internally between the id, ego, and superego, and it produces anxiety.

Anxiety is painful and therefore we automatically try to reduce the tension it produces. Freud first used defense as a psychoanalytic term (1899), but he focused primarily on one type of defense mechanism involving denial and repression. His daughter, Anna Freud, distinguished some of the other major defense mechanisms recognized today (A. Freud, 1936)—discussed in the next chapter.

Psychodynamic theorists emphasize that when a threat becomes especially serious, it may lead to intense inhibitions and defenses. In the psychodynamic view, such defensive inhibition is desperate and primitive. It is a massive, generalized, inhibitory reaction rather than a specific response to the particular danger. This **denial** defense occurs when the person can neither escape nor attack the threat. If the panic is sufficient, the only possible alternative may be to deny it. Outright denial may be possible for the young child, who is not yet upset by violating the demands of reality testing. When the child becomes too mature to deny objective facts in the interests of defense, denial becomes a less plausible alternative and repression may occur.

Defense: Denial and Repression

In psychodynamic theory, **repression** usually refers to a particular type of denial: ". . . the forgetting, or ejection from consciousness, of memories of threat, and especially the ejection from awareness of impulses in oneself that might have objectionable consequences" (White, 1964, p. 214).

Repression was one of the initial concepts in Freud's theory and became one of its cornerstones. Freud (1920) believed that the mechanisms of denial and repression were the most fundamental or primitive defenses and played a part in other defenses. Indeed, he thought that other defenses started with a massive inhibition of an impulse.

5.11 How did Freud use his concept of repression to explain hysterical disorders?

Freud based his ideas concerning repression and defense on his clinical observations of hysterical women at the turn of this century. Recall that he noted that some of these patients seemed to develop physical symptoms that did not make sense neurologically. For example, in a hysterical difficulty called "glove anesthesia," the patient showed an inability to feel in the hands—a symptom that is impossible neurologically. In their studies of hysteria, Freud and his associate Breuer hypnotized some of the patients and found, to their great surprise, that when the origins and meanings of hysterical symptoms were talked about under hypnosis, the symptoms tended to disappear. This finding proved beyond any doubt that the symptoms were not caused by organic damage or physical defects.

Partly to understand hysteria, Freud developed his theory of unconscious conflict and defense. In his view, such symptoms as hysterical blindness and **hysterical anesthesia** (loss of sensation) reflected defensive attempts to avoid painful thoughts and feelings by diversionary preoccupation with apparently physical symptoms. Freud thought that the key mechanism in this blocking was unconsciously motivated repression. Through repression, the basic impulses that are unacceptable to the person are rendered unconscious and thereby less frightening. Because such diversionary measures are inherently ineffective ways of dealing with anxiety-provoking impulses, these impulses persist. The impulses continue to press for release in disguised and distorted forms that are called "symptoms."

Libido

Freud thought that each person contained finite amount of energy, called libido, a term for the total energy that drives id impulses. **Libido** is attached or fixed on aspects of the internal and external environment. The energy available to the organism may be continuously transformed, fixed onto different "objects" (note that "objects" was a term that for Freud included people and not just inanimate things). However, the total amount of energy is conserved and stable. Freud's energy system thus was consistent with the hydraulic models of nineteenth-century physics.

The id was seen as a kind of dynamo, and the total mind (or psyche) was viewed as a closed system motivated to maintain equilibrium: any forces that were built up required discharge. The discharge could be indirect. Instinctual impulses could be displaced from one object to another, for instance, from one's parents to other authority figures or more remotely, from the genitals, for example, to phallic symbols.

▶ NEUROSIS

When Defenses Fail: Neurotic Anxiety and Conflict

Sometimes the defenses that disguise basic motives may become inadequate and denial and repression no longer work. Even under the usual circumstances of everyday life, the defenses are occasionally penetrated and the person betrays himself (Freud, 1901). Such betrayals of underlying motives are seen when defenses are relaxed, as in dream life or in jokes and slips of the tongue. The defense process involves **distortion** and **displacement,** which occur when private meanings develop as objects and events become transformed into symbols representing things quite different from themselves. It is believed that these meanings are partially revealed by behavioral "signs" or symptoms that may symbolize disguised wishes and unconscious conflicts. For example, phobias such as the fear of snakes may reflect basic sexual conflicts; in this case, the feared snake has symbolic meaning.

5.12 What is neurotic anxiety, and what is its role in neurotic symptoms?

Development of Neurotic Anxiety. It is now possible to consider the Freudian conception of how neurotic anxiety and problems may develop. The sequence here (depicted in Fig. 5.1) begins with the child's aggressive or sexual impulses that seek direct release. These efforts at discharge may be strongly punished and blocked by dangers or threats (for example, intense parental punishment such as withdrawal of love). Hence, they lead to objective anxiety. The child may become especially afraid that these impulses will lead to loss of parental love and in time, therefore, may come to fear his or her own impulses. Because this state is painful, the child tries to repress

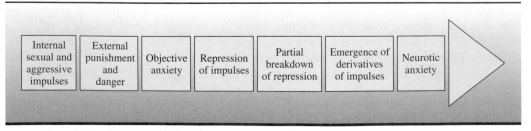

Figure 5.1 Sequence in Freudian conception of neurotic anxiety.

these impulses. If the ego is weak, the repression is only partly successful and the instinctual impulses persist. Unless expressed in some acceptable form, these impulses become increasingly "pent up," gradually building up to the point where they become hard to repress. Consequently, there may be a partial breakdown of repression, and some of the impulses may break through, producing some neurotic anxiety. Anxiety, in this view, functions as a danger signal, a warning to the individual that repressed impulses are starting to break through the defenses. Rather than emerging directly, however, the unacceptable impulses express themselves indirectly in disguised and symbolic ways.

The Meaning of Neurotic Acts. Freud felt that the symbolic meaning of behavior was clearest in neurotic acts. He cited the case of a girl who compulsively rinsed out her wash basin many times after washing. Freud thought that the significance of this ceremony was expressed in the proverb, "Don't throw away dirty water until you have clean." He interpreted the girl's action as a warning to her sister, to whom she was very close, "not to separate from her unsatisfactory husband until she had established a relationship with a better man" (Freud, 1959, vol. 2, p. 28).

Another patient was able to sit only in a particular chair and could leave it only with much difficulty. In Freud's analysis of her problem, the chair symbolized the husband to whom she remained faithful. Freud saw the symbolic meaning of her compulsion in her sentence "It is so hard to part from anything (chair or husband) in which one has once settled oneself" (Freud, 1959, vol. 2, p. 29). Thus, the important object of conflict—the husband—was transformed into a trivial one—the chair. Freud cited these and many similar cases as evidence for the view that neurotic behaviors express unconscious motives and ideas symbolically.

The clinician's task, then, is to decipher the unconscious meaning of the patient's behavior and to discover the conflicts and dynamics that might underlie seemingly irrational behavior patterns (see Table 5.2).

Origins of Neuroses

In Freud's view, serious problems, such as the neuroses, and the roots of the symptoms that characterize them, begin in early childhood:

> . . . It seems that neuroses are acquired only in early childhood (up to the age of six), even though their symptoms may not make their appearance till much later. The childhood neurosis may become manifest for a short time or may even be overlooked. In every case the later neurotic illness links up with the prelude in childhood.

5.13 At what developmental period do neuroses develop and what factors produce them?

TABLE 5.2 Possible Meanings of Some Behavioral Signs in Freudian Theory

Behavioral Sign	Possible Underlying Meaning
Fear of snakes	Sexual conflict regarding genitals
Compulsive cleanliness	Reaction against anal impulses
Obsessive thought: "My mother is drowning"	Imperfectly repressed hostility toward mother
Paranoid jealousy	Homosexual wishes
Preoccupation with money	Problems around toilet training

> . . . *The neuroses are, as we know, disorders of the ego; and it is not to be wondered at if the ego, so long as it is feeble, immature and incapable of resistance, fails to deal with tasks which it could cope with later on with the utmost ease. In these circumstances instinctual demands from within, no less than excitations from the external world, operate as 'traumas,' particularly if they are met halfway by certain innate dispositions (Freud, 1933, pp. 41–42).*

As these quotations indicate, neuroses were seen as the products of early childhood traumas plus innate dispositions. But even the behavior of less disturbed persons was believed to reflect expressions of underlying unconscious motives and conflicts. These manifestations could be seen in the "psychopathology of everyday life"—the occurrence of meaningful but common unconscious expressions, as discussed next.

The Psychopathology of Everyday Life: "Mistakes" That Betray

5.14 How do everyday "slips" reveal the unconscious? Provide some examples.

Some of Freud's most fascinating—and controversial—ideas involved the elaboration of possible hidden meanings that might underlie such common occurrences as slips of the tongue, errors in writing, jokes, and dreams. In Freud's (1901, 1920) view, "mistakes" may be unconsciously motivated by impulses that the individual is afraid to express directly or openly. To show that mistakes may really be motivated by underlying wishes, Freud pointed out many instances in which even the attempt to "correct" the error appears to betray a hidden, unacceptable meaning. In one case, for example, an official introduced a general as "this battle-scared veteran" and tried to "correct" his mistake by saying "bottle-scarred veteran." Other examples are summarized in Table 5.3. Some common Freudian dream symbols are shown in Table 5.4.

Motivational Determinism: Unconscious Causes

5.15 What is motivational determinism?

According to Freud's principle of motivational determinism, all behavior is motivated, and the causal chain that links wishes to actions can be complex and indirect.

TABLE 5.3   Examples of Behaviors Motivated by Unconscious Wishes

Behavior Involved	Unconscious Wish	Transformation
Slip of the tongue: May I "insort" (instead of escort) you?	To insult	Condensation: (insult + escort = "insort")
Slip of the tongue: "Gentlemen, I declare a quorum present and herewith declare the session *closed.*"	To close the meeting	Association of opposites: (open = closed)
Dream of disappointment in quality of theater tickets, as a result of having gotten them too soon.	I married too soon; I could have gotten a better spouse by waiting.	Symbolism: (getting tickets too soon = marrying too soon)
Dream of breaking an arm	Desire to break marriage vows	Conversion into visual imagery: (breaking vows = breaking an arm)

Source: Freud, S. (1920). *A general introduction to psychoanalysis.* New York: Boni and Liveright.

**TABLE 5.4 Some Freudian Dream Symbols
and Their Meanings**

Dream Symbol	Meaning
King, queen	Parents
Little animals, vermin	Siblings
Travel, journey	Dying
Clothes, uniforms	Nakedness
Flying	Sexual intercourse
Extraction of teeth	Castration

Source: Freud, S. (1920). *A general introduction to
psychoanalysis.* New York: Boni and Liveright.

Does a dream of a broken
arm imply a desire to
break one's wedding
vows?

Suppose, for example, a man fights with his wife about money, is personally fussy about
his appearance, and becomes very upset when he loses his umbrella. These seemingly
different bits of behavior might actually be motivated by a common cause. Much of
psychoanalytic assessment and therapy is a search for such underlying causes. A psychodynamic explanation of behavior consists of finding the motives that produced it.
The focus is not on behavior, but on the motivations that it serves and reflects. And
usually these motives are disguised in their expressions and unconscious, rooted in
early experiences.

▶ PERSONALITY DEVELOPMENT

Freud believed that every person normally progresses through five **psychosexual
stages.** During the first five years of life, pleasure is successively focused on three
zones of the body as the oral, anal, and phallic stages unfold. Then comes a quiet
latency period of about five or six years. Finally, if progress through each stage has been
successful, the person reaches the mature or genital stage after puberty. But special
problems at any stage may retard or arrest (fixate) development and leave enduring
marks on the person's character throughout life.

5.16 Describe the five psychosexual stages and indicate how unresolved conflicts at the early stages create personality traits.

Stages of Development

Oral.　The **oral stage** occurs during the first year of life when pleasure is focused on the mouth and on the satisfactions of sucking, eating, and biting in the course of feeding (but see In Focus 5.2). The dependent, helpless person is said to be fixated at this stage, when the infant is totally dependent upon others for satisfaction of his or her needs.

According to Freud, the oral stage is divided into two periods: (1) sucking and (2) biting and chewing. Later character traits develop from these earliest modes of oral pleasure. More specifically, oral incorporation (as in sucking and taking in milk in the first oral period) becomes the prototype of such pleasures as those gained from the acquisition of knowledge or possessions. In his view, the gullible person (who is "easily taken in") is fixated at the oral, incorporative level of personality. The sarcastic, bitingly argumentative person is fixated at the second oral period—the sadistic level associated with biting and chewing.

Anal.　In the second year of life, the **anal stage** is marked by a shift in body pleasure to the anus and by a concern with the retention and expulsion of feces. According to Freud, during toilet training, the child has his first experience with imposed control. The manner in which toilet training is handled may influence later personal qualities and conflicts. For example, extremely harsh, repressive training might produce a person characterized by obstinacy, stinginess, and a preoccupation with orderliness and cleanliness.

5.17 How does the *Oedipus complex* promote male sex role development?

Phallic.　The **phallic stage** is the period in which the child observes the difference between male and female and experiences what Freud called **the Oedipus complex.** This complex, symbolized in the father–son conflicts of ancient Greek myths, occurs at about age five.

Freud thought that both boys and girls love their mother as the satisfier of their basic needs and resent their father as a rival for their mother's affections. In addition, the boy fears castration by the father as punishment for desiring his mother sexually. This **castration anxiety** is so terrifying that it results in the repression of the boy's sexual desire for his mother and hostility toward his father. To reduce the anxiety of possible castration by the father, the boy tries to become like him or to identify with him. In this identification, he gradually internalizes the father's standards and values as his own, becoming more like his father rather than battling him.

Identification with the father in turn helps the boy gain some indirect satisfaction of his sexual impulses toward his mother. In this last phase of the Oedipus complex of the male, the superego reaches its final development as the internalized standards of parents and society, and the opposition to incest and aggression becomes part of his own value system.

In the female, **penis envy,** resulting from the discovery that she lacks the male organ, is the impetus to exchange her original love object—the mother—for a new object—the father. Unlike the boy's Oedipus complex, which is repressed through fear, the girl—having nothing to lose—persists in her sexual desire for her father. This desire does, naturally, undergo some modification because of realistic barriers.

Latency.　After the phallic stage, a **latency period** develops. Now there is less overt concern with sexuality; the child represses his or her memories of infantile sexuality and forbidden sexual activity by making them unconscious.

Genital. This is the final, mature stage of psychosexual development. Now the person is capable of genuine love for other people and can achieve adult sexual satisfactions. No longer characterized by the selfishness (narcissism) and mixed, conflicting

5.18 Does research support Freud's conception of the infant as primarily "oral"?

HOW ORAL IS THE INFANT?

Although the feeding situation is a critical phase of early development, it is only one part of the total relationship between the growing organism and the world. Thus, the baby is more than an "oral" creature. Babies respond to stimulation of the mouth, lips, and tongue, but in addition, they see, hear, and feel, obtaining stimulation visually, aurally, and from being handled.

Convinced that in spite of an abundance of theories personality psychology has much too little real data, Professor Burton L. White of Harvard University began by carefully observing infants as they lay in their cribs. (The participants were physically normal infants in an orphanage.) He and his colleagues recorded the quantity and quality of visual–motor activity to study the babies' attention. On the basis of these observations, they plotted the development of the infants' tendency to explore the visual surroundings, as depicted in Figure 5.2. The findings surprised the investigators:

> *One important revelation for me which resulted from these weekly observations was that, contrary to my academically bred expectations, infants weren't really very oral during the first months of life. In fact, between two and six months, a far more appropriate*

description would be that they are visual-prehensory creatures. We observed subject after subject spend dozens of hours watching first his fists, then his fingers, and then the interactions between hands and fingers. Thumb-sucking and mouthing were rarely observed except for brief periods when the infant was either noticeably upset or unusually hungry (White, 1967, p. 207).

These observations point up how much more we need to know about the details of the infant's activities before we can reach conclusions about what events characterize early development. It may be, as this investigator's comments imply, that the "oral" infant will turn out to be much more attentive and active, and less oral and passive, than was believed in early formulations. Indeed, close observation of young children suggests a dramatic increase in the infant's competence by the second or third month. More wakefulness and alertness, greater receptivity to stimulation, more directed attention and less fussing begin to characterize the baby (Sroufe, 1977). Stimulation becomes less unsettling and may be sought out actively as the baby becomes more and more attentive, even to its own movements.

Figure 5.2 The development of the tendency to explore the surroundings.
Source: Adapted from White, B. L., & Held, R. (1966). Plasticity of sensorimotor development in the human infant. In J. F. Rosenblith and W. Allinsmith (Eds.), *The Causes of Behavior II*, pp. 60–70. Boston: Allyn and Bacon.

feelings that marked the earlier stages, he or she can relate to others in a mature, heterosexual fashion. But before he or she reaches the **genital stage,** excessive stress or overindulgence may cause the person to become fixated at earlier levels of psychosexual development.

Fixation and Regression

5.19 How do fixation, regression, and identification enter into personality development?

The concepts of **fixation** and **regression** are closely connected with Freud's conceptualization of psychosexual stages of development. Fixation means that a sexual impulse is arrested at an early stage. Regression is reversion to an earlier stage in the face of unmanageable stress. Fixation occurs when conflict at a particular stage of psychosexual development is too great. Severe deprivation or overindulgence at a particular stage, or inconsistent alterations between indulgence and deprivation, may lead to fixation.

In sum, personality is intimately related to the individual's mode of coping with problems at each stage of psychosexual development. The result is reflected in the nature of character formation, symptoms, and relations with other people. When individuals' resolution of problems at any stage of development is inadequate, later stress may cause them to regress to that earlier stage. They then display behavior typical of that less mature period.

Freud's Theory of Identification

Parts of Freud's theory of psychosexual stages have been modified and even rejected in recent years. Some of his closely related concepts regarding identification, however, have continued to be influential.

Early personality development occurs in the setting of the family. In that context, you saw Freud strongly emphasize the child's attachment to the mother and the rivalry between son and father for her attentions. This triangle of relations, called the Oedipal situation, is the basis for identification with the standards of the parent. This identification process Freud attributed to two mechanisms that operate during psychosexual development.

Anaclitic identification is based on the intense dependency of a child on the mother, beginning early in the course of the infant's development. Because of the helplessness of the infant, the dependency upon the caretaker is profound. Identification for girls is based mainly on this early love or dependency relation with the mother. In anaclitic identification, the child must first have developed a dependent love relationship with her caretaker (usually the mother). Later, when the mother begins to withdraw some of her nurturant attention, the child tries to recapture her by imitating and reproducing her in actions and fantasy.

For boys, dependency or anaclitic identification with the mother is followed later by **identification with the aggressor.** The "aggressor" is the father during the Oedipal phase of development. Identification with the aggressor is motivated by fear of harm and castration by the punitive father in retribution for the son's fantasies and his sexual wishes toward the mother. Freud described the situation vividly:

. . . When a boy (from the age of two or three) has entered the phallic phase of his libidinal [sexual] development, is feeling pleasurable sensations in his sexual organ and has learnt to procure these at will by manual stimulation, he becomes his mother's lover. He wishes to possess her physically in such ways as he has divined from his observations and

intuitions about sexual life, and he tries to seduce her by showing her the male organ which he is proud to own. In a word, his early awakened masculinity seeks to take his father's place with her; his father has hitherto in any case been an envied model to the boy, owing to the physical strength he perceives in him and the authority with which he finds him clothed. His father now becomes a rival who stands in his way and whom he would like to get rid of (Freud, 1933, p. 46).

The hostile feelings that the boy experiences in the Oedipal situation create great anxiety in him; he desires the mother but fears castration from the father. To defend against the anxiety, he resolves the Oedipal conflict, repressing his aggressive wishes against his father and trying to become more like him. It is as though the boy believes that if he "*is*" the father, he cannot be hurt by him. Identification with the aggressor requires that the boy have a strong (but ambivalent) relation with the father. In this relationship, love for the father is mixed with hostility because the father possesses the mother and interferes with the son's urges. Freud thought that through identification with the aggressor, boys develop a stricter superego.

▶ IMPACT OF FREUD'S THEORIES

Image of the Person

Freud built a dramatic image of what a person might be, inventing a sweeping and novel theoretical system. Freud saw the person as struggling with himself and the world, blocked by anxieties, conflicted, and plagued by his own unacceptable wishes and unconscious secrets. This picture has captivated the imagination of many laymen as well as clinicians. Consequently, it has had an enormous impact on philosophical as well as psychological conceptions of human nature. In Freud's view, humans are not the unemotional, rational beings that Victorian society thought they were. Instead, people are torn by unconscious conflicts and wishes that push them in seemingly puzzling ways.

Freud's emphasis on unconscious impulses as the most basic determinants of behavior is seen in an analogy in which the relation of the id and the ego is likened to that between a horse and its rider:

> . . . *The horse provides the locomotive energy, and the rider has the prerogative of determining the goal and of guiding the movements of his powerful mount towards it. But all too often in the relations between the ego and the id we find a picture of the less ideal situation in which the rider is obliged to guide his horse in the direction in which it itself wants to go (Freud, 1933, p. 108).*

Thus, in Freud's psychology the id is stubborn and strong and often the ego cannot really control it effectively.

Freud believed that the environment is less important than inborn instincts in the dynamics of personality. He thought that external stimuli make fewer demands and, in any event, can always be avoided. In contrast, one's own impulses and needs cannot be escaped. Consequently, he made instinctual impulses the core of personality. Psychodynamic theories also have shaped ideas about adaptation, deviance, and personality change. And they have done this more than any other psychological approach.

5.20 Describe Freud's conception of the human being and relate it to your own beliefs.

The Healthy Personality

5.21 What is Freud's conception of healthy personality functioning?

For Freud, a healthy personality showed itself in the ability to love and work and required a harmony among id, ego, and superego. Referring to the goal of psychotherapy, Freud wrote, "Where id was, there shall ego be." He meant that, for the healthy personality, rational choice and control replace irrational, impulse-driven compulsion. A healthy personality also required mature (genital) psychosexual development.

From the psychodynamic perspective, adequate adaptation requires insight into one's unconscious motives. Persons who can cope adequately are the ones who can face their impulses and conflicts without having to be extremely defensive. Symptoms represent the return of unsuccessfully repressed materials, reemerging to torture the person in disguised forms. Breakdowns reflect the inadequacy of defenses to deal with unconscious conflicts. Symptoms and mental problems develop when the ego does not have the strength to cope with the conflicting demands of external reality and the internal pressures of id and superego. In Freud's words (1940, pp. 62–63), when:

> . . . the ego has been weakened by the internal conflict, we must come to its aid. The position is like a civil war which can only be decided by the help of an ally from without. The analytical physician and the weakened ego of the patient, basing themselves upon the real external world, are to combine against the enemies, the instinctual demands of the id, and the moral demands of the superego. We form a pact with each other. The patient's sick ego promises us the most candor, promises, that is, to put at our disposal all of the material which his self-perception provides; we, on the other hand, assure him of the strictest discretion and put at his service our experience in interpreting material that has been influenced by the unconscious. Our knowledge shall compensate for his ignorance and shall give his ego once more mastery over the lost provinces of his mental life. This pact constitutes the analytic situation.

The pact to which Freud refers above is also the basis for the close relationship between therapist and client that develops over the course of the analysis. It is called **transference.** The name reflects the view that the patient transfers onto the therapist many of the feelings experienced initially with the parents. In the course of the therapy, these feelings are examined closely and "worked through" until they become resolved.

Behaviors as Symptoms

The Freudian approach views an individual's problematic behavior as symptomatic (rather than of main interest in its own right). It searches for the possible causes of these symptoms by making inferences about the underlying personality dynamics. For example, an individual who has a bad stutter might be viewed as repressing hostility, one with asthma as suffering from dependency conflicts, and one with snake fears as victimized by unconscious sexual problems. This focus on the meaning of behavior as a symptom (sign) guides the psychodynamic strategy for understanding both normal and abnormal behavior. Thus, the psychodynamically oriented clinician seeks to infer unconscious conflicts, defense structure, problems in psychosexual development, and the symbolic meaning and functions of behavior.

SUMMARY

BASIC ASSUMPTIONS

- Freud's work was based on clinical observations of neurotic persons and self-analysis. This led him to posit the unconscious as a key component of personality.
- Freud used dreams and free association to tap into unconscious wishes.

PSYCHIC STRUCTURE

- The id, ego, and superego form the psychodynamic structure of the personality.
- The id is the primary, instinctual core, obeying the "pleasure principle."
- The ego mediates between the instinctual demands of the id and the outer world of reality, utilizing "secondary processes": logical thinking and rational planning.
- The superego represents the internalized moral standards of the society and parental control.

CONFLICT, ANXIETY, AND PSYCHODYNAMICS

- Personality dynamics involve a perpetual conflict between the id, ego, and superego.
- The desire for immediate gratification of sexual and aggressive instincts puts the person in conflict with the environment and ultimately the superego. This struggle produces anxiety.
- Defenses such as denial and repression may be used by the ego when it is unable to handle anxiety effectively. The person's unacceptable impulses and unconscious motives are transformed into "symptoms."
- The total mind (or psyche) is seen as a closed system motivated to maintain equilibrium: any forces that build up require discharge.

NEUROSIS

- When defenses fail, the conflicts may build up into neurotic anxiety, revealed indirectly through symbolic behavior.
- Neuroses are a product of early childhood trauma combined with innate predispositions.
- Small mistakes or slips of the tongue may reveal an unconscious need to express undesirable impulses.
- All behavior, even the seemingly insignificant or absurd, is motivated and significant.

PSYCHOSEXUAL STAGES AND PERSONALITY DEVELOPMENT

- Personality development includes a series of psychosexual stages: oral, anal, phallic, and genital.
- Later personality traits develop according to the individual's experience at each of these stages of maturation.
- In fixation, a sexual impulse is arrested at an early stage.
- Regression is a reversion to an earlier stage of development in the face of stress.
- Anaclitic identification and identification with the aggressor are two Freudian identification mechanisms.

IMPACT OF FREUD'S THEORIES

- Healthy individuals achieve a kind of truce within themselves by substituting rational choice for id impulse and arriving at the final stage of psychosexual development.
- The Freudian approach views an individual's problematic behavior as symptomatic and searches for the unconscious causes of these symptoms.

KEY TERMS

anaclitic identification 108
anal stage 106
castration anxiety 106
conscious 95
denial 101
distortion/displacement 102
ego 99
fixation 108
free association 97
genital stage 108
hysteria 95
hysterical anesthesia 101

id 98
identification with the aggressor 108
latency period 106
libido 102
motivational determinism 95
Oedipus complex 106
oral stage 106
penis envy 106
phallic stage 106
pleasure principle 98
preconscious 95

primary process thinking 99
psychodynamics 100
psychosexual stages 105
reality principle 99
regression 108
repression 101
sensory anesthesia 95
superego 99
transference 110
transformation of motives 100
unconscious 95

6

POST-FREUDIAN PSYCHODYNAMICS AND MOTIVES

"Psychoanalysis was a well-guarded fortress, and most psychologists had little interest in scaling its walls . . . [in contrast] today . . . 'pluralism' characterizes contemporary psychoanalysis" (Westen, 1990, p. 21).

The psychodynamic level of analysis has expanded and diversified in the many years since Freud's original concepts were first expressed. This chapter presents some of the main ideas of theorists who were influenced by Freud and retained much of Freud's psychodynamic orientation, but transformed its focus and shape in crucial ways. These "neo-Freudians" or "post-Freudians" or "ego psychologists" represent a wide range of innovations, and have been given many different labels. They began with Freud's own followers at the start of the twentieth century and moved on to some radical departures from his ideas. Their unifying theme is that they retained a focus on the psychodynamic-motivational level of analysis. But they went on to call attention to the diversity of human motives and to mental and emotional processes in personality development after early childhood that had been neglected before.

▶ TOWARD EGO PSYCHOLOGY AND THE SELF

6.1 Describe four changes in emphasis from classical psychoanalysis that occurred among neo-Freudian theorists.

Although each neo-Freudian writer has made a distinctive contribution, certain common themes emerge, especially in recent years. These themes suggest a gradual shift in focus, summarized in Table 6.1. Less attention is paid to Freud's ideas about the basic sexual and aggressive instincts of the id, and the id itself is given a less dominant role. More attention is on the concept and functions of ego and "self," to the point where the newer theoretical trends have been named **ego psychology** and its practitioners often are called *ego psychologists.*

Ego psychologists recognize that the ego has crucial functions that may be relatively independent of underlying unconscious motivations. The ego deals often with "higher order" motives and goals, such as the striving for competence, for achievement, and for power, to name a few of the many motives that may drive human behavior. The ego psychologists see these motives are part of normal ego functions as people form and pursue their life goals. In short, with this growth of the role of ego, and expansion of the range of human motives, the person is viewed as a more competent, potentially creative problem solver, engaged in much more than the management of instincts that press for discharge.

The neo-Freudians, as Table 6.1 suggests, also saw human development as a more continuous process that extends throughout the life span. More than the product of early psychosexual experiences, personality began to be viewed as a lifelong development. Personality is rooted in social and interpersonal relations and in the context of culture and society. It is not isolated within the psyche of the individual and in the drama of the relations with the immediate family in the first few years of life.

Let us now consider some of the major relevant theorists at this level of analysis to illustrate the range and nature of their ideas about personality

Anna Freud and the Ego Defense Mechanisms

As noted in the last chapter, it was Freud who identified and focused on the mechanism of denial and repression. But it was another psychoanalyst, his own daughter, Anna Freud, who provided important analyses of the various forms of defense mechanisms that the ego uses, summarized in Table 6.2.

6.2 How are defense mechanisms involved in the energy exchanges that occur in psychodynamic processes?

Most analysts view the defense mechanisms as the core of psychodynamics. These are the processes through which the ego does much of its peace-keeping work. They are the mechanisms through which the ego tries to subordinate the impulses, test reality,

TABLE 6.1   Post-Freudian Developments: Some Characteristics of the Neo-Freudians

Less Attention to	More Attention to
Id and instincts	Ego and self; ego defenses; higher order motives
Purely intrapsychic causes and conflicts	Social, interpersonal causes; relationship issues
Earliest childhood	Later developments throughout the life span; adult functioning
Psychosexual stages	Social forces and positive strivings; the role of the culture and society

Anna Freud (1895–1982)

and accommodate the demands of the superego in the lifelong war within the psyche. The process of defense involves a continuous conflict between impulses seeking discharge and defenses designed to transform these wishes into an acceptable form for the ego. In the course of these transformations, energy is exchanged and directed toward different objects, mediated by the mechanisms of defense.

Transformation of Motives. For example, if sadistic aggressive impulses cannot be repressed but still are too threatening to self-acceptance, they might be transformed into a more socially sanctioned form, such as an interest in surgery (see Figure 6.1). Likewise, sexual wishes toward the mother might be displaced into a career of painting

TABLE 6.2   Definitions and Examples of Some Defense Mechanisms

Mechanisms	Definition	Example
Repression	Massive inhibition of a threatening impulse or event by rendering it unconscious (beyond awareness)	Guilt-producing sexual wishes are "forgotten"
Projection	Unacceptable aspects of oneself are attributed to someone else	Projecting one's own unacceptable sexual impulses by attributing them to one's boss
Reaction formation	Anxiety-producing impulse is replaced by its opposite in consciousness	Unacceptable feelings of hate are converted into "love"
Rationalization	Making something more acceptable by attributing it to more acceptable causes	Blaming an aggressive act on "being overworked" rather than on feeling angry
Sublimation	Expression of a socially unacceptable impulse in socially acceptable ways	Becoming a soldier to hurt others; becoming a plumber to indulge in anal desires

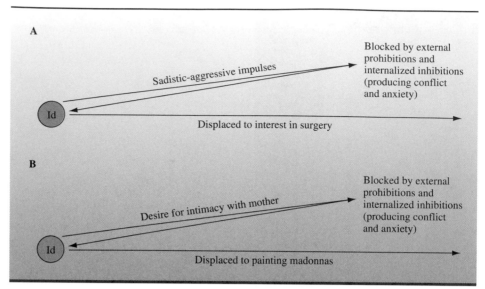

Figure 6.1 The psychodynamic transformation of motives: Examples of displacement in the form of sublimation.

madonnas, as some Freudians think happened among certain Renaissance painters. Freud (1909) himself suggested such dynamics in the case of Leonardo da Vinci.

> **6.3** What are the major signs that repression is occurring?

Freud in his original work was concerned with extreme examples of the mechanism of repression, but its workings also may be seen in many mild forms, as in the following illustration. Jim, a thirteen-year-old, has a girlfriend with whom he has had a few happy "dates," but she fails to show up at the movie after having promised to be there. Jim says that he feels no anger, is not annoyed, and just "doesn't care." Yet he explodes later at dinner with his family and gets into a squabble with his little sister. Is Jim using repression? If Jim privately knows he is just trying to cover his irritation and upset, then repression is not a relevant explanation for what he is doing. On the other hand, if his anger is evident to those who know him well, but truly hidden from his own awareness, then repression may be at work as a defense. This hypothesis is strengthened if Jim also shows resistance to efforts by his mother to suggest, for example, that he may be upset by the broken date. In genuine repression, if you push the person to face the underlying feelings that are being avoided unconsciously, it may only increase the defensive attempts to reject the interpretation and avoid the emotion. That tends to make the defense more elaborate and even irrational. In this type of example, when the person is no longer a young child and the threat is relatively mild, repression is unlikely to be very deep. The depth and desperation of the defenses tend to be much greater in infancy or early childhood, or when the threats are profoundly frightening and the individual is highly vulnerable.

> **6.4** How are unacceptable impulses masked by projection, reaction formation, rationalization, and sublimation?

Projection. In **projection,** the person's own unacceptable impulses are inhibited and the source of the anxiety is attributed to another person. For example, one's own angry feelings are attributed to one's innocent friend. Or a man who is attracted to his brother's wife sincerely believes she is trying to seduce him at a family gathering. Projection presumably gives relief because it reduces anxiety.

Reaction Formation. Another defense, termed **reaction formation,** occurs when a person transforms an anxiety-producing impulse into its opposite. For example, people frightened by their own sexual impulses and desires for unusual sexual adventures may become actively involved in a "ban the filth" vigilante group. They use their energy to vigorously censor books and movies they consider obscene, while secretly and unconsciously attracted to them. Through projection and reaction formation, the id impulses are expressed, but in a disguise that makes them acceptable to the ego: desire becomes disdain and hate.

A mother who was a leading psychoanalyst describes reaction formation as a mechanism shown by her own children in their early development (Monro, 1955). As a psychoanalyst, she was especially sensitive to the possible problems faced in the anal stage and the impulses activated then. She therefore allowed her children considerable freedom to express their infantile anal interests with few inhibitions. After experiencing that early phase of freedom, however, the children seemed to spontaneously develop an opposite pattern. Now they began to exhibit over-cleanliness to the point of finickiness, wanting everything to be "super clean," orderly, and neat. They found dishwater disgusting, for example, and insisted on refilling the sink with clean water repeatedly in spite of an extreme water shortage in the county. Likewise, they refused to clean up the puppy's "mistakes," and, as their insightful mother put it, "The reaction of finicking disgust, very genuinely experienced, was clearly related to the positive pleasures recently renounced. Housekeeping became much smoother as reaction formation involving an extreme if somewhat spotty orderliness also gave way to advancing maturity" (Monro, 1955, p. 252).

Rationalization. **Rationalization** is a defense that involves trying to deceive oneself by making rational excuses for unconscious impulses that are unacceptable. For example, a man who has unconscious, deeply hostile impulses toward his wife might invent elaborate excuses that serve to disrupt and even destroy their relationship without ever admitting his true feelings. He might invoke explanations such as "pressures at the office," "a hectic schedule," or "worrying about inflation and politics" as reasons for staying away from home. In doing so, he experiences little guilt over (and might even feel justified in) ignoring, avoiding, and frustrating his wife.

Sublimation. **Sublimation** is an ego defense that is particularly significant in the development of culture. It consists of a redirection of impulses from an object (or

The concept of sublimation suggests that sexual and aggressive impulses may be redirected from their original objects and displaced to socially acceptable activities and careers.

target) that is sexual or aggressive to one that is social in character. Suppose that aggressive urges become too threatening to the young boy, for example the desire to kill the father while struggling with the Oedipus complex. He (or she) may sublimate (or transform) these impulses into socially acceptable forms that in the course of development evolve into the choice of surgery as a career.

Carl Jung

While Anna Freud remained basically loyal to the ideas proposed by her father, Carl Jung was a much more controversial figure who initiated a different form of the psychodynamic approach. Born in 1875, Carl Jung was raised in Basel, Switzerland, the son of a pastor in the Swiss Reformed Church. Upon earning his medical degree from the University of Basel, he began his career in psychology at the Psychiatric Institute in Zurich. Jung began as an admirer and associate of Freud but later became a dissenter and developed his own theory of psychoanalysis and his own method of psychotherapy. His approach became known as analytical psychology. Although it retains Freud's unconscious processes, it claims a **collective unconscious**—an inherited foundation of personality. The contents of the collective unconscious are **archetypes** or "primordial images." Unlike the personal unconscious, whose contents were once conscious but have been forgotten or repressed, the contents of the collective unconscious have never been in consciousness. Therefore the contents of the collective unconscious are not individually acquired; they are due to heredity. Examples of archetypes include God, the young potent hero, the wise old man, the Earth Mother, the Fairy Godmother, and the hostile brethren. They occur in myths, art, and dreams of all mankind.

In Jung's view, the psyche included not only a conscious side but also a covert or **shadow aspect** that is unconscious. Personal growth involves an unfolding of this shadow and its gradual integration with the rest of the personality into a meaningful, coherent life pattern. The unconscious of every female includes a masculine, assertive element

6.5 How did Jung's notion of the unconscious mind differ from Freud's conception?

Carl Gustav Jung (1875–1961)

TABLE 6.3   Examples of Jungian Concepts

The Collective Unconscious:	Found in everyone and said to contain inherited memories and ancestral behavior patterns
Archetypes:	Basic elements or primordial images forming the collective unconscious, manifested in dreams and myths (e.g., Earth Mother, the wise old man)
The Animus:	The masculine, assertive element in the unconscious of every woman
The Anima:	The feminine, passive element in the unconscious of every man
The Mandala:	Usually a circular shape, symbolizing the self, containing designs often divided into four parts

(the **animus**). The unconscious of every male includes a feminine, passive element (the **anima**). To be constructively masculine or feminine, individuals of each sex must recognize and integrate these opposite sex elements within themselves (see Table 6.3).

Jung described four basic ways of experiencing the world: *sensing, intuition, feeling*, and *thinking*, summarized in Table 6.4. According to Jung, people differ consistently in the degree to which they emphasize each way of experiencing. One person, for example, might typically prefer intuition to abstract thinking, choosing to become a psychoanalyst rather than a mathematician. Another might know the world mostly through his or her senses with little use of either intuition or reason. In addition, Jung was concerned with extraversion–introversion.

6.6 Describe Jung's four basic ways of experiencing the world.

Like the four ways of experiencing, extraversion–introversion for Jung are divided: one is dominant in the conscious life while the other influences the unconscious side of the personality.

Jung broadened the concept of psychic energy. He did not exclude the sexual instinct of Freudian theory but thought it was only one among many instincts. For Jung, the meaning of behavior became fully intelligible only in terms of its end products or final effects; we need to understand humans not only in terms of their past but also in the light of their purposes and goal strivings.

Jung, like Freud, emphasized symbolic meanings. He believed, for example, that "abnormal behaviors" are expressions of the unconscious mind. Also like Freud, Jung thought that abnormal behaviors were merely one way in which the contents of the unconscious may reveal themselves. More often, he felt, they are expressed in dreams. Jung went beyond Freud, however, in his increasing fascination with dreams as unconscious expressions of great interest in their own right. This contrasts with their use merely as starting points for saying whatever comes to mind, that is, "free associations" (discussed in Chapter 5). As Jung put it: ". . . I came increasingly to disagree with free

TABLE 6.4   Jung's Four Ways of Experiencing the World

Ways of Experiencing	Characteristics
Sensing	Knowing through sensory systems
Intuition	Quick guessing about what underlies sensory inputs
Feeling	Focus on the emotional aspects of beauty or ugliness, pleasantness or unpleasantness
Thinking	Abstract thought, reasoning

association as Freud first employed it; I wanted to keep as close as possible to the dream itself, and to exclude all the irrelevant ideas and associations that it might evoke" (Jung, 1964, p. 28).

In the same direction, Jung became intrigued by the unconscious for its own sake. He viewed the unconscious not just as the source of instincts. For him it was a vital, rich part of everyone's life, more significant than the conscious world, full of symbols communicated through dreams. The focus of Jungian psychology became the study of people's relations to their unconscious. Jung's method taught individuals to become more receptive to their own dreams and to let their unconscious serve as a guide for how to live.

Jung's conception of personality is complex, more a set of fascinating observations than a coherent theory. His observations often dwelled on the multiple, contradictory forces in life: "I see in all that happens the play of opposites" (1963, p. 235). Yet he also was one of the first to conceptualize a *self* that actively strives for oneness and unity. Jung saw the self (the striving for wholeness) as an archetype that is expressed in many ways. The expressions of the striving for wholeness include the **mandala** (a magic circle archetype shown in Figure 6.2) and various religious and transcendental experiences. He devoted much of his life to the study of these expressions in primitive societies, alchemy, mythology, dreams, and symbols. To achieve unity and wholeness, the individual must become increasingly aware of the wisdom available in his or her personal and collective unconscious and must learn to live in harmony with it. His ideas continue to fascinate many psychologists and are being applied to topics that range from "feminist consciousness" (Lyons, 1997) to the role of the spiritual in healing

6.7 How did Jung's conception and use of dreams differ from Freud's?

Figure 6.2 A mandala.

(Molina, 1996). However, his ideas remain difficult to study with the methods most psychologists favor.

Alfred Adler

Like Freud, Alfred Adler also was born in Austria, 14 years after Freud—in 1870. He earned his degree as doctor of medicine in 1895. After a brief period as an ophthalmologist, he practiced psychiatry, joining Freud's Vienna circle of associates at the turn of the century. A highly independent, even rebellious person, Adler broke from Freud after 10 years and began his own psychoanalytic movement, ultimately as a founder of the Society for Individual Psychology.

Adler's contributions have suffered an ironic fate. Much of what he said has become so widely accepted, and seems so plausible, that it has been incorporated into the everyday ideas and terms, the ordinary wisdom that we intuitively have about psychology. Some of these concepts are so common as to risk becoming cliches. Nevertheless, while the popularity of Adler's ideas makes them less distinctive, they remain important even in contemporary thinking about personality.

It is often said that every personality theory captures best the personality of the theorist who created it. Adler's own childhood was marked by chronic illness and hostile relations with his five siblings. Interestingly, both these themes—physical weakness, or **organ inferiority,** and **sibling rivalry**—became central concepts in his theory. Adler's theory begins with a recognition of the infant's profound *helplessness,* a state that makes him or her especially vulnerable to any biological *organ inferiority* or weakness. This biological vulnerability becomes the root for a psychological state that endures in the person and that has central importance in Adler's theory: feelings of inferiority.

6.8 How are Adler's own life experiences reflected in his theory?

It is the struggle to overcome these inferiority feelings that provides the underlying motivation for lifelong compensatory strivings. Throughout the life course, the person tries to make up for this perceived deficit by striving for perfection and superiority. The particular attitude the person adopts toward the inevitable state of inferiority, rather than the deficit itself, was most important for Adler; given a courageous attitude, a perceived deficit can become a positive asset. We all know dramatic examples of personal victories in overcoming biological deficits. Demosthenes was the ancient Greek who achieved fame as a great orator, overcoming a childhood stutter, and more than one great athlete reached the Olympics after long efforts to compensate for early concerns with physical weakness or illness. This **compensatory motivation** contrasts sharply with the id impulses, sexual and aggressive in nature, featured as the driving forces in Freud's theory. It is a much more social psychological view of motivation. It is rooted in the person's feelings about a biological deficit but goes much beyond that origin. The striving to compensate can have many constructive healthy outcomes when pursued with courage. If compensatory efforts fail, however, the person may develop an **inferiority complex,** continuing to feel extremely inadequate about the perceived inferiority and failing to grow beyond it.

Adler also showed a more social orientation in other parts of his theory in which he is alert to cultural influences and social, interpersonal situations. He saw the rivalry between siblings within the family as an important part of development. Thus he viewed the family as the context for significant relationships and conflicts beyond those captured in the Oedipal triangle of mother–father–child that was central for Freud. Indeed, Adler's ideas were notable as a major break from concern with inborn impulses and hereditary

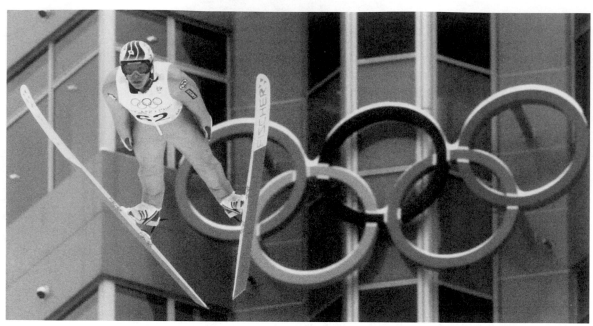

In Adler's view of compensatory motivation, the striving to excel may be a way of overcoming early feelings of inferiority.

6.9 Which concepts in Adler's theory reflect his positive view of human nature?

causes to focus on the environmental forces and the social world as determinants of personality development. Although the individual functions with consistency and unity, the pattern that makes up the style of life can be modified. This happens when the person changes the goals toward which the whole pattern of striving is directed.

The striving for perfection plays a great role for Adler, but it is matched by his concern for the individual's social feeling or *social interest*. This focus on the positive, adaptive aspects of personality development is also seen in two other Adlerian concepts: courage and common sense. Taken together, social feeling, courage, and common sense constitute the set of characteristics that mark well-functioning, healthy persons.

Such persons cope with the realities of life, including their inevitable helplessness and inferiority, with confidence and constructive strivings, without excessive fear but also without unrealistic fantasies. In contrast, the unhealthy personality abandons appropriate effort and avoids facing realistic difficulties by a retreat into increasingly grandiose fantasies. These fantasies are maladaptive if they widen the gap to reality and provide an unrealistic avoidance of failure.

The positive qualities of social feeling, courage, and common sense are natural states: every person is capable of having them spontaneously unless they are blocked or frustrated in the course of development. For example, the excessively *pampered child* may develop a style of life characterized by being extremely demanding, while the severely *rejected child* may live life in a world seen as dangerous and hostile.

To help overcome this type of damage, the therapist in the Adlerian approach provides the encouragement and sympathetic understanding that allows the patient to face life more realistically and effectively. In this supportive atmosphere, the patient can abandon "mistaken" strivings for fantastic superiority and stop the retreat from reality to begin to face life with common sense, courage, and social feeling.

Erich Fromm (1900–1980)

Erich Fromm

Erich Fromm (1941, 1947) helped to expand Freudian concepts to take account of the important role of society in the development and expression of personality.

For Fromm, people are primarily social beings to be understood in terms of their relations to others. According to Fromm, individual psychology is fundamentally social psychology. People have psychological qualities, such as tendencies to grow, develop, and realize their potentialities. These basic tendencies lead them to freedom and to want to strive for justice. Thus, human nature has a force of its own that influences social processes.

Fromm's explanation of character traits illustrates the difference between Freud's biological orientation and Fromm's social orientation. Fromm criticized Freud's idea that fixation at certain pleasure-giving stages is the cause of later character traits. According to Fromm, character traits develop from experiences with others. Psychosexual problems are the body's expressions of an attitude toward the world that is socially conditioned. According to Freud, culture is the result of society's efforts to suppress instinctual drives. For Fromm, culture is molded by the structure and substance of a given society. Another major point of departure from Freud is Fromm's belief that ideals like truth, justice, and freedom can be genuine strivings and not simply rationalizations of biological motives. Freud's psychology is a psychology of instinctual drives that defines pleasure in terms of tension reduction. Fromm's psychology tries to make a place for positive attributes, such as tenderness and the human ability to love, and the desire for freedom as basic aspects of human nature.

6.10 Contrast Fromm's views on the origin of character traits and positive ideals with those of Freud.

Erik Erikson

The psychoanalyst Erik Erikson (1963) has proposed stages of development that call attention to problems of social adaptation (Table 6.5). As children grow up, they face

6.11 Describe Erikson's psychosocial stages and the psychosocial crisis expressed at each stage.

Erik H. Erikson (1902–1994)

a wider range of human relationships and new challenges. The solution of the specific problems at each of eight **psychosocial stages** (rather than psychosexual stages) determines how adequate they will become as adults. Erikson's focus on psychosocial development reflects the growing neo-Freudian emphasis on broad social and cultural forces, rather than instinctual drives alone.

TABLE 6.5   Erikson's Stages of Psychosocial Development

Stage and Age	Psychosocial Crisis	Optimal Outcome
I. Oral-sensory (1st year of life)	Trust vs. Mistrust	Basic trust and optimism
II. Muscular-anal (2nd year)	Autonomy vs. Shame	Sense of control over oneself and the environment
III. Locomotor-genital (3rd through 5th year)	Initiative vs. Guilt	Goal-directedness and purpose
IV. Latency (6th year to start of puberty)	Industry vs. Inferiority	Competence
V. Puberty and Adolescence	Identity vs. Role Confusion	Reintegration of past with present and future goals, fidelity
VI. Early Adulthood	Intimacy vs. Isolation	Commitment, sharing, closeness, and love
VII. Young and Middle Adult	Generativity vs. Self-absorption	Production and concern with the world and future generations
VIII. Mature Adult	Integrity vs. Despair	Perspective, satisfaction with one's past life, wisdom

Source: Adapted from Erikson, E. (1963). *Childhood and society.* New York: Norton.

At each stage of development, Erikson hypothesizes a **psychosocial crisis.** This crisis arises from the person's efforts to solve the problems at that stage. For example, in the first stage of life (the "oral-sensory" stage of the first year), the crisis involves "trust versus mistrust." Erikson hypothesizes that at this stage the child's relation to the mother forms basic attitudes about "getting" and "giving." If the crisis is properly resolved, the experiences at this stage lay the foundation for later trust, drive, and hope.

Erikson's stages extend beyond infancy to include crises of adolescence and adulthood. He sees development as a process that extends throughout life, rather than being entirely determined in the early years. In this developmental process, **ego identity** is central:

> The integration . . . of ego identity is . . . more than the sum of the childhood identifications. It is the accrued experience of the ego's ability to integrate all identifications with the vicissitudes of the libido, with the aptitudes developed out of endowment, and with the opportunities offered in social roles (Erikson, 1963, p. 261).

The underlying assumptions of his view of development are:

> (1) that the human personality in principle develops according to steps predetermined in the growing person's readiness to be driven toward, to be aware of, and to interact with, a widening social radius; and (2) that society, in principle, tends to be so constituted as to meet and invite this succession of potentialities for interaction and attempts to safeguard and to encourage the proper rate and the proper sequence of their enfolding (Erikson, 1963, p. 270).

Erikson's ideas have become popular in many parts of our culture. His thoughts concerning the "identity crises" of adolescence, for example, are discussed widely. Indeed the phrase **identity crisis** has become a part of everyday speech. Erikson's ideas have influenced concepts of human nature and the general intellectual culture. He believed that all young people must generate for themselves some central perspective that gives them a meaningful sense of unity and purpose. This perspective integrates the remnants of their childhood with the expectations and hopes of adulthood (Erikson, 1968). The sense of identity involves a synthesis of how individuals have come to see themselves and their awareness of what the important other people in their lives expect them to be. The stages of development that he discussed are summarized in Table 6.5.

▶ OBJECT RELATIONS THEORY AND THE SELF

Over many decades, psychodynamic theory and practice have undergone particularly important transformations. While many psychologists remain within an essentially psychoanalytic framework, many have moved far beyond Freud and his immediate followers. These innovators further changed how they think about personality, the roots of mental health, and ways to help troubled people.

The basic orientation of this approach has emerged clearly in an integrative review of this movement (Cashdan, 1988; Greenberg & Mitchell, 1983). There have been different variations in this shift. Leaders include such psychoanalysts as Melanie Klein (one of the earliest innovators) in England and, more recently, Otto Kernberg (1976, 1984) and Heinz Kohut (1971, 1977) in the United States. In this section, we will emphasize the common themes of change that seem to characterize this movement.

The developing self is defined from the start in relational, interpersonal terms in Kohut's theory.

6.12 What is the central emphasis within object relations theories?

The approach is called **object relations theory** and therapy (Cashdan, 1988), and the first point to note is that the "objects" in the language of this theory are simply other human beings. The term "objects" is a leftover from classic psychoanalysis, and the phrase "significant others" essentially could substitute for it. The important shift from classic psychoanalysis to object relations theory is that while the former focused on the instinctual drives, the latter focuses on the relationships to significant other people (i.e., object relations).

The most important object for the developing child generally, and unsurprisingly, is the mother. It is in the young child's relationship with the mother that the **relational self** begins to originate and emerge. Note that the self is defined from the start in relational or interpersonal terms.

"Good–Bad Splitting"

Within psychodynamic theory, one of the first to address the mother–child relationship in great depth was Melanie Klein, a British psychoanalyst who was Freud's contemporary. A theme that still persists from Klein's work is her clinical observation that the young child tends to divide the world into good and bad. Klein saw the core conflict throughout life as a struggle between positive feelings of love and negative feelings of hate. Her insight that in this conflict people tend to "split" the world into benevolent and malevolent components has been integrated into much current relational theorizing about personality structure and development.

Klein spoke of a nourishing good breast and an empty bad breast in the child's conflict-ridden representation of the mother. This notion has remained in a variety of contemporary psychodynamic ideas about "good" and "bad" self-representations, internal representations of the self and of other people. It is part of the belief that from infancy on there is a tendency to somehow "split" or partition experiences in good–bad, gratifying–frustrating terms (Cashdan, 1988), fragmenting rather than integrating them into a coherent whole. When these splits are severe, therapy seeks to help the person to integrate them.

The Development of Self

Briefly, development is seen as a process in which the newborn begins in a world that is experienced as split into good (gratifications) and bad (tensions) feelings. In this early world, other people, including the mother, are not yet differentiated. Emotional splitting of experiences and people (objects) in good–bad, positive–negative terms continues throughout later life.

6.13 How is splitting involved in the development of the self concept and in a person's level of self-esteem?

The most important object, the mother, soon begins to be represented by the young child internally as an image. With cognitive development and the growth of language skills, the child can start to internalize not only a maternal image but also maternal conversation in the form of an inner dialogue. Some of these early conversations are audible. You know this if you have ever heard the conversations youngsters sometimes have with themselves as they praise or scold their own performance, saying "good boy" or "no, no" aloud to themselves. This internal dialogue is especially evident during toilet training and other early exercises in the development of self-regulation.

In time, the internalizations of maternal images and conversations become the foundations of the developing self. You can see this development, for example, in the increasing use of "I" in the child's speech. The child's utterance changes from "Jane wants ice cream" to the personal pronoun in which "I" want it, "I" eat it, "I" am bad.

In this conception, emotional splitting continues as an aspect of the developing self: "Just as early splitting of the mother creates a split in the maternal presence, so the split in the inner maternal presence creates a split in the self. Early splits give birth to later splits" (Cashdan, 1988, p. 48). In time, individuals come to view themselves as good or bad depending on their earlier good–bad emotional experiences of splitting. The sense of self-esteem that ultimately emerges characterizes how persons feel about themselves. It is both the consequence of the earlier experiences and the determinant of much of what is experienced later in the course of life.

As the splitting process continues, a variety of identity splits occur. They yield such important categories as one's sexual identity, career identity, identity as a parent, and so on. Each is colored emotionally in good–bad terms. The emotional splitting represented by the enduring concern with goodness–badness never ends. When it is tilted toward a badness imbalance, it continues to corrode the person's relationships and is not adaptive. The therapeutic process, in turn, is viewed as the method for undoing the imbalance, recognizing and overcoming inner conflicts, and developing a more integrated and positive image of the self.

▶ ATTACHMENT: THE ROOTS OF OBJECT RELATIONS

Like Freud, object relations theorists focus on the importance of the early years. Unlike Freud's emphasis on how the instinctual drives are expressed and managed in the first few years, however, these theorists stress the type of relationship that develops with the early caretaker, usually the mother. This early relationship becomes the basic framework for the perception and experience of later relationships. The details of this developmental process have received increasing research attention by child psychologists. They study the quality and varieties of early attachment relations between mother and child (Ainsworth, Blehar, Waters, & Wall, 1978) and trace how these early relationships link to subsequent development (Sroufe & Fleeson, 1986). Much of this work was influenced by the attachment theory proposed by a British psychiatrist, John Bowlby, discussed next.

Attachment Theory

Bowlby was seeing a 3-year-old boy in psychotherapy. It was half a century ago, and he was being supervised by the psychoanalyst Melanie Klein, who refused to allow him to meet with the boy's mother. Frustrated by this experience, as well as by the unscientific nature of psychoanalytic theorizing, Dr. Bowlby developed his now-famous attachment theory (Holmes, 1993). This theory is consistent with object relations theory, giving center stage to the relationship between the young child and the primary caregiver (Bowlby, 1982). For Bowlby, however, the psychological characteristics of the "object"—particularly the mother—were crucial, and he emphasized the experienced relationship between child and the mother as the primary caregiver.

6.14 What is the role of working models in Bowlby's theory? How do these develop?

According to Bowlby, based on experiences in this relationship, the child develops **internal working models.** These are mental representations of others, of the self, or of relationships that guide subsequent experience and behavior. Children who have had positive, gratifying experiences with significant others in their environment will develop internal working models of others as responsive and giving, and of themselves as competent and worthy of affection; those who have painful or unsatisfying experiences develop internal models that reflect those troubled relationships. The basic message in attachment theory is that caregivers who are responsive to the infant and its needs provide a **secure base,** a safe haven of dependable comfort in the young child's life from which the world can then begin to be explored with trust, without fear of abandonment.

Early Attachment Relations: Secure/Insecure Attachment Patterns

Mary Ainsworth (1989) developed the "Strange Situation" to examine patterns of infant–parent attachment in everyday situations among 8 1/2 to 12-month-olds (e.g., Stayton and Ainsworth, 1973; Ainsworth et al., 1978). The **Strange Situation** assesses individual differences in the baby's relationship with the mother. Ainsworth chose to conduct her study in a "strange" setting, that is, one unfamiliar to the baby, because she found that most American children were accustomed to the frequent comings and goings of their mothers throughout the day. Placed in an unfamiliar setting, however, children were expected to exhibit their characteristic attachment behaviors in response to stress.

6.15 Describe the *Strange Situation* and what it has revealed about children's attachment patterns. How are these patterns related to childhood behavior?

In this situation, the toddler (about age 18 months) is introduced to a novel playroom environment with the mother and a stranger. Then the toddler is exposed to different levels of availability of the mother, from present and involved with the child, to present and mildly preoccupied, to absent. The child is separated from the mother twice during the Strange Situation; once left with the stranger and once left alone.

Three main patterns of behavior have been identified in this situation. Toddlers who avoided the mother throughout the paradigm, as well as on reunion, were considered **insecure–avoidant,** or A babies. Some were able to greet the mother positively upon reunion, and then return to play, and they attended to the mother and desired interaction with her throughout the procedure. These were termed **securely attached,** or B babies. Those whose reunion behavior combined contact-seeking and anger, and who were difficult to comfort upon reunion, were classified as the C or

Is early attachment the preface to adult romantic love?

insecure–ambivalent babies. Home visits revealed that the different types of babies experienced different patterns of maternal responsiveness. For example, mothers of infants rated as securely attached were most responsive toward their babies. Mothers of resistant babies were inconsistent in their responsiveness. The responsiveness of mothers of avoidant children varied with the context: they were unresponsive to bids for contact and comfort, but they were controlling and intrusive in reponse to their children's attempts at independent play. Likewise, children rated secure are more likely to remain confident and flexibly organized when faced with an insurmountable task as preschoolers (Arend et al., 1979) and suggest strategies for coping with the absence of a parent as 6-year-olds (Main, Kaplan, & Cassidy, 1985). Additionally, 5-year-olds with a history of a secure relationship with the mother are less likely to exhibit negative interactions with a peer (Youngblade & Belsky, 1992). Likewise, toddlers who at 18 months were able to cope effectively with separation from the mother in the strange situation, for example by distracting themselves and exploring the toys in the environment to reduce distress, were also more likely to become able to cope effectively with frustration in later childhood (Sethi and colleagues, 2000). Specifically, these toddlers also were able, at age 5, to delay immediate gratification longer for more valued rewards.

Attachment in Adult Relationships

Many other links have been found with infant attachment style and some of these may extend into adulthood. Studies of adult attachment suggest that individuals may carry specific attachment styles with them in relationships throughout life (e.g., Fraley & Shaver, 1997; Kobak & Sceery, 1988). For example, college students rated secure (by interview measures) were rated by their friends as warm and nurturant (Bartholomew & Horowitz, 1991).

Studies of adult attachment styles generally classify participants into one of three categories, based on their self-reports: secure, avoidant, and ambivalent. Participants also are asked about their childhood experiences within the family, and their past and current romantic relationship history and satisfaction. Studies try to link the self-reported attachment styles to the participants' reports about their personal relationships. Table 6.6 gives examples of the kinds of relationships found.

6.16 Describe the three adult attachment patterns found in self-report studies. How do these patterns relate to measures of adjustment?

TABLE 6.6   Some Correlates of Adult Relationship Style

Relationship Style	Associated with
Secure	Report they had supportive families; trusting, warm, happy parents; can tolerate separations from partners without high anxiety; have partners who tend to be satisfied with the relationship; able to give partners emotional support when they need it; generally construct positive romantic relationships; believe romantic love is real and can last.
Avoidant	Report they had aloof, emotionally distant parents, did not feel warmth, closeness or trust in family; tend to fear intimacy, find emotional commitment difficult; unable to be highly emotionally supportive of partner; cynical about romantic love and doubt that it lasts.
Ambivalent	Report they have many romantic relationships that don't last long; anxiously fearful of losing partners; ready and eager to change self to please partner; stressed by separations from partner. Believe falling in love is easy but does not last.

Source: Based on Hazan & Shaver, 1987, 1994.

As the table indicates, adults who see themselves as secure about relationships also report themselves to have had happier, more positive relationship histories, including in their families as children, and in their past and current relationships with romantic partners. Unsurprisingly, these differences are seen particularly when the secure adults are compared to those who describe themselves as avoidant in relationships. A study of adults at age 52 also used a more objective measure of relationship success, namely marriage and divorce statistics. It found the adults who were secure (self-described) also were almost all married (95 percent), whereas only 72 percent of the avoidant adults were married and half of them had been previously divorced (Klohnen & Bera, 1998). As the table also indicates, the three groups differ in their beliefs about romantic love, with the secure being believers, the avoidant more cynical, and the ambivalent thinking it comes easily but does not last.

What conclusions do these findings allow? On the one hand, people clearly differ in how secure they feel themselves to be in close relationships, both currently and in the past, and how they feel about those relationships. These feelings are associated also with what they expect to find in relationships, and what they are likely to experience within them, and how their partners will feel about them. Much less clear is the degree to which adult attachment patterns are directly linked to those observed in toddlers and young children. Although object relations theory generally assumes that the adult patterns are a direct outgrowth and continuation of those found in early life, the data are open to alternative interpretations and have been strongly questioned (e.g., Lewis, 1999, 2002).

Specifically, after an extensive and detailed review of the massive research on this topic Lewis (1999, p. 341) concludes that attachment patterns do not show continuity over long periods of time (e.g., from 1 year of age to age 18 years) in the course of development. However, at any given period of time, there are links between current attachment patterns and important indicators of functioning. In Lewis' view, this pattern—not stable forever but significant and meaningful at any given moment in life—points to the importance of the current social environment in which the individual is functioning. But it does not support the idea that the attachment styles of infancy become the model for all that follows.

Rather, individuals seem to acquire multiple mental representations of others, perhaps based on various significant people with whom they come in contact throughout

6.17 How much temporal stability did Lewis find in attachment styles from childhood through adulthood? What are the implications of his findings?

their lives. These mental representations differ in the degree to which they are readily "accessible" or become easily activated in the person's mind. In that case, everything else being equal, the representation that has been activated most in the past is likely to guide their perception of others as well as their thoughts and behaviors in response to them. But everything is often not equal. In any given person's life, there are a variety of people who differ in their expression of love, availability, and supportiveness. Thus, different people could activate different attachment representations (Shaver & Mikulincer, 2002).

In addition, a person's current motives or mood can also affect the attachment representation that is most easily activated at a given moment (Shaver, Collins, & Clark, 1996). In short, the past experiences in earlier attachment relationships may or may not play a major role in the person's current relationships. To the many people in the world whose early childhood was not a picture of ideally experienced security, this is good news, even though it is disturbing to the classic theory of object relations and makes their assumptions of continuity tentative at best.

Kohut's Theory

> . . . *man can no more survive psychologically in a psychological milieu that does not respond empathically to him, than he can survive physically in an atmosphere that contains no oxygen (Kohut, 1977, p. 85).*

The object relations theorists share several themes, as the last section showed. One leader in this movement, Heinz Kohut, is selected in this section for further attention, because his work is seen as especially influential for changing views of the healthy and the disturbed personality. Kohut, a psychiatrist who received his medical training at the University of Vienna, went on to psychoanalytic training and teaching in Chicago where he gained recognition as a theorist and clinician in the 1970s.

In Kohut's view, throughout the century profound changes in the family and culture have occurred: psychoanalysis and psychodynamic theory must be responsive

6.18 According to Kohut, what changes in family life have occurred since Freud's era, and how have they influenced the nature of psychological problems?

Heinz Kohut (1913–1981)

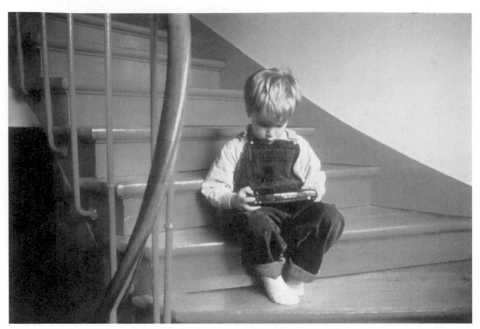

For Kohut, the modern child's life is characterized not by too much parenting and intimacy but by loneliness.

to them. An important change, he believes, is that Freud's patients typically came from a Western civilization in which life was concentrated in the home and family unit. Families tended to expose their children to **emotional overcloseness** (Kohut, 1977, p. 269), and these intense emotional relations in turn often produced neurotic problems involving internal conflicts such as those in the Oedipus complex. The developing child was likely to be trapped in too much intimacy, too much stimulation, too much intrusiveness.

In contrast, children now are more likely to see parents at most in leisure hours and to develop much less clear role definitions and models: "The environment which used to be experienced as threateningly close, is now experienced more and more as threateningly distant . . ." (Kohut, 1977, p. 271). While personal problems used to arise from being too stimulated emotionally by parents (Freud, 1963), now youngsters tend to be *under*-stimulated and may search for erotic sensations and other strong experiences to fill the emotional emptiness of their lives and to try to escape loneliness and depression.

Kohut's thinking has led the way for a new psychoanalytic interest in the self and for the treatment of problems such as disorders of the self. Rather than being driven by unconscious conflicts and impulses, Kohut sees patients today as often deprived of **empathic mirroring** and ideal "objects" (people) for identification. Because their parents were walled off from them emotionally, or too involved with their own narcissistic needs, they did not provide the necessary models for healthy development of the self and for the formation of meaningful, responsive relationships in adulthood.

People fear the destruction of the self when they don't feel the empathic human responses from the important others ("self objects") in their lives. Kohut compares this state to being deprived of **psychological oxygen.** The availability of empathic reactions from self objects is as vital to the survival of the self as the presence of oxygen is to the survival of the body:

> *What leads to the human self's destruction is its exposure to the coldness, the indifference of the nonhuman, the nonempathical responding world (Kohut, 1984, p. 18).*

What is feared most is not so much physical death, but a world in which our humanness would end forever (Kohut, 1980, 1984). In the same vein, Kohut does not see Freud's castration anxiety as the ultimate human anxiety: ". . . the little boy's manifest horror at the sight of the female genitals is not the deepest layer of this experience . . . behind it and covered by it lies a deeper and even more dreadful experience—the experience of the faceless mother, that is, the mother whose face does not light up at the sight of her child" (Kohut, 1984, p. 21).

This type of anxiety about being in a totally uncaring, unresponsive world is experienced in a dream that one of Kohut's patients had (Kohut, 1984, p. 19). In his "stainless steel world" dream, Mr. U was in an ice tunnel with walls from which large glistening strands of ice went down to the ground and up to the ceiling. It was like an enormous model of the human heart, large enough to be walked around in (like one in a museum the patient knew well). Walking within this icy heart, Mr. U felt the anxiety of an oncoming but unnamed danger to which he was exposed, all alone, except for a shadowy figure to whom he appealed but who was unresponsive. In a flash, he was pulled through a crack in the wall into a cityscape that was blindingly bright—a landscape that was utterly unreal, with busy but completely unapproachable people all around: a "stainless steel world" in the patient's own words, in a science fiction scene with no escape, no communication, trapped forever, unreachable in a world of cold-heartedness.

Kohut's theory also leads to a reinterpretation of such Freudian constructs as the "Oedipal period." In his view, during this period the boy fears confrontation from a mother who is nonempathic and sexually seductive rather than affectionate and accepting of him. He also fears confrontation from a father who is competitive and hostile with him rather than pleased and proud. In parallel fashion, during the same period the girl fears confrontation from a father who is nonempathic and sexually seductive instead of affectionate and accepting. At the same time, she also fears a mother who is competitive and hostile rather than reflecting that she is proud of the child and pleased by her.

In Kohut's theory, if parents fail to respond empathically and healthily to their child in this phase of development, it sets up a defect in the self. As a result, the child develops a tendency to experience sexual fantasies and the fragments of love rather than love. Likewise, the child with a defective self also tends to experience hostile fantasies and only the fragments of assertiveness rather than appropriate assertiveness. The individual's typical internal reaction to these experiences becomes great anxiety. These characteristics of the defective self contrast with those of a healthy, normal personality, which, instead of anxiety and fragmented experiences, feels the glow of appropriate sexual functioning and assertiveness, as summarized in Table 6.7.

TABLE 6.7 Kohut's Characteristics of the Self and Mental Health

Defective Self	Healthy Personality
Fragmented experience of love (sexual fantasies)	Feels glow of healthy pleasure in appropriate sexual functioning
Fragmented assertiveness (hostile fantasies)	Able to be self-confidently assertive in pursuit of goals

▶ MURRAY, THE HARVARD PERSONOLOGISTS, AND HIGHER MOTIVES

The psychodynamic approach stimulated many innovations in personality theory and assessment. One of the most extensive and imaginative efforts unfolded under the leadership of Henry A. Murray, Robert W. White, and their many colleagues at the Harvard Psychological Clinic in the 1940s and 1950s. This group, which became known as the **Harvard personologists,** provided a new model called **personology** for the intensive psychodynamic study of individual lives, and devoted itself to the portrayal of persons in depth. The Harvard personologists were influenced strongly by Freud and the post-Freudian ego psychologists. They also were influenced by "biosocial" organismic views that emphasized the wholeness, integration, and adaptiveness of personality. In turn, they trained and influenced a group of students who went on to study a variety of important human motives that are useful for understanding the goals that different people enduringly pursue with varying degrees of intensity.

Higher Order Motives

Perhaps most important for the advancement of personality theory, Henry Murray called attention to the finding that sex and aggression were by no means the only basic motives revealed by the in depth study of fantasies with methods that he helped to develop. His influential investigation, *Explorations in Personality* (1938), suggested that a comprehensive understanding of personality required taking account of the following points:

6.19 How do Murray's higher order needs differ from biological drives? How do needs and presses conform to a person × situation perspective?

In-depth studies of lives revealed many human needs and motives. Although sex and aggression have retained an important place among the human motivations recognized by Freud's successors, Murray believed additional motives and needs have to be hypothesized to capture the complexity of personality. He and the Harvard personologists advanced the modern study of personality dynamics by identifying a wide range of such human motives that go far beyond the id impulses of classic Freudian theory.

The motives that the Murray group identified are called **higher order motives.** They used that name because unlike such basic biological needs as hunger and thirst, they do not involve specific physiological changes (such as increased salivation or stomach

TABLE 6.8   Some Nonphysiological Human Needs Hypothesized by Henry Murray

Abasement (to comply and accept punishment)	Humiliation avoidance
Achievement (to strive and reach goals quickly and well)	Nurturance (to aid or protect the helpless)
Affiliation (to form friendships)	Order (to achieve order and cleanliness)
Aggression (to hurt another)	Play (to relax)
Autonomy (to strive for independence)	Rejection (to reject disliked others)
Counteraction (to overcome defeat)	Seclusion (to be distant from others)
Defendance (to defend and justify)	Sentience (to obtain sensual gratification)
Deference (to serve gladly)	Sex (to form an erotic relationship)
Dominance (to control or influence others)	Succorance (to ask for nourishment, love, aid)
Exhibition (to excite, shock, self-dramatize)	Superiority (to overcome obstacles)
Harm avoidance (to avoid pain and injury)	Understanding (to question and think)

Source: Based on Murray, H. A., Barrett, W. G., & Homburger, E. (1938). *Explorations in personality.* New York: Oxford University Press.

contraction). Instead, they are psychological desires (wishes) for particular goals or outcomes that the person values. Table 6.8 shows examples of the diverse needs inferred by Henry Murray and associates (1938) in their classical listing. Many of these motives have been investigated in detail (e.g., Emmons, 1997; Koestner & McClelland, 1990).

Motives in Murray's view do not operate regardless of the context or situation and its pressures, which he called **environmental presses.** Because Murray theorized that these situational presses influenced personality and its expressions, he and his colleagues developed intensive observational techniques that tried to assess them and take them into account.

The Harvard model for studying personality stimulated many research programs that helped clarify and specify the types of nonbiological higher needs that Murray's group identified. One good example was the motivation for competence—the need to be effective in its own right—described first by Robert White.

Competence Motivation

A variety of higher order motives such as curiosity, the need for stimulation, and the desire for play and adventure all may be seen as parts of a more basic motive: the desire for competence (White, 1959). According to Robert White, who also was a Harvard personologist working with Murray, everyday activities such as a child's exploring, playing, talking, and even crawling and walking reflect the desire for mastery and effective functioning; they are satisfying for their own sake (intrinsically) and create in the person a feeling of efficacy. White argues the point in these words:

6.20 What is the origin of competence motivation? How does it influence behavior?

If in our thinking about motives we do not include this overall tendency toward active dealing, we draw the picture of a creature that is helpless in the grip of its fears, drives, and passions; too helpless perhaps even to survive, certainly too helpless to have been the creator of civilization. It is in connection with strivings to attain competence that the activity inherent in living organisms is given its clearest representation—the power of initiative and exertion that we experience as a sense of being an agent in the living of our lives. This experience may be called a feeling of efficacy (White, 1972, p. 209).

Competence motivation is a desire for mastery of a task for its own sake and may apply to such diverse tasks as running, piano playing, juggling, chess, or the mastery of a new surgical procedure. According to White, the desire for mastery arises independently of other biological drives (such as hunger and sex) and is not derived from them. Moreover, people engage in activities that satisfy competence needs for the sake of the activity, not for the sake of any external reward such as the praise, attention, or money to which it may lead. The concept of competence motivation is valuable in emphasizing the enormous range of creative activities that humans pursue and appear to enjoy in their own right, and it has played a major role in research on motivation and adaptive problem solving (e.g., Dweck, 1990). It is, however, only one of many motives that influence human behavior.

Diverse other higher order nonphysiological motives and needs have been identified in personality research. These include the need for achievement (McClelland et al., 1953; McClelland, 1985), the need for affiliation (McAdams & Constantion, 1983), the need for control (Glass, 1977), and the need to endow experience with meaning, called need for cognition (Cacioppo & Petty, 1982). In addition, researchers are examining individual differences in a large array of other goals, motives, and personal projects that motivate behavior (e.g., Emmons, 1997).

To study motives, the Harvard personologists wanted measures that would get beyond direct self-reports to tap underlying needs of which the participant might not be aware, or which might be uncomfortable to acknowledge. With this goal, they developed a new projective test that examined the person's fantasies as revealed by stories told to a set of pictures, described in In Focus 6.1.

Need for Achievement

David C. McClelland and his colleagues (1953), also working at Harvard University, used the TAT to explore the **need for achievement (n Ach)**. They defined this need as *competition with a standard of excellence.* To study it, they examined fantasies from stories told on the TAT by systematically scoring the occurrence of achievement imagery in the stories. They assumed that the more the stories told involved achievement themes and concerns, the higher the level of the achievement motive.

McClelland (1961) found intriguing relations between TAT achievement themes and many economic and social measures of achievement orientation in different cultures. He devised special TAT cards showing work-relevant themes (see Figure 6.4) to assess the achievement motive. If, for example, the person creates stories in which the hero is studying hard for a profession and strives to improve, to compete against standards of excellence, and to advance far in a career, the story gets high n Ach scores. This technique has become an important way of measuring the motive to achieve in an indirect or implicit way that avoids simple self-report and its potential biases. It has

---

IN FOCUS 6.1

THE THEMATIC APPERCEPTION TEST (TAT)

The **TAT** consists of a series of pictures and one blank card (see Figure 6.3 with TAT-like card). Scenes show, for example, a mother and daughter, a man and a woman in the bedroom, a father and son. The test was developed by Henry Murray in collaboration with Christina Morgan as part of the studies of lives and motivations conducted by the Harvard personologists (Murray et al., 1938). It was used to study a variety of motives.

If you take this test, you will be told that it is a story-telling test and that you are to make up a story for each picture: "Tell what has led up to the event shown in the picture, describe what is happening at the moment, what the characters are feeling and thinking, and then give the outcome." You are encouraged to give free reign to your imagination and to say whatever comes to mind. It is expected that people will interpret the ambiguous pictures presented according to their individual readiness to perceive in a certain way ("apperception"). The themes that recur in these imaginative productions are thought to reflect the person's underlying needs, as well as potential conflicts and problems. Various scoring manuals have been developed that make it possible to objectively code the stories into various categories in research on motives. Good examples of such coding systems are found in studies of the need for achievement described in the text.

Figure 6.3 Picture similar to those in the TAT.

Figure 6.4 A TAT card developed by David C. McClelland for measuring the "Need to Achieve".

been used often in research for many years beginning in the 1950s (Atkinson, 1958) and yielded a rich network of meaningful relationships (McClelland, 1985).

For example, the level of achievement motivation exhibited by unemployed blue-collar workers was related to how they dealt with their unemployment situation and tried to find work again. Those higher in measured achievement motivation used more strategies in their job search, and began to look for a job sooner after being laid off, than did those lower in this motive (Koestner & McClelland, 1990).

It is also noteworthy that achievement motivation, like most other motivations, is influenced by socialization experiences, especially those in childhood. Parents who set standards that challenge their children to compete and excel, who make their expectations clear, provide goals and standards that the child can meet, and who offer support along the work route toward attaining those goals, also tend to have children whose achievement motivation is higher.

Need for Power

Achievement motivation may be the most extensively researched motive, but it is only one of many that has received attention and yielded interesting findings. David Winter (1973), influenced by the work and methods of McClelland, focused on the **need for power,** defined in terms of the impact one wants to have on people. Individual differences are measured by scoring the power themes that appear in the stories people tell

6.21 What relations to behavior have been demonstrated in research on need for power?

to the TAT (e.g., expressed concern with the status of the characters and the strength and impact of their actions). An extensive network of personal qualities and preferences—from greater risk-taking and more leadership activity to more visible indicators of status—is associated with this motive. People high on power motivation express more concern with impact on others, status, and reputation in their stories. To get the image that engages and reflects the power motive, think here of glossy advertisements for luxury automobiles shown glistening in the driveways of elegant mansions. As the image suggests, the advertisement industry is fully aware of the power motive, and seeks to engage it effectively in those who are likely to be responsive to it.

Research on the power motive has found connections between power imagery in political communications, such as the speeches and writings of political leaders, and the warfare that follows at various points in history (Winter, 1993). Winter examined power images in the leaders' communication, for example between Britain and Germany at the time of the First World War. These images also were analyzed in leaders' communications between the United States and the Soviet Union during the Cuban missile crisis in the 1960s. These analyses showed that power images increase before military action and threat erupts. In contrast, power images tend to decrease preceding a decrease in actual threat levels and warfare. The analysis of these images promises to have practical value for predicting important political events.

Need for Intimacy

6.22 How does McAdams's research on need for intimacy relate to Kohut's theory?

The **need for intimacy** was examined by Dan McAdams (1990) and revealed a common human desire: people are motivated to warmly and closely connect, share, and communicate with other people in their everyday life. Also a student of McClelland, and like him, using the TAT, McAdams found that individuals who are high in this motive make more eye contact, and laugh and smile more (McAdams, Jackson & Kirshnit, 1984). In social and group interactions, rather than dominating they tend to be oriented to the communal in their focus and goals (McAdams & Powers, 1981). They prefer close interactions with a few friends with whom they can communicate intimately, and they are not the typical extravert life-of-the party. Consequently, they are more likely to be seen as caring, loving, and sincere, rather than dominant (McAdams, 1990).

Implicit Methods for Assessing Motives

The needs discussed here—from competence and achievement to power and intimacy—merely illustrate the diverse array that continues to be studied in the search for important individual differences. A common theme runs through them all.

Namely, as Freud first noted, people often are unaware of all of their motivations, particularly when they are driven by motives that they do not like to see in themselves. That is why *indirect* and projective methods—like the TAT—are used to study motives rather than relying on simple self-reports on the traditional personality scales. Sometimes also called **implicit methods,** they provide a glimpse into human motives that bypasses the problems found on explicit measures that ask people about the self more directly. Namely, on explicit self-report measures and in face to face interviews, people try to make their responses socially desirable and appropriate, for example, by presenting themselves in a more positive light and hiding their vulnerabilities. Unsurprisingly, the two types of measures, implicit and explicit, often are not closely related so that responses on one do not predict responses on the other (e.g., Greenwald et al, 2002).

SUMMARY

COMMON THEMES: TOWARD EGO PSYCHOLOGY AND THE SELF

- The psychoanalytic followers of Freud deemphasized the role of instincts and psycho-sexual stages.
- They concerned themselves more with the social milieu and the ego.
- Anna Freud described defense mechanisms that may serve the ego in coping with anxiety and life tasks. These mechanisms include repression, projection, reaction formation, rationalization, and sublimation.
- Jung emphasized the collective unconscious and its symbolic and mystical expressions. He focused on dreams and on the need to achieve unity through awareness of the collective and personal unconscious.
- Adler saw individuals as struggling from birth to overcome profound feelings of helplessness and inferiority by striving for perfection.
- According to Adler, people are social beings who are influenced more by cultural influences and personal relations than by sexual instincts.
- Fromm likewise saw people primarily as social beings who can be understood best in relation to others. Culture does not exist to stifle instinctual drives; instead, it is a product of the people in the society.
- Erikson views social adaptation, not unconscious sexual urges, as the key force underlying development that takes place over an entire lifetime. Most critical during this development is the evolution of "ego identity."

OBJECT RELATIONS THEORY AND THE SELF

- In object relations theory, the developing self is defined in relation to other "objects" or human beings.
- Kernberg and Kohut emphasize the mental representation of the self and other persons that develop in the early relationship with the primary caregiver.

ATTACHMENT: THE ROOTS OF OBJECT RELATIONS

- In attachment theory, the early relationship between the individual and his or her caregiver becomes the basic framework for the perception and experience of later relationships.
- Ainsworth's "Strange Situation" study assessed individual differences in attachment relations (insecure–avoidant, securely attached, or insecure–resistant) by putting the toddler in an unfamiliar setting with different levels of exposure to his or her mother.
- Kohut theorized that in Freud's time, families tended to expose their children to excessive emotional closeness, whereas children in the 21st century are more likely to have less parental exposure and emotional support, hence they may lack "empathic mirroring."
- Psychotherapy in this framework tries to provide empathic care, to improve self-esteem and to help find suitable objects for identification.

MURRAY AND THE HARVARD PERSONOLOGISTS

- Henry Murray and the Harvard Personologists focused on the intensive psychodynamic study of individual lives.
- Murray proposed that there are higher order needs and motives, such as competence motivation, need for achievement, need for power, and need for intimacy, which are purely psychological and have no specific physiological basis.

KEY TERMS

anima   118
animus   118
archetypes   118
collective
   unconscious   118
compensatory
   motivation   121
competence
   motivation   135
ego identity   125
ego psychology   114
emotional
   overcloseness   132
empathic mirroring   132
environmental
   presses   135
Harvard
   personologists   134

higher order
   motives   134
identity crisis   125
implicit methods   138
inferiority complex   121
insecure–
   ambivalent   129
insecure–avoidant   128
internal working
   models   128
mandala   120
need for achievement
   (n Ach)   136
need for intimacy   138
need for power   137
object relations
   theory   126
organ inferiority   121

personology   134
projection   116
psychological
   oxygen   132
psychosocial
   crisis   125
psychosocial stages   124
rationalization   117
reaction formation   116
relational self   126
secure base   128
securely attached   128
shadow aspect   118
sibling rivalry   121
Strange Situation   128
sublimation   117
Thematic Apperception
   Test (TAT)   136

PSYCHODYNAMIC PROCESSES

In this chapter, we will focus on research relevant to the psychodynamic level of analysis. This research tells an important story for personality psychology because some of it
has led to conclusions different from original hypotheses, and all of it has stimulated
and challenged later developments throughout the field. Many of those ideas continue
to influence how both professional psychologists and laypersons think about the nature
of personality and the complexities of the mind.

▶ ANXIETY AND UNCONSCIOUS DEFENSES

The psychodynamic view originally saw **anxiety** as the emotional fear triggered when unacceptable impulses begin to push themselves into consciousness. More recently, other theorists have liberalized the definition and recognize that anxiety can be experienced for many different reasons. In spite of the many varieties of anxiety that people experience, the following three elements often are found (Maher, 1966):

7.1 What three elements typically occur in anxiety responses? How can internal processes produce them and defend against them?

- A conscious feeling of fear and danger, without the ability to identify immediate objective threats that could account for these feelings.

- A pattern of physiological arousal and bodily distress that may include miscellaneous physical changes and complaints (Cacioppo et al., 1996). Common examples include *cardiovascular* symptoms (heart palpitations, faintness, increased blood pressure, pulse changes); *respiratory* complaints (breathlessness, feeling of suffocation); and *gastrointestinal* symptoms (diarrhea, nausea, vomiting). If the anxiety persists, the prolonged physical reactions to it may have chronic effects on each of these bodily systems. In addition, the person's agitation may be reflected in sleeplessness, frequent urination, perspiration, muscular tension, fatigue, and other signs of upset and distress.

- A disruption or disorganization of effective problem-solving and cognitive (mental) control, including difficulty in thinking clearly and coping effectively with environmental demands.

An outstanding characteristic of human beings, emphasized in psychodynamic theories, is that they can create great anxiety in themselves even when they are not in any immediate external danger. A man may be seated comfortably in his favorite chair, adequately fed and luxuriously sheltered, seemingly safe from outside threats, and yet torture himself with anxiety-provoking memories of old events, with terrifying thoughts, or with expectations of imagined dangers in years to come. He also can eliminate such internally cued anxiety within his own mind without altering his external environment, simply by avoiding or changing his painful thoughts or memories.

Does such avoidance of anxiety also occur unconsciously, outside the range of one's awareness? A core assumption of the psychodynamic view is that the answer to the question is clearly affirmative. After years of research, however, that answer still remains controversial.

Defense mechanisms are attempts to cope mentally (cognitively) with internal anxiety-arousing cues. Usually it has also been assumed, in line with Freudian theory, that these efforts are at least partly unconscious—that is, they occur without the person's awareness. Because this assumption is so basic, research in the psychodynamic approach has tried to clarify this process. Especially important have been studies of unconscious processes and mechanisms of defense, which are a focus of this chapter. The greatest attention has been devoted to repression, probably because it is the most important one for Freud's theory.

The Concept of Unconscious Repression

Most people sometimes feel that they actively try to avoid painful memories and ideas and struggle to "put out of mind" thoughts that are aversive to them. Common examples are trying not to think about a forthcoming surgical operation and trying to prevent yourself from thinking about the unknown results of an important test. Psychologists often call such efforts to avoid painful thoughts "cognitive avoidance."

Cognitive avoidance obviously exists and everyone is familiar with it. No one doubts that thoughts may be inhibited. However, the mechanisms underlying cognitive avoidance have been controversial. The basic controversy is whether or not cognitive avoidance includes an unconscious defense mechanism of "repression" that forces unacceptable material into an unconscious region without the person's awareness.

Repression versus Suppression. The psychoanalytic concept of **repression** as a defense mechanism is closely linked to the Freudian idea of an unconscious mind. The early Freudians saw the unconscious mind as a supersensitive entity whose perceptual alertness and memory exceeded the conscious mind (Blum, 1955). A chief function of the unconscious mind was to screen and monitor memories and the inputs to the senses. This screening served to inhibit the breakthrough of anxiety-arousing stimuli from the unconscious mind to the conscious, or from the outside world to consciousness. Just as the conscious mind was believed capable of deliberately (consciously) inhibiting events by **suppression,** so the unconscious was considered capable of inhibition or cognitive avoidance at the unconscious level by repression.

Suppression occurs when one voluntarily and consciously withholds a response or turns attention away from it deliberately. Unconscious repression, in contrast, may function as an automatic guardian against anxiety, a safety mechanism that prevents threatening material from entering consciousness. Psychoanalysts have offered clinical evidence for the existence of repression in the form of cases in which slips of the tongue, jokes, dreams, or free associations seemed to momentarily bypass the defenses and betray the person, revealing a brief glimpse of repressed unconscious impulses.

Studying Repression. Repression has remained a cornerstone for most psychoanalysts (Erdelyi, 1985; Grunbaum, 1984), and it has been the subject of a great deal of research for many years. The early efforts to assess whether or not particular findings demonstrated the truth of Freud's concepts created more controversy than clarity. In more recent years, it has been recognized that well-designed experiments on the topic of cognitive avoidance can provide useful information about cognitive processes and personality regardless of their direct relevance to the Freudian theory of repression (Kihlstrom, 1999; Westen & Gabbard, 1999).

Early experiments on repression studied the recall of pleasant and unpleasant experiences (Jersild, 1931; Meltzer, 1930). These investigators assumed that repression showed itself in a tendency to selectively forget negative or unpleasant experiences rather than positive ones. Critics soon pointed out, however, that the Freudian theory of repression does not imply that experiences associated with unpleasant affective tone are repressed (Rosenzweig & Mason, 1934; Sears, 1936). Freudian repression, instead, depends on the presence of an "ego threat" (e.g., a basic threat to self-esteem) and not on mere unpleasantness.

Later researchers also recognized that to study repression adequately they should be able to demonstrate that when the cause of the repression (the ego threat) is removed, the repressed material is restored to consciousness (Zeller, 1950). This assumption was consistent with the psychoanalytic belief that when the cause of a repression is discovered by insight in psychotherapy, the repressed material rapidly emerges into the patient's consciousness. In other words, if the threat is eliminated, it becomes safe for the repressed material to return to awareness. Reports by psychoanalysts often have cited cases in which a sudden insight supposedly lifted a long-standing amnesia (memory loss).

7.2 Differentiate between suppression and repression of anxiety-producing thoughts.

7.3 Summarize some of the challenges in studying repression experimentally and in attributing results to repression.

Experiments to show repression effects have been inconclusive. For example, when college students were threatened by taking a test described as measuring their unacceptable unconscious sexual conflicts, they tended to recall anxiety-arousing words less well. When the threat was removed (by revealing that the test was really not an index for such conflicts), recall improved (D'Zurilla, 1965). Does this mean that repression occurred? After much debate, it has become clear that the answer is "not necessarily"; other interpretations are at least equally plausible.

Reduced recall for threat-provoking information may simply reflect that the person is upset. Therefore, other thoughts, produced by the anxiety as the person worries, may interfere with recall. If the recall improves later when the threat is removed, it may only mean that the competing, anxious thoughts now no longer interfere with recall. It does not necessarily mean either that unconscious repression occurred or that awareness returned when the threat was removed (Holmes & Schallow, 1969; Kihlstrom, 2003; Tudor & Holmes, 1973).

Perceptual Defense

If unconscious repression is a mechanism that keeps painful material out of consciousness, one might also expect it to screen and block threatening perceptual inputs to the eyes and ears. Indeed, clinical reports from psychoanalysts suggest that in some cases of hysteria, massive repression may prevent the individual from perceiving (consciously registering) threatening stimuli such as sexual scenes or symbols.

One very severe instance of this would be hysterical blindness. In these cases, the individual seems to lose his or her vision, although no physical damage to the eyes or to the perceptual system can be detected. Case reports have suggested that such psychological failures to see might be linked to traumatic sexual experiences with resulting repression of stimuli that might unleash anxiety. Although clinical case reports often provide suggestive evidence, they are never conclusive. To go beyond clinical impressions, researchers have tried to study possible anxiety-reducing distortions in perception experimentally. Because it was obviously both unfeasible and unethical to induce sexual traumas in human participants, considerable ingenuity was needed to find ways to study perceptual defense in experiments.

7.4 What methods were used in perceptual defense research, what results were obtained, and what alternative explanations were offered?

The Long History of Perceptual Defense. In the 1940s and 1950s researchers reasoned that persons who did not give sexual or aggressive responses to ambiguous stimuli must be defending against this type of ideation, especially if the same stimuli generally elicited many such responses from most normal people. Consequently, if a person fails to identify potentially threatening inputs to the senses, such as anxiety-arousing sexual words or threatening scenes, it might indicate perceptual inhibition or defense.

To study this process, researchers presented threatening perceptual stimuli in decreasing degrees of ambiguity. They began at a point at which participants could tell what the words were and could reasonably interpret them in many ways, to a point of definiteness that permitted only one clearly correct interpretation. A helpful device for this purpose was the **tachistoscope,** a machine through which potentially threatening words (e.g., "penis," "whore") and neutral words (e.g., "house," "flowers") could be flashed at varying speeds. These stimulus words were presented on a screen very rapidly at first and then gradually exposed for increasingly long durations. The length of time required before each person correctly recognized the stimulus served as the "defensiveness" score; the longer the time required to recognize threatening stimuli, the greater the individual's defensive avoidance tendencies were assumed to be.

In one classic study, college students viewed words presented tachistoscopically so rapidly that they could not perceive them consciously. The words were either emotional or neutral in meaning (McGinnies, 1949). Each student was asked what word had been seen after each exposure. If the answer was wrong, the same word was presented again at a slightly longer exposure time, and the participant again tried to recognize it. It was predicted that such "taboo" words as "penis" or "raped" would be anxiety laden and therefore more readily inhibited than neutral words such as "apple." The results confirmed this prediction, showing greater perceptual defense (longer recognition times) for taboo words than for neutral words.

But these results also can be interpreted quite differently. As was noted long ago (Howes & Solomon, 1951), the perceptual situation places the participant in an embarrassing predicament. In the typical procedure, an undergraduate was brought to the laboratory by a professor or an assistant and then exposed to brief and unclear stimulus presentations by the tachistoscope. The task is essentially a guessing game in which the partcipant tries to discern the correct word from fleeting fragments. On the first trial of a word, for example, something like an "r" and "p" may be seen and the participant may guess "rope." On the next trial, the participant may think "good grief, that looked something like 'rape'!" But rather than make this guess to a professor or an assistant in the academic atmosphere of a scientific laboratory, the participant may deliberately suppress the response. Instead of saying "rape," "rope" is offered again, and the taboo word is withheld until the participant is absolutely sure that this perception is correct.

In sum, a major problem in interpreting results from such studies is that it is extremely difficult to know whether individuals are slower to report some stimuli because they are unconsciously screening them from awareness. Even without such an unconscious mechanism, they may be inhibited about reporting such stimuli until they are absolutely sure, just to avoid embarrassment.

Limitations of Early Laboratory Studies. Psychoanalytically oriented critics have been quite skeptical of the relevance of many of these studies for their theory (Erdelyi, 1993; Erdelyi & Goldberg, 1979). They argue that it is confusing and misleading to study single processes (such as repression) in isolation, outside the context of the person's total psychic functioning. They see these experimental studies at best as suggestive, but clinically irrelevant. They doubt that long-term psychodynamic processes like unconscious reactions to traumatic events in early childhood can be studied under the artificial conditions of the typical laboratory experiment (e.g., Erdelyi, 1993; Madison, 1960). It is also risky to generalize from college sophomores in a laboratory to clinical populations and clinical problems. The mild anxiety induced by experimental threats to college students may have little relevance for understanding the traumas experienced by the young child trying to cope with Oedipal fantasies or the severely disturbed patient in the clinic. On the other hand, the clinician's judgments and intuitive procedures for inferring unconscious dynamics, for example, from projective tests, also have serious limitations (Kihlstrom, 2003; Rorer, 1990). There have been many studies of unconscious repression and unconscious perception, but the conclusions that may be drawn from them have long remained controversial.

7.5 Psychoanalysts have been critical of experimental studies of unconscious processes. What are their major criticisms?

▶ THE COGNITIVE UNCONSCIOUS

Although research on the unconscious remains controversial, some clear themes have emerged (e.g., Kihlstrom, 1999), and we examine them next.

Experimental Evidence for Unconscious Processes

Experiments that try to demonstrate repression and unconscious perception have been difficult to interpret (Erdelyi, 1985; D'Zurilla, 1965; Kihlstrom, 1999). Most of the early studies yielded unclear results. After more than 25 years of experiments, for example, one influential review of experimental research on repression led the reviewer to conclude that "there is no evidence to support the predictions generated by the theory of repression" (Holmes, 1974, p. 651). Two decades later, another review led him to the same conclusion (Holmes, 1992). But it is just as easy to conclude that all these studies were flawed.

The two main ways of looking at the research results are well summarized by Erdelyi (1985, pp. 104–105):

> One may begin to understand why experimental psychology, in contrast to dynamic clinical psychology, has taken such a different stance on phenomena such as repression. Experimental psychology, in the service of simplification and control, has studied manifest events, specific memory episodes, or percepts (as in perceptual defense). It is not typical, however, for a normal college subject to resort in the laboratory to such drastic defenses as to block out a clear memory episode or perceptual experience. Consequently, experimental psychology has had great difficulty in demonstrating repression in the laboratory and has understandably taken a skeptical attitude towards this phenomenon. Clinicians, on the other hand, deal continually with latent (hidden) contents, and in this realm the selective blocking or distortion of information through context manipulation is utterly commonplace. The clinician shakes his head in disbelief at the experimental psychologist, whose paltry methodology cannot even demonstrate a phenomenon as obvious and ubiquitous as repression. The experimentalist similarly shakes his head at the credulity of the psychodynamic clinician, who embraces notions unproven in the laboratory and which, moreover, rest on the presumed existence of unconscious, indeed, physically non-existent, latent contents.

In sum, most clinicians remain convinced that evidence for the unconscious is almost everywhere; in contrast, many experimental researchers have had trouble finding it anywhere. On the other hand, new data have come from experiments by social psychologists into the "automatic processing" of social information at levels that are at least partly outside our awareness. For example, information related to racial and sexual stereotypes can affect our judgments and actions even when we are not aware of ever having seen that information (Bargh, Chen, & Burrows, 1996; Kunda, 1999). After reviewing the extensive evidence rapidly accumulating on the topic of information processing outside awareness, Kunda (1999, pp. 287–288) concludes: ". . . there is considerable evidence that our judgments, feelings, and behaviors can be influenced by factors that we have never been aware of, by factors that we were aware of at one time but can no longer recall, and by factors that we can still recall but whose influence we are unaware of."

The Repressed Memory Debate

7.6 What evidence is there that long-forgotten memories of abuse that suddenly reappear may in some cases be "false" memories? What is the risk of concluding that all are false?

Based on the Freudian premise that the human mind purposefully but unconsciously hides frightening or potentially damaging memories, repression is seen by many clinicians and researchers as a major root of psychological dysfunction. But skeptics see it more as a fiction created by a biased theoretical perspective through which therapists may unwittingly damage their patients and their families (Loftus, 1993, 1994; Ofshe & Watters, 1993). While repressed memory continues to remain a controversial academic topic in psychology, it now also has become the center of a public debate that has spread into the media.

Return of the Repressed.   The public debate began in recent years when many people claimed that they had been the victims of childhood abuse. They asserted that they had been unaware of these abuses until their repressed memories for the traumatic event were recovered, usually in the course of psychotherapy. Often they then tried to bring criminal charges against the alleged perpetrators of these abuses. The question raised then was: are these recovered memories accurate or might they be **false memories**?

The reported recovered memories of abuse have often produced great personal pain and been the bases for lawsuits and punishment of the alleged abusers. As the defense lawyers are quick to point out, however, the existence of repression itself remains controversial. On the one hand, a review of over 60 years of research led Holmes (1992) to still conclude that ". . . at the present time there is no controlled laboratory evidence supporting the concept of repression" (p. 95). Likewise, in a study of children (ages 5–10) who witnessed the murder of one of their parents, Malmquist (1986) reported that none of the children seemed to repress the memory: instead they frequently focused on it.

Nevertheless, most sophisticated and highly experienced clinicians still remain convinced that case studies compellingly document the existence of repression (Erdelyi, 1993). Supporting that view, some researchers make the case that memories for traumatic events from the early years of life, even after they have been forgotten, may reappear in adulthood under conditions of high stress (Jacobs & Nadel, 1985; Schooler, 1994, 1997; Schooler, Bendiksen, & Ambadar, 1997).

Did It Really Happen?   But even assuming that a defensive mechanism of repression occurs and in some cases is activated as a way of coping with traumatic events such as sexual abuse, there is a major problem in determining accurately whether a particular memory for a traumatic event is accurate or instead invented or grossly distorted. Modern memory research makes it clear that memories are not stored like videotapes on a shelf and later replayed. Rather, they are reconstructions of the past, and they are subject to being influenced by suggestions and cues from the outside world and the inside of one's mind, including one's own fantasies and speculations (e.g., Loftus, 1993, 1994; Ofshe, 1992). In short, memories can be created in people by suggestion and self-suggestion, or by telling them that something occurred, often in ways that can even give the person confidence that they are based on reality.

The Power of Suggestion.   One worry is that false memories may be unwittingly strengthened by therapists, particularly if they believe, as Freud did, that problems tend to stem from the abuse that the patient suffered as a child. Guided by that belief, some therapists may too easily encourage their patients to explore their unconscious minds, searching for repressed memories that may not exist. In this search, they may do what is sometimes called "memory work," using hypnosis, suggestive questioning, guided visualization, and dream interpretation (Loftus, 1994). Such exploration risks coming up with memories of traumatic events that may have been imagined or fantasized but that did not actually occur. In that case, instead of helping victims to reclaim lost pieces of their lives, they may hurt innocent people and create rather than reduce distress.

The Risk of Excessive Skepticism

The debate about repressed memory raised important questions but also may risk creating excessive skepticism leading people to doubt all reports about repressed memories that become accessible. The danger is that by making the topic so controversial, many victims of abuse and trauma in childhood and later life may be ignored or undermined in their efforts to find and express the truth. Relevant here is the discovery that when people have had traumatic experiences, it can greatly help them to discuss those memories candidly, rather than to try to hide or suppress them. The process of talking or writing about these traumatic experiences not only helps one feel better by "getting it off your chest," as folk wisdom has long suggested, but also can profoundly improve one's health. For example, by simply writing about their traumatic experiences during a period of four days, essentially healthy college students improved their health following the study, with fewer visits to the health center and improved blood pressure and immune system functioning (Pennebaker, 1993; Pennebaker, Kiecolt-Glaser, & Glaser, 1988). It would therefore be unfortunate if trauma victims failed to use opportunities to appropriately air rather than conceal their experience.

Optimistic Prospects for the Future of the Unconscious

In conclusion, what can be said about the role of the unconscious in modern personality psychology? This question was addressed in a special series of articles in which research experts in the area reviewed what is known about the nature of the unconscious (e.g., Bruner, 1992; Erdelyi, 1992; Greenwald, 1992). Although there was no consistent agreement about how to characterize unconscious processes in terms of their precise role and significance, there was ". . . absolute agreement that exciting times, both in research and theory, are ahead for the unconscious" (Loftus & Klinger, 1992, p. 764). This optimism seems justified because methods and concepts in the research on this topic are becoming more sophisticated (e.g., Lewicki, Hill, & Czyzewska, 1992). There is also growing attention to how motivational factors, such as the person's goals and needs, influence memory (e.g., Kihlstrom, 1999, 2003; Kunda, 1990, 1999; Singer & Salovey, 1993).

▶ PATTERNS OF DEFENSE: INDIVIDUAL DIFFERENCES IN COGNITIVE AVOIDANCE

Cognitive avoidance of anxiety-provoking information is not only a basic process, it also is a dimension of personality on which people differ substantially and interestingly. Some people react to stimuli that arouse anxiety by avoiding them cognitively, but other people do not. For many years, individual differences in "defensive" patterns have been found (Bruner & Postman, 1947; Lazarus, 1976; Miller, 1987; Paulhus, Fridhandler, & Hayes, 1997).

Repression–Sensitization

The dimension on which these differences seemed to fall was a continuum of behaviors ranging from avoiding the anxiety-arousing stimuli to approaching them more readily and being extra vigilant or super-sensitized to them. The former end of the continuum included behaviors similar to the defensive mechanisms that psycho-analysts called denial and repression; the latter pattern—vigilance or sensiti-zation to anxiety-provoking cues—seemed more like obsessive worrying. This dimension has become known now as the **repression–sensitization** continuum. Repression–sensitization became the focus of much research both as a dynamic process and as a personality dimension on which individuals might show consistent patterns.

In general, individuals show some consistency in their cognitive avoidance of anxiety-provoking cues such as threatening words (Eriksen, 1952; Eriksen & Kuethe, 1956). In one study, reaction time and other measures of avoidance were obtained in the auditory recognition of poorly audible sentences that had sexual and aggressive content. People who were slow to recognize such sentences also tended to avoid sexual and aggressive materials in a sentence completion test (Lazarus, Eriksen, & Fonda, 1951). People who more readily recalled stimuli associated with a painful shock also tended to recall their failures; those who forgot one were more likely to forget the other (Lazarus & Longo, 1953). A tendency for some consistency in cognitive avoidance may exist at least when ex-tremely high and low groups are selected (Eriksen, 1966). Correlations between cognitive avoidance on experimental tasks and various other measures of repression–sensitization also imply some consistency in these patterns (Byrne, 1964; McFarland & Buehler, 1997; Weinberger, 2002).

In short, in spite of disagreement about the concept and role of repression, there now is agreement that people do use a mechanism of mentally distancing themselves from awareness of threatening and negative thoughts or emotions. In modern research, the term repression currently often refers to that meaning. In Focus 7.1 illustrates that the expressions of individual differences in repressive tendencies depend on the interaction between the individual's disposition and the particular situation.

7.7 What is meant by repression and sensitization? What research evidence exists that this is a meaningful personality dimension that relates to other behaviors?

IN FOCUS 7.1

PERSON–SITUATION INTERACTION IN REPRESSIVE TENDENCIES

Current work on individual differences in the expressions of repressive tendencies tries to take into account both its dispositional determinants and its situational determi-nants in a Person × Situation interaction model. It thus addresses both overall individual differences in the ten-dency to distance oneself, and the particular types of situ-ations in which these differences will, and will not, be seen. To illustrate, Mendolia, Moore, and Tesser (1996) in one study assessed college students on self-report measures of anxiety and repressive tendencies (Wein-berger, 2002). They then observed their reactions in a series of experiments measuring their attentiveness to the emotional details of positive and negative situations—in this case, success or failure on a task claiming to identify their level of intelligence. After these experiences, partic-ipants were given a word familiarity task designed to measure how much emotion they were feeling. They

were asked to recall emotion (e.g., angry, happy) vs. non-emotion (swift, interstate) words, and a variety of other measures.

Briefly, the researchers found that repressors are more attentive to the emotional details of both positive and neg-ative situations, in this case both when seeming to succeed or to fail on the supposed test of intelligence. Further, three factors differentiate when people will exhibit repres-sive behavior and when they will not: (1) they must possess an increased sensitivity to both positive and negative emo-tional events (i.e., be high in this disposition); (2) there must be situational information that poses a threat to their self-concept; and (3) the situation must provide them with the opportunity to distract or distance themselves from the self-threatening information. According to the researchers, without all of these factors, repressors and nonrepressors may respond in the same manner.

Selective Attention

Individual differences in repression–sensitization have often been measured on a self-report questionnaire (Byrne, 1964). On this scale, **repressors** are people who describe themselves as having few problems or difficulties. They do not report themselves as highly sensitive to everyday stress and anxieties, whereas those with an opposite pattern are called **sensitizers.** Individual differences on this scale can predict selective attention to important personal information about the self. In one study, college students were exposed to personal information about themselves supposedly based on their own performance on personality tests they had taken earlier (Mischel, Ebbesen, & Zeiss, 1973). The results were made available to students in individual sessions in which each was left alone to look at descriptions of his or her personal liabilities (in one computer file) and personal assets (in another file). For example, the personality assets included such feedback as, "Affiliative, capable of cooperating and reciprocating deeply in relations with others. . . ." In contrast, the personality liabilities information included such descriptions as, "Nonperseverative, procrastination, and distractibility . . . resultant failures lead to greater and greater apathy. . . ." (Actually, all students received the same feedback, but in the debriefing session in which they were told the truth, it became clear that they had been convinced that the test results really described them; in fact, they believed the information had captured much about their personalities.)

The question was: Would repressors and sensitizers (as measured on the self-report questionnaire) exhibit different attentional patterns for the positive, self-enhancing information versus the negative, threatening information about themselves? There were clear differences.

These results are summarized in Figure 7.1. Sensitizers attended more to their liabilities and spent little time on their assets; in sharp contrast, repressors attended as much to their assets as to their liabilities. Later research suggests that repressors may

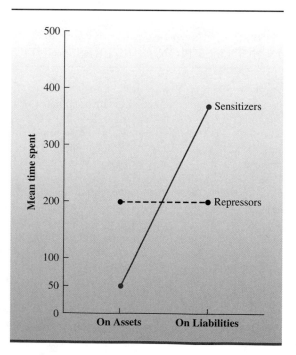

Figure 7.1 Attention deployment by sensitizers and repressors. Mean amount of time (in seconds) spent on assets and liabilities by sensitizers and by repressors.

Source: Based on data in the control condition from Mischel, W., Ebbesen, W. B., & Zeiss, A. R. (1973). Selective attention to the self: Situational and dispositional determinants. *Journal of Personality and Social Psychology, 27,* 129–142. (Figs. 1 and 2, p. 136.)

be people who are especially sensitive to criticism and threat, and use their defense to protect themselves against this vulnerability (Baumeister & Cairns, 1992).

In sum, the repressors and the sensitizers differed in how they dealt with positive and negative ego-relevant information. But these differences seem linked to their attentional strategies, not to unconscious distortions in their memory: both groups are able to recall threatening information about themselves with equal accuracy if they are made to attend equally to that information (Mischel, Ebbesen, & Zeiss, 1976). Normally, however, the sensitizers tended to focus on negative self-relevant information, whereas the repressors tended to avoid it and preferred to think about happier things. When the situation prevents repressors from simply ignoring the threat, they do begin to attend to it and worry anxiously about it (Baumeister & Cairns, 1992).

The two groups also differed in their self-descriptions: while repressors described themselves in positive, socially desirable terms, representing themselves consistently in a more favorable light, sensitizers painted a much more critical and negative self-portrait (Alicke, 1985; Joy, 1963). Most interesting, however, is that it is the repressor, not the sensitizer, who better fits the picture of the optimistic personality with a good mental and physical health prognosis.

This is surprising for psychodynamic theory, which has long assumed that accurate self-awareness and being in touch with one's personal limitations, anxieties, and flaws (i.e., sensitization) were important ingredients of the healthy personality. In contrast, repression and cognitive avoidance of negative information and threat were the hallmark of the brittle, vulnerable personality. It is, of course, likely that the massive emotional repression to which Freudians refer is quite different from the self-enhancing positive bias that seems to characterize repressors as identified on this scale. Likewise, the growth of self-awareness and accessibility of personal anxieties to which psychodynamic theory refers may also be different from "sensitization" measures on this scale. But as the next section also suggests (Miller, 1987), and as a great deal of work shows (Bonanno, 2001; Seligman, 1990; Taylor & Brown, 1988; see Chapter 13), under many circumstances an attitude of emotional blunting that deliberately avoids threatening information may be highly adaptive, a sign of mental health rather than of a fragile personality in need of insight.

Blunting versus Monitoring Styles

In a related direction, it has been shown that people differ considerably in their disposition to blunt and distract themselves or to monitor for (be alert to) danger signals (Miller, 1996). One promising scale tries to identify information avoiders and information seekers as two distinct coping styles. The **Miller Behavioral Style Scale (MBSS)** consists of four hypothetical stress-evoking scenes of an uncontrollable nature (Miller, 1981, 1987; Miller & Mangan, 1983). On this measure, people are asked to imagine vividly scenes like "you are afraid of the dentist and have to get some dental work done"; or "you are being held hostage by a group of armed terrorists in a public building"; or "you are on an airplane, 30 minutes from your destination, when the plane unexpectedly goes into a deep dive and then suddenly levels off. After a short time, the pilot announces that nothing is wrong, although the rest of the ride may be rough. You, however, are not convinced that all is well."

Each scene is followed by statements that represent ways of coping with the situation, either by **monitoring** or by **blunting.** Half of the statements for each scene are of a monitoring variety. For example, in the hostage situation: "If there was a radio present, I would stay near it and listen to the bulletins about what the police were doing";

7.8 Distinguish monitoring versus blunting responses to threatening events. How are MBSS scores related to information search under anxiety-arousing conditions?

Some people cope with unpleasant events by mentally "blunting" (distracting themselves).

or, in the airplane situation: "I would listen carefully to the engines for unusual noises and would watch the crew to see if their behavior was out of the ordinary." The other half of the statements are of the blunting type. For example, in the dental situation: "I would do mental puzzles in my head"; or, in the airplane situation: "I would watch the end of the movie, even if I had seen it before." The individual simply marks all the statements following each scene that might apply to him.

College students were threatened with a low probability shock and allowed to choose whether they wanted to monitor for information or distract themselves with music (Miller, 1981). As expected, the amount of time spent on information rather than on music was predicted reasonably well by an individual's MBSS score. In particular, the more blunting items endorsed on the scale, the less time the person spent listening to the information and the more time listening to the music. In sum, individuals differed in the extent to which they chose to monitor or distract themselves when faced with aversive events (possible electric shocks) in the experiment. These differences in coping style were related to their questionnaire scores, supporting the validity of the MBSS.

The Role of Control: When Don't You Want to Know?

7.9 How does the controllability of aversive stimuli influence the adaptiveness of approach–avoidance tendencies?

Whether or not persons react to negative stimuli by avoiding them "defensively" in their cognitions and perceptions may depend on whether or not they believe that they can somehow cope with them by problem solving and action. If adaptive action seems impossible, cognitive avoidance attempts become more likely. But if the painful cues can be controlled by the person's actions, then greater attention and vigilance to them may occur. This point is illustrated in the same blunting-monitoring study that gave individuals a choice between stress-relevant information or distraction just discussed (Miller, 1979). The information was a warning signal for when an electric shock would come; the distraction was listening to music. Half the participants were led to believe

TABLE 7.1 Number of Participants Who Seek Information (Warning Signal) or Distraction (Listen to Music) When Avoidance Is or Is Not Possible

	Information Seeking	Distraction Seeking
Avoidance Possible	24	10
Avoidance Not Possible	11	23

Source: Based on Miller, S, M. (1979). Coping with impending stress: Physiological and cognitive correlates of choice. *Psychopathology.* 16, 572–581.

the shock was potentially avoidable; the rest believed it was unavoidable. As Table 7.1 shows, when participants believed avoidance was possible, they preferred information; when they thought it was unavoidable, they preferred distraction. Other research has documented the many circumstances under which coping with problems is improved by the selective avoidance of threatening information (Janis, 1971; Lazarus, 1976, 1990; Lazarus & Folkman, 1984).

Matching the Medical Information to the Patient's Style

In a real-life application to a medical situation, Miller and Mangan (1983) gave the MBSS to gynecologic patients about to undergo colposcopy, a diagnostic procedure to check for the presence of abnormal (cancerous) cells in the uterus. Based on scale scores, patients were first divided into monitors or blunters. Half the women in each group were then given extensive information about the forthcoming procedure, and half were given (the usual) minimal information. Psychophysiological reactions (like heart rate), subjective reports, and observer ratings of arousal and discomfort were taken before, during, and after the procedures. The results revealed, again as expected, that monitors showed more arousal overall than blunters (e.g., see Fig. 7.2 for the physician's rating of patients' tension during the exam).

Most interesting, physiological arousal was reduced when the level of preparatory information was consistent with the patients' coping style. That is, physiological arousal was reduced for blunters who received minimal information and for monitors who received extensive information. The total results clearly show strong individual differences in informational preferences during the coping process when people are faced with threats. Most important, they showed that when monitors are told more, and blunters are told less, about an impending stress each type is likely to cope with it best: matching the information to the style can reduce the stress experienced and enhance resources.

Figure 7.2 Doctor's report—Tension during exam.

Source: Miller, S. M., & Mangan, C. E. (1983). Cognition and psychopathology. In K. Dobson & P. C. Kendall (Eds.), *Cognition, stress, and health.* Reprinted with permission from Elsevier.

▶ PERSONALITY ASSESSMENT

Freudian psychology was especially exciting because it promised a way to understand and to treat each complex individual with the depth that he or she deserves. The last two chapters gave you a sense of some of the main concepts that underlie the psychodynamic approach to personality. Guided by these concepts, one tries to help the person to reveal unconscious motives, conflicts, and other dynamics. In this approach, the objective is to uncover disguises and defenses, to read the symbolic meanings of behaviors, and to find the unconscious motives that underlie action. In this way, the clinician tries to find the distinctive qualities that characterize the individual.

The Core Beneath the Mask

Psychodynamic theorists recognized that a person's overt actions across seemingly similar situations often seem inconsistent. They felt, however, that these inconsistencies in behavior were merely superficial, because beneath them were underlying motives that actually drove the person consistently over the years. The basic motives persist across diverse settings, but their overt expressions are disguised. Therefore, the task is to find the person's fundamental motives and dynamics under the defensive distortions of the overt behavior. The challenge is to discover the basic core hidden behind the mask, to find the truth beneath the surface. But how?

Relying on the Clinician

Psychodynamic interpretations depend more on intuitions than on tests. The rules for relating behavioral signs to unconscious meanings are not spelled out and require clinicians to form their own judgments based on clinical experience and the "feel" of the case. The merit of such assessments depends on two things. First, it depends on the evidence supporting the techniques upon which the psychologist relies. Second, it depends on the value of clinical judgment itself. Because psychodynamic theories rest on the belief that the core of personality is revealed by highly indirect behavioral signs, evidence for the value of these indirect signs of personality is most important. We next review some of the main clinical methods that have been studied in the search for valuable signs of personality. Probably the most important of these methods are the projective techniques.

Projective Methods

7.10 What are the major features of projective tests, and the rationale underlying their use? Why are they favored by psychodynamic clinicians?

The main characteristic of **projective methods** is the way in which the testing situation is usually structured so that the task is ambiguous. Typically, there are also attempts to disguise the purpose of the test (Bell, 1948; Exner, 1993), and the person is given freedom to respond in any way that he or she likes. In projective testing, assessors present you with ambiguous stimuli and ask ambiguous questions. For example, they ask, "What might this be?" "What could this remind you of?" [while showing an inkblot] or say, "Create the most imaginative story that you can [showing a picture], including what the people are thinking and feeling, what led up to this situation, and how it all comes out." Or they read words and ask you to "say the first thing that comes to mind."

Psychoanalytically oriented assessors favor projective techniques, because they assume that the "unconscious inner life" is at least partially "projected" and revealed in responses to the ambiguous projective test situation. The two most influential and popular projective techniques have been the Rorschach, and the Thematic Apperception Test (TAT) described below. Both the reliability and the validity of the Rorschach have been heavily disputed and generally found to be problematic. In a comprehensive review, Kihlstrom (2003) concludes that even in the few cases in which projective techniques had some validity, there was no evidence that the findings reflected the person's *unconscious* mental states.

Nevertheless, a 1995 survey with replies from over 400 clinical psychologists across a variety of settings indicated that both the Rorschach and TAT still remain among the most commonly used personality assessment procedures in everyday clinical practice (Watkins et al., 1995).

The Rorschach Test

Developed by the psychiatrist Hermann Rorschach in 1921, the **Rorschach test** consists of a series of inkblots on 10 separate cards (Figure 7.3). Some of the blots are black and white, and some colored. The individual is instructed to look at the inkblots one at a time and to say everything that the inkblot could resemble or look like. The examiner then generally conducts an inquiry into the details of the person's interpretation of each blot.

7.11 How are responses to the Rorschach and TAT analyzed and used to infer psychodynamics?

Responses may be scored for location (the place on the card that the response refers to) and such determinants as the physical aspects of the blot, such as shape, color, shading, or an expression of movement (Exner, 1993). The originality of the responses, the content, and other characteristics also may be scored and compared to

Figure 7.3 Taking a Rorschach test.

those of other people of similar age. The interpreter may try to relate these scores to aspects of personality, such as creative capacity, contact with reality, and anxiety.

Gary's Reactions to Two of the Rorschach Inkblot Cards

Response: This looks like two dogs, head-to-foot (laughs), licking each other. That's about it, that's all.

Inquiry answers (to the question "What about the inkblot made you think of two dogs?"): They're sort of fuzzy . . . kinda shapeless. It was the dark skin and the furry effect that made me think of it.

Response: Didn't we have this one already? This could be an ogre laughing—his head thrown back and he's laughing, his eyes and mouth wide open.

These over here look like insects, tsetse flies in fact, with tiny, tiny legs, and small, delicate and rather beautiful wings. That's it, that's enough.

Inquiry answers: It's the shaggyness and the hugeness, the massiveness of the shape. The wings over here, head here.

Assessment with the TAT

As noted in Chapter 6, the Thematic Apperception Test or TAT was developed in the Harvard Psychological Clinic research program during the 1930s, and used extensively to study motives like need for achievement. The TAT is a projective test in the sense that it is expected that people will interpret the ambiguous pictures presented according to their individual readiness to perceive in a certain way ("apperception"). The themes that recur in these imaginative productions are thought to reflect the person's underlying needs, as well as potential conflicts and problems. Special scoring keys have been designed for use with the TAT (Bellack & Abrams, 1997; McClelland et al., 1953; Mussen & Naylor, 1954). In clinical work, the stories usually are not scored formally, however, and instead the clinician interprets the themes intuitively in accord with his or her personality theory (Rossini & Moretti, 1997). On the other hand, formal scoring is often used in research applications. Two of Gary's answers to TAT cards are shown in In Focus 7.2.

IN FOCUS 7.2

GARY'S TAT STORIES

Card depicting two men: Two men have gone on a hunting trip. It is dawn now and the younger one is still sound asleep. The older one is watching over him. Thinking how much he reminds him of when he was young and could sleep no matter what. Also, seeing the boy sleeping there makes him long for the son he never had. He's raising his hand about to stroke him on the forehead. I think he'll be too embarrassed to go ahead with it. He'll start a fire and put on some coffee and wait for the younger man to wake up.

Card depicting young man and older woman: This depicts a mother–son relationship. The mother is a strong, stalwart person. Her son is hesitating at the doorway. He wants to ask her advice about something but isn't sure whether it's the right thing to do. Maybe he should make up his own mind. I think he'll just come in and have a chat with her. He won't ask her advice but will work things out for himself. Maybe it's a career choice, a girlfriend. I don't know what, but whatever it is, he'll decide himself. He'll make his own plans, figure out what the consequences will be, and work it out from there.

Studying Lives in Depth

Using the TAT and a large variety of other methods, Henry Murray and the Harvard Personologists developed a distinct research-based approach to personality and an assessment style that became widely respected by other psychologists and is still influential. As you saw in the last chapter, it opened the way to studying diverse human motives. It also provided a new research style: the intense study of lives in depth over time.

The Harvard group focused on intensive long-term studies of relatively small samples of people. In one classic project (Murray et al., 1938) called *Exploration in Personality,* researchers studied Harvard college undergraduates over a period of many years and gathered data on their personality development and maturation at many points in their lives. They administered tests of many kinds, obtained extensive autobiographical sketches, observed participants' behavior directly, and interviewed them in great detail. These methods probed thoroughly into many topics and most facets of their lives. They included, for example, inquiries into the individual's personal history and development, school and college, major life experiences, family relations, childhood memories, and sexual development (e.g., earliest recollections, first experiences, masturbation). They also assessed abilities and interests. A sampling of these topics is summarized in Table 7.2. The results often provided rich narrative accounts of life histories, as in Robert White's *Lives in Progress* (1952), which traced several lives over many years.

Assessment Strategy: Diagnostic Council

The researchers in the Harvard clinical studies were experienced psychologists who interpreted their data clinically. Usually a group of several assessors studied each individual participant. To share their insights, they pooled their overall impressions at a staff conference or "diagnostic council." These councils became a model for clinical practice. In them, a case conference was conducted in detail and in depth about each individual. On the basis of the council's discussions, inferences were generated about each participant's personality. They inferred basic needs, motives, conflicts, and dynamics; attitudes and values; main character strengths and liabilities. Each piece of information served as a sign of the individual's personality and was interpreted by the council of assessors.

7.12 How was the diagnostic council used by Harvard personologists in the in-depth study of individuals over time?

TABLE 7.2 Examples of Topics Included in the Study of Lives by the Harvard Personologists

Personal history (early development, school and college, major experiences)

Family relations and childhood memories (including school relations, reactions to authority)

Sexual development (earliest recollections, first experiences, masturbation)

Present dilemmas (discussion of current problems)

Abilities and interests (physical, mechanical, social, economic, erotic)

Aesthetic preferences (judgments, attitudes, tastes regarding art)

Level of aspiration (goal setting, reactions to success and failure)

Ethical standards (cheating to succeed, resistance to temptation)

Imaginal productivity (reactions to inkblots)

Musical reveries (report of images evoked by phonograph music)

Dramatic productions (constructing a dramatic scene with toys)

Source: Based on Murray, H. A., Barrett, W. G., & Homburger, E. (1938). *Explorations in Personality.* New York: Oxford University Press.

Selecting U.S. Spies: The OSS Assessment Project

7.13 How were situational tests used by diagnostic councils in the OSS Assessment Project?

This strategy is illustrated in one of the important applied projects of the personologists—their effort to select officers for the supersensitive Office of Strategic Services (OSS) during World War II. OSS officers in World War II had to perform critical and difficult secret intelligence assignments, often behind enemy lines and under great stress. The personologists obviously could not devote the same lengthy time to studying OSS candidates that they had given to Harvard undergraduates in the relaxed prewar days in Cambridge. Nevertheless, they attempted to use the same general strategy of global clinical assessment. For this purpose, teams of assessors studied small groups of OSS candidates intensively, usually for a few days or a weekend, in special secret retreats or "stations" located in various parts of the country. Many different measures were obtained on each candidate.

One of the most interesting innovations was the **situational test.** In this procedure, participants were required to perform stressful, lifelike tasks under extremely difficult conditions. For example, "The Bridge" task required building a wooden bridge under simulated dangerous field conditions and under high stress and anxiety. But such situational tests were not used to obtain a sample of their bridge-building skills. Instead, the clinicians made deep inferences, based on the behavior observed during the task, about each person's underlying personality. It was these inferences of unobserved attributes or dispositions, rather than the behavior actually observed in the sampled situation, that entered into the assessment report and became the bases for clinical predictions. In this fashion, behavior samples and situational tests were transformed into inferences about underlying dispositions and motives.

To illustrate, in the *Assessment of Men* by the OSS staff (1948), the bridge-building situation was used to answer questions like these (p. 326):

> *Who took the lead in finally crossing the chasm? And why did he do it? Was it to show his superiority? Why did each of the others fall back from the trip? Did they fear failure?*

It is obvious that the chief value of this situation was to raise questions about personality dynamics which required an explanation on the basis of the personality trends already explored. If these could not supply a reasonable explanation, then new information had to be sought, new deductions made.

In the situational test, just as on the projective test, behavior was interpreted as a clue revealing personality. Although behavior was sampled and observed, the observations served mainly as signs from which the researchers inferred the motives that prompted the behaviors.

From Situational Tests to Psychodynamic Inferences

In the global clinical assessment strategy, the assessors form their impressions of the person from performance on various projective and objective tests, the autobiography and total personal history, and reactions to thorough interviews. Several assessors study the same person and each generates his or her own clinical impressions. Later, at a conference, the assessors discuss and share their interpretations and pool their judgments. Gradually they integrate their impressions of each person's overall personality structure and dynamics. To predict the person's behavior in a new situation (for example, under attack behind enemy lines), they try to infer, from the personality they have hypothesized, how such an individual would probably react to the stresses of that situation. This global

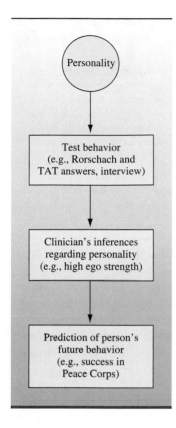

Figure 7.4 Global psychodynamic assessment. The clinician infers the participant's personality from his or her test behavior and predicts future behavior by judging how a person with that personality would probably react to specific future situations.

assessment model is schematized in Figure 7.4. It depicts the strategy of using test behavior to generate inferences about the underlying personality. The prediction of future behavior is based on judgments of how a person with that particular personality would probably act. The test behavior itself is used as a sign of the underlying personality.

▶ TREATMENT AND CHANGE

The psychodynamic approach to treatment has had an enormous influence on American psychiatry and clinical psychology. Its major version is **psychoanalysis** or psychoanalytic therapy, a form of psychotherapy originally developed by Freud and practiced by psychoanalysts.

7.14 What is the basic goal in psychoanalytic treatment? What methods are used to achieve positive outcomes?

Traditionally, in psychoanalysis several weekly meetings, each about an hour long, are held between the therapist and client (or "patient"), often for a period of many years. The treatment is based on the premise that neurotic conflict and anxiety are the result of repressed (unconscious) impulses. The aim is to remove the repression and resolve the conflict by helping patients achieve insight into their unconscious impulses.

Free Association and Dream Interpretation

To uncover unconscious material (or lift the repression), the techniques of **free association** and **dream interpretation** are used in traditional psychoanalysis. As was noted before, in free association the patient, usually reclining on a couch, is instructed to report whatever comes to mind without screening or censoring his or her thoughts in any way. Here is a fragment of free association from a psychotherapy session as an example:

> *I wonder how my mother is getting along. You know how she and I don't get along. Once when I was about twelve, she and I were having an argument—I can't remember what it was about—argument 1001. Anyway, the phone rang and one of her darling friends offered her two tickets to the matinee performance of a ballet that day. What a day. She refused them to punish me. For a change! I don't think I even saw a ballet until I was grown up and married. Joe took me. I still get sad when I think about it. I could cry. All blue. It reminds me of all the times when I felt. . . .*

Any difficulties or blocks in free association are considered as important as the material that is easily produced. These difficulties are interpreted as **resistance,** caused by unconscious defenses blocking access to material central to the patient's problems, and the person is encouraged to continue with the free association.

According to psychoanalytic theory, the ego's defense mechanisms are relaxed during sleep, making dreams an avenue to express repressed material. But the defenses still operate to distort the content of dreams, so interpretation is necessary to unravel their meaning. In treatment, the interpretations of blocks in association, and dreams, are done carefully so that the patient continues to relax the defenses. The therapeutic goal is to make the unconscious conscious as the patient gradually relaxes and overcomes resistances to facing unconscious conflicts and motives. For a more contemporary approach to some of Freud's key concepts, see In Focus 7.3.

7.15 In what ways do contemporary studies on trauma support Freud's views and suggest more effective methods of treatment?

TODAY'S VIEW OF FREUD'S THEORY OF TRAUMA

Freud's theory of trauma and neurosis illustrates how his ideas have remained influential, but only with substantial modifications. Freud's theory of the origin of neurosis emphasized the importance of childhood traumas—intense emotional experiences that the person cannot deal with and that "exert a disintegrating effect on the mind" (Spiegel, Koopman, & Classen, 1994, p. 11). Freud held that traumatic experiences can induce not only severe anxiety but also dissociative states of the sort he reported in his clinical observations of hysterical patients who developed physical symptoms (like "glove anesthesia") that made no sense neurologically.

Although these ideas continue to be controversial, they also have stimulated extensive contemporary research on reactions to acute stress, called **traumatic experiences.** These are experiences that abruptly and severely disrupt the person's normal daily routine, threatening him or her with physical injury or death, as happens under war conditions, in earthquakes, or to victims of violent crimes or terrorism. In contemporary research, it has been possible to document and study these experiences systematically. The results of these

new studies in part support many of Freud's insights, and in part serve to modify and improve the treatment procedures to help the victims deal with their traumas more effectively (e.g., Roth & Newman, 1990; Spiegel & Cardena, 1990, 1991).

In the contemporary view, consistent with Freud, when traumas profoundly endanger the victim's core beliefs about oneself and the world, dissociative reactions may occur to keep the threat outside full awareness, split off from the rest of one's experience. Consequently, treatment is aimed at helping the person to integrate the experience and to manage the painful emotions. Freud originally emphasized simply helping the person to reexperience and repeat the event and its emotions and to express them in the therapy relationship.

Current approaches take another step. Called **cognitive restructuring,** the focus is on reinterpreting the meaning of the event in a way that allows the person to deal with it. It involves helping the person to give up the sense of control over the event that often creates inappropriate guilt:

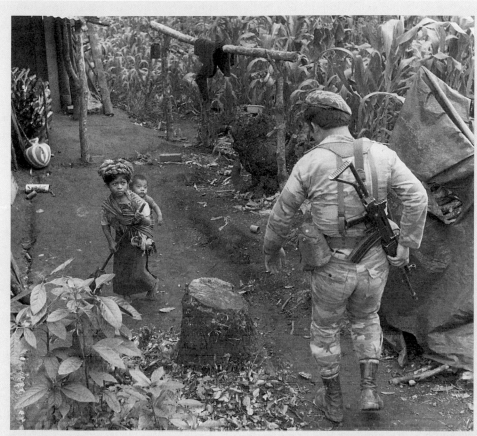

Traumatic experiences may be induced by such extreme events as wars that shatter normal life routines.

A soldier who survived a rocket attack may feel he traded his safety for that of a comrade who died. . . . Therapy is aimed at helping the victim acknowledge and bear the emotional distress which comes with traumatic memories, grieving the loss of control which occurred at the time and thereby admitting the uncomfortable sense of helplessness (Spiegel et al., 1994, p. 18).

In short, in contemporary applications of Freud's ideas about traumas and disassociation, the focus is on helping the person to: acknowledge the trauma itself; bear and reinterpret the memories of the traumatic events; and cast them into a more meaningful perspective with less self-blame. In these efforts, hypnosis, which Freud originally explored deeply but then abandoned as a technique, is often used. Support is given and encouraged, for example, by strengthening interpersonal relationships. These treatment features are characteristic of the "ego psychology" which grew out of, and built upon, Freud's work, and remain influential in current clinical practice.

The Transference Relationship and Working Through

The therapist in psychoanalysis is supposed to create an atmosphere of safety by remaining accepting and noncritical. Therapists deliberately reveal little about themselves and remain shadowy figures who often sit behind the patient and outside his view in order to facilitate a **transference** relationship. Transference is said to occur when the patient responds to the therapist as if he or she were the patient's father,

7.16 Why is the transference relationship so important in psychoanalytic treatment? What is involved in the working-through process?

mother, or some other important childhood figure. Feelings and problems initially experienced in childhood relations with these figures are transferred to the relationship with the therapist. Transference is regarded as inevitable and essential by most psychoanalysts. It is a concept that has been revitalized in current research on memory that shows how early feelings about a person can be reactivated later in life by other people who are perceived to be similar (Andersen & Chen, 2002) as discussed in Chapter 13. In the transference, the therapist demonstrates to patients the childhood origins of their conflicts and helps them to work through and face these problems. Here in the words of a distinguished psychoanalyst (Colby, 1951) is an example of how the transference is used and interpreted:

> *The manner in which a patient acts and feels about his therapist is a bonanza of psychological information. In subtracting the inappropriate from appropriate responses the therapist has a first-hand, immediately observable illustration of the patient's psychodynamics in an interpersonal relationship. . . .*
>
> *A woman from an old Southern family broke away in late adolescence from family ties and values. She became a nomadic Bohemian vigorously opposed to all authority. She expressed her feelings by zealous work in Anarchist societies and other radical movements. In therapy she often told of fearlessly challenging policemen and openly sneering at successful businessmen.*
>
> *Yet her behavior toward the therapist was in marked contrast to this. She was very respectful, non-aggressive and acquiescent—all attitudes she faintly remembers having as a child toward her parents until adolescence. The therapist's concept was that the patient unconsciously saw him as a feared and loved parent who must not be antagonized. She really feared authority as a source of punishment (p. 113).*

The insight to be achieved by the patient in psychoanalysis is not a detached, rational, intellectual understanding. People must work through their problems in the transference relationship. **Working through** involves repeated reexamination of basic problems in different contexts until one learns to handle them more appropriately and understands their emotional roots.

Relational Therapy and Restoration of the Self

7.17 How does relational therapy differ from classical psychoanalytic treatment?

Led by theorists like Kohut, **relational therapy** (also called "object relations therapy") has emerged as a coherent approach to treating personality problems. It is a psychodynamic approach in the sense that its roots are in earlier psychoanalytic theories. Like them, its focus is on the individual's often unconscious, long-standing conflicts and defenses. It is distinctive, however, in three ways. It sees the history of these problems in early relationships, especially with the mother. It sees their expression in current relationships. Finally, it treats them by focusing on the interpersonal relationship within the therapy context.

In this approach, the therapist actively and empathically "engages" the patient to build a close therapeutic relationship. Interpretation and confrontation of basic relational problems occur in this supportive context. Note that this focus on the carefully nurtured empathic relationship contrasts with the "blank screen" image of the traditional Freudian analyst. The Freudian patient free associates while reclining on a couch, with the therapist sitting behind the patient. In relational therapy, the two face each other and interact actively, as the therapist provides empathic support as well as gradual confrontation.

Alternative Psychodynamic Interpretations of Gary W.

One concrete implication of these results is that the psychodynamic meaning of the same information may be interpreted quite differently depending on the specific theory and biases of the particular psychologist. This is especially likely when broad inferences are made about a person's deep, unobservable psychodynamics. For example, if a disciple of Alfred Adler assesses Gary W., he may find evidence for an inferiority complex and sibling rivalry from the same observations that lead a Freudian to infer castration anxiety and an Oedipal complex. Likewise, in the same set of responses, Kohut's student may see Gary's fragmented self and his cry for empathic mirroring of his feelings.

Many psychologists now see such alternative views as a welcome development. It encourages the frank recognition that the same "facts" about a person are indeed open to multiple interpretations from different perspectives. Each view may contribute a somewhat different vision of the individual from a different angle, and no one view is necessarily exclusively correct or absolute. Critics of this approach, however, are understandably concerned that there are no clear standards for selecting among alternative interpretations. There also is no strong evidence to help decide how to select those that might be most useful for different goals. Fortunately, work at the levels of analyses that are presented in the subsequent parts of this text have helped to overcome these limitations.

SUMMARY

ANXIETY AND UNCONSCIOUS DEFENSES

- Conscious and unconscious defense mechanisms can be used to cope with anxiety-arousing stimuli.
- The nature and mechanisms of unconscious repression remain controversial.
- "Perceptual defense" may reduce anxiety by altering sensory perceptions, as in hysterical blindness.
- The length of time required to recognize threatening stimuli may be interpreted as a measure of defensive avoidance.
- Many psychoanalysts warn against generalizing from experiments with college students to clinical populations and problems.
- It is difficult to determine whether a particular memory for a traumatic event is accurate or invented or grossly distorted.

PATTERNS OF DEFENSE: INDIVIDUAL DIFFERENCES IN COGNITIVE AVOIDANCE

- Individuals tend to respond to stress in one of two ways: either avoidance or hypersensitization. This is the repression–sensitization personality dimension.
- These two types do not differ in their recall for positive or negative information.
- Repressors attend more to positive feedback, see themselves more favorably, and are more mentally and physically healthy, whereas sensitizers are preoccupied with negative feedback and are often self-critical.
- There are individual differences in the tendency toward blunting (self-distraction) versus monitoring (increased alertness) in stressful situations.
- If adaptive action in the face of a threat seems impossible, cognitive avoidance or blunting may be more likely. If the potentially painful events can be controlled by the person's actions, then greater attention and vigilance to them may be found.

PERSONALITY ASSESSMENT

- Psychodynamic assessment tries to find the person's fundamental motives and dynamics, and relies on the clinician.
- Projective methods such as the TAT (Thematic Apperception Test) or the Rorschach test are used often.
- In the Rorschach test, the individual is shown a series of inkblots and is asked to say what the inkblots resemble.
- The TAT consists of a series of ambiguous pictures for which the test-taker is asked to make up a story.
- Harvard personologists provided a model for the intensive clinical study of individuals.
- The OSS Assessment project analyzed individuals while they performed tasks under highly stressful situations to infer each person's personality.

TREATMENT AND CHANGE

- Psychoanalytic treatment aims to reduce unconscious defenses and conflicts by helping patients gain insight into their unconscious motivations, using methods like free association and dream interpretation.
- Patients "work through" their problems in the transference relationship with the therapist.
- In relational therapy, the therapist actively and empathically "engages" the patient to build a close working relationship.

KEY TERMS

anxiety 142
blunting 151
cognitive
  restructuring 160
dream interpretation 159
false memories 147
free association 159
Miller Behavioral Style
  Scale (MBSS) 151

monitoring 151
projective methods 154
psychoanalysis 159
relational therapy 162
repression 143
repression–
  sensitization 149
repressors 150
resistance 160

Rorschach test 155
sensitizers 150
situational test 158
suppression 143
tachistoscope 144
transference 161
traumatic
  experiences 160
working through 162

PART II

THE PSYCHODYNAMIC-MOTIVATIONAL LEVEL

▶ OVERVIEW: FOCUS, CONCEPTS, METHODS

Some of the essentials of work at the psychodynamic level are summarized in the Overview table. The table reminds you that unconscious motives and psychodynamics within persons are viewed as the basic causes of their behavior, including their feelings, conflicts, and problems. Clinicians working at this level of analysis try to infer and interpret these causes from their overt "symptom-like" expressions in the individual's behaviors. Dreams, free associations, and responses to unstructured situations such as projective stimuli (for example, the Rorschach inkblots), are especially favored sources of information. The responses from the person serve as indirect signs whose meaning and significance the clinician interprets. The role of the situation is deliberately minimized, guided by the belief that the more ambiguous the situation, the more likely it is that the individual's basic, underlying psychodynamics will be projected in how he or she interprets it and reacts.

The focus of research, like the focus of personality assessment and of psychotherapy at this level of analysis, is on the person's unconscious psychodynamics and defenses. Those defenses disguise the underlying motives and conflicts that must be revealed and confronted in order for the individual to function well. Personality change requires insight into the disguised (unacceptable to the person) unconscious motives and dynamics that underlie the behavioral symptoms, so that they can be made conscious, accepted, and managed more rationally. When that occurs, the symptoms should diminish. In more

Overview of Focus, Concepts, Methods: The Psychodynamic-Motivational Level

Basic units:	Inferred motives and psychodynamics
Causes of behavior:	Underlying stable motives and their unconscious transformations and conflicts
Behavioral manifestations of personality:	Symptoms and "irrational" patterns of behavior (including dreams, "mistakes," and fantasies)
Favored data:	Interpretations by expert judges (clinicians)
Observed responses used as:	Indirect signs
Research focus:	Personality dynamics and psychopathology; unconscious processes; defense mechanisms; the fragmented self
Approach to personality change:	By insight into the motives and conflicts underlying behavior, by making the unconscious conscious
Role of situation:	Deliberately minimized or ambiguous

recent work, however, increasing attention is being given to such concepts as the self, self-perception, and interpersonal relationship problems with significant others.

► ENDURING CONTRIBUTIONS OF THE PSYCHODYNAMIC-MOTIVATIONAL LEVEL

The impact of Freud's theory on society and on philosophy, as well as on the social sciences, is almost universally hailed as profound; its significance is frequently compared with that of Darwin. Freud's monumental contributions have been widely acknowledged. He opened the topic of childhood sexuality, revolutionized conceptions of the human psyche, provided strikingly powerful metaphors for the mind and human condition, and pioneered twentieth-century psychiatry with his approach to the treatment of psychological problems. The evidence relevant to Freud's theory as a scientific psychological system, however, has been questioned persistently (e.g., Grunbaum, 1984).

Although Freud attempted to create a general psychology, his main work was with conflict-ridden persons caught up in personal crises. Freud observed these tortured individuals only under extremely artificial conditions: lying on a couch during the psychotherapy hour in an environment deliberately made as nonsocial as possible. This drastically restricted observational base helped to foster a theory that originally was almost entirely a theory of anxiety and internal conflict. It paid little attention to the social environment and to the interpersonal context of behavior. We have already seen that many of Freud's own followers attempted to modify that initial emphasis and to devise a more ego-oriented and social approach. That trend is continuing.

This newer "ego psychology" and more "cognitive clinical psychology" is characterized by a greater focus on development beyond early childhood to include the entire life span. It attends more to the role of interpersonal relations and society, and to the nature and functions of the concepts of ego and self and how the person thinks rather than to the id and its impulses. Freud's ideas thus have been going through a continuing revolution that goes beyond his own writings to the extensions introduced by his many followers over the years. The object relations theories of analysts such as Kohut and Kernberg are especially important innovations that seem to be changing psychodynamic theories substantially. They emphasize the self (rather than the instincts and the unconscious defenses against their expression) and thus have some similarity to the self theories discussed in later parts of this text.

One of the main criticisms of Freud's theory is that it is hard to test. Unfortunately, this criticism also applies (although to a lesser degree) to most of the later psychodynamic thinkers. That is true in part because psychodynamic constructs tend to have both the richness and the ambiguity of metaphors; while they may seem compelling intuitively, they are hard to quantify. Rooted in clinical experience and clinical language, the terms often are loose and metaphoric and convey different meanings in different contexts. The theory also requires the user to have available a clinical background with much experience and training as the framework and language on which the constructs draw.

These criticisms notwithstanding, many of the key concepts from the theory are still central in different areas of contemporary psychology, psychiatry, and clinical practice, and some of these have been modified and extensively researched, leading to many new insights and discoveries (e.g., Andersen, Chen, & Miranda, 2002; Bargh, 1997; Kihlstrom, 1999; Miller, Shoda, & Hurley, 1996). Especially vigorous efforts have been made to deal with defense mechanisms and conflict, and to submit them to experimental study (e.g., Blum, 1953; Erdelyi, 1985; Holmes, 1974; Sears, 1943, 1944; Silverman, 1976; Westen & Gabbard, 1999). You already saw some of the research that psychoanalytic ideas have influenced, and you will see many more examples throughout the text.

Particularly exciting in recent years is the renewed interest in psychodynamic concepts such as the unconscious, in light of new discoveries about mental processes (e.g., attention, thinking, and memory) emerging from the study of cognitive psychology. There are many interesting parallels, and people certainly are not aware of all the things that happen in their minds. Modern cognitive psychology has understandably stimulated a sympathetic reexamination of the nature of unconscious processes (e.g., Kihlstrom, 1999).

There is evidence that unconscious processes and events influence us massively. For example, individuals with amnesia continue to be affected by previous experiences although they cannot remember them (Kihlstrom, Barnhardt, & Tataryn, 1992). All sorts of information that influences how different individuals encode (interpret) and evaluate their social environments is acquired unconsciously (e.g., Lewicki et al., 1992). And most of what we feel and believe and do may be elicited or triggered automatically without conscious control or awareness (e.g., Bargh, 1997). Thus, the reality of unconscious processes is now accepted as a fact. Its significance, however, continues to be debated (Loftus & Klinger, 1992), and firm conclusions cannot be reached until further research explores more directly the relevance of nonconscious information processing for Freud's concepts about the unconscious mind (e.g., Erdelyi, 1992).

In sum, when these contributions are put in perspective, they are most impressive. Especially notable is the continued recognition of the importance of motives and conflicts often operating at levels outside the person's full awareness. Likewise, work at this level called attention to the self-protective nature of the mind, and the diverse defense operations people use to reduce anxiety and to try to make themselves feel better about themselves, often with substantial long-tem costs to themselves and others. This list merely hints at the enormous contributions made by a genius and his colleagues, beginning more than a hundred years ago, and still being vigorously pursued in current thinking, theory, research, and clinical applications.

PART

III

THE PHENOMENOLOGICAL LEVEL

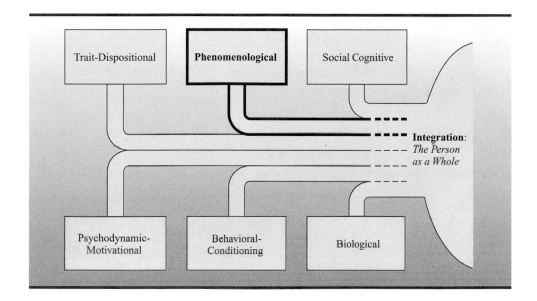

▶ PRELUDE TO PART III: THE PHENOMENOLOGICAL LEVEL

The phenomenological level is devoted to understanding the individual's inner psychological experiences as perceived and understood by that person. Its focus is on how we see and experience ourselves, other people, and the social world. It is also concerned with the nature of the self, and the relationships between self, other people, and the social world. Work at this level began in the late 1940s and in the 1950s mostly as a protest against the psychoanalytic work of Freud and his followers which was dominant in clinical psychology and psychiatry at that time. Unlike the beginnings of the Freudian movement, there was no single leader. Instead, a number of different psychologists who cared about personality and psychotherapy began to raise questions that challenged basic assumptions that were accepted by many in the field at that time.

George Kelly, for example, proposed that what is most important about personality is that each person views or "construes" the world in distinctly different ways. It is these personal "construals" or appraisals that guide what people think, do, and become. They may even lead the person to develop maladaptive, self-defeating, and self-destructive problems like those shown by Freud's patients. Most important, Kelly believed that people are free to change how they construe and appraise themselves and their world, and they can do so in constructive ways that enhance their freedom. In other words, we do not have to be victims of the past, of our genes, and of our life situations. At the same time that Kelly was making his contributions and even in the same place—Ohio State University's Psychology Department—Carl Rogers, a former minister who also became a psychology professor, developed a new theory of personality that focused on the individual's potential for personal growth and genuineness and on the nature of the self.

The contributions at the phenomenological level are diverse and significant and remain vibrant in somewhat modified forms. For example, a great deal of current work is devoted to understanding the "self" and its role in personality (Part V), building directly on the contributions first made at the phenomenological level. In hindsight, although work at the phenomenological level began as a protest against earlier work, much of it turned out to be compatible with some of those earlier contributions and built constructively on them. But it evolved in new directions that added to the understanding of the self and the importance of interpersonal relationships for personality and personal growth, as discussed throughout this part.

The Personal Side of the Science

Some questions at the phenomenological level you might ask about yourself:

▶ Who do I want to become?

▶ How do I see myself? How do I see my parents?

▶ What do I feel about myself when I don't meet my parents' expectations?

▶ How is my real self different from the self I would ideally like to be?

▶ What is my ideal self?

▶ How am I different from my mother but similar to my father?

8

PHENOMENOLOGICAL CONCEPTIONS

Each person sees the world subjectively in his or her own personal way. To understand this privately experienced side of personality, we must examine the nature of subjective experience; we must see how people perceive their world. For example, we cannot understand anxiety as an aspect of personality fully without understanding how the individual experiences it. We begin with a sample of such personal experience in the form of a self-description by a college student about to take a final examination:

> When I think about the exam, I really feel sick . . . so much depends on it. I know I'm not prepared, at least not as much as I should be, but I keep hoping that I can sort of snow my way through it. He [the professor] said we would get to choose two of three essay questions. I've heard about his questions . . . they sort of cover the whole course, but they're still pretty general. Maybe I'll be able to mention a few of the right names and places. He can't expect us to put down everything in two hours . . . I keep trying to remember some of the things he said in class, but my mind keeps wandering. God, my folks—What will they think if I don't pass and can't graduate? Will they have a fit! Boy! I can see their faces. Worse yet, I can hear their voices: "And with all the money we spent

on your education." Mom's going to be hurt. She'll let me know I let her down. She'll be a martyr: "Well, Roger, didn't you realize how this reflects on us? Didn't you know how much we worked and saved so you could get an education? . . . You were probably too busy with other things. I don't know what I'm going to tell your aunt and uncle. They were planning to come to the graduation you know." Hell! What about me? What'll I do if I don't graduate? How about the plans I made? I had a good job lined up with that company. They really sounded like they wanted me, like I was going to be somebody. . . . And what about the car? I had it all planned out. I was going to pay for it and still have enough left for fun. I've got to pass. Oh hell! What about Anne [girlfriend]? She's counting on my graduating. We had plans. What will she think? She knows I'm no brain, but . . . hell, I won't be anybody. I've got to find some way to remember those names. If I can just get him to think that I really know that material, but don't have time to put it all down. If I can just . . . if . . . too goddamn many ifs. Poor dad. He'll really be hurt. All the plans we made—all the . . . I was going to be somebody. What did he say? "People will respect you. People respect a college graduate. You'll be something more than a storekeeper." What am I going to do. God, I can't think. You know, I might just luck out. I've done it before. He could ask just the right questions. What could he ask? Boy! I feel like I want to vomit. Do you think others are as scared as I am? They probably know it all or don't give a damn. I'll bet you most of them have parents who can set them up whether they have college degrees or not. God, it means so much to me. I've got to pass. I've just got to. Dammit, what are those names? What could he ask? I can't think . . . I can't. . . . Maybe if I had a beer I'd be able to relax a little. Is there anybody around who wants to get a beer? God, I don't want to go alone. Who wants to go to the show? What the hell am I thinking about? I've got to study. . . . I can't. What's going to happen to me? . . . The whole damn world is coming apart (Fischer, 1970, pp. 121–122).

Feelings and thoughts like those reported by this student are the raw materials of theories that deal with the self and with the person's subjective, internal experiences and personal concepts. These are the theories that traditionally have guided much of the work at this level of analysis. There are many complexities and variations in the orientation to personality presented in this chapter. In spite of these variations, however, a few fundamental themes emerge.

8.1 What is the focus of the phenomenological level of analysis?

We call the level of analysis in this chapter phenomenological, a term that refers to the individual's experience as he or she perceives it, because that is its most basic element. Some of the orientations guiding the work here have been given other labels also, such as "self" theories, "construct" theories, "humanistic" theories, "cognitive" theories, and "existential" theories. Most phenomenological theories are distinctive both in the concepts they reject and in the ones they emphasize. They tend to reject most of the dynamic and motivational concepts of the psychoanalytic level and also most of the assumptions of the trait level. Persons thus are viewed as experiencing beings rather than as the victims of their unconscious psychodynamic conflicts. Most of the approaches discussed in this chapter also stress people's positive strivings and their tendencies toward growth and self-actualization.

Most of the theories presented here are concerned broadly with how we know and understand the world and ourselves. They have tried to understand how the individual perceives, thinks, interprets, and experiences the world; that is, they have tried to grasp the individual's point of view. Their focus is on persons and events of life as seen by the perceiver. In sum, they are most interested in the person's experience as he or she perceives and categorizes it—the person's **phenomenology.** Ideally, they would like to look at the world through the "participant's" eyes and to stand in that person's shoes, to experience a bit of what it is to *be* that person. This phenomenological view is the main concern of the present chapter.

▶ SOURCES OF PHENOMENOLOGICAL PERSPECTIVES

The orientation presented in this chapter has numerous sources. Among the many early theorists who were fascinated with the self were William James, George H. Mead, and John Dewey. Another early theorist concerned with the self was Carl Jung. As early as the start of the century, Jung called attention to the organism's strivings for self-realization and integration. He believed in creative processes that go beyond the basic instincts of Freudian psychology. It is also noteworthy that in the psychodynamic tradition, Heinz Kohut and other "object relations" theorists (Chapter 7) also make the self a central concept.

Allport's Functional Autonomy

Gordon Allport (1937) was one of the first to emphasize the uniqueness of the individual and of the integrated patterns that distinguish each person. He also noted the *lack of motivational continuity* during the individual's life and criticized the Freudian emphasis on the enduring role of sexual and aggressive motives.

8.2 What did Allport mean by functional autonomy? How does this concept relate to a phenomenological approach to behavior?

According to Allport, behavior is motivated originally by instincts, but later it may sustain itself indefinitely without providing any biological gratifications. Allport saw most normal adult motives as no longer having a functional relation to their historical roots. "Motives are contemporary. . . . Whatever drives must drive now. . . . The character of motives alters so radically from infancy to maturity that we may speak of adult motives as *supplanting* the motives of infancy" (1940, p. 545). This idea has been called **functional autonomy** to indicate that a habit, say practicing the violin at a certain hour each day, need not be tied to any earlier motive of infancy. The extent to which an individual's motives are autonomous is a measure of maturity, according to Allport.

Allport thus stressed the **contemporaneity of motives** (1961): motives are to be understood in terms of their role in the present regardless of their origins in the past. In his view, the past is not important unless it can be shown to be active in the present. He believed that historical facts about a person's past, while helping to reveal the total course of the individual's life, do not adequately explain the person's conduct today. In his words, "Past motives explain nothing unless they are also present motives" (1961, p. 220). In sum, Allport emphasized that later motives do not necessarily depend on earlier ones. Although the life of a plant is continuous with that of its seed, the seed no longer feeds and sustains the mature plant. A pianist may have been spurred to mastery of the piano through the need to overcome inferiority feelings, but the pianist's later love of music is functionally autonomous from its origins. Allport focused on the individual's currently perceived experiences, his or her phenomenological self and unique pattern of adaptation. He also favored a holistic view of the individual as an integrated, biosocial organism, rather than as a bundle of traits and motives. Table 8.1 summarizes some of Allport's main ideas about individuality.

Lewin's Life Space

Still another important post-Freudian influence came from field theories (Lewin, 1936). These theories saw behavior as determined by the person's psychological life space — by the events that exist in the total psychological situation at the moment — rather than by past events or enduring, situation-free dispositions. The most elegant formulation of this position was Kurt Lewin's **field theory.** In field theory, the way in which an object is perceived depends upon the total context or configuration of its surroundings. What is

TABLE 8.1   Some Distinguishing Features of Individuality According to Allport (1961)

1. Motives become independent of their roots (*functional autonomy*).
2. A *proprium* or self develops, characterized by:

    | Bodily sense | Self-esteem |
    | Self-identity | Rational thought |
    | Self-image | |

3. A *unique*, integrated pattern of adaptation marks the person as a whole.

perceived depends on the *relationships* among components of a perceptual field, rather than on the fixed characteristics of the individual components.

8.3 What are the major components of Lewin's life space? Describe his classic formula for the causes of behavior.

Lewin defined **life space** as the totality of facts that determine the behavior (B) of an individual at a certain moment. The life space includes the person (P) and the psychological environment (E), as shown in Figure 8.1. Behavior is a function of the person and the environment, as expressed in the formula

$$B = f(P, E)$$

Ordinary cause, based on the notion of causation in classical physics, assumes that something past is the cause of present events. Teleological theories assume that future events influence present events. Lewin's thesis is that neither past nor future, by definition, exists at the present moment and therefore neither can have an effect at the present. Past events have a position in the historical causal chains that create the present situation, but only those events that are functioning in the present situation need to be taken into account. Such events are, by definition, current or momentary. In other words, only present facts can cause present behavior.

To represent the life space, Lewin therefore took into account only that which is contemporary. He termed this the **principle of contemporaneity** (Lewin, 1936). This does not mean the field theorists are not interested in historical problems or in the effects of previous experience. As Lewin (1951) pointed out, field theorists have enlarged the psychological experiment to include situations that contain a history that is systematically created throughout hours or weeks. For example, college students in an experiment might be given repeated failure experiences (on a series of achievement tasks) during several sessions. The effects of these experiences on the students' subsequent aspirations and expectations for success might then be measured.

The boundaries between the person and the psychological environment and between the life space and the physical world are **permeable boundaries,** that is,

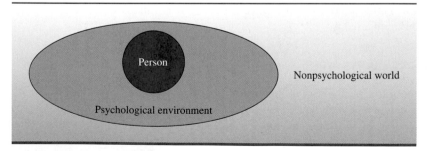

Figure 8.1   Lewin's life space. The life space contains the person in his or her psychological environment, which is delineated by a boundary (the ellipse) from the nonpsychological world.

they can be crossed easily. That makes prediction difficult because one cannot be sure beforehand when and what facts will permeate a boundary and influence a fact from another region. Lewin asserts that the psychologist might therefore concentrate on describing and explaining the concrete psychological situation in terms of field theory rather than trying to predict the future.

Lewin (1935) rejected the notion of constant, entity-like personality characteristics such as unchanging traits. As a result of dynamic forces, psychological reality is always changing. The environment of the individual does not serve merely to facilitate tendencies that are permanent in the person's nature (1936). Habits are not frozen associations, but rather the result of forces in the organism and its life space.

Lewin was similarly dissatisfied with the usual concept of needs. In descriptions of psychological reality, Lewin said, the needs that are producing effects in the momentary situation are the only ones that have to be represented. A need in Lewin's theory corresponds to a tension system. Lewin was also interested in reward and punishment. He saw rewards as devices for controlling behavior in momentary situations by causing changes in the psychological environment and in the tension systems of the person.

For Lewin, behavior and development are functions of the same structural and dynamic factors. Both are a function of the person and the psychological environment. In general, with increasing maturity there is greater differentiation of the person and the psychological environment.

Lewin's field theory had a major impact on experimental social psychology. His students extended his ideas and pursued them through ingenious experiments designed to alter the participant's life space—by altering perceptions about the self, about other people, about events. The effects of these alterations on attitudes, aspirations, and other indices were then examined carefully. Until recently Lewin's influence on personality psychology has been less extensive. There is now, however, an increasing recognition of the importance of the psychological situation in studies of traits and motives (e.g., Magnusson, 1999; Mischel & Shoda, 1999).

Kurt Lewin (1890–1947)

Phenomenology and Existentialism: The Here and Now

George A. Kelly and Carl Rogers developed views of personality in which private experiences, subjective perceptions, and the self all have an important part. Abraham Maslow put his emphasis on human growth motivation. In his view, growth motivation moves the individual through hierarchically ordered degrees of health to ultimate self-actualization. "Every person is, in part, his own project, and makes himself" (Maslow, 1965, p. 308). Behavior is goal directed, striving, purposeful, and motivated by higher needs to realize or **self-actualize** one's human potential rather than by primary biological drives alone.

The ideas of most of these theorists have much in common with the existential philosophical position developed by such European thinkers and writers as Kierkegaard, Sartre, and Camus and by the Swiss psychiatrists Binswanger and Boss. The key features of their orientation are expressed by Rollo May, an American proponent of existential psychology. Thinking about a patient of his in psychotherapy, May recognizes that he has available all sorts of information about her, such as hypotheses from her Rorschach and diagnoses from her neurologist. He then comments (1961, p. 26):

> But if, as I sit here, I am chiefly thinking of these whys and hows of the way the problem came about, I will have grasped everything except the most important thing of all, the existing person. Indeed, I will have grasped everything except the only real source of data I have, namely, this experiencing human being, this person now emerging, becoming, "building world," as the existential psychologists put it, immediately in this room with me.

8.4 What is the role of immediate experience in existential theories? Where are the true causes of behavior?

May's remarks point to the existentialist's focus on phenomenological experience, on the "here and now" rather than on distant historical causes in the person's early childhood. Furthermore, the existential orientation sees the human being as capable of choice and responsibility in the moment rather than as the victim of unconscious forces or of habits from the past.

The Swiss existential psychiatrist Binswanger commented that Freudian theory pictured human beings not yet as people in the full sense, but only as creatures buffeted about by life. Binswanger believes that for a person to be fully himself— that is, to be truly realized or actualized as a human being—he must "look fate in the face." In his view, the fact that human life is determined by forces and conditions is only one side of the truth. The other side is that we ourselves "determine these forces as our fate" (cited in May, 1961, p. 252). Thus, in the phenomenological and existential orientation, humans are seen as beings whose actualization requires much more than the fulfillment of biological needs and of sexual and aggressive instincts.

The existentialists propose that we are inevitably the builders of our own lives and, more specifically, that each person is:

1. a *choosing* agent, unable to avoid choices throughout the course of life
2. a *free* agent, who freely sets life goals
3. a *responsible* agent, accountable personally for his or her life choices

Our existence in life is given, but our essence is what we make of life, how meaningfully and responsibly we construct it. This is an often painful, isolated, agonizing enterprise. To find satisfying values, to guide our lives accordingly, to give life meaning—these goals are all part of the existential quest. They require the "courage to be"—the courage to break from blind conformity to the group and to strive instead for self-fulfillment by seeking greater self-definition and authenticity.

Finally, to grasp what it means to *be* also requires being in constant touch with the awareness of nonbeing, of alienation, of nothingness, and ultimately of the inevitability of death, everyone's unavoidable fate. The awareness of this inevitable fate and what that implies produces **existential anxiety.** The antidote for such anxiety is to face and live our lives responsibly, meaningfully, and with courage and awareness of our potential for continuous choice and growth.

To understand some of the main features of the existential and phenomenological orientation more closely, we shall consider the ideas of one of its most articulate proponents in the next sections.

8.5   What is meant by existential anxiety?

▶ GEORGE KELLY'S PSYCHOLOGY OF PERSONAL CONSTRUCTS

To the humanist every man is a scientist by disposition as well as by right, every subject is an incipient experimenter, and every person is by daily necessity a fellow psychologist (G. A. Kelly, 1966, in B. A. Maher, 1979, p. 205).

In addition to acting as motivated organisms, people also are perceivers and construers of behavior: they give meaning to their experience and interpret events. They generate abstractions about themselves and others, just like psychologists do. These hypotheses and constructions have long intrigued psychologists interested in subjective states, phenomenology, and the experience of the self.

The Person's Constructs

In the psychodynamic approach, the motive is the chief unit, unconscious conflicts are the processes of greatest interest, and the clinical judge is the favored instrument. Kelly's (1955) personal construct theory, in contrast, seeks to illuminate the person's own constructs rather than the hypotheses of the psychologist. Its main units are personal constructs—the ways we represent or view our own experiences. Rather than seeing people as victimized by their impulses and defenses, this position views the human being as an active, ever-changing creator of hypotheses.

According to Kelly, trait psychology tries to find the person's place on the *theorist's* personality dimension. **Personal construct theory** instead tries to see how the person sees and aligns events on *his or her own* dimensions (Fransella, 1995). It is Kelly's hope to discover the nature of the personal construct dimensions rather than to locate the individual's position on the dimensions of the psychologist's theory. If next week's test is important to you, Kelly wants to explore how you see it, what it means to you, not what your score is on a scale of test-taking anxiety.

Suppose that you see a person quietly letting herself be abused by someone else. You might conclude that the person is "submissive." Yet the same behavior might be construed by other observers as sensitive, cautious, intelligent, tactful, or polite. Thus Kelly emphasized that different people may construe the same event differently and that every event can be construed in alternative ways.

The **personal construct** is the central unit of George Kelly's theory. Kelly's operation for measuring a construct is best seen in his **Role Construct Repertory Test** or **"Rep" Test.** On the Rep Test, you are asked to list many people or things that are important to you (for example, self, mother, brother). After these items are listed (or the assessor lists them), you are asked to consider them in groups of three. In each

8.6   What are personal constructs? How does Kelly's orientation and measurement approach differ from the trait approach? What did Kelly's approach reveal about Gary W.?

George A. Kelly (1905–1967)

triad you have to indicate how two items are similar to each other and different from the third. In this way the subjective dimensions of similarity among events, and the subjective opposites of those dimensions, may be evoked systematically (Table 8.2). It is also possible to study the characteristics of the people's construct systems—for example, the number of different constructs they have in their construct repertory.

The Rep Test is a flexible instrument that can be adapted for many different purposes, and it provides a convenient and fairly simple way to begin the exploration of personal constructs. Some examples, taken from the study of Gary W., are shown in Table 8.2 (which illustrates the general type of procedure that may be used to elaborate personal constructs).

Research on the temporal stability of personal constructs from Kelly's Rep Test indicates a good deal of consistency over time (Bonarius, 1965). For example, a high

---

TABLE 8.2   Elaboration of Personal Constructs: Examples from Gary W.

1. List the three most important people in your life:

   Me, my brother, my father

   How are any two of these alike and different from the third?

   My brother and I both know how to be tough and succeed, no matter what—my father is soft, knocked out, defeated by life.

2. Think of yourself now, five years ago, and five years from now. How are any two of these alike and different from the third?

   Five years ago I was warmer, more open and responsive to others than I am now. Now I'm mostly a scheming brain. Five years from now I hope to have recaptured some of that feeling and to be more like I was five years ago.

retest correlation (.79) was found for constructs after a two-week interval (Landfield, Stern, &Fjeld, 1961), and factor analyses of the Rep Test suggest that its main factor is stable (Pedersen, 1958), and thus that an individual's main constructs may be relatively permanent.

According to Kelly, the individuals' personal constructs gradually become elaborated through their answers on the Rep Test and through their behaviors in the interview and on other tests. To illustrate some features of the assessment of personal constructs, here is an analysis of our case based on how Gary spontaneously elaborates and contrasts the constructs with which he views the world. What follows are excerpts from an attempt by an assessor to summarize some of Gary's main conceptions.

A Personal Construct Conceptualization of Gary W.

Rationality–Emotionality. This is a construct dimension that seems to be of considerable importance for Gary. He elaborates what this construct means to him most clearly when he is discussing his interpersonal relationships. He describes a sexual relationship with a woman in such terms as "spiritual," "instinctive," "sublime," and "beyond rationality." It is characterized by intense feeling and the primacy of emotions, and it is based on physical attraction. Real friendships, in contrast, are based upon rational grounds—such as interests and ways of thinking that are common to both parties.

The distinction between the rational and the emotional is echoed when Gary describes his worries in terms of those that are "rational" versus those that are "immediate and threatening." In discussing anger, he says that he has learned to cover up his feelings, but that his emotions sometimes "surface." He no longer gets violently angry, as he did when he was a child, but is "controlled," "stony," and "devious." He gives the most positive evaluation to reason, and contrasts what is reasonable with what is "worthless."

Transposed onto a time line, his distinction between reason and emotion forms part of the contrast between adults and children. After he was about 12 years old, Gary "psyched out" his father, so the latter was no longer his "enemy" but instead became his "friendly, rational adviser." He also describes shifts in his relations with his mother and with his brother that apparently involve handling his feelings toward them in a less explosive way.

Power and Control versus Dependence and Weakness. This seems to be a major dimension on which adults and children differ. Adults are the enemies of children. In his interview, descriptions of his childhood experiences, what parental figures require of a child, are typically the opposite of what the child wants. Gary describes life as a child as involving "denial, helplessness, nothing and nobody on my side." It was a time when he "couldn't control events," when he was being "manipulated" and "shamed." Gary contrasts foresight, and events that he can plan and control, with accidents, terror, and the unpredictable.

Defeat–Success. Defeat–Success is a closely related dimension around which a number of constructs are clustered. Defeat is defined in terms of lack of money, passivity, compliance, dependence, frustration, undermined masculinity, and physical pain. Success means money, activity, freedom, independence, control, and being a "real" man.

Security–Liberty. This is another major dimension for Gary. In describing jobs, acquaintances, and life styles, he talks in terms of "the ordinary 9 to 5 job complete with wife, kids, and mortgage," versus the "free and easy life." "Blind obedience" is contrasted to "judging the issues for oneself." Gary describes himself as being "uncertain," and contrasts being freewheeling with plodding determination. He sees himself as being currently without "acceptance" and "success" and he feels "cut off." His own "procrastination" hinders his "drive," but he hopes his "ambition will win out" and gain him both security and liberty.

As far as *role conceptions* are concerned, Gary now sees his father as "emasculated" and "knocked out," although once he saw him as "a giant" and as his "enemy." The father seems to have moved along the conceptual continuum from "power and control" to a point where he is seen as inadequate and as being competition no longer. He dislikes his father for the middle-class values that he feels he represents and for his passivity. There is also the implication that he resents his father for not comparing favorably with his mother. The turning point in Gary's feelings for his brother, whom he disliked for sharing many of their father's qualities, came when his brother was smashed up in a car crash. He now sees him as less conventional, more humorous and self-examining.

Gary sees his mother, and ideal women in general, as "independent partners" rather than "devouring" sources of affection. Instead of making their families central in importance, they achieve success and recognition in work outside their home. They keep the male "alive" by providing stimulation through their competence, which extends even to athletics, rather than being dependent and "clinging." Gary sees himself as similar to his mother and says he loves her best, next to himself. On the more negative side, he sees his mother as frigid and incapable of expressing affection. However, in view of his own evaluation of emotionality, this criticism is a highly qualified one. He sees his mother as having in many ways been the cause of his father's defeat, but constantly adds that she did not intend this result and feels bad about it, that it was a byproduct of other admirable qualities she possesses.

His relationship with his mother is characterized by control of expression of both anger and love. He sees her dominating tendencies as dangerous, as evidenced by his childhood conception of her as omniscient and omnipotent. This fear seems to have generalized to his grandmother and to other women, as evidenced by his TAT stories.

In his relationships with women, there seems to be a general distinction between sex objects and companions. In describing a sexual relationship that he felt had no potentialities for friendship, Gary says, "If we hadn't been able to 'make it' we would have stopped seeing each other." He generally prefers women who are stimulating and challenging, though he fears all forms of domination, through either authority or emotional ties.

In his relationships with men outside his family, Gary prefers distance and respect and finds that closeness leads to friction, as with his present roommate. At school he found two older men whom he could look up to: a teacher to whom he was grateful for not being "wishy-washy" and another person whom he describes as being a "real man."

Behavioral Referents for Personal Constructs

8.7 How are behavioral referents used to clarify personal constructs? How does this differ from a psychodynamic approach?

Some of Gary's main personal constructs emerged from his self-descriptions and verbalizations. When people start to express their constructs, they usually begin with very diffuse, oversimplified, global terms. For example, Gary called himself "shrewd," "too shy," "too sharp." He also said he wanted to "feel more real," to "adjust better," and to "be happier."

What can the construct assessor do with these verbalizations? As we have seen in earlier chapters, psychodynamically oriented clinicians rely chiefly on their intuitive inferences about the symbolic and dynamic meanings of verbal behavior. Personal construct assessors recognize that talk about private experiences and feeling tends to be ambiguous. For example, statements of the kind commonly presented in clinical contexts, like "I feel so lost," generally are not clear. Instead of inquiring into why the person feels "lost," personal construct assessments try to discover referents for just what the statement means. An adequate personal construct assessment of what people say involves the analysis of what they mean. For this purpose, the assessor's initial task is like the one faced when we want to understand a foreign language. A personal construct analysis of language tries to decipher the content of what is being conveyed and to discover its meaning for the person. Its aim is not to translate what is said into signs of underlying motives, of unconscious processes, or of personality dimensions. Often it is hard to find the words for personal constructs. Just as the psychologist interested in such concepts as extraversion, identity, or anxiety must find behavioral referents to help specify what he or she means, so must the client find such referents for his or her private concepts, difficulties, and aspirations.

In sum, Kelly urged a specific and elaborate inquiry into personal constructs by obtaining numerous behavioral examples as referents for them. Kelly (1955) has described in detail many techniques to explore the conditions under which the individual's particular constructions about emotional reactions may emerge and change. His ideas still influence current work to explore the meanings that underlie puzzling behavior patterns and seeming inconsistencies in the expressions of personality.

Exploring the Meaning Underlying Puzzling Behavior Patterns

Contemporary work that was inspired by Kelly also tries to understand the personal meaning that may underlie puzzling patterns of behavior. Consider Mary, a senior attorney at an international corporate law firm, who is concerned about the performance of one of her new staff attorneys, John. Before becoming a corporate lawyer, Mary had done graduate work in psychology many years ago at Ohio State University where she was influenced by one of her professors, George Kelly.

Mary has been puzzled by the variability in John's work and wants to find a way to improve his sense of well-being and productivity. Is he always distracted, or does it depend on situations? What are the situations in which he's less distracted and can concentrate? In short, Mary is trying to assess the *if . . . then . . .* patterns that constitute his behavioral signature (see Chapter 4) so that she can understand their meaning and implications. After she learns that John tends to be particularly distracted in meetings at the corporate headquarters but not when he travels to branch offices, she begins to wonder: What exactly is the important difference between the meetings at the headquarters and those at branch offices? In essence, Mary wants to know the personal meaning of the situations, seen from John's point of view. This is also one of the central questions for the science of personality. In particular, researchers have been asking: can personal meanings of situations be assessed in a systematic, objective fashion?

George Kelly anticipated this challenge, and in his personal construct theory offered a general strategy. Although his strategy was originally proposed for individual therapeutic settings, it is being extended to a method for systematically and objectively assessing the meaning of a situation to a given individual (e.g., Mischel & Shoda, 1995; Shoda, LeeTiernan & Mischel 2002). For example, meetings at company headquarters may be characterized by such features as the presence of the boss, the authority whose

8.8 How does selective attention to psychologically meaningful features of situations provide information about a person's constructs?

opinions directly influence promotion and salary decisions. Another feature might be the presence of highly competitive "career climbers" who focus only on advancement of their individual careers.

The subjective meaning of the situations may be understood by a person's tendency to selectively attend to particular types of features. While some people may not even notice the career-advance focus of their colleagues at headquarters, for others, like John, it is highly salient. Individuals also may differ reliably in the psychological impact of attending to these features. In this example, John's perception of his colleagues' focus on selfish career advancement reminds him that he feels himself losing sight of the sense of purpose that initially attracted him to his career. Now suppose that John has a stable tendency to attend to and react to the presence of these features in distinctive ways, for example by becoming upset and less motivated in his own work. If so, it is important to identify the features that are influencing him if one wants to understand their meaning for him and the ways they are affecting what he is thinking, feeling, and doing.

People as Scientists

8.9 In what sense is each individual a "personal scientist"? What are the "operational definitions" for personal constructs?

The psychology of personal constructs explores the maps that people generate in coping with the psychological terrain of their lives. Kelly emphasizes that, just like the scientist who studies them, human participants also construe behavior—categorizing, interpreting, labeling, and judging themselves and their world: Every person is a scientist.

The individuals assessed by psychologists are themselves assessors who evaluate and construe their own behavior; they even assess the personality psychologists who try to assess them. Constructions and hypotheses about behavior are formulated by all persons regardless of their formal degrees and credentials as scientists. According to Kelly, it is these constructions, and not merely simple physical responses, that must be studied in an adequate approach to personality. Categorizing behavior is equally evident when a psychotic patient describes his personal, private ideas in therapy, and when a scientist discusses her favorite constructs and theories at a professional meeting. Both people represent the environment internally and express their representations and private experiences in their psychological constructions. Personal constructions, and not objective behavior descriptions on clear dimensions, confront the personality psychologist.

Kelly noted that most psychological scientists view themselves as motivated to achieve cognitive clarity and to understand phenomena, including their own lives. Yet the "subjects" of their theories, unlike the theorists themselves, are seen as unaware victims of psychic forces and traits that they can neither understand nor control. Kelly tries to remove this discrepancy between the theorist and the participant and to treat all people as if they were scientists.

Just like the scientist, participants generate constructs and hypotheses with which they try to anticipate and control events in their lives. Therefore, to understand the participant, one has to understand his or her constructs or private personality theory. To study an individual's constructs, one has to find behavioral examples or "referents" for them. We cannot know what another person means when she says, "I have too much ego," or "I am not a friendly person," or "I may be falling in love," unless she gives us behavioral examples. Examples (referents) are required whether the construct is personal, for example the way a patient construes herself "as a woman," or theoretical, as when a psychologist talks about "introversion" or "ego defenses." Constructs can become known only through behavior.

Constructive Alternativism: Many Ways to See

If one adopts Kelly's approach to understanding people, then:

Instead of making our own sense out of what others did we would try to understand what sense they made out of what they did. Instead of putting together the events in their lives in the most scientifically parsimonious way, we would ask how they put things together, regardless of whether their schemes were parsimonious or not (Kelly, 1962, in B. A. Maher, 1979, p. 203).

8.10 Define constructive alternativism. How do anticipations guide behavior?

The same events can be alternatively categorized. While people may not always be able to change events, they can always construe them differently (Fransella, 1995). That is what Kelly meant by **constructive alternativism.** To illustrate, consider this event: A boy drops his mother's favorite vase. What does it mean? The event is simply that the vase has been broken. Yet ask the child's psychoanalyst and he may point to the boy's unconscious hostility; ask the mother and she tells you how "mean" he is; his father says he is "spoiled"; the child's teacher may see the event as evidence of the child's "laziness" and chronic "clumsiness"; his grandmother calls it just an "accident"; and the child himself may construe the event as reflecting his "stupidity." While the event cannot be undone—the vase is broken—its interpretation is open to alternative constructions, and these may lead to different courses of action.

Kelly's theory began with this fundamental postulate: "A person's processes are psychologically channelized by the ways in which he anticipates events" (Kelly, 1955, p. 46). This means that a person's activities are guided by the constructs he or she uses to predict events. Like other phenomenological theories, this postulate emphasizes the person's subjective view, but it is more specific in its focus on how the individual predicts or anticipates events. Although the details of the theory need not concern us here, several of the main ideas require comment.

Kelly was concerned with the **convenience of constructs** rather than with their absolute truth. Rather than try to assess whether a particular construct is true, his approach attends to its convenience or utility for the construer. For example, rather than try to assess whether or not a client is "really a latent homosexual" or "really going crazy," one tries to discover the implications for the client's life of construing himself in that way. If the construction is not convenient, then the task is to find a better alternative—that is, one that predicts better and leads to better outcomes. Just as psychologists may get stuck with an inadequate theory, so their patients also may impale themselves on their constructions and construe themselves into a dilemma. Individuals may torture themselves into believing that "I am not worthy enough" or "I am not successful enough," as if these verdicts were matters of indisputable fact rather than constructions and hypotheses about behavior. The job of psychotherapy is to provide the conditions in which personal constructs can be elaborated, and tested for their implications. And, if they prove to be not helpful to the person, they then can be modified, just as a scientist can change a theory or idea that turns out not to work well. Like the scientist, every person needs the chance to test personal constructs and to validate or invalidate them, progressively modifying them in the light of new experience.

8.11 Why are constructs not evaluated in terms of truth or falsity? What did Kelly view as the goal for therapy?

Roles: Many Ways to Be

Rather than seeing humans as possessing fairly stable, broadly generalized traits, Kelly saw them as capable of enacting many different roles and of engaging in continuous

8.12 What is a role as defined by Kelly? How was role-taking used therapeutically?

change. A **role,** for Kelly, is an attempt to see another person through the other's glasses—that is, to look at a person through *his or her* constructs—and to structure one's actions in that light. To enact a role requires that behavior be guided by perception of the other person's viewpoint. Thus, to "role play" your mother, for example, you would have to try to see things (including yourself) as she does, "through her eyes," and to act in light of those perceptions. You would try to behave as if you really were your mother. Kelly used the technique of role playing extensively as a therapeutic procedure designed to help persons gain new perspectives and to generate more convenient ways of living.

People Are What They Make of Themselves: Self-Determination

Like other phenomenologists, Kelly rejected the idea of specific motives. His view of human nature focuses on how people construe themselves and on what they do in the light of those constructs (Fransella, 1995). Kelly (like Rogers) believed that no special concepts are required to understand why people are motivated and active: Every person is motivated "for no other reason than that he is alive" (Kelly, 1958, p. 49).

Like many existentialists, Kelly believed that the individual *is* what he *does* and comes to know his nature by seeing what he is doing. Starting from his clinical experiences with troubled college students in Fort Hays, Kansas, where he taught for many years, Kelly independently reached a position that overlaps remarkably with the views of such European existential philosophers as Sartre. In Sartre's (1956) existentialist conception, *"existence precedes essence"*: There is no human nature—man simply *is*, and he is nothing else but what he makes of himself.

▶ CARL ROGERS' SELF THEORY

Carl Rogers and George Kelly overlapped briefly when both held positions as professors at Ohio State University in the middle of the last century, and while their views shared many similarities, they developed them in quite different directions. Whereas Kelly as you saw earlier put the focus on personal constructs and alternative ways of finding more constructive ways of viewing the world, Rogers went on to develop a theory of the self and the conditions that allow its optimal growth and fulfillment.

Unique Experience: The Subjective World

At the start just like Kelly, Rogers' theory of personality emphasizes the unique, subjective experience of the person. He believed that the way you see and interpret the events in your life determines how you respond to them. Each person lives in a subjective world, and even the so-called objective world of the scientist is a product of subjective perceptions, purposes, and choices. Because no one else, no matter how hard he tries, can completely assume another person's "internal frame of reference," the person himself has the greatest potential for awareness of what reality is for him. In other words, each person potentially is the world's best expert on himself and has the best information about himself.

In Rogers' view, "behavior is typically the goal-directed attempt of the organism to satisfy its needs as experienced, in the field as perceived" (1951, p. 491). The emphasis is on the person's perceptions as the determinants of his or her actions: How one sees and interprets events determines how one reacts to them.

Carl Rogers (1902–1987)

Self-Actualization

Like most phenomenologists, Rogers wanted to abandon specific motivational constructs and viewed the organism as functioning as an **organized whole.** He maintained that "there is one central source of energy in the human organism; that it is a function of the whole organism rather than some portion of it; and that it is perhaps best conceptualized as a tendency toward fulfillment, toward actualization, toward the maintenance and enhancement of the organism" (1963, p. 6). Thus the inherent tendency of the organism is to actualize itself. "Motivation" then becomes not a special construct but an overall characteristic of simply being alive.

8.13 What is meant by self-actualization? What does it imply about the nature of the human being, and how does this conception differ from Freud's?

In line with his essentially positive view of human nature, Rogers' theory asserts that emotions are beneficial to adjustment: "emotion accompanies and in general facilitates . . . goal-directed behavior, . . . the intensity of the emotion being related to the perceived significance of the behavior for the maintenance and enhancement of the organism" (1951, p. 493).

In the course of actualizing itself, the organism engages in a valuing process. Experiences that are perceived as enhancing it are valued positively (and approached), while experiences that are perceived as negating enhancement or maintenance of the organism are valued negatively (and avoided). "The organism has one basic tendency and striving—to actualize, maintain, and enhance the experiencing organism" (Rogers, 1951, p. 487). The idea and implications of self-actualization are discussed more fully in In Focus 8.1.

The Self

The self is a central concept for most phenomenological theories, and it also is basic for Rogers—as it was for many of the post-Freudians working at the psychodynamic level. Indeed, his theory is often referred to as a self theory of personality. The self or

SELF-ACTUALIZATION AS A NEED (MASLOW)

Abraham Maslow (1968, 1971) was one of the most influential spokespersons for the importance of becoming "in touch" with one's true feelings. He considered this a core ingredient of well-being and self-fulfillment. Maslow also emphasized human beings' vast positive potential for growth and fulfillment, and believed that the striving toward actualization of this potential is a basic quality of being human:

> *Man demonstrates in his own nature a pressure toward fuller and fuller Being, more and more perfect actualization of his humanness in exactly the same naturalistic, scientific sense that an acorn may be said to be "pressing toward" being an oak tree, or that a tiger can be observed to "push toward" being tigerish, or a horse toward being equine . . . (Maslow, 1968, p. 160).*

Maslow's commitment was to study optimal man and to discover the qualities of those people who seemed to be closest to realizing all their potentialities. In his view one has **higher growth needs**—needs for self-actualization fulfillment—that emerge when more primitive needs—physiological needs, safety needs, needs for belongingness and esteem—are satisfied (see Fig. 8.2). Maslow wanted to focus on the qualities of feeling and experience that seem to distinguish self-actualizing, fully functioning people. Therefore, he searched for the attributes that seemed to mark such people as Beethoven, Einstein, Jefferson, Lincoln, Walt Whitman, as well as some of the individuals he knew personally and admired most. These positive qualities are an essential part of the humanistic view of the "healthy personality."

Maslow called the special state in which one experiences a moment of self-actualization a **peak experience.** It is a temporary experience of fulfillment and joy in which the person loses self-centeredness and (in varying degrees of intensity) feels a nonstriving happiness, a moment of perfection. Words that may be used to describe this state include "aliveness," "beauty," "ecstasy," "effortlessness," "uniqueness," and "wholeness." Such peak experiences have been reported in many contexts, including the aesthetic appreciation of nature and beauty, worship, intimate relationships with others, and creative activities.

8.14 How did Maslow study optimal human functioning? What were the most notable characteristics of highly functioning people?

The peak experience is characterized by a feeling of fulfillment and joy.

Figure 8.2 Maslow's hierarchy of needs. Maslow arranges motives in a hierarchy ascending from such basic physiological needs as hunger and thirst through safety and love needs to needs for esteem (e.g., feeling competent), and ultimately, self-actualization—the full realization of one's human potential, as in creativity. The lower needs are more powerful and demand satisfaction first. The higher needs have less influence on behavior but are more distinctly human. Generally, higher needs do not become a focus until lower ones have been at least partly satisfied.

In sum, in spite of its many different versions, the phenomenological-humanistic orientation tends to view "healthy people" as those who:

1. Become aware of themselves, their feelings, and their limits; accept themselves, their lives, and what they make of their lives as their own responsibility; have "the courage to be."
2. Experience the "here-and-now"; are not trapped to live in the past or to dwell in the future through anxious expectations and distorted defenses.
3. Realize their potentialities; have autonomy and are not trapped by their own self-concepts or the expectations of others and society.

To help achieve these ideals, several avenues for constructive personality change have been favored by advocates of the phenomenological approach, as discussed next.

self-concept (the two terms mean the same thing for Rogers) is an organized, consistent, whole. It consists of perceptions about oneself and one's relationships to others and to diverse aspects of life, and these all have values attached to them (Rogers, 1959, p. 200). As a result of interaction with the environment, a portion of the perceptual field gradually becomes differentiated into the self. This perceived self (self-concept) influences perception and behavior. That is, the interpretation of the self—as strong or weak, for example—affects how one perceives the rest of one's world.

The experiences of the self become invested with values. These values are the result of direct experience with the environment, or they may be taken over from others. For example, a young child finds it organismically enjoyable to relieve himself whenever he experiences physiological tension in the bowel or bladder. However, he may sometimes also experience parental words and actions indicating that such behavior is bad, and that he is not lovable when he does this. A conflict then develops that may result in distortion and denial of experience. That is, the parental attitudes may be experienced as if they were based on the evidence of the child's own experience. In this example, the satisfaction of defecating may start to be experienced as bad even though a more accurate symbolization would be that it is often experienced as organismically satisfying. Rogers goes on to suggest that in bowel training, denial or distortion of experience may be avoided if the parent is able genuinely to accept the child's feelings and at the same time accepts his or her own feelings.

8.15 What is the self? How does it develop, acquire values, and influence behavior?

Consistency and Positive Regard

Rogers proposes two systems: the **self** or **self-concept** and the organism. The two systems may be in opposition or in harmony. When these systems are in opposition or

8.16 How does the need for positive regard cause inconsistencies between self-concept and experience?

incongruence, the result is maladjustment, for then the self becomes rigidly organized, losing contact with actual organismic experience and filled with tensions. Perception is selective: we try to perceive experiences in ways consistent with the self-concept. The self-concept thus serves as a frame of reference for evaluating and monitoring the actual experiences of the organism. Experiences that are inconsistent with the self may be perceived as threats, and the more threat there is, the more rigid and defensive the self structure becomes to maintain itself. At the same time, the self-concept becomes less congruent with organismic reality and loses contact with the actual experiences of the organism.

Rogers (1959) assumed a universal need for positive regard. This need develops as the awareness of the self emerges and leads the person to desire acceptance and love from the important people in his life. Sometimes they may accept him conditionally (i.e., depending on his specific behavior), or they may accept him in his own right and give him unconditional regard. The person needs positive regard not only from others but also from his self. The need for self-regard develops out of self-experiences associated with the satisfaction or frustration of the need for positive regard. If a person experiences only unconditional positive regard, his self-regard also would be unconditional. In that case, the needs for positive regard and self-regard would never be at variance with **organismic evaluation.** Such a state would represent genuine psychological adjustment and full functioning.

Most people do not achieve such ideal adjustment. Often a self-experience is avoided or sought only because it is less (or more) worthy of self-regard. For example, a child may experience anger toward her mother but avoids accepting that feeling because she wants to be a "good girl." When that happens, Rogers speaks of the individual's having acquired a **condition of worth.** These are the conditions that other people, usually the parents, implicitly make a requirement for being loved and worthwhile. For example, a parent may lead a child to feel that to be worthy she has to get outstanding grades at school, or that the boy in the family has to be a robust athlete even if he is naturally inclined to become someone quite different. Experiences that are in accord with the individual's conditions of worth tend to be perceived accurately in awareness, but experiences that violate the conditions of worth may be denied to awareness and distorted grossly. When there is a significant amount of incongruence between the individual's self-concept and her evaluation of an experience, then defenses may become unable to work successfully. For example, if a young woman persistently experiences herself as painfully dissatisfied and "unhappy" in her efforts at schoolwork, but views herself as having to "succeed at college" in order to be an adequate person, she may experience great strain in her defensive efforts.

Rogers' theory, like Freud's, posits that accurate awareness of experiences may be threatening to the self. Anxiety in Rogers' theory might be interpreted as the tension exhibited by the organized concept of the self when it senses (without full awareness) that the recognition of certain experiences would be catastrophic to the self (1951). If a person's concept of the self has been built around his "masculinity," for example, experiences that might imply that he has some stereotypically feminine tendencies would threaten him severely. Anxiety thus involves a basic threat to the self, and defenses are erected to avoid it. Consistent with Rogers' theory, a great deal of research has demonstrated that people in fact engage in diverse strategies to protect their self-esteem when it is severely threatened. For example, they readily attribute important failures to chance rather than to themselves, but see success as due to their own abilities (Snyder & Uranowitz, 1978; Weiner, 1995).

8.17 What role do conditions of worth play in anxiety and perception?

Rogers assumed a need for unconditional positive regard not only from others but from the self.

Client-Centered Therapy

Rogers' ideals led to a new and still influential form of thinking about personality change and conducting therapy to facilitate positive change. **Client-centered,** or **person-centered (Rogerian), therapy** seeks to bring about the harmonious interaction of the self and the organism. The warm and unconditionally accepting attitude of the counselor hopefully enables the client to perceive and examine experiences that are inconsistent with the current self-structure. The client can then revise this self-structure to permit it to assimilate these inconsistent experiences. According to Rogers, the client gradually reorganizes the self-concept to bring it into line with the reality of organismic experience: "He will *be*, in more unified fashion, what he organismically *is*, and this seems to be the essence of therapy" (1955, p. 269).

In his therapy, Rogers rejected most of Freud's concepts regarding the nature of psychodynamics and psychosexual development. He also avoided all diagnostic terms, refusing to put his labels on the client. He maintained, however, the interview format for psychotherapy (using a face-to-face arrangement rather than the orthodox psycho-analyst's couch for the client). Rogers and his students focused on the client–clinician relationship. Usually they required many fewer sessions than did psychoanalytic therapy, and they dealt more with current than with historical concerns in the client's life.

For Rogers (1959), the therapist's main task is to provide an atmosphere in which the client can be more fully open to her own **organismic experience.** To achieve a growth-conducive atmosphere, the clinician must view the client as intrinsically good and capable of self-development. The clinician's function is to be nonevaluative and to convey a sense of unconditional acceptance and regard for the client (Brazier, 1993). To reach the client effectively the clinician must be "genuine" and "congruent"—an open, trustworthy, warm person without a facade (Lietaer, 1993). The **congruent therapist,** according to Rogers, feels free to be himself or herself and to accept the client fully and immediately in the therapeutic encounter, and conveys this openness to the client. When a genuinely accepting, unconditional relationship is established, the client will become less afraid to face and accept his or her own feelings and experiences. Becoming open to the experience of herself as she is, she can reorganize her

8.18 What is the objective in client (person)-centered therapy? Which therapist qualities contribute to a positive outcome?

self-structure. Now, it is hoped, she will accept experiences that she had previously denied or distorted (because they did not fit her self-concept) and thus achieve greater internal congruity and self-actualization.

Rogers thus sought an empathetic, interview-based relationship therapy. He renounced the Freudian focus on psychodynamics and transference. Instead, he wanted to provide the client an unconditionally accepting relationship—an atmosphere conducive to "growth" (self-actualization). In this relationship, the focus is on empathic understanding and acceptance of feelings rather than interpretation, although the latter is not excluded. The clinician is relatively "nondirective"; the objective is to let the client direct the interview while the clinician attempts to accurately reflect and clarify the feelings that emerge.

In client-centered therapy, now also called person-centered therapy, permissiveness and unqualified acceptance on the part of the therapist provide an atmosphere favorable to personal honesty. Psychologists are urged to abandon their "objective" measurement orientation and their concern with tests. Instead, they should try to learn from the client how he or she thinks, understands, and feels. "The best vantage point for understanding behavior is from the internal frame of reference of the individual himself" (Rogers, 1951, p. 494). Although their focus is on empathy, the Rogerians have not neglected objective research into the relationship, as was noted earlier in this chapter in the context of interview research. As a result, Rogerians have helped to illuminate some of the processes that occur during client-centered therapy and also have provided considerable evidence concerning its effectiveness (e.g., Truax & Mitchell, 1971).

8.19 Compare and contrast person-centered and psychoanalytic therapy.

Rogers' client-centered psychotherapy differs in many ways from Freudian psychotherapy. Indeed, when Rogers first proposed his techniques, they were considered revolutionary. Sometimes his approach to psychotherapy is even described as the polar opposite of Freud's. While there are major differences between Freudian and Rogerian approaches to psychotherapy, on closer inspection there also are some fundamental similarities. Both approaches retain a verbal, interview format for psychotherapy; both focus on the client–clinician relationship; both are primarily concerned with feelings; both emphasize the importance of unconscious processes (defense, repression); both consider increased awareness and acceptance of unconscious feelings to be major goals of psychotherapy.

To be sure, the two approaches differ in their focus. They differ in the specific content that they believe is repressed (for example, id impulses versus organismic experiences), in the motives they consider most important (such as sex and aggression versus self-realization), and in the specific insights they hope will be achieved in psychotherapy (the unconscious becomes conscious and conflict is resolved versus organismic experience is accepted and the self becomes congruent with it). But these differences should not obscure the fact that both approaches are forms of relationship treatment that emphasize awareness of hypothesized unconscious feelings and the need for the client to accept those feelings.

Rogers Reflects on His Own Work

Looking back at the almost 50 years of his contributions to psychology, Rogers (1974) tried to pinpoint the essence of his approach. In his view, his most fundamental idea was that:

the individual has within himself vast resources for self-understanding, for altering his self-concept, his attitudes, and his self-directed behavior—and that these resources can be tapped if only a definable climate of facilitative psychological attitudes can be provided (Rogers, 1974, p. 116).

Such a climate for growth requires an atmosphere in which feelings can be confronted, expressed, and accepted fully and freely. His continued emphasis on the person's potential freedom, the hallmark of a humanistic orientation, remains unchanged:

> *My experience in therapy and in groups makes it impossible for me to deny the reality and significance of human choice. To me it is not an illusion that man is to some degree the architect of himself . . . for me the humanistic approach is the only possible one. It is for each person, however, to follow the pathway—behavioristic or humanistic—that he finds most congenial (Rogers, 1974, p. 119).*

In the same humanistic vein, he regretted modern technology and called for autonomy and self-exploration:

> *Our culture, increasingly based on the conquest of nature and the control of man, is in decline. Emerging through the ruins is the new person, highly aware, self-directing, an explorer of inner, perhaps more than outer, space, scornful of the conformity of institutions and the dogma of authority. He does not believe in being behaviorally shaped, or in shaping the behavior of others. He is most assuredly humanistic rather than technological. In my judgment he has a high probability of survival (Rogers, 1974, p. 119).*

In sum, Rogers' theory and the therapy he developed highlights many of the chief points of the phenomenological and humanistic approach to personality. It emphasizes the person's perceived reality, subjective experiences, organismic striving for actualization, the potential for growth and freedom (Rowan, 1992). It rejects or deemphasizes specific biological drives. It focuses on the experienced self rather than on historical causes or stable trait structures. A unique feature of Rogers' position is his emphasis on unconditional acceptance as a requisite for self-regard.

Other phenomenological theorists have emphasized different aspects in their formulations. For example, the **gestalt theory** (meaning completeness or fullness) of Fritz Perls focuses on awareness of one's own experience in dynamic interaction with the environment (e.g., Van De Riet, Korb, & Gorrell, 1989). Perls' theory continues to influence some psychotherapists.

▶ COMMON THEMES AND ISSUES

The conceptions surveyed in this chapter are quite diverse and far more complex than a brief summary suggests. In spite of their diversity, they share a focus on the self as experienced, on situations as perceived, on personal constructs, on feelings, and on the possibility of freedom. They search for data and methods that explore how people can reveal themselves more fully and honestly. They also see greater self-awareness, consistency, and self-acceptance as crucial aspects of personal growth and actualization (Spinelli, 1989).

8.20 What major assumptions and commonalities characterize the various phenomenological approaches to personality?

Potential for Growth and Change

The existential belief that "man is what he makes of himself" and what he conceives himself to be is extremely appealing to many people. It recognizes the human potential for growth and change, and for alternative ways of construing and dealing with life's challenges. It is optimistic in its belief that people do not have to be victimized by their biographies (as George Kelly put it). While emphasizing the potential for freedom and choice, it also is sensitive to the constraints and limitations of the human condition.

Psychologists who appreciate the attractiveness of these beliefs, but who are committed to a deterministic view of science, also have to ask, however: what are the causes that govern what individuals make of themselves and conceive themselves to be? And how do individuals come to make themselves and conceive themselves in particular ways? While philosophers may put the springs of action and cognition into the will (as Sartre does), the scientifically oriented psychologist seeks to understand the psychological mechanisms that underlie the will (Mischel, Shoda, & Rodriguez, 1989). Many psychologists accept the idea that individuals are what they make of themselves. However, as scientists they want to go further and search for the conditions and processes that make that possible. For example, they want to identify the influences that determine the person's self-conceptions and ability to choose. These challenges began to be addressed by work at the phenomenological level, as you will see in the next chapter, and it continues to be on the agenda of all levels in the rest of the text.

The existential idea that the person has potential control and responsibility for himself or herself, and that people are what they make of themselves, has profound implications for the study of personality. Instead of a search for where the individual stands with regard to the assessor's dimensions, the assessor's task is to help clarify what the individual is making of himself or herself, and the "projects" and goals and plans of that person (Cantor, 1990) as they unfold in the course of life (Emmons, 1997; Mischel, Cantor, & Feldman, 1996). The next chapter illustrates some of the main steps taken in this direction at the phenomenological level.

SUMMARY

SOURCES OF PHENOMENOLOGICAL PERSPECTIVES

- Phenomenological theories focus on the immediate perceived experience and concepts of individuals, and on their strivings toward growth and self-actualization.
- Allport stresses the functional autonomy of motives—current motives may be independent of their historical roots.
- Lewin's field theory introduces the notion of life space and the importance of the psychological environment. He stresses the immediate relationships between the person and the psychological environment.
- The existentialists focus on the "here and now." They emphasize that we build our own lives, and that each person is a choosing, free, responsible agent.

GEORGE KELLY'S PSYCHOLOGY OF PERSONAL CONSTRUCTS

- George Kelly focuses on how the individual views his or her own experiences. His Role Construct Repertory (Rep) Test is used to study personal constructs.
- Kelly emphasizes that all individuals think much like the scientists who study them.
- "Constructive alternativism" refers to the individual's ability to construe the same event in different ways, leading to different courses of action.
- Role play may help the person to select more satisfactory modes of construing the world.

CARL ROGERS' SELF THEORY

- Rogers' theory emphasizes the person's unique, subjective experience of reality. He proposes that the inherent tendency of the organism is to actualize itself.
- Maslow saw self-actualization as a basic human need.

- In Roger's theory, the *self* (self-concept) develops as the result of direct experience with the environment and may also incorporate the perceptions of others. The experienced self in turn influences perception and behavior.
- Maladjustment occurs when the self-concept and a person's experiences are in opposition.
- Client-centered therapy seeks to bring about the harmonious interaction of the self and the organism through unqualified acceptance by the therapist.
- Rogers emphasizes unconditional acceptance as a requisite for self-regard.

KEY TERMS

client-centered (person-centered) therapy 189
condition of worth 188
congruent therapist 189
constructive alternativism 183
contemporaneity of motives 173
convenience of constructs 183
existential anxiety 177
field theory 173

functional autonomy 173
gestalt theory 191
higher growth needs 186
life space 174
organismic evaluation 188
organismic experience 189
organized whole 185
peak experience 186
permeable boundaries 174

personal construct 177
personal construct theory 177
phenomenology 172
principle of contemporaneity 174
role 184
Role Construct Repertory Test ("Rep" Test) 177
self-actualize (self-actualization) 176
self-concept (self) 187

THE INTERNAL VIEW

The phenomenological theories discussed in Chapter 8 deeply influenced personality theory, assessment, and change. To be useful, these theories require ways to access the person's perceived internal experience. In Kelly's own words, if a person's private domain is ignored, "it becomes necessary to explain him as an inert object wafted about in a public domain by external forces, or as a solitary datum sitting on its own continuum" (1955, p. 39). On the other hand, if individuals are to be understood within the framework of scientific rules, methods have to be found to reach those private experiences and to bring them into view. In this chapter, we will consider some of the methods used to examine the internal view of other people.

▶ EXPLORING INTERNAL EXPERIENCE

Phenomenologists like Rogers and Kelly wanted to go beyond introspection and anchor their theories to scientific methods. In Rogers' view, for example, the therapist enters the internal world of the client's perceptions not by introspection but by observation and inference (1947). The same concern with objective measurement of subjective experience characterized George Kelly's approach to assessment. This chapter considers some of the main efforts that have been made by psychologists working at this level to study experience objectively. Beyond finding such methods, they also have developed new strategies for personal growth and awareness. Although much of this work was begun more than 50 years ago, it has remained important in current work (e.g., Higgins, 1996; Lamiell, 1997; Leary & Tangney, 2003).

Why Self Matters: Consequences of Self-Discrepancies

The theories presented in Chapter 8 make a compelling case for the importance of subjective experience and of the self for personality. Going beyond theory to data, contemporary research is showing the powerful role of the individual's self-concepts, self-perceptions, and feelings about himself or herself (e.g., Hoyle, Kernis, Leary, & Baldwin, 1999; Leary & Tangney, 2003). The results show that the internal experiences on which the theorists in the last chapter focused change what people become and influence the types of problems and coping strategies they develop.

One of the most notable findings is that people experience different types of discrepancies between different aspects of the self, and these discrepancies influence their subsequent emotions and behaviors in predictable ways (see Table 9.1). It was Carl Rogers who first suggested that, beginning early in life, discrepancies develop between various mental representations of the self. For example, your **actual self,** that is, the representation of yourself as you are (e.g., a good basketball player) may be discrepant with your **ideal self,** the representation of who you would like to be (a great basketball player). Likewise, the actual self may be discrepant with the **ought self,** the representation of who you believe you should be (e.g., a doctor).

According to E. Tory Higgins (1987), such discrepancies may be experienced not only from one's own vantage point, but also from that of significant others, such as

9.1 Describe three types of self-discrepancies and the emotions to which they give rise according to Higgins.

E. Tory Higgins

TABLE 9.1   Types of Concepts about the Self

Self-Concept	Definition	Example
Actual	One's representation of oneself: the belief about the attributes one actually has	I am a caring and warm person, athletic and attractive
Ideal	One's representation of who one would hope, wish, or like to be: the beliefs about the attributes one would like to have ideally	I would love to be generous and giving, successful, popular, brilliant, and loved
Ought	One's representation of who one should be, or feels obligated to be: the beliefs about the attributes one is obligated to have, i.e., that are one's duty to possess	I should be more ambitious and tough, hardworking and disciplined

Note: In addition to one's own standpoint, each concept also can be represented from the viewpoint of a significant other. For example, your perception of who your father thinks you should be (e.g., strong-willed instead of caring) is an "ought/other" representation of the self.

Source: Based on Higgins, E. T. (1987). Self-discrepancy: A theory relating self and affect. *Psychological Review, 94,* 319–340.

a parent or an older sibling (see Table 9.2). An example of a discrepancy between the actual self and ought self would be a disagreement between the self you believe yourself to be and the "ought self" that you perceive your father thinks you should be. This could take a form like the thought: "I'm afraid my father will be angry with me because I didn't work as hard on my exams as he believes I should." That in turn can lead to feelings of agitation, such as fear and worry. In contrast, a perceived discrepancy between the actual self and ideal self makes an individual more vulnerable to feelings of dejection, such as disappointment and dissatisfaction. In short, Higgins

TABLE 9.2   Illustrative Self-Discrepancies

Types of Self-Discrepancies	Induced Feelings	Example
Actual/Own: Ideal/Own	Disappointment and dissatisfaction	I'm dejected because I'm not as attractive as I would like to be.
Actual/Own: Ideal/Other	Shame and embarrassment	I'm ashamed because I fail to be as kind a person as my parents wished me to be
Actual/Own: Ought/Own	Guilt and self-contempt	I hate myself because I should have more willpower
Actual/Own: Ought/Other	Fear or feeling threatened	I'm afraid my father will be angry with me because I didn't work as hard as he believes I should

Note: "Own" refers to the person's vantage point, "other" to the vantage point of another significant person (e.g., the father).

Source: Based on Higgins, E. T. (1987) Self-discrepancy: A theory relating self and affect. *Psychological Review, 94,* 319–340.

proposed and found evidence that various discrepancies like those shown in Table 9.2 have predictable emotional consequences.

Furthermore, different emotions lead to different patterns of coping with the perceived self-discrepancies (Higgins, 1987). Suppose for example that Gary experiences a discrepancy between the actual self and ought self and feels distressing negative emotions. If the discomfort associated with these negative feelings becomes too great, he may try to reduce or eliminate it in various ways. For example, to deal with a discrepancy between the perceived actual self and the own ideal self, one can reevaluate the negative interpretation of past painful events. For example, the high school student who feels rejected by others ("nobody likes me") because he was not elected class president then might think about the many close friends he has to reduce the negative feelings produced by the experienced actual-ought self-discrepancy.

Alternatively, to remove discrepancies people may change their actual behavior to match an important standard. Suppose an undergraduate studies very little for a midterm and receives a low grade on the exam. For the final, she may study very hard. In doing so, she relieves her guilt for not living up to what she herself perceives to be her responsibility to work diligently in college and receive exemplary grades. In this approach, regardless of the form the change actually takes, the motivation for the change arises from the conflicts each individual feels among his or her various representations of the self. These discrepancies, according to Higgins, cause specific types of emotional discomfort that individuals are motivated to reduce as best they can.

The key point from this is that the work on self-discrepancies makes clear that the self matters. It matters because the internal experiences that people have when they perceive such discrepancies are consequential for the emotions they experience and for the coping patterns they use to try to deal with them. For the scientist concerned with the experienced self and the internal view, the work by Higgins and colleagues also is interesting because it offers a way to study these experiences rigorously using the methods of the science. This work is also having practical applications for understanding serious personality problems, like eating disorders, as discussed in In Focus 9.1.

9.2 What kinds of methods are used to cope with the various self-discrepancies?

Actual–Ideal self discrepancies can be painful.

EFFECTS OF SELF-DISCREPANCY: ANOREXIA

Alarmed by the growing number of cases of eating disorders especially among adolescents and young adult women, researchers and clinical psychologists have been trying to understand this self-destructive, potentially fatal behavior. Explanations offered for eating disorders range from maladaptive interactions among family members to perceptual distortions in the way victims actually see their own bodies. Eating disorders also may reflect discrepancies among the individual's self-concepts, which impact his or her self-evaluation and can disturb self-regulation (Strauman et al., 1991). This explanation stems from self-discrepancy theory (Higgins, 1987) in which different kinds of negative feelings typically are associated with particular kinds of perceived self-discrepancies. As discussed in the text, according to the theory, **actual/ideal discrepancies** make one vulnerable to feelings of dejection. In contrast, **actual/ought discrepancies** make an individual susceptible to feelings of agitation. In Higgins' theory, the person's **self-evaluative standards** (self-guides) are represented by the ideal self and the ought self. When the actual self falls short of these self guides, the individual becomes prone to negative emotions and motivational states. These negative feelings, in turn, can produce distress and maladaptive behavior (Strauman and associates, 1991). Some of the negative effects may be seen in eating disorders.

Thus, **anorexic behavior** (self-starvation) has been linked to actual/ought discrepancies (Strauman et al., 1991). According to these researchers, anorexic behaviors tend to be more characteristic of individuals whose actual self-concepts are discrepant from their representations of how significant others believe they ought to be. The anorexic behaviors seem to be part of a pattern of self-punitive, self-critical efforts to meet what these individuals see as the demands and expectations of significant others. In contrast, bulimic eating problems, such as binging, tend to be more associated with discrepancies between people's actual self-concept and their own ideal self-concepts. Emotionally, those suffering from bulimia experience dejection and related feelings as a reflection of the discrepancy between the body types they perceive themselves to have and their ideals. Interestingly, this seems to be the case irrespective of the person's actual body mass.

Self-discrepancy theory also suggests another insight into eating disorders. The fact that eating disorders are much more prevalent among adolescent girls than boys has led to speculation that women are more commonly socialized to derive feelings of self-worth from their physical appearance. Because modern society mainly considers thin women to be beautiful, many women feel compelled to constantly monitor their body weight and thus are more prone to eating disorders. An alternative explanation, however, is that girls typically are more restricted and controlled than boys. Consequently, prior to adolescence they develop more rigid self-guides, that is, more clearly defined ideal and ought selves. The stronger the self-guides, the more vulnerable the individual is to experience self-discrepancy and negative feelings (Strauman et al., 1991, p. 947). According to the theory, then, women are more likely than men to develop disordered eating habits.

9.3 How has self-discrepancy theory contributed to our understanding of anorexia?

The View Through the Person's Eyes

Phenomenological study begins with the person's own viewpoint. To approach that viewpoint, one may begin with the individual's self-presentation, as expressed in the person's own self-description. Some of the raw data of phenomenology were illustrated in the self-description recorded by Gary W. when he was asked to describe himself as a person, which was presented in Chapter 2, In Focus 2.1. If you look back at it, you will see that it gives at least a preliminary sense of Gary looking at himself and his world through his own eyes, using his own phrases, beginning to show some of his perceptions, thoughts, beliefs, and feelings.

How can we begin to interpret Gary's self-portrait? It is possible to proceed in terms of one's favorite theory, construing Gary's statements as reflections of his traits, or as signs of his dynamics, or as indicative of his social learning history, or as clues to the social forces that are molding him. But can one also make Gary's comments a bridge for understanding his private viewpoint, for glimpsing his own personality theory and for seeing his self-conceptions?

Because each of us is intimately familiar with his own conscious, perceived reality, it may seem deceptively simple to reach out and see another person's subjective world. In fact, we of course cannot "crawl into another person's skin and peer out at the world through his eyes," but we can "start by making inferences based primarily upon what we see him doing rather than upon what we have seen other people doing" (Kelly, 1955, p. 42). That is, we can try to attend to him rather than to our stereotypes and theoretical constructs.

A most direct way to inquire about another person's experience is to ask him, just as Gary was asked, to depict himself. Virtually all approaches to personality have asked people for self-reports. Usually, these reports have served primarily as cues from which to infer the individual's underlying personality structure and dynamics. Perhaps because of the assumption that people engage in extensive unconscious distortion, the client's own reports generally have been used as a basis for the clinician (or the test) to generate inferences and predictions about her, rather than as a means of conveying the client's view of herself.

Uses of Self-Assessments

Can people be "experts" about themselves? Can their reports serve as reliable and valid indices of their behavior? For example, in his self-appraisal Gary predicts that he can succeed in the job for which he is being considered. Is this self-assessment accurate, or is it a defensive hope?

One way to address these questions is to examine whether people's self-assessments can predict their own future behavior. To establish the utility of a person's direct report about himself, you must compare it with the predictions about him that can be made from other data sources. For example, you may compare the individual's self-reports with the statements drawn from sophisticated psychometric tests or from well-trained clinical judges who use such techniques as the interview and the projective test to infer the individual's attributes.

9.4 What evidence exists that simple self-reports can have predictive validity that equals or exceeds that of more complex methods?

It has been a surprise for many psychologists to learn that simple self-reports may be as valid as, and sometimes better predictors than, more sophisticated, complex, and indirect tests designed to disclose underlying personality. In a pioneering study, researchers tried to predict future adjustment for schizophrenic patients (Marks, Stauffacher, & Lyle, 1963). They found that simple self-reports on attitude scales yielded better predictions than did psychometrically more sophisticated scales. Such attitude statements have also been one of the best predictors of success in the Peace Corps; they have been more accurate than far more costly personality inferences. Interviews and pooled global ratings from experts did not prove nearly as accurate as self-reports were (Mischel, 1965). In sum, useful information about people may be obtained most directly by simply asking them (e.g., Cantor & Kihlstrom, 1987; Emmons, 1997). These conclusions seem to hold for such diverse areas as college achievement, job and professional success, treatment outcomes in psychotherapy, rehospitalization for psychiatric patients, and parole violations for delinquent children (e.g., Emmons, 1997; Mischel, 1981; Rorer, 1990).

In sum, under some conditions, people may be able to report and predict their own behavior at least as accurately as experts. Of course, people do not always predict their own behavior accurately. Sometimes individuals lack either the information or the motivation to foretell their own behavior, or are motivated to not reveal it even if they know it. If a criminal plans to steal again, we cannot expect him to say so to the examining prosecutor at his trial. Moreover, many future behaviors may be determined by variables not in the person's control (for example, other people or accidents). The obtained findings do suggest that self-estimates and self-predictions are useful assessment tools.

The Q-Sort Technique

9.5 Describe the Q-sort technique, and the various aspects of the self that it can assess.

One problem with self-descriptions, however, is that different individuals may use different words, phrases, and expressions to describe the same experience, and therefore it becomes difficult to compare one person's self-description with another person's. To compare people, they need to use the same standard language to describe themselves. An especially useful technique for achieving this goal is the **Q-technique** or **Q-sort,** a tool that also has been used in work at other levels of analysis, including the trait-dispositional (Block, 1961, 1971). This technique consists of many cards, each with a printed statement such as "I am a submissive person," "I am likable," and "I am an impulsive person." Or the items might be "is a thoughtful person," "gets anxious easily," "works efficiently."

The Q-sort may be used for self-description, for describing how one would like to be (the ideal self), or even to describe a relationship. For a self-sort, clients would be instructed to sort the cards to describe themselves as they see themselves currently, placing cards in separate piles according to their applicability, ranging from those attributes that are least like them to those that are most like them. For example, the terms that Gary W. had indicated as most self-descriptive were: "haughty, determined, ambitious, critical, logical, moody, uncertain."Or people might be instructed to use the cards to describe the person they would most like to be—their ideal person. To describe a relationship, they would sort the cards into piles ranging from those that are most characteristic of the relationship to those least characteristic. As these examples indicate, the method asks one to sort the cards into a distribution along a continuum from items that are least characteristic (or descriptive) to those that are most characteristic of what one is describing.

The Q-sort is also used to describe the characteristics associated with successful performance in a given task. For example, one can find the profile of qualities "most characteristic" of people who succeed in a particular situation. One can then search for those individuals who best match that profile when trying to predict who will or will not do well in that type of situation (Bem & Funder, 1978). Likewise, Q-sorts are often used to characterize changes in development, for example by comparing people's Q-sort profiles at different stages (Mischel, Shoda, & Peake, 1988).

At this level of analysis, for many psychologists, self-statements from Q-sorts may be of interest in themselves. The phenomenologist simply wants to see the person's self-characterization for its own sake. Unlike other measures that compare individuals with each other along a given dimension to obtain *between-person* differences, the goal of Q-sort assessment is the pattern of the various characteristics *within each person*.

Because the Q-sort requires arranging the cards into a predetermined distribution (e.g., 5 cards in the "least characteristic," 5 cards in the "most characteristic," and 20 cards in the "neither characteristic nor uncharacteristic" piles), if one averages across all the characteristics, everyone will have the same score. This is like giving different painters tubes of red, blue, green, and yellow watercolor paint, and they are asked to paint while making sure they use up all the paint they are given. If you "average" all the colors on each canvas, they will be all the same. What is different is the spatial configuration of the colors on the canvas. Similarly, what is different in the Q-sort depiction of an individual is the *arrangement* among the set of characteristics. With this focus on intraindividual arrangement or configuration, Q-sort has been used to determine how similar, or dissimilar, persons' descriptions are of themselves as they really view themselves ("real self") and as they would like to be ("ideal self"). For example, using a Q-sort that contains 100 cards, individuals can "paint" the picture of their real self. Using the same set of 100 cards, they also paint the picture of their ideal self. Now, the similarity between these two pictures of self can be indexed by the correlation between the two, because both real and ideal selves are described using the same 100 descriptors. As you'll see later, often the degree of similarity between these two descriptions is informative.

Interviews

Most modern phenomenologists have recognized that self-reports may not reveal everything important about behavior and may not give a complete picture of personality. Persons may be conscious of the reasons for their behavior but be unable or unwilling to report them, for example, if they are uncomfortable or ashamed about aspects of their own feelings, perceptions, and behaviors. Or they may not be conscious of all of their experiences, in which case, they cannot communicate them no matter how hard they try. Rather than considering that as a limitation, phenomenologists such as Rogers focus on the person's frame of reference as an important vantage point for understanding him or her. To illustrate this point, imagine two people who, objectively, are both good singers. But while the first thinks she is a great singer, the second thinks he is often out of tune and believes that others are only being polite when they say he sings well. Obviously these differences in their subjective views of themselves make them quite different people even though both sing equally well.

9.6 How is the interview used to assess personality characteristics?

The psychologist's task, in Rogers' view, is to provide conditions that are conducive to growth and that facilitate free exploration of feelings and self in a therapeutic context. This is because one cannot expect people to be honest about themselves when they fear that their statements may incriminate them or lead to negative decisions about their future. In order to become more aware of and articulate private feelings, one needs an unthreatening atmosphere that reduces anxieties and inhibitions, and fosters self-disclosure (Jourard, 1967; Lietaer, 1993). Phenomenologically oriented psychologists therefore try to create conditions of acceptance, warmth, and empathy in which the individual may feel more at ease for open self-exploration (Vanaerschot, 1993). These conditions of acceptance are illustrated vividly in "client-centered" (Rogerian) therapy, discussed later in this chapter.

Rogerians have not only tried to create conditions conducive to personal growth, they also have studied these conditions through methods such as the interview (e.g., Rogers, 1942; Rogers & Dymond, 1954). They use the interview to observe how the individual interprets himself and his experiences, regardless of the validity of the data he provides. This is done in an atmosphere conducive to genuine self-disclosure in which self-revelation and honest self-reports are actively encouraged (e.g., Cantor, 1990; Fodor, 1987; Jourard, 1974).

The Semantic Differential

The **semantic differential** is used to study what different stimuli, events, or other experiences mean to the individual—that is, their personal significance. If you take the semantic differential you are asked to indicate the meanings of diverse words, phrases, and concepts by rating them on many scales (Osgood, Suci, & Tannenbaum, 1957). You

9.7 Describe the
semantic differential
method. What three
underlying factors
consistently emerge
from such ratings?

are given a stimulus word like "feather," or "me," or "my father," or a phrase like "my ideal self," and are asked to rate each stimulus on a seven-point, bipolar scale. Polar adjectives like "rough-smooth" or "fair-unfair" are the extremes of each scale, and you mark the point that most nearly indicates the meaning of the stimulus concept for you. For example, you might be asked to rate "my ideal self" on scales like those shown in Table 9.3. To see what that is like, you should try it for yourself, both for the concepts suggested and for any others you find interesting for yourself. The technique is both objective and flexible. It permits investigation of how people describe themselves and others, as well as how special experiences (for example, psychotherapy) affect them.

A great deal of research has repeatedly indicated that three main factors tend to emerge when the results are analyzed. A primary **evaluative (good-bad) factor** seems to be the most important (Kim & Rosenberg, 1980). In other words, evaluations in such terms as "good-bad" enter most extensively into how people characterize themselves, their experiences, and other people (Ross & Nisbett, 1991). The two other factors are **potency,** represented by scale items like hard-soft, masculine-feminine, strong-weak, and **activity,** tapped by scales like active-passive, excitable-calm, and hot-cold (Mulaik, 1964; Vernon, 1964).

Nonverbal Communication

9.8 What is the
significance of nonverbal
behavior in assessing
inner experiences?

Techniques like the semantic differential and the Rep Test sample what people say—that is, their verbal behavior. But significant communication among people is often nonverbal—it can involve facial expressions, movements, and gestures. Nonverbal expressions have intrigued psychologists of many theoretical orientations who are interested in the individual's perceptions and inner states. Researchers explore the possible meanings and effects of such nonverbal expressions as eye contact and the stare.

For example, when an interviewer evaluates participants positively they increase eye contact with him but when he evaluates them negatively, they decrease eye contact

TABLE 9.3   Examples of Concepts and Rating Scales from the Semantic Differential

Concepts whose meanings are rated:
  My Actual Self
  My Ideal Self
  Masculinity
  Foreigner
  Mother

Scales for rating the meaning of each concept:

Strong	___:___:___:___:___:___:___	Weak
Pleasant	___:___:___:___:___:___:___	Unpleasant
Hard	___:___:___:___:___:___:___	Soft
Safe	___:___:___:___:___:___:___	Dangerous
Fair	___:___:___:___:___:___:___	Unfair
Active	___:___:___:___:___:___:___	Passive

Note: As an exercise, provide these ratings yourself for each concept.
Source: Based on Osgood, C. E., Suci, G. J., & Tannenbaum, P. H. (1957). *The measurement of meaning.* Urbana, IL: The University of Illinois Press.

with him (Exline & Winters, 1965). The effects of eye contact seem to interact with the verbal content conveyed in the relationship. One study varied whether an interviewer looked at the participant frequently or hardly at all, and whether the conversation was positive or threatening (Ellsworth & Carlsmith, 1968). When the verbal content was positive, more frequent eye contact on the part of the inteviewer produced more positive evaluations of the interviewer. In contrast, when the verbal content was negative, more frequent eye contact produced more negative evaluation.

Although much is still unknown about nonverbal communication, many results have been encouraging. It has been shown, for instance, that "when people look at the faces of other people, they can obtain information about happiness, surprise, fear, anger, disgust/contempt, interest, and sadness. Such information can be interpreted, without any special training, by those who see the face . . ." (Ekman, Friesen, & Ellsworth, 1972, pp. 176–177). In short, phenomenological, "inner" experiences may be visible in the form of nonverbal behaviors.

Studying Lives from the Inside

The Whole Person: Psychobiography.   The phenomenological approach has many of its deepest roots in the psychotherapies of theorists like Rogers and Kelly, but it also has been extended in other directions. Most notably, the approach has been adapted and combined with other methods to study lives in depth and over long periods of time (Runyan, 1997). Called **psychobiography,** the intensive study of individual lives has become a specialty area in its own right. These studies attempt to provide a comprehensive psychological understanding of one person, often selecting public figures like Adolf Hitler or Ghandi. As its advocates note, personality psychology has many sides, and does not have to be confined to quantitative comparisons between people or groups (Lamiell, 1997; Runyan, 1997). Instead, the study of lives focuses on one person at a time, and tries to cover the whole of his or her life in all its complexity over the life course. The methods employed borrow from biography, history, and other social sciences as well as from psychology and the phenomenological approach. As one of its most enthusiastic practitioners put it, there is a "softer human science end of psychology" whose advice to students is "Learn all you can about people and lives, including yourself" (Runyan, 1997, p. 61).

9.9 How have the methods of psychobiography and personal narrative been used to study people's lives?

Life Stories: Personal Narratives.   In a closely related vein, but with its own guiding philosophy and methodology, Dan McAdams (1999) has developed an approach to understanding persons and the ways in which they construct their lives. His focus is on the **personal narratives**—the stories—that people tell themselves as they try to make sense of their own lives and experiences. McAdams (1999, p. 488) proposes that "The I apprehends experience in narrative terms, casting the Me as one or more characters in an ongoing sequence of scenes." Essentially the I is a storyteller, and the story each person tells—both to himself or herself and to other people varies with time and circumstances. The stories you tell in a college application, a job interview, when building a relationship with a potential romantic partner, or in a private diary entry to yourself will vary. The contents and structure of the story will change, and as life is lived the stories of one's life are progressively edited, revised, rewritten, reconstructed. The core of this message is that regardless of their validity by any external standard, these stories people tell about themselves are worth hearing, and personality psychologists—as well as nonprofessionals—can benefit by listening closely.

▶ ENHANCING SELF-AWARENESS: ACCESSING ONE'S EXPERIENCES

Given that people's subjective experiences of the self have far-reaching implications for their emotions, behavior, and their well-being, it should not be surprising that changing the subjective views of the self can have significant impact on individuals' well-being. Probably the most dramatic and controversial manifestation of the effort to alter the subjective experience of self on a massive scale was by means of psychedelic drugs, and in some ways it created at least a short-term cultural revolution in much of the western world. Initially, drugs such as psilocybin and LSD were advocated most energetically by Timothy Leary and Richard Alpert when they were psychologists at Harvard University in 1961 and 1962. In the 1960s, the "mind-expanding" movement through drug-induced "trips" or psychic "voyages" gained many enthusiastic participants throughout the western world. Such drugs as LSD undoubtedly produce major alterations in subjective experience, including the intensification of feelings (Leary, Litwin, & Metzner, 1963), but enthusiasm for them was soon tempered by the recognition that they entail serious risks. The trend became to search for greater awareness without the aid of any drugs by means of psychological experiences and changes within the self and in how life is lived.

Historically, routes to increasing awareness that rely on psychological experiences rather than on drugs include meditation (Ornstein, 1972), encounter groups, and "marathons" of the type developed originally at the Esalen Institute in Big Sur, California (Schutz, 1967). While meditative techniques were based mainly on Eastern religious sources (Ornstein & Naranjo, 1971), the encounter or "sensitivity training" movement drew on various role-play and psychodrama techniques, existential philosophy, and Freudian psychodynamic theory.

The resulting syntheses were seen in the ideas of the **Gestalt therapy** of Fritz Perls (1969), in the efforts to expand human awareness and to achieve "joy" and true communication (Schutz, 1967), and in the pursuit of "peak experiences" and "self-actualization" (Maslow, 1971). In its early versions, Gestalt therapy included confrontations and "encounters" that quickly challenged the person's self-reported experiences, sometimes interpreting them as superficial and defensive. Often the "leader" tried rapidly and directly to stimulate and probe the deeper feelings that might underlie what the person disclosed (Polster & Polster, 1993). In more recent versions, there is less rapid and dramatic confrontation and a slower, more empathic attempt to explore the person's internal experiences in his or her own terms. The aim is to focus awareness on what is being felt fully and honestly. The process of enhancing both self-awareness and interpersonal awareness becomes the center of the therapeutic relationship, encouraging the person to be more closely in touch with what is experienced and freer to experiment interpersonally (Fodor, 1987; Wheeler, 1991).

9.10 Indicate how gestalt therapy and T-groups are used to explore and alter internal experience? What anecdotal and scientific evidence is there for their effectiveness?

Group Experiences

As part of the search for growth and expanded awareness, in the 1960s and 1970s a variety of group experiences became popular. Encounter groups have had many different labels, such as **human-relations training group (T-group),** and **sensitivity training group,** but in this discussion the focus is on their common qualities. Schutz (1967) in his book *Joy* noted that encounter group methods involve doing something, not just talking. In this quest, he advocated a host of group methods that include body exercises, wordless meetings, group fantasy, and physical "games." Elliot Aronson (1972, p. 238), a pioneer of experimental social psychology and a major contributor to the science, described what is learned in group experiences this way: ". . . in a psychology course I learn how people behave; in a T-group I learn how I behave. But I learn much more than that: I also learn how others see me, how my behavior affects them, and how I am affected by other people." Referring to the process through which such learning occurs, Aronson (p. 239) emphasizes learning-by-doing; ". . . people learn by trying things out, by getting in touch with their feelings and by expressing those feelings to other people, either verbally or nonverbally." Such a process requires an atmosphere of trust so that members learn not how they are "supposed" to behave but rather what they really feel and how others view them.

At a theoretical level, the encounter group movement involved a complex synthesis of both Freudian and Rogerian concepts with a focus on nonverbal experiences and self-discovery. The psychodynamic motivational framework was largely retained and was used in many of the interpretations, but it was implemented by direct "acting-out" procedures for expressing feelings through action in the group, by body contact designed to increase awareness of body feelings, and by games to encourage the expression of affection and aggression. Thus, many of Freud's and Rogers' ideas were transferred from the consulting room to the group encounter, and from verbal expression to body awareness and physical expression. Indeed, Carl Rogers (1970) developed and extended many of his theoretical concepts to the encounter experience, and he became one of its leading advocates. Rather than talking about impulses, feelings, and fantasies, the individual is encouraged to act them out in the group. For example, rather than talk about repressed feelings of anger toward his father, the individual enacts his feelings, pummeling a pillow while screaming "I hate you, Dad, I hate you." Many people have reported positive changes as a result of group experiences. To illustrate, consider this testimonial cited by Rogers (1970, p. 129):

I still can't believe the experience that I had during the workshop. I have come to see myself in a completely new perspective. Before I was "the handsome" but cold person insofar as personal relationships go. People wanted to approach me but I was afraid to let them come close as it might endanger me and I would have to give a little of myself. Since the institute I have not been afraid to be human. I express myself quite well and also am likeable and also can love. I go out now and use these emotions as part of me.

While such reports were encouraging, they are not firm evidence, and they were offset in part by reports of negative experiences (Lieberman et al., 1973). Some behavior changes did seem to emerge, but their interpretation is beset by many methodological difficulties (Campbell & Dunnette, 1968). When careful control groups were used, doubt was raised if the gains from encounter experience reflect more than the enthusiastic expectancies of the group members. For example, people in weekend encounter groups showed more rated improvement than did those who remained in an at-home control group, but improvement in the encounter groups did not differ from that found in an on-site control group whose participants believed they were in an encounter group although they only had recreational activities (McCardel & Murray, 1974).

Nevertheless, a number of experimental studies indicated specific changes that may occur in some types of groups. These changes include a decrease in ethnic prejudice (Rubin, 1967; Saley & Holdstock, 1993), an increase in empathy (Dunnette, 1969) and susceptibility to being hypnotized (Tart, 1970), and an increased belief by individuals that their behavior is under their own control (Diamond & Shapiro, 1973). This evidence is accompanied by a greater awareness on the part of therapeutic group enthusiasts that not all groups are for all people, that bad as well as good experiences may occur (Bates & Goodman, 1986), and that coerciveness in groups is a real hazard that needs to be avoided (Aronson, 1972).

Particularly important is the finding that **self-disclosure** and sharing of stressful, traumatic experiences, either in groups or in other forms (e.g., in diaries) can have dramatically beneficial effects on well-being and health (Pennebaker, 1993, 1997). An illustration of the value of sharing traumatic experiences comes from work with patients suffering from advanced breast cancer (Spiegel et al. 1989). The patients were divided into two conditions, both conditions receiving the usual medical care for cancer. However, people in the intervention received weekly supportive group therapy for a period of one year, sharing their experiences with others openly. The patients who had this experience survived almost twice as long (37 months) as those who did not.

Meditation

As Eastern cultures have long known, and as Western cultures have only recently learned, meditation can have powerful effects on subjective experience. The term "meditation" refers to a set of techniques that are the product of another type of psychology, one that aims at personal rather than intellectual knowledge. As such, the exercises are designed to produce an alteration in consciousness. It is a shift away from the active, outward-oriented mode and toward the receptive and quiescent mode. Usually it is a shift from an external focus of attention to an internal one (Ornstein, 1972, p. 107).

Students, businessmen, athletes, ministers, senators, and secretaries were among the more than 600,000 people in the United States alone who enthusiastically endorsed one version of meditation called **transcendental meditation (TM).** Introduced into the United States in 1959 by Maharishi Mahesh Yogi, a Hindu monk, TM has changed over the years in the public's mind from counterculture fad to mainstream respectability. TM is defined as a state of restful alertness from which one is said to emerge with added energy and greater mind-body coordination. It is practiced during two daily periods of 20 minutes each. The meditator sits comfortably with eyes closed and mentally repeats a Sanskrit word called a **mantra.**

Maharishi, his movement, and more recent followers maintain that the technique of TM can be learned only from specially trained TM teachers who charge a substantial fee. One of the pioneer researchers into the effects of TM, Herbert Benson, a Harvard cardiologist, disagreed (1975). He believed that the same kind of meditation can be self-taught with a one-page instruction sheet, achieving the same measurable results (see Table 9.4).

TABLE 9.4   The Mechanics of Meditation

1. Sit in a comfortable position in a quiet environment, eyes closed.
2. Deeply relax all muscles.
3. Concentrate on breathing in and out through your nose. As you breathe out, repeat a single syllable, sound, or word such as "one" silently to yourself.
4. Disregard other thoughts, adopt a passive attitude, and do not try to "force" anything to happen.
5. Practice twice daily for 20-minute periods at least two hours after any meal. (The digestive process seems to interfere with the elicitation of the expected changes.)

Source: Adapted from Benson, H. (1975). *The relaxation response.* New York: Morrow.

Scientific research indicates that there are direct physical responses to meditation (Alexander, Robinson, Orme-Johnson, Schneider, & Walton, 1994). These changes include decreased rate of metabolism (decreased oxygen consumption), and an increase in alpha waves (slow brain-wave patterns). Although meditation was initially introduced as a technique for expanding consciousness, the current emphasis is on reducing stress, lowering blood pressure, alleviating addictions (O'Connell & Alexander, 1994), and increasing energy and powers of concentration.

9.11 What physiological and psychological effects occur from meditation?

The research publicized by the TM movement is open to criticism. The fact that many of the researchers are dedicated meditators themselves makes it possible that their results and interpretations may be unintentionally biased. Perhaps most important, the characteristic brain-wave pattern that the TM movement claims to be a sign of the "alert reverie" produced by meditation does not appear to be unique to meditation (Pagano, Rose, Stivers, & Warrenburg, 1976). It can occur, for example, in hypnosis when a state of deep relaxation is suggested. And Benson's (1975) relaxation technique (see Table 9.4) produces the same reductions in oxygen consumption and respiration rate that are produced during transcendental meditation without the expense and the complex rituals of meditation training. In reply, those committed to the movement argue that TM produces a wide range of more fundamental changes than relaxation, including a tremendous improvement in the quality of life. Perhaps because the subjective experience produced by meditation may appear unique to the meditators, they often continue to claim that meditation is a distinct state of consciousness in spite of the contradictory physiological evidence.

The Person's Experience and the Unconscious

For many years, most psychologists did not consider subjective experiences as phenomena of interest in their own right. They preferred, instead, to infer what dispositions and motives might underlie the person's behavior. The historical neglect of the individual's viewpoint probably has many reasons. One was the belief that because of unconscious distortions and defenses, people's self-appraisals were biased and inaccurate. Some psychologists thus refrained from studying the person's perceptions, concepts, and intentions because they felt such data were not really scientific. But it is entirely legitimate philosophically and logically to take account of individuals' reported subjective perceptions—the rules they use and the reasons they give to explain their own actions (Lamiell, 1997; T. Mischel, 1964). It is not legitimate, however, to assume that these rules and reasons are useful bases for predicting what individuals will do—their behavior—in other situations. The links between persons' reported feelings and beliefs and their other behaviors have to be demonstrated empirically.

9.12 Why have some psychologists minimized the clinical and scientific value of subjective self-reports?

Although the phenomenological orientation focuses on the individual's viewpoint, in some of its variations it also seeks to infer his or her unconscious characteristics and conflicts. For example, Carl Rogers in some of his formulations (1963) has emphasized integration, unity, and achieving congruence with their "inner organismic processes." Rogers thought that these organismic processes were often unconscious. As a result of socialization procedures in our culture, persons often become dissociated, "consciously behaving in terms of static constructs and abstractions and unconsciously behaving in terms of the actualizing tendency" (Rogers, 1963, p. 20).

To the extent that psychologists accept the idea that unconscious processes are key determinants of personality, and rely on clinical judgment to infer them, they face all the challenges previously discussed in the context of psychodynamic theory. But methodological difficulties should not deter psychologists from listening more closely

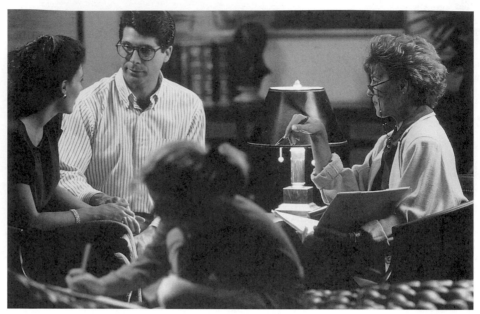

Family therapy analyzes the transactions in a relationship, helping each partner to see the viewpoint of the other.

to what their "participants" can tell them; the caution applies to the interpretation process, not to the value of listening and empathizing. **Family therapies** have been influenced extensively by this perspective, and try to sensitize the members of a family to see each other's viewpoints and take them into account in their daily transactions within the family system.

Accessing Painful Emotions: Hypnotic Probing

9.13 How is hypnosis used to help people access dissociated experiences? What limitations of hypnotic probing have emerged?

In one direction, hypnosis is being used to help individuals access the painful feelings and memories that may become difficult to recall in the aftermath of traumatic experiences (Spiegel et al., 1994). Such mental avoidance may follow potentially life-threatening events and losses of the sort experienced by victims of disasters, violent crimes, or war. But they may also occur in the course of everyday life especially in early childhood when people have experiences and feelings that they may find traumatic and too difficult to deal with, as Freud stressed in his theory. The dissociated state itself is characterized by being out of touch with one's feelings, sometimes with amnesia, depression, a sense of numbing, detachment, and withdrawal.

In this type of therapy, hypnosis may be used within a highly supportive, structured setting to induce a trance state. While the person is in this state, memories of the painful events may be re-experienced in the safe therapeutic setting. Recall of the traumatic events is stimulated by the careful guidance and suggestions of the therapist, designed to elicit vivid images that make the memories more accessible (Spiegel, 1981, 1991). It may then become possible for the person to try to place the traumatic experience into perspective and to accept it emotionally. In this process, the person is encouraged to grieve for what has been lost rather than continue to "split off" the painful feelings and run away from them. According to this approach ". . . a loss not grieved leads to a life not lived— to a kind of numbing or withdrawal and depression . . ." (Spiegel, 1981, p. 35).

While this approach has received much attention, in recent years its limitations and hazards also have become clear. Hypnosis is not a magic route to the truth: what is re-experienced and reported is subject to all sorts of influences, including implicit suggestions from the therapist and expectations about what will be revealed. As a result, the reports that follow are not at all above suspicion (Loftus, 1994, 1993).

Peering into Consciousness: Brain Images of Subjective Experiences

Interestingly, it was Freud who initially thought that hypnosis would provide a window into the unconscious, but who soon decided to abandon it in favor of other techniques—a choice that now seems like a mistake to some of his critics. Especially exciting is that new functional brain imaging techniques are helping to specify the brain locations that become activated during hypnotic concentration and that underlie different types of mental states and events (e.g., Spiegel, 1991; Schachter, 1995). For example, these imaging techniques show that the practice of meditation activates distinctive brain structures involved in attention and control of the autonomic nervous system (e.g., Lazar and associates, 2000).

The Value of Self-Disclosure about Subjective Experiences

Over the course of many years, Jamie Pennebaker and his colleagues have been studying how writing about stressful and traumatic experiences influences people's mental and physical well-being (Pennebaker & Graybeal, 2001). In Pennebaker's typical method, volunteer participants, usually college undergraduates, are brought into the laboratory and asked to write about either traumatic experiences from their past or superficial topics (for comparison purposes) for 15 minutes a day for 3 to 4 consecutive days.

9.14 Summarize the research of Pennebaker on self-disclosure of painful events and its effects? How does Pennebaker account for the positive results?

As was noted in the discussion of psychodynamic process, these studies demonstrated that when people write about their traumatic and stressful experiences, they dramatically improve their well-being and health. Relative to people who are told to write about superficial topics, people who write about their emotional experiences subsequently make fewer visits to the doctor, at least in short-term follow-up studies (Smyth, 1998; Pennebaker, Colder, & Sharp, 1990; Pennebaker, Kiecolt-Glaser, & Glaser, 1988). They also show improved hormonal activity and immune function (Petrie et al. 1995). In addition, people who self-disclose their subjective experiences by writing about them tend to show a number of other behavioral improvements. College students who self-disclosed improved their grades (Pennebaker and associates, 1990), and unemployed workers got new jobs faster (Pennebaker, 1997).

Contrary to classical psychoanalytical theory, Pennebaker does not believe that the power of writing is a function of catharsis or the release of pent-up negative feelings. Instead, he and his collaborators have evidence that writing about emotional experiences influences people's health and behavior by changing the way they think about their emotions and themselves. Writing allows them to construct mental narratives—literally stories—of their experiences. The specific psychological processes that make writing about emotional experiences lead to such positive outcomes still needs more research and many studies are under way. Finally, note also that while it helps to write about one's negative feelings, brooding and ruminating about them can have the opposite effect, as discussed in In Focus, 9.2.

IN FOCUS 9.2

CAUTION: RUMINATION CAN INCREASE DEPRESSION

Being in touch with, and expressing, what you really think and feel, including with regard to painful emotions, may have considerable value, but thinking about the negative too much also has its hazards. Although many people believe that they should focus inward and attend in detail to their feelings, ruminating about the negative can become a pattern that makes depressive feelings even worse.

Going against the grain of popular wisdom, Susan Nolen-Hoeksema and colleagues have found that **rumination** tends to enhance angry and depressed moods rather than to foster improvements. People who ruminate are more likely to generate more negative memories, make more pessimistic predictions about the future, and interpret present situations more negatively than people who do not ruminate (Lyubomirsky & Nolen-Hoeksema, 1993, 1995). By ruminating about negative feeling it can

become more difficult to focus on and solve the problems that underlie one's distress and depression. In a study of people who lost a loved one to a terminal illness, those who ruminated more at the time of their loss were more depressed 18 months later than those who ruminated less (Nolen-Hoeksema, Parker, & Larson, 1994).

In moderation, the tendency to ruminate is a relatively common and stable coping style that is more prevalent among women than men (Butler & Nolen-Hoeksema, 1994; Nolen-Hoeksema et al., 1994). But chronic ruminators— people who reflexively ruminate in response to stress— experience more distressing thoughts and feelings compared to people who do not ruminate when under distress (Rusting & Nolen-Hoeksema, 1998). In fact, the tendency to ruminate may be an indicator that predicts future diagnoses of depression and anxiety (Nolen-Hoeksema, 2000).

9.15 How does rumination go beyond Pennebaker's approach? What negative effects result?

▶ CHANGE AND WELL-BEING

The Meaningful Life, the Healthy Personality

The phenomenological orientation implies a "humanistic" view of adaptation, personal health and "deviance." There are many variations, but in general personal genuineness, honesty about one's own feelings, self-awareness, and self-acceptance are positively valued. **Self-realization,** the ultimate in fulfillment in this perspective, involves a continuous quest to know oneself and to actualize one's potentialities for full awareness and growth as a human being. Denouncing "adjustment" to society and to other people's values as the road to dehumanization, the quest is to know oneself deeply and to be true to one's own feelings without disguise or self-deception. Human problems are seen as rooted in distortions of one's own perceptions and experiences to please the expectations of society, including the demands of one's own self-concept (Chapter 8).

9.16 What kinds of characteristics did Maslow identify in self-actualized people?

Maslow (1968) offered a description of the **healthy personality** from a humanistic viewpoint, and his view of the qualities of the **self-actualizing person** is summarized in Table 9.5.

In recent years, research has identified many of the key psychosocial ingredients that enhance well-being (e.g., Aspinwall & Staudinger, 2002), summarized in Table 9.6. The results are generally consistent with the expectations of the Phenomenological Approach. Namely, human resilience and strength—including physical well-being and health—in dealing with serious stressors is enhanced when the individual can find **meaning in life** and in the experience of living it. This is the case even when (or perhaps especially when) the experience is tragic, such as the loss of a life partner or the development of a life-threatening illness (O'Leary, 1997). A dramatic example is seen in how the actor Christopher Reeve, who had starred as Superman in the movies, dealt with his sudden paraplegic condition after an accident. He managed to construe this experience not as an occasion for self-pity but as an opportunity to make a contribution, becoming a dedicated spokesperson to increase research for spinal cord injury.

9.17 What psychosocial factors seem to contribute to physical and psychological well being? Cite relevant research results.

TABLE 9.5   Some Qualities of Maslow's "Self-Actualizing" People

1. Able to perceive reality accurately and efficiently.

2. Accepting of self, of others, and of the world.

3. Spontaneous and natural, particularly in thought and emotion.

4. Problem-centered: concerned with problems outside themselves and capable of retaining a broad perspective.

5. Need and desire solitude and privacy; can rely on their own potentialities and resources.

6. Autonomous: relatively independent of extrinsic satisfactions, for example, acceptance or popularity.

7. Capable of a continued freshness of appreciation of even the simplest, most commonplace experiences (for example, a sunset, a flower, or another person).

8. Experience "mystic" or "oceanic" feelings in which they feel out of time and place and at one with nature.

9. Have a sense of identification with humankind as a whole.

10. Form their deepest ties with relatively few others.

11. Truly democratic; unprejudiced and respectful of all others.

12. Ethical, able to discriminate between means and ends.

13. Thoughtful, philosophical, unhostile sense of humor; laugh at the human condition, not at a particular individual.

14. Creative and inventive, not necessarily possessing great talents, but a naive and unspoiled freshness of approach.

15. Capable of some detachment from the culture in which they live, recognizing the necessity for change and improvement.

Source: Based on Maslow, A. H. (1968). *Toward a psychology of being.* New York: Van Nostrand.

Beyond such vivid single cases, there is a great deal of evidence that the ingredients of well-being, summarized in Table 9.6, significantly improve the biological response to illness (Ickovics, 1997). To illustrate, Shelly Taylor found that HIV positive gay men who had lost a life partner but construed the experience as giving new meaning to their life maintained their level of immune functioning longer than did those who did not find meaning in the same experience (O'Leary 1997; Taylor, 1995).

A second ingredient of resilience is an **optimistic orientation** (as contrasted to a pessimistic, hopeless, helpless orientation), and a focus on the positive in oneself and in human nature (e.g., Aspinwall & Staudinger, 2002). Scheier and colleagues compared optimists and pessimists (identified through a self-report measure) on a well-researched measure of coping styles in dealing with stress (Scheier & Carver, 1992). Optimists characteristically tend to use more active coping and planning, seek emotional support

TABLE 9.6   Some Key Ingredients for Well-Being

- finding meaning in life
- optimism (versus helplessness/hopelessness)
- self-efficacy/agency (beliefs that one can do things effectively)
- social support (relatedness: groups or friends that share experience caringly)

The star of Superman became heroic also in real life.

more, use religion, and attempt to grow constructively with the adverse experience they are having. They also are less likely than pessimists to use negative kinds of coping strategies. For example, when dealing with breast cancer, optimists are less likely to deny that they had cancer, tend to disengage less, and use generally positive ways of coping with their disease. In turn, such active coping styles and realistic acceptance of the illness tend to be predictive of survival. As the table indicates, beliefs that one can do things effectively, called **self-efficacy,** and having relationships that provide support and connectedness also are important ingredients for effective coping and well-being.

SUMMARY

EXPLORING INTERNAL EXPERIENCE

- Discrepancies develop between various mental representations of the self and they have emotional consequences. People use various strategies to reduce these discrepancies.

- Research indicates that self-assessment sometimes can yield predictions as accurate as those from sophisticated personality tests.

- In the Q-sort procedure, participants are asked to sort attribute cards from most descriptive to least descriptive to describe, for example, the self, the ideal self, or a relationship.

- Phenomenologists use the interview to explore the person's feelings and self-concepts and to see the world from his or her framework and viewpoint.

- The "semantic differential" is a rating technique for the objective assessment of the meaning of the rater's words and concepts.

- Personal narratives and psychobiographies are other useful methods of exploring individuals at this level of analysis.

ENHANCING SELF-AWARENESS: ACCESSING ONE'S EXPERIENCES

- Methods to enhance self-awareness and interpersonal awareness include Gestalt therapy, meditation and encounter groups, and generally emphasize emotional aspects of experience and existence.

- Researchers have also examined the effects of self-disclosure (e.g., by writing about traumatic experiences) and of rumination on diverse positive and negative outcomes.

CHANGE AND WELL-BEING

- In this perspective, the healthy personality is characterized by personal genuineness, honesty about one's own feelings, self-awareness, self-acceptance, and self-realization, without destorting one's self-perceptions.

KEY TERMS

activity   202
actual self   195
actual/ideal
   discrepancies   198
actual/ought
   discrepancies   198
anorexic
   behavior   198
evaluative factor   202
family therapy   208
Gestalt therapy   204
healthy
   personality   210

human-relations training
   group (T-group)/
   sensitivity training
   group   204
ideal self   195
mantra   206
meaning in life   210
optimistic orientation   211
ought self   195
personal narratives   203
potency   202
psychobiography   203
Q-sort (Q-technique)   200

rumination   210
self-actualizing
   person   210
self-disclosure   206
self-efficacy   212
self-evaluative standards
   (self-guides)   198
self-realization   210
semantic
   differential   201
systems therapy   215
transcendental
   meditation (TM)   206

PART III

THE PHENOMENOLOGICAL LEVEL

▶ OVERVIEW: FOCUS, CONCEPTS, METHODS

As this part concludes, we again take stock and seek an overview of this level of analysis. Many psychologists welcome the emphasis on the person's cognitions, feelings, and personal interpretations of experience stressed by the contributors at this level of analysis. This concern with how individuals construe events and see themselves and the world has been a most influential force, and it has generated a great deal of research. The resulting contributions are widely acknowledged. Some of the main features of phenomenological approaches are summarized in the next table, which shows some of their shared characteristics.

Overview of Focus, Concepts, Methods: The Phenomenological Level

Basic units:	The experienced self; personal constructs and self-concepts; subjective feeling and perceptions; self-discrepancies
Causes of behavior:	Self-concepts, personal construal (appraisal), feelings and conflicts, free choices
Manifestations of personality:	Private internal experiences, perceptions, and interpretations, self-actualization
Favored data:	Self-disclosure and personal constructs (about self and others); self-reports
Observed responses used as:	Signs (of the person's inner states, perceptions, or emotions)
Research focus:	Personal constructs; self-concepts, self-awareness and expression; human potential and self-actualization; emotion
Approach to personality change:	By increased awareness, personal honesty, internal consistency, and self-acceptance; by modifying constructs; by alternative construals (appraisals)
Role of situation:	As the context for experience and choice; focus on the situation as perceived

As the table indicates, the basic unit of personality is the experienced self and the personal concepts and feelings of the individual. These feelings and concepts and the conflicts experienced in relation to them are seen as basic causes of behavior, but the person has choice and responsibility for what he or she does. The favored data are people's reports and self-disclosures about their personal feelings and constructs. They provide the assessor with a glimpse of the person's inner states, perceptions, and emotions, and an empathic sense of what it is like to view the world through that person's eyes. The goal of research is to explore the individual's private feelings and concepts and examine their implications. It is assumed that by increasing self-awareness and "being in touch with" one's genuine experienced feelings, persons will enhance their perceived coherence, realize their potential for growth, and self-actualize. The effect of situations can be substantial but always depends on how they are perceived subjectively by the person.

► ENDURING CONTRIBUTIONS OF THE PHENOMENOLOGICAL LEVEL

Work at this level, begun by pioneers in the middle of the twentieth century, that focuses on how people construe or appraise themselves and their experiences is still timely today. There is a renewed research interest in personal constructs and construal, the self, and the nature of selfhood (e.g., Hoyle et al., 1999; Leary & Tanguey, 2003; Mischel & Morf, 2003), as discussed in Part V and in the final chapters on the integration of levels.

Work at the phenomenological level looked beyond the individual's previous history, or early life traumas and conflicts, or traits, to offer a more positive, optimistic view of the human condition and the prospects for personal growth and constructive change. This focus also has encouraged movement toward a more positive psychology directed at enhancing human potential (Aspinwall & Staudinger, 2002). It proposed that people do not forever have to be victims of their past and can move beyond the less constructive aspects of their personalities toward much more positive ways of fulfilling themselves.

One enduring practical application from work at this level came in the form of family therapy or **systems therapy** (e.g., Minuchin, Lee, & Simon, 1996). These therapies try to understand how the problems of an adolescent, for example, are interpersonal and reflect conflicts and issues in the family system within which he or she lives. Treatment therefore needs to take account of what is going on in the family as a whole, not just in the adolescent's mind. It examines for example, the role that was established for the "problem person" within the context of the larger system (e.g., "Anne's the one you can't count on"), and the ways in which that role feeds into the conflicts currently experienced. The goal is to help the family members to see each other more constructively. The hope is to reconstrue the "problem" to move beyond old stereotypes and essentially create new narratives that work better and fit the changing circumstances and the contexts of the family and all its members as they evolve and try to deal with each other. The same would be true if the case was one of an abused woman. Treatment would focus on understanding the abusive relationship and the ways in which it was maintained, not just on the personality of the abused person.

In sum, the applications of this approach have been broad, and have ranged from working to help overcome the psychological consequences of child abuse, battering, and incest to the trauma of HIV infection and AIDS (e.g., Walker, 1991; White & Epston, 1990) to modern family therapists (e.g., Minuchin, Lee, & Simon, 1996), to help for women in abusive relationships with violent men (Goldner et al., 1990). These applications have made clear that many key phenomenological concepts can help in understanding and treating some of the most difficult problems of contemporary life. They also illustrate how well the ideas of George Kelly and Carl Rogers, articulated half a century ago, have stood the test of time.

Theorists like Rogers and Kelly at first were lone voices calling for a new kind of personality psychology, and sketching some of its components and outlines. It is a tribute to the early theorists working at this level that many of the topics they championed are being built upon decades later with fresh and intense new interest. Stimulated by the explosion of interest in cognitive approaches to personality, the self and its perceptions and cognitions are receiving unprecedented attention in personality psychology, as you will see in later chapters. In fact they have become a centerpiece for current work at the social cognitive level (Part V). Before we get there however, we turn to a level of analysis that added a very different focus to the study of personality: the role of learning and conditioning as determinants of human action and personality.

PART

IV

THE BEHAVIORAL-CONDITIONING LEVEL

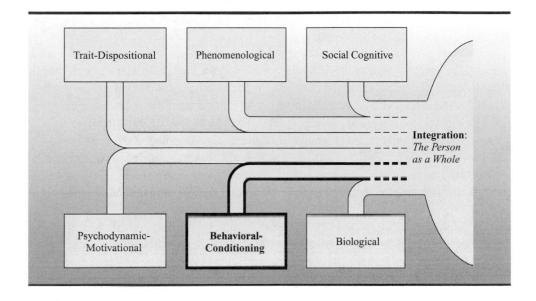

▶ PRELUDE TO PART IV: THE BEHAVIORAL-CONDITIONING LEVEL

Mr. Z was institutionalized in a large midwestern state mental hospital for psychotic patients in the 1950s. Pacing in a day-room with broken chairs and filled with the screams of disturbed people, he was a portrait in distress and isolation. At the center of this huge bleak room was a glassed-in, walled nursing station, behind which the staff and occasional visiting physician took shelter. The ward was high security, and medications for helping to deal with psychotic outbursts and aggressive rages were still in their infancy. In this kind of bedlam, some psychologists formed a hypothesis. They thought that the patients' wild behavior might in part be a function of the fact that the only time staff emerged to have any contact with them was when they began to act up: might there be a relationship between the display of disturbed behavior and the conditions under which they received any kind of human attention? Might psychotic behavior actually be inadvertently strengthened by the hospital conditions under which they lived and the contingencies under which they received attention? Systematic studies over the years showed that even under less extreme conditions in human relationships, people reinforced and strengthened in each other the very behaviors that they were trying to control.

While Freud and his followers were capturing the attention of the clinical world with their fresh approaches to the treatment of personality problems in Europe, psychologists in the United States were committing themselves to the scientific, experimental study of behavior under well-controlled laboratory conditions. Often they used animals as subjects so that experimental manipulations were possible. Committed to building a science of personality, they wanted to only study phenomena that they could observe directly and objectively. Therefore, they deliberately avoided asking questions about anything that they felt they could not test experimentally. So they did not want to deal with questions about what people are like (Trait-Dispositional Level), or what their motives might be (Psychodynamic-Motivational Level), or what their "real" selves could be (Phenomenological Level).

Instead, they insisted on studying what organisms—whether people or rats— actually *do,* and linking it to the conditions under which they do it. If they could not do this with people, they did it with animals. At the same time, however, some of these scientists were personally intrigued by Freud's clinical work, and its potential value for helping troubled people. Two pioneers, Neal Miller and John Dollard, devoted themselves to make his ideas testable in experiments. As a first step, they translated the core ideas about conflict and anxiety into the language of learning theory and conditioning in ways that could be tested in experiments with animals. Their attempts to study Freud's ideas in rigorous experiments with rats are presented at the start of the first chapter in this part.

To apply the principles of learning to the study of personality, researchers also drew on earlier work in experimental psychology. That work, beginning with Pavlov in Russia, had shown how emotional reactions, both positive and negative, to previously neutral stimuli may be acquired through simple conditioning principles. The excitement here was that the analysis of learning promised to become a more scientific way of understanding some of the complex phenomena that had been discovered by Freud and his followers.

Learning, of course, occurs in various ways, and another breakthrough came in the contributions of the behaviorist B.F. Skinner and his many disciples. Not unlike Freud, Skinner also was often attacked, and often with good reason. Nevertheless, he provided a novel way for thinking about personality and above all for applying the principles of learning to improve the human condition, as described in this part of the text.

Because of the intense focus on behavior in the work done at this level, one may ask: The behavioral level seems to be all about *behavior,* but what about personality? For researchers at this level, the route to changing anything on the "inside"—feelings, cognitions, personality—is by understanding the person's behavior and the "conditions that control it," and then using that knowledge to help the individual to behave in more adaptive, functional ways (e.g., O'Donohue and associates, 2001). They assume that if problematic behaviors like stutters, tics, debilitating fears, or inappropriate patterns of impulsive or over-controlling behaviors are modified appropriately, then the internal states and stable qualities of the individual will essentially "catch up" and also change. A person who could not speak in public but now can is likely to feel and become less shy, for example.

Work at the behavioral-conditioning level originated in experimental psychology and remained isolated from mainstream work in personality research for many years. More recently, as part of the emerging integration among the various levels of analysis, these contributions are being connected to developments at the other levels of analyses, as you will see in subsequent parts of the text, particularly when we turn to the social cognitive level that builds directly on it.

The Personal Side of the Science

Some questions at the behavioral-conditioning level you might ask about yourself:

▶ How are important behavior patterns, including emotions and fears, learned?

▶ How does what I do and feel depend on my earlier experiences?

▶ How can my behavior and feelings be modified by new learning experiences?

▶ Do aspects of my personality depend on the contexts in which I find myself?

▶ How am I different when with a good friend at school and when with my family at home for the holidays? Why?

10

BEHAVIORAL CONCEPTIONS

Within the broad boundaries set by human genes, what people become is influenced importantly by learning. Through learning, things that attract one person may come to repel another, just as one individual's passions may become another's nightmares. Much is known about human learning, and it can be harnessed to influence people for good or for ill.

In this chapter and in the next, you will find some approaches to personality that focus on the level of learning through conditioning. These approaches are called behavioral theories, or learning-conditioning theories, and several different varieties have been formulated. In this chapter, we will consider some of the original classic concepts of this approach; in later chapters, we will examine its more recent developments and applications.

Work relevant to personality conducted at this level has been done primarily by psychologists dedicated to the rigorous, scientific study of psychology, who were heavily influenced by research on the nature of the learning process. In work that began more than 75 years ago, they devoted themselves to the development of an experimental methodology. Their goal was to conduct research that was experimental and yet relevant to understanding complex social behavior and individual differences. Guided by strategies in other natural sciences, they began with careful study of learning and performance in lower animals in highly controlled laboratory situations. While some were fascinated by the bold speculations about the mind that were coming at the same time from theorists like Sigmund Freud, most were skeptical about the use of informal clinical methods. Rather than probe the dreams and free associations of neurotic patients or theorize broadly about human nature and society, these researchers sought a system that would be objectively testable, preferably by laboratory techniques.

Psychologists working at this level studied the learning mechanisms through which certain events—"stimuli"—become associated with particular behaviors or responses. Like all scientific theorists, they wanted to understand causes—in this case, learning or the ways in which stimuli become associated with responses. The basic assumptions of the learning theories may appear at first glance quite different from those of psychodynamic theories. Yet they try to provide complementary accounts of many of the same basic personality phenomena. To illustrate this fundamental interrelatedness of these different levels of analyses, we begin this chapter with what may be the most systematic attempt to translate some of Freud's ideas into the concepts and language of learning.

10.1 What causal factors in personality are the focus of the behavioral level of analysis?

▶ THE BEHAVIORAL APPROACH TO PSYCHODYNAMICS: DOLLARD AND MILLER

In this section, we will concentrate on the theory developed at Yale University in the late 1940s by John Dollard and Neal Miller, who were fascinated by Freud's bold speculations about the mind. But they were also skeptical about his informal clinical methods and were motivated to really test his ideas. We will call their orientation **psychodynamic behavior theory** because it is the major effort to integrate some of the fundamental ideas of Freudian psychodynamic theory with the concepts, language, and methods of experimental laboratory research on behavior and learning. Although this work began as a translation of Freud's core concepts into the language and ideas of theory, it went much beyond translation by also opening the way to extensive experimental research into the basic processes involved.

Primary Needs and Learning

In this learning reinterpretation, the newborn infant begins life with a set of *innate* or **primary biological needs,** such as the need for food and water, oxygen, and warmth. Satisfaction of these needs to some minimal degree is essential for the organism's survival. But although these needs are innate, the behaviors required to satisfy them involve learning.

The most casual observation of other cultures quickly reveals that there are almost endless ways to fulfill even such primary needs as hunger and thirst. Through learning, great variability develops in the ways in which needs are fulfilled. Consider, for example, food preferences: The gourmet dishes of one culture may be the causes of nausea in another. The same learned variability seen in food preferences is also found in standards of shelter, clothing aesthetics, and values when one compares different cultures.

Most human behaviors involve goals and incentives whose relations to innate needs are extremely remote. People seem to strive for such exceedingly diverse goals as money, status, power, love, charity, competence, mastery, creativity, self-realization, and so on—as was discussed in earlier chapters. These and many more strivings have been characterized and classified as human motives. Neal Miller and John Dollard explored the learning processes through which such motives may evolve from primary needs.

10.2 Describe the four central concepts in the learning process, according to Dollard and Miller.

Starting with the basic assumption that behavior is learned, Dollard and Miller (1950) constructed a learning theory to explain the wide range of behavior involved in normal personality, neurosis, and psychotherapy. In their view, the four important factors in the learning process are drive (motivation), cue (stimulus), response (act or thought), and reinforcement (reward). In its simplest form, their idea is that

> *In order to learn one must want something, notice something, do something, and get something (Miller & Dollard, 1941, p. 2).*

These four events correspond respectively to "drive," "cue," "response," and "reward" ("reinforcement"). Learning, in their view, is the process through which a particular response and a cue stimulus become connected.

Think of an animal in the psychologist's laboratory. Motivated by the *drive* of hunger, the animal engages in diffuse activity. At one point, the animal happens to see a lever *(cue)*. Its *response*, at first accidental, is to press the lever, and this action releases food into his cup. The animal eats the food at once, thereby reducing tension of his hunger drive *(reward* or *reinforcement)*. Now in the future when the animal is hungry, it is more likely to press the lever again: The association between the cue stimulus (the lever) and the response (pressing it) has been strengthened. On subsequent trials, the hungry animal will press the lever sooner. Let us consider each of the four components separately.

Drive. For Dollard and Miller (1950), any strong stimuli (internal or external) may impel action and thus serve as drives. The stronger the stimulus, the greater its **drive** or motivating function. A mild stimulus (such as the faint sound of a distant horn) does not motivate behavior as much as a strong stimulus (the blare of the horn near one's ear). Examples of strong stimuli are hunger pangs and pain-inducing noise—they motivate behavior. While any stimulus may become strong enough to act as a drive, certain classes of stimuli (such as hunger, thirst, fatigue, pain, and sex) are the primary basis for most motivation. These stimuli are "primary" or innate drives. The strength of the primary drives varies with the **conditions of deprivation:** The greater the deprivation, the stronger the drive. Like Freud, Dollard and Miller's theory of drives was based on a "hydraulic" or steam boiler model. The build up of a drive, like the steam in a boiler as the temperature rises, increasingly presses for release of discharge. When release occurs, the drive is reduced. Drive reduction is satisfying or "reinforcing" (as discussed further in the concept of "reinforcement" below).

10.3 Differentiate between primary and secondary drives. In what sense is fear both a learned response and a learned drive that can result in reinforcement?

Often the operation of primary drives is not easy to observe directly. Society generally protects its members from the unpleasant force of strong primary drives by providing for their reduction before they become overwhelming. Moreover, social inhibitions—for example, in the area of sex—may further prevent the direct or complete public expression of primary drives. Consequently, much visible behavior is motivated by already altered "secondary" or **learned drives.** It is these transformed motives that are most evident under conditions of modern society and that are important in civilized human behavior.

According to Dollard and Miller, these learned drives are acquired on the basis of the primary (unlearned, innate) drives and are elaborations of them. The acquisition of fear as a learned drive has been studied carefully. (Some of the specific mechanisms of such learning are discussed in detail in the next chapter.) A fear is learned if it occurs in response to previously neutral cues (e.g., a white room). A learned fear is also a drive in the sense that it motivates behavior (e.g., escape from the room), and its reduction is reinforcing.

In one study, rats were exposed to electric shock in a white compartment and were permitted to escape to a black compartment where there was no shock (Miller, 1948). Eventually the rats responded with fear to the white compartment alone (that is, without the shock). Even when the shock (primary drive stimulus) was no longer present, the animals learned new responses, such as pressing a lever or turning a wheel, in order to escape from the harmless white compartment. In commonsense terms, they behaved as if they were afraid of an objectively harmless stimulus. The motivation for this new learning lies, according to Miller and Dollard, in the learned fear of the white compartment. Thus, fear is conceptualized as both a learned response and a learned drive, and its reduction is considered to be a reinforcement.

Dollard and Miller's emphasis on drives, both "primary" and "secondary," is reminiscent of the Freudian emphasis on motives and impulses as the forces underlying behavior. While Freud's conceptualization stresses instinctual wishes, however, Dollard and Miller's makes room for many learned motives, whose roots are in primary drives.

Cue. "The drive impels a person to respond. Cues determine when he will respond, where he will respond and which response he will make" (Dollard & Miller, 1950, p. 32). The lunch bell, for example, functions as a **cue** for hungry schoolchildren to put away their books and get their lunchboxes. Cues may be auditory, visual, olfactory, and so on. They may vary in intensity, and various combinations of stimuli may function as cues. Changes, differences, and the direction and size of differences may be more distinctive cues than is an isolated stimulus. For example, a person may not know the absolute length of an unmarked line but yet be able to tell which of two lines is longer.

Response. Before a **response** to a cue can be rewarded and learned, it must of course occur. Dollar and Miller suggest ranking the organism's responses according to their probability of occurrence. They call this order the "initial hierarchy." Learning changes the order of responses in the hierarchy. An initially weak response, if properly rewarded, may come to occupy the dominant position. The new hierarchy produced by learning is termed the "resultant hierarchy." With learning and development, the hierarchy of responses becomes linked to language, and is heavily influenced by the culture in which social learning has occurred.

Reinforcement. A **reinforcement** is a specific event that strengthens the tendency for a response to be repeated. For Miller and Dollard, reinforcement involved **drive reduction** or tension reduction. Guided by their hydraulic or boiler model of drives, they believed that drives that are not released continue to build up like steam in the boiler, creating tension and pressing for discharge, as noted above. It is the reduction of tension—drive-reduction—that is the organism's goal: when it happens, it is reinforcing or rewarding.

A reduction of a drive reinforces any immediately preceding response. The reduction or avoidance of painful stimulation, and of learned fears or anxieties associated with pain and punishment, also may function as a reinforcement (Miller, 1948). Reinforcement is essential to the maintenance of a habit as well as to its learning.

10.4 According to Dollard and Miller, how do reinforcement and extinction occur?

Extinction is the gradual elimination of a tendency to perform a response; it occurs when that response is repeated without reinforcement. The time required to extinguish a habit depends on the habit's initial strength and on the conditions of the extinction situation. According to Dollard and Miller, extinction merely inhibits the old habit; it does not destroy it. If new responses performed during extinction are rewarded, they may be strengthened to the point where they supersede the old habit. For example, if a child is praised and rewarded for independent, autonomous play but consistently unrewarded (extinguished) when he or she dependently seeks help, the independent pattern will become predominant over the dependent one.

Later, Miller (1963) speculated about possible alternatives to his drive-reduction concept of reinforcement learning. His hypothesis of an alternative to drive reduction includes the tentative assumption of "activating" or "go" mechanisms in the brain. These "go" mechanisms, Miller conjectured, could be activated in a variety of ways (such as by thinking), not merely by the reduction of drives or noxious stimuli.

10.5 What is the basis for conflicts? What major forms do they take?

Conflict.   Individuals may experience **conflict** when they want to pursue two or more goals that are mutually exclusive. For example, a person may want to spend the evening with a friend but thinks he should prepare for an examination facing him the next morning; or she may want to express her anger at her parents but also does not want to hurt them. When an individual must choose among incompatible alternatives, he or she may undergo conflict.

Neal Miller's (1959) conceptualization of conflict, which is influenced by Lewin (1935), hypothesizes **approach** and **avoidance tendencies.** For example, in an **approach–approach conflict,** the person is torn, at least momentarily, between two desirable goals. Conversely, people often face **avoidance–avoidance conflicts** between two undesirable alternatives: to study tediously for a dull subject or flunk the examination, for example. The individual may wish to avoid both of these aversive events, but each time he starts to move away from his desk, he reminds himself how awful it would be to fail the test.

Some of the most difficult conflicts involve goals or incentives that are both positive and negative. These are the goals or incentives that are mixed feelings or ambivalent attitudes. For example, we may want the pleasure of gourmet treat but not the calories, or we may desire the fun of a vacation spree but not the expense, or we may love certain aspects of a parent but hate others.

Recall that approach–avoidance conflicts had a predominant place in Freud's hypotheses regarding intrapsychic clashes—for example, between id impulses and inhibitory anxieties. Just as conflict is central to Freud's conception of personality dynamics, so it is the core of Dollard and Miller's theory. But whereas Freud developed his ideas about conflict from inferences regarding id–ego–superego clashes in his neurotic patients, Dollard and Miller tested their ideas in controlled experiments with rats (e.g., Brown, 1942, 1948; Miller, 1959).

Briefly, the drive-conflict model proposes the simultaneous existence of drive-like forces (approach tendencies) and of inhibitory forces (avoidance tendencies). Predictions about behavior in an approach–avoidance conflict involve inferences about the strength of the approach tendencies and of the inhibiting forces, the resulting behavior being a function of their net effect. Within this general framework of drive-conflict theory, many formulations have been advanced that are similar to the intrapsychic conflicts between id impulses and ego defenses that are crucial in Freud's theory. Some of these ideas are still relevant in current work on approach and avoidance behaviors and will be discussed in that context (Chapter 17).

Neurotic Conflict: The Core

Freud conceptualized conflict and anxiety as fundamental for understanding personality, both normal and abnormal, and saw them as the core ingredients of neurotic behavior. In Freud's formulation, **neurotic conflict** involves a clash between id impulses seeking expression and internalized inhibitions that censor and restrain the expression of those impulses in accord with the culture's taboos. Dollard and Miller state the same basic ideas in the language of learning theory.

In their view of neurosis, strong fear (anxiety) is a learned drive that motivates a conflict concerning "goal responses" for other strong drives, such as sex or aggression—the impulses that also were basic for Freud. Specifically, when the neurotic person—or even the young child—begins to approach goals that might reduce such drives as sex or aggression, strong fear is elicited in him or her. Such fear may be elicited by thoughts relevant to the drive goals, as well as by any overt approach attempts. For example, sexual wishes or hostile feelings toward a parent may be frightening; hence a conflict ensues between the wishes and the fear triggered by their expression. These inhibitory fearful responses further prevent drive reduction, so that the blocked drives (such as sex and aggression) continue to "build up" to a higher level. The person is thus trapped in an unbearable neurotic conflict between frustrated, pent-up drives and the fear connected with approach responses relevant to their release.

The neurotic person in this dilemma may be stimulated simultaneously by the frustrated drives and by the fear that they evoke. The high drive state connected with this conflict produces "misery" and interferes with clear thinking, discrimination, and effective problem solving. The "symptoms" shown arise from the build up of the drives and of the fear that inhibits their release.

Anxiety and Repression. Like Freud, Dollard and Miller accept unconscious factors as critically important determinants of behavior, and, again like Freud, they give anxiety (or learned fear) a central place in dynamics. In their view, repression involves the learned response of **not-thinking** of something and is motivated by the secondary drive of fear. That is, due to past experiences, certain thoughts may have come to arouse fear as a result of their associations with pain or punishment. By not-thinking these thoughts, the fear stimuli are reduced and the response (of not-thinking) is further reinforced. Eventually, not-thinking (inhibiting, stopping, repressing) becomes anticipatory, in the sense that the individual avoids particular thoughts before they can lead to painful outcomes. This formulation is similar to Freud's idea that repression is the result of anxiety caused when unacceptable material starts to emerge from the unconscious to the conscious.

Dollard and Miller's account thus serves as a clear translation of the psychodynamic formulation of anxiety, repression, and defense into the terms of reinforcement learning theory. Defenses and symptoms (e.g., phobias, hysterical blindness) are reinforced by the immediate reduction of the fear drive. While the temporary effect of the symptom is drive reduction and momentary relief, its long-range effects may be debilitating. For example, a phobic symptom may prevent a person from working effectively and hence create new dilemmas, fear, guilt, and other conditions of high drive conflict.

Psychodynamic Behavior Theory. As was noted earlier, Freud constructed a theory of development without the benefit of learning concepts. He adopted a body of language and invented new terms that made it difficult to coordinate his theory with experimental psychology. Dollard and Miller demonstrated that this coordination could be achieved.

10.6 How did Dollard and Miller translate Freud's concept of neurotic conflict into learning theory terms?

10.7 How are anxiety and repression translated into learning theory terms? How does this approach explain repression?

10.8 Summarize the major contributions and criticisms of psychodynamic learning theory.

They drew on laboratory research with animals to devise a personality theory in learning terms that closely paralleled, and in many respects translated, Freudian theory. The psychodynamic emphasis on motives, on unconscious processes, and on internal conflicts and defenses, such as repression, remained largely unchanged. Many psychologists found Freud's basic ideas more congenial and easier to adopt when they were put into the language of learning and experimental psychology. Consequently, these concepts stimulated much research.

Other psychologists were troubled because the research by Miller and his colleagues was based mainly on animal studies. Indeed, this fact has earned it some of its greatest criticism over the years. Careful investigation carried out with a lower species, such as the rat, whose behavior is far removed from human problems, may not hold up when extrapolations are made to people. Many critics have objected that human social behavior is fundamentally different than the behavior of animals in the laboratory and therefore requires a different methodology. Some critics were repelled by the analogies between rat and person and believed that in the transition from the clinic to the laboratory, some of the most exciting features of Freud's view of people were lost. Of course the real test of a position is not its appeal to friends and critics, but the research and conceptual advances it produces.

We now turn to the basic research that provided the foundation for Miller and Dollard's theory, and that still is a basis for understanding how some important aspects of personality may develop, are maintained, and sometimes can be changed dramatically. It also offered a way of making irrational fears and some of the other phenomena Freud identified less mysterious and more open to scientific testing.

▶ CLASSICAL CONDITIONING: LEARNING EMOTIONAL ASSOCIATIONS

Strong human emotions, often seemingly irrational, including negative emotions such as intense fears, and positive feelings, as in attraction, love, and patriotism, may be acquired through the simple processes of classical conditioning. It is therefore important to understand the basic rules of conditioning because they help to take the mystery out of many of the complex emotions we all experience. Knowing these rules is especially useful because we often experience strong negative emotions without awareness of why and how they originated, or how we might be able to change our feelings when they create serious problems for us—like being unable to take a desired job because it happens to be on a high floor.

Classical conditioning or **conditioned-response learning** is a type of learning, first demonstrated by the Russian psychologist Ivan Pavlov, in which a neutral stimulus (for example, a bell) becomes conditioned by being paired or associated with an unconditioned stimulus (one that is naturally powerful).

How Classical Conditioning Works

A dog automatically salivates when food is in its mouth. The response of salivation is a **reflex** or **unconditioned response (UCR):** it is natural and does not have to be learned. Like most other reflexes, in humans and in animals alike, salivation helps the organism adjust or adapt: the saliva aids in digesting the food. Stimuli that elicit unconditioned responses are called **unconditioned stimuli (UCS).** The unconditioned stimulus (food in this example) can elicit behavior without any prior learning.

Any dog owner knows that a hungry dog may salivate at the mere sight of food, before it gets any in its mouth. The dog may even begin to salivate at the sight of the empty dish in which the food is usually served. Salivating at the sight of the empty dish that has been associated with food is an example of a learned or **conditioned response (CR)**. The stimulus that elicits a conditioned response is called a **conditioned** (learned) **stimulus (CS)**: its impact on behavior is not automatic but depends on learning.

Pavlov discovered some of the ways in which such neutral stimuli as lights and metronome clicks could become conditioned stimuli capable of eliciting responses like salivating. His pioneering experiments with dogs began with his repeatedly making a certain sound whenever he gave his dogs their food. After a while he found that the dogs salivated to the sound even when it was no longer followed by food: conditioning had occurred. This type of learning is what we now call classical conditioning.

To sum up, in classical conditioning the participant is repeatedly exposed to a neutral stimulus (that is, one that elicits no special response) together with an unconditioned stimulus that elicits an unconditioned response. When this association becomes strong enough, the neutral stimulus by itself may begin to elicit a response similar to the one produced by the unconditioned stimulus. (See Tables 10.1 and 10.2 for basic definitions and examples.)

10.9 Define UCS, UCR, CS, and CR. How are conditioned responses learned?

Higher-Order Conditioning

We have seen that when a previously neutral stimulus, such as a light, a bell, or a face, has become a conditioned stimulus through its association with an unconditioned stimulus, such as food or pain, it can in turn modify one's reactions to another neutral stimulus by being associated with it. This process is called **higher-order conditioning.** It was demonstrated when Pavlov found that after a metronome sound had

10.10 How does higher-order conditioning underlie many of our likes and dislikes?

Ivan Pavlov (1849–1936)

TABLE 10.1   The Language of Classical Conditioning

Term	Definition
Unconditioned stimulus (UCS)	A stimulus to which one automatically, naturally responds without learning to do so.
Unconditioned response (UCR)	The unlearned response one naturally makes to an unconditioned stimulus. The response may be positive or negative (e.g., salivating when food is placed in the mouth; jerking one's hand away from a hot stove).
Conditioned stimulus (CS)	A previously neutral stimulus to which one learns to respond after it has been paired or associated with an unconditioned stimulus.
Conditioned response (CR)	The learned response to a conditioned stimulus. This response was previously made only to an unconditioned stimulus, but now it is made to a conditioned stimulus as a result of the pairing of the two stimuli.

become a conditioned stimulus (by being paired with food), it could itself be paired with a neutral stimulus (such as a black triangle) and, as a result of that association, the neutral stimulus would also elicit the unconditioned response of salivation. In people, words and other complex symbols can be powerful conditioned stimuli capable of evoking emotional responses through higher-order conditioning.

A wide variety of stimuli, including activities, individuals, groups, and events, are valued according to their associations with positive or negative outcomes and even mere labels. For example, when neutral items are paired with words like "dirty" and "ugly," they take on negative valuations, but the same items become positively evaluated when they have been associated with words like "beautiful" and "happy" (Staats & Staats, 1957). Likewise, the names of countries and political parties and the sight of national flags, or the sounds of national anthems can come to arouse intense positive or negative feelings depending on their earlier associations.

TABLE 10.2   Examples of Possible Effects of Classical Conditioning

Before Conditioning	After Conditioning
Dog knocks child over (UCS) Child cries (UCR)	Dog approaches (CS) Child cries (CR)
Mother feeds and cuddles baby (UCS) Baby relaxes (UCR)	Baby smells mother's perfume (CS) Baby relaxes (CR)
Car accident injures woman (UCS) Woman is afraid (UCR)	Woman thinks about getting in car (CS) Woman is afraid (CR)
Man drives across swaying bridge (UCS) Man is afraid (UCR)	Man approaches another bridge (CS) Man is afraid and avoids bridge (CR)
Mother discovers her daughter masturbating, scolds her, slaps her hands (UCS) Daughter is hurt and afraid (UCR)	Daughter looks at her nude body (CS) Daughter feels anxious and negative about her body, particularly her genitals (CR)

Most experiments in classical conditioning are performed in the laboratory, but the knowledge they have generated may help us to understand many things that happen outside the laboratory, such as the development of affections and attractions (Byrne, 1969; Lott & Lott, 1968). For example, a liking for particular people and things may depend on the degree to which they have been associated with positive or pleasant experiences (Griffitt & Guay, 1969). If so, one's affection for a friend may be directly related to the degree to which he or she has been associated with gratifications for oneself.

Now consider the development of fear. How do initially neutral (or even positive) stimuli acquire the power to evoke fear? Suppose, for example, a person repeatedly sees a light and experiences an electric shock simultaneously. In time, the light by itself may come to evoke some of the emotional reaction produced by the shock. Neutral stimuli that are closely associated in time with any pain-producing stimulus then become conditioned stimuli that may elicit fear and avoidance reactions. Thus, the seemingly irrational fears that some people have may reflect a conditioned association between previously neutral stimuli and painful events.

Classical conditioning may influence development throughout a person's life. If, for example, sexual curiosity and fear-producing experiences (such as severe punishment) are closely associated for a child, fear may be generated by various aspects of the individual's sexual behavior even after there is no longer any danger of punishment. And conditioning can spread as well as persist: the child who is made to feel bad about touching the genitals may also become anxious about other forms of sexual expression and may even develop broader fears.

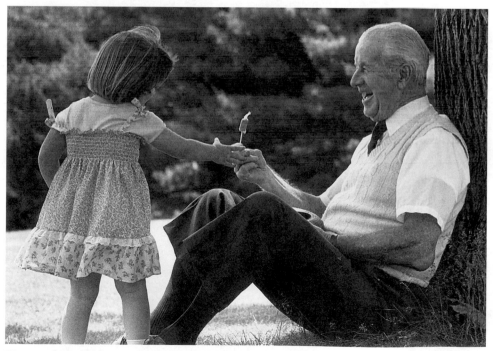

How much we like a person may depend on the degree to which he or she has been associated with gratification.

In a classic study, following a strategy that would not be tolerated now because of the ethical issues it raises, Watson and Rayner (1920) induced a severe fear of rats in a little boy named Albert, who had not been afraid of rats before. This was done by classical conditioning: just as Albert would reach for the rat, the experimenters would make a loud noise that frightened him. After he had experienced the rat and the aversive noise several times in close association, he developed a strong fear of the rat.

Albert's fear generalized so that later, when shown a variety of new furry stimuli such as cats, cotton, fur coats, human hair, and wool, he responded with obvious fear to them as well. His fear had spread to these new objects even though they had never been paired with the noise. This is a human example of the kind of learning found when rats who were shocked in a white compartment began to respond fearfully to the compartment itself even when the shock no longer occurred (Miller, 1948). The case of Little Albert has become one of the first bases for applications of classical conditioning to the analysis and treatment of human problems.

10.11 Compare Freud's analysis of Little Hans with the behavioral reinterpretation of the case.

As the In Focus 10.1 example illustrates, the behavioral view of neurosis is concerned with anxiety and avoidance no less than the psychodynamic view, but it tries to link them to external circumstances rather than to internal conflicts (Redd, 1995; Redd, Porterfield, & Anderson, 1978). Through direct or vicarious frightening experiences, people often develop anxiety in response to particular objects, persons, or

---

IN FOCUS 10.1

A BEHAVIORAL CHALLENGE TO THE PSYCHODYNAMIC THEORY OF NEUROSIS

Differences between theoretical approaches are seen most clearly when applied to the same case. Behavior theorists have strongly challenged Freud's theory of neurosis by reanalyzing in learning terms a case that he presented. Recall that Freud's view of how neuroses develop begins with the child's aggressive or sexual impulses, which seek direct, immediate release. Because expression of these impulses may be punished severely, the child may become anxious about his own impulses and try to repress them. But the impulses continue to seek release and become increasingly pent up. Eventually they may be impossible to repress, and components of them may break through, creating further anxiety. To reduce this anxiety, the person may attempt a variety of defense mechanisms. In neurosis, these defenses begin to break down: the unacceptable impulses start to express themselves indirectly and symbolically in various disguised forms, such as in phobias or obsessive–compulsive thoughts and actions. The roots of neurosis, in Freud's view, are always in childhood:

It seems that neuroses are acquired only in early childhood (up to the age of six), even though their symptoms may not make their appearance till much later. The childhood neurosis may become manifest for a short time or may even be overlooked. In every case the later neurotic illness

links up with the prelude in childhood (Freud, 1933, pp. 41–42).

An example from Freud's (1963) theory is his published case of Little Hans. Hans was a five-year-old boy who developed a horse phobia. He was afraid of being bitten by a horse and, after seeing a horse hitched to a wagon slip and fall on a street near his home, began to dread going out. Freud interpreted the phobia as an expression of the child's psychodynamic conflicts. These conflicts included his desires to seduce his mother and replace his father. These desires, in turn, made him fear castration by the father; symbolically, the horse came to represent the dreaded father.

A behavioral analysis of this case, however, explains Hans's phobia without invoking any internal conflicts or symbolism (Wolpe, 1997; Wolpe & Rachman, 1960). Namely, the scene Hans witnessed of a horse falling down and bleeding on the street was sufficiently frightening to the young child to produce fear. In turn, the fear generalized to all horses and resulted in Hans's avoidance behavior. Thus, a simple conditioning process might explain a phobia: since the horse was part of an intensely frightening experience, it became a conditioned stimulus for anxiety, and the anxiety generalized to other horses. The process is the same as in the case of Little Albert whose fear was induced by conditioning, as discussed in the text.

situations. Not only encountering these events in reality but even just thinking about them may be upsetting. These emotional reactions may generalize and take many forms. Common examples include muscle tensions, fatigue, and intense fear reactions to seemingly neutral stimuli.

Psychodynamic and behavioral theorists do agree that the neurotic individual may make all sorts of efforts to escape and avoid painful feelings. Many of his avoidance attempts may be maintained persistently because they serve to terminate the pain. For example, such elaborate avoidance defenses as obsessive–compulsive rituals, in the form of handwashing for many hours, may be maintained because they reduce the person's anxiety (Wolpe, 1963). In addition, attention and sympathy from relatives and friends for being sick or relief from pressures and obligations can also serve to maintain the anxious person's avoidance patterns by providing reinforcement for them.

From Trauma to Anxiety

Some of the clearest examples of anxiety reactions occur after the individual has experienced a threatening danger or trauma. A near-fatal automobile accident, an almost catastrophic combat experience, an airplane crash—such intense episodes of stress are often followed by anxiety. After the actual dangers have passed, stimuli that remind the individual of those dangers, or signs that lead him or her to expect new dangers, may reactivate anxiety and distort perceptions (e.g., Rachman & Cuk, 1992).

After severe trauma, the victim is more likely to respond anxiously to other stress stimuli that occur later in life (Archibald & Tuddenham, 1965; Milgram, 1993). Surviving victims of Nazi concentration camps, for example, sometimes continued for years to be hypersensitive to threat stimuli and to react to stress readily with anxiety and sleep disturbances (Chodoff, 1963). These observations support the idea that anxiety involves a learned fear reaction that is highly resistant to extinction and that may be evoked by diverse stimuli similar to those that originally were traumatic. That is, the fear evoked by the traumatic stimuli may be reactivated and also may *generalize* to stimuli associated with the traumatic episode. For example, after a child has been attacked and bitten by a dog, her fear reaction may generalize to other dogs, animals, fur, places similar to the one in which the attack occurred, and so on (Fig. 10.1). Moreover, if the generalization stimuli are very remote from the original traumatic stimulus, the person may be unable to see the connection between the two and the anxiety may appear (even to her) particularly irrational. Suppose, for example, that the child becomes afraid of the room in which the dog bit her and of similar rooms. If the connection between her new fear of rooms and the dog's attack is not recognized, the fear of rooms now may seem especially bizarre.

From a learning point of view, anxieties after traumas, like other learned fears, may be acquired through simple association or conditioning principles. If neutral stimuli have been associated with aversive events or outcomes, then they also may come to elicit anxiety in their own right. Such aversively conditioned emotional reactions may also generalize extensively to new stimuli (Fig. 10.1). Clinical examples of aversive arousal and avoidance include many phobic and anxious reactions to objects, people, and social and interpersonal situations. Not only external events, but also their symbolic representations in the form of words or of thoughts and fantasies, may create painful emotions. In our example of the child traumatized by the dog, even thinking about the incident, or the room in which it occurred or similar rooms may terrify the youngster.

Stimuli closer or more relevant to those associated with emotional arousal tend to elicit stronger reactions. In one study, novice sports parachutists and members of the control group took a specially constructed word association test (Epstein & Fenz, 1962;

10.12 Why are trauma victims more reactive to later life stresses?

Figure 10.1   From trauma to anxiety.

Fenz, 1964). The words contained four levels of relevance to parachuting. Throughout the word association tests, participants' physiological reactions (*galvanic skin response*, or *GSR*, which as discussed earlier is a change in electrical activity of the skin due to sweating) were recorded to measure their emotional arousal in response to the various stimulus words. One testing occurred two weeks before the scheduled jump, another testing was done the day before the jump, and a final test was on the day of the parachute jump.

The results showed more arousal in parachutists for parachute-relevant words. The effect was greatest for the words most relevant to parachuting, and their arousal was highest when the testing time was closer to the emotion-arousing parachute jump itself.

▶ INSTRUMENTAL (OPERANT) CONDITIONING: LEARNING FROM RESPONSE CONSEQUENCES

The work of Pavlov and the many others who explored the implications of classical conditioning showed how emotional reactions, both positive and negative, to previously neutral stimuli may be acquired through the process of close association with unconditioned stimuli. But learning takes place in more than one form, and a second type, called instrumental or operant conditioning, provides another foundation for understanding the role of experience and social learning for the development of personality.

How Instrumental or Operant Conditioning Works

10.13 How does operant conditioning differ from classical conditioning?

Behavior is modified by its consequences: the outcome of any response (or pattern of responses, often called **operants** for how the organism "operates" on the environment) determines how likely it is that similar responses will be performed in the future. If a response has favorable (reinforcing) consequences, the organism is more likely to perform it again in similar situations. Contrary to some widespread misconceptions, reinforcers or favorable outcomes are not restricted to such primitive rewards as food pellets or sexual satisfactions. Almost all events may serve as reinforcers, including such cognitive gratifications as information (Jones, 1966) or the achievement of competence. Such learning, based on the consequences produced by responses, is called **operant conditioning** (or, in earlier usage, trial-and-error or **instrumental learning**).

TABLE 10.3   Summary of Two Types of Learning

Type	Arrangement	Effect	Example	Interpretation
Classical conditioning	A neutral stimulus (e.g., a bell) repeatedly and closely precedes a powerful unconditioned stimulus (e.g., food).	The originally neutral stimulus becomes a conditioned stimulus—that is, acquires some of the impact of the powerful unconditioned stimulus.	Bell begins to elicit a salivary response, even when not paired with food.	Organism learns that the conditioned stimulus (bell) signals (predicts) the occurrence of the unconditioned stimulus (food).
Instrumental (Operant) conditioning	A freely emitted response (operant) is repeatedly followed by a favorable outcome (reinforcement).	The operant increases in frequency.	If crying is followed by attention, its frequency is increased.	Organism learns that this response will produce that particular outcome.

When the consequences of a response pattern change, the probability of it and of similar response patterns occurring again also changes (Nemeroff & Karoly, 1991). If a little boy whines and clings to his mother and she drops everything in an attempt to appease him, the chances increase that he will behave in this way in the future. If she systematically ignores the behavior, however, and consistently fails to react to it, the chances decrease that the child will continue to behave this way.

Summary of Two Types of Learning

Table 10.3 summarizes the two types of learning discussed so far: classical conditioning and operant conditioning. There is much overlap between these types of learning, but each has some relatively distinct features, as indicated in the table, and each has a place within current social learning theory.

▶ B. F. SKINNER'S INFLUENCE ON PERSONALITY

The motivational-drive theory of Miller and Dollard provided an account of human personality that gave motivation an important role. It also allowed a learning reinterpretation of many of the motivational concepts that Freud invoked in his psychoanalytic theory. But while the motivational focus of Miller and Dollard spoke to the interests of many clinical psychologists, it was rejected within learning theory by the highly influential American behaviorist, B. F. Skinner. Skinner and his followers wanted to find a level of analysis that was entirely objective and required no inferences about underlying mental processes.

In Skinner's view of science, we can know people only by examining their behavior—the things they say and do. In a sense, all psychological approaches are based on the study of behavior, but they differ in how the behavior is used. For example, in analyses at the trait level, behaviors are used as signs for inferring the person's traits or attributes from the observable things the individual does. In the behavioral approach favored by B. F. Skinner and many of his students, however, the observed behavior is the basic unit, and the interest is in specifying the conditions and stimuli or situations that "control" it. The concept that the stimulus controls the response is called **stimulus control.**

In this tradition, behaviorists tried to sample the individual's behaviors directly but generally were reluctant to interpret them as signs (indicators) of the person's motives or other attributes. For example, from this perspective one might try to sample Gary's behaviors to find out just what he does before speeches, without drawing any inferences from them about his underlying anxiety, insecurity, or other personal qualities. To the degree that theorists limit themselves to behavior, their definition of personality itself becomes equated with the whole of an individual's behaviors: *the person "is" what the person "does."*

Importance of the Situation

10.14 What is meant by stimulus control of behavior?

Work at this level of analysis gives particular importance to the role of stimuli and situations in the regulation of behavior, including behaviors indicative of personality. Because the strategy used is often experimental, these stimuli are simply green or red lights or tones that have become associated with certain qualities through manipulated learning experiences. But evidence for the important role of the situation in social behavior and even as a determinant of how we perceive other people also comes from more naturalistic social experiments.

Psychologists guided by this approach point out that often behavior may be predicted simply from knowledge about relevant conditions. Consider, for example, studies that tried to predict the post-hospital adjustment of mental patients. Accurate predictions of post-hospital adjustment required knowledge of the environment in which the ex-patient would be living in the community—such as the availability of jobs and family support—rather than any measures of person variables or in-hospital behavior (e.g., Fairweather, 1967; Fairweather et al., 1969; Holahan & Moos, 1990).

Likewise, to predict intellectual achievement it helps to take into account the degree to which the child's environment supports (models and reinforces) intellectual development (Wolf, 1966). And to predict whether or not people respond to stress with illness, it helps to know the degree to which they have social supports (e.g., spouse, family) in their environments (Holahan & Moos, 1990; Nilson et al., 1981). Finally, when powerful treatments are developed, predictions about outcomes may be useful when based simply on knowing the treatment to which the individual is assigned (e.g., Bandura, Blanchard, & Ritter, 1969; Bandura, 1986).

In daily life, different people are exposed to extremely different kinds of situations, often in stable ways. The life of a college student contains sets of situations that may importantly influence not only what the students do but also in time, through their interactions with those situations, what they become (Cantor et al., 2002). Imagine a day in the life of a New York City taxi driver, or that of a monk, a professor, a company executive, or a hairdresser, and the differences in the kinds of situations they must encounter, day in and day out. Such differences are not limited to occupational and social role differences. A person with an irritating, defensive style of social interaction is likely to provoke different reactions from others compared to a person with a more agreeable style.

A dramatic illustration of the power of the situation and the social role it assigns to one is seen in a natural experiment that was considered shocking at the time (Rosenhan, 1973). Normal individuals (doctors, psychologists, and graduate students from Stanford University) admitted themselves to the local mental hospital by complaining of various psychiatric symptoms. Then, during their confinement, they proceeded to behave rationally, which they normally were. From the moment that they were admitted to the hospital, these individuals were consistently treated by the professional hospital staff (who did not know their true identity) as if they were insane, and labeled psychotic. Their rational, normal behavior not withstanding, they were still treated as insane by the staff, although some of the other patients suspected that they did not really belong there. Staff observations of the Stanford group included notes about their obsessive intellectualizing—frantically scribbling notes, and so on.

Rejection of Inferred Motives

To explain behavior, many earlier theorists hypothesized a wide range of human motives. Theories concerning motivation have helped to reveal the variety and complexity of human strivings, and also have contributed to the development of research about their causes. Investigators of motives originally were inspired by the model of experimental research on biological drives in animals. In animal studies of motivation, the hypothesized need of the animal (its hunger or sex drive, for example) has been linked clearly to observable conditions manipulated in the laboratory. For example, the strength of the hunger drive may be inferred in part from the amount of time that the animal has been deprived of food. When a dog has not been fed for two days, we may safely say that it has a high hunger drive. In such cases, references to drives and motives are straightforward. Likewise, some careful investigations of hypothesized higher-order motives in people have specified clearly the objective conditions that define the motive (e.g., Emmons, 1997; McClelland, 1992; McClelland et al., 1953).

10.15 Why did Skinner reject motives and inner conflicts as causes of behavior?

Less rigorous applications of motivational theory to personality, however, may use motives loosely (e.g., as "wishes" or "desires"), and their value as explanations of behavior is open to question—and Skinner took the lead in raising those questions for many years. In his view, the tendency to invoke motives as explanations of why people behave as they do is understandable, because that is how we "explain" behavior in commonsense terms. To explain why a child spent an unusual amount of time cleaning and grooming himself neatly, we easily might say "because he had strong cleanliness needs" or "because he had a compulsive desire for order."

Such hypotheses about motives may sound like explanations, but they tell us little unless the motive is defined objectively and unless the causes of the motive itself are established. What makes the child have "cleanliness needs"? What determines his "compulsive desires"? Why does she "wish" to be clean? These are the kinds of questions raised by B. F. Skinner, who worked for many years at Harvard University.

A pioneer in the behavioral approach, Skinner criticized many concepts regarding human needs as being no more than motivational labels attached to human activities. Thus, orderly behavior may be attributed to a motive for orderliness, submissive behavior to submissiveness needs, exploratory behavior to the need to explore, and so on. To avoid such circular reasoning and to untangle explaining from naming, behaviorally oriented psychologists like Skinner prefer to analyze behaviors in terms of the observable events and conditions that seem to vary with them. Hence, they refuse to posit specific motivations for behavior. Rather, they try to discover the external events that strengthen its future likelihood and that maintain or change it. This approach leads to questions like: When does that child's cleaning activity increase, and when does it decrease in relation to observable changes in the environment? For example, how do the reactions of the parents influence the behavior?

For Skinner, psychology is the science of behavior: inferences about unobservable states and motives are not adequate explanations, and they add nothing to a scientific

B. F. Skinner (1904–1990)

account of the conditions controlling behavior. "Motivation" is simply the result of depriving or satiating an organism of some substance such as water or food for a given period of time. Thus, a "drive" is just a convenient way of referring to the observable effects of such deprivation or satiation. Likewise, Skinner avoids any inferences about internal "conflicts," preferring an experimental analysis of the stimulus conditions that seem to control the particular behavior in the situation. In his words:

> *Man, we once believed, was free to express himself in art, music, and literature, to inquire into nature, to seek salvation in his own way. He could initiate action and make sponta-neous and capricious changes of course. . . . But science insists that action is initiated by forces impinging upon the individual, and that caprice is only another name for behavior for which we have not yet found a cause (Skinner, 1955, pp. 52–53).*

The essence of Skinner's behavioristic view is the belief that our behavior is shaped by the external environment, not by motives, dispositions, or "selves" that are "in" the person.

Identifying Stimuli (Situations) Controlling Behavior

10.16 What is involved in a functional analysis of behavior?

Skinner's work is based on the premise that a genuine science of human behavior is not only possible but desirable. In his view, science should try to predict and determine experimentally the behavior of the individual organism (Skinner, 1974).

Skinner proposed a **functional analysis** of the organism as a behaving system. Such an analysis tries to link the organism's behavior to the precise conditions that control or determine it. Skinner's approach therefore concentrates on the observable covariations between independent variables (stimulus events) and dependent variables (response patterns). The variables in a functional analysis, according to Skinner, must be external, observable, and described in physical and quantitative terms. It will not do to say that a child becomes concerned with cleanliness when she "fears her father's disapproval"; one must specify the exact ways that changes in the father's specific behavior (e.g., his praise) are related to specific changes in what the child does (e.g., how much she washes her hands per hour).

Skinner contends that the laboratory offers the best chance of obtaining a scientific analysis of behavior; in it, variables can be brought under the control of experimental manipulation. Furthermore, the experimental study of behavior has much to gain from dealing with the behavior of animals below the complex human level. Science, Skinner points out, advances from the simple to the complex and is constantly concerned with whether the processes and laws discovered at one stage are adequate for the next.

Skinner incorporated into his position many concepts regarding classical conditioning, but he concentrated on another kind of learning that is different in some ways from classical conditioning. He contends (1953) that most human social behavior consists of freely emitted response patterns, or operants. Even a little baby shows much spontaneous behavior: it reaches up to a mobile, turns its head, looks at objects, cries and gurgles, and moves its arms and legs. Through such operants, the organism operates on its environment, changing it and, in turn, being changed by it.

In research on operant conditioning, the typical experiment involves an animal or a person freely performing (emitting) operant responses. The experimenter has preselected a particular class of responses to reinforce (e.g., a young child successfully using a potty-training chair or an adult using personal pronouns in an interview). When the selected operant response is made (the child urinates in the potty or the adult says, "I," "you," "she," and so on), the reinforcement occurs: the child gets a small toy; the interviewer nods or murmurs "good." Figure 10.2 illustrates what happens in operant conditioning.

The outcomes a person obtains for a particular behavior influence his or her future behavior. A child's refusal to eat may gain attention from a father usually too busy to pay the child much attention. Since the child's behavior is reinforced by the attention, she may refuse to eat again. If she is offered special treat foods in an effort to tempt her,

	Operant responses	Consequences
Stage 1	R_1	None
	R_*	Reward
Person A in Situation 1	R_2	None
	R_3	None
	R_4	None
Stage 2		
Person A in Situation 1 —— Increased probability ——	R_*	

Figure 10.2 Operant conditioning: Skinner's view. A person performs (emits) many operant responses in any given situation. If one operant is followed by a favorable outcome (reward) in that situation, the person will be more likely to perform that operant again in a similar situation.

she may quickly turn into a finicky eater with limited food preferences. By changing the outcomes of responses, reinforcing previously unreinforced behaviors or discontinuing reinforcement for other behaviors, even behavior patterns that seem deeply ingrained may be changed.

10.17 How are operant techniques used to change behavior?

Influenced by Skinner, many psychologists have tried to modify maladaptive behavior by altering the consequences to which it leads. Working with people who have severe behavioral problems, they attempt to remove reinforcement for disadvantageous behavior and to make attention, praise, or other reinforcement contingent on the occurrence of more adaptive advantageous behavior. Learning programs of this type follow a set of definite steps. First, the problem behaviors are carefully defined and their frequency in a naturalistic context is measured. Next, one observes and records the reinforcing consequences that seem to maintain the behaviors. Guided by this analysis, the relearning program is designed and put into effect. Finally, the resulting changes are assessed over a period of time.

For example, in one case, parents sought help because their three-year-old daughter developed regressive behaviors and reverted to crawling rather than walking. This regression produced serious problems for the child and the family. An analysis of the girl's behavior suggested that her regressive, babyish actions were being encouraged and maintained unwittingly by the attention they brought her. Therefore, an effort was made to rearrange the response–reinforcement patterns so that crawling and infantile acts were not rewarded by the attention of worried adults. Instead, attention and other rewards were made contingent on more adaptive and age-appropriate behaviors, such as jumping, running, and walking, thereby increasing these desirable behaviors while the infantile ones decreased (Harris et al., 1964).

Conditioned Generalized Reinforcers

10.18 How are conditioned generalized reinforcers created?

As noted before, neutral stimuli may acquire value and become conditioned reinforcers when they become associated with other stimuli that already have reinforcing properties. **Conditioned reinforcers** become generalized when they are paired with more than one primary reinforcer. A good example of a conditioned generalized reinforcer is money, because it can provide so many different primary gratifications (food, shelter, comfort, medical help, and alleviation of pain). Gradually, generalized reinforcers may become quite potent even when the primary reinforcers upon which they were initially based do not accompany them any more. Some people, for example, seem to learn to love money for its own sake and work to amass "paper profits" that they never trade in for primary rewards.

Some generalized reinforcers are obvious—like money—but others are subtle and involve complex social relationships. Attention and social approval from people who are likely to supply reinforcement—such as parents, a loved one, or a teacher—often are especially strong **generalized reinforcers.**

Discrimination and Generalization in Everyday Life

10.19 Define generalization and discrimination. Provide an example of a discriminative stimulus in your own life.

Discriminative stimuli indicate when an operant response will or will not have favorable consequences. Without such signals we would not know in advance the outcomes to which different behaviors are likely to lead and life would be chaotic. With the help of discriminative stimuli we learn to stop the car when coming to a railroad crossing; to eat certain foods with forks and spoons and to continue to eat others with our fingers; to shout and cheer at football games, but not at course examinations; to wear warmer clothes when the temperature starts to drop and to shed them when it becomes hot; to stop at red traffic lights and to go when they turn green.

When a particular response or pattern of responses is reinforced in the presence of one stimulus but not in the presence of others, discrimination occurs. It may be all right to belch in your own room when alone or with close friends but less acceptable to do so when talking to a faculty advisor in her office, and people soon get feedback that makes this clear to them. Discrimination results from the reinforcement or condoning of behavior in some situations but not in others. The individual is more likely to display the behavior in those situations in which it will probably be reinforced than in those in which it is unlikely to be reinforced.

If a response pattern is uniformly rewarded in many conditions or situations, **generalization** occurs. For example, a child is likely to develop generalized aggressive patterns if he is encouraged or allowed to behave aggressively with his parents and teachers as well as with his siblings and classmates both when he is at school and at home. Generalization depends on the similarity among stimulus situations. Stimuli that are physically similar or that have similar meanings result in the greatest generalization.

From the behavioral perspective, the socialization of children is based on discrimination training. For example, children must learn to control their bowel and bladder functions so that defecation and urination occur only in some situations and not in others. Active exploration of the toy box or the sandbox is permitted and encouraged, while forays into the medicine chest or mother's jewel box have quite different outcomes. As a result of such **discrimination training,** the child's behavior begins to depend on the specific conditions in which it unfolds.

When behavior yields similar consequences in a broad variety of settings, it can be expected to generalize from one situation to another. For example, if a little girl easily gets help in solving problems at home, at school, with parents, teachers, and siblings, she may develop widespread dependency. In contrast, when certain behaviors, such as

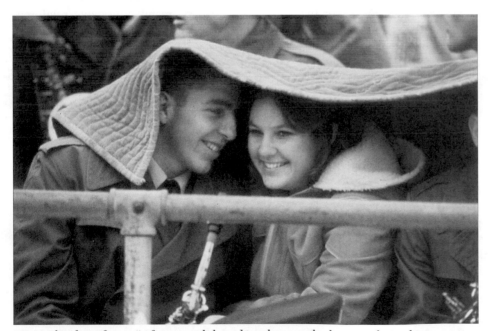

"Generalized reinforcers" often are subtle and involve complex human relationships.

curiosity, are punished in some situations but not in others, consistencies across the different situations should not be expected. A child becomes increasingly discriminating as the various roles of sibling, student, lover, and many more are learned. Each of these roles implies its own distinct set of appropriate behaviors in particular situations.

Shaping Behavior by Successive Approximations

10.20   How is shaping of behavior accomplished?

Before a response can be reinforced, it must occur. Extremely complex responses, such as saying new words in a foreign language, are unlikely ever to be performed spontaneously by the learner. If you do not know how to say "How do you do?" in Greek, you are unlikely ever to come out with the right phrase spontaneously, no matter how many sounds you utter. To try to overcome this problem, and to help an organism form new responses, Skinnerians often use a procedure called "shaping."

Shaping is a technique for producing successively closer approximations to a particular desired behavior. It consists of carefully observing and immediately rewarding any small variations of the behavior in the desired direction as they are spontaneously performed by the organism. At first, a large class of responses is reinforced; then gradually the class is narrowed, and reinforcement is given only for closer approximations to the final form of the desired behavior. For example, when teaching a pigeon to stand only in the center of a large bull's-eye target painted on the floor, one might reward the bird for standing increasingly close to the center.

The Patterning of Outcomes: Schedules of Reinforcement

10.21   Describe the effects of schedules of reinforcement on learning and extinction of behaviors.

The patterning, sequencing, or scheduling of reinforcement affects the future occurrence and strength of the reinforced behavior (Ferster & Skinner, 1957). Sometimes the scheduling of reinforcement may be even more important than the nature of the reinforcer (Morse & Kelleher, 1966). Continuous reinforcement usually increases the speed with which responses are learned. Intermittent reinforcement tends to produce more stable behavior that is more persistently maintained when reinforcement stops. For example, rewarding temper tantrums intermittently (by occasionally attending to them in an irregular pattern) may make them very durable. Since many potentially maladaptive behaviors, such as physical aggression and immature dependency, are rewarded intermittently, they can become very hard to eliminate (Plaud & Gaither, 1996).

Different schedules have different influences on operant responses. Operant strength is measured by the rate of responses: the more frequently a response is made in a given period of time, the greater its rate (and inferred strength).

Continuous reinforcement (CRF) is a schedule on which a behavior is reinforced every time it occurs. Responses are usually learned most quickly with continuous reinforcement. A child would become toilet trained more quickly if he were praised and rewarded for each successful attempt. While continuous reinforcement is easy to create in a laboratory, in life it is a rare experience; a partial reinforcement or intermittent schedule, in which a response is reinforced only some of the time, is much more common. We see partial reinforcement when a child's bids for attention succeed only occasionally in getting the parent to attend, or when the same sales pitch produces a sale once in a while, or when the gambler hits the jackpot but only in between many losing bets.

Behavior that has received **partial reinforcement** or **intermittent reinforcement** often becomes hard to eliminate even when reinforcement is withdrawn altogether. A mother who intermittently and irregularly gives in to her child's nighttime bids for attention (crying, calling for a drink of water, or for just one more story) may find the child's behavior very durable and unresponsive to her attempts to stop it by ignoring it. Many potentially maladaptive behaviors (facial tics, physical aggression, immature dependency) are hard to eliminate because they are rewarded intermittently.

The child with a speck of grit in her eye who successfully follows her father's instruction to blink to get it out may keep on blinking periodically long after the eye is clear of irritation. If her blinks are further reinforced by her parents' occasional attention (whether troubled concern or agitated pleas to "stop doing that!"), she may develop an unattractive facial tic that is extremely resistant to extinction. Likewise, as has often been noted, the gambler who hit a jackpot once may persist for a long time even when the payoff becomes zero. The persistence of behavior after partial reinforcement suggests that when one has experienced only occasional, irregular, and unpredictable reinforcement for a response, one continues to expect possible rewards for a long time after the rewards have totally stopped.

Superstitions: Getting Reinforced into Irrationality

The relationship between the occurrence of an operant response and the reinforcement that follows it is often causal. For example, turn the door knob and the door opens, the outcome reinforcing the action. Consequently, in the future, we are likely to turn door knobs to enter and leave rooms, and our behavior at the door seems rational. Often, however, the response–reinforcement relationship may be quite accidental, and then bizarre and seemingly superstitious behavior and false beliefs may be produced (Matute, 1994). For example, a primitive tribe may persist in offering human sacrifices to the gods to end severe droughts because occasionally a sacrifice has been followed by rain.

The development of superstition, according to Skinner, may be demonstrated by giving a pigeon a bit of food at regular intervals—say every 15 seconds—regardless of what he is doing. Skinner (1953, p. 85) describes the strange rituals that may be conditioned in this way:

> When food is first given, the pigeon will be behaving in some way—if only standing still— and conditioning will take place. It is then more probable that the same behavior will be in progress when food is given again. If this proves to be the case, the "operant" will be further strengthened. If not, some other behavior will be strengthened. Eventually a given bit of behavior reaches a frequency at which it is often reinforced. It then becomes a permanent part of the repertoire of the bird, even though the food has been given by a clock which is unrelated to the bird's behavior. Conspicuous responses which have been established in this way include turning sharply to one side, hopping from one foot to the other and back, bowing and scraping, turning around, strutting, and raising the head. The topography of the behavior may continue to drift with further reinforcements, since slight modifications in the form of response may coincide with the receipt of food.

Punishment

Skinner focused on the role of rewards, but punishment or **aversive stimulation** is also important. In laboratory studies of anxiety, the unconditioned stimulus is usually a painful electric shock and the stimulus to be conditioned is a discrete event such as a distinctive neutral tone or a buzzer. Generally, human life is not that simple and neat. Often "aversive stimuli" involve punishments that are administered in less obvious and less controlled

10.22 How are superstitious behaviors established? Why is it so difficult to abolish them?

10.23 Describe advantages and possible disadvantages of punishment involving aversive stimulation. What is the preferred approach to eliminating undesirable behavior?

ways. These punishments may be conveyed subtly, by facial expressions and words rather than by brute force, and in extremely complicated patterns, by the same individuals who also nurture the child, giving love and other positive reinforcement. Moreover, the events that are punished often involve more than specific responses; they sometimes entail long sequences of overt and covert behavior (Aronfreed, 1994).

The behaviors that are considered inappropriate and punishable depend on such variables as the child's age and sex as well as the situation. Obviously the helplessness and passivity that are acceptable in a young child may be maladaptive in an older one, and the traits valued in a girl may not be valued in a boy. While the mother may deliberately encourage her son's dependency and discourage his aggressiveness, his school peers may do the reverse, ridiculing dependency at school and modeling and rewarding aggression and self-assertion. Given this, the influence of punishment on personality development is, not surprisingly, both important and complex (Aronfreed, 1968, 1994).

A careful review of research on the effects of punishment upon children's behavior concluded, in part, that:

> . . . *aversive stimulation, if well timed, consistent, and sufficiently intense, may create conditions that accelerate the socialization process, provided that the socialization agents also provide information concerning alternative prosocial behavior and positively reinforce any such behavior that occurs (Walters & Parke, 1967, p. 218).*

The important point to remember here is that when punishment is speedy and specific it may suppress undesirable behavior, but it cannot teach the child desirable alternatives. Therefore, parents should use positive techniques to show and reinforce appropriate behavior that the child can employ in place of the unacceptable response that has to be suppressed (Walters & Parke, 1967). In that way, the learner will develop a new response that can be made without getting punished. Without such a positive alternative, the child faces a dilemma in which total avoidance may seem the only possible route. Punishment may have very unfortunate effects when the child believes there is no way in which he or she can prevent further punishment and cope (Linscheid & Meinhold, 1990). If you become convinced that no potentially successful actions are open to you, that you can do nothing right, depression, hopelessness, and negative thinking may follow (Nolen-Hoeksema, 1997; Seligman, 1975).

SUMMARY

THE BEHAVIORAL APPROACH TO PSYCHODYNAMICS: DOLLARD AND MILLER

- Dollard and Miller fused psychoanalytic concepts with the more objective language and methods of laboratory studies of animal learning.
- Their theory emphasizes drive, cue, response, and reinforcement as the basic components of learning. Events that reduce a drive serve as reinforcements.
- Conflict exists when two or more goals are mutually exclusive. This conflict can create anxiety and repression.

TWO TYPES OF CONDITIONING

- Classical conditioning principles have been extended to explain some complex social phenomena and neurotic or abnormal behaviors, such as irrational fears.
- Traumatic fear may generalize so that events and cognitions closely associated with the original traumatic experiences may later evoke anxiety even after the objective danger is gone.

- In operant conditioning, behavior patterns may be modified by changing the consequences (reinforcements) to which they lead. Information and attention, as well as food and sexual gratification, are among the many outcomes that can serve as reinforcers.

B. F. SKINNER'S INFLUENCE ON PERSONALITY

- Analysis of the stimulus conditions controlling behavior replaces inferences about internal conflicts and underlying motives in Skinner's conceptualization.

- Discrimination in learning is fundamental in the socialization process. When behavior yields similar consequences under many conditions, generalization occurs, and the individual may display similar behavior patterns across diverse settings.

- Behavior may be shaped by reinforcing successively closer approximations to a particular desired behavior.

- While continuous reward or reinforcement for behavior may result in faster learning, irregular or intermittent reinforcement often produces more stable behavior that persists even when reinforcement is withdrawn. Many potentially maladaptive behaviors are rewarded irregularly and may therefore become very resistant to change.

- Irrational behavior may be created by accidental/noncausal pairings of behavior and response.

- The influence of punishment is complex and depends on many conditions, such as its timing.

KEY TERMS

11

ANALYZING AND MODIFYING BEHAVIOR

Many psychologists recognized that the principles of classical and operant conditioning, discussed in the last chapter, might be useful for treatment of at least some human behavioral problems, such as specific fears. Most psychologists, however, were concerned that the early behavioral work was based largely on studies with animals constrained in artificial laboratory situations. Elegant experiments were done on the behavior of rats running in mazes and of pigeons pecking on levers as food pellets dropped down. But how could one meaningfully extend the results from these studies to personality and the complex lives of people?

At the same time (before the 1970s), most clinicians saw behavioral concepts as too superficial for understanding the complexities of personality and irrelevant for helping people with personality problems. Partially in response to these challenges, behaviorally oriented workers tried to apply their ideas and methods to people and to issues relevant to personality and personality change. For several decades, they began to treat some of the most difficult behavioral and personality problems that had resisted other forms of therapy (e.g., O'Donohue et al., 2001). For example, they were allowed to try to treat hospitalized people who were so severely disturbed that there was little to lose by attempting experimental innovations with them after other available methods had proved to be unsuccessful. This chapter gives you a sense of their main strategies for assessment and change that are still relevant in various forms. By learning about some of these procedures, you will also get a better picture of the underlying philosophy that guides work at this level.

▶ CHARACTERISTICS OF BEHAVIORAL ASSESSMENTS

Rather than trying to infer the person's broad traits and motives, behavioral approaches focus on the specific conditions and processes that might govern his or her behavior.

Keep in mind again that all scientific psychological approaches are based on behavioral observation: giving answers on personality inventories or saying what an inkblot looks like are behaviors just as much as crying or running or fighting. However, in most personality assessment, the observed behaviors serve as highly indirect *signs* of the traits or motives that might underlie them. In contrast, in behavior assessments, the observed behavior is treated as a *sample,* and interest is focused on how the specific sampled behavior is affected by alterations in conditions (Mischel, 1968). For example, if the interest is in a child's physical and verbal aggression when relating to peers at preschool, then that is the type of behavior and situation that will be observed and assessed directly, rather than relying on teacher's or parent's reports, or scores on personality tests (O'Donohue et al., 2001).

11.1 How does behavioral assessment differ from trait measures of personality?

Case Example: Conditions "Controlling" Gary's Anxiety

To illustrate the general strategy of behavior assessment, let's again consider the case of Gary W. An assessment of Gary at this level obviously would focus on his behavior in relation to stimulus conditions. But what behaviors, and in relation to which conditions? Rather than seek a portrait of Gary's personality and behavior "in general," or an estimate of his "average" or dominant attributes, the focus is much more specific at the behavioral level of analysis. The behavior patterns selected for study depend on the particular problem that requires investigation. In clinical situations, the client indicates the priorities; in research contexts, they are selected by the investigator.

During his first term of graduate school, Gary found himself troubled enough to seek help at the school's counseling center. As part of the behavioral assessment that followed, Gary was asked to list and rank in order of importance the three problems that he found most distressing in himself and that he wanted to change if possible. He listed "feeling anxious and losing my grip" as his greatest problem. To assess the behavioral referents for his felt "anxiety," Gary was asked to specify in more detail just what changes in himself indicated to him that he was or was not anxious and "losing his grip."

He indicated that when he became anxious he felt changes in his heart rate, became tense, perspired, and found it most difficult to speak coherently. Next, to explore the covariation between increases and decreases in this state and changes in stimulus conditions, Gary was asked to keep an hour-by-hour diary sampling most of the waking hours during the daytime for a period of two weeks and indicating the type of activity that occurred during each hour. Discussion with him of this record suggested that anxiety tended to occur primarily in connection with public speaking occasions—specifically, in classroom situations in which he was required to speak before a group. As indicated by the summary shown in Table 11.1, on only one occasion that was not close in time to public speaking did Gary find himself highly anxious. That occasion turned out to be one in which he was brooding in his room, thinking about his public speaking failures in the classroom.

TABLE 11.1   Occurrence of Gary's Self-Reported Anxiety Attacks in Relation to Public Speaking

Occurrence of Anxiety	Hours with Anxiety (10)	Hours without Anxiety (80)
Within 1 hour of public speaking	9 (90%)	0 (0%)
No public speaking within 1 hour	1 (10%)	80 (80%)

Having established a covariation between the occurrence of anxiety and public speaking in the social-evaluative conditions of the classroom, his assessors identified the specific components of the public speaking situation that led to relatively more and less anxiety. The purpose here was to establish a hierarchy of anxiety-evoking stimuli ranging from the mild to the exceedingly severe. This hierarchy then was used in a treatment designed to gradually desensitize Gary to these fear stimuli.

Note that this behavioral assessment of Gary is quite specific: It is not an effort to characterize his whole personality, to describe "what he is like," or to infer his motives and dynamics. Instead, the assessment restricts itself to some clearly described problems and tries to analyze them in objective terms without going beyond the observed relations. Moreover, the analysis focuses on the stimulus conditions in which Gary's behavior occurs and on the covariation between those conditions and his problem. Behavior assessment tends to be focused assessment, usually concentrating on those aspects of behavior that can be changed and that require change. Indeed, as you will see often in this chapter, behavior assessment and behavior change (treatment) are closely connected.

The assessment of Gary's anxiety illustrates one rather crude way to study stimulus–response covariations. Of course there are many different ways in which these covariations can be sampled. This chapter illustrates some of the main tactics developed for the direct measurement of human behavior at this level of analysis.

Direct Behavior Measurement

For many purposes in personality study, it is important to sample and observe behavior in carefully structured, lifelike situations. In clinical applications, direct observation may give both client and assessor an opportunity to assess life problems and to select treatment objectives. Direct observation of behavior samples also may be used to assess the relative efficacy of various treatment procedures. Finally, behavior sampling has an important part in experimental research on personality.

The types of data collected in the behavioral approach include situational samples of both nonverbal and verbal behavior, as well as physiological measurements of emotional reactions. In addition, a comprehensive assessment often includes an analysis of effective rewards or reinforcing stimuli in the person's life. Examples of all of these measures are given in the following sections.

11.2   Describe how behavioral assessment has been used to assess anxieties and psychotic behavior.

Situational Behavior Sampling.   You already saw examples of **behavior sampling** in Chapter 2; such sampling is basic for much of the work at this level. Given the important role of fears and avoidance behavior, much attention has been given to assessing in detail the strength of diverse avoidance behaviors reliably in clinical situations. This was done, for example, by exposing fearful individuals to a series of real or symbolic fear-inducing stimuli. For example, fear of heights was assessed by measuring the distance that the phobic person could climb on a metal fire escape (Lazarus, 1961).

The same people were assessed again after receiving therapy to reduce their fears. In this phase, they were invited to ascend eight stories by elevator to a roof garden and to count the passing cars below for two minutes. Claustrophobic behavior—fear of closed spaces—was measured by asking each person to sit in a cubicle containing large French windows opening onto a balcony. The assessor shut the windows and slowly moved a large screen nearer and nearer to the person, thus gradually constricting her space. Of course each person was free to open the windows, and thereby to terminate the procedure, whenever she wished, although she was instructed to persevere as long as possible. The measure of claustrophobia was the least distance at which the person could tolerate the screen. As another example, Table 11.2 shows a checklist for performance anxieties before making a public speech.

Direct behavior sampling has also been used extensively in the analysis of psychotic behavior. One study, for instance, employed a time-sampling technique. At regular, 30-minute intervals, psychiatric nurses sought out and observed each hospitalized patient for periods of one to three minutes, without directly interacting with him (Ayllon & Haughton, 1964). The behavior observed in each sample was classified based on the occurrence of three experimenter-defined behaviors (for example, psychotic talk), and the time-check recordings were used to compute the relative frequency of the various behaviors. This time-sampling technique was supplemented by recordings of all the interactions between patient and nurses (such as each time the patient entered the nursing office). The resulting data served as a basis for designing and evaluating a treatment

TABLE 11.2   Timed Behavioral Checklist for Performance Anxiety

Behavior Observed	Time Period 1 2 3 4 5 6 7 8
1. Paces	
2. Sways	
3. Shuffles feet	
4. Knees tremble	
5. Extraneous arm and hand movement (swings, scratches, toys, etc.)	
6. Arms rigid	
7. Hands restrained (in pockets, behind back, clasped)	
8. Hand tremors	
9. No eye contact	
10. Face muscles tense (drawn, tics, grimaces)	
11. Face "deadpan"	
12. Face pale	
13. Face flushed (blushes)	
14. Moistens lips	
15. Swallows	
16. Clears throat	
17. Breathes heavily	
18. Perspires (face, hands, armpits)	
19. Voice quivers	
20. Speech blocks or stammers	

Source: Paul, Gordon. *Insight vs. desensitization in psychotherapy.* © 1966 by The Board of Trustees of the LeLand Stanford Jr. University, renewed 1994. With the permission of Stanford University Press, www.sup.org.

program. Similar ways of sampling and recording family interactions have been developed by others (Patterson, 1976; Ramsey et al., 1990). They studied highly aggressive children in the course of everyday family life, for example, at dinner. The attempt was to analyze the exact conditions under which aggression increased or decreased.

Verbal Behavior. As illustrated in the assessment of Gary's public speaking anxieties, a daily record may provide another valuable first step in the identification of problem-producing stimuli. Many behaviorally oriented clinicians routinely ask their clients to keep specific records listing the exact conditions under which their anxieties and problems seem to increase or decrease (Wolpe & Lazarus, 1966). The person may be asked to prepare by himself lists of all the stimulus conditions or events that create discomfort, distress, or other painful emotional reactions.

Finding Effective Rewards

11.3 How can direct observation be used to identify reinforcers that control behavior? How have tokens been used to change behavior and to identify reinforcers?

So far, we have considered the direct measurement of various responses. Behavior assessments, however, analyze not just what people do (and say and feel), but also the conditions that regulate or determine what they do. For that reason, behavior assessments have to find the rewards or reinforcers that may be influencing a person's behavior. If discovered, these reinforcers also can serve as incentives in therapy programs to help modify behavior in more positive or advantageous directions. Psychologists who emphasize the role of reinforcement in human behavior have devoted much attention to discovering and measuring effective reinforcers. People's actual choices in lifelike situations, as well as their verbal preferences or ratings, reveal some of the potent reinforcers that influence them. The reinforcement value of particular stimuli also may be assessed directly by observing their effects on the individual's performance (Daniels, 1994; Weir, 1965).

Primary reinforcers such as food, and **generalized conditioned reinforcers** such as praise, social approval, and money, are effective for most people. For example, in one case study, researchers and teachers attempted to reduce the disruptive behaviors of a blind, learning-disabled boy (Heitzman & Alimena, 1991). His behaviors were problematic because they disrupted the class and also prevented the boy from achieving optimal academic success. Differential reinforcement was used to reduce the amount of inappropriate behaviors to a socially acceptable level. In this procedure, the boy could not exceed a certain amount of disruptive or inappropriate behaviors in one day if he wanted to be rewarded. Examples of rewards were listening to a favorite tape, free time to talk to friends, and sitting in the teacher's car (he liked the feel of velour seats). After 26 days, there was an 88 percent reduction in target behaviors.

Sometimes, however, it is difficult to find potent reinforcers that would be feasible to manipulate. With disturbed groups (such as hospitalized schizophrenic patients), for example, many of the usual reinforcers prove to be ineffective, especially with people who have spent many years living in the back wards of a mental hospital. Ayllon and Azrin (1965) have shown how effective reinforcers can be discovered even for seemingly unmotivated psychotic patients. These reinforcers then can serve to motivate the patients to engage in more adaptive behavior.

As a first step, the patients were observed directly in the ward to discover their most frequent behaviors in situations that permitted them freedom to do what they wished. Throughout the day, observers carefully recorded the things the patients did, or tried to do, without pressures from the staff. The frequency of these activities provided an index of their potential values as reinforcers.

Six categories of reinforcers were established on the basis of extensive observation. These categories were: privacy, leave from the ward, social interactions with the staff, devotional opportunities, recreational opportunities, and items from the hospital canteen. "Privacy," for example, included such freedoms as choice of bedroom or of eating group, and getting a personal cabinet, a room-divider screen, or other means of preserving autonomy. "Recreational opportunities" included exclusive use of a radio or television set, attending movies and dances, and similar entertainment.

The patients could obtain each of the reinforcers with a specific number of **tokens** which they earned by participating in such rehabilitative functions as self-care and job training. A sensitive index of the subjective reinforcement value of the available activities is obtained by considering the outcomes for which the patients later chose to exchange most of their tokens. Over 42 days, the mean tokens exchanged by eight patients for the available reinforcers are shown in Table 11.3. Note that chances to interact socially with the staff and opportunity for recreation and spiritual devotion are most unpopular. These results suggest that, with chronic hospitalized patients such as these, therapy programs that rely primarily on social motivations would not fare well. Instead, such reinforcers as privacy, autonomy, and freedom might be the most effective incentives.

Assessing Conditions Controlling Behavior

To assess behavior fully, behavior theorists believe that we have to identify the conditions that control it. But how do we know whether or not a response pattern is really controlled or caused by a particular set of conditions? Behaviorally oriented psychologists test the conditions by introducing a change and observing whether or not it produces the expected modification in behavior. They ask: Does a systematic change in stimulus conditions (a "treatment") in fact change the particular response pattern that it supposedly controls? If we hypothesize that a child's reading problem is caused by poor vision, we would expect appropriate treatment (such as corrective eye glasses or corrective surgery) to be followed by a change in the behavior (i.e., an improvement in reading). The same should be true for psychological causes. For example, if we believe that the child's reading difficulty is caused by anxiety about pressure to read from her mother, we should try to show that if the mother reduces her pressure, it will yield the expected improvement in reading. That is, to understand behavior fully, we need to know the conditions that cause it. We can be most confident that we understand those conditions when we can show that a change in them yields the predicted change in the response pattern.

TABLE 11.3   Mean Tokens Exchanged for Various Available Reinforcers (by 8 Patients During 42 Days)

Reinforcers	Mean Tokens Paid	Number of Patients Paying Any Tokens
Privacy	1352.25	8
Commissary items	969.62	8
Leave from ward	616.37	8
Social interaction with staff	3.75	3
Recreational opportunities	2.37	5
Devotional opportunities	.62	3

Source: Based on Ayllon, T., & Azrin, N. H. (1965). The measurement and reinforcement of behavior of psychotics. *Journal of the Experimental Analysis of Behavior, 8,* 357–383.

A rigid distinction between behavior assessment and treatment (i.e., behavior change) thus is neither meaningful nor possible. Indeed, some of the most important innovations in behavior assessment have grown out of therapeutic efforts to modify problematic behavior. A main characteristic of these assessment methods is that they are linked closely to behavior change and cannot really be separated from it.

The close connection between behavior assessment and behavior change is most evident in **functional analyses**—that is, analyses of the precise covariations between changes in stimulus conditions and changes in a selected behavior pattern. Such functional analyses are the foundations of behavior assessments, and they are illustrated most clearly in studies that try to change behavior systematically. The basic steps may be seen in a study that was designed to help a girl in nursery school.

Functional Analyses: Case Example

11.4 What was the usefulness of a reversal design in the functional analysis of Ann's problem behaviors?

Ann was a bright four-year-old from an upper-middle-class background who increasingly isolated herself from children in her nursery school (Allen et al., 1964). At the same time, she developed various ingenious techniques to gain prolonged attention from the adults around her. She successfully coerced attention from her teachers, who found her many mental and physical skills highly attractive. Gradually, however, her efforts to maintain adult attention led her to become extremely isolated from other children.

Soon Ann was isolating herself most of the time from other youngsters. This seemed to be happening because most of the attention that adults were giving her was contingent, quite unintentionally, upon behaviors that were incompatible with Ann's relating to other children. Precisely those activities that led Ann away from play with her own peers were being unwittingly reinforced by the attention that her teachers showered on her. The more distressing and problematic Ann's behavior became, the more it elicited interest and close attention from her deeply concerned teachers.

Ann was slipping into a vicious cycle that had to be interrupted. A therapeutic plan was formed where Ann no longer received adult attention for her withdrawal from peers and her attempts at solitary interactions with adults. At the same time, the adults gave her attention only when she played with other children. That is, attention from adults became contingent on her playing with her peers.

As part of the assessment, two observers continuously sampled and recorded Ann's proximity to and interactions with adults and children in school at regular 10-second intervals. The therapeutic plan was instituted after five days of baseline data had been recorded. Now, whenever Ann started to interact with children an adult quickly attended to her, rewarding her participation in the group's play activities. Even approximations to social play, such as standing or playing near another child, were followed promptly by attention from a teacher. This attention was designed to further encourage Ann's interactions with other children. For example: "You three girls have a cozy house. Here are some more cups, Ann, for your tea party." Whenever Ann began to leave the group or attempted to make solitary contacts with adults, the teachers stopped attending to her.

Figure 11.1 summarizes the effects of the change in the consequences to Ann for isolate behavior with her peers. Notice that in the baseline period before the new response–reinforcement contingencies were instituted, Ann was spending only about 10 percent of her school time interacting with other children and 40 percent with adults. For about half the time she was altogether solitary. As soon as the **contingencies of reinforcement** were changed and adults attended to Ann only when she was

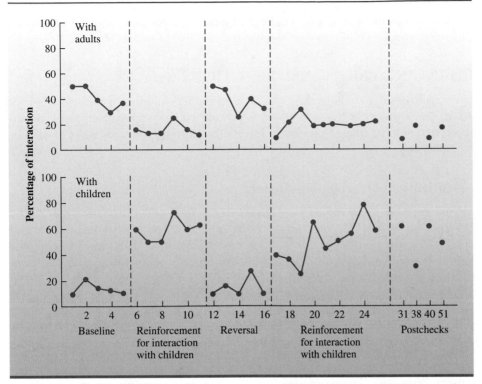

Figure 11.1 Percentages of time spent by Ann in social interaction during approximately two hours of each morning session.

Source: From Allen, E. K., Hart, B., Buell, J. S., Harris, F. R., & Wolf, M. M. (1964). Effects of social reinforcement on isolated behavior of a nursery school child. *Child Development, 35,* p. 515.

near children, her behavior changed quickly in accord with the new contingencies. When adult–child interactions were no longer followed by attention, they quickly diminished to less than 20 percent. On the first day of this new arrangement (day six), Ann spent almost 60 percent of her time with peers.

To assess the effects of reinforcement more precisely, the procedures were reversed on days 12 to 16. Adults again rewarded Ann with their attention for interacting with them and disregarded her interactions with children. Under these conditions (the "reversal" days in Figure 11.1), Ann's previous behavior reappeared immediately. In a final shift (beginning on day 17), in which attention from adults again became contingent upon Ann's interacting with children, her contact with peers increased to about 60 percent. After the end of the special reinforcement procedures (day 25), periodic postchecks indicated that Ann's increased play behavior with peers tended to remain fairly stable.

A complete analysis also must consider the total relations among stimulus conditions rather than focus on single aspects of reinforcement in isolation. These assessments showed, for example, that this child was highly discriminating in the very particular times and circumstances during which she became self-destructive. For example, massive withdrawal of attention—as when the experimenter withheld attention from an entire session—did not affect her self-destructive behavior. In contrast, the removal of smiles and attention *only* for previously reinforced responses changed her behavior (also see

Smith et al., 1992). Note that in this approach, assessment and behavior change become inextricably fused: the assessments guide the therapeutic program, and the efficacy of the treatment program is in turn continuously assessed (e.g., Frank & Hudson, 1990).

► CHANGING EMOTIONAL REACTIONS

Next we will consider some of the main techniques and findings of behavior therapy based on the concepts of the classic learning-conditioning theories. First we focus on methods designed to change previously learned disadvantageous emotional reactions, such as anxiety.

Desensitization: Overcoming Anxiety

11.5 What behavior change principle underlies systematic desensitization? Describe the three procedural steps in the treatment.

For many years, most therapists were afraid that symptom substitution would occur if they tried to remove the problematic behaviors. This concern stemmed from the Freudian assumption that attempts to change problematic behavior without first getting at the unconscious causes would lead to other problems that would be even worse than the original ones. This belief was based on the medical model of illness in which it is important to distinguish the observed behavior (e.g., pain in a leg) and its potential cause (e.g., a malignant tumor). Treating the symptoms with pain-killers rather than the cancer of course would soon be disastrous. Joseph Wolpe, a psychiatrist who became skeptical about psychoanalytic theory, took the risk of attempting

Systematic desensitization has been used effectively to treat anxiety about public speaking and many other fears.

direct behavior modification with many of his patients. In 1958 he published a book describing a method of **systematic desensitization** based on the principle of classical conditioning.

Wolpe was impressed by the work of such early learning theorists as Pavlov and believed that neurosis involves maladaptive learned habits, especially anxiety (fear) responses. In neurotic behavior, he hypothesized, anxiety has become the conditioned response to stimuli that are not anxiety-provoking for other people. He reasoned that therapy might help the neurotic individual to inhibit anxiety by counterconditioning him to make a competing (antagonistic) response to anxiety-eliciting stimuli. In his words, "If a response antagonistic to anxiety can be made to occur in the presence of anxiety-evoking stimuli so that it is accompanied by a complete or partial suppression of the anxiety responses, the bond between these stimuli and the anxiety response will be weakened" (Wolpe, 1958, p. 71). His attempt to desensitize the individual to anxiety-evoking stimuli includes three steps (summarized in Table 11.4):

1. *Establishing the anxiety stimulus hierarchy.* First the therapist helps the client identify the situations that evoke distressing emotional arousal and avoidance, usually in the course of interviews. Sometimes a person has many areas of anxiety, such as fear of failure, self-doubts, dating, guilt about sex, and so on. Regardless of how many areas or "themes" there are, each is treated separately.

For each theme, the person grades or ranks the component stimuli on a **hierarchy of severity of anxiety** ranging from the most to the least intensely anxiety-provoking events (see Table 11.5). For example, a person who is terrified of public speaking might consider "reading about speeches while alone in my room," a mildly anxiety-provoking stimulus, while "walking up before the audience to present the speech" might create severe anxiety in him (Paul, 1966). In Gary's case, "the minute before starting a formal speech" was the most anxiety-provoking, while "watching a friend practice a speech" and "taking notes in the library for a speech" were only moderately disturbing. As another example, a woman who sought treatment for sexual dysfunction indicated that "being kissed on cheeks and forehead" evoked merely mild anxiety but thinking about items like "having intercourse in the nude while sitting on husband's lap" produced the most intense anxiety in her (Lazarus, 1963).

TABLE 11.4   Three Basic Steps in the Desensitization of Anxiety

Step	Example
1. Establishing the anxiety stimulus hierarchy; anxiety-evoking situations ranked from least to most severe	*Low anxiety:* reading about speeches alone in your room *Intermediate anxiety:* getting dressed the morning on which you are to give a speech *High anxiety:* presenting a speech before an audience
2. Learning an incompatible response	Learning deep muscle relaxation by tensing and relaxing various muscle groups (head, shoulders, arms), deep breathing techniques, and similar methods
3. Counterconditioning: learning to make the incompatible response to items in the hierarchy	Practicing relaxation responses to the lowest item on the hierarchy and moving gradually to the higher items

Note: These items are examples from much longer hierarchies.

TABLE 11.5   Items of Different Severity from Four Anxiety Hierarchies*

Severity (Degree of Anxiety)	Anxiety Hierarchies (Themes)			
	1 Interpersonal Rejection	2 Guilt About Work	3 Test-Taking	4 Expressing Anger
Low	Thinking about calling Mary (a new girlfriend) tonight	Thinking "I still haven't answered all my mail"	Getting the reading list for the course	Watching strangers quarrel in street
Intermediate	Asking for a date on the telephone	Taking off an hour for lunch	Studying at my desk the night before the final	My brother shouting at his best friend
High	Trying a first kiss	Going to a movie instead of working	Sitting in the examination room waiting for the test to be handed out	Saying "No! I don't want to!" to mother

*These items are examples from much longer hierarchies.

2.   *Training the incompatible response (relaxation).* After identifying and grading the stimuli that evoke anxiety, the person needs to learn responses that can be used later to inhibit anxiety. Wolpe prefers to use **relaxation responses** because they can be taught easily and are always inherently incompatible with anxiety: no one can be relaxed and anxious simultaneously. The therapist helps the client to learn relaxation by elaborate instructions that teach first to tense and then to relax parts of the body (arms, shoulders, neck, head) until gradually an almost hypnotic state of total calm and deep muscle relaxation is achieved. Most people can learn how to relax within a few sessions. The critical problem is to learn to relax to anxiety-evoking stimuli, and that task is attempted in the next phase.

3.   *Associating anxiety stimuli and incompatible responses.* In the critical phase, **counterconditioning**, the client is helped to relax deeply, and then is presented with the least anxiety-arousing stimulus from the previously established hierarchy. Usually the stimulus event is described verbally or presented symbolically (in a picture) while the client is deeply relaxed and calm. As the therapist says the words for the item (e.g., "walking down a fire escape from the 6th floor") the client with a fear of heights tries to generate the most vivid image of it that his or her imagination can form. As soon as the client can concentrate on this item while remaining calm, the next, more severe item from the hierarchy is introduced until, step by step, the entire hierarchy is mastered (e.g.,"looking down from the roof of a skyscraper").

If at any point in the procedure the client begins to become anxious while presented with an anxiety stimulus, he or she signals the therapist. The client is promptly instructed to discontinue the image of the stimulus until calm again. Then a somewhat less severe item from the hierarchy is presented so that he or she can concentrate on it without anxiety. After that, the client is ready to advance to the next item in the anxiety hierarchy and the step-by-step progress up the list can be resumed.

In sum, the **desensitization** (counterconditioning) procedure attempts to have responses incompatible with anxiety (such as relaxation) occur in the presence of mildly anxiety-evoking stimuli. The incompatible response then will at least partially prevent the anxiety response. In that way, the association between the aversive stimulus and anxiety becomes reduced, while the association of the stimulus with the relaxation reaction becomes strengthened (Guthrie, 1935; Wolpe, 1958).

McClanahan (1995), for example, treated a woman who suffered from severe habitual nail-biting. McClanahan noted that the nail-biting was almost always precipitated by anxiety which included feeling overwhelmed, apprehensive, nervous, and worried. The desensitization techniques used were deep muscle relaxation and Transcendental Meditation. Systematic desensitization reduced anxiety and decreased the frequency and duration of nail-biting significantly. Clinical reports of successful desensitization may be encouraging, but more conclusive evidence comes from controlled experiments, and many studies indicate that desensitization is a valuable method for modifying phobias and reducing anxiety (Kazdin & Wilson, 1978; Wilson & O'Leary, 1980).

Conditioned Aversion: Making Stimuli Unattractive

While some people suffer because they have learned to react negatively to certain situations, others are plagued because they become pleasurably aroused by, or even addicted to, stimuli that most people in the culture find neutral or even aversive. One example of this problem is fetishistic behavior, in which the person may become sexually excited by such objects as undergarments. In these cases, things that are neutral or even disgusting for most people have acquired the power to produce pleasurable emotional arousal. Another example is drug addiction for which the arousal may have a significant and necessary physiological component to it. Such reactions can provide the person with some immediate reduction of pain, but they often have severely negative and destructive long-term consequences (Baker et al., 2003).

A positively valued stimulus may be neutralized by counterconditioning if it is presented with stimuli that evoke extremely unpleasant reactions. Gradually, as a result of repeated pairings, the previously positive stimulus acquires some of the aversive emotional properties evoked by the noxious events with which it has been associated.

11.6 What conditioning procedures are used in aversion therapy? What are some limitations of this approach?

An Example: Treating Cocaine Dependency

Chemical aversion therapy was used to treat cocaine addicts who volunteered to participate in a two-week study (Frawley & Smith, 1990). The stimulus used to represent cocaine was a mixture of chemicals which tasted and smelled like "street cocaine." In the treatment room, there were pictures of paraphernalia for cocaine use, as well as the utensils used to snort cocaine. The patients were instructed to "snort" the "cocaine" in their normal fashion. They then were given an injection of nausea-inducing drugs and were instructed to continue to "snort" the "cocaine." Afterwards, the patients were encouraged to focus on paraphernalia, pictures of cocaine, and to pair the cocaine use with negative consequences, all while experiencing nausea.

At 6 months posttreatment, more than half of the cocaine addicts had totally abstained from cocaine since the treatment. As predicted, the pairing of the nausea with the cocaine use produced a conditioned aversion for the recovering addicts and helped them break their habit. Systematic counterconditioning has also been attempted with other addictions such as alcoholism (Bandura, 1969, 1986).

Psychologists are reluctant to use **aversion therapies** like this one because they inflict aversive experiences on a troubled person. However, aversion therapies usually are attempted only after other forms of help (such as interview therapies) have been tried unsuccessfully. In some cases, aversion treatments have come as a last resort in lieu of more drastic treatments, such as long imprisonment or irreversible brain surgery (Rachman & Hodgeson, 1980; Raymond, 1956). And usually they are not imposed on the client: they are voluntary and the person submits to them with full knowledge and consent.

Indeed, it is this very dependence on the client's cooperation that limits the efficacy of the treatment. That is, after the initial counterconditioning trials, the client often may revert to his or her fetish without submitting voluntarily to further treatment. Since it becomes impractical to hospitalize him continuously or remove him from exposure to the problematic stimuli, he must learn to administer aversive stimulation to himself whenever necessary. For example, he may be taught to administer electric shock to himself from a small portable, battery-operated apparatus concealed in his clothing, or to induce aversive thoughts or imagery whenever he experiences the problematic urges. Thus, counterconditioning procedures ultimately provide the individual with a form of *self*-control. Whether or not he continues to practice and seek this self-control is up to him. And whether or not he practices self-control determines how effectively his new behavior will be maintained (Mischel et al., 1996).

▶ CHANGING BEHAVIOR

Many psychologists have tried to modify maladaptive behaviors by changing the consequences to which those behaviors lead. Guided to a large extent by B. F. Skinner's ideas about learning, they try to withdraw reinforcement for undesired behavior and to make attention, approval, or other reinforcement contingent on the occurrence of more appropriate, advantageous behavior (e.g., Haring & Breen, 1992). Their basic procedure is well illustrated in the work of Hawkins and his colleagues (1966).

Case Example: Hyperactivity

11.7 How have operant procedures been used to treat autistic children?

Hawkins' case was Peter, a young child of low intelligence. Peter was brought to a clinic by his mother because he was "hyperactive" and "unmanageable." Because the problems seemed to involve the relations between Peter and his mother, he was assessed and treated directly in his home. His mother served as a therapist under the guidance of the professional workers.

A first task was to specify the problematic behaviors. Direct observations of Peter in the home revealed the following problems to be among the most common and disturbing ones:

1. Biting his shirt or arm.
2. Sticking his tongue out.
3. Hitting and kicking himself, other people, or objects.
4. Using derogatory names.
5. Removing his clothing and threatening to remove it.

The frequency of these and similar behaviors was carefully recorded at 10-second intervals during one-hour observation sessions in the home. After the first assessments were completed, the researcher helped the mother to recognize the occurrence of Peter's nine most objectionable behaviors. Whenever these occurred during subsequent one-hour sessions at home, she was taught to respond to them with definite steps. These steps involved signaling to Peter when his behavior became disruptive and, if a verbal warning failed, isolating him briefly in a separated, locked "time out" room without toys and other attractions. Release from the room (and reinstatement of play, attention, and nurturance) was contingent on Peter's terminating the tantrum and showing more reasonable, less destructive behavior. This arrangement was opposite to the one the mother may have inadvertently used in the past, when she became increasingly concerned and attentive (even if distressed) as Peter became increasingly wild. Subsequent assessment revealed that the new regimen was effective in minimizing Peter's outbursts. While apparently helpful to Peter's development, reducing his tantrums may have been just one step toward the more extensive help he needed.

Using a combination of modeling and reinforcement procedures, Lovaas and his coworkers (Lovaas et al. 1966, 1991) modified the deficient speech and social behaviors of severely disturbed ("autistic") children who were unable to talk. First the therapist modeled the sounds himself. He rewarded the child only for vocalizing the modeled sounds within a specified time interval. As the child's proficiency increased, the therapist proceeded to utter more complicated verbal units. Gradually, training progressed from sounds to words and phrases. As the training continued, rewards from the therapist became contingent on the child's reproducing increasingly elaborate verbalizations more skillfully (i.e., more quickly and accurately). The combination of modeling and reinforcement procedures gradually helped the child to learn more complex meanings and complicated speech. Research like this shows the value of wisely used reinforcement; but rewards also may be hazardous, as discussed in In Focus 11.1.

11.8 How can overjustification effects be avoided in behavior change attempts involving the use of positive reinforcers?

IN FOCUS 11.1

REWARDS MAY BACKFIRE

Rewards are important for effective behavior, but they can be used unwisely. A major purpose of effective therapy (and socialization) is to wean the individual away from external controls and rewards so that his behavior becomes increasingly guided and supported by intrinsic gratifications—that is, satisfactions closely connected with the activity itself. Therefore, it is essential to use rewards or incentives only to the extent necessary to initiate and sustain prosocial (adaptive, desirable) behavior.

External incentives may be important in order to encourage a person to try activities that have not yet become attractive for him or her. When rewards are used to call attention to a good job, or to an individual's competence at an activity, they may actually bolster interest. They provide positive performance feedback and supply tangible evidence of excellence (Harackiewicz, Manderlink, & Sansone, 1984). Approval and praise from parents for trying to play a violin, for example, may be helpful first steps in encouraging the child's earliest musical interest. But when the youngster begins to experience activity-generated satisfactions (for example, from playing the music itself), it becomes important to avoid excessive

external rewards. Too much reward would be unnecessary and possibly harmful, leading the child to play for the wrong reasons and making him or her prone to lose interest easily when the external rewards are reduced or stopped altogether (Lepper, Greene, & Nisbett, 1973). Likewise, children need to be encouraged to develop sense of fairness, empathy, and helpful responsiveness to the needs of other people. To become a social being requires attention to the long-term consequences of one's behavior and not just to its immediate payoffs. While such sensitivities might initially be encouraged by external rewards, ultimately they need to be sustained by gratification from the activities themselves.

In sum, **overjustification** of an activity by excessive external reward may interfere with the satisfactions (intrinsic interests) that would otherwise be generated by the activity itself. Excessive external rewards may even have boomerang effects and lead the recipient to devalue and resist the rewarded activity. Children who get paid to do their homework may develop a feeling that school work is an aversive chore rather than a route to learning and self-development.

People often are judged to be maladjusted mainly because they have not learned how to perform the behavior patterns necessary to effectively meet the social or vocational demands they encounter. They cannot behave appropriately because they lack the skills required for successful functioning. For example, the socially deprived, economically underprivileged person may suffer because he or she never has acquired the response patterns and competencies needed to obtain success in vocational and interpersonal situations. Similarly, the high school dropout in our culture does indeed carry an enduring handicap. Such **behavioral deficits,** if widespread, may lead to many other problems, including severe emotional distress and avoidance patterns to escape the unhappy consequences of failure and incompetence. Many special learning programs have been designed to teach people a variety of problem-solving strategies and cognitive skills (Bijou, 1965), and to help them achieve many other positive changes in behavior (e.g., Kamps et al., 1992; Karoly, 1980).

Contingency Contracting

11.9   Describe the use and effectiveness of contingency contracting in self-control programs.

A move to enroll the person actively in his or her own behavior change program whenever possible is reflected in the use of **contingency contracting** (Rimm & Masters, 1974; Thoresen & Mahoney, 1974). An example was the treatment of "Miss X" for drug abuse as described by Boudin (1972). Miss X, a heavy user of amphetamines, made a contingency contract with her therapist. She gave him $500 (all of her money) in 10 signed checks of $50 each and committed him to send a check to the Ku Klux Klan (her least favorite organization) whenever she violated any step in a series of mutually agreed-upon specific actions for curbing her drug use. After applying the contract for three months, a follow-up for a two-year period indicated that Miss X did not return to amphetamine use. The principle of contingency contracting can be extended to a wide variety of commitments in which the client explicitly authorizes the therapist to use rewards to encourage more advantageous behaviors in ways formally agreed upon in advance.

Symptom Substitution?

11.10   What controversy gave rise to the concept of symptom substitution? What research evidence exists for symptom substitution?

Do behavior therapies neglect the causes of the person's problematic behavior and thus leave the "roots" unchanged while modifying only the "superficial" or "symptomatic" behaviors? It is often charged that behavior therapists ignore the basic or underlying causes of problems. Advocates of behavior therapy insist that they do seek causes but that they search for *observable* causes controlling the current problem, not its historically distant antecedents or its hypothesized but unobservable psychodynamic mechanisms. Traditional, insight-oriented approaches have looked, instead, for historical roots in the person's past and for theoretical mechanisms in the form of psychodynamics. The difference between these two approaches thus is not that one looks for causes while the other does not: Both approaches search for causes but they disagree about what those causes really are.

> *All analyses of behavior seek causes; the difference between social behavior and [psychodynamic] analyses is in whether current controlling causes or historically distant antecedents are invoked. Behavioral analyses seek the current variables and conditions controlling the behavior of interest. Traditional [psychodynamic] theories have looked, instead, for historical roots . . . (Mischel, 1968, p. 264).*

Traditional approaches ask about the patient, "Why did she become this kind of person?" Behavioral approaches ask, "What is now causing her to behave as she does and what would have to be modified to change her behavior?"

Does a neglect in treatment of the psychodynamics hypothesized by traditional therapies produce **symptom substitution**? In spite of many initial fears about possible symptom substitution, behavior change programs of the kind discussed in the preceding sections tend to be the most effective methods presently available. Researchers have found that the changed behaviors are not automatically replaced by other problematic ones (Bandura, 1986; Kazdin & Wilson, 1978; Lang & Lazovik, 1963; Paul, 1966; Rachman, 1967; Rachman & Wilson, 1980). On the contrary, when people are liberated from debilitating emotional reactions and defensive avoidance patterns, they generally tend to become able to function more effectively in other areas as well. As was noted years ago:

> Unfortunately, psychotherapists seem to have stressed the hypothetical dangers of only curing the symptoms, while ignoring the very real dangers of the harm that is done by not curing them (Grossberg, 1964, p. 83).

On the other hand, some enthusiastic proponents of behavior modification overlook the complexity of the client's problems. They may oversimplify the difficulties into one or two discrete phobias when in fact the client may have many other difficulties. In that case, it would not be surprising to find that even after removal of the initial problem, the individual still is beset with such other psychological troubles as self-doubts, feelings of worthlessness, and so on. Such a condition, of course, would imply that the person had an incomplete treatment rather than that symptom substitution had occurred. It would be extremely naïve to think that reducing Gary's public speaking anxiety, for example, would make his life free of all other problems. Whatever other difficulties he might have would still require attention in their own right.

In sum, to avoid the emergence of disadvantageous behaviors, a comprehensive program must provide the person with more adaptive ways of dealing with life; such a program may have to go beyond merely reducing the most obvious problems. Behavior modification does not automatically produce generalized positive effects that remove all the person's troubles.

Evaluating the Consequences of Behavior, Not the Person

The behavioral approach avoids evaluating the health, adequacy, or abnormality of the person or personality as a whole. Instead, when judgments are made, they focus on evaluation of the individual's specific behaviors. Behaviors are evaluated on the basis of the kinds of consequences that they produce for the person who generates them and for other people who are around him or her. Evaluations about the positive or negative consequences of behavior are social and ethical judgments that depend on the values and standards of the community that makes them. Advantageous behaviors are those judged to have positive personal and interpersonal consequences (for example, helping people "feel good," or increasing constructive, creative outcomes) without any aversive impact on others. Behaviors that have negative, life-threatening, destructive consequences, or those that endanger the full potentialities of the person or other people (for example, debilitating fears, homicidal attempts), would be considered maladaptive.

The behavioral approach also implies a high value for the development of the individual's total competencies and skills so that he or she can maximize opportunities and options. Similarly, the person must be able to discern the important contingencies and rules of reinforcement in his or her life in order to maximize satisfactions and minimize aversive, disadvantageous outcomes. To be able to overcome unfavorable environments and life conditions, it is especially important to develop effective strategies for self-control.

Does Changing Behavior Change Personality?

11.11 Under what conditions can changes in specific behaviors foster personality change?

There is much controversy with regard to the depth and endurance of behavior change. Basically, the question is whether behavior change entails genuine, durable change or whether it is limited to relatively minor, specific behaviors that have little applicability to major life problems.

To facilitate transfer from treatment to life, workers at this level of analysis introduce into treatment stimulus conditions that are as similar as possible to the life situations in which the new behaviors will be used. For example, if the patient is afraid of going into elevators, the treatment may be conducted in elevators, not in the therapist's office.

The question remains: When fears and other emotional problems are reduced, and social competence improves through more adaptive, functional patterns of social behavior, does personality change? The answer depends on the definition of personality. There is considerable evidence that changing disadvantageous behaviors, such as a severe stutter or uncontrolled facial tics, and eliminating distressing, fear-producing emotional reactions, also improves how people feel about themselves, and their self-concepts (e.g., Bandura, 1997; Meichenbaum, 1995). Self-concepts, and self-esteem, tend to reflect at least in part the individual's actual competencies and how the person's behavior is seen by others (e.g., Leary & Downs, 1995). Our self-perceptions include the information that we get about the adequacy of our own behaviors, and if these self-perceptions are part of personality, then personality changes when behavior becomes more adaptive and gratifying. The individual who learns to perform more competently achieves more gratification and is also likely to develop a more positive attitude toward himself or herself. As a result of being able to overcome fears and anxieties, one should also become more confident. Reducing Gary's fears of public speaking would not be a cure-all, but it might certainly help him to feel more positively about himself and would open alternatives (for example, in his career opportunities) otherwise closed to him. Ultimately, if enough anxious behavior is brought under control, shyness may decrease, creating a cycle of improved behavior leading to improved confidence and positive expectations, leading to further personality change. At least, that is the rationale of much work at this level of analysis.

But while this may often be true, it does not always happen. Indeed, critics of behavior therapy note that people may suffer not because their behavior is inadequate but because they evaluate it improperly. That is, some people have problems with distorted self-concepts more than with performance. Often people label themselves and react to their own behaviors very differently than do the people around him and the rest of society. An esteemed financier, for example, may receive the rewards and praise of society while he is privately unhappy enough to commit suicide. Or a popular student who is the prom queen of her school might have secret

People's standards affect their reactions to performance outcomes. To some, an A− can feel like a failure.

doubts about her sexual adequacy and femininity and might be torturing herself with these fears.

Many personal problems involve inappropriate self-evaluations and self-reactions. In these cases, the difficulty often may be the person's appraisal of his or her performances and attributes rather than their actual quality and competence level. For example, a student may react self-punitively to his scholastic achievements even when their objective quality is high. The student who is badly upset with himself for an occasional grade less than an A may need help with self-assessment rather than with school work. Fortunately, work at the social cognitive level, reviewed in the next part of the text, goes on to address those issues.

Unexpected Similarities: Behavior Theory and Existentialism

Psychological theories sometimes have unexpected similarities. The behavioral approaches discussed in this part focus on what the person is *doing* in the here and now, rather than on reconstructions of personal history or inferences about hypothesized traits and motives. In this way, they have some unexpected similarities with work at the phenomenological level described in the previous part. The irony is that many leaders of the phenomenological approach were motivated originally to protest against behavioral-learning-conditioning approaches, just as the behavioral approaches were a protest against speculating about internal states and experiences that could not be directly observed. After the heat of the battles cools, however, one can see a surprising common theme. Thus, the behavioral focus on what the person is *doing*, rather than on attributes or motives, is compatible with the views of the famous existentialist thinker, Sartre, who declared: "existence precedes essence." He meant by that phrase that:

> . . . *man first of all exists, encounters himself, surges up in the world—and defines himself afterwards. If man as the existentialist sees him is not definable, it is because to begin with he is nothing. He will not be anything until later, . . . Thus, there is no human nature. . . . Man simply is (Sartre, 1965, p. 28).*

11.12 What similarities exist between behavioral and existential theories? What is their major area of disagreement?

A rejection of preconceptions about motives and traits was also true for George Kelly in his "personal construct theory" (Chapter 8), and it is what he meant when he said, "I *am* what I *do*," and urged that to know what one is, one must look at what one does. Skinner the arch behaviorist would have agreed with him on this point at least, and probably on a few others. The possible compatibility between aspects of behavior theory and of the existential-phenomenological movement hinge on several common qualities, summarized below.

The behavior level and the existential-phenomenological level are similar in that:

- Both share a focus on the here and now.
- Both emphasize what the person is doing rather than the constructs of the psychologist who studies the person.
- Both share a lack of interest in distant historical reconstruction in favor of a concern with new action possibilities for the individual.

These commonalities violate many common stereotypes about both approaches. They suggest that each is enriched by taking account constructively of the other's work. The similarities, although only partial, are impressive, the more so because philosophically it is hard to imagine two positions that on the surface would seem more incompatible.

However, the two positions may have one critical incompatibility. The existentialist takes the philosophical position that the individual is responsible and attributes to the person's choices the ultimate causes of behavior. In Sartre's phrase, a person "is what he wills to be" (1956, p. 291). A behavior theorist may share Sartre's desire to put "every man in possession of himself" rather than allow him to be possessed by unconscious psychic forces. But a behavioral analysis of causation cannot begin with the person's will as the fundamental cause of what he does, nor can it end with his constructs as a final explanation of his behavior.

George Kelly (personal communication, 1965) once emphasized his belief that personal constructs are the basic units and that it is personal constructs, rather than stimuli, that determine behavior. He recalled vividly from his Navy experience during World War II how very differently he related to the same officer on different occasions depending on how he construed him at the time. He remembered that the captain seemed different to him in an informal role, chatting with his jacket off, from the way he seemed when he wore his officer's coat. "You see," Kelly said, "it is not the stimulus—the captain—but how I construed him that [led] to my reactions to him."

But B. F. Skinner would find this story an excellent example, not of "construct control," but of "stimulus control": With his four stripes on, you see the captain one way; without his four stripes, you see him differently. To understand the change in the construct, in the behavioral view, you have to include in your understanding how those four stripes came to control it. The phenomenological and behavioral positions differ in their focus of attention. The phenomenologist wants to know and understand the person's experience; the behaviorally oriented psychologist wants to clarify the conditions that control the ultimate behavior.

The approaches to which we turn in the rest of the text seek to reconcile and integrate the two within a more comprehensive system that draws on contributions from each of the levels of analysis discussed throughout the text.

IN FOCUS 11.2

DEPRESSION: MORE THAN INSUFFICIENT REINFORCEMENT

According to one influential behavioral theory, depression may be understood as a result of a persistent lack of gratification or positive outcomes (reinforcement) for the person's own behavior (Lewinsohn, 1975; Lewinsohn, Clarke, Hops, & Andrews, 1990). That is, depressed persons feel bad and withdraw from life because their environments are consistently unresponsive to them and fail to provide enough positive consequences for what they are doing. The situation is analogous to an **extinction schedule** in which reinforcement for a behavior is withdrawn until gradually the behavior itself stops. In the case of the depressed person, the only reinforcement that does continue tends to be in the form of attention and sympathy from relatives and friends for the very behaviors that are maladaptive: weeping, complaining, talking about suicide. These depressive behaviors are so unpleasant that they soon alienate most people in the depressed person's environment, thus producing further isolation, lack of reinforcement, and unhappiness in a vicious cycle of increasing misery and increasing withdrawal.

Behavioral View of Depression. Depressed people, according to this theory, may suffer from three basic problems. First, they tend to find relatively few events and activities gratifying. Second, they tend to live in environments in which reinforcement is not readily available for

their adaptive behaviors. For example, they may live highly isolated lives, as often happens with older people living alone, or with younger people in large universities that make them feel lost. Third, they lack the skills and behaviors they need to get positive reactions and feedback from other people. For example, they may be shy and socially awkward, making gratifying relationships with others very difficult. It follows that they in turn develop feelings such as "I'm not likable," or even "I'm no good." The essentials of the theory are shown schematically in Figure 11.2.

Although the theory has not been tested conclusively, a good deal of evidence is consistent with it. For example, depressed people do seem to elicit fewer behaviors from other people and thus presumably get less social reinforcement from them. Depressed people also tend to engage in fewer pleasant activities and enjoy such events less than individuals who are not depressed (Lewinsohn, 1975).

This concept of depression immediately suggests a treatment strategy (Lewinsohn et al., 1990): increase the rate of positive reinforcement for the depressed person's adaptive efforts. Note that such a plan would require increasing the rate of positive outcomes received by depressed people contingent on their own behavior; it does not mean simply giving more rewards regardless of what the individual does.

11.13 Describe the behavioral theory of depression and its implications for treatment.

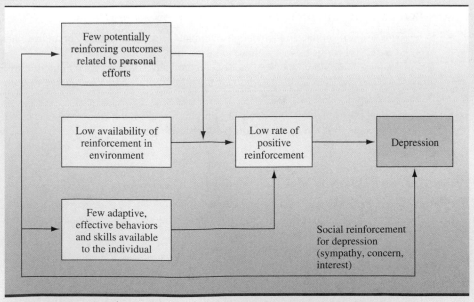

Figure 11.2 Schematic representation of Lewinsohn's theory of depression.
Source: Based on Lewinsohn, P. M. (1975). The behavioral study and treatment of depression. In M. Hersen (Ed.), *Progress in behavior modification.* Reprinted with permission from Elsevier.

SUMMARY

CHARACTERISTICS OF BEHAVIORAL ASSESSMENTS

- Behavioral approaches to personality all carefully measure behavior in relation to specific stimulus conditions. They treat observed behavior as a sample, and the focus is on how the specific sample is affected by variations in the stimulus conditions.
- The case of Gary W. illustrates the behavioral assessment of anxiety.

DIRECT BEHAVIOR MEASUREMENT

- Behavior may be measured directly by sampling it, both verbally and in performance, and by measuring physiological and emotional reactions.
- The reinforcing value of stimuli may be assessed from an individual's choices in lifelike situations, verbal preferences, and ratings, or the observed effects of various stimuli on actual behavior.
- In clinical work, it may be especially important to discover rewards that are effective for the individual to facilitate therapeutic progress.

ASSESSING CONDITIONS CONTROLLING BEHAVIOR

- Functional analyses, the foundations of behavior assessments, require careful observation of the behavior in question as it naturally occurs to specify the conditions that maintain this behavior.
- Then systematic changes are made in those conditions until the problem behavior no longer occurs and more satisfying behaviors are substituted.
- Behavior therapies attempt to modify disadvantageous behavior by planned relearning experiences and by rearranging stimulus conditions.

CHANGING EMOTIONAL REACTIONS

- Systematic desensitization can help people overcome fears or anxieties. The individual is exposed cognitively (e.g., in imagination) to increasingly severe samples of aversive or fear-arousing stimuli; simultaneously she is helped to make responses incompatible with anxiety, such as muscle relaxation. Gradually the anxiety evoked by the aversive stimulus is reduced and the stimulus is neutralized.
- In conditional aversion, a positive arousing stimulus (for example, cocaine for a cocaine addict) may be neutralized by repeatedly pairing it with one that is very aversive (such as chemically induced nausea).

CHANGING BEHAVIOR

- Maladaptive behaviors such as hyperactivity may be modified by changing the consequences to which they lead. Attention, approval, or other positive consequences are withdrawn from the maladaptive behavior and rewards become contingent instead on the occurrence of more advantageous behavior.
- The overuse of external rewards may backfire.
- In contingency contracting, the person makes a contract with another individual to self-reward for increasing positive behaviors (or self-punish for performing negative behaviors), as specified in the contract.
- To facilitate transfer from treatment to life, treatment samples the relevant situations and occurs in the same life setting in which improvement is desired. New behavior change

methods encourage self-management so that individuals may gain relative independence and control of their own behavior as rapidly as possible.

- A promising theory of depression suggests that depressed people are caught in a vicious cycle of lack of reinforcement for their own efforts, leading to greater withdrawal from other people and, in turn, increased depression.

KEY TERMS

aversion therapy 255
behavior sampling 246
behavioral deficits 258
contingencies of
   reinforcement 250
contingency
   contracting 258
counterconditioning
   (desensitization) 254

extinction
   schedule 263
functional analysis 250
generalized conditioned
   reinforcers 248
hierarchy of anxiety
   (grading the
   stimuli) 253
overjustification 257

primary
   reinforcers 248
relaxation
   responses 254
symptom
   substitution 259
systematic
   desensitization 253
tokens 249

PART IV

THE BEHAVIORAL-CONDITONING LEVEL

▶ OVERVIEW: FOCUS, CONCEPTS, METHODS

The next table summarizes the main characteristics of work at the behavioral-conditioning level of analysis. As the table indicates, these approaches focus on the individual's behavior in its context. Prior learning and cues in the situation are seen as important determinants of behavior. Preferred data consist of direct observations of behavior as it changes in relation to changing situations. Responses are used as samples of behavior, not as indirect indicators of hypothesized inner states, motives, or traits. Research seeks to analyze the conditions that influence or control the behavior of interest, including the conditions that allow persons to enhance and control their own behavior, for example, by rearranging their environments. To change the person's behavior, therapy is directed at identifying and modifying the consequences behavior produces or the outcomes associated with it. The situation is treated as an integral aspect of behavior; it provides cues and outcomes that impact the maintenance and modification of behavior. Thus, the situation cannot be removed from the assessment of behavior or from attempts to change behavior.

Overview of Focus, Concepts, Methods: The Behavioral-Conditioning Level

Basic units:	Behavior-in-situation
Causes of behavior:	Prior learning and cues in situation (including behavior of others); reinforcement contingencies
Behavioral manifestations of personality:	Stable behavior equated with personality
Favored data:	Direct observations of behavior in the target situation; behavior change as a function of changing the situation (stimulus conditions)
Observed responses used as:	Behavior samples
Research focus:	Behavior change; analysis of conditions controlling behavior
Approach to personality change:	By changing conditions; by learning experiences that modify behavior
Role of situation:	Extremely important: regulates much behavior, elicits emotional reactions and behavior patterns

▶ ENDURING CONTRIBUTIONS OF THE BEHAVIORAL-CONDITIONING LEVEL

The contributions of behavioral approaches for applied purposes were widely applauded for identifying many effective, if incomplete, ways to help think about and improve diverse problems in everyday life (O'Donohue et al., 2001). Dollard and Miller translated many key psychodynamic concepts into learning terms in ways that encouraged experimental research. Work at the behavioral level helped take the mystery out of many of the "abnormal" phenomena that had long puzzled earlier workers. Notably, it showed how seemingly inexplicable and irrational behaviors—such as intense anxieties and bizarre behavior patterns—may be shaped by the circumstances of life and the ways in which learning and reinforcement occur. Over the years, much of this work became the basis for current "cognitive behavior therapies" which directly address issues in personality change and the coping processes of normal individuals (Meichenbaum, 1993). Gradually, these therapies have integrated discoveries from the behavioral level with those from more recent work on social cognition and mental processes, which are discussed in later sections.

Likewise, findings from research at the behavioral level on the responses of animals in laboratory conditions became the basis of later studies of complex social learning and personality at the social cognitive level (Part V). Recent breakthroughs at the biological level that identify brain centers involved in emotional reactions and those fundamental for other types of learning and memory functions also have given new life to work at the behavioral level. Brain processes and their links to behavior now can be studied experimentally, particularly in laboratory studies with animals. Consequently, the "black box" of the brain and the processes that occur within it, previously treated as "fictions" and off limits for a scientific psychology, have now become the arena for extensive research (e.g., LeDoux, 1996, 2001), at the vanguard of the science, as discussed in the final chapters of the text.

In the past, work at this level was faulted for overemphasizing the "stimulus" or "situation" and the role of rewards, and for missing much of the essentials of human personality, including the human potential for freedom and self-control: people are not just victims of their situations but also can actively create and change them, if not in the laboratory then certainly in real life. Critics saw behavioral work as reflecting a focus on the importance of the situation that minimizes the importance of dispositional or intrapsychic determinants such as traits and motives (Bowers, 1973; Carlson, 1971). A great deal of research in recent years has again demonstrated the power of stimuli to trigger automatically all sorts of cognitive, emotional, and behavioral reactions, leading practitioners to question the importance of the person's consciousness or internal thought processes (e.g., Bargh, 1996, 2001). The question of the degree to which the person can actually exert "agency" and intervene to change the ways in which stimuli impact on him or her remains one of the great open issues, actively pursued by a wide range of scientists and philosophers. We will revisit these big questions in the final sections of this text.

Historically, one of the persistent concerns about behavioral approaches is whether they really contribute to an understanding of the phenomena of interest to personality psychologists. An early worry about behavioral approaches was that they did not even try to study complex and distinctively human qualities, such as the emotions and internal states that seem so basic for understanding personality and appreciating its complexity. Indeed, some critics charged that behavioral psychologists only study what is easy to study with available methods. They accuse them of looking only under the light. Addressing this concern, researchers at the social cognitive level discussed in the next part of the text introduced some of the important missing pieces.

PART

V

THE SOCIAL COGNITIVE LEVEL

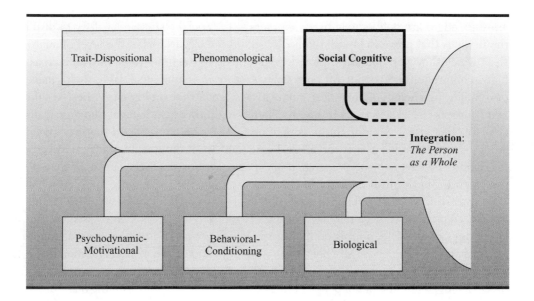

▶ PRELUDE TO PART V: THE SOCIAL COGNITIVE LEVEL

In the l960s and 1970s, Albert Bandura and Walter Mischel were both young psychologists at Stanford University with offices across from each other. They both had been trained as researchers in approaches to personality that made learning and conditioning a cornerstone of personality development. But they both also had been trained as clinical psychologists interested in helping people deal with their life problems. As clinicians working with people in real-life situations, they saw the limitations of the simple forms of behavioral conditioning that were based mostly on experiments with rats or pigeons in the laboratory. Consequently, they tried to connect findings from the behavioral approach with new insights coming from research on social cognition and the extraordinary mental capacities of human beings. In time, their work and that of others (e.g., Rotter, 1954) led to a radically different social and cognitive approach to learning that had more direct relevance to personality. It also addresses the specific mechanisms that enable people to use both social learning and cognitive principles to enhance their own abilities to self-regulate and to pursue their chosen life goals as effectively and happily as possible.

Currently, researchers at the social cognitive level focus on the importance of social cognition for personality. *Social cognition* refers to the person's social knowledge of the world, to how we see and make sense of ourselves and other people, and how we use this knowledge in dealing with the world, with ourselves, with our relationships. These researchers are concerned with the links between what goes on in the mind of the person—their social cognitions, emotions, goals—and their social behaviors. Their aim is to understand both what people think and feel and want and what they actually do. With these broad goals, the social cognitive level tries to integrate contributions coming from the behavioral level, the phenomenological level, and from the study of social cognition, to form a more complete view of the person.

Thus, a distinctive feature of work at this level of analysis is that it is explicitly integrative: rather than building a single unique theory or approach with distinct boundaries, its edges are deliberately fuzzy. Workers at the social cognitive level try to distill the findings that prove to be valid, reliable, and useful, regardless of the level of analysis at which they were initially explored. And they try to integrate them into an increasingly comprehensive model of personality. An overarching goal is to help make personality psychology a genuinely cumulative science that builds on its best results and concepts, regardless of their origins. Therefore, in this part, you will see numerous concepts that also are important in work at other levels of analysis, and that have been enriched and extended in new directions by researchers at the social cognitive level.

Efforts to integrate social cognition and personality originally began more than 40 years ago in the form of a "social learning theory" approach (Bandura, 1969; Mischel, 1968; Rotter, 1954). These theorists took from the behavioral level a focus on what people actually do, not just on what they say. Some also took from the phenomenologists, particularly from George Kelly, a focus on the ways in which people construe or appraise themselves and their experience (Mischel, 1973). And they all increasingly paid attention to the role of the person's expectancies, goals, and values in how information is interpreted and processed by different types of people. Further advance came rapidly with the onset of the cognitive revolution in psychology in the 1970s, and was stimulated by progress in recent years in the understanding of brain functions coming from related disciplines.

The next chapter discusses the development and emergence of the social cognitive approach. The second chapter in this part then illustrates the social cognitive processes that are being studied and their implications for understanding personality.

The Personal Side of the Science

Some questions at the social cognitive level you might ask about yourself:

▶ What is the role in personality of what people know, think, and feel?

▶ How does what I know, think, and feel about myself and the social world influence what I do and can become?

▶ What can I do to change how I think and feel?

▶ Will that change my personality and behavior?

▶ How much of who and what I am and do is "automatic"?

▶ How much is open to "willpower" and self-regulation?

▶ How do willpower and self-regulation work?

▶ How can I enhance my control over my life?

12

SOCIAL COGNITIVE CONCEPTIONS

▶ DEVELOPMENT OF THE SOCIAL COGNITIVE PERSPECTIVE

For more than four decades, psychology has experienced a cognitive revolution that has made the mind and how it works the focus of the field. It made exciting discoveries about how people think, and how they selectively attend to, manipulate, transform, store, and generate information. The findings soon made it clear that cognition has a central role in personality (Bandura, 1986; Mischel, 1973, 1990; Pervin & John, 1999), clinical psychology (Arkowitz, 1989; Beck, 1976), and social psychology (e.g., Higgins & Kruglanski, 1996).

Historical Roots

The social cognitive approach to personality began in the late 1960s. It was conceived by many psychologists who were in rebellion, frustrated by the limitations of earlier theories. At that time, the field of personality was divided into three theoretical camps. In one were enthusiastic Freudians guarding Freud's original work against anyone who sought to revise or criticize it. In a second camp were students of individual differences searching for broad personality trait dimensions. In the third camp were radical behaviorists concerned with conditioning and the relations between stimuli and responses, not with the internal ways an organism mediates between them. This third camp opposed any constructs that invoked the mind or mental activity in any form that could not be directly or simply measured. Except for occasional exchanges to attack each others' work, there was little communication among the camps. It was a milieu unresponsive to any "constructive alternatives."

You have already seen one protest movement in response to this state of affairs in the humanistically oriented ideas developed by theorists at phenomenological level, such as Carl Rogers and George Kelly. In their focus on the concepts and constructs of the individual, as perceived and understood by that person, they were anticipating the cognitive revolution. But these voices were treated more as a sideline protest movement than as a route for redirecting mainstream theory and research. Major disturbances were needed in that mainstream before serious attention would be paid to possible alternatives, and they occurred in the late 1960s.

Cognitive Processes Underlying Behavior

In the 1960s, some personality psychologists were drawn to the behavioral perspective, attracted by its rigorous scientific emphasis (Bandura, 1969; Mischel, 1968; Rotter, 1954). In their theorizing, they drew heavily on principles of learning established originally in experimental work with animals, as in the operant and classical conditioning studies (reviewed in Chapter 10). Nevertheless, much as they tried to stretch existing behavioral concepts, these personality psychologists encountered more and more new research findings that forced a change in their view and required moving beyond behaviorism, as discussed next.

12.1 How did delay of gratification research illustrate the important role of cognitive transformations?

Traditional behavioral approaches asserted that stimuli control behavior. But in fact, the perceiver's mental representations and **cognitive transformations** of the stimuli can determine and even reverse their impact. Such transformations were illustrated in research on the factors that influence how long preschool children will actually sit still alone in a chair waiting for a desired but delayed outcome (e.g., tempting pretzels or marshmallows) that has been placed in front them (Mischel, Ebbesen, & Zeiss, 1972). The question was: how long will children voluntarily continue to delay and what makes it hard or easy? It turned out that the answer depends importantly on how the children mentally represent the rewards (Mischel, 1974; Mischel et al., 1996).

For example, if a young child is left during the waiting period with the actual desired objects—the pretzels, for example—in front of her, it becomes extremely difficult to wait for more than a few moments. But through self-instructions they can cognitively transform the objects in ways that permit them to wait for long periods of time. For example, if they think about the stick pretzels they want now as little logs, or think about the marshmallows as round white clouds or as cotton balls, they often can wait for the whole required time. In short, what is in the children's heads—not what is physically in front of them—determines their ability to delay. Through self-instructions about what to imagine during the delay period, it is possible to completely alter (indeed, to reverse) the effects of the physically present temptations in the situation.

This was important because at that time behaviorism was still the dominant view. These findings with the little children made clear that it's what's in the head that is influencing behavior. Therefore, how people think and represent the world has to be taken into account to understand what they are doing and why they are doing it. George Kelly and Carl Rogers were right.

▶ OBSERVATIONAL LEARNING (MODELING): ALBERT BANDURA

At about the same time, new discoveries in learning research revealed a third type of learning process independent both of classical conditioning and of reinforcement. It was recognized, of course, that reward or reinforcement has a powerful influence on behavior in a great variety of situations. But it also became clear that people learn by observing others, not merely by experiencing rewards for what they do themselves. Much social learning occurs through observation without any direct reinforcement administered to the learner. Classical and operant conditioning remain important types of learning. However, it is now also clear that some of the most important human learning occurs through observation.

Learning Through Observation

Observational learning, sometimes called **modeling,** is learning that occurs without the learner's receiving direct external reinforcement. Such learning occurs even without the person's ever performing the learned response at all. You can learn a lot about how to kill people, for example, just by watching how it's done on television.

Observational learning occurs when people watch others or when they attend to their surroundings, to physical events, or to symbols such as words or pictures. Albert Bandura (1969, 1986) for the last four decades has led the way in the analysis of observational learning and its relevance for personality. Much human learning, from table manners, interpersonal relations, including cooperation and aggression, to school and work, depends on observation of this kind rather than on direct reinforcement for a particular action.

12.2 What is required for observational learning to occur?

Albert Bandura

Children learn partly through observation and imitation.

Figure 12.1 Photos depicting children spontaneously imitating a previously viewed model's aggressiveness.
Source: Bandura, A. (1965). Vicarious processes: A case of no-trial learning. In L. Berkowitz (Ed.), *Advances in experimental social psychology* (Vol. 2, pp. 1–55). New York: Academic Press.

Observational learning is often indirect. We learn much from what others observe and then tell us about. The mass media, which are highly effective means of communicating experiences and observations, contribute heavily to the enormous amount we learn about the environment and the behavior of others.

The influence of observational learning through the mass media is seen in the contagion of aggression that has spread through the United States as a result of so many people's watching television violence. Although the television networks are reluctant to accept it, watching violence on television can have definite negative effects on viewers (Liebert, 1986; Murray, 1973). For example, after observing films of an aggressive model who punched, pummeled, and hurled a Bobodoll, children spontaneously imitated the model's aggressiveness when put in a similar situation (Bandura, 1965). (See Figure 12.1 for an illustration.) Similarly, after watching violent cartoons for some time, children became more assaultive toward their peers than did other youngsters who had viewed nonviolent cartoons for the same period of time (Steuer, Applefield, & Smith, 1971).

Completely new response patterns can be learned simply by observation of others performing them. Observation is especially important for learning a language. Bandura (1977) emphasizes the advantages of observation for language learning compared to direct reinforcement for uttering the right sounds. He notes that exposure to models who speak the language leads to relatively rapid acquisition, while shaping would take much longer.

Observing Other People's Outcomes: What Happens to Them Might Happen to You

People learn about the possible consequences of various behaviors from observing what happens to others when they engage in similar behaviors. Your expectations about the outcomes of a particular course of action depend not only on what has happened to you in the past, but also on what you have observed happening to others.

We are more likely to do something if we have observed another person (model) obtain positive consequences for a similar response. Seeing other children praised for cooperative play, for example, makes a child more likely to behave cooperatively in similar situations. If, on the other hand, models are punished for a particular pattern of behavior such as cooperation, observers are less likely to display similar behavior (Bandura, 1965).

Although laboratory studies offer clear demonstrations of the importance of expected consequences, examples from life are more dramatic. Consider, for instance, the role of modeling in airline hijackings (Bandura, 1973). Air piracy was unknown in the United States until 1961. At that time, some successful hijackings of Cuban airliners to Miami were followed by a wave of hijackings, reaching a crest of 87 airplane piracies in 1969 that intermittently continued and, in tragically altered form, were seen again in the disaster of the September 11, 2001 terrorist attack on the United States.

In sum, you do not have to perform particular actions yourself in order to learn about them and their consequences; the observed as well as the directly experienced consequences of performances influence subsequent behavior. You do not have to rob a bank to learn that it is punishable; you do not have to be arrested for hijacking to learn about its consequences; and you do not have to rescue a burning child from a fire or return found money to discover that such acts are considered good. Information that alters what people expect will happen as result of a behavior changes the probability that they will perform it. Models inform us of the probable consequences of particular behaviors and thus affect the likelihood that we will perform them.

Observation also influences the emotions we experience. By observing the emotional reactions of others to a stimulus, it is possible vicariously to learn an intense emotional response to that stimulus. Suppose you see someone wincing from a painful electric shock each time a red light goes on in the machine to which he is attached. Soon you will wince when the red light comes on. Thus, you may become "vicariously conditioned" when you observe repeatedly the close connection between a stimulus (red light on) and an emotional response (pain cues) exhibited by another person, and this happens without your receiving any direct aversive stimulation yourself.

This point was demonstrated in a study in which adults observed another person making fear responses in reaction to the sound of a buzzer supposedly associated with the onset of an electric shock. (Actually the person was a confederate of the experimenter and only feigned pain and fear without getting any shocks.) Gradually, after repeatedly watching the pairing of the buzzer and the responses made by the confederate, the observers themselves developed a measurable physiological fear response to the sound of the buzzer alone (Berger, 1962).

Rules and Symbolic Processes. Many studies showed that people did not seem to need trial by trial "shaping" but rather seemed to be helped most by the rules and self-instructions they use to link discrete bits of information meaningfully to learn and remember materials (Anderson & Bower, 1973). Likewise, studies with children indicated that it helps not only to reward appropriate behavior but also to specify the

12.3 How do observed consequences affect the likely occurrence of behaviors learned through modeling?

12.4 What evidence exists that emotional responses can be acquired through observation alone?

12.5 How are symbolic processes involved in learning?

relevant underlying rules and principles so that children can more readily learn the standards that they are supposed to adopt (Aronfreed, 1966). When children understand that particular performance patterns are considered good and that others are unsatisfactory, they adopt the appropriate standards more easily than when there are no clear verbal rules (Liebert & Allen, 1967). Beginning early in life, the young child is an active thinker and perceiver who forms theories about the world, not a passive learner shaped by external rewards (Bruner, 1957; Flavell & Ross, 1981).

Cognition plays a role even in classical conditioning. Suppose, for example, that a person has been conditioned in an experiment to fear a light because it is repeatedly paired with electric shock. Now if the experimenter simply informs her that the light (the conditioned stimulus) will not be connected again with the electric shock, her emotional reactions to it can quickly extinguish (Bandura, 1969). On later trials, she can see the light without becoming aroused. Findings like these forced both researchers and behavior therapists to pay more attention to the individual's mental processes. In the development of therapeutic methods to change behavior, they began to more directly engage the person's thought processes and social knowledge for therapeutic ends (Davison & Neale, 1990; Davison, Neale, & Kring, 2004).

New Directions.   These sorts of findings suggested that a more cognitive approach to personality was required that takes into account how the individual characteristically deals mentally and emotionally with experiences. The search began for a theory of the cognitive-emotional-motivational processes that underlie the person's characteristic behavioral expressions and conflicts. As such, these efforts are in the tradition pioneered by Sigmund Freud, Henry Murray, and George Kelly, advanced over the century by many theorists reviewed in earlier chapters.

▶ SOCIAL COGNITIVE PERSON VARIABLES

12.6 Describe the five basic "person variables" in the social cognitive conception of personality.

Growing out of these contributions, a basic set of psychological **person variables** for describing individual differences in personality was proposed (Mischel, 1973), summarized in Table 12.1. These person variables try to capture the differences between people in the characteristic ways in which they interpret aspects of themselves and of their social worlds. It includes how they react to their own interpretations cognitively and emotionally, and in their behavior patterns.

TABLE 12.1 Types of Person Variables

- *Encodings (Construals, Appraisals):* Categories (constructs) for the self, people, events, and the situations (external and internal).

- *Expectancies and Beliefs:* About the social world, about outcomes for behavior in particular situations, about self-efficacy, about the self.

- *Affects:* Feelings, emotions, and affective responses (including physiological reactions).

- *Goals and Values:* Desirable outcomes and affective states; aversive outcomes and affective states; goals, values, and life projects.

- *Competencies and Self-Regulatory Plans:* Potential behaviors and scripts that one can do, and plans and strategies for organizing action and for affecting outcomes and one's own behavior and internal states.

Source: Mischel, W., & Shoda, Y. (1995). A cognitive-affective system theory of personality: Reconceptualizing situations, dispositions, dynamics, and invariance in personality structure. *Psychological Review, 102,* 253.

Walter Mischel

As the table shows, the person variables include encodings or construals, expectancies and beliefs, affects (feeling states and emotions), subjective values and goals, as well as competencies and self-regulatory strategies. These variables interact, but each provides distinctive information about the individual.

Encodings (Construals): How Do You See It?

People differ greatly in how they **encode** (represent, construe, appraise, interpret) themselves, other people and events, and their experiences. The same hot weather that upsets one person may be a joy for another who views it as a chance to go to the beach. The same stranger in the elevator who is perceived as dangerous by one person may be seen as interesting by another. Individuals differ stably in how they encode and categorize people and events, and these interpretations influence their subsequent reactions to them.

Suppose Mark, a teenager, tends to encode (construe, perceive) peers in terms of their hostile threats, and is highly sensitive to their possible attempts to challenge, manipulate, and control him. If he cognitively represents his world in such terms, Mark will be vigilant to threats and primed to defend himself. He therefore may see an innocent accident, such as having someone push against him in the crowded staircase, as a deliberate affront or violation (Cantor & Mischel, 1979; Dodge, 1986).

Different persons group and encode the same events and behaviors in different ways (Argyle & Little, 1972) and they selectively attend to and seek out different kinds of information (Bower, 1981; Miller, 1987). For example, some individuals tend to encode ambiguous negative events as instances of personal rejection (e.g., Downey & Feldman, 1996) and keep looking for clues that they are being rejected, which then makes them depressed and withdrawn. Other people, however, may easily feel disrespected and become angry and hostile even when they hear a mumbled greeting (e.g., Dodge, 1993).

12.7 What is meant by encoding? How does encoding affect other thoughts, feelings, and behaviors?

Different individuals may encode the same situation in different ways.

How people encode and appraise events and selectively attend to what they observe also greatly influences what they learn. For example, people who have poor social skills tend to encode situations in terms of the degree to which they might feel self-conscious versus self-confident in them. In contrast, more socially skilled individuals encode the same situations in terms of other dimensions such as how interesting or pleasant they might be (Forgas, 1983).

Expectancies and Beliefs: What Will Happen?

This analysis of personality does not stop with a description of what people know and how they interpret events. It also seeks to predict and understand actual performance in specific situations. Research on learning made it clear that the actions people perform depend on the consequences they expect (Bandura, 1986; Rotter, 1954). To predict specific behavior in a particular situation, one has to consider the individual's specific expectancies about the consequences of different behavioral possibilities in that situation (Mischel, 1973).

12.8 Differentiate between self-efficacy and behavior–outcome expectancies. How do they affect goals, behavior, and behavior change?

A particularly important type of expectancy consists of **self-efficacy expectations:** the person's belief that he or she *can* perform a particular behavior, like handling a

The development of self-efficacy takes many forms.

IN FOCUS 12.1

SELF-EFFICACY AND ITS IMPLICATIONS

Self-efficacy refers to the individual's belief that he or she can successfully execute the behaviors required by a particular situation. Perceptions of one's own efficacy importantly guide and direct one's behavior. The close connection between high self-efficacy expectations and effective performance is illustrated in studies of people who received various treatments to help reduce specific fears. A consistently high association was found between the degree to which persons improved from treatment (becoming able to handle snakes fearlessly) and their perceived self-efficacy (Bandura, 1977). If we assess perceived self-efficacy (asking people to specifically predict their ability to do a given act successfully), according to Bandura we can predict whether or not they will be able to perform it—for example, whether they now can pick up and play with the previously feared snake. (Bandura & Adams, 1977). Results of this kind suggest some clear links between self-perceptions of one's competence and the ability to actually behave competently.

Perceived self-efficacy influences the goals people set for themselves and the risks that they are willing to take: the greater their perceived self-efficacy, the higher the goals they choose and the stronger their commitment and perseverance in pursuing them (Bandura, 1997, 2001). Conversely, people who view themselves as lacking efficacy for coping with life tasks are vulnerable to anxiety and may develop avoidance patterns designed to reduce their fears. People who see themselves as lacking in essential efficacy also may become prone to depression. They may even show impairments in their immune system when coping with stressors that they believe they cannot control (Wiedenfeld et al., 1990).

The Role of Self-Efficacy. Although many different therapy techniques may produce changes in behavior,

might they all work through the same basic mechanism? Bandura (1978, 1982) has proposed that there is such a common mechanism: people's expectations of self-efficacy. Behavior therapy works, according to Bandura, by increasing efficacy expectations and thus leading people to believe that they can cope with the difficult situations that threatened them before. In this view, individuals will try to overcome a particular fear to the extent that they expect they can do so successfully. Any methods that strengthen expectancies of personal efficacy will therefore help the person perform the relevant behavior. The best methods will be the ones that give the person the most direct, compelling success experiences in performing the particular behavior, thereby increasing efficacy expectancies most. For example, actually climbing a fire escape successfully is a better way to overcome a fear of heights than just thinking about it, because it provides a more complete success experience and a stronger expectation for future mastery.

In sum, diverse processes of behavior therapy in Bandura's view exert their beneficial effects mainly by enhancing the individual's sense of self-efficacy. Thus, he sees each of the major behavioral strategies for inducing change as sharing one crucial ingredient: They improve perceived self-efficacy, thereby freeing the individual to perform actions that previously were not possible.

Self-efficacy is Bandura's most basic construct for understanding human motivations and emotional reactions. People with a sense of self-efficacy about their intended actions are more able to carry them out. High efficacy expectations thus help the individual to persist in the pursuit of goals, even in the face of adversities that would derail or depress persons who are less sure of their relevant personal competencies.

---

snake or taking an exam. Measures of these expectations predict with considerable accuracy the person's actual ability to perform the relevant acts. Efficacy expectancies guide the person's selection of behaviors from among the many that he or she is capable of constructing within any situation (Bandura, 1986). (See In Focus 12.1 for a detailed discussion of self-efficacy.)

Another type of expectancy concerns **behavior–outcome** relations. These behavior–outcome expectancies (hypotheses, contingency rules) represent the expected *if . . . then . . . relations* between behavioral alternatives and expected probable outcomes in particular situations. In any given situation, we generate the response pattern that we expect is most likely to lead to the most subjectively valuable outcomes in that situation (Bandura, 1986; Mischel, 1973; Rotter, 1954). In the absence of new information about the behavior–outcome expectancies in any situation, behavior will depend on one's previous behavior–outcome expectancies in similar situations (Mischel & Staub, 1965). That is, if you do not know exactly what to expect in a new situation (a first job interview, for example), you are guided by your previous expectancies based on experiences in similar past situations.

For example, we generate behavior in light of our expectancies even when they are not in line with the objective conditions in the situation. If you expect to be attacked, you become vigilant even if your fears later turn out to have been unjustified. If you expect to succeed, you behave quite differently than if you are convinced you will fail. Indeed, we sometimes behave in ways that directly help to confirm our expectations, thus enacting self-fulfilling prophecies (Buss, 1987). The person who is easily suspicious, angry, and ready to aggress is likely to extract reciprocal hostility and defensiveness from others that will, in turn, confirm his beliefs about them.

Affects: Feelings and "Hot" Reactions

12.9 Why are "hot" cognitions" so named?

What we feel—our affects and emotions—profoundly influences other aspects of behavior (e.g., Contrada, Cather & O'Leary, 1999; Smith & Lazarus, 1990; Zajonc, 1980). They also impact on the person's efforts at self-regulation and the pursuit goals (e.g., Mischel et al., 1996). It has long been known that such cognitions as beliefs about the self and one's personal future are themselves **hot cognitions,** that is, thoughts that also activate strong emotion (Ayduk & Mischel 2002; Metcalfe & Mischel, 1999). As Smith and Lazarus (1990) noted, anything that implies important consequences, harmful or beneficial, for the individual can trigger an emotional reaction. For example, when one is feeling bad or sad—what is called a negative affective state—and gets negative feedback about performance (e.g., a disappointing test score), it is easy to become demoralized and to over-interpret the feedback, resulting in depression (Wright & Mischel, 1982).

Affective reactions to situation features (such as faces) may occur immediately and automatically (e.g., Murphy & Zajonc, 1993; Niedenthal, 1990), outside of awareness (Gollwitzer & Bargh, 1996). These emotional reactions in turn can trigger closely associated cognitions and behaviors (Chaiken & Bargh, 1993). The affective states and moods experienced are easily influenced by situational factors, even by such simple events as finding a coin on the street (e.g., Isen, Niedenthal, & Cantor, 1992; Schwarz, 1990). But what we feel also reflects stable individual differences which may be related to temperament and biological variables (Rothbart et al., 1994).

Goals and Values: What Do You Want? What Is It Worth?

12.10 Describe the organizational functions of goals and values. What is intrinsic motivation?

Goals and values drive and guide the long-term projects people pursue, the situations and outcomes they seek, and their reactions to them (e.g., Linville & Carlston, 1994; Martin & Tesser, 1989). They serve to organize and motivate the person's efforts, providing the direction and structure for the life tasks and projects they pursue (Grant & Dweck, 1999). Motives, such as achievement, power, intimacy, and others studied by the Harvard personologists, are also represented in the personality system by the person variable of goals.

Goals influence what is valued, and values also influence performance. For example, even if two individuals have similar expectancies, they may act differently if the outcomes they expect have different personal values for them (Rotter, 1954, 1972) or if they are pursuing different goals (e.g., Cantor, 1994). If everyone in a group expects that approval from a teacher depends on saying certain things the teacher wants to hear, there may be differences in how often they are said due to differences in the perceived value of obtaining the teacher's approval. Praise from the teacher may be important for a student striving for grades, but not for a rebellious adolescent who rejects school. What delights one person may repel his or her neighbor. That makes it necessary to consider the individual's goals and the subjective value of particular classes of events, that is, his or her preferences and aversions. These goals and values are particularly important because much human behavior is driven by **intrinsic motivation:** the gratification the individual receives from the activity or task itself (Cantor, 1990; Deci & Ryan, 1987). Such motivation is reflected in the life goals that the person pursues, as will be discussed in detail in later chapters (Chapters 16, 17).

What Can You Do? Overcoming Stimulus Control

People regulate their own behavior by self-imposed goals and self-produced consequences. Even in the absence of external constraints and social monitors, we set performance goals for ourselves. We react with self-criticism or self-satisfaction to our behavior depending on how well it matches our expectations and standards (Bandura, 1986; Higgins, 1990). The expert sprinter who falls below his past record may condemn himself bitterly; the same performance by a less experienced runner who has lower standards may produce self-congratulation and joy. To predict Mark's reaction to being pushed, for example, it helps to know the personal standards he uses to evaluate when and how to react aggressively. Will he react aggressively even if the peer who pushed him is much younger? Likewise, can he regulate his own response strategically, or will he react explosively and automatically?

People also differ in the types of plans that guide their behavior in the absence of, and sometimes in spite of, immediate external situational pressures. Such plans specify

12.11 How do self-regulation processes counteract external stimulus control of behavior?

Self-observation plays an important role in the acquisition of skills and competencies.

the kinds of behavior appropriate under particular conditions, the performance levels (standards, goals) that the behavior must achieve, and the consequences of attaining or failing to reach those standards (Mischel et al., 1996). Plans also specify the sequence and organization of behavior patterns (Gollwitzer & Moskowitz, 1996; Schank & Abelson, 1977). Individuals may differ with respect to each of the components of self-regulation (e.g., Baumeister & Heatherton, 1996).

Self-regulation provides a route through which we can influence our interpersonal and social environment substantially. We can actively *select* many of the situations to which we expose ourselves, in a sense creating our own environment, choosing to enter some settings but not others (Buss, 1987; Ross & Nisbett, 1991). Such active choice, rather than automatic responding, may be facilitated by thinking and planning and by rearranging the environment itself to make it more favorable for one's goal (e.g., Gollwitzer & Moskowitz, 1996). Even when the environment cannot be changed physically (by rearranging it or by leaving it altogether and entering another setting), it may be possible to *transform* it psychologically, as discussed in Chapter 17.

In this section, we have summarized the person variables that are the basic units of the theory that we next describe. But first look at the long history of these person variables, as described in In Focus 12.2.

12.12 Which of the five person variables were especially influenced by the theories of Rotter and Kelly?

IN FOCUS 12.2

ON THE HISTORY OF PERSON VARIABLES

The development of person variables (Mischel, 1973; Mischel & Shoda, 1995) has a long history. These variables reflect an attempt to integrate contributions from two quite different theoretical perspectives that at first may seem incompatible. One was the personal construct theory of George Kelly (discussed in Chapter 8) and the other was the social learning theory developed by Julian B. Rotter (1954). Both Rotter and Kelly were professors in the graduate training program in clinical psychology at Ohio State University in the early 1950s, and both were important mentors for Walter Mischel. In the early 1950s, Mischel did his doctoral dissertation with Rotter, but most of his clinical psychology training was with Kelly. Although Professor Kelly's and Professor Rotter's offices were across the hall from each other, the two men were as different as their theories. They had little direct contact, and little influence on each other, although they both greatly influenced any students who were at Ohio State in those years. Their ideas were expressed in two extremely important books, Rotter's *Social Learning and Clinical Psychology*, published in 1954, and Kelly's two-volume *The Psychology of Personal Constructs* (1955). Together, these two pioneers contributed much to modern personality and clinical psychology.

The person variable of "encoding strategies" explicitly reflected George Kelly's core point—the importance of how individuals construe their experience and themselves. This construal or appraisal characterizes the first phase of how people make sense of incoming social information and interpret its personal meaning. The conceptualization of personality in cognitive social terms, however, sought a personality theory that includes not only how people perceive and interpret but also what they actually choose and do (Mischel 1973). For that purpose, it explicitly drew on expectancy-value concepts which had been given a central place by Rotter (1954). In Rotter's early social learning theory, the probability that a particular pattern of behavior will occur was a joint function of the individual's outcome expectancies and the subjective value of those outcomes.

In the late 1940s and early 1950s, Rotter introduced the expectancy construct to personality psychology and made it a centerpiece of his version of social learning. He had argued convincingly for the importance of both expectancies and values as basic building blocks for a theory of social learning that he wanted to speak more directly to the assessment and treatment of clinical problems. While his theory was extremely elegant, it was, like his colleague George Kelly's theory of personal constructs, apparently ahead of its time: the impact of both these theorists seems to be felt more decades later in indirect forms than when Rotter and Kelly first advanced their ideas.

Julian B. Rotter

▶ THE COGNITIVE–AFFECTIVE PERSONALITY SYSTEM (CAPS)

Structure and Dynamics

The **cognitive–affective personality system,** abbreviated as **CAPS** (Mischel & Shoda, 1995, 1998; Shoda & Mischel, 1998), focuses on how the person variables are organized and function within the individual. The personality system consists of a distinctive stable organization of person variables whose interactions generate the patterns of behavior that characterize the person.

When a person experiences certain features of a situation, a characteristic pattern of cognitions and affects becomes activated. The personality structure—the person's stable organized system of interconnections among the person variables—guides their further activation. In other words, given the occurrence of particular situational features, a cascade of interpretations, expectations, feelings, goals, and possible behavior scripts becomes activated in a pattern that is distinctive and stable. You saw examples in the descriptions of the narcissistic and rejection sensitive personality types given in Chapter 4. For example, the rejection sensitive person is likely to perceive the partner's "need for space to devote more time to work" as a sign of potential rejection. In turn, fears of abandonment, feelings of anxiety, impulses of anger, and so on become activated internally and expressed in aggressive behavior in a distinctive sequence.

Personality processing dynamics in this theory consist of such stable distinctive sequences of thoughts, feelings, and behaviors that become activated by particular types of situations. These are the stable *if . . . then . . .* patterns, or personality signatures, discussed in Chapter 4. *If* Gary sees himself as being rejected, *then* he thinks about abandonment, feels panic, and erupts with anger, aggression, and insults against his partner. The pattern is self-defeating because his hostility in response to his own rejection fears is likely to lead to actual rejection even when there was none before, making his worst fears come true (Downey et al., 1997).

You can see the implications of the CAPS model and the social cognitive approach to personality more concretely if you look at how it is applied to understanding a particular life, rather than people in general or even different types. We therefore focus again on Gary W.

View of the Person: Gary W.

12.14 Describe how the CAPS model guided the personality assessment of Gary W.

To give a richer sense of how this level of analysis sees the person as a whole, we next apply it to Gary W.

Assessing Person Variables and Dynamics. The assessments of Gary on each of the person variables used many sources: his own self-reports, diary notes based on daily self-observations, and interviews. The focus was on each of the person variables and on the situations in which they were expressed. Diverse measures, including questionnaires, were devised to sample a wide range of information about Gary and his personal world.

These measures drew on recent research which has provided relevant strategies for such assessments of experiences and behaviors that take account of the situations in which they occur (Cervone & Williams, 1982; Mischel et al., 1996; Mischel & Shoda, 1998). The methods include time sampling of tasks, behavior, and perceptions (e.g., Cantor et al., 1991; Moskowitz, Suh, & Desaulniers, 1994), and self-reports of reactions to daily stressors (e.g., Bolger & Schilling, 1991). They also include sampling of physical symptoms and of emotional reactions to them (Larsen & Kasimatis, 1991), as well as records of personal strivings and well-being (Emmons, 1991). All these methods allow systematic analyses of the types of *ifs* and *thens* significant in the lives of individuals in which their characteristic behavioral patterns unfold.

The assessments of Gary were intended to obtain answers to questions such as the following:

1. **Encodings.** What are Gary's enduring views of himself (self-concepts) and of his relations to the significant people in his life that are most important for him? In which of these is he particularly vulnerable? How does he assign causal responsibility for the positive and negative events and outcomes experienced in different domains (e.g., work, interpersonal)?

2. **Expectancies and beliefs.** What are Gary's self-efficacy beliefs and expectations in the domains that matter most to him? What are the major anticipated consequences (outcomes) of different alternative courses of action that he is considering for dealing with his current life goals?

3. **Affects.** What are his characteristic "hot" reaction patterns? What triggers them?

4. **Goals and values.** What values seem to be guiding his behavior? What life goals motivate Gary and shape the direction of his efforts?

5. **Competencies and self-regulatory strategies.** What strategies and competencies are available and readily activated by him? How do they help him to sustain long-term effort and self-control in the pursuit of his goals? What standards does he use in self-evaluation?

Note that the assessment of Gary in this approach does not address each person variable in isolation. Rather, it seeks to clarify how they interact, that is, their organization. For example, how do Gary's expectations affect his mood, and how does his mood, in turn, influence the strategies that are activated? It's these interactions of person variables within the system that generate the distinctive, stable patterns of *if . . . then . . .* signatures that characterize the person.

Gary's Ways of Encoding Experience and Himself.   Gary tends to encode situations on the basis of their potential threat for him. He views himself as a person who needs and wants a warm and caring relationship with a woman but he also sees women as a source of threat and provocation who "can't really be trusted."

For example, he views his new girlfriend's bids for "more emotional space"—for example, when she says "I feel like you're strangling me"—as "cold" and "rejecting." He becomes quickly infuriated when she expresses her feelings of anger and frustration with his demands and expectations and feels it means "she doesn't really love me." He says he tries to control himself on such occasions but in fact he quickly loses his temper. He then becomes enraged, although he claims to have overcome his childhood tendency toward emotional outbursts. He justifies and dismisses this behavior as an inevitable result of his girlfriend's lack of understanding and sympathy for him. Thus, he sees his explosions of anger as not in his control, attributes them to her "cold and rejecting style" and his "temper"—"I got it from my dad"—and exempts himself from responsibility.

Gary sees himself as shrewd and analytic, able to persist tenaciously in pursuit of a work goal. He seems to be exceptionally sensitive to the reactions of other people. Although Gary often seems to devalue many of his work achievements, particularly those that are in a verbal form, he actually has high regard for his quantitative abilities and work (e.g., priding himself on an innovative financial software program he developed). In the quantitative domain, he takes appropriate credit for his achievements ("with numbers I have a mind like a sharp razor"). Here he accurately evaluates himself as exceptionally talented and sometimes even inflates the magnitude of his contribution (when compared to its assessment by his peers).

Affect and Distress Reactions.   When dealing with public speaking situations, Gary is prone to becoming swamped with debilitating anxiety, followed by some depressive feelings. Most important, Gary becomes easily upset by any feedback short of complete approval and applause, especially in close romantic relationships. Unless he gets rapt attention and praise from his girlfriend, he feels she is rejecting him. He then becomes angry and hostile. After only several months, his relationship with his new girlfriend is in danger of being soured by the same conflicts that ended his relationship with his former girlfriend.

Gary's Rejection Sensitivity Dynamics (Interpersonal Domain).   Figure 12.2 shows Gary's **rejection sensitivity (RS)** dynamics, which are typical of rejection sensitivity in the domain of interpersonal relations. These dynamics are shown in abstract terms in the figure. The solid arrows show the activation paths in the dynamics, the broken arrows indicate deactivation. Gary's rejection sensitivity dynamics become activated when he perceives and encodes rejection cues, which he does easily and for which he scans persistently. He anxiously expects and vigilantly looks for signs that he is being criticized, "violated," ignored, or rejected. He easily interprets even ambiguous events, like the partner's momentary wandering attention or preoccupation with other concerns, as if they were intended to hurt him deliberately. His anger and even rage become easily and automatically activated.

12.15 Describe how Gary's rejection sensitivity reflects the interaction of CAPS elements.

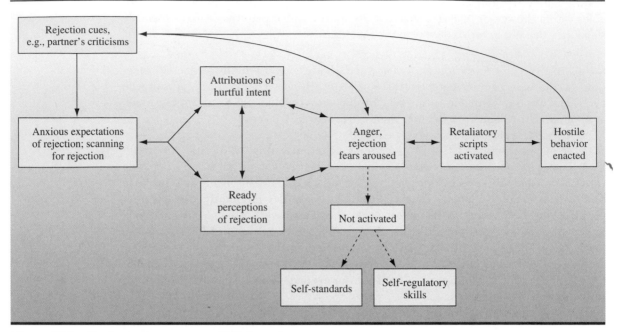

Figure 12.2   Gary's rejection sensitivity (RS) dynamics.

Note that the path to the activation of self-standards and values that might help him control his rage are not activated (broken arrows), nor are his self-regulatory skills accessed. Bypassing these, he becomes increasingly distressed, activating retaliatory hostile scripts and behaviors that he acts out. These lead to real rejection from his girlfriend, and the cycle is ready to be repeated again, spiraling into destruction of the relationship that he is so anxious to preserve. Although this dynamic is activated mostly in relations with the romantic partner, Gary's sensitivity to rejection sometimes is also visible in the domain of work and relations with authority. For example, he can suddenly become angry, impulsive, and hostile when he believes his work, especially quantitative, is not sufficiently respected and appreciated, once even starting a physical scuffle that later embarrassed him greatly.

Expectancies, Values, and Goals.   At first, Gary tries to present the self-confidence expected of an ambitious business student, but on closer examination he has many self-doubts. His genuine high self-efficacy expectations in the quantitative domain are an important exception to these self-doubts.

Most of Gary's goals, even in business school, seem to be directed at avoiding negative reactions from other people. Rather than being characterized by learning goals and motivated by the intrinsic satisfaction of mastering a given activity itself, Gary seems driven by concerns about the evaluative reactions of other people, particularly male peers, and is oriented to preventing himself from getting hurt. He becomes especially anxious and even depressed at the prospect of intimate relations with women. This raises conflicts for him because he values and seeks such intimacy. Unfortunately, at present he does not seem to see clearly how his behavior, specifically his temper outbursts, impacts his closest relationships and therefore assumes no responsibility for it. As was noted in the discussion of his rejection sensitivity dynamics, when these become activated, he bypasses his own standards, values, and goals. Instead, automatic impulsive outbursts of anger become enacted without self-censorship, although they are followed by self-blame and self-criticism after they are enacted.

These excerpts from the case of Gary illustrate concretely how the CAPS personality system operates. To summarize, in CAPS theory, the personality system interacts continuously and dynamically with the social world in which it functions (Mischel et al., 1996; Shoda & Mischel, 1998). The interactions with the external world involve a two-way reciprocal interaction process. Gary is responding to his girlfriend, interpreting her expressed needs as rejections of him. His ways of reacting automatically with hurt, retaliation, and anger alienate her, and she in fact becomes increasingly rejecting. Ultimately, his expectations of abandonment are confirmed, but he was instrumental in shaping that outcome.

In the CAPS model, the behaviors that the personality system generates impact the social world, partly shaping and selecting the interpersonal situations the person subsequently faces. In turn, these situations influence the person (e.g.,Bandura, 1986; Buss, 1987). The personality system actively selects and changes situations. Thus it is *proactive* insofar as it does not just respond to the environment but generates, selects, modifies, and shapes situations in its reciprocal transactions with them (see Dodge, 1997a,b; Mischel & Shoda, 1995).

12.16 What is meant by the concept of reciprocal interactionism? How do we see it at work in Gary W.'s case?

▶ COMMON THEMES

The perspective that is illustrated by CAPS includes many different themes and variations. Some of the main shared features of this still-evolving approach are summarized below.

Work at this level of analysis has a social cognitive focus. It is social in its concern with patterns of social behavior and the interpersonal aspects of life. It is cognitive in its emphasis on mental processes and on understanding how different people process incoming information (Higgins & Kruglanski, 1996). It examines how people process and use information about themselves and their social worlds, and studies the cognitive strategies they develop for coping with important life challenges. Research tries to see how individuals differ in their distinctive encoding (appraisal) of different features of situations. It also examines how those encodings activate and interact with other cognitions and affects in the personality system to generate the person's distinctive patterns of behavior.

The situation is important in work at this level because the personality system is in continuous interaction with situations: the behaviors that are generated depend on the situation involved in the particular interaction. But this is a two-way relationship: the effect of the situation also depends on the characteristics of the personality system. The personality system in part creates the situations themselves through its own interpretations, thoughts, and actions (Bandura, 2001; Mischel & Shoda, 1998). Sometimes this two-way interaction process is called **reciprocal interactionism** (Bandura, 1977), to refer to the chain of causes. In this causal chain, the qualities of a person (including cognitive social person variables), the behaviors generated by the person, and the environment all interact with each other, and each influences the others.

Theory at this level is influenced by information processing models about how the mind works. Although originally based on simple computer systems, in recent years these models have gained more of the depth and complexity essential for a dynamic conception of personality. First, modern information processing models are more like biological and cognitive neuroscience models of how the brain works (e.g., Anderson,

1996; Churchland & Sejnowski, 1992; Shoda & Mischel, 1998). Their focus now is not just on how much of a particular quality (e.g., of self-efficacy expectations) a person has. Rather, it is on the way the person's internal mental representations—the specific cognitions and feelings that become activated—are related to each other and interconnected within the total network of the mental and emotional system. In this view, it is the person's distinctive network that makes up the structure of personality.

The metaphor for this network now tends to be the systems of connections within the human brain through which the neurons are interconnected and process information. This type of processing system operates rapidly and functions at multiple levels often outside conscious awareness (Kihlstrom, 1999, 2003). Theoretically, it is able to deal with the fact that personally important information processing is emotional and often automatic and unconscious. Models that deal with these processes now try to go beyond merely "cool" cognitions to "hot" affect-laden representations and feeling states (e.g., Metcalfe & Mischel, 1999; Smith & Lazarus, 1990; Kahneman & Snell, 1990).

Many researchers at this level of analysis also hope that their ideas and work will help people to enhance their options and decrease their personal vulnerabilities. Put most simply, they would like their work to ultimately help optimize human well-being, freedom, and choice. Thus, they also emphasize human potential and assume that people can change constructively and extensively under appropriate conditions. With that goal in mind, often they study such real-life problems as overcoming anxious, depressive, and health-threatening mental states (Aspinwall & Taylor, 1997; Cantor & Kihlstrom, 1987; Taylor & Armor, 1996). Much of this work tries to improve people's sense of mastery and competence so they can better fulfill their potential. The commitment is to enhancing the human potential for alternative, more constructive ways of coping, consistent with the phenomenological perspectives of such earlier theorists as George Kelly.

The emphasis on stimulus conditions in early behavioral approaches often implies a passive view of people—an image of organisms that are empty except for sets of automatic responses to external stimuli. In contrast, social cognitive approaches emphasize that people are active and agentic—that is they actively shape their worlds and social environments. Consequently much of the research at this level deals with issues of self-regulation and self-control and is designed to see how people can more effectively regulate their behavior to "take charge" of their lives (e.g., Bandura, 2001; Mischel et al., 1996).

Recall that trait theories emphasize differences *between* people in their response to the same situation or even regardless of the situation. Cognitive social theories also address these differences. However, they go on to try to understand the unique ways an individual's behavior may change in response to even slight changes in conditions, as indicated in Figure 12.3. They focus on these enduring within-individual differences (intra-individual stability) as an important aspect of the difference between individuals. Understanding the psychological impact or meaning of particular events and conditions in the person's life requires observing how changes in those conditions alter what he or she expects, thinks, and feels.

Work at this level also draws on the behavioral level of analysis to the degree that it asks: Why and when will individuals *do* what they do? That is, it goes from social cognition, feelings, and motivation to a focus on human action (e.g., Gollwitzer & Bargh, 1996). But although the approach includes a focus on behavior, its primary goal is to clarify the psychological processes that underlie the particular behavior of interest.

Figure 12.3   The same person behaves in distinctive but stable ways in response to various psychological situations.

SUMMARY

DEVELOPMENT OF THE SOCIAL COGNITIVE PERSPECTIVE

- The social cognitive level seeks to understand the cognitive, affective, and social processes that characterize the individual. It was stimulated by the finding that the perceiver's mental representations and cognitive transformations of stimuli can determine their impact on the individual.

OBSERVATIONAL LEARNING (MODELING): ALBERT BANDURA

- Albert Bandura called attention to the importance of observational learning for personality development and change.
- Observational learning can help create or remove fears and other strong emotional reactions.
- Human performance is dramatically improved by awareness of the rules or principles that influence the outcomes for behavior.

SOCIAL COGNITIVE PERSON VARIABLES

- In social cognitive theory, a set of *person variables* (cognitive–affective units or CAUs) is used to describe individual differences.
- They consist of *encodings, expectancies and beliefs, affects, goals and values, and self-regulatory strategies and competencies.*

THE COGNITIVE–AFFECTIVE PERSONALITY SYSTEM (CAPS)

- In CAPS theory, individual differences reflect (1) differences in the chronic accessibility of person variables, and (2) differences in their organization.
- In the CAPS system the person and the situation are in continuous interaction, influencing each other reciprocally.
- The system's structure is reflected and expressed in the person's stable patterns of *if . . . then . . .* relationships which form distinctive behavioral signatures.
- Gary's personality dynamics illustrate how CAPS interacts continuously and dynamically with the social world.

COMMON THEMES

- Social cognitive approaches focus on how individuals select, attend to, and process information about the self and the world and react to it.
- *Reciprocal interactionism* suggests that people's attributes and actions interact with the social environment continuously, each influencing the other.

KEY TERMS

behavior–outcome
relations   279
cognitive transformations
(of stimuli)   272
cognitive–affective
personality system
(CAPS)   283

encoding   277
hot cognitions   280
intrinsic motivation   281
modeling   273
observational
learning   273
person variables   276

personality processing
dynamics   283
reciprocal
interactionism   287
rejection sensitivity   285
self-efficacy
expectations   278

CHAPTER

13

SOCIAL COGNITIVE PROCESSES

When Jana told her partner Rodolfo she had to spend the evening preparing for a work assignment due the next day he became upset, interpreting it as another sign of her increasingly uncaring attitude toward him. He felt rejected, and then quickly became irritated and angry, starting an argument. His interpretation of her behavior as rejecting him was of course only one way to encode it. Compare him with Mike who is less sensitive to rejection. When Mike heard a similar comment from his partner he took it at face value, respecting her need to concentrate on her work.

To explain individual differences in reactions to the same event, researchers at the social cognitive level of analysis begin by seeing how the different individuals construe and interpret its meaning and significance. These interpretations and the emotions and behavioral reactions that unfold are, in turn, influenced by the "self."

The importance of the self in psychology has had many dramatic ups and downs. For many years at the height of behaviorism it was almost totally down. There were, however, some notable exceptions, discussed earlier in this text. The self was important for the phenomenologists, and likewise in the clinical work of some of the post-Freudians and object relations theorists. But these remained lone voices for decades, muted by the dominance of behaviorists who judged the self to be a confusing fiction outside the realm of science. Currently, interest in the self is again extremely high (e.g., Leary & Tangney, 2003). After its long slumber, the self is attracting the attention of many theorists and researchers because new methods for studying social cognition have opened it to systematic study. The self now has become a core topic in personality at the social cognitive level of analysis. This chapter examines the self and self-relevant processes, focusing on concepts and research from the social cognitive level of analysis.

▶ THE SELF

At a common sense level, everyone knows what the self is: we have a sense of ourselves, refer to ourselves, talk about ourselves, evaluate ourselves—sometimes blaming ourselves, sometimes praising ourselves—and we often control ourselves—with varying degrees of success. The "self" has been central in personality psychology since the start of the field, reflected in concepts like "self-actualization," "self-evaluation," "self-regulation" and "self-control." For many researchers, the self has become a prefix for practically every important process and function in a personality system.

The "I" and the "Me"

13.1 In what two ways do we use the term "self"?

An important distinction between two different aspects of the self was originally made a century ago by America's pioneering psychologist William James (1890), and it still guides much of the work on the self.

The self as an "I" is an agent, actor, or doer, an executive who conducts basic psychological functions. The **"I" as an agent** engages in such functions as self-regulation (as in impulse control and planning for the future), and self-evaluation to assess progress along the way.

The self has a second important aspect that James also recognized: the "Me" that is observed and perceived. It is the Me that one sees when attention is focused on the self, the **"Me" as an object,** represented in self-concepts, in how we see ourselves. Each person develops a self-theory about his or her Me. This theory is a construction, a set of concepts about the self (Epstein, 1973, 1983; Harter, 1983; Wiley, 1979).

The Self as a Basic Schema

Intuitively the "I," "me," or "self" is a basic reference point around which experiences and the sense of personal identity itself seem to be organized. At the social cognitive level of analysis, the self is viewed not as a "thing" but as a schema or cognitive category that serves as a vital frame of reference for processing and evaluating experiences (e.g., Baumeister, 1997; Markus, 1977; Markus & Cross, 1990; Markus, Kitayama, & Heiman, 1996).

Schemas in social cognitive theories are important for understanding mental functioning because they are basic units for organizing information. You can think of them as knowledge structures made up of collections of attributes or features that have a "family resemblance" to each other. These structures often have clear exemplars or "best examples" (e.g., a sparrow is a better or more prototypic example of a bird than an ostrich). Schemas help one to make sense of new events by recognizing what they are like in terms of their similarity to the structures that already exist. That happens, for example, when you see a flying object of a type you don't recall having seen before, but nevertheless have no trouble deciding it must have been a bird—not a plane, or a stone, or a balloon. The "self" that develops also consists of interconnected knowledge structures of many different sorts.

In the course of development, the child acquires an increasingly rich concept of himself or herself as an active agent, an "I" separate from other people and objects. A sense also develops of a "Me" that has defining features and qualities reflected in multiple self-concepts.

Self-Schemas. Self-concepts or **self-schemas** (Markus, 1977) include generalizations about the self, such as "I am an independent person" or "I tend to lean on people." These cognitions arise from past experiences and, once formed, guide how we deal with new information related to the self. To illustrate, if you have strong self-schemata about being extremely dependent, passive, and conforming, you would process and remember information relevant to those schemata more quickly and effectively than do people for whom those schemata are not personally relevant (Markus, 1977). People have better recall for information about traits that they believe describe them than for traits that are not self-descriptive (Rogers, 1977; Rogers, Kuiper, & Kirker, 1977). Thus, we give information relevant to the self special cognitive treatment, for example, by being more attentive toward it.

Self-schemas are highly accessible personal constructs that a person is ready to use for encoding information. People differ stably in their self-schemas (Higgins, 1996; Higgins, King, & Mavin, 1982). These self-concepts also have motivational implications. For example, most people desire to maintain positive views of themselves, are motivated to pursue self-knowledge, and want to enhance and improve themselves (Baumeister, 1996).

Each person develops a **self-theory** about his or her Me. This theory is a construction, a set of concepts about the self. It is created by the child from experience, but it in turn affects future experience (Epstein, 1973, 1983; Harter, 1983, 1999; Wiley, 1979). The individual's self-concepts are not a simple mirror-like reflection of some absolute reality. Self-concepts, like impressions of other people and of the world, involve an integration and organization of a tremendous amount of information. Self-concepts are not a mirror of reality, but they are correlated with the reactions and outcomes that the person has experienced throughout the past and expects to obtain in the future (Leary & Tangney, 2003; Wiley, 1979). Although the concepts change over time, their foundations form early in life, and they influence what that future becomes (Markus & Cross, 1990; Markus et al., 1996).

13.2 Describe the meaning and functions of the self-schema.

The Relational Self and Transference

In recent years, the self has been reconceptualized in light of current theory and findings on social cognition and specifically on how memory works.

The Relational Self. Self-knowledge includes all the thoughts (cognitions) and feelings (affects) that develop about oneself. It consists of information that is stored and organized in memory as a cognitive–affective (mental and emotional) representation. This knowledge representation is closely connected in the memory system to knowledge

13.3 In what sense is the self inherently relational? What do social cognition researchers mean by transference, and how does this compare with Freud's use of the term?

representations about the significant other people in one's life (e.g., Andersen & Chen, 2002; Linville & Carlston, 1994), making these two types of information directly associated. Consequently, when the representation of a particular significant other is activated (e.g., you think about your mother), aspects of your own self-representation also become activated mentally. These close connections in memory make the self intrinsically *relational* and interpersonal: in a sense, the significant others to whom one is close become part of one's personal identity. Thus, the self evolves from, and is linked to, the important relationships in one's life: in this sense, the self that emerges is intrinsically entangled with significant others.

As the self develops in relation to a particular significant other person, expectations also develop about the most likely interactions that will occur with him or her. For example, an adolescent may come to expect that interactions with her mother about smoking are likely to play out along predictable lines (e.g., more hassles, more guilt, more avoidance). These scripts become reactivated in future interactions with the significant other or with other people who remind you of that person (Andersen, Reznik, & Chen, 1997).

Transference Reconsidered. The notion of the *relational self,* conceptualized in terms of memory representations that connect self-knowledge with representations of significant others, also allows a fresh view of psychodynamic concept of transference. Transference, as discussed in earlier chapters, plays an important role in psychoanalytic theory and psychotherapy beginning with Freud, and in the ideas of Kohut and the object relations theorists. The concept of transference has now been recast in social-cognitive terms, and this is not just a renaming: it informs the process in light of findings from memory research. In the social cognitive reinterpretation by Susan Andersen and colleagues (2002), when one develops relationships with new people, transference readily occurs. This happens to the degree that

The self is interpersonal.

Susan Anderson

representations of significant others in memory are activated by the newly encountered person.

Feeling attracted to—or repelled by—a newly encountered person, and easily making all sorts of inferences about his or her qualities (that may or may not turn out to be accurate), can be understood in terms of the particular significant other representation that is being triggered by, and applied to, the new person (Andersen et al. 1997; Andersen & Chen, 1998). If the psychiatrist's manner reminds the patient of her father, the cognitive–affective representation of the father, and of the patient's self in relation to him, also may become easily activated and brought to mind.

Note that this view of transference is compatible with Freud's (1912/1958) claim that the individual's mental representations of significant others, most notably the parents in early childhood, profoundly influence relationships to new people, including the psychoanalyst in the treatment process. It is different, however, because it sees this process in terms of social-cognitive information processing rather than as a reflection of the psychosexual drives and conflicts favored in psychodynamic theory.

Perceived Stability of Self and Potential for Change

Perhaps the most compelling quality of the self is its perceived continuity. The experience of **subjective continuity** in oneself—of basic oneness and durability in the self—seems to be a fundamental feature of personality. Indeed, the loss of a feeling of consistency and identity may be a chief characteristic of personality disorganization, as is seen in schizophrenic patients who sometimes report vividly experiencing two distinct selves, one of them disembodied (Laing, 1965).

13.4 What psychological mechanisms enable us to maintain consistency and continuity in the self-schema?

Each person normally manages to reconcile seemingly diverse behaviors into one self-consistent whole. A man may steal on one occasion, lie on another, donate generously to charity on a third, cheat on a fourth, and still readily construe himself as "basically honest and moral." People often seem to be able to transform their seemingly discrepant behaviors into a constructed continuity, making unified wholes out of diverse actions. How does this integration work?

Many complex factors are involved (Harter, 1983; Markus & Cross, 1990). One answer to this question may be that people tend to reduce cognitive inconsistencies and, in general, simplify and integrate information so that they can deal with it (Ross & Nisbett, 1991; Tversky & Kahneman, 1974). The human mind may function like an extraordinarily effective reducing valve that creates and maintains the perception of continuity even in the face of perpetual observed changes in actual behavior (Festinger, 1957; Mischel, 1973). The striving for self-consistency that the phenomenologists emphasized (Rogers, 1951) has received support in the work of other researchers working on related topics (Aronson & Mettee, 1968; Cooper & Fazio, 1984).

Another basis for perceived consistency is that people often know a good deal about their own characteristic *if . . . then . . . ,* situation–behavior patterns. There is a strong relationship between the intra-individual stability of those patterns and the person's self-perception of consistency. This finding was discussed in Chapter 4. It was found that college students who perceived themselves as consistent with regard to their "conscientiousness" had much more stable patterns of situation–behavior relations in their conscientious behavior than did those who saw themselves as not highly consistent (Mischel & Shoda, 1995). For example, students who always conscientiously prepared for tests, but were not conscientious about keeping appointments on time would see themselves as consistent. Note that their consistency was in their stable *pattern*, rather than from one type of situation (test preparation) to another (punctuality).

In general, the self-concepts and personal constructs that people have seem to show a good deal of stability (Byrne, 1966; Gough, 1957; Mischel, 1968). Thus our personal theories about ourselves and the world tend to be relatively stable and resistant to change (Nisbett & Ross, 1980), as are our attitudes and values (E. L. Kelly, 1955). This perceived stability, however, coexists with the equally compelling fact that throughout the life course, people modify and transform their self-concepts as they envisage and construct "alternative future selves" (Cantor, 1990, p. 735) and strategically adapt to diverse life challenges (Mischel & Morf, 2003).

Multiple Self-Concepts: Possible Selves

The self traditionally has been viewed as unitary: a single self that is relatively consistent (Allport, 1955; Snygg & Combs, 1949). More recently, it is increasingly common to characterize the self as a multifaceted, dynamic set of concepts consisting of multiple selves. These different peceived selves reflect different aspects of an individual's total personality.

Consider a woman who seems hostile and fiercely independent some of the time but passive and dependent on other occasions. What is she really like? Which one of these two patterns reflects the woman that she really is? Must she be a really aggressive person with a facade of passivity—or is she a warm, passive-dependent woman with a surface defense of aggressiveness? In theory, at the social cognitive level, it is possible for her to be all of these: a hostile, fiercely independent, passive, dependent, aggressive, warm person all in one (Mischel, 1969). Indeed, each of these aspects may constitute a different **possible self** or potential way of being (Markus & Cross, 1990).

Hazel Markus

Of course, which of these selves she is at any particular moment would not be random; it would depend on who she is with, when, and why, and most importantly on how she construes and interprets the situation, that is, its meaning to her. But each of these aspects of her self may be a quite genuine and real aspect of her total being, part of her own unique but stable patterning of person variables (Mischel & Morf, 2003).

The self-concepts that encode different aspects of the person vary, depending on particular contexts, on the type of behaviors that are self-assessed, and on the culture. The beliefs and values of one's culture and group profoundly influence how individuals construe themselves and their future possibilities (e.g., Stigler, Shweder, & Herdt, 1990), and even the conception and definition of the "self" varies greatly across cultures. Thus, the self may be a more central concept for societies like ours that value self-enhancement and see the self as an entity, than for societies like the Japanese that value the relations between the person and other people rather than oneself alone (e.g., Markus et al., 1996; Markus & Kitayama, 1991).

The concepts of the self that the person can access easily comprise what has been called the **working self-concept** (Markus & Nurius, 1986), which derives from various self-conceptions that are present in thought and memory. According to Markus and her colleagues, this working self-concept includes ever-changing combinations of *past selves* and *current selves,* as well as the imagined *possible selves* that we hope to become or are afraid of becoming. These possible selves serve as guides for behavior and can have significant impact on one's emotional and motivational states. A schematic representation of some components of a working self-concept is shown in Figure 13.1.

Self-Esteem and Self-Evaluation

One of the most critical aspects of the self-concept is **self-esteem** (Harter, 1983). Self-esteem refers to the individual's personal judgment of his or her own worth (Coopersmith, 1967; Epstein, 1973, 1990). Self-esteem is such an important aspect of

13.5 How does self-esteem develop and influence behavior?

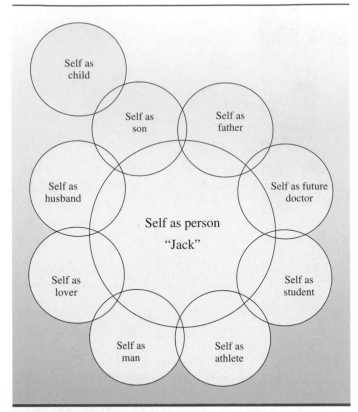

Figure 13.1 Schematic representation of a working self-concept. The working self-concept contains mental representations of diverse aspects of the self, from the present and the past, as well as imagined possible future selves.

the self-concept that the two terms are often used as if they were the same. Although self-esteem is sometimes discussed as if it were a single entity, persons may evaluate their functioning in different areas of life discriminatively (Crocker, 2002).

Self-esteem and self-evaluations are influenced by the feedback that people continuously get from the environment as they learn about themselves, beginning in the early course of development (Leary & Downs, 1995; Leary, 2002). In their self-appraisal, individuals are guided by their memories and interpretations of earlier experiences, and by the framework of self-concepts, self-standards, and self-perceptions through which they view and filter their experiences. People compare themselves to their own standards, as well as to their perceptions of the performance of relevant others (Bandura, 1986; Higgins, 1996; Norem & Cantor, 1986). For example, people who greatly value achievement and who are motivated to achieve tend to react quite differently to failure experiences than do those who are low in achievement striving (Heckhausen, 1969; Koestner & McClelland, 1990). However, the same outcome that is a discouraging "wipe out" for one may be a motivating challenge for the other.

People adopt many different strategies to cope with performance feedback relevant to self-esteem. For example, the impact of success and failure experiences depends on whether the person construes or "frames" the outcomes as reflecting on the self as a whole, or in terms that are more circumscribed and specific to the particular success or failure situation (Mendoza-Denton and associates, 2001). So if the experience of failure is framed in terms of being about the self as whole without any situational qualifiers (e.g., "I am a failure"), the emotional fall-out and consequences generalize much more broadly than when the experience is framed in situation-specific, *if . . . then . . .* terms (e.g., "I fail if I take this kind of test on this topic.")

Self-evaluation processes are basic for understanding how people see themselves and respond to their own experiences. They reflect each person's compromises between the need for accurate perception of his or her performance in the real world and the self-protective desire to maintain a favorable self-image. Personality theorists have long recognized that in this self-evaluation process, we generally manage to combine a mix of "thorough realism" and "protective maneuvering" (Cantor & Kihlstrom, 1987, p. 152).

Costs of Self-Esteem Pursuit. People with high as compared to low overall levels of self-esteem generally seem to function better in many aspects of their lives, and to feel better about themselves in many domains (Hoyle et al., 1999). However, while having genuinely high self-esteem may have its substantial benefits, its active pursuit can have high costs (e.g., Crocker, 2002). The risk in the pursuit of self-esteem is that it can lead people to focus too much on themselves while neglectful of the feelings and needs of others. This can encourage competitiveness rather than cooperation (e.g., Carver & Scheier, 1998). It can lead to preoccupation with "how am I doing?" rather than attention to "how are you?"—and a neglect of other people while busily trying to build up one's own self-esteem. The costs of pursuing self-esteem tend to be especially high for people who see high self-esteem as essential for feeling that they are worthy. For them, threats to self-esteem may trigger anxiety followed by negative defensive reactions to reduce the discomfort. These defensive reactions can range from hostility and aggression to withdrawing from relationships or creating emotional distance that undermines important connections with other people (e.g., Baumeister, 1998).

13.6 How can the pursuit of high self-esteem create maladjustment?

Features and Functions of the Self: Overview

The explosion of research on the self in the last few decades is leading to a consensus about its essential features (Hoyle et al., 1999; Mischel & Morf, 2003). In contemporary views on the self, the self is seen as having the following qualities:

13.7 Describe three important features of the self.

- *The self is essentially social and interpersonal—it arises out of social experiences with significant other people and is expressed in relation to them (e.g., Andersen & Chen, 2002).*

In earlier forms this social view of the self was seen in the discussion particularly of Carl Rogers and the later work of Tory Higgins. It is seen clearly in current work, for example, on the relational self and the reinterpretation of transference in social cognitive terms.

- *The self is important for understanding the processes of adaptation and coping—that is the doing or executive functions of personality (e.g., self-regulation, self-defense). In performing these functions it is a dynamic, motivated system (e.g., Baumeister, 2002; Derryberry, 2002; Leary, 2002).*

Many of these qualities and functions were emphasized in earlier forms by the ego psychologists, stemming originally from the psychodynamic Freudian tradition. It was seen, for example, in Anna Freud's focus on ego defenses and in the theories and clinical practice of Alfred Adler and Carl Jung (Chapter 6).

- *Closely related to the above is the view that the self has evaluative functions, and it is basic for the concept of identity (e.g., Crocker, 2002; Eisenberg, Spinrad, & Morris, 2002). It is motivated to protect self-esteem (Leary, 2002). These features were important in the theories of Erik Erikson, Heinz Kohut (1971), and Otto Kernberg (1976, 1984), which you already encountered in this text in Chapter 6. They are again being given new life in the work on self-regulation and goal pursuit discussed later in the text (e.g., Chapters 16 and 17).*

▶ CAUSAL ATTRIBUTIONS, HELPLESSNESS, AND MASTERY

Perceptions about one's adequacy and self-efficacy can have either self-enhancing or self-destructive consequences. In this section we consider how these positive and negative patterns develop and play out.

Causal Attributions Influence Emotions and Outcomes

13.8 What two kinds of causal attributions do people make? Define the self-enhancing attributional bias.

Did I do it? Was it my fault? Did I really deserve it? Was it just luck? Did he spill the milk on me on purpose? Is she mean or just upset today? The different ways in which individuals answer these kinds of questions about causation reflect some extremely interesting individual differences. *Causal attributions* are the explanations people make of the causes of events and they have predictable implications for how they feel about themselves and other people (Weiner, 1990). For example, we may see the same event—say, getting an A on an exam—as due to *internal causes* (such as high ability or hard work) or as due to *external causes* (such as the ease of the task or good luck). How we feel about the grade depends on whether we see it as due to internal or external causes (Phares, 1976; Rotter, 1966).

Pride and Shame. Generally, "pride and shame are maximized when achievement outcomes are ascribed internally, and minimized when success and failure are attributed to external causes" (Weiner, 1974, p. 11). In other words, a success that is perceived to be the result of one's ability or effort (internal causes) produces more positive feelings about oneself than does the same success when it is viewed as merely reflecting luck or an easy task (external causes). Conversely, we feel worse (for example, experience "shame") when we perceive our failure as reflecting low ability or insufficient effort than when it is seen as due to bad luck or the difficulty of the particular task. For example, being fired from a job for one's incompetence has a different emotional impact than does being fired because the firm went bankrupt (see In Focus 13.1 for discussion).

As noted in the In Focus 13.1, in most people, perceptions of causes tend to be biased in self-enhancing ways (Greenwald, 1980; Harter, 1983; Leary, 2002). This bias can have beneficial effects, although in the extreme it can be self-deluding. But at the other extreme, to lack the self-enhancing, self-protective bias completely may risk developing a depressive orientation (Lewinsohn and colleagues, 1980).

Learned Helplessness and Apathy

13.9 How does learned helplessness develop and affect behavior?

When people believe that there is nothing they can do to control negative or painful outcomes, they may come to expect that they are helpless (Seligman, 1975) and encode themselves in helpless terms. They expect that the aversive outcomes are uncontrollable, that there is nothing they can do. In this state, called **learned**

IN FOCUS 13.1

THE PERCEPTION OF CONTROL AND MEANINGFULNESS

There is a strong bias to see events and behavior as meaningful, orderly, and controllable even when they are random. You have seen this attributional bias if you have ever watched behavior in a casino. If you observed closely, you probably noticed how often gamblers act as if they can control chance by shaking the dice just right, or waiting to approach the roulette wheel at the perfect moment, or pulling the slot machine levers with a special little ritual. Gamblers are not unique in believing they can control chance events.

Even when something is clearly the result of chance (like the cards one draws in a poker game), people may see it as potentially controllable and not just luck. There is a deep human tendency to see the world as predictable and fair. We expect a "just world" (Heider, 1958), a world in which the things that happen to people are deserved and caused by them—even things like whether or not they win a lottery, get cancer, or are raped and murdered. Much research (reviewed by Langer, 1977) suggests that people often do not discriminate between objectively controllable and uncontrollable events. Instead they seem to have the "illusion of control," acting as if they can even control events that actually are pure chance.

In most people, this is part of a **self-enhancing bias**: we are more likely to see ourselves as causally responsible for our actions when they have positive rather than negative outcomes. When we do well or win, it is to our personal credit; when we do badly or lose, we could not help it (e.g., Fitch, 1970; Urban & Witt, 1990). Even when outcomes are negative, as in a tragic accident, we may find it hard to cope with events unless we somehow can see them as "just," meaningful, and orderly (e.g., Taylor & Armor, 1996; Taylor & Brown, 1988). Although this finding was first seen as evidence for a simple self-enhancing bias by perceivers, more recently it has been shown to have important, potentially beneficial and therapeutic effects for personality (e.g., Seligman, 1990; Seligman, Reivich, Jaycox, & Gillham, 1995; Taylor & Armor, 1996).

helplessness, they also may become apathetic and despondent and that state may generalize and persist.

The concept of learned helplessness originally was based on findings from some experiments with animals exposed to extreme frustration. Consider, for example, a dog placed in a situation where he can do nothing to end or escape an electric shock delivered to his feet through an electrified grid on the floor. Later he may sit passively and endure the shocks even though he can escape them now by jumping to a nearby compartment (Seligman, 1975, 1978). These findings on learned helplessness with animals also were consistent with less rigorous observations of humans forced to face extreme and persistent frustration. Withdrawal, listlessness, and seeming emotional indifference are often found among war prisoners and inmates of concentration camps, for example. The victims seem to have given up totally, presumably overwhelmed by their inability to do anything that will change their desperate lot.

Dramatic examples of learned helplessness may be found among the children of America's migrant families whose plight was described by Coles (1970). He notes that unlike typical children in the middle class, migrant children soon discover that their shouts and screams will not necessarily bring any relief from their pains and frustrations. Consider this description by a migrant mother of her own helpless feelings in the face of her children's suffering:

My children, they suffer, I know. They hurts, and I can't stop it. I just have to pray that they'll stay alive, somehow. They gets the colic, and I don't know what to do. One of them, he can't breathe right and his chest, it's in trouble. I can hear the noise inside when he takes his breaths. The worst thing, if you ask me, is the bites they get. It makes them unhappy, real unhappy. They itches and scratches and bleeds, and oh, it's the worst. They must want to tear all their skin off, but you can't do that. There'd still be mosquitoes and ants and rats and like that around and they'd be after your insides then, if the skin was all gone. That's what would happen then. But I say to myself it's life, the way living is, and there's not much to do but accept what happens. Do you have a choice but to accept? That's what I'd like to ask you, yes sir. Once, when I was little, I seem to recall asking my uncle if there wasn't something you could do, but he said no, there wasn't, and to hush up. So I did. Now I have to tell my kids the same, that you don't go around complaining—you just don't (Coles, 1970, pp. 9–10).

In sum, a good deal of research now suggests that when people believe they cannot control events and outcomes, they gradually develop a sense of helplessness (Wortman & Brehm, 1975; Seligman, 1990) and even severe depression. In the extreme, when people feel they cannot tolerate the frustrations in their lives, they may lose interest in all activities and virtually stop behaving, often spending a great deal of time in bed. They tend to become very sad and feel worthless, often suffering a variety of physical complaints.

13.10 What four classes of symptoms characterize depression?

There is general agreement that the behaviors listed in Table 13.1 characterize depressed people as a group. Each depressed individual displays his or her own combination of any of these behaviors, often including deep unhappiness, emotional numb-

---

TABLE 13.1   Some Indicators of Depression

Mood
  Feel sad and blue most of the time
  No longer enjoy things they used to
  General loss of feeling
  Fatigue, apathy, boredom
  Loss of interest in eating, sex, and other activities

Physical symptoms
  Headaches
  Difficulty sleeping
  Gastrointestinal symptoms (indigestion, constipation)
  Weight loss—loss of appetite
  Vague physical complaints

Behaviors
  Unsociable—often alone
  Unable to work, less sexual activity
  Complaining, worrying, weeping
  Neglect appearance
  Speak little (speech is slow, monotonous, soft)

Ideation
  Low self-esteem ("I'm no good")
  Pessimism ("Things will always be bad for me")
  Guilt, failure, self-blame, self-criticism
  Feel isolated, powerless, helpless
  Suicidal wishes ("I wish I were dead." "I want to kill myself.")

Source: Based on Lewinsohn, P.M. (1975). The behavioral study and treatment of depression. In M. Hersen (Ed.), *Progress in behavior modification* (pp. 19–64). New York: Academic Press.

ness and loss of interest, withdrawal from normal activities, and profoundly negative feelings about oneself and life. In contrast, when people believe that they can make an impact on their environment, that they can influence and control events, they become more alert, happier—and may even live longer (Seligman, 1990).

Pessimistic Explanatory Styles

Persons are most vulnerable to perceiving themselves as helpless when they see the bad things that happen in life as due to their own internal qualities rather than to more momentary, external, or situational considerations (Abramson, Seligman, & Teasdale, 1978). They explain why they failed the test, for example, by thinking "I'm incompetent" rather than as due to the flu they had and the fact that they could hardly see the page. People who do this consistently have a distinctive, essentially *pessimistic explanatory style*.

Pessimism is defined as an explanatory style that has three components: the person sees bad events as enduring, widespread, and due to the self. At an early age, this style can be a predictor of poor health for the future (Peterson, Seligman, & Vaillant, 1988). In one study, a group of healthy 25-year-old college graduates filled out questionnaires asking them to tell about difficult personal experiences in their lives. Researchers then analyzed the way the students explained the bad events that had occurred to determine whether or not their explanatory styles were generally pessimistic. Judges rated the explanations according to three criteria: the level of *stability* (seeing an event as having no end in sight; for example, "it won't ever be over for me"), *globality* (generalizing the event to many aspects of one's life), and *internality* (accepting one's self as causing or central to the problem rather than attributing it to some external factor or just plain circumstances). The more consistently stable, global, and internal the explanations, the higher the "pessimistic" style score.

Over a span of 35 years, the group was followed up with health examinations, and measures of illnesses were recorded. For about 20 years after college, there were no significant differences in the health of the participants. By the time they reached the ages of 45 through 60, however, those who at age 25 had been more pessimistic in their responses were more likely to be suffering from illness.

Researchers of optimistic–pessimistic explanatory styles also studied newspaper interviews with ballplayers from the Baseball Hall of Fame, published throughout the first half of the century. The interviews quoted the players' explanations of good and bad events as they discussed how and why they won or lost games. Players who attributed their losses to their own personal, stable qualities and thus saw them as their own fault, but saw their wins as due to momentary external causes (e.g., "the wind was right that afternoon") tended to live less long than those who used more optimistic explanatory styles to construe their good and bad experiences (Peterson & Seligman, 1987).

Learned Optimism

The opposite of the learned helplessness pattern is a pattern of experience and thinking called **learned optimism** (Seligman, 1990). To develop this style the person is helped to encode the daily hassles and setbacks in life by deliberately using self-enhancing explanations. Now negative experiences become viewed as momentary, specific, and not due to one's one failings. This optimistic, positive way of interpreting experience tends to be associated with a wide range of positive outcomes, as assessed by self-reports of feeling happier and evidence of more effective functioning and work success (also see In Focus 13.2).

13.11 Describe the three attributional elements of the pessimistic explanatory style. How does pessimism relate to physical well-being?

13.12 Contrast learned optimism with learned helplessness. How are optimism and self-enhancing illusions related to psychological adjustment?

THE ILLUSORY WARM GLOW OF OPTIMISM

Traditionally, psychologists have considered an accurate perception of self as essential for mental health (Jahoda, 1958). Researchers, however, have found that most psychologically healthy people have somewhat unrealistically positive illusory self-views, whereas those who perceive themselves more accurately tend to be the less mentally healthy (Taylor & Brown, 1988). For example, people with realistic self-perceptions are more likely to experience low self-esteem and depression, while more stable individuals tend to see positive personality traits as being most descriptive of themselves (Alicke, 1985; Brown, 1986).

The exaggeratedly positive self-perceptions that most people have became apparent in a study comparing depressed patients with nondepressed psychiatric and normal controls (Lewinsohn et al., 1980). Patients who had interacted in small group situations were asked to rate both themselves and each other with regard to personality characteristics. Nondepressed individuals' self-ratings were considerably more favorable than the ratings others had given them. Self-ratings of depressed individuals were consistent with the ratings given them by others,

suggesting that the nondepressed people had unrealistically positive self-views, seeing themselves through rose-colored glasses.

Individuals biased by such self-enhancing illusions also tend to feel they have an unrealistically large amount of control in pure chance situations, where in fact they cannot influence the outcome (Langer, 1975). In a study involving dice-throwing, for example, nondepressed participants felt that they would have greater control when throwing the dice themselves than when someone else did it for them (Fleming & Darley, 1986). The opposite state is found in depressed persons, who are likely to have a more realistic perception of the amount of control they have in chance situations—which in the case of dice-throwing is zero. Likewise, people in a depressed state tend to be reasonably accurate when predicting the future, while the nondepressed display an unrealistic optimism (Alloy & Ahrens, 1987). These results are clear, interesting, and consistent but, of course, they should not be misread as suggesting that gross distortions of reality characterize nondepressed individuals.

The depressed may perceive themselves *more* accurately than the non-depressed perceive themselves.

Similar results were found with different measures based on self-reported optimism in one's orientation to, and interpretation of, life events. For example, the degree of optimism in the person's orientation to life predicts recovery from coronary bypass surgery in patients; it also predicts fewer physical symptoms in college students (Scheier & Carver, 1987). People with an optimistic orientation to life seem to face stressful situations by thinking about them constructively to deal with them as effectively as possible, essentially trying to make the best of the situation even if it is an extremely difficult one. In contrast, the pessimistic orientation is associated with withdrawal, which automatically prevents problem solutions or constructive reinterpretation (Scheier, Weintraub, & Carver, 1986).

Helpless versus Mastery-Oriented Children

Following failure on a task, some individuals seem to fall apart and their performance deteriorates. But other people actually improve. What causes these two different types of responses to failure? The answer to this question again requires understanding how the person construes or interprets the reasons for the experience. Consistent with the work on learned helplessness, children who believe their failure is due to lack of ability (called *helpless children*) were found to perform more poorly after they experienced failure than did those who see their failure as due to lack of effort (called *mastery-oriented children*). Indeed, the **mastery-oriented** children often actually performed better after failure (Dweck, 1975).

When faced with failure, helpless children seem to have self-defeating thoughts that virtually guarantee further failure. This became clear when groups of helpless and mastery-oriented fifth-graders were instructed "to think out loud" while solving problems. When children in the two groups began to experience failure, they soon said very different things to themselves. The helpless children made statements reflecting their

13.13 Compare the attributional patterns of helpless and mastery-oriented children, and their effects on performance.

Carol Dweck

TABLE 13.2   Coping Strategies of Helpless and Mastery-Oriented Children

Helpless Children	Mastery-Oriented Children
Attributions for failure to self "I'm getting confused" "I'm not smart"	*Self-instructions to improve performance* "The harder it gets, the harder I need to try"
Solution irrelevant statements "There's a talent show this weekend, and I am going to be Shirley Temple"	*Self-monitoring statements* "I'm really concentrating now"
Statements of negative affect "This isn't fun anymore"	*Statements of positive affect* "I love a challenge"

Source: Based on Diener, C. I., & Dweck, C. S. (1978). In analysis of learned help-lessness: Continuous changes in performance, strategy, and achievement cognitions following failure. *Journal of Personality and Social Psychology, 36,* 451–462.

loss or lack of ability, such as "I'm getting confused" and "I never did have a good memory" (Diener & Dweck, 1978, p. 458). None of the mastery-oriented children made lack-of-ability statements. Instead, these children seemed to search for a remedy rather than for a cause for their failure. They gave themselves instructions that could improve their performance, such as "I should slow down and try to figure this out" and "The harder it gets, the harder I need to try."

The helpless children made many statements that were irrelevant to the solution and that usually were ineffective strategies for problem-solving (see Table 13.2). For example, one helpless male repeatedly chose the brown-colored shape, saying "chocolate cake" in spite of the experimenter's repeated feedback of "wrong." Finally, the attitudes of the two groups toward the task differed markedly. Even after several failures, mastery-oriented children remained positive and optimistic about the possibility of success, while helpless children expressed negative feelings and resignation, declaring, for example, "I give up."

Incremental versus Entity Theories: Your Own Personality Theory Matters

13.14 Compare entity with incremental theories. How do they affect the goals people choose and their achievement outcomes?

Not just psychologists but everyone—including the young child—has theories. Often their theories are not spelled out and thus only implicit theories of personality, but they can have profound effects on daily life. Carol Dweck and colleagues have shown that people's implicit theories or beliefs about the malleability or fixedness of personality and character predict many of their reactions to others as well as to their own performance and feelings. This work began when Dweck and Leggett (1988) found that children who display the helpless pattern see their intelligence as a fixed trait or static entity that they cannot change or control. In contrast to such an entity interpretation, youngsters who are mastery-oriented tend to view their intelligence more flexibly as something they can increase and develop.

These different views or theories about intelligence also orient them toward different types of goals. The **entity theorists** seem to choose goals motivated by the desire to avoid unfavorable judgments and to gain approval about their competence.

The **incremental theorists** choose goals motivated by the desire to increase their competence, for example, seeking opportunities to learn new things and enhance their mastery.

These differences in children's theories about their intelligence also predict important real-life outcomes in their development. Children were tracked from sixth to seventh grade in their transition to junior high school (Henderson & Dweck, 1990). The most impressive gains in grades during this transition were found for the incremental theorists. In sharp contrast, children who saw their intelligence as fixed tended to remain low achievers if they had been low achievers before and, most distressing, among these entity theorists ". . . many of those who had been high achievers in sixth grade were now among the lowest achievers" (Dweck, 1990, p. 211). Clearly, our self-concepts and theories about our important qualities, our way of "encoding" or construing ourselves, impact our subsequent development (see In Focus 13.2).

Going further, Erdley and Dweck (1993) divided late grade school children into those who held entity versus incremental theories and showed them slides depicting some negative behaviors of a "new boy at school" For example, he lied about his family background, cheated from a classmate's paper, and stole a classmate's left-over art materials. They also received information about situational factors (the boy had moved in the middle of the school year to the new school) and about possible psychological mediators (the boy was nervous about making a good impression).

As predicted, entity theorists made significantly stronger judgments about the boy's global moral traits (e.g., bad, mean, nasty) than did incremental theorists. Furthermore, entity theorists did not revise their trait judgments of the boy when positive information was provided whereas incremental theorists responded to the inconsistent information. Entity theorists also expected their first impression of the boy to remain valid forever whereas incremental theorists predicted that the boy might act differently in the future. Once they have rendered a negative moral judgment, entity theorists generally recommend punishment for the transgressor (Chiu, Dweck, Tong, & Fu, 1997; Erdley & Dweck, 1993), whereas incremental theorists recommend education or rehabilitation, consistent with their belief in the possibility of personality change even in wrongdoers.

The implications of these two types of theories for other attitudes and behaviors also have been explored across different cultures. For example, although Hong Kong college students were significantly more "collectivistic" than U.S. students, the entity theorists in both cultures made stronger dispositional inferences than did incremental theorists, apparently assuming that what people do even in a single instance reflects their stable fixed traits. (Chiu, Hong, & Dweck, 1997). Likewise, entity theorists, in another study, endorsed both positive and negative stereotypes about ethnic groups (African–Americans, Asians, Latinos) and occupational groups (lawyers, politicians) more strongly than did incremental theorists in studies with college students (Levy, Stroessner, & Dweck, 1998). In short, one's implicit personality theory shows itself in many forms, influencing how one judges people and interprets behavior.

Is the entity theory or the incremental theory better? Although an entity view has so far been linked with more maladaptive outcomes, neither view necessarily reflects the truth. And each theory has advocates convinced of its greater value.

▶ PERSONALITY ASSESSMENT

The social cognitive level of analysis has made diverse contributions to personality assessment and personality change.

13.15 Describe three characteristics of social cognitive personality assessment. What kinds of measures are typically employed, and how do they differ from trait measures?

First, assessments at this level tend to be specific, focused on specific cognitions, feelings, and behavior in relation to particular types of situations, rather than in terms of situation-free broad trait terms. Recall, for example, that self-efficacy refers to individuals' beliefs that they can do what is required in a particular type of situation or task (such as if asking for a pay raise, or on a specific achievement task, or in approaching a dangerous object), not their overall efficacy expectations in general. This focus reflects the view that the expressions of the personality system and the person's goals and motivations are seen in *if . . . then . . .* personality signatures, not just in the overall levels of different types of behavior.

Second, assessments whenever possible also try to identify the implications for constructive personality change or treatment. They thus are aimed at identifying the psychological person variables which might be modified, for example by enhancing efficacy expectancies through exposure to relevant efficacy-building experiences. Such assessments, always closely linked to change or treatment programs, are being done effectively in areas that range from weight control in anorexic patients to recovery of sexual functioning after massive coronary problems, to overcoming debilitating fears.

Personality assessors in this approach also seek to identify the underlying person variables and processes that seem to account for the individual's stable behavior patterns. They tend to conceptualize these underlying variables in relatively specific (rather than global) terms.

Researchers and assessors therefore obtain self-reports, ratings, and other data to infer the particular person variable as directly and specifically as possible within these contexts. Some also try to sample and observe behavior as it occurs naturally. For example, they ask people to provide daily diary reports of what they actually did and experienced within specific situations (e.g., Ayduk and associates, 2003; Bolger & Schilling, 1991; Cantor et al., 1991). There have been many applications, and we illustrate these with the example of the measurement of self-efficacy expectations.

Measuring Self-Efficacy Expectancies

Given the importance of the self-efficacy construct in social cognitive theories it is also a person variable that is used extensively in personality assessment at this level of analysis (Bandura, 1978, 1986; Cervone, Shadel, & Jencius, 2001; Merluzzi, Glass & Genest, 1981). Self-efficacy is assessed by asking the person to indicate the degree of confidence that he or she can do a particular task. For example, Bandura et al. (1985) wanted to assess the recovery of patients who had suffered heart attacks. Many tasks were described to the patients. These included such potentially stressful things as driving a few blocks in the neighborhood, driving on a freeway, and driving on a narrow mountain road. They also included situations that would induce other kinds of emotional strain, as illustrated in Table 13.3. For each item the respondent indicates the confidence level for being able to do the task.

13.16 How is self-efficacy measured? How well do these measures predict behavior?

Self-efficacy measures are particularly useful because they tend to predict the relevant behaviors at high levels of accuracy. For example, a consistently strong association was found between rated self-efficacy and the degree to which people showed increased approach behavior toward previously feared objects after they had received treatment for their fears (Bandura, Adams, & Beyer, 1977). Note that a distinguishing feature of self-efficacy measurement is that it is always about a specific domain, such as the ability to approach a type of feared object, or to control your weight, or efficacy about college course work in your major. This specificity contrasts with global measures, for example when you are asked to rate your "over-all level of self-esteem."

TABLE 13.3   Measuring Self-Efficacy Expectancies

Listed below are situations that can arouse anxiety, annoyance, and anger. Imagine the feelings you might have in each situation, such as your heart beats faster and your muscles tense. Indicate whether you could tolerate now the emotional strain caused by each of the situations.

Under the column marked *Can Do,* check (✓) the tasks or activities you expect you could do *now.*

For the tasks you check under *Can Do,* indicate in the column marked *Confidence* how confident you are that you could do the tasks. Rate your degree of confidence using a number from 10 to 100 on the scale below.

10	20	30	40	50	60	70	80	90	100
Quite Uncertain				Moderately Certain			Certain		

	Can do	Confidence
Attend a social gathering at which there is no one you know.	_____	_____
At a social gathering, approach a group of strangers, introduce yourself, and join in the conversation.	_____	_____
At a social gathering, discuss a controversial topic (politics, religion, philosophy of life, etc.) with people whose views differ greatly from yours.	_____	_____
Be served by a salesperson, receptionist, or waiter whose behavior you find irritating.	_____	_____
Complain about poor service to an unsympathetic sales or repair person.	_____	_____
When complaining about bad service, insist on seeing the manager if you are not satisfied.	_____	_____
In a public place, ask a stranger to stop doing something that annoys you, such as cutting in line, talking in a movie, or smoking in a no-smoking area	_____	_____
Ask neighbors to correct a problem for which they are responsible, such as making noise at night, not controlling children or pets.	_____	_____
At work, reprimand an uncooperative subordinate.	_____	_____

Source: Examples reprinted from *American Journal of Cardiology, Vol 55,* Bandura, A., Taylor, C. B., Ewart, C. K., Miller, N. M., & Debusk, R. F., "Exercise testing to enhance wives' confidence in their husbands' cardiac capability soon after clinically uncomplicated acute myocardial infarction", 635–638 (1985), with permission from Excerpta Medica Inc.

The focus on the context, situation, or contingency (e.g., *if . . . then . . .*) is of course a key characteristic of assessment at this level in which person qualities are directly linked to contexts and situations. It is also well illustrated in the work discussed next.

Individual Differences in *If . . . then . . .* Signatures

Advances also are being made in assessments of individual differences that take close account of the situation. Iven Van Mechelen and his colleagues (Van Mechelen & Kiers, 1999; Vansteelandt & Van Mechelen, 1998) are using the concept of *if . . . then . . .* signatures to classify people into different types based on the kind of responses they give in specific types of situations, such as those that are especially frustrating, as discussed in Chapter 4. The results are encouraging for building a classification system for types of people that is both theory-guided and specific enough to predict behavior in different contexts. Recall that the ultimate goal of such typologies is to predict the probability of certain type of individuals exhibiting certain types of behavior when faced with certain types of situations. The hope would be that this could allow a level of precision not possible with typologies based on characterizations in broad trait terms like "disagreeable" or "unsociable." In their recent work, these researchers took the additional step of linking their typology to measures of social cognitive person variables. Using a questionnaire that asked about the participant's encodings, expectancies, and whether they kept their anger in or let it out, they demonstrated meaningful links between such person variables and types of *if . . . then . . . behavior signatures.*

The Implicit Association Test (IAT)

13.17 What kinds of cognitive processes are implicit measures designed to assess?

Behavioral measures have the advantage of being objective, in that most people would agree that a child hit another child when they see the behavior in front of them. But what about assessing thoughts and feelings, especially those that are not within the person's awareness? We could, of course, ask people to tell us what's on their mind. But then we will learn what they *think* are their thoughts or feelings. What if these are not their *true* thoughts and feelings? And what exactly would one mean by "true" thoughts and feelings? These are the issues that are central for researchers at the psychodynamic-motivational level of analysis, and they also are important for the social cognitive level of analysis. The CAPS system described in the last chapter, for example, assumes that many of the thoughts and feelings in the personality system may not be accessible to the person's awareness. In recent years there have been important advances in assessing such aspects of personality outside awareness. Consider the following scenario:

A boy goes fishing with his father, but slips on a slippery rock and suffers a serious head injury. When the ambulance takes him to the ER, the doctor there turns pale, and exclaims "Oh, my god, it's my son!"

What's going on here? Is there something strange about this scenario? How do you explain this? Wasn't the boy's father with the boy when the accident occurred? In fact, nothing may be unusual with the scenario, and the most likely, and mundane, interpretation is that the doctor at the ER is the boy's mother. If you didn't think of that possibility right away, that may be because in your mind you may have associated doctors in emergency rooms more strongly with men than women, reflecting gender stereotypes in our society.

Such an association is *implicit* when people have no awareness of making it and being influenced by it as they process social information such as this scenario. It may be like a mental habit, not necessarily a motivated bias, which is applied automatically, without much awareness. Several ways to assess implicit associations have been developed (Greenwald et al., 2002). Here we will describe one, called the **Implicit Association Test (IAT),** for the assessment of **implicit self-esteem,** developed by Greenwald and Farnham (2000).

The IAT requires participants to make a series of judgments about each of the words presented to them briefly, one at a time, in quick succession.

Specifically, the words presented come from four distinct categories, and the participants' task is to indicate the category of the word presented, as quickly as possible, by pressing an appropriate computer key. One category of words refers to *self* such as "I," "me," and "mine." As soon as these words appear, participants press a particular computer key (e.g., the "A" key located on the left side of the keyboard). Another category represents *not self,* and so when they see words such as "they," "theirs," "it," they press a different computer key (e.g., the "5" key in the numerical keypad located on the right side of a keyboard). The remaining two categories refer to obviously good and obviously bad concepts. So when they see words such as *health, joy,* and *kindness,* they press one computer key, and when they see words such as *ugly, failure,* and *awful,* they press another.

If participants were given four separate keys to indicate each of the four categories, the task would be relatively simple. But the crucial innovation in the design of IAT is that there are only two keys available to press on the keyboard. Therefore two concepts must "share" a key. This is done in one of two ways. In the "self = bad" condition, participants press the same key (e.g., "A") to indicate that the word they see refers to either "self" or "bad," and they press another key (e.g., "5") when the word refers either to "not self" or "good." Most participants find this combination of keys very difficult to master, and their responses are slow, in order to prevent making mistakes. In contrast, in the "self = good" condition, in which the concepts are combined in a different way, they find it much easier to do this task. Namely, when they use the same key to indicate they saw a word that referred to either "self" or "good," and the other key to indicate they saw a word that referred to either "not self" or "bad," they are much faster in completing the task.

The difference in the impact of these two ways of combining the concepts on the difficulty of the task, reflected in the time needed to complete it, is taken to indicate the strength of association between "self" and "good" (and "not self" and "bad"). This is a measure of self-esteem, because a central element of the concept of self-esteem is how positively or negatively one regards oneself. And it is an implicit measure because the associations being measured do not rely on people's own awareness and report of how strongly they associate self with good, but rather based on an automatic response that has been shown to be difficult to control consciously. In fact, the implicit and explicit measures of self-esteem were largely unrelated to each other. In the Greenwald and Farnham (2000) study, those who had a high implicit self-esteem as measured by IAT were no more likely than those who had low implicit self-esteem to describe themselves as "good" when they were asked to rate themselves on a "good"–"bad" continuum.

Because the self-report measures used in this study were well-established in the field, one may be tempted to conclude that the implicit measure was not a good measure. However, the measure of implicit self-esteem also was able to predict a phenomenon that has been well-established as related to self-esteem (Brown & Dutton, 1995; Dodgson & Wood, 1998; Greenberg et al., 1992). Namely, people who were high in self-esteem, as determined by the implicit measure, were relatively unaffected by experience of failure, while those who were low in self-esteem by the implicit measure took the failure to heart (Greenwald & Fahnham, 2000, Study 3).

Since its introduction in 1998, the IAT has become widely used to measure not only implicit self-esteem, but also implicit attitudes, beliefs, and values in a number of domains. One very interesting finding is that IAT measures of anti-Black prejudice predicted the White participants' behaviors toward Black people on indicators such as body openness, eye contact, and friendly laughter (McConnell & Leibold, 2001).

▶ PERSONALITY CHANGE AND THERAPY

Work at the social cognitive level has had an important influence on current forms of therapy for a wide range of personality problems. These range broadly from fears and depression through difficulty in relationships, to troubles dealing with work challenges. Other examples include the treatment of impulsive and aggressive tendencies, and help

13.18 What are the objectives of social cognitive approaches to therapeutic behavior change?

for overcoming addictions and improving self-control in adhering to crucial health and medical regimens. Many psychologists who work at the social cognitive level also explore the links between personality and health (e.g., Miller, Shoda, & Hurley, 1996). In recent years they have been investigating individual differences in vulnerability to severe psychological disorders, such as depression, as well as to physical diseases, such as cancer and coronary–pulmonary disease. Social cognitive approaches are also being applied to understanding social and cultural differences (Mendoza-Denton, Shoda, Ayduk & Mischel, 1999).

Social Cognitive Influences

Therapists within this approach try to help clients to identify their disadvantageous ways of thinking about themselves, other people, and their problems. In the safety of the therapy situation, therapist and client interact to experiment and explore ways of reconstruing and modifying basic assumptions in thinking and the automatic emotional reactions that are not working well for the client. A fundamental aim is to increase the client's perceived and real freedom to change in desired directions. One route is to provide experiences that enhance efficacy expectations. Change becomes easier when clients begin to expect that they can cope more effectively and that they can face previously terrifying situations more calmly. Therapy includes a wide range of actual and imagined (symbolic) experiences designed to develop more effective strategies and plans for setting, and achieving, desired goals, for functioning more comfortably and effectively interpersonally, and for reducing anxiety, depression, and perceived stress.

The social cognitive approach to personality has influenced contemporary approaches to constructive educational and therapeutic change in many domains. They range from the treatment of all sorts of fears to the conduct of psychotherapy and the development of mass public education programs to improve health-enhancing behaviors, such as reduction of tobacco and other drug use, dieting, and reduction of high-risk sexual practices. These programs often use exposure to models who display the desired behaviors as part of their efforts to effect change (e.g., Bandura, 1986; Cervone et al., 2001).

13.19 How are modeling and role playing used in social skills training?

Modeling has been used, for example, to help people overcome shyness and assert themselves more effectively when they feel they should. Assertiveness skills may be sought by anyone who wishes to be more effective with other people, whether roommates, a boss, spouse, or parent. People who are unable to be assertive, who cannot stand up for their rights, may not only be exploited and deprived by others but may feel ineffective and incompetent and lack self-esteem. Thus, **assertiveness training** may have many positive effects on one's life. The procedure may include observation of models who assert themselves effectively. This step may be followed by role playing with the therapist and by rehearsing more assertive responses, first in safe situations and ultimately in real life when the assertive responses are needed.

Improvement in assertive behavior may be achieved by observation of models who display assertiveness. In **covert modeling,** this is done in imagination, as unassertive individuals visualize scenes in which a model performs assertively when it is appropriate. Here is a typical scene:

The person (model) is dining with friends in a restaurant. He (she) orders a steak, instructing the waiter that it be rare. The steak arrives and as the person cuts into it, it is apparent that something is wrong. He (she) signals the waiter, who comes to the table. The person says, "This steak is medium; I ordered it rare. Please take this back and bring me a rare one"·(adapted from Kazdin, 1974, p. 242).

Cognitive Behavior Therapy

Because so many behavioral approaches in clinical psychology and therapy have become cognitive, their more accurate new name within the profession is **cognitive behavioral therapy** or CBT. Indeed they may more accurately be called "social cognitive behavioral therapy" except for the fact that it's much too cumbersome a label. Donald Meichenbaum (1995, p. 141), a CBT leader, describes how cognitive-behavioral therapists challenged the earlier behaviorists this way:

> They [cognitive-behavioral therapists] questioned the tenets of classical learning theories and psychoanalytic formulations, and caused the field to question how best to conceptualize the clients' thoughts and feelings. Moreover, they raised questions of how the clients' thoughts influence and, in turn, are influenced by their feelings, behaviors, resultant consequences, and physiological processes. They emphasized that individuals not only respond to their environments but are also the architects of those environments.

Within the last four decades, the cognitive-behavioral model has evolved into a prominent force in psychology (Dobson & Craig, 1996). CBT is currently used to treat conditions such as depression, anxiety, phobias, obsessional disorders, aggression, and hypochondriasis (Dunford, 2000; Kendall & Panichelli-Mindel, 1995; Rachman, 1996). Its growth reflects many changes and reasons, as summarized in Table 13.4. It also gives increasing attention to the client's personal feelings, to experiences as seen by the client, and to developing as well a balanced, internally harmonious life. In that sense it shows similarity to many of the therapeutic values and practices first emphasized in the phenomenological–humanistic approaches, for example in the work of Carl Rogers and Abraham Maslow.

Donald Meichenbaum

TABLE 13.4   **Some Reasons for the Growth of Cognitive Behavior Therapy**

Recognition of problems that go beyond specific behaviors (e.g., career conflict, depression)

Helps people interpret and construe experiences constructively

Address affect (feelings and emotions) as well as action

Deals with interactions between thoughts, feelings, and action

Uses and combines diverse methods and concepts that prove useful

Conceptually and historically, CBT is rooted deeply within behavioral approaches. But its growth also was influenced by other contributions, and it now integrates work from the behavioral and social cognitive levels with insights and methods from most of the other levels of analysis. At a theoretical level it has considerable similarity to George Kelly's work on personal constructs, particularly for the treatment of depression.

Beck's Cognitive Therapy

13.20   What are the goals and procedures in Beck's cognitive therapy?

The social-cognitive trend in therapeutic practice is reflected in their labels; for example, Aaron T. Beck's **cognitive restructuring.** Working as a psychiatrist in Philadelphia, Beck developed one of the most influential and well-articulated versions of cognitive therapy. His approach is directed at changing how people encode or construe their experiences and themselves, and he has applied it systematically to the treatment of depression (Young, Weinberger, & Beck, 2001). He defines cognitive therapy this way:

Cognitive therapy is an active, directive, time-limited, structured approach used to treat a variety of psychiatric disorders (for example, depression, anxiety, phobias, pain problems, etc.). It is based on an underlying theoretical rationale that an individual's affect and behavior are largely determined by the way in which he structures the world. His cognitions (verbal or pictorial "events" in his stream of consciousness) are based on attitudes or assumptions (schemas), developed from previous experiences. For example, if a person interprets all his experiences in terms of whether he is competent and adequate, his thinking may be dominated by the schema, "Unless I do everything perfectly, I'm a failure." Consequently, he reacts to situations in terms of adequacy even when they are unrelated to whether or not he is personally competent (Beck, Rush, Shaw, & Emery, 1979, p. 3).

There are five basic steps in Beck's version of cognitive therapy:

1. Clients first learn to recognize and monitor their negative, automatic thoughts. These thoughts are "dysfunctional," that is, ineffective, and lead to serious dilemmas.

2. They are taught to recognize the connections between these negative thoughts (cognitions), the emotions they create, and their own actions. (See Figure 13.2 for examples of connections between thoughts and emotions.)

3. They learn to examine the evidence for and against their distorted automatic thoughts.

4. They substitute for these distorted negative thoughts more realistic interpretations.

5. They are taught to identify and change the inappropriate assumptions that predisposed them to distort their experiences. Examples of such assumptions are shown in Figure 13.3.

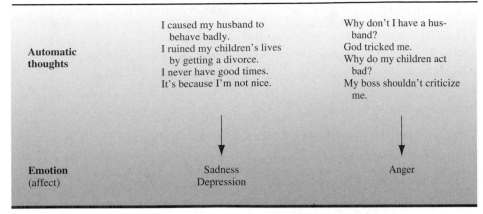

Figure 13.2 Examples of connections between negative automatic thoughts and emotion.

Source: Adapted from Beck, A. T., Rush, A. J., Shaw, B. F., & Emery, G. (1979). *Cognitive therapy of depression* (p. 250, fig. 3). New York: The Guilford Press.

A variety of ingenious techniques have been developed to encourage people to undertake these five basic steps and to use them effectively to alter their actions, thoughts, and feelings. Cognitive therapy of this sort appears to be a promising part of treatment for depression and related emotional and behavioral problems. Its value has been explored in a large number of studies with subjects ranging from those with mild problems to hospitalized, severely depressive patients. The results seem to be consistently encouraging (Beck et al., 1979; Wright & Beck, 1996).

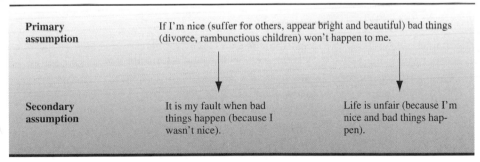

Figure 13.3 Examples of assumptions that encourage depression

Source: Adapted from Beck, A. T., Rush, A. J., Shaw, B. F., & Emery, G. (1979). *Cognitive therapy of depression* (p. 250, fig. 3). New York: The Guilford Press.

SUMMARY

THE SELF

- William James distinguished between two aspects of the self: the "I" and the "Me."
- Self-concepts or self-schemas are knowledge structures developed from the person's perceived life experiences. They influence how new information relevant to the self will be processed.

- The relational self is a representation of the self that is connected to representations of the significant other people in one's life. In new relationships, representations of significant others may be activated by the newly encountered person.

- The working self-concept comprises the most salient concepts of the self.

- Self-esteem refers to the individual's personal judgment of his or her own worth.

- Self-evaluation reflects the individual's performance, as well as earlier experiences and personal self-standards.

CAUSAL ATTRIBUTIONS, HELPLESSNESS, AND MASTERY

- Causal attributions influence emotions and behavioral reactions. Events that are attributed to *internal causes* are more likely to produce pride or shame than are results attributed to *external causes.*

- People with learned helplessness believe they have no control over negative outcomes in their lives and may become apathetic and depressed.

- Pessimism is an explanatory style in which bad life outcomes are attributed to one's own internal qualities. Learned optimism is an opposite, self-enhancing explanatory style that often has positive effects.

- *Helpless children,* who perceive their intelligence as unchanging, tend to perform poorly after failure. Conversely, *mastery-oriented children,* who feel they can improve their intelligence, cope better with failure.

- Entity theorists choose safe goals to avoid negative outcomes but incremental theorists prefer goals that enhance their competence.

PERSONALITY ASSESSMENT

- Assessments at the social-cognitive level of analysis tend to be specific and connected to treatment efforts, as exemplified in self-efficacy expectancy measures.

- The Implicit Association Test (IAT) uses a word-association task to evaluate participants' implicit level of self-esteem and diverse attitudes.

PERSONALITY CHANGE AND THERAPY

- Therapies at this level try to identify the person's disadvantageous ways of thinking and to encourage more adaptive ways of thinking, feeling, and solving problems.

- Aaron Beck's cognitive behavioral therapy (CBT) treats personal problems and depression by changing the way people encode themselves and their experiences to find more constructive ways of thinking and behaving.

KEY TERMS

assertiveness
  training   312
cognitive behavioral
  therapy (CBT)   313
cognitive
  restructuring   314
covert modeling   312
entity theorists   306
"I" as an agent   292

Implicit Association
  Test (IAT)   310
implicit self-esteem   310
incremental
  theorists   307
learned helplessness   300
learned optimism   303
mastery-oriented   305
"Me" as an object   292

pessimism   303
possible self   296
schemas (schemata)   292
self-enhancing bias   301
self-esteem   297
self-schemas   293
self-theory   293
subjective continuity   295
working self-concept   297

PART V

THE SOCIAL COGNITIVE LEVEL

▶ OVERVIEW: FOCUS, CONCEPTS, METHODS

As Part Five, the Social Cognitive Level of Analysis, concludes, the next table summarizes its main characteristics and enduring contributions.

Overview of Focus, Concepts, Methods: The Social Cognitive Level

Basic units of personality:	Underlying person variables and processes: Encoding (construing, including self-concepts and explanatory styles), expectancies and beliefs, affects, values and goals, self-regulatory competencies
Causes of behavior:	Reciprocal interaction between person and situation, mediated by the person variables interacting within the personality system
Behavioral manifestations of personality:	Stable patterns of person–situation interactions; distinctive signatures of *if . . . then . . .* relationships (she does *X* when *Y*, but she does *A* when *B*)
Favored data:	Self-reports, diaries, ratings, and behavior samplings relevant to person variables; outcome information (such as symptoms, later school grades) within specific situations
Observed responses used to:	Infer underlying person variables and cognitive, emotional, motivational processes. Assess and predict behavior and outcomes (such as proneness to disease, well-being)
Research focus:	Refining theories about underlying processes, clinical implications (for health, for risk prevention in vulnerable individuals, for therapy, for enhancing self-efficacy)
Approach to personality change:	By changing person variables and mediating processes (dynamics), modifying expectations, developing effective self-regulatory strategies and plans for goal-attainment
Role of situation:	Important; provides psychological cues and interacts with person variables

As the overview table indicates, the social-cognitive level focuses on the psychological variables that underlie the differences between individuals in their cognitions, emotions, and actions. For that purpose, psychologists study the diverse person variables discussed in this section of the text. They see these variables as basic units of personality and as important—but not exclusive—determinants of the patterns of behavior that characterize individuals distinctively and enduringly. They try to understand 1) the processes through which the variables operate and exert their effects, and 2) the unique patterns through which different persons manifest these variables in their behavior. These behavioral expressions of personality are found in stable patterns of *if . . . then . . . ,* person–situation interaction.

▶ ENDURING CONTRIBUTIONS OF THE SOCIAL COGNITIVE LEVEL

Work on personality at the social cognitive level began in the early 1970s by building on the foundations provided by earlier behaviorally oriented theorists, particularly social learning theory (e.g., Bandura, 1969; Rotter, 1954), and George Kelly's focus on personal constructs as guides for behavior and social perception. Going beyond the "stimulus-response" concepts developed in simple learning experiments with animals, more complex social learning was studied, and social cognitive theories of personality were expanded to include the role of both cognitive and social variables (e.g., Bandura, 1969, 1986; Mischel, 1973, 1990; Rotter, 1954). Work at this level moved away from a focus on external stimuli and rewards and explicitly rejected the idea that situations are the only (or even the main) determinants of behavior. Instead, personality was conceptualized in terms of cognitive and social person variables. The reciprocal (mutual) interaction between the person and the situation was emphasized, recognizing that people select, create, and change situations actively and are not merely passively "shaped" by them (Bandura, 1977, 1986; Mischel, 1973, 1984).

In the last few decades, social cognitive theories still include principles of social learning as a centerpiece for understanding many aspects of personality and social behavior. But they now give an even greater role to cognition, emotion, and motivation, and address an increasingly wide range of personality phenomena. In one direction, work at this level of analysis is building on and revitalizing the contributions of phenomenological approaches and self-theorists, reopening many of the topics the self theorists pioneered more than thirty years ago. This renewal has already proved to be fruitful. Decades ago, phenomenological approaches were criticized because they relied heavily on people's perceptions, which are subject to all sorts of biases and, therefore, are potentially inaccurate sources of information. Researchers at the social cognitive level in recent years have turned this so-called problem into an exciting research topic. Instead of dismissing the individual's perceptions because of their possible biases, they have made those biases major topics in the study of social cognition, investigating how they influence social judgment and decisions.

The realization that how people perceive themselves and their experiences crucially influences their behavior, previously the distinctive hallmark of phenomenological approaches, is now also a central assumption within social cognitive approaches. Because researchers now use more sophisticated methods of measurement, difficult topics that previously resisted objective research are being opened. For example, the "self" in personality psychology has gone from an abstract concept about which theorists speculated to become an active research topic about which much has been learned. The same can be said for emotions, whose nature is becoming much clearer. Thus researchers at the social cognitive level are seeking ways to link social cognition and social perception to other aspects of personality and social behavior. We saw, for example, some of the determinants of perceptions of personal control, and that changes in those perceptions can influence behavior for good or ill. The results ultimately should help clarify the relations between what people perceive and think and what they feel and do.

The classic humanistic commitment to enhance personal growth and the human potential has long been a key feature of phenomenological approaches. Now it also seems to be absorbed increasingly into some forms of cognitive behavior therapy. Personality psychologists within this framework devote much attention to the therapeutic implications of their work for both psychological and physical health and well being (e.g., Contrada and associates, 1990).

Traditionally, most approaches to personality have proposed certain basic assumptions about the nature and causes of personality (e.g., in terms of unconscious psychodynamics and motives). Their proponents have devoted themselves to trying to prove the truth and importance of those assumptions, usually ignoring findings from other approaches. As a science progresses, however, it tends to develop a more cumulative strategy in which concepts are modified, deleted, and incorporated in light of new research findings, regardless of the theoretical orientation that guided the original researchers. The field then matures into one in which the contributions of individual theorists become moments in a larger history of continuous change and evolution. In time, the best of what proves useful and valid is retained; the rest is left behind.

The social cognitive level of analysis helps to provide a foundation for a cumulative science of individuals because it deliberately drew on earlier work that had proved promising rather than trying to emerge with a totally novel approach. A review of much of the work at the social cognitive level suggests the emerging "convergence and complementarity of theoretical conceptions and empirical findings" that may be seen as a basic indicator of the field's progress (Cervone, 1991, p. 371). The degree to which the various levels of analysis do in fact complement and add to each other will become especially clear in the final part of the text that focuses on the integration among all the levels.

VI

THE BIOLOGICAL LEVEL

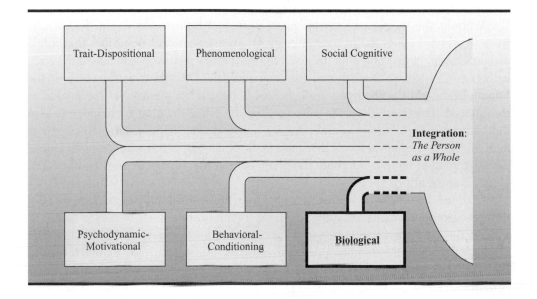

▶ PRELUDE TO PART VI: THE BIOLOGICAL LEVEL

Two identical twin girls were separated at birth, adopted and raised apart in different families from birth on. Nahid's life was spent in the capital of Iran while Jane grew up on a farm in rural Iowa. As identical twins, the two shared the same genetic heritage equally at the outset and consequently started their development with essentially identical brains and physical-biological structures. Nevertheless, the two girls grew up and experienced their lives in very different families, social worlds and cultures. One was reared by loving parents in a family that adored her, surrounded by six siblings, four older than she and two much younger. The other twin grew up as the only child with a neglectful, depressed mother and an alcoholic, abusive stepfather. If the twins are reunited at age 30 and tested extensively, how similar will their personalities turn out to be?

At the biological level of analysis researchers want to answer the age-old question: how much of personality reflects nature, and how much nurture—and how do these two sources of influence interact in shaping human characteristics?

A second question also springs from the recognition that we humans are biological beings. It asks: what are the consequences of having evolved as creatures within the animal kingdom? Evolution endowed us with a host of biological characteristics, constraints, and possibilities that influence who and what we are and do and can become—from eating, drinking, and breathing, to fighting, mating, socializing, and creating. Work at this level shows that people are not simply a blank slate; we are born with a wide range of mechanisms that make it possible to perform an impressive array of complex feats of information processing that facilitated the evolutionary fitness of our species. Like other species, we are the products of the evolutionary processes that shaped us. Consequently, a major goal at this level of analysis is to examine the ways in which personality may have evolved in response to the evolutionary pressures and history that shaped our species over the span of time.

Work at the biological level for many years had little to say about the specific ways in which biology influences individuals' experiences and behaviors that interested personality psychologists. In just a few years that picture has changed dramatically: new ways have been found for examining the links between activity in the human brain and the thoughts, feelings, and behavioral tendencies of the person as they occur. The most dramatic advances are in brain imaging technology. These methods now allow studies of the relations between what happens at the brain level and all the psychological levels that have been discussed in the text. These relations are beginning to be traced as both the brain and the psychological processes are activated concurrently.

Chapter 14 discusses genes, heredity, and the interplay of genetic and social influences on personality. Chapter 15 considers the evolutionary processes that have shaped the genes over the course of the species' development, and examines the implications for understanding personality at that level of analysis. Then we turn to the specific biological processes and brain mechanisms that link each individual's genetic background to central aspects of personality and social behavior, such as emotion and motivation.

The Personal Side of the Science

Some questions at the biological level you might ask about yourself:

▶ What in my personality comes from my parents and the genes I inherited?

▶ How is my personality a reflection of my life experiences?

▶ How does my personality reflect my basic biological predispositions?

▶ Can my experiences change my biology; for instance, does my brain change when I'm depressed?

▶ How do the same experiences affect people with different genetic predispositions?

▶ Why is my personality so different from (or similar to) that of my siblings?

▶ How does my biology influence my pursuit of life goals?

14

HEREDITY AND PERSONALITY

Our genes dictate whether we will be male or female, blue eyed or brown eyed, curly haired or straight haired. To some extent they also influence height and weight. But do the genes also underlie aspects of personality? If the answer is that they do, the next question is "how much?" Do they affect sexual preferences and choice of partners? Are they reflected in tendencies to develop severe mood disorders and mental illness?

The rapidly growing field of **behavior genetics** studies the role of genes in social behavior and personality. Current work on these topics is vigorous and moving in many new directions. It is propelled by better methods for studying the inheritance of personality characteristics and by rapid advances in genetics research. In this chapter, we examine the genetic and biochemical roots of personality, including temperament and attitudes, beliefs and behavior. We next consider the interplay between genetic determinants and social factors, such as the family and culture in which the child develops, as influences on personality.

▶ GENETIC BASES OF PERSONALITY

The Human Genome: The Genetic Heritage

As scientists race to map out the human genome, controversies sprout about the implications and the hazards of each new claim. The arguments become especially heated as they speak to the heritability of personality characteristics and behavioral tendencies—from thrill-seeking, alcoholism, and criminal tendencies to sexual attitudes and political conservatism. The conclusions reached influence how we judge other peoples' behavior and our own. If genes underlie antisocial and violent behavior, can one hold criminals responsible for their crimes? Can reform and change be possible? Is biology destiny? How you see the role of heredity in personality affects not just your view of human nature. It also can change your personal sense of your own possibilities and limitations in trying to build a life.

14.1 What is the human genome? How does it contribute to human similarities and differences?

The genetic heritage of each human being—the **human genome**—consists of roughly 30,000 to 40,000 genes. Each gene consists of DNA sequences contained in 23 pairs of chromosomes. In each chromosome pair, one set comes from the mother, the other from the father. Each of about a trillion cells in the human body houses within its nucleus this genetic inheritance.

The vast majority of human genes are the same for every human being, resulting in the enormous similarities that people share—10 toes, 10 fingers, 32 teeth, two arms, two legs, two eyes, two ears, one heart, and so on. But a relatively small minority of genes are different for different persons and these make the individual distinctive genetically. They are the ones that influence the diverse variations among people in such characteristics as eye color and height—and perhaps in aspects of personality and social behavior not anticipated until recently. The question to which we turn here is the role of these genetic differences between individuals as influences on personality.

Most of what is known about the genetic roots of personality comes from studies that compare the similarity in personality shown by individuals who vary in the degree to which they share the same genes and/or the same environments. Therefore, the "genetic" and "environmental" influences on personality discussed next do not refer to the effects of specific genes and specific environments. Rather, they refer to the overall effects of these two types of determinants on individual differences on average. A great deal has already been discovered in recent years about the effects of heredity and environment on personality and the results have profound implications for how one thinks about human nature.

To anticipate what you will see in this chapter, genetic research on personality is producing a huge and complex literature, but it has a clear message: Genes play a role in personality, and it appears to be a larger one than earlier research had suspected (e.g., Eaves, Eysenck, & Martin, 1989; Loehlin, 1992; Loehlin & Nichols, 1976; Plomin et al., 1997). For example, it is now widely believed that such dispositions as extraversion–introversion (Chapter 3) have a biological-genetic basis (Bouchard et al., 1990; Eysenck, 1973; Plomin & Caspi, 1999; Tellegen et al., 1988). Now let us look at some of the evidence that leads to that conclusion.

The Twin Method

14.2 How do twin studies shed light on genetic factors in personality?

Most often, these studies use the **twin method** to assess genetic influence. This method simply compares the degree of similarity on measures of personality obtained for genetically identical twins—those who are from the same egg or **monozygotic (MZ)**—as opposed to twins who are fraternal or **dizygotic (DZ),** that is with each from a different fertilized egg (Plomin et al., 1997). Identical twins are virtually clones, that is, they are genetically identical, but fraternal twins—like other siblings—are only 50 percent similar genetically. To the degree that genetic factors affect personality, it follows that identical twins must be more similar than fraternal twins with regard to that characteristic.

Studies comparing identical twins and fraternal twins help specify the role of genes in personality.

Results of Twin Studies

A pioneering study with nearly 800 pairs of adolescent twins and measuring dozens of personality traits reached a conclusion that has stood the test of time (Loehlin & Nichols, 1976): Identical twin pairs are much more alike than fraternal twin pairs. The resemblance within identical twin pairs tends to be strongest for general ability and is less strong for special abilities. The resemblance is somewhat lower for personality inventory scales and lowest for interests, goals, and self-concepts (see Table 14.1). For personality, twin correlations are about .50 for identical twins and .25 for fraternal twins. This same study also found that nearly all personality traits measured by self-report questionnaire show moderate genetic influence.

14.3 In general, what do twin studies find regarding the degree of resemblance in personality as compared with other characteristics?

The Big Five. Genetic research on personality has focused on five broad dimensions of personality—the Big Five (Goldberg, 1990), discussed in Chapter 3. Extraversion and neuroticism have been studied most. Extraversion includes sociability, impulsiveness, and liveliness. Neuroticism (emotional instability) includes moodiness, anxiousness, and irritability. Table 14.2 summarizes results for extraversion and neuroticism (Loehlin, 1992). Results from five twin studies in five different countries, using a

TABLE 14.1 **Resemblance of Identical and Fraternal Twin Pairs: Typical Correlations within Pairs**

Trait Area	Identical Twins	Fraternal Twins
General ability	.86	.62
Special abilities	.74	.52
Personality scales	.50	.28
Ideals, goals, interests	.37	.20

Source: Adapted from *Heredity, Environment, and Personality: A Study of 850 Sets of Twins* by John C. Loehlin and Robert C. Nichols, Copyright © 1976. By permission of the University of Texas Press.

TABLE 14.2   Resemblance of 24,000 Pairs of Reared-Together Twins in Five Countries and Identical Twins Reared Apart

	Correlations within Twin Pairs		
	Identical Twins Reared Together	Fraternal Twins Reared Together	Identical Twins Reared Apart
Extraversion	.51	.18	.38
Neuroticism	.46	.20	.38

Source: Adapted from Loehlin, J. C. *Genes and environment in personality development.* © 1992, reprinted by permission of Sage Publications, Inc.

total of 24,000 pairs of twins, consistently indicate moderate genetic influence. Correlations are about .50 for identical twins and about .20 for fraternal twins.

The role of heritability in extraversion and neuroticism has been studied extensively, but much less genetic research has been done for the other three Big Five traits, namely, agreeableness (likeability, friendliness), conscientiousness (conformity, will to achieve), and culture (openness to experience). These qualities have been investigated with diverse measures (rather than standardized tests) that also make it more difficult to compare results across different studies. Nevertheless, results of twin and adoption studies with measures related to these three traits also suggest genetic influence for agreeableness, conscientiousness, and culture at least to a moderate degree (Loehlin, 1992).

Temperaments.   The term **temperaments** refers to traits that are visible in early childhood (Buss & Plomin, 1984), and seem especially relevant to the individual's emotional life (Allport, 1961; Clark & Watson, 1999). Dispositions usually considered temperaments include the general level of emotionality, sociability, and activity. These temperaments are usually assessed through parental reports about their children on temperament rating scales (Rothbart et al., 1994). In adults, they typically are assessed by self-report measures (e.g., Buss & Plomin, 1984), with items like those shown in Table 14.3.

TABLE 14.3   Self-Report Items to Assess Temperament in Adults (Buss & Plomin, 1984)

EMOTIONALITY (easily aroused physiologically to experience negative emotions)
  Many things annoy me.
  I get emotionally upset easily.

SOCIABILITY (seeks social interaction)
  I prefer working with others rather than alone.
  I like to be with other people.

ACTIVITY (overall energy level, tempo/speed, intensity or vigor)
  My life is fast-paced.
  I usually seem to be in a hurry.

Note: Participants rate on five-point scales the degree to which items like these apply to them, from "not typical" of me to "very typical" of me. Based on Buss, A. H. & R. Plomin. (1984). *Temperament: Early developing personality traits* (Table 7.3). Hillsdale, NJ: Erlbaum. Copyright, 1984, reprinted by permission.

Emotionality is often defined as the tendency to become aroused easily physiologically (by ready activation of the autonomic nervous system) and especially to experience frequent and intense negative emotions such as anger, fear, and distress (Buss & Plomin, 1984). Not all researchers agree with this definition, however. They find that the intensity with which an individual experiences emotions is independent of how often he or she has such feelings (Larsen, Diener, & Emmons, 1986). That suggests that these two components of emotionality need to be considered separately, and that both need to be taken into account. For example, if Jane rarely experiences fear but becomes unbearably fearful in some situations, her emotional life would be quite different from someone who is often moderately fearful but never intensely afraid. Further, positive and negative emotions can function independently and they need to be measured separately. For example, people who often experience positive emotions may or may not also experience negative emotions often. In spite of these variations, there is agreement that emotionality is an important aspect of temperament.

Sociability refers to the degree to which the person seeks to interact with others and to be with people. (As such, it overlaps with the concept of extraversion versus introversion introduced in Chapter 3.)

Activity may be defined with regard both to the vigor or intensity of responses and their tempo or speed. It refers to individual differences on a dimension that ranges from hyperactivity to extreme inactivity.

In these dispositions genetic endowment seems to have a significant part (e.g., Thomas & Chess, 1977), and the evidence is increasingly strong (e.g., Plomin, 1990; Rowe, 1997; Clark & Watson, 1999). Figure 14.1 illustrates these types of results more concretely. It shows that on the dimension of emotionality, identical twins are rated as much more similar by their mothers than are fraternal twins.

Although the results are impressive, they are not easy to interpret. Some of the greater similarity found may reflect that the mothers themselves may treat the identical twins more similarly, as might other people in the environment. The mothers also may

14.4 In twin studies, how strongly do genetic factors seem to influence temperament? Why are these results difficult to interpret?

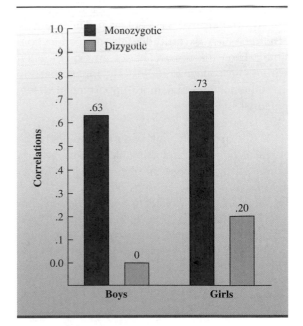

Figure 14.1 Similarity of emotionality: mother's ratings of monozygotic and dizygotic twin pairs.
Source: Correlation coefficients for degree of similarity from data in Buss, Plomin, & Willerman (1973).

have been influenced in their ratings not only by the twins' behavior but by their own expectations and preconceptions for identical versus fraternal twins. Nevertheless, results like these tend to be obtained so consistently that they suggest a significant genetic role in personality with regard to the temperaments of emotionality, activity, and sociability (Buss & Plomin, 1984; Plomin et al., 1997). A comprehensive review of this research concluded that: ". . . one-third to one-half of individual differences in temperamental traits can be attributed to genetic variation among children" (Rowe, 1997, p. 378).

Genetic researchers investigating differences between children in temperament could not use self-report questionnaires with their young participants and therefore used other measures, such as direct ratings of the children's behavior by observers (e.g., Cherny et al., 1994; Goldsmith & Campos, 1986; Saudino et al., 1996). With few exceptions (confined to the first few days of life), observational studies of young twins show genetic influence for diverse characteristics in both twin and adoption studies. These characteristics include the degree to which the child's behavior is inhibited—an aspect of fearfulness (e.g., Robinson et al., 1992); shyness both when observed at home and in the laboratory (Cherny et al., 1994); activity level (Saudino & Eaton, 1991); and empathy (Zahn-Waxler, Robinson, & Emde, 1992). Findings from these studies are notable because they supplement those that rely on self-reports—which are by far the most common.

14.5 How strongly are attitudes influenced by genetic factors? Which attitudes seem most strongly influenced?

Attitudes and Beliefs. Genetic influences also seem to play a role in individual differences in attitudes and beliefs. Results come from a number of twin studies (Eaves et al., 1989), including one of twins who were adopted and reared apart (Tellegen et al., 1988). To illustrate, a substantial genetic influence was found on *traditionalism,* a general orientation which taps conservative (as opposed to liberal) attitudes on diverse topics and many other attitudes also seem to show genetic influence (Eaves et al., 1989; see Plomin et al., 1997).

Attitudes that are more heritable may differ from those that are less heritable systematically, and examining such differences sheds some light on the nature of genetic influences. For example, in one study the researcher separated many specific attitudes into two sets (Tesser, 1993). One set contained those that twin studies had found were more heritable (such as attitudes about the death penalty and about jazz). The other set consisted of those that were less heritable (such as attitudes about coeducation, straightjackets, and the truth of the Bible). Then the researcher set up experimental situations designed to change these attitudes in college students. He found that the more heritable attitudes were harder to influence and also more important in determining the person's judgments of interpersonal attraction.

Aggressive and Altruistic Tendencies. Research with adult twins also points to the influence of genes on other aspects of social behavior. For example, self-reports on aggressiveness questionnaires were obtained from a large number of twin pairs in England (Rushton et al., 1986). The twins answered such questions as: "I try not to give people a hard time," and "Some people think I have a violent temper." The altruism questionnaire asked for the frequency of such behaviors as "I have donated blood," and "I have given directions to a stranger." Within the identical (monozygotic) twin pairs, the answers were more similar than would be expected by chance whereas between fraternal twins, the correlation was merely at a chance level. These results occurred both for the males and for the females. Using sophisticated statistical techniques, the researchers estimated that genetics accounted for approximately 50 percent of the individual differences in test answers.

Romantic Love. Although genes seem to directly or indirectly influence individual differences on most measures of personality, as well as on social attitudes, including peoples' self-esteem (e.g., McGuire et al., 1994), one area that seems to be beyond DNA is romantic love. A behavior genetic twin family study focused on the genetic versus environmental influences on individual differences in adult romantic love styles. The participants were drawn from 890 adult twins and 172 spouses from the California Twin Registry and they had been married for an average of a dozen years (Waller & Shaver, 1994). Six different love styles were measured, ranging from one that values passion, excitement, intimacy, self-disclosure and "being in love from the start," to one that values a relationship that is affectionate and reliable and has companionship and friendship (with items like "It is hard for me to say exactly when our friendship turned into love.").

The findings showed that how people love is almost completely due to the environment and essentially unaffected by genetic influences. In fact, this is one domain in which it is the family environment that turned out to be particularly important (Waller & Shaver, 1994). As the researchers noted ". . . love styles may be learned during early familial or shared extra-familial interactions and subsequently played out in romantic relationships" (p. 272–273).

Twins Reared Apart

To try to separate the role of genetics and environment, it is especially informative to assess identical twins who have been reared apart in different families. Reports have come from two large-scale studies of twins reared apart in Minnesota (Bouchard et al., 1990; Tellegen et al., 1988) and in Sweden (Pedersen et al., 1988; Plomin et al., 1988). The results surprised even many of the researchers who have long been convinced that genes affect personality.

In this research, Bouchard, Tellegen, and their associates for more than a decade studied a sample of identical (monozygotic) twin pairs reared apart who were separated early in life (on average before the end of the second month). They grew up in different families, but mostly in English-speaking countries. As adults, their responses were assessed on many medical and psychological measures, including personality questionnaire scales and intelligence tests (as seen in Table 14.4). Most had not seen each other

14.6 What is the special value of comparing twins raised together and apart? What general result occurs in such studies that strengthens genetic explanations?

TABLE 14.4 Names of Personality Scales in Studies of Twins Reared Apart and Together

Well-being	Control
Social Potency	Harm Avoidance
Achievement	Traditionalism
Social Closeness	Absorption
Stress Reaction	Positive Emotionality
Alienation	Negative Emotionality
Aggression	Constraint

Note: On most scales, identical twins reared apart were as similar to each other as those reared together. The main exception was "social closeness" (on which those raised together were more similar).

Source: Tellegen, A., Lykken, D., Bouchard, T., Wilcox, K., Segal, N., & Rich, S. (1988). Personality similarity in twins reared apart. *Journal of Personality and Social Psychology, 54,* 1035 (Table 3).

for an average of about 30 years, although some had contact over the years. Comparisons were made with a larger sample of twin pairs who had been reared together and grew up in Minnesota.

There were instances of dramatic psychological similarities within the twin pairs, even for twins who grew up in radically different environments for 30 years or more in many cases. These twins seemed to share some quite distinctive mannerisms, postures, attitudes, and interests. For example, in some cases they posed alike for photos. Some turned out to have virtually the same height, the same weight, the same number of marriages and children, the same drinking and smoking habits, the same mannerisms, the same clothes, food, and jewelry preferences, similar physical symptoms—and similar scores on personality tests (e.g., Segal 1999). Many also quickly felt a close emotional connection with each other even though they had spent their entire lives apart.

There also were strong similarities in many of the test results of the identical twins. Especially interesting, the similarity was almost as high for the monozygotic twins who grew up in different homes as it was for those raised within the same family (as was seen in Table 14.2). Bouchard and colleagues (1990) attributed approximately 70 percent of the individual differences found in intelligence to heredity. They interpreted the effects of heredity on personality (as assessed on their questionnaires) to be approximately 50 percent and the effects of family environment to be trivial (Tellegen and associates, 1988). Likewise, twin studies of the Big Five factors suggest "The shared genes, not the shared experiences, mainly determine the family resemblance of 'blood relatives'" (Rowe, 1997, p. 380).

Beyond Self-Report Measures

14.7 What difficulties attend the use of self-report measures to assess heritability? How have researchers addressed these difficulties?

One of the most surprising findings from genetic research on self-report personality questionnaires is that of the many traits that have been studied virtually all show genetic influence. That may be because all these traits in fact reflect genetic predispositions. But at least some of the similarity may lie in the eyes of the beholder. For example, identical twins who have a higher level of frustration tolerance may *think* and honestly say that they experience less negative emotions than others, worry less, and rarely feel anxious, not because they experience these feelings less than others, but because they are less bothered by them. It is therefore particularly important to use measures of personality other than self-report questionnaires to investigate whether or not this result is somehow due to biases in the self-report measures themselves.

To address this, researchers gave a measure of the Big Five personality factors to almost a thousand pairs of twins (Riemann, Angleitner, & Strelau, 1997) in Germany and Poland. They also obtained ratings of each twin's personality by two different peers (who agreed reasonably with each other in their ratings about each twin's personality).

On average, ratings by the peers correlated .55 with the twins' self-report ratings, providing moderate validity for those ratings. Table 14.5 shows twin correlations for the "Big Five" personality traits, which are similar to those summarized in Table 14.2, with average correlations of .52 for identical twins and .23 for fraternal twins. The fact that the peer ratings also indicated genetic influence helps support the conclusions reached earlier based on self-report questionnaires.

So far in this chapter we have reviewed some of the main findings that show significant effects of one's genetic heritage on the personality that develops. Most of these studies use the heritability index to estimate the size of these effects. Because the method and the conclusions it allows are easy to misunderstand they need to be examined carefully. In Focus 14.1 discusses these misunderstandings and clarifies the meaning of this index.

TABLE 14.5 Twin Study Using Self-Report and Peer Ratings of "Big Five" Personality Traits

| | Correlations within Pairs | | | |
| | Self-Report Ratings | | Peer Ratings | |
	Identical Twins	Fraternal Twins	Identical Twins	Fraternal Twins
Extraversion	.56	.28	.40	.17
Neuroticism	.53	.13	.43	−.03
Agreeableness	.42	.19	.32	.18
Conscientiousness	.54	.18	.43	.18
Culture	.54	.35	.48	.31

Source: Riemann, R., Angleitner, A., & Strelau, J. (1997). Genetic and environmental influences on personality: A study of twins reared together using the self- and peer report NEO-FFI scales. *Journal of Personality, 65,* 449–476. With permission from Blackwell Publishing.

14.8 How are heritability coefficients computed? What do such estimates mean? What misconceptions and difficulties occur in interpreting them?

IN FOCUS 14.1

UNDERSTANDING HERITABILITY AND THE HERITABILITY INDEX

Attempts to understand the implications of heritability for personality have been undermined by widespread misconceptions. Let's address some of the most common.

The Heritability Index. Correlations like those shown in Table 14.5 are used by behavioral geneticists to estimate the percent of the variation in scores measuring individual differences that is attributable to genetic factors. The computation of this index is straightforward, but its interpretation is not. To compute it, pairs of same-sex fraternal and identical twins are compared on particular variables. For each type of twin, the researchers compute a correlation among pairs of identical twins to index their similarity, as well as a correlation among pairs of fraternal twins. Subtracting the latter from the former, and then multiplying the result by 2, results in the heritability index. It is an estimate of the role of heritability in accounting for individual differences on the variable studied. Results using these estimates to date suggest that heritability plays an important role in many aspects of personality.

The Meaning of High Heritability. Twin studies are a valuable first step toward answering whether genetic factors contribute to individual differences in personality. But the hertiability indexes they compute have to be interpreted cautiously for several reasons (e.g., Dickens & Flynn, 2001):

- First, **heritability estimates** always are limited to the specific population that was studied in the

research reported and for which they were computed. This is a crucial caution that behavioral geneticists generally emphasize but that many readers often fail to appreciate. (Goldsmith, 1991). Heritability estimates *do not* provide an absolute index of the degree to which a given characteristic is influenced by the genes. It is nonsense to think for example that Joe's aggressiveness is made up of 30 percent genetic influence and 70 percent environmental influences or that Susan's ballet skills are 20 percent genetic and 80 percent ballet school and practice. If all children took ballet lessons, then a greater portion of the differences among the children in ballet skills may be due to their variations in their genetic endowment. But if only some children took ballet lessons, then how well children can perform *pirouettes* may depend largely on the availability of ballet lessons. In general, the heritability index depends on the variations in the environment that exist within a given society in which the study is conducted. The more homogenous the environments are, the greater is the heritability index. Thus the heritability index reflects characteristics of a population, rather than of an individual. If the psychological environments to which children are exposed become more homogeneous across different cultures, for example due to global communication and media influences, the result would be an increase in the relative proportion of the genetic influences in the observed variations among people.

Heritability estimates *do* index the portion of the individual *variability* related to the genetic *variability* that exists in the population. If the characteristic is so important that any variation in the genes that affect it can reduce the evolutionary fitness of the individual, the heritability index would be close to 0. That happens because all individuals are likely to be identical with regard to that gene, and any variability observed in that characteristic is likely to come from environmental differences.

- Second, even when identical twins are reared apart, their similarities on personality measures are not necessarily due to their genes for personality itself. For example, similar interests and values in identical twins may in part reflect their similar physiques and appearance, constitutions, abilities, skills, and physical characteristics rather than any genes for personality. These physical qualities may lead other people to treat them similarly even when the twins live in different environments. A shared interest in becoming a fashion model, for example, may say more about the inheritance of faces than of personality. Their similar physical qualities also may lead each twin to see himself or herself in a somewhat similar way, for example, as highly attractive or unattractive, or as physically strong and skilled and competent or as weak and ineffective. This in turn could influence such aspects of personality as self-concepts and self-confidence and a host of related characteristics.

- Third, as mentioned earlier, many studies that compare the similarity of identical and fraternal twins who grow up together draw mostly on their answers on self-report personality questionnaires (the measure most often used). On these tests the identical twins might give more similar answers not just because they have the same genes but also because they might identify more closely with each other and emulate each other more, or might be treated more alike by parents and other people, and therefore become more alike in all sorts of ways. For example, they might often wear more similar clothes and share more activities and time together. Just as greater similarity in dress among identical twins does not necessarily imply that clothing tastes are genetically determined, it is important also to be cautious before concluding that similarity in answers to self-report questionnaires about an attribute necessarily implies the specific genetic heritability of that attribute.

- Fourth, high heritability coefficients do *not* imply that the particular characteristic cannot be changed significantly. Even when genetics importantly influence individual differences in a trait, the trait may be modified by environmental influences. For example, substantial genetic influence for height means that height differences among the sampled individuals are largely due to genetic differences. But even when a trait is highly heritable it may be influenced importantly by the environment. The average height of Europeans has climbed more than 20 cm in the past 150 years (*TIME*, October 14, 1996 Volume 148, No. 16; see http://www.vwl.unimuenchen.de/ls_komlos/covereu.html). Thus, although height is highly heritable, such environmental interventions as improving children's nutrition and health can affect it. Indeed, environmental factors seem to account for the average increase in height across generations, although within each generation individual differences in height are highly heritable. As another example, consider the role of inheritance in intelligence. Research with twins raised in various environments (either together or apart) suggests that intelligence measured on standard tests tends to be increasingly similar to the degree that the individuals have an increasing proportion of genes in common (Cartwright, 1978; Plomin et al., 1997; Vandenberg, 1971). But whereas a person's genetic endowment may set an upper limit or ceiling on the degree to which his or her intelligence can be developed (Royce, 1973) it is the environment that may help or hinder achievement of that ceiling (e.g., Cantor & Kihlstrom, 1987).

- Finally, the heritability index itself does not address the mechanisms through which the genetic influences on personality operate and exert their effects on the individual.

Heredity versus Environment: Another False Dichotomy

Debates about heredity and environment have raged for years. Unfortunately, they readily turn into either/or competitions to see which one is more important. As a leader in research on the role of inheritance in behavior points out: ". . . evidence for significant genetic influence is often implicitly interpreted as if heritability were 100%, whereas heritabilities of behavior seldom exceed 50%" (Plomin, 1990,

p. 187). Plomin notes that this should make it clear that "non-genetic sources of variance" are also of self-evident importance. Indeed, Bouchard and colleagues in their studies of identical twins raised apart acknowledge that in their own results, "in individual cases environmental factors have been highly significant" (1990, p. 225), as with the case, for example, of a 29-point difference in the IQs of two identical twins.

In short, regardless of the exact percent used to estimate the influence of genetic factors, clearly their influence is considerable, especially given that few findings in personality account for as much as 20 percent of the variance. Just as noteworthy, however, is the other side of that finding: namely, the fact that the same data show that at least half of the variance of personality is *not* due to genetic factors and thus also attest to the importance of the environment for personality. The recurrent theme throughout this research is clear: unquestionably one's genetic endowment has extensive influences on one's life and personality development, and so also does the environment. The challenge will be to untangle the mechanisms through which both genes and experience interact throughout the life course to influence what we become. That will require specifying the mechanisms that produce these effects and clarifying the nature of the characteristics that are heritable and the specific aspects of the environment that are important.

Summary

Taken collectively, the findings support the view that genetic factors play a significant role in personality, in attitudes and values, as well as in self-esteem (e.g., McGuire et al., 1994). In some cases, genetic influences seem to account for as much as half of the individual differences observed. The magnitude of these effects may be exaggerated, however, particularly when the findings are based on self-reports. Plomin and colleagues (1990), critically reviewing twin studies of personality based on self-reports, point out certain method problems in these studies that may systematically overestimate the role of genetics. They believe the biases can be corrected if results from adoption studies are appropriately taken into account. When corrections are made for the erroneous inflation of the heritability estimates (see subsection, Stress Is Bad for Your Brain): "The true heritability estimate for self-reported personality is closer to the adoption study estimate of 20% than to the twin study estimate of 40%" (Plomin et al., 1990, p. 233). It is also clear, however, that even when one goes beyond self-reports the role of genetics in personality is still significant and has to be taken seriously. The task ahead is to understand the mechanisms through which these effects play out.

14.9 Compare heritability estimates derived from twin studies with those obtained in adoption studies.

▶ GENE–ENVIRONMENT INTERPLAY

Assuming that both nature (genetics) and nurture (environment) are important influences on personality, the next step is to understand the developmental interplay between them. This interplay is seen in the course of life as the personality of the person, partly influenced by genetics, interacts with and to some degree selects and shapes the situations in his or her psychological world. The causal relations go in both directions because those situations over time, in turn, exert their impact on what the person becomes. Let's examine this interplay and its implications for personality.

The Unique (Nonshared) Psychological Environment of Each Family Member

14.10 Differentiate between shared and unshared environmental influences within the family. Why is it difficult to interpret the causal influences between environmental and genetic factors?

Twin studies have inquired into the environmental influences that make genetically identical "clones"—identical twins—different from one another. For many years, it was widely thought that children growing up in the same family would be similar to one another in personality for environmental reasons because they shared the "same" family situation. Genetic researchers now believe that this assumption is false. They contend that family members resemble each other in personality largely because of genetic influences, and that the environment seems to make members of a family different (e.g., Plomin et al., 1997). Their reasoning is based on two findings. First, twins reared apart are only somewhat less similar in personality than twins who grew up in the same family. In addition, in studies of adoptive families that have more than one adopted child, the genetically unrelated children show little similarity in personality even though they had the same **shared environment,** that is, they were raised within the same family (Plomin, Chipuer, & Neiderhiser, 1994).

Note that the shared or **family environment** in the twin studies was treated as a global entity, as if families treat all the siblings in them the same way. The psychological environments experienced by each member of the family, however, may be quite different and each may receive distinctively different treatments within the same family. Each parent may relate differently to each child. In fact, findings of birth order effects suggest that children in the same family encounter quite different psychological environments (Sulloway, 1996). Moreover, much of the psychological environment experienced by individuals involves continuing significant encounters outside the family (with peers, school, spouse, and in the broader group and culture), the nature and effects of which may change with different phases of development.

Environmental Influences Within the Family. The **nonshared** or **unique environment** exerts its effects on each person through many routes, beginning in prenatal development and birth order effects. It includes biological events such as illness and nutrition, as well as psychosocial events such as interpersonal experiences that may range from parental reactions to peer influences, romantic partners, and mates (see Table 14.6). For example, earlier-born children are larger, more powerful, and more privileged than later-born children and that, in turn, may affect their personality development (Sulloway, 1996). From the start, each child is born into a slightly different family psychologically and structurally because parents treat siblings differently, and siblings treat each other differently.

It is understandable that most parents find it hard to admit that they treat their children differently, given the social norms that press for them to treat each one the

TABLE 14.6 Some Environmental Influences that Siblings in the Family Do Not Share Equally

Position in the family

Parental reactions

Accidents

Prenatal events, Illness

Peer group reactions and support

Other interpersonal experiences (e.g., mates)

Educational and occupational experiences

same. But children correctly believe that their parents do treat them differently—an impression confirmed by observational studies (Reiss and colleagues, 2000). So, for example, parents are likely to react differently to their first and their fifth child, perhaps hovering over their first baby and swamped by the time the fifth one arrives. On close examination, children growing up in the same family lead remarkably separate lives (Dunn & Plomin, 1990). Even such variables as parental divorce tend to affect children within the family differently, depending, for example, on the child's age and role in the family as well as many other variables (Hetherington & Clingempeel, 1992). In short, siblings growing up in the "same" family experience it differently so that psychologically it is not the same.

Research that traces how differences in such experiences lead to differences in outcomes is still just beginning, but some links have already been shown (Reiss et al., 2000). Most of these associations connect negative aspects of parenting (such as conflict) with such negative outcomes as antisocial behavior later in development. It is especially interesting that some associations (of modest strength) have been reported between differences in parental negativity toward identical twins and their adolescent maladjustment on such indices as depression and antisocial behavior (Reiss et al., 2000). Obviously such differences cannot be due to genetic factors and thus must be due to the nonshared environment (Pike et al., 1996). Generally weaker correlations are found between positive aspects of parenting (such as affection) and positive outcomes.

The correlations between measures of the children's nonshared environment and their personality also raise the old chicken and the egg question, that is, the direction of the effects: Does parental negativity cause negative outcomes in personality? Or do parents treat some of their children more negatively than others in reaction to the child's personality, responding more harshly, for instance, to siblings who are more difficult to deal with? If the latter holds, the differential treatment siblings receive may be due in part to each child's distinctive genetics (Plomin, 1994). In other words, differential parental treatment of siblings may be due to genetically influenced differences between the siblings, including in their personality.

Environmental Influences Outside the Family. The nonshared environment includes, but goes far beyond, differences in siblings' unique experiences within the family (see Table 14.6). Some of the most important aspects of the nonshared environment unfold in the experiences children have outside the family as they interact with their expanding worlds, most notably in relationships with peers and in school and play contexts. If you reflect on your own life, you will not find it difficult to come up with examples of relationships and experiences outside the immediate family that influenced your development. In these interactions even siblings living in the same family form quite different relations with peers, encounter different types of social support, build different lives with different educational, occupational, and interpersonal experiences and events along the route (Plomin, 1994). Further, such factors as accidents and illnesses, as well as chance encounters and experiences, may initiate significant differences between siblings (Dunn & Plomin, 1990). While such events initially may be relatively minor they can snowball and become compounded over time into large outcome differences years later.

To recapitulate, we saw that environmental influences that affect personality development do not seem to operate on a family-by-family "on the whole" basis, but rather on an individual-by-individual basis. That suggests that environmental effects on personality are specific to each child rather than general for all children in a given family.

It makes the unit of analysis each child as he or she distinctively interacts with relevant specific environmental situations, including with particular family members. Environmental influences on personality development seem to operate mostly in a nonshared manner, making children growing up in the same family different from one another. As was discussed, attempts to identify specific sources of nonshared environment indicate that many sibling experiences differ substantially. Even such seemingly shared variables as parental attitudes about childrearing and parents' marital relationship might not be experienced the same way and might, in fact, be subtly different for each sibling.

Interactions Among Nature-Nurture Influences

14.11 What research results suggest genetic effects on experience within the family? Describe some ways in which genetic factors influence nonshared aspects of the environment.

There are continuous complex interactions between the expressions of genetic influences and the situations and events that the person experiences (e.g., Rutter and colleagues, 1997). These interactions make it difficult to isolate the contribution of genetics versus environmental influences because their interplay becomes virtually indivisible.

For example, adult twins reared apart rated the family environments in which they grew up more similarly than did fraternal twins reared apart (Rowe, 1981, 1983). Presumably this happened for at least two possible reasons. First, identical twins even reared apart may be more alike in how they perceive and interpret their experiences. Second but equally important, they may have been treated more similarly due to their genetically-influenced shared characteristics such as their more similar physical appearance, abilities, skills, and temperaments, for example (Plomin et al., 1988). Likewise, beyond the family environment, genetic similarity may lead to greater similarity in the experienced environments in peer groups (e.g., Manke et al., 1995), in the classroom (Jang, 1993) and in work environments (Hershberger, Lichteinstein, & Knox, 1994). It may also influence such other life events as proneness to childhood accidents or illness (Phillips & Mathews, 1995), exposure to trauma (Lyons et al., 1993), or to drugs (Tsuang et al., 1992).

Perhaps the clearest evidence for genetic effects on experience comes from observational studies that also show such genetic effects (although often of lower magnitude), making it plain that they do not just depend on self-reports and questionnaires. For example, the Home Observation for Measurement of the Environment or HOME is a widely used measure of the home environment that combines observations and interviews (Caldwell & Bradley, 1978). It assesses aspects of the home environment such as parental responsiveness and encouraging developmental advance. In an adoption study with this measure, the home environment of each sibling was assessed when the child was one year old and again when each child was two years old (Braungart, Fulker, & Plomin, 1992). HOME correlations for genetically unrelated children adopted into the same home (adoptive siblings) were compared to those for genetically related siblings in nonadoptive homes (nonadoptive siblings). HOME scores were more similar for nonadoptive siblings than for adoptive siblings at both one and two years, suggesting genetic influence on this measure (see Table 14.7).

In another observational study, O'Connor and associates (1995) obtained videotaped observations of adolescents' interactions with their mothers or their fathers in 10-minute discussions of problems and conflicts within each parent–adolescent dyad. The adolescent participants included six groups of siblings: identical twins, fraternal twins, full siblings in nondivorced families, and full siblings, half siblings, and unrelated siblings in step-families. Using sophisticated estimates of heritability the researchers found some significant genetic influences both on the positive and negative interaction with both the mothers and fathers.

TABLE 14.7 HOME Score Correlations for Nonadoptive and Adoptive Siblings at Ages 1 and 2 Years

	Sibling Correlations	
Environmental Measure	Nonadoptive	Adoptive
1 year	.58	.35
2 years	.57	.40

Note: Adoptive = genetically unrelated, adopted into same home;
Nonadoptive = genetically related in nonadoptive homes

Source: Braungart, J. M., Fulker, D. W., & Plomin, R. (1992). Genetic influence of the home environment during infancy: A sibling adoption study of the HOME. *Developmental Psychology, 28,* 1048–1055.

Genes Also Influence Environments

Genetic factors may contribute to the experienced environment in several ways (Plomin et al., 1997; Rutter and colleagues, 1997). First, people encounter the environments that their genetic relatives, in part, make for them. Take activity level, for example, which seems to have a heritable component and is thus shared to some degree between the child and the parents (Saudino & Plomin, 1996). From the start, parents construct aspects of their child's early environment, and tend to make it more (or less) stimulating and activity-filled in a way that is consistent with both their own and their child's genetic propensities. Thus highly active children are likely to have active parents who model and reward high activity and who also provide them with both genes and an environment conducive to the development of high activity.

Second, the individual's genetically influenced characteristics affect how other people will react to him or her. For example, highly active children might receive more positive reactions from their peers or, in the opposite direction, more negative reactions from their schoolteachers.

Third, and most important, individuals actively seek and create situations and social environments in ways congruent with their genetically influenced dispositions and qualities. Whereas extremely active children are likely to create a high-energy environment by actively selecting highly active friends and activities, less active children are apt to make their environment less energy demanding. This self-directed process of selecting and creating one's own situations is the most central for personality; it is literally the seat of the sort of dynamic Person × Situation interactions through which dispositions and the environment reciprocally influence each other.

Given the multiple paths through which genetic influences impact on the environment, it is understandable that genetic factors often contribute substantially to measures of the environment in research. But while it is clear that genetic factors influence the environments we experience and select, the effects are complex and the direct genetic influence is only one part of the variance, and does not account for most of it.

These findings suggest that researchers need to move away from passive models of how the environment or the genes separately affect individuals and turn to models of person-environment interaction. These interaction models recognize the active role that persons play in selecting, modifying, and creating their own environments. In this process there is a continuous interaction between dispositions (partly influenced by genetics, partly by environmental influences) and situations as the individual deals with his or her world in the course of development. Such interaction implies that some of the most important questions in genetic research will involve the environment and some of the most important questions for environment research will involve genetics (Rutter et al., 1997).

The interplay of biological and psychological processes is evident at every level of analysis. It is apparent even at the molecular level: the synapses in the brain change physically when new learning occurs. In this interaction, genes are switched on to make new proteins that are crucial in long-term memory, wherein the person's history resides. Furthermore, even relatively small heritable differences in qualities of temperament, such as activity and energy levels, emotionality, and sociability, which appear to be visible in early childhood (Buss & Plomin, 1984), can be biological foundations for diverse enduring behavioral tendencies that may develop from these roots (Kagan, 2003).

For example, temperamentally more active, energetic children tend to explore and interact more vigorously and forcefully with their environments, rapidly encountering its challenges and gratifications as well as its dangers and frustrations. In time they also are likely to become more aggressive than children who are temperamentally inhibited from exploring the unfamiliar and thus inclined toward shyness (e.g., Daniels et al., 1985). Heritable variations in arousal thresholds in certain loci of the brain also could influence such behaviors as shyness (e.g., Kagan, Reznick, & Snidman, 1988). Heritable differences in sensitivity and physiological reactivity in response to sensory stimulation partly predispose people to become introverted rather than extroverted (Stelmack, 1990). In turn, introverts may be more disposed to avoid the types of social stimulation that extroverts desire and actively select for themselves (Plomin, Manke, & Pike, 1996).

Search for Specific Gene–Behavior Connections

Given the evidence for genetic influence on personality traits that has been found in recent years, researchers in the vanguard of the field are now trying to become more precise and to identify specific genes that might connect to specific characteristics. They are beginning to go much beyond demonstrations that genetic influences are important for personality.

In earlier research, specific genetic defects have been linked to various abnormalities such as mental deficiencies. **PKU** is a case in point (see Table 14.8). **PKU (phenylketonuria)** disease is an inherited disorder in which a genetic abnormality results in the lack of an enzyme necessary for normal metabolism. Because of this enzyme deficiency, a toxic chemical accumulates in the body and results in central nervous system damage and mental retardation. Diagnosis of PKU disease is now possible immediately after birth, and highly successful treatment has been devised. The child is

TABLE 14.8   Effects of Some Genetic Abnormalities: Two Examples

Name of Disorder	Description	Cause
Down Syndrome	Severe mental retardation	A third, extra chromosome in the twenty-first chromosome pair
	Physical appearance: small skull, sparse hair, flat nose, fissured tongue, a fold over the eyelids, short neck	Appears to be associated with advanced age in the mother
PKU (phenylketonuria)	Results in mental retardation if not treated soon after birth	A gene that produces a critical enzyme is missing

placed on a special diet that prevents the toxic substance from building up in the bloodstream. When the biological mechanisms underlying other forms of mental deficiency are known, equally effective cures may be possible.

Some psychological characteristics are determined by an individual's specific genetic structure. For example, when the twenty-first chromosome in the body cell of an individual has a third member instead of occurring as a pair, the individual will have **Down Syndrome,** a form of mental retardation. A technique for drawing amniotic fluid from the uterus of the pregnant mother enables doctors and prospective parents to know in advance if the developing fetus has this chromosome abnormality. This procedure is performed routinely for pregnant women 35 years of age or older because women in this age group are more likely to give birth to children with Down Syndrome.

To link genes to personality, promising examples include the report that a gene for a dopamine receptor was correlated with novelty-seeking in two studies (Benjamin et al., 1996; Ebstein et al., 1996), with other researchers finding that the same gene was related to hyperactivity (LaHoste et al., 1996). While such findings are exciting for genetic researchers, they must be interpreted with much caution and still be treated as tentative and suggestive rather than conclusive.

These reservations are necessary because findings of associations between personality and specific genes in the past have failed to replicate. That happened, for example, for the reported correlation between neuroticism and a gene important in the functioning of the chemical neurotransmitter serotonin (Lesch et al., 1996), which two other studies could not reproduce (Ball et al., 1997; Ebstein et al., 1997). Perhaps even more important, personality traits involve extremely complex patterns of characteristics and behaviors such that an association with any specific gene probably will have only a small effect (Plomin, Owen, & McGuffin, 1994). That is, genetic influence on personality involves the action of many genes, each of which has a small effect rather than the direct effect of any single major gene.

Given this great but unsurprising complexity, it can be valuable to use the sorts of promising methods for identifying genes in lower animals that cannot be employed with people (Plomin & Saudino, 1994). For example, in such animal studies it is possible to use powerful techniques that alter specific genes, called knock-outs, to test just how they influence behavior (Capecchi, 1994). In mice, for instance, several genes that, if disrupted, would result in fearfulness have been located (Flint et al., 1995). As predicted, mice display greater aggression when the researchers knock out the genes for an important neurotransmitter (Saudou et al., 1994) or enzyme (Nelson et al., 1995). The limitation of course is that it is difficult to generalize results from studies with mice to humans. But there are exciting prospects for discoveries in molecular genetics that do speak to the human condition and will prove generalizable to personality (Hamer & Copeland, 1998). However, that is the story that is not yet written but that should unfold in the next few years.

14.12 Have researchers been able to link specific genes to personality variables?

Causal Mechanisms: The Role of Neurotransmitter Systems

As discussed above, genetic and environmental influences are always in close interaction. The question then becomes: What are the causal mechanisms that underlie this interaction? To address that question at the molecular biological level of analysis, researchers now try to examine how genetic variability underlying neurotransmitter systems can be linked to variability in personality traits and behavioral patterns (e.g. Grigorenko, 2002).

Neurotransmitter systems are the physiological pathways that communicate and carry out the functions of signal detection and response via chemical receptors (neurotransmitters). The variability of each of these neurotransmitters is dictated by the variants of its corresponding gene. There are nine neurotransmitter systems, but based on their biochemical functions, some are more relevant to the carrying out of psychological functions than others. In general, personality psychologists have focused on three primary systems involved in behavioral functions (the dopaminergic, seritonergic, and GABAergic systems).

Researchers have been analyzing how certain behavioral patterns correlate with specific genetic variants. Originally, researchers aimed to show direct, one-to-one correlations between specific traits or behavioral attributes and specific genetic mutations. So far these studies have provided mixed results. Many of the experiments that seemed to exhibit this kind of direct correlation could not be repeated. Though it is clear that neurotransmitter systems are linked to the expression of behavioral patterns, it is also evident that these neurotransmitter systems do not necessarily act alone in producing their affect on behavioral attributes. In fact, recent studies have revealed that the various neurotransmitter systems work together very closely, and many of the behavioral functions originally attributed to specific neurotransmitter systems are actually a function of the interaction of more than one of these systems.

As we begin to understand more about these neurotransmitter systems and the genetic variations that effect their functioning, it is clear that the task of correlating genes to behavior is not as simple as was originally believed. The interaction between genetic expression and the phenotypic expression of personality is complex. Specifically, researchers must take into account that the genetic variability that underlies human behavior is influenced not only by the additive and interactive factors on the genetic level, but also by characteristics in the surrounding environment.

14.13 What were the results of Grigorenko's review of genetics and personality? What conclusions did she reach?

Let us look in detail at a comprehensive review of research on genes and personality (Grigorenko, 2002). The results challenge some of the basic, commonly accepted assumptions of recent years. Take the claim that genetic factors contribute extensively to the similarity of MZ twins, whereas the family–environment plays no serious role, discussed earlier in this chapter. Elena Grigorenko's review and research makes it clear that *it really all depends.* She reports a recent behavior–genetic analysis conducted with more than 700 Russian families in which shared family–environment factors contributed significantly to variation in the majority of the traits studied. Note that this contrasts with the fact that in a large subsample of the population (218 families in which at least one parent had a criminal record), genetic factors did *not* contribute significantly to variation in 13 of 15 traits. Why?

There are good biological reasons for these puzzling results. The main point here is that neurotransmitter systems interact with one another. Consequently, personality characteristics will not reflect the action of a single neurotransmitter system. The complexities get even greater because gene expression and surface-level behavioral characteristics are not stable, and instead tend to fluctuate across development in interaction with environmental conditions.

The fundamental message from all this for the student of personality is that the links between our biochemistry and our personality characteristics reflect interactions both within and between systems. These are not simple one-way causal influences—a message very much like the one that emerged in our review of the "person versus situation" debate at the trait level of analysis (Chapter 4). One specific implication is that it is unlikely that there will be either simple or direct relationships between particular genetic factors and very broad categories of personality traits like those represented by the Big Five. Thus, any expectation that a few genes might account for qualities like "open-mindedness" is probably unjustified.

Genetic and Environmental Influences on Person × Situation Interactions

The interplay of genes as well as the environment also is reflected in the kinds of **Person × Situation interaction patterns** and *if . . . then . . .* personality signatures discussed in earlier chapters. These signatures may reflect both genetic and environmental influences, depending on the specific type of behavior involved. An early study using an adult twin sample showed, for example, that the person × situation interaction patterns for anxiety were influenced significantly by genetics whereas for dominance shared sibling-environmental influences were found (Dworkin, 1979). The results supported the general conclusion that an individual's behavior shows characteristic, meaningful patterns across situations that partly reflect genetic influences.

14.14 How might genetic factors influence Person × Situation interactions?

More recent studies with larger samples and other methods provide further and even stronger evidence for the same basic point (Cherney et al., 1994; Plomin et al., 1997, p. 202). An important implication is that genetic influences may be expressed not simply in how much of a given trait a person "has." Genetics also may influence the characteristic pattern in which that trait-relevant behavior is typically expressed in relation to particular types of situations (Wright & Mischel, 1987, 1988; Mischel & Shoda, 1995).

Social Environments Change the Expression of Genes, the Brain, and Personality

Researchers pursuing the genetic approach to personality readily acknowledge that even highly heritable traits can be constrained or limited in their full expression. We see that, for example, when the person's growth and ultimate height is affected by nutrition or disease in development. But although they refer to the interplay of genes and environment often they do *not* see this interplay as a two-way reciprocal or mutual influence process. Obviously social environments and the experiences in the world (barring extreme radiation or other biochemical effects on the genes directly) cannot affect the structure of your DNA. So in that sense the interplay between genes and environment in these analyses refers to a one-way influence process from genes to environment, in which genetic influences impact through various routes on the environments experienced with no modification of the genetic structure itself.

14.15 Can the environment change genes? Cite results from stress research.

But it is also the case that social-psychological environmental influences can and do affect the expression of the genes: just by reading this paragraph you increase DNA transcription rates of certain neurotransmitters. And environmental influences also change the hardwiring of the brain—the neuronal structures themselves—and thus produce stable changes within the person at an organic level, even though they do not alter the structure of the DNA. This is evident for example in the finding that stress actually shrinks the size of the hippocampus—a brain structure basic for higher-order mental functions (e.g., Sapolsky, 1996).

Stress Is Bad for Your Brain

Sapolsky reviewed studies showing that sustained stress increases glucocorticoids (GCs), a chemical substance that at high rates can have negative effects on health.

Figure 14.2 Relation between Hippocampal volume and duration of depression among individuals with a history of major depression.

Reported in: Sapolsky, R. M. (1996). Why stress is bad for your brain. *Science, 273,* 749–750. Figure is referenced as adapted from Sheline, Y., Wang, P. W., Gado, M. H., Csernansky, J. G., & Vannier, M. W. (1996). Hippocampal atrophy in recurrent major depression. Proceedings of the National Academy of Sciences of the United States of America. 93(9):3908–13.

Consistent with this finding, Sapolsky (1996) reports research with rodents showing that exposure to excessive amounts of GCs can impair the brain, with particularly unfortunate effects on the hippocampus, a brain structure crucial for learning and memory. Studies with depressed patients (as summarized in Fig. 14.2) also showed that the volume of this brain structure was significantly reduced, and the longer the depression the greater the amount of brain atrophy (Sapolsky, 1996). Furthermore, combat veterans suffering from post-traumatic stress reactions (e.g., after terrifying war experiences) also displayed not only greater exposure to GCs but also substantial reduction in their hippocampi on both sides of the brain.

In short, although the social environment does not influence the structure of the genes it can influence their expression, the brain, and the person's personality. As other sections of the text discuss, situations and environments importantly influence what people experience and do in stable relationship to those contexts. When the situations remain stable, so does their characteristic pattern of social behavior; when the situations change, the behavior pattern also does so predictably (e.g., Mischel & Shoda, 1995, 1998). And as was just noted, such environmental events as stress levels not only impact dramatically on behavior and experience, but also change the hardwiring, i.e., the structures in the brain. Person–environment interactions are two-way interactions in which the person's characteristics show some change over time, just as the characteristics also in part change the environment (Rutter et al., 1997).

In sum, environmental, genetic, and brain influences are in continuous interaction. These interactions affect what we feel and do, which, in turn, produces further changes. The challenge in future research on the interplay of genes, brain, and environment will be to clarify the complex and dynamic processes that lie between genes, brain, and behavior.

SUMMARY

GENETIC BASES OF PERSONALITY

- Twin studies examine the separate role of genetics and environment by comparing the similarities between identical and fraternal twins raised together and raised apart.

- In these studies, answers on self-report personality questionnaires typically yield correlations of about .50 for the similarity of identical twins reared together and about .25 for fraternal twins reared together. For identical twins reared apart, correlations are only slightly lower. About 40–50 percent of the self-reported personality differences among individuals may be accounted for by their genetic differences.

- The genetic contribution to personality is considerable, particularly to such temperaments as emotionality, activity level, and sociability.

- Most twin data on personality come from self-report personality questionnaires and are open to criticism. However, in recent twin studies such measures as ratings by peers or observational measures also indicate a strong genetic influence.

- The meaning of heritability estimates and their uses and misuses were discussed.

GENE–ENVIRONMENT INTERPLAY

- Nonshared environmental influences on personality development are substantial and children growing up in the same family experience it differently.

- Individual differences in what is experienced and in the environments one encounters are partly influenced by genetic factors that exert their impact through several routes. One's personality, itself influenced by genetics as well as environment, also affects the situations that one selects, influences, and creates in the course of development.

- Even highly heritable traits can be constrained or limited by aspects of their social environment. Although the social environment does not influence the structure of the genes it can change the brain and thus produce stable changes within the person at an organic level.

- Stable Person × Situation interaction patterns also reflect both genetic and environmental influences.

KEY TERMS

activity 327
behavior genetics 323
dizygotic twins 324
Down Syndrome 339
emotionality 327
heritability estimates
  (index) 331
human genome 324

monozygotic twins 324
neurotransmitter
  systems 340
nonshared (unique)
  environment 334
person × situation
  interaction patterns
  341

PKU (phenylketonuria)
  338
shared environment
  (or family environment)
  334
sociability 327
temperaments 326
twin method 324

CHAPTER

15

EVOLUTION, BRAIN, AND PERSONALITY

▼ EVOLUTIONARY THEORY AND PERSONALITY

The Evolutionary Approach

Implications of Evolution for Personality

    Mate Selection

    Sexual Jealousy

    Explanations Are Not Justifications

    Altruism

Evolutionary Theory and Inborn Constraints on Learning

    Biological Preparedness

    Evolution of Fears

Specificity of Psychological Mechanisms

The Value of Discriminativeness in Coping with Stress

▼ BRAIN–PERSONALITY LINKS

IN FOCUS 15.1 An Early Effort: Physique and Personality?

Biological Bases of Extraversion–Introversion
    (H. J. Eysenck)

The Behavioral Inhibition and Activation Systems

Brain Asymmetry and Emotional Reactivity

Summary and Implications

Sensation Seeking: A Trait with a Specific Biological Basis?

IN FOCUS 15.2 Testosterone and the Antisocial Personality

▼ BIOLOGICAL ASSESSMENT AND CHANGE

New Windows on the Brain

Biological Therapies

    Antidepressants

    Antipsychotics

    Tranquilizers

    Other Common Drugs

SUMMARY

KEY TERMS

▼ TAKING STOCK PART VI: THE BIOLOGICAL LEVEL OF ANALYSIS

OVERVIEW: FOCUS, CONCEPTS, METHODS

ENDURING CONTRIBUTIONS OF
    THE BIOLOGICAL COGNITIVE LEVEL

▶ EVOLUTIONARY THEORY AND PERSONALITY

15.1 How does the evolutionary approach differ from the genetics approach?

Both evolutionary theory and the genetics approach try to link personality to its biological foundations, but there is a distinctive difference. The genetics approach focuses on the genetic influences that shape the specific biological processes and brain mechanisms underlying personality and social behavior. The evolutionary approach focuses on the processes that have shaped the genes over the long course of the species' development.

The Evolutionary Approach

The evolutionary approach is based on Charles Darwin's well-established theory of the evolution of the species (e.g., Buss, 1991, 1997, 1999, 2001; Cosmides & Tooby, 1989). In this view, the important personality differences between people reflect the process of natural selection through which change takes place in all organic forms over the course of evolution. The processes of adaptation and selection help to

344

What personality attributes allowed our
ancestors to survive and reproduce?

explain the evolution of organisms and to understand *why* they become what they
are (e.g., why kidneys, larynxes, feet, and keen sight develop). These attributes are
in us now because, in the evolutionary view, they allowed our ancestors to survive
and reproduce.

The focus on reproduction and on passing forward one's own genes, rather than
those of genetic competitors, has many implications for social life and personality. It
suggests, for example, that such traits as dominance, conscientiousness, emotional stability, and sociability would have an especially significant role because they facilitate
reproduction and survival (e.g., Kenrick, Sadalla, Groth, & Trost, 1990). Through the
evolutionary process, people also should develop mechanisms that predispose them to
be particularly fine-tuned to potential mates' indicators of health and various types of
abilities, because they impact on their survival and reproductive success (McCrae &
Costa, 1989, 1997; Wiggins, 1979, 1997). These mechanisms become stable and robust
because of their evolutionary value (Buss, 1997).

In the evolutionary view, it is not surprising if, as language developed in the relatively recent evolutionary past, many personality trait terms have become established
that describe the variations of the most important features of the social terrain—the
landscape—to which human beings have to adapt (Buss, 1989). In fact, the lexicon
contains thousands of trait terms that describe these features, summarized in taxonomies like the Big Five. People use these terms to try to answer questions about the
status of others in the social hierarchy, their value for providing or sharing needed
resources, their potential harmfulness or helpfulness, and so on.

15.2 What are the
roles of directional
selection and adaptation
in evolutionary theory?

These functions of trait terms make it understandable that the dimensions captured in trait taxonomies like the Big Five are both highly evaluative and interpersonal. They seem intuitively to summarize the types of judgments people tend to make as they try to know others within their "adaptive landscape." Looked at from this perspective, these dimensions provide a map of potential resources. They identify, for example, who to go to for advice and help (those with high intellect, the open-minded), or who to avoid (the unstable, the unconscientious, the hostile), or who to choose as a mate or partner.

In evolutionary theory, the focus is not on the survival of the individual but on the fate of the gene pool that is distributed in groups across a population. The groups that survive, thrive and rapidly reproduce will pass their genes forward into future generations. The characteristics that are passed on include many variations on which individuals differ—from height and weight through diverse abilities and social-personal traits. Over the course of many generations, the variations in characteristics that are transmitted are influenced by **directional selection.** Through directional selection, versions of the characteristics that enhance survival and reproduction gradually become increasingly represented, while those that handicap survival and reproduction tend to fade out. Such selection has a directional effect, leading ultimately to more adaptive qualities in future generations.

If that were the whole story, in time, individual differences would disappear and everyone in the surviving group would have the ideal qualities for survival. The script becomes complicated by the fact that the characteristics that may be highly adaptive in some contexts and environments may be dysfunctional and even catastrophic in others—and the species has to deal with all kinds of changing environments and challenges. Hence the maintenance of genetic variability and intermediate values of certain characteristics is often adaptive for functioning under ever-changing life conditions. When it is adaptive to have characteristics that are not at the extreme ends of dimensions, genetic variability may be maintained through a mechanism of **stabilizing selection** (Plomin, 1981).

Implications of Evolution for Personality

Evolutionary theory has potentially great implications for personality (e.g., MacDonald, 1998). It provides provocative but often speculative insights and reinterpretations of everyday phenomena like human courtship and aggression among males. Consistently, its contributions are guided by the view that passing your genes or your group's genes—rather than those of your genetic competitor—forward to the next generation is much of what life is about.

15.3 How does the major goal of life explain such behaviors as male jealousy, standards for mate selection, and altruism?

Mate Selection.   Evolutionary theory has a lot to say particularly about mate selection and the competition for mates in humans. The theory predicts that in mate selection there will be important sex differences in the desired characteristics. To the degree that some genes predispose males to search for fertile partners, those genes are more likely to be passed on over the generations. If cues for fertility are youth and beauty, males may evolve to seek such features. In contrast, genes will be passed forward if they predispose females to seek partners who will have the resources, status, dominance, and power that provide for and protect their offspring.

Sexual Jealousy.   Consider next the evolution of male sexual jealousy. From this perspective, male sexual jealousy evolved throughout the evolutionary past of the species because those who had such feelings and behaviors prevented competing males from sexual contact with their mates. This mechanism prevented their competitors from interfering with their reproductive success (Buss, 1997) and so it survived.

Likewise, the competition for mating and reproduction among males also may play a role in the violence and killing not infrequently seen among young males, and only very rarely among females. Male aggression is often provoked by disputes about respect, status, and dominance, and it may not be coincidental that the age at which the killing is highest is also the age at which the mating is highest (Wilson & Daly, 1996).

Explanations Are Not Justifications.   At a theoretical level, these explanations may help one understand all sorts of behavior but they do not justify it. Critics of the approach therefore are quick to note that today's abusive, violent, criminal behaviors, or hurtful macho attitudes and biases, cannot be excused by pointing to their possible origins in evolutionary struggles at the dawn of human life. Attitudes and behaviors that may have served prehistoric ancestors can be inappropriate and dysfunctional for many aspects of modern social life. Fortunately, human beings also have the capacity for self-regulation that enables them to modify their behavior adaptively without waiting for the species to evolve further over the eons of time (Bandura, 2001).

With these hedges in mind, the evolutionary approach nevertheless offers insights into social behavior today. Look through the lenses of evolutionary theory at human courtship on a weekend evening at a crowded urban singles bar. The males try to strut and impress with talk and demonstrations about their ambitions, virility, accomplishments, and possessions. In the same scene, the females display their distinctively different strategies for enhancing their appeal. And the motivations that drive the sexes in the courtship dance may also be quite different. The male is eager to mate and reproduce while the female is more motivated to delay reproduction until the resources and opportunities for long-term offspring protection and care are favorable.

Altruism.   Evolutionary theory also speaks to human qualities that at first glance do not seem consistent with evolution, most notably altruism. Why should humans behave altruistically, taking risks that can kill them, as firemen and police officers do daily? Over the course of evolution, shouldn't such risk-taking and unselfishness fade out since it does nothing to increase the chance of passing your genes forward? The answer is again put in terms of the survival of the group, and not of the individual. To the degree that altruistic acts toward members of one's group facilitate their survival and reproduction, the genes from your gene pool will continue to be passed forward, even if you don't survive as an individual. Consistent with the theory, the most altruistic behaviors are often confined to one's own kin and kind, reflected in the phrase "charity begins at home." But the theory even sees an evolutionary basis for altruism toward strangers as a tendency acquired over the course of time as our ancestors discovered **reciprocal altruism.** This is the recognition that if we help others they are likely to reciprocate in kind, in turn, enhancing the potential for survival and reproduction (e.g., Trivers, 1971).

Evolutionary Theory and Inborn Constraints on Learning

Because evolution seems to prepare organisms to learn some associations much more easily than others, evolutionary theory also has implications that need to be considered when thinking about the relations between learning and personality. As you saw in work at the behavioral-conditioning level (Part IV), for many years, psychologists

15.4 How might innate
factors affect organisms'
learning capabilities?
Why might humans
differ from other animals
in preparedness?

searched for general laws of learning which they assumed would hold for all species
and for all types of responses and stimuli. This assumption has been seriously challenged (Seligman, 1971) and the evidence against it has mounted (Marks, 1987;
Marks & Nesse, 1994; Pinker, 1997). By now it will not surprise you that evolutionary
theory proposes that the differences found between species in the types of associations they readily learn reflect differences in what it was necessary to learn in the
evolutionary struggle for survival (Buss, 1996, 1997; Seligman, 1971; Seligman &
Hager, 1972).

Biological Preparedness.   Let's look at evidence that, when organisms learn, not
all associations between stimuli are formed with equal ease. Rats fed a distinctively fla-
vored new food and then made sick to their stomachs will avoid that food even if their
illness does not occur until 12 hours later. If the same food is followed by electric
shock, however, the rat does not learn to avoid eating it, even when the shock is delivered immediately (Garcia, McGowan, & Green, 1972). A rat can be taught in one trial
to avoid shock from a grid floor if it can escape to a compartment with a smooth black
floor. It takes the rat close to 10 trials to learn to avoid the shock when the escape compartment has a grid floor continuous with that of a shock compartment (Testa, 1974).
Little Albert was conditioned by Watson and Rayner to fear rats by pairing the appearance of the animal with a loud noise, as discussed in Part IV. But a student of Watson's
was unable to produce fears when either a block of wood or a dark curtain was paired
with the noise. These variations in the ease of associating different types of events suggest selective **biological preparedness.**

Evolution of Fears.   Evolutionary theory also argues that people are disposed biologically to fear things that have threatened human survival throughout evolution
(Buss, 1997; Seligman, 1971). For example, there are only a small number of common
human fears, and they seem to be virtually universal. Fears of snakes, spiders, blood,
storms, heights, darkness, and of strangers are typical, and they share a common
theme: they endangered our evolutionary ancestors, and now we seem to be prewired
to fear them. As Pinker (1997, p. 387) puts it: "Children are nervous about rats, and
rats are nervous about bright rooms, before any conditioning begins, and they easily
associate them with danger." These findings are only small examples of a wide range of
data that in recent years increasingly point to prewired dispositions in the brain that
arose in the course of evolution. And these dispositions seem to make humans distinctively prepared not only for some fears rather than for others, but also for all sorts of
high-level mental activities, from language acquisition to mathematical skills to music
appreciation to space perception (Pinker, 1997).

On the other hand, evidence that learning in animals, especially lower animals, is
constrained by their biological capacities does not necessarily mean that humans are
innately programmed in favor of specific associations. Such preprogramming in
humans might be very disadvantageous in evolution because of our need to adapt to
more complex and rapidly changing circumstances—circumstances that we ourselves
often create. The human ability to symbolize experience allows enormous potential for
learning. The extraordinary variety of human behaviors is well documented both by
formal evidence and by casual observation. While chickens and pigs may have serious
biological learning constraints, people are generally not so prewired, according to the
counterargument (Bandura, 1986, 2001).

Specificity of Psychological Mechanisms

Some of the most important challenges that required adaptive solutions and that created problems for human survival came not from the physical challenges of nature but from other hostile humans. As Buss (1997) points out, this recognition comes from studies on topics that range from group warfare to the evolution of language and higher mental functions (e.g., Pinker, 1997).

15.5 What is domain specificity? How is it explained by evolutionary theory?

To illustrate, consider the formation of dyadic alliances, such as lifelong mating relationships. These relationships pose problems that demand adaptive social solutions for reproduction and survival. To enable this, we need to accurately assess the resources and characteristics of potential friends and enemies as they initiate efforts to develop friendships and connections to enhance their adaptation and survival. Relevant to this function, it has been suggested that humans have developed a **cheater detector**—a mechanism to detect cheaters who will seek the benefits of social exchange but refuse to reciprocate appropriately (Cosmides, 1989; Cosmides & Tooby, 1989).

The cheater detector mechanism also illustrates another key point of current evolutionary thinking: the concept of **domain specificity.** Because humans face a host of different types of social problems, each of which requires somewhat different strategies and solutions, evolutionary theory proposes that the mechanisms that emerge will be highly domain specific. Thus the psychological mechanisms that evolve were targeted to solve quite specific evolutionary problems like mate choice and mate retention (Buss, 1997). We saw that specificity in mate choice takes a somewhat different form for males and females. In turn, the psychological problem-solving mechanisms in mate choice are different from those needed in other social exchanges, for example, when dealing with potential enemies. Specificity appears to be a necessary requirement for achieving the enormous discriminativeness and flexibility in behavior that has been observed in most domains. In fact, specificity appears to be the rule, as seen in domains that range from the diversity of human motives to the specificity of learning, to the specificity of fears (Buss, 1997), to most patterns of interpersonal behavior (Cantor & Kihlstrom, 1987; Mischel, 1968, 1973; Mischel & Shoda, 1998).

Addressing the question of domain specificity, David Buss puts it this way:

> A carpenter's flexibility comes not from having a single domain-general 'all purpose tool' that is used to cut, saw, screw, twist, wrench, plane, balance, and hammer, but rather from having many, more specialized tools each designed to perform a particular function (Buss, 1997, p. 325).

Evolutionary theory emphasizes that it is the "specificity, complexity, and numerosity of evolved psychological mechanisms" (Buss, 1999, p. 41) that enable the behavioral flexibility crucial for adaptation. The availability of many specific tools, not any single highly elastic tool, gives the carpenter—and the human being—the flexibility required for the diverse challenges encountered.

Taking the analogy of the carpenter and his diverse highly specialized tool kit a bit further, different carpenters are particularly skilled with some tools and less skilled with others and each has tools that vary in quality. Similarly, people differ in the domains in which they are likely to be especially vulnerable and those in which they excel: the pattern of each person is unique and domain-specific in its behavioral expressions. These patterns are the stable *if . . . then . . .* , behavioral signatures of personality discussed in Chapter 4.

The Value of Discriminativeness in Coping with Stress

15.6 How do
coping flexibility and
discriminative facility
relate to successful
adaptation?

To illustrate domain specificity and the discriminative behavior and flexibility it demands, let's look at how people cope with stress effectively. An individual's ability to cope with daily stressors in the psychological and physical environment is fundamental to survival. Psychologists have distinguished two methods of coping with physical and psychological stress: problem-focused and emotion-focused coping (Chan, 1994; Lazarus & Folkman, 1984; Parker & Endler, 1996). The method that works best depends on the nature of the situation. Consequently, adaptive behavior ideally requires people to be flexible in the methods they use, and to discriminate among different types of situations so that they apply the method that best fits the particular context. For example, adaptive coping has to take into account whether or not the situation is controllable (Aldwin, 1994; Miller 1992). If a situation is controllable, then it is more adaptive to respond in a problem-focused manner. In contrast, in an uncontrollable situation, problem-focused coping is ineffectual, and emotion-focused coping is more adaptive.

One of the important factors that influence an individual's ability to successfully cope with stressful situations is **discriminative facility** (Chiu, Hong, Mischel, & Shoda, 1995; Cheng, Hui, & Lam, 2000). Discriminative facility is the ability to appraise situations as they present themselves and to respond appropriately. Cecilia Cheng and her associates found that individuals who had more discriminative facility used more flexible coping strategies in an experimental setting, and they also showed decreased levels of anxiety (Cheng et al., 2000; Cheng, Chiu, Hong, & Cheung, 2001, Study 1; Roussi, Miller, & Shoda, 2000). In short, to cope well, one needs to discriminate carefully and identify the type of situation faced so that one can then use the problem-solving approach that fits it best. Like the carpenter, in addition to having the right specific tools available, people need to select the tool that fits the task.

In short, evolutionary theory emphasizes the adaptive value of flexibly allowing one's behavior to take into account the requirements of the particular context, and carefully discriminate among situations so that one can identify the specific requirements and act accordingly. Knowing when to fight, when to flee, who to trust and rely upon, and who to fear are of long-term value for survival and reproduction (MacDonald, 1998). To illustrate further, in that view, people who are highly prone to intimacy may under some conditions also be highly prone to aggression and hostility. Consequently their relationships become 'compartmentalized.' They may be highly intimate with family and friends, while hostile, aggressive, and exploitative with out-group members or competitors.

▶ BRAIN–PERSONALITY LINKS

Over millions of years, our species has accumulated genes that have proven useful for individual survival and reproductive success, passing them from generation to generation. The result is the set of what is currently estimated to be about 30,000 genes that make up the human genome. Some of these genes are so important to an individual's basic functions that their DNA sequence is believed to be identical for all individuals. Any deviations from the optimal sequence perfected through evolution are likely to reduce adaptability. For other genes, there are variations. For example, there are variations in the genes that influence eye color, and individuals differ in the particular variations of those genes they have. Heritable differences in personality of the kind described in Chapter 14 reflect such variations.

AN EARLY EFFORT: PHYSIQUE AND PERSONALITY?

Attempts to connect the physical-biological aspects of individuals to their personality are hardly new. Long before genetics was a word, people noticed the dramatic differences in the kinds of bodies that different personalities seem to live in, and asked questions about the possible connections between physical make up and personality. In ancient Greece, Hippocrates described four types of personality. In turn, Galen's theory linked each type to the amounts of different types of bodily humors present, with excessive amounts of different humors interpreted as the biological factors underlying the different personality types.

In early versions of personality work at the biological level, formal classifications of the possible connections between mental disorders and body type were developed by the German psychiatrist Kretschmer a century ago. In 1942, an American physician, William H. Sheldon, suggested three dimensions of physique and their corresponding temperaments. These are summarized in Figure 15.1 and for many years received much attention. As

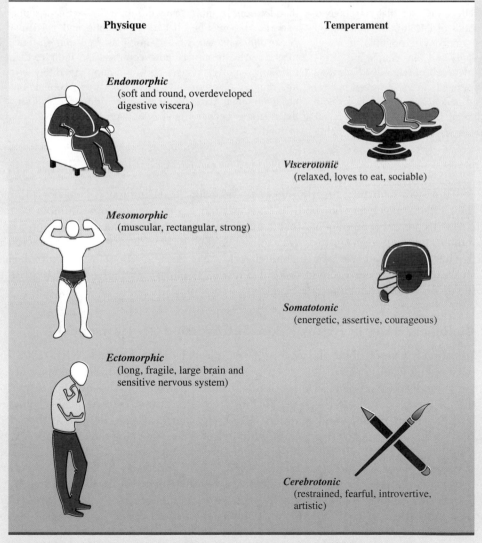

Physique

Endomorphic
(soft and round, overdeveloped digestive viscera)

Mesomorphic
(muscular, rectangular, strong)

Ectomorphic
(long, fragile, large brain and sensitive nervous system)

Temperament

Viscerotonic
(relaxed, loves to eat, sociable)

Somatotonic
(energetic, assertive, courageous)

Cerebrotonic
(restrained, fearful, introvertive, artistic)

Figure 15.1 Sheldon's physique dimensions and their associated temperaments.

Figure 15.1 suggests, according to Sheldon the **endo-morph** is obese, the **mesomorph** has an athletic build, and the **ectomorph** is tall, thin, and stoop-shouldered. Rather than dividing people into three distinct types, Sheldon considered every individual's status on each dimension. He developed a seven-point rating system for measuring body types. For example, a 7-3-1 would be high on endomorphy, moderate on mesomorphy, and low on ectomorphy, presumably with corresponding levels of the associated temperaments. Sheldon's typology thus was quite sophisticated, especially by comparison with earlier attempts.

Sheldon's ideas about the association between body build and temperament get some support when untrained people rate the personality characteristics of others. In part these findings may reflect the fact that stereotyped ideas about the characteristics of fat, athletic, and skinny people are shared by the raters. For example, if raters think most fat people are jolly and thin people are sensitive, they may base their judgments of the individuals they rate on these stereotypes rather than on observed behavior. Thus they may rate a fat person as jolly, no matter how he or she behaves. Studies of behavior that avoid such stereotypes generally provide less evidence for the value

of this system (Tyler, 1956) and leave Sheldon's theory largely unsupported (Herman, 1992).

In addition to such effects from the stereotypes of others, people perceive and interpret their own body types. The thoughts and feelings we develop about our bodies may influence our behavior and who we become, increasing the connections between body types and personality. Thus, physical appearance and physical characteristics certainly affect the ways in which others perceive us, and ultimately even what we feel and experience about ourselves.

Physical characteristics such as strength, height, and muscularity also affect what we can and cannot do easily and thus also influence the situations we select, the work and avocations we pursue, and the interests and values that develop. In short, many different indirect causes may underlie the relations between physique and particular personality characteristics. The links between the two turned out to be much more complex and indirect than the early typologies suggested, and they are difficult to unscramble. Consequently, interest in these connections has gone down, particularly as better routes for exploring the relations between biology and personality have been opened.

15.7 What links did Sheldon propose between physique and personality? What factors could affect such relations?

But genes do not directly influence behavior. They influence behavior through their effects in shaping our body, particularly our brain, and the large number of specialized chemical components that regulate their functioning, such as enzymes, hormones, and neurotransmitters. We experience the world with distinctive brains. In the rest of this chapter, we will explore theories and findings about how our biological structures and processes influence our thoughts, feelings, and behavior, giving rise to the distinctive personalities that characterize each of us.

Biological Bases of Extraversion–Introversion (H. J. Eysenck)

15.8 According to Eysenck, what biological differences underlie extraversion and introversion?

You already learned about the work at the trait level by Hans Eysenck (1916–1997), an outstanding English personality theorist (Chapter 3). Eysenck also was a pioneer in trying to connect psychological dispositions to their biological foundations, focusing on the characteristics of extraverts versus introverts. Recall that extraverts are characterized as active, outgoing, and venturesome, whereas introverts are defined as the opposite: withdrawn, quiet, introspective, with a preference for being alone or with a good friend or two, but an aversion for large groups. According to Eysenck's theory (Eysenck, 1990; Eysenck & Eysenck, 1985, 1995), extraverts differ from introverts because of differences in their physiological **level of arousal** or **LOA** in the brain. Specifically, he proposed that these differences are influenced by the **ascending reticular activation system (ARAS)** of the brain, the system believed to regulate overall arousal in the cortex.

When Eysenck (1967) first developed his theory in the 1960s, the ARAS was viewed as a gateway that controls the level of stimulation into the cortex. In Eysenck's theory, introverts need only small amounts of stimulation to overstimulate them physiologically, which then leads them to become distressed and withdrawn in their behavior. In extraverts, in contrast, according to the theory, the ARAS is not easily stimulated, which leads them to seek activities that will increase the level of stimulation, for example, by socializing more actively and seeking activities—such as parties and adventures—more than introverts.

To test this theory, Eysenck and colleagues conducted studies with extraverts and introverts and measured their brain wave activity and cardiovascular activity. Researchers found, for example, that introverts (compared to extraverts) show greater changes in their brain wave activity in response to low frequency tones, indicating their lower threshold for stimulation to the CNS (central nervous system), as the theory predicted (Stelmack & Michaud-Achorn, 1985). Overall, a good deal of research indicates that while extraverts and introverts don't differ in their level of brain activity at resting levels, for example while sleeping, they do differ as predicted by the theory in their physiological reactivity to stimulation. Many different types of studies suggest this conclusion (e.g., Eysenck, 1983).

The differences between extraverts and introverts in their reactivity to stimulation also should influence their performance under different arousal levels because different activities require different arousal levels to do them well. In earlier work, Hebb (1955) defined the **optimal level of arousal** or **OLA** as the arousal level that is most appropriate for doing a given task effectively, and showed that too much or too little arousal undermines performance. This is intuitively familiar: as you know from your own experience, prepping for an important examination, for example, requires a higher level of arousal and alertness than you need when trying to relax or to go to sleep. The point is that to be able to perform effectively requires a good match between one's arousal level and the optimal arousal level needed for the particular task. Consequently, the differences between extraverts and introverts in their ease of arousal should have important implications for how well they do on many life tasks: they should do well on tasks that require arousal levels that match their own, but not on those where there is a major mismatch.

An extravert faced with monotonous work tasks such as closely monitoring control panels that remain generally stable, or proofreading, is likely to soon become bored and have trouble maintaining attention, becoming underaroused, and apt to tune out or even fall asleep. In this situation, an introvert will probably remain attentive and perform more effectively. Suppose, however, the job is that of a fireman or emergency room worker, and all the alarms and sirens suddenly are ringing, the emergency lights are flashing, the scene is chaotic. Now the situation is reversed in terms of the amount of arousal activated, and the introvert who is easily overaroused has the disadvantage, prone to becoming distressed and ineffective, whereas the extravert may be in his ideal element and functioning at his best.

This point was made in a classic, well-controlled experiment by Geen (1984) whose results supported the expectations from Eysenck's theory. Geen allowed extraverts and introverts to choose their preferred noise level of background stimulation while working on a potentially boring but difficult task (learning paired associations between words). As expected, extraverts chose higher levels of stimulation than did introverts. Under these conditions, according to the theory, both groups will be working under their preferred level of arousal and therefore should perform equally well—and they did. It also follows that when extraverts are given the lower levels of arousal preferred by introverts during the task, they should become underaroused and bored, and therefore do less well. Likewise, when introverts are given the higher arousal levels

15.9 How did Eysenck test his theory? What physiological differences exist between introverts and extraverts?

preferred by introverts, they should become overaroused and upset, and their performance should deteriorate. To test these expectations, Geen in fact reversed the preferred stimulation conditions on the work task, giving the introverts the noise levels chosen by the extraverts and vice versa. Again the results were as predicted: performance was poorer when extraverts worked under the lower stimulation conditions preferred by the introverts, and vice versa.

The Behavioral Inhibition and Activation Systems

15.10 Describe the BIS and BAS, as well as their functions. How do they relate to introversion and extraversion?

Two neurological systems in the brain seem to be closely related to the distinction between the extraversion–introversion personality types. One is the **behavioral inhibition system (BIS),** which causes individuals to withdraw from certain undesirable stimuli or punishments and thus inhibits behavior. You can think of it as a withdrawal–avoidance system that allows one to pause and then contemplate alternatives before taking action. Shakespeare's Hamlet probably would have scored high on measures of the strength of this system. The other is the **behavioral activation system (BAS),** which directs individuals toward certain desirable goals or incentives and thus activates approach behavior. You can think of it as an energizing system that activates and facilitates rapid action.

According to some researchers, the BIS is the more influential, active system in introverts, and the BAS is believed to be the more active system in extraverts (Gray, 1991). The theory suggests, for example, that because BAS is the more active system in extraverts, they tend to focus on rewards and seek situations in which they could find them to actively pursue their desires. This is in contrast to the more passive, avoidant behavior of introverts who are, in the theory, physiologically more sensitized to punishment and threats (e.g., Bartussek, Diedrich, Naumann, & Collet, 1993). Gray's theory and related work also indicates that the BIS is linked to anxiety as a personality dimension, whereas the BAS is related to individual differences in impulsivity or the inability to inhibit and control one's immediate responses and urges.

Although there still is considerable disagreement among theorists about the nature of the exact mechanisms and links to personality (e.g., Cloninger, 1988; Davidson, 1995; Depue & Collins, 1999) several tentative conclusions seem to be emerging from a great deal of work at this level of analysis. Individuals who are extremely reactive in the BIS tend to be especially sensitive to potential threat, punishment, and danger. They therefore may focus more on the potential negative outcomes rather than on the possible gains and rewards when considering alternative action possibilities. For example, they are likely to attend more to how much money they could lose from a business decision than to how much they might gain. They are more prone to anxiety and in the extreme even to panic, more tuned to negative outcomes and punishment, less sensitive to possible rewards, incentives, and gratifications. On the other hand—or more literally, on the other side of the brain—people who are highly reactive in the BAS are likely to show the opposite pattern: they are more responsive to incentives and possible positive outcomes, more ready to experience positive emotions such as eagerness, hope, and excitement. These differences in the nature and meaning of BIS and BAS reactivity are becoming especially clear from studies on brain asymmetry, considered next.

Brain Asymmetry and Emotional Reactivity

In recent years, the implications of the brain's activity for personality also are being illuminated by investigations of the electrical activity in the frontal lobe areas of the cortex that are involved in such positive emotions as eagerness and hope (Davidson & Sutton, 1995), or in negative emotions such as disgust and fear (Davidson et al., 1990). This work begins with the finding that people differ consistently in the degree to which the right versus the left sides of their brains are activated, and that difference is called **brain asymmetry.** In these studies, the brain's electrical activity is assessed by the electroencephalograph (EEG). (This measure was more fully described in Chapter 2.)

To calculate differences in the brain's asymmetry, researchers subtract the level of EEG brain wave activity on the left side of the brain from the level of activity on the right side of the brain. A positive asymmetry measure indicates a relatively higher degree of activity on the right side of the brain; a negative measure indicates a relatively higher degree of activity on the left side of the brain (Sutton, 2002, p. 136). In these studies, stable individual differences have been found repeatedly in the brain's asymmetry in anterior (frontal) brain regions (e.g., Sutton & Davidson, 2000).

You can get a sense of these individual differences and their implications for personality from some experiments in which participants were exposed to videotapes depicting funny or aversive, fear-inducing, and disgusting themes. While they were watching these videos, their EEGs were recorded, their facial and behavioral reactions were filmed, and self-reports of their emotional reactions also were obtained. Individuals who had higher resting levels of activity in their left frontal area of the brain gave more positive responses to happy stimuli (Wheeler, Davidson, & Tomarken, 1993). They also showed higher levels of self-reported BAS sensitivity on questionnaires (Harmon-Jones & Allen, 1997; Sutton & Davidson, 1997). In contrast, higher resting levels of activity in the right frontal area of the brain were indicative of more negative feelings in response to aversive stimuli (Davidson and associates, 1990), as well as higher levels of self-reported BIS sensitivity on the self-report measures of reactivity to threats.

Evidence for the stability of these individual differences in affective styles also comes from studies of very young children. For example, 10-month-old children were exposed to a brief separation from the mother while she left the playroom in an experimental situation. While some infants became greatly distressed, others remained much calmer. Those who cried and were more upset also tended to be the ones who characteristically have more brain wave activity on the right than on the left side, even when they were measured during the resting stage. Thus individual differences in this type of emotional reactivity seem to be a stable quality already seen in the young child (Fox, Bell, & Jones, 1992). Likewise in adults, brain asymmetry is sufficiently stable over time to suggest an enduring disposition that relates to how one deals with different kinds of emotion-inducing events and experiences (Davidson, 1993).

The overall implication from this line of research for personality is clear. Individuals who are dominantly left-side active in their brains experience pleasant, positive emotions more easily when positive stimuli are encountered. People who are dominantly right-side active are more ready to respond with negative emotional reactions and distress when they face unpleasant or threatening events. Some people are more ready to feel and be happy than others; some people are more ready to feel and be distressed and to experience negative emotions than others.

Summary and Implications

In sum, findings on the BAS and BIS and on brain asymmetry suggest that these are specific and distinct incentive and threat systems in the brain that are responsive, respectively, to environmental signals of reward and threat, and that are related, respectively, to positive and negative mood (e.g., Gable, Reis, & Elliot, 2000). This is

15.11 How are hemispheric activation differences related to types of emotions?

important for understanding individual differences in personality because people differ in stable ways in their levels of reactivity in these two brain systems. These differences link to their behavioral dispositions with regard to active positive approach tendencies versus fearful behavioral inhibition and avoidance tendencies. These differences are reflected on measures of the relevant personality dispositions (extraversion, impulsivity for the BAS; inhibition, withdrawal, anxiety, or neuroticism for the BIS). Studies of brain asymmetry likewise suggest stable individual differences in the level of reactivity in different brain areas that are directly correlated with individual differences in positive and negative emotional and behavioral reactions to different types of stimuli. In short, there are clear and meaningful specific links between peoples' characteristic brain activities and their characteristic emotional and behavioral reaction patterns to different types of positive and negative stimulation.

15.12 How is the action of biological systems influenced by situational factors?

It is also noteworthy that brain systems such as BIS and BAS are linked to personality in context-specific ways that again reflect the importance of taking account of the relationship between the expressions of personality and the characteristics of the stimulus situation. You see this in the finding that high BIS reactivity relates to more sensitivity and attention to possible punishments, less to possible rewards, and is essentially diagnosed by the difference between the two. The distinctive dispositional pattern of people high in BIS activity takes the form: *if* threats-punishments are encountered, *then* inhibition, high anxiety-distress, negative emotions. The opposite *if . . . then . . .* pattern seems to characterize those high in BAS. For them, *if* rewards, incentives, *then* approach, eagerness, positive emotions. While the two types also link to broad dispositions like extraversion, their behavioral expressions are especially evident when the relevant "ifs" are present. Once again, we find that the expressions of personality are seen in person-situation interactions as well as in overall behavioral tendencies.

New insights about personality dispositions are coming from studies that probe the relationships that do—and that don't—exist between individual differences with regard to various types of relatively broad trait categories like neuroticism on the one hand, and biological processes on the other. For example, Heller and colleagues (2002) find that anxious emotional arousal and worry may reflect two separate neural networks in the brain. Specifically, these networks are in the left versus right hemispheres, and in the frontal versus posterior regions, as measured by EEG and blood flow indices of cortical activity. Their research suggests that psychological conditions that have long been grouped under the term "neuroticism" may actually consist of two distinct mechanisms that need to be understood separately. These two systems thus may involve different mechanisms that lead to different experiences and life problems, and that require different treatment.

What are the implications? New discoveries from multiple levels of analysis, in this case, the biological level utilizing modern brain assessment techniques, are allowing a greater level of precision in the analysis of broad dispositions like neuroticism. The ability to distinguish the different phenomena covered by a broad term like neuroticism makes it possible to examine their different causes. Then one also can develop distinctive therapies targeted to treat these different disorders more effectively.

Sensation Seeking: A Trait with a Specific Biological Basis?

15.13 How do high and low scorers on the Sensation Seeking Scale differ behaviorally?

Why do some people go parachuting and drive fast, whereas others prefer TV and rarely exceed the speed limit? According to one researcher, Marvin Zuckerman, the answer may lie in a trait called **sensation seeking.** Of particular interest is that this trait also seems to have clear connections with findings from the biological level that point both to the role of brain chemicals and of genetics as determinants. First, let us consider the nature of individual differences in this characteristic. These differences are measured with a **Sensation Seeking Scale (SSS)** which taps into four different aspects: Thrill and Adventure Seeking (engaging in risky sports and fast driving, for example), Experience Seeking (seeking novelty), Disinhibition (seeking sensation through social stimulation and activities), and Boredom Susceptibility (lack of tolerance for repetitive events).

This scale has helped to predict how people cope with situations in which there is a lack of stimulation: in this context, the sensation seekers get more restless and upset. It also predicts reactions to the opposite experience, as when one is placed in close confinement with another person. In that situation, those low in sensation seeking become more stressed, both in their own reports of the experience and on biochemical measures (e.g., Zuckerman, and associates 1968). Sensation seeking now has been related to a wide range of diverse behaviors (Zuckerman, 1979, 1983, 1984, 1994), as the examples in Table 15.1 summarize.

How does this personality characteristic connect to the biological level? As with extraversion, individual differences in sensation seeking also may arise in part from physiological differences in physical arousal, such as cortical activity in reaction to novel and familiar stimuli (Zuckerman, 1990). Hebb's (1955) ideas about optimal level of arousal (OLA) again are relevant here just as they were in our discussion of extraverts and introverts and their very different reactions to different types of situations that require different arousal level for optimal performance. Consistent with Hebb, if individuals differ in their preferred optimal level of arousal, then those with a low optimal level of arousal will attempt to maintain a low level of arousal which requires them to sometimes work toward reducing the stimulation in their environment. Those with a high OLA—the sensation seekers—will work toward increasing the stimulation they get in order to achieve and maintain their optimal level of arousal, and therefore they keep looking for change and searching for novel and complex sensations and experiences. Individuals who are high versus low on Zuckerman's measures of sensation seeking tend to choose occupations and display life patterns that are consistent with these expectations. High compared to low sensation seekers are more likely to be skydivers,

15.14 What is the hypothesized biological basis for differences in sensation seeking?

TABLE 15.1 Characteristics of High Sensation Seekers

Risk-Taking Behaviors:
   More varied sexual experience
   Greater use and variety of illegal drugs
   Risky driving habits
   More risky sports, take risks within sports

Intellectual Preferences:
   Prefer complexity
   Have a high tolerance for ambiguity
   Are more original and creative
   Rich imagery and dreams

Interests and Attitudes:
   Liberal, permissive, and nonconforming attitudes and choice
   Prefer high stimulation vocations (e.g., aircraft controllers; high-risk security officers, war-zone journalists, emergency room doctors)
   May view love more as a game and show less commitment to their relationships

or police officers who prefer riot duty, to take greater risks in gambling situations, to self-report having more diverse sexual experiences and partners (e.g., Zuckerman, 1978, 1984, 1991)—in other words, to behave in ways consistent with their needs for higher arousal states to obtain their "optimal" levels as Table 15.1 indicated.

Sensation seeking also may be linked to impulsiveness. Impulsiveness is a quality that in extreme and unsocialized form characterizes people who are considered antisocial personalities, sometimes also called sociopaths or psychopaths. These are people who frequently engage in criminal and antisocial behavior, seem unable to control their own impulses or to show the type of conscientiousness and adherence to conventions generally expected in social interactions and relationships within the society and culture. Zuckerman (1993) suggests that these may be unsocialized, impulsive sensation seekers—individuals who have difficulty inhibiting their impulses for the sake of social adaptation. They seek sensation even when the long-term costs to them and society are high. Unsurprisingly, such individuals also tend to be low on measures of conscientiousness, and high on measures of aggression.

To find the biological bases for individual differences in sensation seeking, Zuckerman has paid particular attention to the role of the chemicals in the nerve cells of the brain that are crucial for transmitting nerve impulses from cell to cell across the slight space—the synapses—that separates them. The **neurotransmitters** are the chemicals that enable the nerve impulses to jump across the synapses. When their levels are appropriate, the transmission across cells continues, allowing signals to get to their destinations. As with most processes in nature, there is a system of checks and balances, of activation and inhibition. The proper level of neurotransmitters is maintained by **monoamine oxidase (MAO)**, enzymes that break down the neurotransmitters after they have passed along the route. The theory here is that high sensation seekers are the individuals who are low in their MAO levels, and therefore lack the chemical inhibitors required to keep their neurotransmitter levels down.

15.15 How might testosterone interact with socialization factors to influence antisocial personality development?

IN FOCUS 15.2

TESTOSTERONE AND THE ANTISOCIAL PERSONALITY

As an example of the multiple biological factors that may interact and contribute jointly to personality, let us again consider antisocial personalities. You already saw that the MAO inhibitors may play a role here, as does the characteristic of impulsive sensation seeking. Research suggests that hormones, and specifically testosterone levels, may be another biological contributor to such antisocial behaviors. High levels of the sex hormone testosterone relate to, and may possibly promote, such behaviors as assaulting others, going AWOL while on military duty, abusing drugs, having multiple sex partners, or encountering other social problems throughout development and adulthood (Dabbs & Morris, 1990). Also, the higher the levels of this hormone, the lower the level of education attained, and consequently the lower also the ultimate socioeconomic level (Dabbs, 1992). Therefore, the causal chain here may be very complicated, influenced perhaps by a variety of socialization factors such as lower education rather than directly by testosterone.

The point here is like the one Zuckerman (1994) makes in his discussion of the biology of antisocial impulsivity: the interactions between neurotransmitters, enzymes, and hormones that underlie the behavioral and psychological manifestations of personality will probably turn out to be multiple and complex—and these biological factors are likely to also interact with a host of social and psychological factors. Thus, to adequately understand complex patterns of social behavior, whether antisocial or prosocial, one needs to consider determinants from every level of analysis discussed throughout this text.

Some support for these ideas comes from moderate or low correlations found between sensation seeking on the sensation-seeking scale and lower MAO levels in the bloodstream (Zuckerman, 1993). Although the evidence is still limited, this work continues to stimulate exciting developments at the interface of personality and biology that seeks to connect personality characteristics to specific neurotransmitters. Some of these studies are using either pharmacological or psychophysiological techniques to examine the physiological correlates of social behaviors.

The hope of finding such simple and direct links is understandably appealing, but Zuckerman (1994), himself is cautious about the prospects, noting that there are likely to be extremely complex interactions between neurotransmitters, enzymes, and hormones that underlie the behavioral and psychological manifestations of personality (also see In Focus 15.2). Nevertheless, and beyond sensation seeking, there is promising pharmacological work, for example, indicating that the neurotransmitter serotonin and the neurohormone oxytocin may mediate social bonding and affiliation, as well as social dominance and aggression (e.g., Carter, 1998; Taylor et al., 2000). Likewise, there is interesting work suggesting correlations between testosterone levels and antisocial personality (see In Focus 15.2).

Recent research on sensation seeking is itself producing something of a sensation with reports of links to a specific gene. In two studies, associations have been reported between a DNA marker (for a particular neuroreceptor gene) and measures of novelty seeking, an aspect of the broader pattern of sensation seeking (Benjamin et al., 1996; Ebstein et al., 1995). Findings like these await much further research before conclusions can be reached, but they again point to the potentially exciting connections between aspects of behavior and their biological roots which may well be found in the future. They make sensation seeking a particularly promising disposition for linking the biological and the dispositional-psychological levels of analysis.

▶ BIOLOGICAL ASSESSMENT AND CHANGE

Throughout this chapter and the last, you have seen that the interrelationships between biological processes and psychological processes central for personality, such as our emotions and motivations, are becoming increasingly visible. It has become possible to explore the relations between brain, evolution, and personality through the development of assessment methods that now enable researchers at the biological level to investigate these links systematically. In recent years, a revolution has occurred in such measurement that opens new routes for seeing brain–behavior connections.

New Windows on the Brain

Technological advances in brain imaging now allow researchers to use methods that capture even subtle nerve activity in the brain. As noted in Chapter 2, the technique of functional magnetic resonance imaging or fMRI measures the magnetic fields created by the functioning nerve cells in the brain and with the aid of computers depicts these activities as images. These images enable researchers to see the brain areas that are most active as the person performs different kinds of mental tasks and experiences different kinds of perceptions, images, thoughts, and emotions, from fears to anticipated

15.16 Describe fMRI and PET techniques for measuring brain processes.

Woman entering an fMRI brain scanner.

gratifications. Brain imaging makes it possible to trace the relations between activity at the biological level and activity that involves different aspects of the person's mental and emotional representations as studied at the social cognitive, phenomenological, and psychodynamic-motivational levels. In short, the new windows on the brain allow a much more precise and detailed analysis of the links between activity in the brain and at the psychological levels reviewed throughout this text.

A second technique to link brain and behavior is the PET procedure or positron emission tomography method, which also was briefly introduced in Chapter 2. This technique creates images and maps of brain functioning by assessing metabolic activity in different areas. It records the radioactivity in the brain that occurs after the participant has been given a nontoxic but radioactively labeled form of glucose, which is the energy source for the brain's activity. These methods are being used by cognitive neuroscientists, increasingly working in collaboration with psychologists from the areas of social-personality and clinical psychology (e.g., Kosslyn et al., 2002; Ochsner & Lieberman, 2001).

Particularly exciting is the recognition that in these studies individual differences in personality are not "noise" that needs to be removed to decipher the mechanisms involved. On the contrary, attention to personality and the differences between individuals in responsiveness on these brain measures allows a much deeper and more complete understanding. For example, in studies of mental imagery using the amount of blood flow measurable in different areas of the brain, it was found that:

. . . monitoring individual differences in blood flow in relevant areas . . . provides enormous power in predicting behavior . . . individual differences not only can be used to establish that a particular type of representation is used during the task . . . but also can help identify the neural underpinnings of such processing (Kosslyn et al., 2002).

Biological Therapies

As we saw, some psychological dispositions have biological roots. If problematic behaviors, such as severe depression, in part reflect biological dispositions and biochemical problems, might they also respond to biological treatment? Researchers have actively pursued this question.

Biological treatments attempt to change an individual's mood or behavior by direct intervention in bodily processes. Pharmacotherapy, or treatment with drugs, has so far proved to be the most promising biological therapy for psychological problems. The types of drugs used for specific purposes are summarized in Table 15.2.

Antidepressants. The antidepressants, or psychic energizers, are used to elevate the mood of depressed individuals. Two of the largest categories are the cyclics and the monoamine oxidase inhibitors, or MAOIs (Lader, 1980). Fluoxetine (trade name Prozac) is currently one of the most favored and widely used cyclic antidepressants, which increases the chemical neurotransmitter serotonin (Kramer, 1993). Excessively low serotonin levels seem to be related to such feelings as chronic pessimism, rejection sensitivity, and obsessive worry. Antidepressants have been shown to have varying degrees of efficacy and to produce various side effects (e.g., Davis, Klerman, & Schildkraut, 1967; Klein et al., 1980; Levine, 1991). The MAOIs, for example, appear highly effective in certain types of depressed individuals, although their side effects can include a dangerous rise in blood pressure when foods high in tyramine, such as red wine and cheese, are consumed (Howland, 1991; Kayser et al., 1988; Potter, Rudorfer,

15.17 Describe the drugs commonly used for therapeutic purposes.

TABLE 15.2 Some Drugs Used in Pharmacotherapy

Type of Drug	Application	Therapeutic Effects
Antidepressants (cyclics, monoamine oxidase inhibitors)	Depression	Appear effective for elevating mood in some people
Antipsychotics (phenothiazines)	Schizophrenia	Well substantiated: gets patients out of hospitals, have practically eliminated need for restraints in hospitals
Minor tranquilizers (benzodiazepines)	Anxiety, tension, milder forms of depression	Seem to slow down transmission of nerve impulses in the brain
Lithium	Manic behavior	Reduces mood swings
Methadone (a synthetic narcotic)	Heroin addiction	May eliminate craving for heroin; blocks "highs"

Note: These drugs are classified according to their effects on behavior not according to their chemical composition. Chemically dissimilar drugs can produce similar effects.

& Manji, 1991). Lithium, an alkali metal in a drug category of its own, is used to stabilize mood swings and occasionally to treat severe depression (Grilly, 1989).

Antipsychotics. The phenothiazines (most notably chlorpromazine) have proved to be so useful in managing schizophrenic patients that they are referred to as antipsychotic drugs. Their use in mental hospitals has been widespread since the 1950s and has changed the character of many hospitals, eliminating the need for locked wards and straitjackets. Discharged patients are often on maintenance dosages of these drugs and must occasionally return to the hospital for dose level adjustments.

The major tranquilizers have potentially serious side effects that may include motor disturbances, low blood pressure, and jaundice. There are also unpleasant subjective effects such as fatigue, blurred vision, and mouth dryness, which may explain why patients on their own may simply stop taking these drugs and often have to return to the hospital for an extended stay.

Tranquilizers. The barbiturates were the first widely used so-called "minor tranquilizers"—drugs that relieve relatively mild anxiety. However, these drugs were replaced by the benzodiazepines, which proved more effective with fewer side effects (Lader, 1980). For many years, the most widely used of these drugs was a synthetic chemical known by its trade name, Valium. It became the medicine most frequently prescribed in the United States for several years as Americans spent almost half a billion dollars a year on it.

Valium, like its predecessors the barbiturates, acts on the limbic system of the brain and is useful in the treatment of anxiety, panic disorder, and some convulsive disorders (Gitlin, 1990). Although Valium seemed less harmful than the barbiturates, it also proved to have side effects and to be potentially addictive. It can endanger a developing fetus and can have adverse effects of confusion and agitation, especially in the elderly. Now other benzodiazepines such as Xanax, Klonodin, and Ativan are popular alternatives, although their potentially severe side effects also require extremely cautious monitoring. The use of antidepressant medication in treatment of extreme anxiety or panic attacks also may be effective (Gitlin, 1990).

Other Common Drugs. Other widely used drugs include the psychostimulants, such as Ritalin, which are used in treating impulse disorders and severe attention deficits. Methadone, a drug which blocks the craving for heroin and prevents heroin "highs," is often used to overcome heroin addiction, either by weaning the person off it or by maintaining him or her on a fixed dose; however, methadone itself is addictive, and the process can take a long time (Lawson & Cooperrider, 1988).

As this brief survey suggests, some drugs appear to be positive contributors to a treatment program for some disorders. However, no drug by itself constitutes an adequate complete treatment for psychological problems. To the extent that the person's difficulties reflect problems of living, it would be naive to think that drugs can substitute completely for learning and practicing more effective ways to cope with the continuous challenges of life. And the fact that most drugs have negative side effects (Maricle, Kinzie, & Lewinsohn, 1988) makes it all the more important to seek psychological treatment for psychological problems whenever possible, often in conjunction with a medically supervised form of pharmacotherapy.

In spite of the problems encountered by efforts to treat psychological problems chemically, there is much exciting progress, and the new field of neuropharmacology is thriving (e.g., Cooper, Bloom, & Roth, 1986). For example, biological responses in panic disorders are becoming better understood and, in turn, the effects of various chemicals (such as sodium-lactate) on panic states are becoming known (e.g., Hollander et al., 1989). As a result, treatments for a wide range of anxiety and mood disorders are taking into account both biochemical and psychological processes (Barlow, 1988; Klein & Klein, 1989; Simons & Thase, 1992).

SUMMARY

EVOLUTIONARY THEORY AND PERSONALITY

- At the evolutionary level of analysis, personality traits and individual differences reflect the processes of natural selection and adaptation.

- For example, such traits as dominance, emotional stability, and sociability are seen as particularly robust because they have an especially significant role in mate selection and retention.

- The evolutionary perspective provides a fresh view of behaviors from mate selection and jealousy to altruism, aggression, and the development of fears.

- Evolutionary theory emphasizes the adaptive value of flexibly allowing one's behavior to take into account the requirements of the particular context. This requires carefully discriminating among situations.

BRAIN–PERSONALITY LINKS

- William H. Sheldon was an American physician who classified individuals into three different body types and their corresponding temperaments.

- More recently, Hans J. Eysenck measured brain wave and cardiovascular activity in introverts and extraverts to further understand the physiological differences that underlie these types.

- The behavioral inhibition system (BIS) is the neurological system that may dispose individuals to withdraw from negative stimuli. The behavioral activation system (BAS) is the neurological system that may lead individuals to seek out positive stimuli or rewards.

- BAS and BIS research suggests that these are specific and distinct incentive and threat systems in the brain with important links to personality.

- Sensation-seeking behavior has been linked to several biological factors including the level of the MAO enzyme in the brain and the presence of a specific DNA marker.

- The interactions between neurotransmitters, enzymes, and hormones that underlie the behavioral and psychological manifestations of personality seem to be multiple and complex and also interact with a host of social and psychological factors.

BIOLOGICAL ASSESSMENT AND CHANGE

- Personality psychologists utilize magnetic resonance imaging (MRI) and positron emission tomography (PET) scans to examine brain activity during various psychological experiences.

- Biological treatments for psychological disorders favor pharmacotherapy, which makes use of a variety of drugs including antidepressants, antipsychotics, and minor tranquilizers.

KEY TERMS

ascending reticular
   activation system
   (ARAS)   352
behavioral activation
   system (BAS)   354
behavioral inhibition
   system (BIS)   354
biological
   preparedness   348
brain asymmetry   355

cheater detector   349
directional selection   346
discriminative
   facility   350
domain specificity   349
ectomorph   352
endomorph   352
level of arousal
   (LOA)   352
mesomorph   352

monoamine oxidase
   (MAO)   358
neurotransmitters   358
optimal level of
   arousal (OLA)   353
reciprocal altruism   347
sensation seeking   356
sensation seeking
   scale (SSS)   357
stabilizing selection   346

PART VI

THE BIOLOGICAL LEVEL OF ANALYSIS

▶ OVERVIEW: FOCUS, CONCEPTS, METHODS

As summarized in the Overview table, work at the biological level in the last few decades is changing the conception of personality in many crucial ways. It has demonstrated the significant role of heredity in personality, particularly with regard to such qualities as emotionality, activity, sensation seeking, extraversion, and a host of psychosocial traits. It thus has called attention to the important role of biology and the genes in personality and social behavior as well as in human abilities. It has opened the way to studying the activity in the brain, and to linking biological processes to psychological processes—including the person's thoughts, feeling, memories. The breakthroughs that are occurring rapidly in the tools available for studying these links are exciting, and they promise to pave the way for tracing the relationships between what goes on in the body and in the mind with increasing depth and precision.

Overview of Biological Level: Focus, Concepts, Methods

Basic units:	Biological variables: genetics, brain and other biological systems; brain–behavior links; role of biology in social behavior
Causes of behavior:	Biological and evolutionary processes; interactions between biological and environmental-social variables
Behavioral manifestations of personality:	Social behavior, personality traits, mental-emotional states
Favored data:	Physiological measures: PET Scans, EEG, MRI; test responses; trait ratings, adaptive and maladaptive behavior patterns; brain–behavior links, interactions of genetic and environmental factors
Observed responses used as:	Data for linking brain–behavior relations; behavior analyzed in terms of evolutionary theory
Research focus:	Heritability of personality; analyzing brain–behavior relations; effects of biological variables on personality
Approach to personality change:	Personality change is linked to brain/chemical changes; biological treatments for disorders (e.g., medications)
Role of the situation:	Important for evolutionary analyses of social behavior

▶ ENDURING CONTRIBUTIONS OF THE BIOLOGICAL LEVEL

The biological level of analysis is justifiably creating great interest at present on many fronts. As you saw in the discussion in Chapter 14 on studies of identical twins, many qualities of personality, especially as assessed on standardized trait questionnaires, are substantially influenced by genetic-biological determinants. Humans are biological creatures, and personality is importantly influenced by biological processes, beginning with the genes that are our heritage. The findings that genes influence personality have become sufficiently clear and strong to avoid debates about whether or not they are important: they are very important—but so is the environment. Research now is going beyond demonstrations that genes have a substantial impact on personality to identify the specific biochemical and psychosocial processes and their interactions that underlie these effects. Fortunately, such studies are now being pursued vigorously and promise to yield increasingly precise answers.

By discovering new methods for viewing the activity in the brain, work at the biological level of analysis also has opened a new route for personality research. It makes it possible to study the relationship between the individual's psychological activities, such as thoughts, memories, and intense feelings experienced by the person, for example, when exposed to a feared stimulus, and the activation of specific brain areas and centers in the brain. Studies of brain systems like the BIS and BAS, and of brain asymmetry, are already yielding new insights into the biological processes that link to crucial aspects of personality. These features of personality are fundamental, influencing the approach and avoidance dispositions that characterize each person distinctively. They affect one's typical reactions to rewards and incentives versus punishments and threats, and the positive and negative emotions and moods that influence how we experience the world and relate to it.

The challenge ahead for this line of research will be to examine more fully how these biological system relate to, and interact with, relevant aspects of personality assessed at the other levels of analysis, for example, in studies of human motivation, planning, and self-regulation. These new directions are already being pursued and are the topics of the final chapters in the text.

Questions for work at this level in the future will include the ways in which learning and therapeutic and educational experiences might be used to influence the level of activity in different brain areas in constructive directions. Such research ultimately may help liberate individuals from biological burdens of which they may not have to be the victims. The long-term yield from such research may help in the diagnosis and treatment of an array of human problems not yet imaginable in biochemical terms. If so, the approach also may make a great contribution to treatment and improvement of the human condition, but that possibility lies mostly in the years ahead. Concurrently, work on social evolution is providing new models, concepts, and methods for thinking in fresh ways about diverse aspects of social behavior—from mate selection and courtship to aggression, altruism, and human competencies. In the future, it will be important to try to link evolutionary processes to personality at the theoretical level in ways that allow empirical tests of the implications with increasing precision.

VII
INTEGRATION OF LEVELS: THE PERSON AS A WHOLE

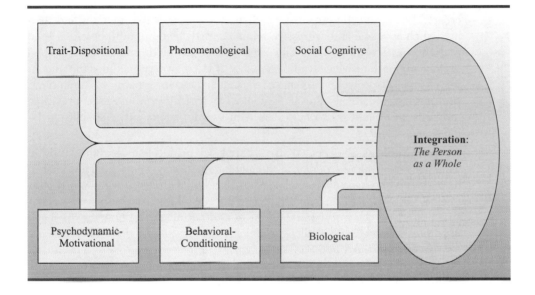

► PRELUDE TO PART VII: THE INTEGRATION OF LEVELS

In this final part of the text we look at the ways in which the levels come together when the person is studied as a whole, drawing on contributions from all levels. As a first step and preview, we begin with a review of the most basic contributions from each level. Even the short summary of these contributions below suggests that each level adds something significant to the others. Thus, far from being incompatible alternatives, the six levels provide insights on different aspects of the whole person. To reiterate a key theme in this text: when the levels are seen together and integrated, they enrich rather than fragment the view of the whole person.

Overview of Contributions from Each Level

    1. **Trait-dispositional level.** Work at this level asks: "What units shall we use to describe the important stable, consistent individual differences in personality?" It has answered with the Five Factor Model (or Big Five) of traits, which pro-

vides a useful map of broad individual differences. Research at this level also has demonstrated that traits may be expressed as consistencies in behavior that take two complementary forms. Type I consistency is seen in overall average differences between people in their levels of different behavioral dispositions. Type II consistency is seen in differences in people's stable *if . . . then . . .* , situation–behavior patterns or personality signatures. The consistencies in personality identified by this level open the way for exploring how these patterns develop.

2. **Psychodynamic-motivational level.** This level identifies some of the possible causes of the consistencies and inconsistencies that characterize the individual. It discovered that people have motives and feelings that are threatening (anxiety-provoking) to them and to other people (e.g., parents) on whom they are dependent. Consequently, self-protective mechanisms and defenses develop to reduce the anxiety and conflicts that these motives and feelings create. As a result, the expressions of socially unacceptable motives and feelings, such as sexual and aggressive impulses, may become indirect and at least partially outside awareness. The contributions from this level have helped build a comprehensive view of personality. It is a view that includes the unconscious and self-protective aspects of personality and its dynamics. The findings profoundly influenced clinical psychologists and other therapists, providing methods and measures to help deal with a wide variety of personality problems and disorders.

3. **Phenomenological level.** Work at this level made clear that the study of what goes on inside the person at the mental-emotional experiential level has to be included in personality psychology and can be investigated with its methods. It called attention to the importance of the ways in which people view (construe, appraise) the world and themselves as determinants of how they feel and how they cope with life challenges and stresses. It showed that individuals are not necessarily the victims of their biology and their biography but can do much to change both their life course and their internal subjective experiences. It also innovated methods both for understanding and influencing the internal states of the person. And it gave center stage to the experience of the self as both an object that "knows itself" and as an active agent that can act to influence the life course. In all these ways, the pioneers at this level were years ahead of the field. Their contributions have been foundation stones for some of the most interesting developments in the evolution of personality psychology as a cumulative science, for example, in current work at the social cognitive level.

4. **Behavioral-conditioning level.** Work at this level began with discoveries about how simple processes of learning and conditioning can help make scientific sense of such phenomena as seemingly irrational fears and impulsive emotional reactions. It provided methods for examining experimentally the relationship between changes in conditions and changes in social behavior, opening the way to research into basic processes of learning. It demonstrated the importance of the environment in the development and modification of even extremely complex patterns of behavior. It insisted that the study of personality has to include what people *do*. It has to examine actual social behavior as it unfolds within particular contexts and interactions, not just what people *say* they do or what they say they are like. Thus, this level provided methods for closely observing and studying behavior and its links to the situations that preceded it and the consequences that

followed. It opened the way for a more rigorous approach that went beyond self-reports and ratings to understand what people really do.

For years, workers at this level, however, were reluctant to even consider the internal mental and emotional processes within the person because they lacked the methods for investigating them objectively. Consequently, their contributions to understanding personality, while important, were limited in scope. This was true especially when behaviorism was at its height in the middle of the last century. In more recent years, advances in ways of studying brain and hormonal processes and emotional reactions are bringing fresh life to work at this level. Currently, it again provides a valuable component for the evolution of an increasingly cumulative science of persons.

5. **Social cognitive level.** Work at the social cognitive level attempts to combine contributions from several of the other levels. First, it expanded the understanding of the role of social learning in personality development, noting the crucial importance of cognition and observation in the learning processes most relevant for personality. It showed that humans learn through what they see and observe and hear and read, and do so often even without making any external response or receiving any external rewards. It went on to integrate these insights with findings on work from other levels, including studies of the self, personal constructs, expectancies, values, and goals. It then applied these integrations to investigate the ways in which individuals can self-regulate and modify their own behavior in light of their long-term goals and values. Work at the social cognitive level also has provided a model for combining the contributions of multiple levels. The goal is to help personality psychology to evolve into an increasingly cumulative, integrated science for understanding the person as a functioning whole, not just piece by piece.

6. **Biological level.** This level links personality to its biological bases. It is exploring genetic-brain-behavior links and analyzing their interactions as they play out in the genesis of individual differences. It also shows the value of applying concepts and methods from the study of human evolution and adaptation to understand a wide range of social phenomena, from mating practices to altruism to coping with threat and stress. Insights, findings, and methods from this level open the way to connecting biological processes with work at all the other levels. For example, the feelings, thoughts, and personal constructs of interest to the phenomenologists now can be studied using fMRI to trace how what we think and understand relates to our brain activities. It is a sign of how far the field has moved that mental phenomena considered beyond the pale of scientific inquiry are now the central subject matter for brain research. Few would have anticipated just a few years ago that the self and consciousness would be the topics for a major conference of leading brain researchers and psychologists in New York City in 2002. Research now illustrates in detail that what people think, feel, and do depends on their genes and their brains, neural networks, and biochemistry. At the same time, the reverse is equally true: what people think, feel, and do changes their genes, brains, neural networks, and biochemistry. The implications are profound, and will become clear as you read the three chapters in this part.

With all the levels in mind as background, this final part of the text illustrates steps toward building a cumulative science of personality. It is based on promising ideas, findings, and methods from all levels of analysis and integrates them to help understand personality as completely as the state of the science allows. With that purpose, we now turn to the question of how people pursue their life goals, and answer it by drawing on contributions from diverse levels and focusing on their interconnections.

Chapter 16 applies the integrated view to understand how people with different personality structures and organizations characteristically pursue their life goals. It is an integration that is built on the field's century-long past but guided in new directions by research findings in the last few decades.

Chapter 17 examines work on personality and the mechanisms that enable self-regulation. Chapter 18 considers the person in context. It examines the diverse aspects of the personality and the multiple influences—from the biological to the cultural—that affect the life trajectories that people construct and the options they have for influencing their own future.

Will the applications from these findings allow people to become more self-directed, effective, fulfilled, and happier? The hope is that what is known about the ways in which the personality system functions will help individuals to "take charge" of their own lives with greater freedom to influence their future in the directions they choose for themselves.

The Personal Side of the Science

Some questions on the integration of levels you might ask about yourself:

▶ How does my gender influence my life goals and the ways in which I pursue them?

▶ How does the culture in which I live affect my answer to the first question?

▶ How do my most important characteristics reflect the interactions between my biological inheritance and the social environment in which I grew up?

▶ What are the various factors from all levels that influence my ability to exert self-discipline, e.g., to study for exams when tempted to head for a movie?

▶ How is my personality more than the sum of its parts?

16

PERSONALITY IN THE PURSUIT OF GOALS

Veronica and Martha are close college friends but could hardly be more different. Veronica "goes for the gold"—she is open to possibilities for new challenges and gratifications every day. This is true for her, whether in the sports world in which she excels already, or in taking on academic challenges, or in her readiness for new weekend adventures. Her roommate Martha is at the opposite pole—she always "plays it safe." When Veronica says "Let's get pizza," Martha says "But it's so full of calories!" Ever ready to worry about the possible downside, Martha sees opportunities more as threats to be avoided than challenges to be taken on. She typically tries out several classes before staying in any, and drops those that look like they could be too much for her—and that is often many of them. Nevertheless, she's an excellent student even in difficult courses and on average her grades are better than Veronica's.

▶ APPROACH–AVOIDANCE DISPOSITIONS IN GOAL PURSUIT

This chapter illustrates how contributions from each different level of analysis supplement and enrich the understanding of the functioning of the whole personality. When taken together, they can help to explain in depth the differences described in the Veronica–Martha example. In this chapter, the focus is on how work from the different levels illuminates the differences between people in how they pursue their goals. The questions here are: how and why do different personalities think, feel, and behave in distinctively different ways in their approach and avoidance patterns?

Individual differences in goal pursuit are seen in the differences among people, for example, in how they make and pursue their New Year's resolutions and try to deal with the frustrations and temptations that get in the way. You see these differences in the goals they set (to diet, to stop smoking, to save more money, to get a new job, to build a better relationship, to have more fun, to get a medical check-up), and in the life projects they pursue (to go to college, to get into business school, to get to know that person, to be a more caring, worthy human being). Dramatic differences are especially evident in the strategies that different individuals use to pursue their goals in the face of the obstacles that arise in daily life. Individuals differ in how they deal with competing and often conflicting life goals, motives, and tasks, and in how they approach or avoid different alternatives in goal pursuit. These differences are a central aspect of personality, and they are this chapter's concern.

The Biological Level: BIS and BAS

At the biological level, there are two distinct neural systems in the brain, one associated with approach, and the other with avoidance behavior (as discussed in Chapter 15). We reintroduce these biological systems here to show their links to the other levels of analysis. One is the behavioral inhibition system (BIS), and its activity leads individuals to withdraw from certain undesirable stimuli or punishments and thus inhibits their behavior. This withdrawal–avoidance motivational system is the one that enhances attention to threats and risks and possible punishment. From an evolutionary perspective, it is adaptive to humans because it is useful for avoiding danger and for surviving. But excessive BIS activity also has its costs. It can potentially deprive one of all sorts of rewarding and life-affirming approach activities in goal pursuit.

In contrast to the BIS, the behavioral activation system (BAS) is the energizing system. In Chapter 15, you saw that activity in this appetitive, positive-approach motivational system enhances attention to reward cues. It facilitates approach behaviors in the search for possible gratifications and positive outcomes in the pursuit of goals. Its downside is that it does not sensitize the person to the potential long-term risks and negative consequences of tempting approach behaviors that can be dangerous.

The Trait-Dispositional Level

16.1 How does BIS or BAS prominence influence people's goals and their strategies for goal attainment?

Some people have more activity in the BIS, whereas some are more active in the BAS. In turn, the degree of activity in these two systems also is linked to individual differences at the broad dispositional-trait level, as assessed for example by the NEO-PI-R and the Five Factor (Big Five) model.

Greater activity in the BAS seems to be more characteristic of extraverts, and greater activity in the BIS is theoretically and empirically linked to introversion and anxiety, and to related measures of temperament beginning early in life (Derryberry &

Rothbart, 1997; Gray, 1991). The BAS also seems to be associated with dominance/sensation seeking and impulsivity, and the BIS with conscientiousness/behavioral inhibition (MacDonald, 1998).

Theoretically, because of their greater reactivity in the BAS, extraverts and those high in dominance/sensation seeking will focus more on rewards, especially immediate rewards, and look eagerly for situations in which they could get them. Think here of a person like Veronica in the chapter introduction who loves adventures, gets easily involved, seizes opportunities, and often can be impulsive and indifferent to the long-term costs. In contrast, the greater reactivity in the BIS of introverts and anxiety-prone persons is related to their focus on threats and potential negative outcomes. The anxious introvert's tendency to be more passive and avoidant may reflect greater physiological sensitivity and alertness to all the possible things that could go wrong and produce trouble. Think here of the person who, like Martha in the chapter opening, foregoes strong temptations and pleasures (from pizzas to potentially dangerous thrills and adventures) out of the fear of the delayed consequences (from upset stomachs to unwanted pregnancies and HIV infections).

The Phenomenological Level: Positive–Negative Moods

Some researchers probe the links of the biological level to the different psychological levels without direct biological measurement. That became possible because reliable and valid self-report measures of BIS and BAS reactivity (Carver & White, 1994) were developed that correlate well with the brain measures (e.g., Gable, Reis, & Elliot, 2000). Table 16.1 lists items from the BIS/BAS self-report scales.

For example, people who had higher resting levels of activity in their left frontal area of the brain (indicative of BAS activity) also self-reported higher BAS sensitivity on items like those shown in Table 16.1. In contrast, higher resting levels of activity in the right frontal area of the brain (indicative of BIS activity) were related to higher self-reported BIS sensitivity (Harmon-Jones & Allen, 1997; Sutton & Davidson, 1997).

Using these self-report measures, some researchers examined the impact of the two systems on college students' emotional experiences in everyday life. They explored the joint effects of dispositional differences in BIS and BAS sensitivities to cues of rewards and punishments on participants' daily experiences. These experiences included the emotions of undergraduate students, specifically, their positive affect (PA) and negative affect (NA), and the positive and negative events that they encountered in their daily lives at college (Gable, Reis, & Elliot, 2000). According to BIS/BAS theory (e.g., Gray, 1991), individuals with high BIS dispositions will seek out and select negative cues and events in their environments. Those high in BAS dispositions will attend to and pursue positive events and possibilities for gratifications. Veronica and Martha again are examples you might have in mind here: one woman anticipates the pleasure of late night pizza and a beer with gusto and goes for it, the other thinks of the calories and even the prospect of an upset stomach and decides to call it a night.

Dr. Gable and her research group wanted to test if people's BIS/BAS dispositions in fact influence their experiences and their daily emotional states (Gable et al., 2000). They hypothesized that because BAS increases sensitivity to positive events, individuals high in BAS will have stronger reactions to them. The reverse should be true for individuals high in BIS: people high in this disposition over time should have magnified reactions to negative events.

16.2 How did Gable study emotional correlates of the BIS/BAS scales? What did she find?

TABLE 16.1   Some Items from the BIS/BAS Scale (Carver & White, 1994)

	1	2	3	4	
	Strongly Agree			Strongly Disagree	

BIS
1. If I think something unpleasant is going to happen, I usually get pretty "worked up."
2. I worry about making mistakes.
3. I feel pretty worried or upset when I think or know somebody is angry at me.
4. Even if something bad is about to happen to me, I rarely experience fear or nervousness.

BAS Reward Responsiveness
1. When I get something I want, I feel excited and energized.
2. When I'm doing well at something, I love to keep at it.
3. When good things happen to me, it affects me strongly.
4. When I see an opportunity for something I like, I get excited right away.

BAS Drive
1. When I want something, I usually go all out to get it.
2. I go out of my way to get things I want.
3. If I see a chance to get something I want, I move on it right away.
4. When I go after something, I use a "no holds barred" approach.

BAS Fun Seeking
1. I will often do things for no other reason than that they might be fun.
2. I crave excitement and new sensations.
3. I'm always willing to try something new if I think it will be fun.
4. I often act on the spur of the moment.

Source: Carver, C. S., & White, T. L. Behavioral inhibition, behavioral activation, and affective responses to impending reward and punishment: The BIS/BAS scales. *Journal of Personality and Social Psychology,* 67, 319–333. © 1994, American Psychological Association.

To test these ideas, participants were divided into BIS and BAS groups based upon their scores on the BIS–BAS Scale (Carver & White, 1994). In a series of studies, they were then asked for daily reports of their positive or negative affect on a 20-item scale to rate how much "you feel from day to day" emotions described by words like happy, distressed, nervous, enthusiastic (Watson, 1988). They also reported the occurrence of positive and negative daily events on a questionnaire consisting of 16 positive events (social and achievement) and 19 negative events (social and achievement), and indicated their frequency and importance for each.

These results show the important role of BIS/BAS as personality dispositions. Dispositional BAS sensitivity magnified peoples' reactions to positive events, and BIS sensitivity magnified their reactions to negative events. Furthermore, in their daily lives, on average, higher BAS people experienced more positive affect, more strongly.

Gable and colleagues also found that, as predicted, the number of positive events that occurred during the day on average was strongly related to participants' positive affect, and their negative affect was strongly related to the number of negative events. However, consistent with the BIS/BAS theory, on the whole, the two types of emotional reactions, positive and negative affect, seem to be functionally independent like the BAS and BIS systems themselves. This finding also fits with other data showing the independence of positive and negative affect (Cacioppo & Gardner, 1999; Watson, 1988).

The Social Cognitive Level: Promotion-Prevention Focus

So far, we have considered dispositions at a level of broad super traits (e.g., overall level of approach versus avoidance tendencies; Big Five dispositions such as extraversion). The dispositional differences illustrated above, however, also are seen in different characteristic self-systems and motivational patterns identified at the social cognitive level of analysis (e.g., Cantor & Mischel, 1977, 1979; Higgins & Kruglanski, 1996; Kunda, 1999) in which personality is expressed in daily life. At that level, one of the most important aspects of individual differences is in the characteristic, distinctive ways in which the person responds to new goals or tasks.

Consistent with work on BIS and BAS, and its related personality dispositions, some people are excited by the prospect of achieving a new goal, while others are more cautious and fear the possibility of failure. At the social cognitive level, a key question is: How are these different achievement attitudes shaped by the individual's personal experiences and cognitive structures? And how do the attitudes that develop in turn influence the person's goal pursuit strategies, motivations, and emotional experiences?

In the mid-twentieth century, researchers working at the motivational level discovered that people differ in their levels of achievement motivation (Chapter 6), and showed that how they view their achievements also influences their emotional experiences. Those who believe that they have generally achieved most of their goals have pride in their achievements—**"achievement pride"**—and are therefore more eager to pursue new goals, while those who believe that they have generally failed to achieve most of their goals are ashamed of their lack of achievement and tend to avoid pursuing new goals (Atkinson, 1964; McClelland, 1951, 1961).

Recently, psychologists working at the social cognitive level have reexamined these findings and reinterpreted them in ways that directly link to discoveries about the BIS and BAS. **Regulatory focus theory** (Higgins 1997, 1998) proposes that all goal-directed behavior is governed by two motivational systems—the **prevention system** and the **promotion system,** and these systems conceptually relate to the BAS and BIS. The promotion system (like the BAS) is focused on obtaining positive outcomes such as accomplishments or rewards. In the promotion system, the presence of positive rewards provides pleasure, and the absence of positive rewards brings pain. In contrast, the prevention system, like the BIS, attends to negative outcomes such as punishment or failure. In this system, the presence of negative outcomes brings pain, and the absence of negative outcomes provides pleasure. So the experience of people characterized either by more BIS sensitivity or by more BAS sensitivity would include both pleasure and pain, but they are experienced in different ways and in different circumstances.

If goal-directed behavior is regulated by these two motivational systems, how do they affect the strategies people use to achieve their goals at the social cognitive level? And, at the level of social learning, how are these motivational systems influenced by people's history of success and failure? The social cognitive level focuses on how people interpret events and their experience. At this level, it is therefore of particular interest to understand how the attributions they make about the causes of those experiences influence their strategies for goal pursuit.

Higgins and colleagues proposed that there are two types of achievement pride—promotion pride and prevention pride (Higgins, Friedman, Harlow, Chen-Idson, Ayduk, & Taylor, 2001). **Promotion pride** would motivate people to eagerly pursue their goals, while **prevention pride** would motivate people to vigilantly avoid factors that may hinder them from achieving their goals. The researchers further proposed that these two types of pride are influenced by the strategies an individual has successfully used to attain his or her goals in the past (thus connecting to the level of learning and past experience).

16.3 Which concepts in regulatory focus theory correspond to the BIS/BAS systems?

16.4 Describe two variants of achievement pride, and the factors that lead to their development.

16.5 What kinds of items are used to measure the two types of achievement pride? How do scores on the RFQ subscales relate to one another and to achievement behaviors?

Above all, the emotions experienced and the strategies preferred for goal pursuit will depend on how the person interprets those experiences. In the examples in the chapter opener, if Martha believes that she has often succeeded because she pays strict attention to the rules and avoids potentially goal-threatening situations, then she will be more likely to exhibit prevention pride and use vigilant means to achieve her goals. If Veronica sees successes as reflecting courageous risk-taking and willingness to take big chances for big prospects, promotion pride and a promotion-focused approach strategy—consistent with dispositional BAS tendencies—should emerge.

Higgins and colleagues examined these ideas in a series of studies. Their findings again underline the close links between the different levels of analysis, and the fact that when they are considered together the level of understanding is enriched. The studies are described in In Focus 16.1.

IN FOCUS 16.1

STUDYING PROMOTION VERSUS PREVENTION PRIDE

To test the propositions discussed in the text, Higgins and colleagues (Higgins et al., 2001)[1] conducted several studies in order to fully explore the relationship between a person's history of achievement and his or her strategy for pursuing goals in the future. The first study included the preparation of a scale to measure promotion versus prevention pride.

They developed the Regulatory Focus Questionnaire (RFQ) which measures how often participants feel that they have experienced success (or failure) through promotion or prevention self-regulation (see Table 16.2). They tested this new questionnaire by examining how well scores on this scale predicted participants' responses on a decision-making task.

TABLE 16.2 Sample Items from the Regulatory Focus Questionnaire

This set of questions asks you about specific events in your life. Please indicate your answer to each question by circling the appropriate number below it.

1. Compared to most people, are you typically unable to get what you want out of life?

1	2	3	4	5
(never or seldom)		sometimes		very often

2. How often have you accomplished things that got you "psyched" to work even harder?

1	2	3	4	5
never or seldom		sometimes		(very often)

3. Growing up, would you ever "cross the line" by doing things that you parents would not tolerate?

1	2	3	4	5
(never or seldom)		sometimes		very often

4. Not being careful has gotten me into trouble at times.

1	2	3	4	5
(never or seldom)		sometimes		very often

Note: Items 1 and 2 measure promotion pride, 3 and 4 prevention pride. Answers in parentheses are scored as high pride.

Source and Permission: Higgins, E. T., Friedman, R. S., Harlow, R. E., Chen-Idson, L., Ayduk, O. N., & Taylor, A. Achievement orientations from subjective histories of success: Promotion pride versus prevention pride. *European Journal of Social Psychology, 31,* 3–23. © 2001, John Wiley & Sons Limited. Reproduced with permission.

There were two decision-making tasks—one in which the correct answer required the participant to take advantage of an opportunity, and the other in which the correct answer required the participant to be more cautious in the approach. Participants also were asked to list their goals, the relative importance of each goal, and up to seven activities they could do to attain each goal, and answered a number of other questionnaires. In still another study, participants were asked to complete the RFQ and the Self-Control Strategies Scale (SCSS; Ayduk, 1999) which measures the self-control tactics a person uses to maintain a diet. The researchers also measured how often participants experienced the motivational states of eagerness vs. apathy and vigilance vs. carelessness. Finally, they examined how often participants felt they had experienced success or failure by using different kinds of strategies in their goal pursuit. Responses on these and other measures were coded and their relationships were analyzed statistically. Higgins and colleagues found that:

- Promotion pride was unrelated to prevention pride—a finding that is consistent with the view of BAS and BIS as independent systems.

- Individuals with high prevention pride experienced vigilance—anxiety and concern with making mistakes—more often in their activities, whereas those with high promotion pride experienced eagerness more often.

- People with a history of promotion success (promotion pride) responded to challenges with approach-oriented strategies. For example, someone with promotion pride will err on the side of trying too many options or taking full advantage of an opportunity. In contrast, people with a history of prevention success (prevention pride) are more vigilant and cautious in their goal-directed behavior. They err on the side of caution and avoid more risky avenues to success.

- When people feel that they have had success in the past due to promotion-related behavior, they practice more eager, approach-oriented behavior to attain their goals. If they feel that they have succeeded because of prevention-related behavior (e.g., their cautiousness), then they practice vigilant, more cautious strategies to attain their goals.

Taken collectively, the studies by Higgins and colleagues indicate that people can succeed in one of two ways. One may succeed by being cautious and avoiding failure at all costs, or one may succeed by eagerly pursuing one's desires. Though these are both positive experiences, they are distinct in their strategic orientation and the way that they influence future behavior and emotions.

The studies of promotion and prevention pride and orientation discussed above illustrate an *if . . . then . . .* analysis of the interaction of persons and situations in approach–avoidance patterns. The findings show the close links between broad personality dispositions and their more specific personality signatures (Chapter 4).

Thus, while people with promotion pride thrive in situations that offer opportunities and challenges, those with prevention pride do best when the tasks require caution and vigilance. Each orientation has its advantages and disadvantages. The individual who is able to flexibly access the orientation that best suits the situation is likely to be able to deal well with the widest possible range of encounters that might be faced in life. Since promotion and prevention are independent dimensions, it is possible for the same individual to be high (or low) in both types of pride.

Convergence with Evolutionary Theory

Evolutionary theory also calls attention to the need for organisms to take the context into careful account in their behavioral responses to the environment. Theoretically, the evolutionary level of analysis, like the social cognitive level, thus emphasizes interactions in the ways in which approach and avoidance tendencies and their associated dispositions are expressed and contextualized in goal pursuit. As noted in the discussion of evolutionary theory (Chapter 15), it is adaptive to flexibly suit one's actions to the requirements of the particular situation—essentially knowing when to approach, and when to avoid, to cope and survive. Consequently, in evolutionary theory (MacDonald, 1998, p. 128), people tend to compartmentalize. As seen in the last chapter, they may seek intimacy and approach under some conditions (e.g., with mates and offspring) but are also ready to flee or to be aggressive and hostile when necessary (e.g., with competitors or perceived enemies). How the patterns are played out in the process of adaptation depends in part on the overall level of broad dispositions like BIS/BAS. But it also depends on the particular domain and on the types of conditions and situations that are being encountered.

Linking Dispositions to Situations

In traditional approaches to dispositions, the "situation" was often treated as a source of measurement noise to be removed in personality assessment. More recently, the need to include situations in the analysis of personality is being recognized even by advocates of the Big Five broad dispositional approaches (e.g., John, 2001). The situation activates the processing dynamics or mechanisms through which a disposition functions and is expressed and in that sense, it becomes part of the disposition itself and its *if . . . then . . .* behavioral signature (Mischel & Shoda, 1998).

In time, individuals who are particularly high or low on factors like the Big Five are likely to actively influence the environments they typically encounter and experience. Just as you saw in Chapter 14, people's genetics in part influence the social environments in which they develop, so do their dispositional preferences in part shape the worlds that they experience. Those who are predominantly reactive in the BAS, for example, may change their personal environment by maximizing opportunities for challenges and rewards. In contrast, those high in BIS will tend to avoid risks and potential danger and threat, and subsequently try to shield themselves from them. In turn, the social world will soon reciprocate and react in distinctively different ways to these different types of individuals, further changing the environments they typically encounter.

You do not invite friends to try new rock-climbing adventures when you know they are risk-averse and will shy away from them. Likewise, high BAS people (think again of extraverts and people like Veronica) are likely to get and accept more party invitations than those high in BIS. Thus, both the brain and the external world interact and contribute jointly to the motivational qualities and emotional dispositions that characterize different individuals and types, which then actively influences the environments they experience and encounter, which further strengthens the dispositional tendencies. Again we see the dynamic interactions between the biological level, the trait-dispositional level, and the social environment. We next illustrate the links between multiple levels by looking at relations between the psychodynamic and behavioral levels when dealing with approach–avoidance conflicts.

Links to the Psychodynamic-Motivational and Behavioral Levels

16.6 How do current approach–avoidance models relate to Dollard and Miller's learning-based model of psychodynamic conflict?

The study of approach–avoidance tendencies and the dilemmas that they can produce has been a core topic of personality psychology ever since Sigmund Freud made conflict the center of his theory a hundred years ago. Because these conflicts create anxiety, the individual, according to Freud, engages in massive unconscious efforts to reduce it, which in turn can produce all sorts of difficulties and symptoms. The problem for scientists early in the last century was that such conflicts were very difficult to study experimentally. To make approach–avoidance conflicts open to experimental research, recall that John Dollard and Neal Miller (1950) working at the behavioral level of analysis years later attempted to rethink psychodynamic conflicts in the language of learning. As noted in earlier chapters, these were pioneering attempts to integrate the levels of analysis in the study of goal pursuit. Given the renewed interest in the approach and avoidance systems as key aspects of personality, the classic work of these pioneers has renewed relevance.

To resummarize, these researchers hypothesized *approach* and *avoidance* tendencies, and analyzed them in careful experiments with animals (Chapter 10). In such conflicts, the organism, at least momentarily, is torn between two desirable goals. Just as conflict was central to Freud's conception of personality dynamics, so it was at the core of Dollard and Miller's theory. But whereas Freud developed his ideas about conflict from inferences regarding id–ego–superego clashes in his neurotic patients, Dollard and Miller tested their ideas in controlled experiments with rats. Their findings shed light on understanding some of the problems of Freud's patients in more objective terms.

Their original theory of conflict was based on a number of animal experiments (e.g., Brown, 1942, 1948; Miller, 1959). In one study, for example, hungry rats learned how to run down an alley to get food at a distinctive point in the maze. To generate **ambivalence** (approach–avoidance tendencies), the rats were given a quick electric shock while they were eating. To test the resulting conflict, the rats were later placed again at the start of the alley. The hungry rat started toward the food but halted and hesitated before reaching it.

Dollard and Miller applied the concept of **goal gradients** to analyze these conflicts. Goal gradients are changes in response strengths as a function of distance from the goal object. To assess the strength of approach and avoidance tendencies at different points from the goal, a harness apparatus was devised to measure a rat's pull toward a positive reinforcement (food) or away from a negative reinforcement or punishment (shock). The harness enabled the experimenter to restrain the rat for a moment along the route to the goal and measure (in grams) the strength of the animal's pull on the harness at each test point (Brown, 1948). In this type of situation, the rats could be given different experiences that led the same response from them to become associated both with approach motivation (the food) and with avoidance motivation (the electric shock). First the hungry rats learned to run the maze to get the food that was waiting for them at the end, thus developing approach tendencies. Then sometimes they also received the electric shock at the end of the maze, which led their maze-running response to also become associated with punishment, analogous to the dilemmas of Freud's patients whose socially unacceptable desires also had become associated with fear of punishment.

When a hungry but now also fearful rat with such a history next gets into this maze he faces an approach–avoidance conflict. This conflict is shown in Figure 16-1. Running toward the goal is associated with hunger reduction and induces approach tendencies. But it is also associated with getting electric shock, which makes running in the opposite direction a way to reduce the fear drive. As a result, the rat would run in both directions, forward toward the food, and then away. Interestingly, the researchers found that when far from the goal, the approach tendency was stronger than the avoidance tendency, hence producing approach behavior. However, as the goal got nearer, the strength of the avoidance tendency increased sharply, leading the rat to run in the opposite direction. The animal stopped at the point where the approach and avoidance pulls became equalized,

16.7 Describe the role of goal gradients in explaining approach–avoidance conflicts. How were the gradients measured in the laboratory?

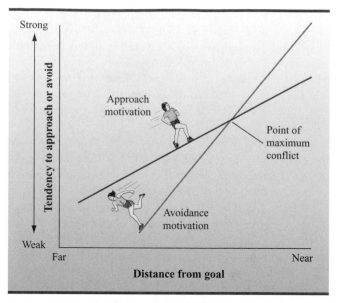

Figure 16.1 According to Neal Miller's analysis of approach-avoidance conflicts, both the tendency to approach and the tendency to avoid grow stronger as one moves closer to the goal. However, the tendency to avoid increases faster than the tendency to approach. Maximum conflict is experienced when the two gradients cross, because at this point the opposing motives are equal in strength.

Source: Smith, R.E. (1993). *Psychology.* St. Paul, MN: West. Reprinted with permission.

essentially torn equally in both directions. And at least by analogy that is also the neurotic dilemma of persons afflicted with intense approach–avoidance conflicts in which they feel psychologically paralyzed.

The work at the various levels of analysis discussed in this section points to some of the many ways in which individuals facing such conflicts are likely to behave. For example, those with much higher BAS reactivity and promotion focus might approach more readily and persistently compared to those with higher BIS reactivity and prevention focus.

▶ THE GOAL PURSUIT PROCESS

Life Tasks, Personal Goals, and Projects

The goals an individual pursues are organized and coherent. They reflect the activity of the entire personality system as the person interacts with the situations within his or her world at any given point in development. The goals of a college student, and the situations, challenges, and threats faced, are obviously different from those experienced in early childhood, or those that will be salient at mid-life and beyond. In this section, we will focus on how personality plays out and influences the mental and emotional processes that unfold, as individuals pursue their important life goals (e.g., Cantor & Kihlstrom, 1987; Cantor, 1990; Zirkel, 1992).

Current life tasks are defined as those central projects to which individuals perceive themselves as being committed during particular periods in their lives, such as in the transition from high school to college (Cantor & Kihlstrom, 1987, p. 168). These self-created tasks help give meaning to the individual's life and provide organization and direction for many more specific activities and goal pursuits that are in their service.

Examples of common life tasks include "getting promoted," "finding the right person and getting married," "making myself more fit," and "taking off a couple of years to do something meaningful for needier people." Life tasks thus constitute significant long-term goals that are meaningful for the individual at some point in his or her life. While they are typically experienced as personally urgent, they are also often ill-defined and loosely formulated.

Certain types of life tasks are shared by many people in the same phase of life. For example, first-year students in an honors college at the University of Michigan often had life tasks like the following ones in common: "Being on my own," "making friends," "establishing an identity," "getting good grades," and "establishing a future direction" (Cantor & Kihlstrom, 1987, p. 172). When the students were encouraged to elaborate their plans, feelings, and specific strategies, some common themes emerged concerning achievement, intimacy, and gaining better self-control. Each student, however, also uniquely construed his or her tasks and focused on somewhat different aspects of the same common themes. For example, while "being on my own" meant learning to cope with personal failures without the help of parental hugs for one student, for another it meant working on how to manage money responsibly.

Investigations of this type (e.g., Cantor and associates, 2002; Harlow & Cantor, 1996; Snyder & Cantor, 1998) help to provide systematic methods for accessing these personally significant, often unique aspects of experience. They draw on the person's own expertise to articulate his or her personal constructs, plans, and problem-solving strategies for dealing with everyday real-life challenges. In addition, they also help identify certain problem-solving strategies that different individuals prefer to guide and monitor their own progress as they pursue their chosen life tasks.

In this section we will illustrate the personality processing dynamics—the flow of interacting thoughts and feelings and potential behaviors—that become activated in goal pursuit. These dynamics are activated in ways that are distinctive for the particular individual's personality organization and structure, as people choose and pursue their life tasks and goals. The goals themselves are organized in their degree of importance for the person in **goal hierarchies** with some life goals at higher-order levels than others, as discussed in the section below on goals and standards.

Table 16.3 shows aspects of the mental and emotional dynamics in the personality system activated in goal pursuit. Goal pursuit in a situation begins with the ways in which the individual encodes—that is, interprets or appraises it. Then expectations, beliefs, feelings, and goals relevant to the appraisal are activated. These all interact within the system in ways that are guided and constrained by its unique organization. It is this distinctive personality organization that is relatively stable. The organization reflects the multiple influences of the person's unique total biological and psychosocial history.

Illustrative Processing Dynamics: Thinking about a Career

To illustrate this more concretely, we take another look at Veronica and Martha, the two women introduced in the chapter opener. In this simple example, the situation is inside the head: it happens when each woman is thinking about her future and a career in medicine.

16.8 How do CAPS dynamics help us explain Veronica and Martha's career goals?

TABLE 16.3 Overview of Personality Dynamics in the Goal Pursuit Process

Encoding (Construal/ Appraisal)	Expectancies/ Beliefs	Affects	Goals/ Values	Regulatory Competencies (Effortful Control)
Self-relevance (personal meaningfulness) appraisal	Perceived regulatory control/ helplessness	Emotional arousal	Goal hierarchy	Self-control
		Fears and desires	Standards	Strategies (distraction/ "cooling")
Automaticity (trigger reactions)	Self-efficacy/ expected outcomes	Feelings states/"hot" (impulsive) automatic responses		Self-monitoring Planning
				Self-instruction

Source: Based in part on material in Mischel, W., Cantor, N., & Feldman, S. (1996). Principles of self-regulation: The nature of willpower and self-control. In E. T. Higgins & A. W. Kruglanski (Eds.), *Social Psychology: Handbook of Basic Principles* (pp. 329–360). New York: Guilford.

What might they think and feel as they consider their futures? Assume that both are equally qualified academically for medical school, and have long had it as a life goal. One plausible script that seems to fit Veronica is in Figure 16.2. It shows that given her highly active BAS, and extraverted dispositional tendencies, she is likely to frame her future in medicine as full of opportunities. Theoretically, this activates her promotion focus and the eager, enthusiastic emotions that this entails. She could even imagine herself discovering or finding something exciting, maybe even a cure for cancer.

Martha's processing dynamic in goal pursuit, shown in Figure 16.3, is a sharp contrast. Given her generally high BIS and readiness to worry, her prevention focus snaps into action and she is anticipating the potential threats. She imagines herself failing,

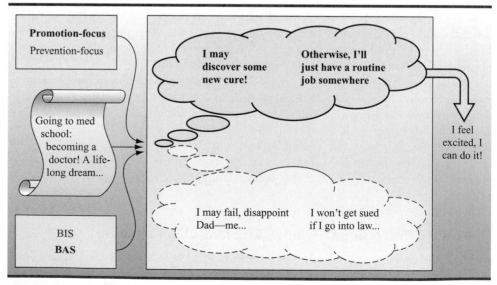

Figure 16.2 Veronica's processing dynamics in goal pursuit. Thinking about medical school activates promotion focus and BAS.

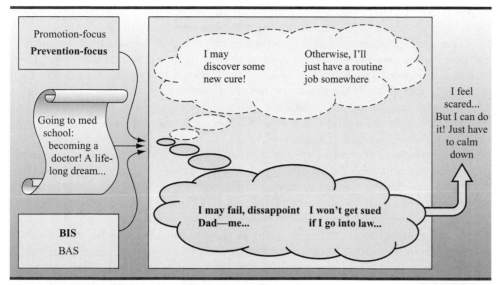

Figure 16.3 Martha's processing dynamics in goal pursuit. Thinking about medical school activates prevention focus and BIS.

disappointing her father and herself, perhaps even inadvertently hurting a patient and being sued for malpractice. She is strongly motivated to prevent these negative outcomes, and eager to not disappoint her father and to not get into trouble. But she also has high efficacy expectancies about her own ability to get into med school and have a successful career in medicine, in spite of her anxieties. And she places high value in having a life in medicine. Therefore, she decides to go forward with med school. Thus in spite of the large differences between Veronica and Martha in personality, both women reach the same decision—to apply to med school. But they do so with very different mental and emotional experiences and processing dynamics that affect how they feel and behave during the long process of trying to create a career in medicine.

We next consider the steps in goal pursuit shown in Table 16.3. This discussion is without sustained reference to the two women, but you might want to speculate about what went on in their heads as they moved forward in their goal pursuit.

Encoding/Appraisal of the Situation

Self-Relevance. The motivation to try to pursue a goal tends to increase to the extent that the activity or situation is encoded or appraised as personally meaningful (Bandura, 1986; Cantor, 1990). Consider, for example, how new mothers try to cope with the often exhausting and sometimes anxiety-provoking or boring chores of parenting. Research showed that they cope better when they view those tasks as fulfilling important self-obligations rather than as taking time away from other modes of self-fulfillment, such as a career (Alexander & Higgins, 1993).

The social interactions of daily life contain such episodes as an argument with parents, a movie with friends, a visit to the doctor, or a shopping trip to the mall. The differences among people in how they encode these events are related to their differences on other measures of personality, perceived social competence, and skills (Forgas, 1983).

Emotional Meanings. To appraise situations, you have to interpret their emotional meanings. Is your father really angry or teasing? Is your roommate being friendly

16.9 How do customary encodings and appraisals influence goal activation? Which encoding factors are particularly important?

or just polite? Usually these interpretations are made automatically, depending on previous experience and expectations. But the automatic appraisal *can* be inaccurate.

This point becomes most evident from anthropological reports of differences in cultural expressions of emotions. Visitors to a strange culture would make many mistakes if they tried to assess the meaning of emotional expressions in terms of their own past experience. A Masai warrior honors a young man who looks promising by spitting in his face; an Andaman Islander greets a visitor by sitting down on his lap and sobbing his salutation tearfully; a scolded Chinese schoolboy takes a reprimand with cheerful grinning as a sign of his respect; and to show anger, Navajo and Apache Indians lower the voice instead of raising it (Opler, 1967). Within each culture, people reach an agreement about the meaning of emotional cues. But certain facial expressions also may have universal meaning. The emotions of anger, happiness, disgust, sadness, fear, and surprise, shown in photographs of faces, tended to be correctly identified in a variety of extremely different cultures (Ekman, 1982).

On visits to extremely different cultures, people usually try to be careful not to misinterpret the emotional signals they observe and to avoid reacting inappropriately. A similar caution may be useful in carefully attending to the emotional signals that come from people in one's own personal life. Focused attention, rather than automatic responding, may allow one to see more clearly what is really going on.

Biological and Trait-Dispositional Levels. As you saw before, at the biological level, the appraisal process reflects the reactivity in the BIS/BAS. As they appraise situations, people with high chronic BIS reactivity are likely to focus on threats and to anticipate and experience them with increased negative emotions and anxiety. At a physiological level, this will be visible in bodily changes. Those who are extremely high in their BAS reactivity are likely to appraise even potentially threatening and stressful situations in ways that focus on what can be gained or maximized from the experience. They are more likely to minimize the downside and to focus on potential benefits.

For example, suppose both Veronica and Martha love cross-country skiing, but fall badly, sustaining serious fractures that greatly interfere with their plans and schedules. Martha is apt to focus on all the things she will not be able to do while in casts, and the negative consequences (e.g., incompletes in courses, disappointing others and herself, missed appointments). Veronica is likely to focus on how she can maximize or create some gains from her mishap. She imagines that soon she will have friends visit, be able catch up with sleep and see some good videos, treating herself to a bit of an unscheduled vacation. These differences between the two women also are reflected at the trait-dispositional level in their scores on measures like the Big Five and the NEO-PI-R: Veronica is likely to be high in extraversion and impulsivity, Martha is apt to be high in anxiety and neuroticism, for example. They are seen at the social cognitive level in their different promotion-focused versus prevention focused styles and behavioral signatures. Again, data from each level enrich the view of the whole person.

Expectancies and Beliefs

16.10 Describe how self-efficacy, perceived control, and behavior-outcome expectancies relate to goal striving and success.

The appraisal of the situation activates various relevant expectations and beliefs. Especially relevant for goal pursuit are efficacy, outcome expectations, and control beliefs.

Self-Efficacy Expectancies. Expectancies and beliefs that one will be able to exert control and successfully execute necessary actions are essential for effective goal pursuit. They support one's efforts and guide whether, where, when, and how one should pursue relevant goals (Mischel et al., 1996). To even try to "take charge" in self-guided goal pursuit requires a representation of the self "as a causal agent of the intended action" (Kuhl, 1984, p. 127). As discussed in Chapter 12, self-efficacy—the belief that "I can do it"—is a foundation for the successful pursuit of a difficult goal, or for changing and improving one's situation or oneself. Its psychological opposite, perceived helplessness, is the route to giving up, apathy, and depression (Chapter 13). Both Veronica and Martha may have equally high self-efficacy expectations about being able to pass the entry tests for getting into medical school—indeed Martha's expectancies may be higher than Veronica's. These expectancies may be good predictors of how well they actually will do on those tests, in spite of the very different thoughts and feelings they have when they think about themselves as becoming physicians (Figs. 16.2 & 16.3).

Perceived Control and Predictability.   Even when the particular task is something aversive that has to be endured and cannot be controlled—like a painful dental procedure—the belief that one can predict or control the event or the stress is an important ingredient for adaptive behavior. For example, in a classic study, college women were exposed to an aversive noise while they worked on a task. The noise either occurred at a predictable time or unpredictably (Glass et al., 1969). Their tolerance for frustration and the quality of their performance on the task were impaired only when the noise was unpredictable. Equally interesting, the negative effects were reduced considerably if during the stress period the participants believed they could do something to control the end of the stress. Generally, most people tend to become less upset when they think they can predict and control stressful or painful events (Staub, Tursky, & Schwartz, 1971), even if the perception is illusory (Taylor & Brown, 1988).

Outcome Expectancies.   Goal striving is also bolstered—or undermined—by outcome expectancies about the likelihood that the time and energy spent on the task will actually result (or not result) in the desired outcome (Brunstein, 1993; Carver & Scheier, 1982; Klinger, 1975). When, and where, and what we choose to wait or work for depends in part on the anticipated consequences. To the extent that the individual believes that self-regulation will lead to desirable consequences, he or she will be more likely to choose to perform it (Feather, 1990; Rotter, 1954).

People base these outcome expectations both on information in the current situation and on information from previous similar situations. Such expectancies strongly influence whether people will try to perform a task that is a prerequisite for attaining a larger reward or instead settle for a smaller reward that is available non-contingently and immediately. Those who expect to succeed on the task are more willing to try to perform it (e.g., Mischel & Staub, 1965). In sum, people are more likely to choose to perform an action that requires effort if they believe that they can perform the action (i.e., have high self-efficacy expectancies) and expect that it will lead to favorable consequences (e.g., Bandura, 1986; Mischel, 1973). A good example comes from studies designed to increase commitment to condom use among inner-city African–American adolescents (e.g., Jemmott and colleagues, 1992). A key component for achieving this goal required raising the participants' self-efficacy beliefs and their outcome expectancies about the positive consequences of using condoms.

Enhancing Self-Efficacy in Goal Pursuit.   People who expect failure are likely to fulfill their prophecy. But if they are led to think they can do better, will their performance actually improve? One study of academically borderline college students examined just this question (Meichenbaum & Smart, 1971) and concluded that students who were led to expect success in fact became more successful in their schoolwork.

The power of positive thinking is shown even more dramatically through "mental practice." In one experiment, participants were instructed to imagine throwing darts at a target (Powell, 1973). Half of them were asked to imagine that their darts were hitting near the target's center; the other half imagined that their darts were striking outside the target area. Dart throwing improved significantly for people who had imagined successful performances during mental practice, but not for those who had imagined poor performances. Numerous studies to increase self-efficacy have shown similar effects (Bandura, 1986). The moral is plain: Think success!

Affects/Emotions

"Hot" Emotions and Impulsive Reactions. The personality system is not a cool information-crunching machine in which calm thoughts about possible outcomes are contemplated thoughtfully and rationally from a detached perspective. In the century since Sigmund Freud and his colleagues began their work at the psychodynamic-motivational level, it has become clear that humans are also emotion-driven creatures who are prey to their emotions, from which they can either benefit or suffer.

Even those who reject many of Freud's ideas recognize that people are intrinsically self-protective and sometimes even severely self-deceiving in how they deal with feelings and conflicts. Consider, for example, the student with public-speaking anxiety who panics at the thought of having to make a presentation to a group. Or take the dilemma of the addict who is trying to quit but is tempted with heroin, or the starving dieter faced with the ultimate chocolate cake. These kinds of hot situations and stimuli tend to automatically trigger hot reactions, rapidly generating the associated feelings of fear or desire and the urge to respond impulsively, bypassing self-regulatory controls just when they are most important.

In situations in which "hot" emotional reactions such as intense fear or cravings are elicited, the person may be subject to what the behaviorists call "stimulus control." If, for example, intense anger is aroused or strong temptations encountered that distract from one's commitments, an impulsive automatic response may follow. These also are the emotional conditions in which self-protective mechanisms, such as extreme avoidance, are automatically triggered, consistent with findings at the psychodynamic-motivation level.

Consider again the Veronica–Martha examples in Figures 16.1 and 16.2. When they imagine their medical futures, Veronica's focus on such positive possible outcomes as finding a new cure, and Martha's worry about possible malpractice risks, illustrate the very different internal states these women are likely to experience in their goal pursuit. The risk for Martha is that her sensitivity to potential problems may create so much anxiety that she ultimately drops out, or becomes extreme in her defenses to cope with those negative feelings. For Veronica, the risk may be that her insensitivity to the potential difficulties and stresses of a medical career may leave her inadequately prepared to cope with them when they do arise. In the next chapter, we will discuss the processes of self-regulation that can allow, or undermine, continued goal pursuit under difficult and emotion-arousing conditions.

16.11 How does anxiety affect goal striving?

Tuning in to the Wrong Thoughts: Anxiety. Effective goal pursuit is severely sabotaged by anxious, self-preoccupying thoughts (e.g., "I'm no good at this—I'll never be able to do it"). These anxious thoughts compete and interfere with task-relevant thoughts (such as, "Now I have to recheck my answers"). The result is that performance (as well as the person) suffers (Sarason, 1979). Self-preoccupying thoughts interfere most when the task to be done is complex and requires many competing responses. One just cannot be full of anxious, negative thoughts about oneself and simultaneously concentrate effectively on difficult work, like preparation for a chemistry final exam. Likewise, as the motivation to do well increases (as when success on the task is especially important), the highly anxious person may become particularly self-defeating. That happens because under such highly motivating conditions, test-anxious people tend to catastrophize, imagining all the terrible things that could happen. They then become even more negatively self-preoccupied, dwelling on how poorly they are doing. In contrast, if one can become less anxious, then attention can be devoted to the task and the person can concentrate on how to master it effectively.

Goals/Values, Motivations

Almost by definition, goals are pursued because the person is motivated to pursue them: the motivation for goal pursuit depends on the importance of the goal within the personality system.

Goal Hierarchies.   A person's goals are organized hierarchically, with some more important or "super-ordinate" than others (e.g., Carver & Scheier, 1998; Vallacher & Wegner, 1987). The goal to be and feel "safe and secure" is a higher-level goal, than "finding a partner I can trust" or "getting a job I can count on." The latter goals are at a lower level than the super-ordinate one, but they are much higher than "making the apartment safer." Making the apartment safe is executed at the even more subordinate level of "going to the hardware store" or cleaning out potential fire hazards. Likewise, the goal of being "a worthy person" is higher in the organization of the system than a goal such as being "kind and caring." Being kind and caring connects to even lower-level goals like "helping the needy person cross the street."

> 16.12 Explain the concept of goal hierarchies and the factors that influence which goals are pursued.

When goal attainment at a given level (e.g., getting a job) is blocked and frustrated, people may continue to strive toward the higher-level goal (being safe and secure) toward which the lower-level activity was directed. They may try, for example, to focus more on building the relationship with the partner now and postponing the job search, as long as it still serves the same higher-level goal (Martin, Tesser, & McIntosh, 1993). Goals are central for understanding the personal and life goals that people pursue, but the processing dynamics of how they pursue them depend on their own standards and self-evaluations as they monitor their progress.

Standards and Self-Evaluation.   In goal pursuit, people evaluate their own behavior and perceived progress, and they reward and punish themselves accordingly, thereby further influencing how they progress—or fail to do so (e.g., Bandura, 1989; Carver & Scheier, 1990). They congratulate themselves for what they see as positive, and they feel good or bad or uncertain about their own achievements. They self-administer psychological, social, and material rewards and punishments. In short, people assess themselves and become their own internal judges and reward–punishment system, using the standards that they have developed for themselves (Bandura, 1986, 2001; Higgins, 1990). Self-praise and censure, self-imposed treats and punishments, self-indulgence and self-laceration are signs of this pervasive human tendency to congratulate and condemn oneself.

> 16.13 How do self-evaluative standards influence striving and emotional responses? What kinds of conditions negate their influence?

You see it when people celebrate their good test scores and their acceptance letters, or kick themselves for what they read as disappointments and setbacks. A critical aspect of goal pursuit thus stems from the fact that beginning early in development, people learn to set their own performance standards and to make their own self-reward contingent upon their achieving these self-prescribed criteria. It's common to make a treat, like going to the movies, contingent on first finishing an assignment.

In this self-evaluation process, people compare their current state of performance with those standards. If they perceive a discrepancy, they tend to be motivated to reduce it or to reset their standards to a lower level (e.g., Carver & Scheier, 1981, 1990). As Bandura explained: "When people make self-satisfaction or tangible gratifications conditional upon certain accomplishments, they motivate themselves to expend the effort needed to attain the requisite performance" (Bandura, 1986, p. 350). By generating consequences for their own actions, individuals can bring them into line with their higher-order values and goals.

16.14 How are modeling and social comparison involved in self-standard development? How does self-awareness activate self-standards?

Acquisition of Standards.   The standards and goals people observe in the behavior of the models they value guide their self-regulatory efforts. In a pioneering series of studies on the acquisition of self-regulatory standards, Bandura and Kupers (1964) examined young children's patterns of self-reward during a rigged bowling game. They found that children who observed adults reward themselves for low levels of performance (i.e., low-standard models) subsequently treated themselves to available rewards after achieving low or moderate scores. In contrast, those who had been exposed to high-standard models adopted a stricter criterion for self-reward, making it contingent on high levels of performance. Social comparisons with peers also influence adult standards and self-regulation. For example, the levels of drinking that college students consider acceptable depend on the standards and values of the groups to which they belong (Prentice & Miller, 1993).

Bypassing Self-Standards.   Self-standards may be bypassed easily under various pressures of the moment (Carver & Scheier, 1978, 1998; Higgins, 1990; Wright & Mischel, 1987). Just as looking at yourself in the mirror makes it harder to bypass your "conscience" (that is, the personal standards and values to which you strive to adhere), listening to the "leader," the "authority," or the "group" can make it easy to forget those standards. Films about lynch mobs, gang rapes, wartime atrocities, the Holocaust, and urban riots document what can happen when personal responsibility is forsaken. Although we become desensitized easily by viewing them repeatedly in the media, they illustrate how often self-standards and careful self-examination are forgotten, with terrible consequences both to the victim and to the perpetrator. Research also has shown how easily people can be urged by authority figures into acts of aggression, failing to access their own self-standards and readily doing to others what they would consider unthinkable for themselves (Milgram, 1974). On the other hand, when self-regulatory scripts and plans for self-control are activated, the person may be able to overcome such pressures.

If you had to predict how easily Veronica and Martha would bypass their self-standards, and whose standards would be more stringent, what would you hypothesize, and why? Who would be more likely to make it through medical training? How sure are you, and on what basis?

Activation of Self-Standards: From Mindlessness to Self-Focus.   Much of what we do as we pursue goals is **mindless** (Langer, 1978), guided by more or less automatic

If the bypasser sees herself in the store window she is more likely to help the sick old man.

behavioral routines or scripts that are familiar and require little active attention or self-regulatory effort (Abelson, 1976). In a fast-food restaurant or at a football game, for example, we tend to act out more or less automatic routines. Under such conditions, active, conscious self-regulation plays little role and we do not experience self-awareness; that is, we do not focus on ourselves and our self-standards, but behave more or less as if on automatic pilot.

Self-standards are more likely to be accessed and brought into play when attention is focused on the self. That happens, for example, when one is observed, or sees oneself in a mirror. Under such self-focus, people become more conscious of their behavior and how it compares to their standards. In turn, awareness of any discrepancies motivates them to modify their actions in order to bring them more into line with their standards and ideals. Thus, a focus of attention on the self motivates the person to try to reduce perceived discrepancies between what he or she is doing and the relevant standards for comparison (Carver & Scheier, 1981; Duval, Duval, & Mulilis 1992; Scheier & Carver, 1988). For example, a self-perceived "caring" person who sees herself reflected in a store window about to pass a sick old man sprawled on a city sidewalk is more likely to bring herself in line with her own standards and pause to try to help.

Alternative Routes in Effective Goal Pursuit

Before ending this discussion, let's look again at the finding by Higgins and colleagues (2001) that people can succeed through either prevention or promotion focus. They concluded that people may succeed in their goal pursuit by being cautious and avoiding failure at all costs, as exemplified by the Martha illustration. Or they can also succeed by eagerly pursuing their desires, like Veronica. Both are potential routes to success, although they are distinctively different strategic orientations. They are experienced very differently in the thoughts and feelings of the individuals, and they influence their future behavior, mental activity, and emotions in quite different ways.

Thus, the two women in our example have extremely different personality systems. These differences are seen at multiple levels of analysis. They differ in their BIS/BAS reactivity and in their Big Five factor scores and profiles especially with regard to extraversion, impulsivity, neuroticism, and anxiety. At the social cognitive level they experience their worlds in dramatically different ways. They contrast in typical moods and feeling states, and in how they mentally and emotionally represent their experiences and their possible futures. This is seen even in how they imagine their possible careers in medicine. They use very different strategies in their pursuit of goals—one "psyches" herself up, imagining the exciting possibilities; the other scares herself about the possible negatives and stressors along the route. Nevertheless, both might be able to persist and succeed in their goal pursuit. What are the probable psychological determinants of those ultimate outcomes?

In Table 16.3 on p. 382, summarizing the processes and person variables that influence goal pursuit, the last column lists regulatory competencies. The nature of those competencies, and their role in personality are discussed in the next chapter. There we will examine how the different levels of analysis discussed throughout the text help clarify the mechanisms of self-regulation and effortful control. These are mechanisms through which goal pursuit, whether motivated for rewards and opportunities or to avoid punishments and reduce fears, can be maintained effectively. Specifically, the next chapter details how individuals can self-regulate their own behavior and internal reactions in ways that allow them to achieve increasing mastery—and to feel better, more in control, and more effective—as they go from pursuing their goals to attaining them.

SUMMARY

APPROACH–AVOIDANCE DISPOSITIONS IN GOAL PURSUIT

- At the biological level, the behavioral inhibition system (BIS) regulates avoidance behavior; the behavioral activation system (BAS) regulates approach behavior.
- At the trait-dispositional level, increased activity in the BAS is linked to extraverted personality characteristics; activity in the BIS is linked to introversion and anxiety.
- At the internal-experiential level, BAS and BIS activity are related respectively to sensitivity to positive (reward) cues and to negative cues (threats, punishment).
- In regulatory focus theory, goal-directed behavior is governed by two motivational systems—the prevention system and the promotion system.
- Evolutionary theory emphasizes the adaptive value of situation-specific behaviors.
- Genetics and dispositional preferences influence the social environments in which people develop.

THE GOAL PURSUIT PROCESS

- During goal pursuit, mental and emotional dynamics are activated. These include encodings, expectancies/beliefs, feelings and emotions, personal goals/values, and regulatory competencies.
- The BIS and BAS biological systems influence how individuals appraise and respond to situations.
- In "hot," emotional situations, the person may be subject to "stimulus control," triggering impulsive, automatic responses.
- Anxious, self-preoccupying thoughts can sabotage goal pursuit.

- When a lower-level goal (e.g., getting a job) is blocked and frustrated, people often continue to strive toward the higher-level goal (being safe and secure).
- In goal pursuit, people influence their own progress by rewarding and punishing themselves.
- Self-standards may be bypassed easily under various pressures of the moment.
- Self-standards are more likely to be accessed when attention is focused on the self.
- People may succeed in their goal pursuit by being cautious and avoiding failure (prevention focus) and/or by eagerly pursuing their desires (promotion focus).

KEY TERMS

achievement pride   375
ambivalence   379
current life tasks   380
goal gradients   379

goal hierarchies   381
mindless   388
prevention pride   375
prevention system   375

promotion pride   375
promotion system   375
regulatory focus
  theory   375

17

SELF-REGULATION: FROM GOAL PURSUIT TO GOAL ATTAINMENT

Veronica and Martha are now in their third year in medical school. They both have successfully finished the grueling coursework in biochemistry, and today, on the first day of class in anatomy, they dissect a cadaver. With their shiny new dissecting kits, dissecting manuals, and scrub suits, each begins dissecting a real human body for the first time. Two classmates leave the lab 15 minutes into dissection, visibly pale and distressed. This semester, they will be spending many hours next to their cadaver learning the seven ins and outs of the pterygopalatine fossa and other structures in the nasal cavity. That evening, Veronica thinks: "Wow, finally, real medical education. I'm a bit uneasy about this right now, but like everyone says, I'm sure I'll get used to it, and who knows, I might be good at this—maybe I'll choose surgery as my specialty." Martha, on the other hand, is thinking: "Ok, this is the real thing. If I can't do this, no matter how many A's I get in biochemistry, I won't make it as a doctor. But the truth is, I almost fainted today. How am I going to get through this semester when we have this class every week?"

In this chapter, we will consider findings that can help Martha answer her question: what can she do if she wants to continue to pursue her goals in medicine to overcome the stress she is experiencing? She is committed to not quitting and does not want to shift to other routes for pursuing her life goals. Given her choice, her personal challenge becomes learning how to self-regulate her own thoughts and emotions to cope more adaptively with the stresses that are sure to arise along the route to her goals. For Martha, who focuses on threats and punishments, this is likely to be very difficult. This chapter examines the cumulative contributions from different levels of analysis in personality theory and research that speak to this fundamental human dilemma: *How can people protect themselves against their own dispositional vulnerabilities when they interfere with their life goals and well-being?*

► SELF-REGULATORY PROCESSES

In the last chapter we looked at individual differences in types of approach–avoidance dispositions at many different levels of analysis, from the biological, to the trait-dispositional, to the phenomenological, to the social cognitive, to the psychodynamic. We then turned to the mental and emotional processes that become activated in the personality system in goal pursuit. This chapter goes beyond such descriptions. Now we will examine the specific mechanisms that make self-regulation possible as individuals engage in their characteristic approach and avoidance patterns. Again we will draw on findings from multiple levels of analysis—from the biological to the social cognitive to the experiential, motivational, and emotional.

When BIS/BAS, approach–avoidance dispositions, or promotion–prevention goals and strategies are activated, people become motivated, pursuing their goals with their preferred strategies. Who perseveres and reaches those goals even when the inevitable obstacles arise along the road? Who fails? And why? The answers show that the differences between people in this regard are large, and the implications for their lives can be profound.

Why Self-Regulate?

Automaticity. Most of what people do in their goal pursuit is virtually automatic. Automatic behavior is seen in routine activities from attending classes and going to work or interacting with friends and family, to dealing with stress and coping with temptation and frustration. Most of the time, these processes appear essentially to run

17.1 How does self-regulation relate to the concept of automaticity?

on their own as if the person were on automatic pilot (e.g., Bargh, 1997, 2001). In this sense, the reactions of both Veronica and Martha to their first experience dissecting a cadaver are their first automatic reactions. They reflect the reactivity of their respective personality systems to the new events encountered. Some of the details of those mental and emotional processes were illustrated in the last section of the previous chapter, and were summarized in Table 16.3.

These automatic mental–emotional processes activated in goal pursuit are adaptive for most life functions. But sometimes what runs off automatically may be exactly what the person is eager to *not* do—for example, to yield to the temptation of the dessert when trying to diet, or to head for the movies soon after deciding to spend the evening working.

Examples of the difficulty of overcoming the usual automatic reactive tendencies are easy to find in daily life. Every dieter knows the quick failure of good intentions when the waiter flashes the chocolate pastry on the dessert tray. Strong motivation is not enough when the temptations are intense and "in your face."

Beyond Automaticity? Self-regulation becomes important—in fact crucial—when the person experiences a distressing conflict between strong approach tendencies and strong avoidance tendencies in goal pursuit. The dieter on the first day of her new health plan experiences such a conflict when she sees her friend consuming the tempting double-chocolate cake. The medical students eager to start becoming real doctors experience such a conflict when facing their first human cadaver.

Approach (Appetitive) and Avoidance (Aversive) Dilemmas

Approach–avoidance conflicts produce dilemmas of two types:

17.2 Distinguish between appetitive and aversive dilemmas in terms of approach and avoidance motives.

1. Approach or **appetitive dilemmas** occur when facing a strong approach temptation (take the cake, grab the money, be selfish in a relationship dispute). The conflict occurs because pursuing these temptations also threatens to interfere with another even more important, higher-order goal (to have self-respect, to be a worthy person). These conflicts are common and difficult to resolve because often the higher-order goal is more abstract and temporally delayed (to stay slim, to stay healthy in the future, to avoid shame or embarrassment later, to be moral, to be caring to your partner or parent). The human paradox is that although the delayed goal is ultimately more important to the self, it also is more abstract and far off. It therefore has less immediate emotional impact and "hot stimulus pull" in the situation compared to the temptation that is staring you in the face (e.g., Trope & Lieberman, 2003; Mischel & Ayduk, 2002).

2. Avoidance or **aversive, anxiety-producing dilemmas** occur when the immediate impulse is to flee because aversive emotions like fear, distress, and anxiety are experienced. The conflict arises when to serve a higher-order goal one needs to remain in the situation and behave rationally within it. The medical students staring at the human cadaver's decomposing face impulsively feel driven to rush away, but they are tortured because they don't want to humiliate themselves, and they do want to become good doctors in the future. Again the conflict is between the impulses and pressures within the immediate situation and the more distant, higher-order outcomes later. If you rely on what comes naturally, often the immediate pull of the situation, not you, becomes the winner.

Willpower. The impressive power of the situation or "stimulus control" is seen in work at the behavioral level, and in more recent studies in social cognition (e.g., Bargh, 1997, 2001). John Bargh and his colleagues have shown that most of what people do runs off automatically without conscious intervention. It is elicited by the particular stimulus conditions in the situation, often without the person's awareness. But these findings coexist with the intuitive conviction that human beings have the capacity to take control and exert willpower at least some of the time (e.g., Ayduk & Mischel, 2002; Derryberry, 2002). Often people do overcome obstacles and temptations along the way to achieving their valued long-term goals, and manage to resist the pull of even strong situational pressures. How do they do it? What makes willpower possible?

Motivation and Competence. Effective self-regulatory behavior and self-control in goal pursuit depends both on the person's *motivation* and on his or her *competencies*. First let's consider the role of motivation. Take the motivation to refuse a slice of double-chocolate fudge cake. The motivational strength of this may depend, for example, on whether the individual construes the cake as "unhealthy and fattening" or as "a great treat." It also depends on how much the person values the long-term super-ordinate goals that are served by eating healthy and being fit. If these self-regulatory behaviors are serving a higher goal central to the self, like being a worthy self-respecting person, their motivational significance will be high and they will be mentally more accessible.

17.3 What besides regulatory motivation is needed in order to manifest willpower?

It is important, however, to distinguish between regulatory motivation and regulatory competence. Often people have one of these but not the other: a good example is a recent president of the United States. His adroit handling of political and foreign affairs showed that he had such skills, yet he either was unable or insufficiently motivated to apply them to himself when it came to his personal affairs, and he was disgraced and almost impeached as a result.

Even when motivation is high, self-control in the face of temptations and frustrations requires more than good intentions. As William James noted more than a hundred years ago, the gap from "desiring and wanting" to "willing" cannot be bridged unless "certain preliminaries" are met (1890). Even in the presence of high regulatory motivation, goal attainment depends critically on the availability and accessibility of effective self-regulatory competencies. **Regulatory competencies** refers to the cognitive and attentional mechanisms that help us execute goal-directed behavior. In the remainder of this chapter, we will examine the processes that underlie these competencies.

The Biological Level: Executive Functions

First, we consider the nature of these regulatory competencies and mechanisms at the biological-brain level. In the last few decades, much has been learned about the neural mechanisms that underlie and enable **executive functions** in self-regulation. A century earlier, Freud and his followers had used the same term "executive functions" to refer to the ways in which the ego enables delay of gratification and impulse control. Findings from cognitive neuroscience now indicate that at the biological level many of these functions involve executive systems in the frontal cortex.

17.4 Define executive functions. Which brain regions are involved?

Brain Mechanisms in Effortful Control. Michael Posner and colleagues have described an "anterior attentional system" that regulates the pathways involved in executive functions throughout the cortex (Derryberry, 2002; Posner & Rothbart, 1991, 1998). These brain systems enable **effortful control,** or in lay language, willpower, in goal pursuit. They do so by allowing people to regulate their attention. This attention regulation process includes the ability to focus attention in perception, to

The same person can have high self-control in some situations but not in others.

switch attention between tasks, and to control thoughts flexibly (Derryberry & Reed, 2002). These processes and brain mechanisms are crucial for effective goal pursuit and self-regulation.

Self-Report Measures.   Self-report measures also have been developed to identify individual differences in the executive attention control mechanisms that are basic for effortful control. These scales (see Table 17.1 for sample items) measure individual differences in attention control ability and capacity for effortful control at the psychological level that are correlated with the brain measures (Derryberry, 2002).

The Trait-Dispositional Level

At the broad dispositional level, attention control scores are related positively to extraversion and negatively to anxiety and impulsivity (Derryberry, 2002). These findings closely parallel those from work on the BAS/BIS, as should be expected theoretically. Individual differences in self-regulation and the ability to exert effortful control are dramatic. While some people adhere to stringent diets or give up cigarettes after years of smoking them addictively, others fail in spite of affirming the same initial good intentions. The ancient Greeks considered a weakness of the will a character trait and called it *akrasia* — the deficiency of the will. To this day, this type of trait remains important in personality theories. It is seen in the factor of "conscientiousness" within the Big Five (Chapter 3) and in the dispositions of "ego resilience" and "ego control" (e.g., Block & Block, 1980; Eisenberg, Spinrad, & Morris, 2002), two personality characteristics discussed next.

Ego Control and Ego Resilience.   **Ego control** refers to the degree of impulse control in such functions as inhibition of aggression and the ability to plan. A related construct, **ego resilience**, refers to the individual's ability to adapt to environmental demands by appropriately modifying his or her habitual level of ego control. Ego resiliency allows functioning with some "elasticity" and "permeability" (Block, 2001, p. 123). Together, these two constructs represent core qualities for adaptive functioning from an influential trait-dispositional perspective (Eisenberg et al., 2002).

TABLE 17.1   Items from the Attention Control Scale

Please read each item below and then indicate how often you experience it, using the following response scale:

1	2	3	4
almost never	sometimes	often	always

_____ 1. It's very hard for me to concentrate on a difficult task when there are noises around.

_____ 2. When I need to concentrate and solve a problem, I have trouble focusing my attention.

_____ 3. When I am working hard on something, I still get distracted by events around me.

_____ 4. My concentration is good even if there is music in the room around me.

_____ 5. When concentrating, I can focus my attention so that I become unaware of what's going on in the room around me.

_____ 6. When I am reading or studying, I am easily distracted if there are people talking in the same room.

_____ 7. When trying to focus my attention on something, I have difficulty blocking out distracting thoughts.

_____ 8. I have a hard time concentrating when I'm excited about something.

_____ 9. When concentrating, I ignore feelings of hunger or thirst.

_____ 10. I can quickly switch from one task to another.

Source: Derryberry, D., & Reed, M. A. (2002). Anxiety-related attentional biases and their regulation by attentional control. _Journal of Abnormal Psychology, 111,_ 225–236.

As Jack Block (2001, pp. 123–124) puts it: "The resilient person anticipates wisely when to stop something unfruitful (like repetitively hitting a large boulder with a tiny hammer) or to continue something that may ultimately prove fruitful

Jack Block

(like shattering a small boulder with a repetitive sledge hammer). In its adaptiveness, resiliency well serves evolution." Note that this illustration also highlights the importance of the ability to discriminate, and the flexibility that this allows—an emphasis now found in the evolutionary approach, in the social cognitive approach, and in findings from the biological level of analysis (e.g., Grigorenko, 2002).

17.5 How have ego-control and ego resilience been measured in children? How are they related to adaptive behavior?

A number of tasks are used to measure the construct of ego control and ego resilience. For example, in one study researchers rated children's tendency to inhibit impulses to infer their level of ego control and also observed their delay behavior in experimental situations (Block & Martin, 1955). They exposed the children to a frustration in which a barrier separated the child from desired and expected toys. The **undercontrolling** children (those who had been rated as not inhibiting their impulses) reacted more violently to the frustrating barrier than did **overcontrolling,** inhibited children. The undercontrolling youngsters also became less constructive in their play.

Individuals who are high (rather than low) on indices of ego control tend to be somewhat more able to control and inhibit their motor activity. For example, they may be able to sit still longer or draw a line more slowly without lifting their pencil. These are only a few examples from much larger networks of correlations that support the constructs of ego resiliency and ego control (Block & Block, 1980; Mischel, 1984; Shoda, Mischel, & Peake, 1990).

In studies of the ego-resiliency construct, toddlers were evaluated for the degree to which they seemed secure and competent (in a problem-solving task). The toddlers who were secure and competent also scored higher on measures of ego resiliency when they reached the age of four to five years (Gove, Arend, & Sroufe, 1979; Matas, Arend, & Sroufe, 1978). As another example, ego-resilient children at age three are also viewed as more popular, interesting, and attractive at later ages (Block & Block, 1980). The resilience concept also is related to delay of immediate gratification for the sake of more valued but delayed outcomes (Shoda, Mischel, & Peake, 1990), discussed below. In short, both the concepts of ego control and ego resiliency offer useful characterizations of important individual differences (Eisenberg et al., 2002). These differences remain stable over many years in the course of development (e.g., Caspi, 1987; Caspi & Bem, 1990; Mischel, Shoda, & Rodriguez, 1989).

The Social Cognitive and Phenomenological Levels

17.6 What questions about self-regulation are explored at the social cognitive level of analysis?

In sum, work at the biological level is identifying the brain centers that enable executive skills and self-regulation. Work at the dispositional level on characteristics like ego resilience provides useful descriptions of what a person with self-regulatory competence is like. What about the social cognitive and phenomenological levels? Work at these levels currently tries to understand the mental mechanisms—the thoughts and strategies—that enable self-regulatory competence.

Cognitions, Emotions, and Attention in Self-Regulation. Specifically, the question asked is:

How does what you think, or where you focus your attention, enable or undermine your ability to self-regulate in emotion-arousing dilemmas?

Applied to the dieter who has resolved to forego the double-chocolate cake tonight, how will what he thinks and how he deploys his attention make it possible for him to stick to his goal? Applied to Martha's dilemma as she tries her first dissection, how will what she says to herself and thinks make it possible for her to appropriately dissect the cadaver?

To answer such questions, researchers at this level have examined how mental activities—cognition and attention—during goal pursuit influence the ability to persist and reach the goal when there are strong approach–avoidance conflicts (e.g., Mischel & Ayduk, 2002). To orient you to those findings, let's anticipate their gist before they are discussed next in more detail. Briefly, they show that how the person construes and interprets the situation, and deploys attention while attempting effortful control, has effects on effortful control ability that directly parallel and complement those identified at the brain level in the work of Posner and his colleagues.

▶ EMOTION REGULATION IN APPROACH (APPETITIVE) DILEMMAS

In this section, we will examine how certain mental processes enable—or undermine—self-regulation and goal pursuit in approach or appetitive dilemmas, as in the dieter's struggles with dessert temptations. Then in the section that follows, we will do the same with regard to avoidance and aversive dilemmas like the one Martha faced in her anatomy exercise. In both types of dilemmas people need willpower, or rather, the mental processes that make willpower possible. One of the clearest examples of the need for willpower, or in scientific terms, effortful control, is seen when people try to defer immediate gratification for the sake of important but delayed consequences.

Delay of Gratification as a Basic Human Task

The ability to voluntarily delay immediate gratification, to tolerate self-imposed delays of reward, is at the core of most concepts of willpower, ego strength, and ego resilience. It is hard to imagine civilization without such self-imposed delays, and it was Freud who called attention to the great importance of this ability as a requirement for ego development a century ago. Learning to wait for desired outcomes and to behave in light of expected future consequences is essential for the successful achievement of long-term, distant goals.

Beginning with toilet training, every person must learn to defer impulses and needs and to express them only under special conditions of time and place. To achieve educational and personal life goals, such as a college degree or a professional or business career, the route requires a continuous series of delays of gratification. This is seen in the progression from one grade to the next, and from one barrier to another in the long course from occupational choice to occupational success. In social relationships, the culture also requires delays, for example, the expectation that people should postpone sexual relations, marriage, and children until they are "ready for them." The importance of self-control patterns that require delay of gratification has been widely recognized by theorists from Freud to the present. It is personally familiar to every

17.7 Why is delay of gratification an essential self-regulation skill? Describe the methods used to study this ability in children.

student who has tried to persist with school work due the next day when greater temptations were available at the moment. The challenge for self-regulation research is to answer the question: Given that one has chosen to wait or work for a larger deferred goal, how can the delay period be managed and the impulse to take the immediate reward be resisted?

The Goal-Directed Delay Situation. A good method for the study of willpower in such "hot" approach–appetitive situations has proved to be the preschool delay of gratification paradigm (see Figure 17.1). It is a method that has been used extensively to study self-regulatory processes at early periods in development when they begin to emerge in the young child (Mischel and associates, 1989; Mischel & Ayduk, 2002).

In this method, the experimenter deliberately creates a dilemma for the young child. Imagine that a four-year-old is shown some desired treats, for example, marshmallows or little pretzel sticks. The child faces the following conflict: wait until the experimenter returns and get two of the desired treats, or, ring a bell, and the experimenter will come back immediately—but then the child gets only one treat. After the child chooses to wait for the larger outcome, the delay soon becomes very difficult and the frustration grows quickly. This situation has become a prototype for studying the conflict between an immediate smaller temptation and a higher-order but delayed larger goal, the bigger treat that will come later (when the experimenter returns). In this type of situation, more than 500 preschoolers in the Stanford University community were studied systematically through observation and experiments (e.g., Ayduk & Mischel, 2002; Mischel et al., 1989).

One of the most striking delay strategies used by some youngsters was as simple as it was effective. These children seemed to manage to wait for the preferred reward for long periods apparently by converting the aversive waiting situation into a more pleasant, nonwaiting one. They seemed to do this by elaborate self-distraction techniques through which they spent their time psychologically doing something (almost anything) other than waiting. Rather than focusing prolonged attention on the objects for which they were waiting, they avoided looking at them. Some of these children covered their eyes with their hands, rested their heads on their arms, or found other similar techniques for averting their eyes from the reward objects. Others seemed to try to reduce the frustration of delay of reward by generating their own diversions: they talked to themselves, sang little songs, invented games with their hands and feet, and when all

17.8 What methods were used by children able to delay gratification? How was this strategy studied experimentally, and with what results?

Figure 17.1 Waiting for delayed gratification.
Source: Based on Mischel, W., Ebbsen, E. B., & Zeiss, A. R. (1972). Cognitive and attentional mechanisms in delay of gratification. *Journal of Personality and Social Psychology, 21,* 204–219.

other distractions seemed exhausted, even tried to fall asleep during the waiting situation—as one child successfully did.

These observations suggested that diverting yourself from attention to the delayed reward stimulus (while maintaining behavior directed toward its ultimate attainment) may be a key step for effective delay of reward. That is, learning *not* to attend to or think about what you are awaiting may enhance effective delay of gratification much more than focusing attention on the outcomes. When hungry, for example, it seems easier to wait for supper if one is not confronted with the sight and smell of food. A series of experiments summarized next tested these hypotheses.

Cooling Strategies: It's How You Think That Counts

Strategic Self-Distraction.   Directing attention away from the rewards turned out to be an excellent strategy. For example, Figure 17.2 shows results of an experiment that manipulated the extent to which children could attend to the reward objects while they were waiting (Mischel, Ebbesen, & Zeiss, 1972). As shown in the figure, in one condition, the children waited with both the immediate (less preferred) and the delayed (more preferred) reward facing them in the experimental room so that they could attend to both outcomes. In another group, neither reward was available for the child's attention, both having been removed from sight. In the remaining two groups, either the delayed reward only or the immediate reward only was available for attention while the child waited. The measure was the length of time before each child voluntarily stopped waiting. As the graph shows, the child waited much longer when the rewards were not available for attention, supporting the observations and hypotheses discussed above.

Many experiments have demonstrated that voluntary delay of gratification can be aided by activities that serve as distractions from the rewards and thus from the

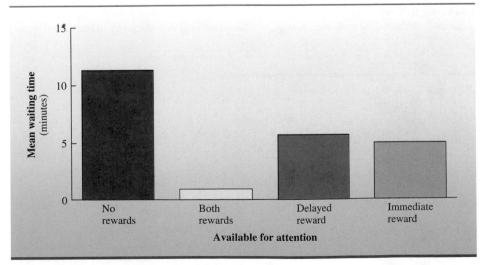

Figure 17.2   Effects of attention on delay of gratification.
Source: Based on data from Mischel, W., & Ebbsen, E. B. (1970). Attention in delay of gratification. *Journal of Personality and Social Psychology, 16,* 239–337.

aversiveness of wanting them but not having them. Through such distraction, it is possible to convert the frustrating delay-of-reward situation into a psychologically less aversive condition. For example, children waited much longer for a preferred reward when they were distracted cognitively from the goal objects than when they directly attended to them (Mischel, Ebbesen, & Zeiss, 1972; Mischel, Shoda, & Rodriguez, 1989). In contrast, distracting oneself from the rewards, overtly or cognitively (e.g., by thinking of "fun things") made it possible to wait longer for them. These results showing the value of self-distraction for avoiding temptation are consistent with the old saying "Satan, get thee behind me."

Rather than trying to maintain aversive activities such as delay of reward through "acts of will" and focused attention, effective self-control is helped by mentally *transforming* the difficult into the easy, the aversive into the pleasant, and the boring into the interesting, while still maintaining the activity on which the ultimate reward depends. Rather than "willing" oneself to heroic bravery, one needs to enact the necessary "difficult" response while engaging in another one cognitively (Mischel et al., 1996; Peake, Hebl, & Mischel, 2002). To do this effectively, when the task is complex, the individual may need to extensively rehearse and plan to implement the necessary actions (Gollwitzer & Moskowitz, 1996).

17.9 How do hot and cool construals of rewards differ? How can they be used to maintain motivation and resist immediate gratification?

Hot and Cool Construal. The outcomes or rewards in this type of situation may be construed in terms of their "hot," consummatory properties, or in terms of their "cool," informative properties. A hot representation of a reward such as a desired treat activates the behaviors associated with experiencing or consuming it. When young children look at the actual rewards, or think about them, they may focus spontaneously on these hot, arousing qualities. If they do this, they increase their own frustration and arousal, making it more difficult to continue to wait (e.g., Mischel & Ebbesen, 1970; Mischel, et al., 1972; Toner, 1981). In contrast, a psychologically distant or cool representation of the rewards has the opposite effect on self-regulation, enhancing goal-directed waiting (see Figure 17.3). Thus, presenting children with a picture of the rewards (e.g., in the form of life-size slide-projected images) or instructing them to cognitively transform them (e.g., by turning the pretzels into thin, brown logs in their imagination) actually facilitates waiting (Mischel, Shoda, & Rodriguez, 1989). In short, just how one thinks about the rewards (hot or cool) in the contingency crucially

Figure 17.3 Effects of hot–cool thinking on delay time.

Source: Based on studies reported in Mischel, W., Shoda, Y., & Rodriguez, M. L. (1989). Delay of gratification in children. *Science, 244,* 933–938.

influences how long one can wait or work to attain them (Metcalfe & Mischel, 1999; Peake et al., 2002).

The children's behavior during the delay period (Mischel & Ebbesen, 1970) also suggested how they support their efforts at self-control. At points throughout the waiting period, most of the children's spontaneous attempts at self-distraction wavered. Those children who persisted often used strategies such as verbalizing self-instructions to remind themselves of the contingency (e.g., "If I wait I get [the preferred reward] but if I ring the bell I get [the less preferred reward]") and of their goal. In short, in effective delay of gratification the child tunes out the hot properties of the reward. Instead, to sustain her waiting behavior she focuses on its cool properties and the contingency.

Flexible Attention. Adaptive self-regulation involves more than application of cooling strategies. Successful delay and goal pursuit often require shifting attention flexibly rather than unconditional use of cooling strategies. Experiments confirm that some of the children who delay best seem to focus briefly on the hot features in the situation to sustain motivation but then quickly switch back to the cool features and self-distraction to avoid excessive arousal and frustration (Peake et al., 2002).

Effective self-regulation requires sensitivity to the demands, constraints, and opportunities of the particular situation. Such **discriminative facility**—taking into account characteristics of each situation and responding accordingly—may play a central role in coping, self-regulation, and social-emotional competence in general (see Cheng, 2003; Chiu, Hong, Mischel, & Shoda, 1995). Distraction, or cooling, then, is likely to be adaptive when applied to coping in aversive or frustrating situations that must be tolerated for goal attainment, but not in many other types of situations. The key is to know when to cool, when to stay warm, and to be able to do so when you need to. The mechanisms described underlie the kind of flexible, discriminative behaviors that Jack Block (2001) also saw as the essence of the resilient person.

In sum, in this section we have focused on voluntary delay of gratification when trying to control impulses in the process of waiting or working for a positive delayed outcome or goal. The findings also fit those from many other areas of self-regulation (Harter, 1983; Kopp, 1982; Kuhl, 1985), as illustrated next.

▶ EMOTIONAL REGULATION IN AVOIDANCE (AVERSIVE) DILEMMAS

The strategies that help people deal with the control of appetitive impulses as in the delay situation also apply to emotional self-regulation for dealing with aversive stimulation, fears, and stress-inducing situations. An example to keep in mind is the anxiety-producing situation in the anatomy room in which Veronica and Martha faced the dissection of their first human cadaver.

In a study that directly speaks to the self-regulatory problem these students had at the anatomy table, researchers interviewed medical students witnessing a medical autopsy for the first time (Lief & Fox, 1963). They found that many aspects of the autopsy procedure appear to have been designed as an institutionalized ritual to help students cope with their distress by making it easier for them to detach themselves

17.10 Describe some advantages and undesirable consequences of cognitive detachment in aversive situations.

emotionally. The autopsy room itself is arranged to provide a sterile, clinical, impersonal atmosphere. The face and genitalia of the corpse are kept covered unless they are being examined, and so on. But beyond the physical arrangements, it is a detached, emotionally distanced scientific stance that further helps to keep the whole procedure abstract and impersonal, helping to reduce emotional arousal. But as is always the case, adopting such a stance is easier for some people than for others. For Martha, with her readiness to scan for potential troubles down the road and to become anxious at the prospects of all the things that can go wrong, both in the lesson and in her career, dealing with this was particularly challenging.

Experimental research confirms that an attitude of detachment helps people react more calmly when exposed to gory scenes portraying bloody accidents and death (Koriat et al., 1972) or when expecting electric shock (Holmes & Houston, 1974). These results are consistent with reports showing that soldiers may immunize themselves against emotion by distancing themselves psychologically from their victims, for example, by calling them "gooks" and labeling them as subhumans. While highly effective for reducing feeling, a detachment strategy to reduce emotionality can be misused, producing callous, insensitive attitudes and cold-bloodedness toward others, in war, in medical practice, and in much of social life. On the other hand, in many life situations, detachment through cognitive reappraisal to attain emotional cooling provides a basic route for effective emotion regulation, as discussed in In Focus. 17.1.

Cognitive Transformations to Deal with Stress

Not surprisingly, a good deal of related research leads to the conclusion that self-distraction, when possible, can be an excellent way to manage unavoidable stresses like unpleasant medical examinations (Miller, 1987; Miller & Green, 1985) and coping with severe life crises (Taylor & Brown, 1988). Self-distraction (e.g., watching travel slides or recalling pleasant memories) increases tolerance of experimentally induced physical pain (e.g., Berntzen, 1987; Chaves & Barber, 1974). Similarly, distracting and relaxation-inducing activities such as listening to music reduce anxiety in the face of uncontrollable shocks (Miller, 1979, 1996), helps people cope with the daily pain of rheumatoid arthritis (Affleck et al., 1992) and even with severe life crises (e.g., Taylor & Brown, 1988). "Cooling" strategies generally can help one to transform potentially stressful situations to make them less aversive. For example, if surgical patients are encouraged to reconstrue their hospital stay as a vacation to relax a while from the stresses of daily life, they show better postoperative adjustment (Langer, Janis, & Wolfer, 1975), just as chronically ill patients who reinterpret their conditions more positively also show better adjustment (Carver et al., 1993). In sum, when stress and pain are inevitable, the adage to look for the silver lining and to "accentuate the positive" seems wise.

The type of cognitive strategy that helps one to deal best with stress also depends on the individual (Miller, 1987). Recall, for example, individual differences in the tendency to use distraction or "blunt" rather than to sensitize or "monitor," discussed in the chapter on repression as a mechanism of defense (Chapter 6). The point to remember is that such preferences in the type of information sought for dealing with stress affect how the person copes best with stress; while one strategy may help some people, the opposite strategy may help others. The task is to get the right match.

COOLING UNWANTED EMOTIONS: COGNITIVE REAPPRAISAL IS BETTER THAN DENYING NEGATIVE FEELINGS

When people are trying to hide their secret thoughts, or reduce the pain and fear of viewing a horrible event, what processes allow them to regulate their negative emotions? Stanford University psychologist James Gross and his colleagues have focused on two specific emotion regulation strategies. One is **cognitive reappraisal,** the other is **suppression.**

In a typical study, Gross brings participants into the laboratory and informs them that they will be watching a movie. The film they will see shows detailed, close-up views of severe burn victims or of an arm amputation. Participants then are divided into one of three different groups and given different instructions prior to viewing the film. In the cognitive reappraisal condition, they are asked to use a cooling strategy. Specifically, they are asked to try to think about the movie in a detached unemotional way, objectively, and to focus attention on the technical details of the event, not feeling anything personally (e.g., pretend that you're a teacher in medical school). In the suppression condition, participants are asked to try to hide their emotional reactions to the film as they watch it so that anyone seeing them would not know that they were feeling anything at all. In the control condition, participants are simply asked to watch the movie.

This and similar studies find that cognitive reappraisal is an overwhelmingly more adaptive way to regulate negative emotions. It is much better than suppression in which people hide the feelings they are experiencing. These differences are seen in how the two strategies influence the intensity of people's experiences as well as their effect on the person's level of physiological autonomic nervous system arousal and distress. Specifically, people who are told to think about the movie in a way that cools the emotional content (reappraisal condition) experience fewer feelings of disgust and less physiological activation (evidenced by less blood vessel constriction) when compared to people who are asked to try to hide and suppress their emotional responses to the film so that no one could see their real feelings on their faces (Gross, 1998).

Cognitive reappraisal and suppression produce differences at the cognitive level of analysis as well. In a variation of the study described above, participants saw a slide show instead of a movie and were later asked how much of the information from the slide show they remembered. People who suppressed during the experiment performed more poorly on the memory task relative to people who engaged in cognitive reappraisal (Richards & Gross, 2000). In addition, people who have a tendency to suppress perform more poorly on memory tasks than those who don't tend to suppress (Gross & John, 2003). Specifically, people who score high on the suppression scale of the Emotion Regulation Questionnaire perform more poorly than those who score low on the suppression scale.

Finally, note that the results from this work on emotion regulation are consistent with a psychodynamic level view of the relative ineffectiveness of emotional denial: trying to hide one's feelings is a poor defense mechanism (Chapters 6 and 7).

▶ INTERACTION AMONG LEVELS: HOT AND COOL SYSTEMS IN SELF-REGULATION

17.11 How did James Gross study the relative effectiveness of emotional suppression and cognitive restructuring? What were the results?

So far, we have considered the findings on self-regulation from each level of analysis, one at a time. This can create a somewhat misleading impression that these are independent sources of influence. In fact, the biological brain system and the social cognitive system of processing dynamics activated in the particular situation are in a continuous dynamic two-way interaction process. What Martha thinks when dealing with the dissection, and where she focuses her attention (on the ghastly tortured expression on the face, on the intricate ways in which the capillary system is organized) influence what becomes activated in the brain, which influences what she next feels and thinks, on and on. To reiterate, the psychological system and the biological system interact: to understand them requires attention to how they play out jointly.

Specifically, with regard to both approach and avoidance dilemmas, the person's thoughts, cognitive appraisals, and attention deployment are related to, and influence, what happens in the relevant brain systems. That process, in turn, influences what is experienced emotionally and cognitively in continuous interaction. At the social cognitive level, cooling operations make it easier to activate long-term goals and reduce the hot pull of the immediate emotion-producing triggers in the situation. Consequently, what becomes activated in the brain and at the neural level is modified as well. To understand this more deeply, we have to examine the relevant interactions.

The Emotional (Hot) Brain/The Rational (Cool) Brain

To reiterate, the situations in which people most need and want to control their impulses often are those in which it is most difficult for them to do so. These are the situations that elicit "hot" emotional reactions such as intense fear and anxiety, or strong appetites and cravings. These were seen in miniature form in the studies of little children trying so hard to wait for bigger treats but unable to hold out as the temptation to "get it now" becomes too strong. These kinds of hot situations tend to automatically trigger hot reactions—to eat the dessert, take the drug, grab the hundred-dollar bill dropped in your path. Such situations rapidly generate the associated feelings of fear or desire and the urge to respond impulsively. They lead people to bypass self-regulatory controls and self-standards just when they need them most. Why does that happen so easily?

Bodily Changes: Emotion in Stress.   When an event triggers automatic fear reactions or is perceived as stressful, physiological reactions in the body are triggered at the biological level. Such feelings as "makes my heart race," and "choked up with rage" or "ready to vomit" are experienced psychologically in emotional states that involve bodily changes. It is the activation of the sympathetic division of the autonomic nervous system that produces many of the physiological changes that are experienced in reaction to perceived stress. They include a cascade of events such as channeling of the blood supply to the muscles and brain, slowing down of stomach and intestinal activity, increase in heart rate and blood pressure, and the pupils in the eyes widen. There is an increase in rates of metabolism and respiration, increase in sugar content of the blood, decrease in electrical resistance of the skin, increase in speed of the blood's ability to clot, and even "goose pimples" resulting from the erection of hairs on the skin.

17.12   How can stress responses have evolutionary value but be maladaptive in today's world?

Fight or Flight Reactions.   These changes are referred to as parts of the automatic **fight or flight reaction,** because they are considered to be the body's emergency reaction system to threat and danger. At an evolutionary level, this automatic reaction pattern reflects an adaptive system developed over the course of the species' history for getting ready to cope with environmental challenges. These biological reactions enable the organism to cope rapidly and effectively with diverse environmental dangers, in part by providing the alertness and energy necessary for survival in the face of attack. This mechanism was crucial for survival in earlier ages in the species' history when physical dangers lurked everywhere.

Activation of this system can save your life when you face a real emergency—for example, when about to be assaulted in a dark alley, or in the midst of a sudden fire.

However, in contemporary life, it is often elicited in response to situations that do not objectively endanger survival. When you face a French examination, or a cadaver you have to dissect in an anatomy class, or walk into the boss's office to ask for a raise, it may feel high risk; but adaptive behavior in dealing with such challenges requires more fine-grain reactions—like thinking and planning—rather than fight or flight. In these situations, automatic hot emotional reactions, particularly intense fears, become debilitating rather than adaptive (e.g., Le Doux, 1996, 2001). And when individuals have these experiences persistently over long periods of time, they can become dangerous to physical health and well-being. The Type A pattern used to illustrate a dispositional typology in Chapter 3 is an example.

In sum, hot reflexive reactions may be part of the overall arousal state that helps initiate quick adaptive action, as in an emergency response to sudden dangers that mobilize the body's resources like a fire alarm. In the course of human evolution they are sure to have had important adaptive advantages for survival. However, this alarm system can make reflection and self-regulation most difficult (Metcalfe & Mischel, 1999).

The Hot Amygdala.   A small almond-shaped region in the forebrain, buried under the prefrontal cortex called the **amygdala** (which means "almond" in Latin), is crucially important in emotional reactions, particularly fear (LeDoux, 1996). The central nucleus of this brain structure reacts almost instantly to signals that warn of danger, immediately sending out behavioral, physiological (autonomic), and endocrine responses. It mobilizes the body for action, readying it to flee or flight. As noted above, presumably this reflexive emergency reaction was useful for adaptation. From an evolutionary perspective, it had survival value to be able to react automatically to the snake in the grass without having to think about it, or to fight the opponent who is ready to strike when flight is not possible. The amygdala also seems to play an important role in strong appetitive behaviors, leading to impulsive approach behaviors, as when the sizzling pizza becomes irresistible to the hungry dieter, or the preschooler can't resist the tempting immediately available treat in the delay experiments.

17.13   What brain areas underlie the hot and cool behavior regulation systems, and how do they interact with one another?

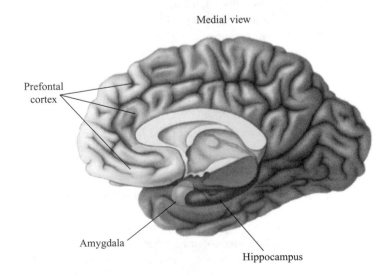

Medial view

Prefontal cortex

Amygdala

Hippocampus

The amygdala is important in fear and emotional reactions.

The Rational Cool Brain. But these automatic reactions are only a "quick fix" that actually doesn't work well for most situations people face in modern life (LeDoux, 1996, p. 176). Unlike lower animals on the evolutionary ladder, human beings have the capacity to take control with higher-level brain centers (the prefrontal cortex). This makes it possible for the person to start cool rational thinking to try to solve the problem that the amygdala has already begun to respond to automatically and emotionally. How you think—hot or cool—can change the attention control centers activated, which in turn makes self-regulatory efforts either more or less difficult (Derryberry, 2002; Posner & Rothbart, 1998). In short, humans have an emotional brain. But they also have other areas of the brain that are crucially important for the more rational higher-level processes that make the species human. While part of the brain is emotional, there also is a thoughtful part that can be rational and used to solve problems effectively. Both areas of the brain interact in dealing with emotion-arousing dilemmas. The Hot System/Cool System Interaction model of self-regulation considered next was designed to understand these interactions.

Biosocial Model of Self-Regulation: Hot System/Cool System Interaction

To understand how the person's thoughts and feelings interact to enable or prevent self-control, a two-system biosocial model of willpower was developed. In this model, self-regulation is a function of a balance between two processing systems: the **emotional, hot system** and the **cognitive, cool system** (Metcalfe & Mischel, 1999). The theory proposes that the emotional, hot system generates automatic approach–avoidance or fight-or-flight responses. Biologically it is based primarily in the amygdala. In contrast, the cognitive cool system, based in the **hippocampus** and frontal lobe, is the locus of cognitive thought processes, generating thoughtful reflective reactions and plans. At relatively low levels of stress, the two systems work in concert, but as stress levels and aversive arousal (e.g., frustration) increase, hot-system processing begins to dominate the cool system. Thus, effective self-regulation hinges on being able to access cooling mechanisms to reduce negative arousal and suppress hot system activation when needed (Metcalfe & Mischel, 1999).

The *cool cognitive system* is specialized for complex mental and spatial representation and thought. It is cognitive, emotionally neutral, contemplative, flexible, integrated, coherent, slow, strategic—the seat of self-regulation and self-control. The *hot system* is specialized for quick emotional processing and automatic responding to "hot" trigger stimuli, as when rejection cues elicit abusive behavior from highly rejection sensitive people. It is quick and automatic, and is the basis of emotionality. It activates fears as well as passions, and it is impulsive and reflexive. This system is fundamental for emotional (classical) conditioning, but its activation undermines efforts at self-control, reflective thought, and planfulness.

The balance between the hot and cool systems is influenced both by stress and by the person's level of development. Stress—both chronic and situational—enhances the hot system and reduces activity in the cool system. With maturation beginning at about age 4 years, the cool system becomes more developed and active, and the hot system becomes more manageable (see In Focus 17.2 for discussion of the brain mechanisms involved as maturation normally occurs).

Attention Control. How does all this translate into what people have to do for effective goal pursuit and resistance to temptations when dealing with the kinds

IN FOCUS 17.2

NEURAL MECHANISMS IN IMPULSIVE VIOLENCE

Recent advances in brain imaging technology have allowed researchers to understand how impulsive "hot" behavioral tendencies, seen for example in outbursts of violence and impulsive aggression, play out in underlying neural processes at the brain level of analysis. Among the many scientists that are active in this area of research, University of Wisconsin psychologist Richard Davidson and his colleagues have been pinpointing specific patterns of brain activation that underlie the self-regulation of impulsive behavior (Davidson et al., 2000).

Drawing on both animal and human brain research, Davidson and his colleagues have found that emotion is normally regulated in the human brain by a complex circuit of brain structures involving several interconnected regions. Brain imaging studies suggest that in a typical sequence of events, threatening behaviors (staring eyes, shouting, etc.) are conveyed to the amygdala, which then sends information to other higher regions of the brain that are responsible for initiating behavioral reactions.

In normal people, however, this pattern of events (threatening stimuli → amygdala activation → response) does not always lead to impulsive emotional responses. A number of prefrontal brain regions connect to the amygdala and interact to constrain the impulsive expression of emotional behavior. These connections provide people with the ability to self-regulate their emotional responses. It is the prefrontal brain regions that seem to constitute the core structures underlying the process of emotion regulation and are thus essential for achieving emotional restraint at the biological level. Consequently, functional or structural abnormalities in one or more of these regions, or in the interconnections among them, are believed to increase people's impulsive tendencies. Indeed, Davidson and his colleagues' research suggest that individuals who are predisposed to aggression and violence many suffer from an abnormality in this prefrontal circuitry.

---

of dilemmas discussed throughout this chapter? Extrapolating from the delay of gratification research and other studies on self-regulation (Mischel et al., 1996; Derryberry, 2002), effective self-regulation requires guiding the automatic hot emotional responses. When the person thinks of the rewards that can be obtained right away in a "hot" way, they become irresistible. But through mental transformations and strategic self-distractions, one can effectively continue to delay by "cooling" the hot pull of the immediate gratifications (Mischel et al., 1989). In Martha's case, she is struggling to reduce the aversive arousal created in the dissection situation, and to control herself from automatically dashing out of the room. For that goal, she has to shift attention away from her distressing feelings and focus instead on the complex technical details of the brain structures to prevent her from messing up her dissection.

Cool cognitions focused on the technical details of the procedures allow her to regulate her feelings adaptively, and shift them away from her distress and empathy with a dead human on to the medical task that needs doing. But that can change in a millisecond if suddenly something in the face reminds her that it looks a little like her father when he died.

When people manage to cool their impulsive hot reactions by attention control, they can make use of the vast cognitive resources that give humans their evolutionary advantage (Metcalfe & Jacobs, 1998; Metcalfe & Mischel, 1999). In other words, the trick is to think cool when your impulse is to act hot, and reduce hot ideation so that automatic hot responses are not made. Then problems can be dealt with more rationally, allowing long-term goals to be pursued effectively even in the face of strong momentary temptations to forget them. The ability to use attention control effectively in this manner is related closely to mechanisms that are activated in the brain. The first

17.14 How can voluntary attentional control guide hot and cool systems in an adaptive fashion?

chapter of this text described the case of Charles Whitman, the Texas Tower killer who suddenly massacred people on the college campus below him. Many years later it now is becoming possible to understand what may go wrong in such cases at the biological level, as discussed in In Focus 17.2.

Social Emotions Enable Self-Regulation: Links to Evolution

17.15 Why are social emotions an important evolutionary mechanism for human life? What is their relation to Freud's superego?

The discussion so far might easily create the impression that self-regulation always requires cooling one's emotions so that rational, problem-focused thinking can proceed effectively. In fact, it all depends on which emotions are involved. There are many social emotions that activate feelings like loyalty to the group or a partner. Such emotions can support self-regulation by calling attention to the long-term consequences of behaving, for example, in selfish or disloyal ways. Observations of life in diverse cultures throughout the world lead anthropologists and other social scientists to that conclusion as well (e.g., Fiske, 2002; Nesse, 2001). Their analysis again draws on evolutionary theory.

For example, the anthropologist-psychologist Alan Fiske (2002) proposes that from an evolutionary perspective, certain emotions have developed and are universally experienced because they are useful for self-regulation and make social life and long-term relationships possible in human society everywhere. The emotions that are experienced, however, also are shaped by the local demands and structures of the particular culture. Fiske argues that people need to have emotions that represent their important relationships, reflected in such feelings as empathy, affection, and loyalty.

Further, because humans are naturally impulsive and self-serving creatures driven to immediate gratification, they need to experience these essentially social and moral emotions, including guilt and shame, that allow them to take account of the long-term consequences of their actions. Such emotions help people to curb their appetites and prevent themselves from acting in impulsive, relationship-destructive and community-destructive ways. They are experienced as quick internal signals that help activate rapidly the self-control necessary for cooperation, for resisting temptation, and for maintaining duties and obligations. In short, this evolutionary and anthropological view casts what Freud called the superego in a new light. It sees the social-moral emotions as reflecting adaptive evolutionary processes. The basic point is that humans have intense social and moral emotions because they motivate them to "curb their non-social appetites in the interest of the relationships that are so crucial to their survival, reproduction, and welfare" (Fiske, 2002, pp. 173–174). These ideas are still in need of much research before they allow for firm conclusions. However, they help make clear that self-regulation reflects a basic human process shaped by a wide range of interacting influences, and is central for understanding the nature of personality.

▶ SELF-REGULATORY COMPETENCE

So far, we examined the processes that make self-regulation possible and that underlie individual differences in this ability. Much research also documents that self-regulatory competence is a person variable that has substantial stability and significantly predicts many aspect of the person's future.

A Stable Person Variable

Long-Term Stability of Self-Regulatory Competence. Self-regulatory competence as assessed in the delay of gratification paradigm in early childhood turns out to be a reliable index of a stable competence basic for many aspects of personality. First of all, it predicts important outcomes in development, adolescence, and adulthood. Studies with children tested in preschool showed that the number of seconds the child was able to delay gratification as a preschooler predicted positive social and cognitive outcomes many years later, including in adulthood.

To illustrate, those who waited longer in this situation as preschoolers were described by their parents as more socially and cognitively competent teenagers. They were perceived as more able to manage stress and exert effective self-control in diverse frustrating situations in adolescence (Mischel et al., 1989). They also had substantially higher SAT scores than the children who could not wait (Shoda et al., 1990). In a follow-up conducted when these individuals reached their early thirties, correlations remained significant between their preschool delay behavior and adult-relevant measures of social-cognitive competence, goal-setting, planning, and self-regulatory abilities (Ayduk et al., 2000).

Long-Term Protective Effects. More exciting than these kinds of predictions is the finding that this type of self-regulatory competence can have significant long-term protective effects. Self-regulatory competence helps to protect people from experiencing many of the negative consequences associated with their dispositional vulnerabilities. Consider, for example, the tendency to be highly rejection sensitive (RS) in interpersonal relationships. Often, highly rejection sensitive people in time develop lower self-esteem and become either more aggressive or more depressed which, in turn, undermines the quality of their lives. But that is not necessarily their fate. In an adult follow-up of the preschoolers who had participated in the original delay of gratification studies 20 years earlier, preschool delay ability predicted adult resiliency against the potentially destructive effects of RS (Ayduk et al., 2000, Study 1). Specifically, high RS people who were able to delay gratification longer in preschool were buffered in adulthood against low self-esteem and self-worth, were better able to cope with stress, and had greater ego resiliency. High RS people who were unable to delay gratification in preschool had lower academic achievement and more frequent cocaine/crack use than low RS people. As Fig. 17.1 shows, high RS people who had high preschool delay ability were buffered against such negative outcomes.

A parallel study, conducted among low-income, urban, minority middle-school children who are at higher demographic risk for maladjustment, replicated these findings with population-appropriate measures (Ayduk et al., 2000, Study 2). Again, among children high in RS, delay of gratification ability was associated with lower aggression against peers, greater interpersonal acceptance, and higher levels of self-worth.

Individual differences in attention control are visible already in the behavior of toddlers, and they predict self-regulatory competencies years later in development. In one study, mother–toddler interactions were observed as they unfolded at 19 months of age (Sethi and colleagues, 2000). Some toddlers used effective attention deployment strategies, such as self-distraction, to cope with and "cool" distress while briefly separated from their mothers in a playroom experiment. These tended to become the preschoolers who also significantly used more effective attention strategies to help themselves to delay gratification when tested in preschool 3 1/2 years later. When they were toddlers, they had actively directed attention away from the mother's absence, distracting themselves by exploring the room and playing with toys. In contrast, other toddlers were unable to activate such cooling strategies at 19 months. Instead, they stayed focused on the absence of the mother (e.g., clinging to the door) and became distressed. These tended to be the youngsters who also were less able to effectively

17.16 What is the evidence that self-regulatory competence is a stable personality factor that aids adjustment?

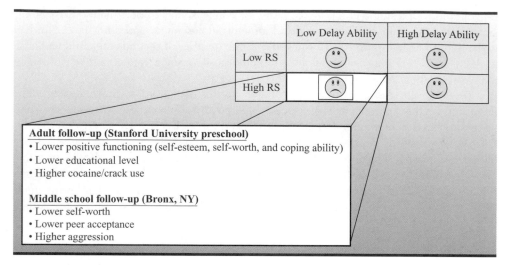

Figure 17.4 Chronic vulnerability (rejection sensitivity) is linked to negative outcomes (☹)
when delay ability is low.

Note: Smiley faces ☺ show positive outcomes, frowning faces ☹ , negative outcomes. High delay ability
protected even high rejection sensitive people from the negative outcomes experienced by equally rejection
sensitive people who also were low in delay ability. Only the combination of High RS, Low Delay predicted
significantly negative life outcomes.

Source: Based on studies in Ayduk, O., Mendoza-Denton, R., Mischel, W., Downey, G., Peake, P. K., &
Rodriguez, M. (2000). Regulating the interpersonal self: Strategic self-regulation for coping with rejection
sensitivity. *Journal of Personality and Social Psychology, 79,* 776–792.

self-distract during preschool delay and were unable to wait to get the bigger treat that
they wanted.

In short, individual differences in the use of effective attention strategies for
reducing stress and making self-regulation easier are seen early in life and seem to
endure. Stable individual differences in attention processes such as eye-gaze aversion,
flexible attention shifting and focusing, also have been documented as early as in
infancy. Further, effective attention control is related to having lower impulsivity and
less negative affect later in life, as seen both in children and in adults (Derryberry,
2002; Derryberry & Rothbart, 1997). Thus, attention control is part of a generalized
self-regulatory competency that enables effective cooling of arousal and self-control of
impulsive behaviors. These skills have adaptive long-term benefits and can protect
against dispositional vulnerabilities.

17.17 In what ways can
excessive self-control be
maladaptive?

The Down-Side of Self-Regulation. On the one hand, cooling operations and
effortful attention control seem to have significant value for the adaptive pursuit of life
goals and effective functioning over time. On the other hand, these competencies may
come with a cost, making some of these "high delay" individuals susceptible to other
kinds of difficulties such as tendencies to become avoidant and withdrawn (Eisenberg
et al., 2002). Likewise, whether or not one *should* or *should not* delay gratification or
"exercise the will" in any particular choice is often everything but self-evident. Lionel
Trilling, a distinguished humanist with much to say about psychology, captured the
risks of too much self-control in a few words. After reminding us of the place of
passion, he said "the will is not everything," and spoke of the "panic and emptiness
which make their onset when the will is tired from its own excess" (Trilling, 1943,

p. 139). An excess of will can certainly be as self-defeating as its absence. Postponing gratification can be an unwise—and even stifling—joyless choice. But unless people develop the competencies to sustain delay and continue to exercise their will when they want and need to do so, the choice itself is lost.

For a clinical description of Gary W's Self-Regulatory System, see In Focus 17.3. It illustrates the multiple factors that influence the self-regulatory system, and the complex ways it plays out in the life of an individual, sometimes in self-defeating ways that undermine attainment of the most important goals.

Conclusions

Putting it together, "willpower" requires a combination of self-regulatory competencies and regulatory motivation: both desire (goals and motivations) and regulatory competencies (e.g., flexible attention deployment strategies) are needed. Both are necessary if one is to go from good but difficult intentions to their realization under frustrating, temptation-filled conditions. Even when regulatory competency is available, it will not be activated in the absence of regulatory motivation. Case studies and dramatic examples abound of individuals, including a recent U.S. president who exerted remarkable self-regulation in many areas of life—but did not do so in other areas, although the consequences were destructive. Presumably these individuals had the ability to control themselves but not sufficient motivation. Conversely, regulatory motivation is unlikely to sustain difficult long-term goal pursuit unless regulatory competency is available and accessible to smooth the journey.

17.18 How does the social cognitive conception differ from the notion of willpower as an internal force that people either have or don't have?

The ingredients of willpower and particularly the processing dynamics that enable regulatory competence have long been mysterious, but some of the essentials now seem clear. Individual differences in self-regulatory ability are visible early in life, and a good deal is also known about the basic attention control mechanisms that enable it. These mechanisms help to demystify willpower and identify some of its key ingredients. Attention control is important in dealing both with fear and with the regulation of appetitive-approach behaviors. The implications of regulatory ability for the self are straightforward. This ability influences self-concepts and self-esteem, interpersonal strategies (e.g., aggression), coping, and the ability to buffer or protect the self against the maladaptive consequences of chronic personal vulnerabilities such as rejection sensitivity.

Potential for Self-Directed Change. Perhaps the most important question remains: can self-regulation be taught to empower the self and improve resilience? We do know that attention control strategies can be briefly modified in experiments (Ayduk, Mischel, & Downey, 2002; Mischel et al., 1989). Moreover, when effective control strategies are modeled, they may be readily adopted and generalize to self-control behavior outside the lab for at least a few months (Bandura & Mischel, 1965). What is not yet known is whether effective attention control to reduce stress and frustration during goal pursuit can be increased long-term via socialization, education, and therapy.

This chapter opened with Martha asking herself what can she do to overcome the stress she experiences when faced with tasks like her first dissection of a human cadaver, and we have tried to address her question. In a case like Martha's, it would not be surprising if on her own she began to more readily access the same self-regulatory competencies that allowed her to progress to this point in her impressive academic career. One can imagine her learning spontaneously to desensitize herself to the aversive emotions in the situation. With more exposure gradually she can detach herself

IN FOCUS 17.3

GARY W'S SELF-REGULATORY SYSTEM

Although Gary is strongly motivated by concerns about how other people—particularly romantic partners—will see him and treat him, he does not seem to acknowledge approval or praise from others. He undermines his own hopes and potential with a pessimistic explanatory style. Privately, he tends to dismiss and trivialize his successes and magnify his perceived shortcomings, on which he focuses much of his attention, ruminating about them obsessively. But he can also flip and present a glowing picture of his abilities in his self-presentation in social situations.

At work or in school, he drives himself harshly. He holds himself to rigid goals for perfectionist performance, setting standards so high they virtually guarantee self-perceived failure. He then criticizes himself severely and ruminates about his shortcomings, depressing himself with his own thoughts. A notable exception to this pattern of stringent self-evaluation is in the domain of aggressive behavior. When he feels highly frustrated and stressed (which is not infrequent), he becomes capable of angry outbursts of temper and rage, particularly in his relations with his current girlfriend. Sometimes this also happens when he is frustrated in work situations with people he sees as less competent, especially when they are his seniors in authority. His hot emotional outbursts undermine his relationships and reflect his poor self-regulatory "cooling" skills for dealing effectively with impulsive angry reactions.

Gary lacks understanding of how his behavior undermines his ability to achieve the caring interpersonal relations he desires. He seems especially immature and vulnerable in this domain and flounders between bursts of anger and a sense of uncontrolled helplessness. He feels unable to influence his relationship or himself in directions that allow effective communication with a partner, a feeling that only furthers his frustration and anger and erodes his relationships.

Gary has excellent academic and cognitive skills. However, there is an obvious and urgent need to assess his social, interpersonal, and self-regulatory competencies, as well as his personal theories about relationships and himself. Many of his problems may reflect disadvantageous styles of interpreting and explaining his experiences. He also lacks interpersonal skills. He would benefit from role-play and practice with alternative ways of construing and solving conflicts when he feels threatened. Although he has self-regulatory competencies, as evident in his schoolwork and achievements, he has to learn to access those skills when he becomes too "hot" and frustrated to cope rationally in interpersonal situations.

Self-improvement efforts for Gary need to be directed at identifying and controlling social and internal cues that signal eruptions of his anger. The focus should be on ways in which he can more effectively regulate those emotions, and overcome the anger and hostility that jeopardize relationships he cares about most. He needs to develop less rigid and obsessive control patterns for coping with anxiety, particularly in public speaking contexts. At the same time, Gary needs to reexamine and rethink his interpersonal assumptions and personal theories. It will be especially important for him to probe alternative ways of construing criticism in order to find more effective ways of coping.

Thus, Gary needs to identify the interpersonal situations in which he feels provoked. He then can explore how his perceptions of rejection in those situations make him vulnerable to eruptions and automatic reactions that ultimately destroy the relations and intimacy that he is trying to build. Likewise he can be helped to see the consequences of his assumptions and habitual reactions in his close relations with women. Alternative ways of thinking likely to generate better outcomes then can be explored and practiced (Meichenbaum, 1995).

After recognizing and understanding the situations he finds most provoking and in which he feels violated, he then can try to reframe them in alternative, more constructive ways that make them less threatening and/or modify his own reactions to them. For example, by understanding the interpersonal situations in which he feels especially vulnerable he can reappraise them and activate his own self-regulatory controls. He can then begin to respond with appropriate assertiveness rather than with massive anxiety or uncontrolled rage. He also can learn to communicate more effectively about his feelings and needs. Developing more adaptive ways of thinking constructively about his relationships can make it easier to stop being destructive with the women he cares about and allow him to get what he wants more effectively.

17.19   How do self-regulation principles help us understand Gary W's adaptive skills and his problems in living?

and begin to cool her anxieties about anatomy, concentrating on the details of the dissecting method and the anatomical structures. In time, one can see her working carefully and patiently with great concentration. She begins to use some self-calming cooling strategies whenever anxiety begins to set in, and is sensitive enough to the cues of their onset to rapidly refocus her attention on where it will serve her best.

In fact, the person on whom the example of Martha is based did well in medical training, excelled working with oncology patients suffering from advanced cancers, and went on to become an expert in pathology, specializing in the diagnosis of brain tumors. This physician is still far from immune or insensitive to the many anxieties that are part of the daily routine, making potential life and death decisions based on reading the slides of brain tissues rushed to the pathology lab from patients still in the midst of surgery, and winning the admiration of colleagues and grateful patients. With intense focus on the many things that can go wrong in the diagnosis, "Martha" carefully scans the slides and tries hard to prevent most of them from happening.

SUMMARY

SELF-REGULATORY PROCESSES

- Approach or appetitive dilemmas occur when facing a strong approach temptation that interferes with one's more important, higher-order goal. Avoidance or aversive dilemmas occur when one is tempted to flee a situation that will ultimately help one to attain a high-order goal.

- Effective self-regulatory behavior and self-control in goal pursuit depends both on motivation and on regulatory competencies. The latter require cognitive and attention control mechanisms that help execute goal-directed behavior.

- Ego control refers to individual differences in the degree of impulse control in such functions as inhibition of impulses.

- Ego resilience is a construct that refers to the individual's stable ability to adapt flexibly to environmental demands by appropriately modifying his or her habitual level of ego control.

EMOTION REGULATION IN APPROACH (APPETITIVE) DILEMMAS

- The ability to voluntarily delay immediate gratification is at the core of most concepts of willpower and ego resilience.

- Successful delay of gratification in goal pursuit involves the ability to prevent oneself from focusing attention on the frustrating, emotion-arousing aspects of difficult situations, and instead strategically shifting attention elsewhere.

EMOTIONAL REGULATION IN AVOIDANCE (AVERSIVE) DILEMMAS

- To cope with aversive situations, individuals who practice cognitive reappraisal (cognitive "cooling" strategies) experience less negative feelings and physiological arousal than individuals who try to suppress their feelings.

- It also helps to cognitively transform or redefine stressful situations in more positive ways.

INTERACTION AMONG LEVELS: HOT AND COOL SYSTEMS IN SELF-REGULATION

- The emotional, hot system, centered in the amygdala, underlies automatic approach–avoidance or fight-or-flight responses.

- The cognitive, cool processing system, based in higher brain centers, particularly the prefrontal cortex, enables thoughtful, reflective thinking and planning.

- Anxious and self-preoccupied thoughts compete and interfere with task-relevant thoughts and undermine effective self-regulation.
- The balance between the hot and cool systems is influenced both by stress and by the individual's level of development. To effectively self-regulate, the individual must prevent or postpone automatic, hot, emotional, impulsive responses and activate cooling strategies by shifting attention and cognitions away from the hot features of the reward or the frustrating features of the conflict.
- "Hot," automatic responses are necessary in some situations. For example, strong social emotions can help people to resist temptation and avoid shirking responsibilities.

SELF-REGULATORY COMPETENCE

- The attention control mechanisms that underlie delay of gratification can help shield individuals against the negative consequences of their chronic personal vulnerabilities.
- Although always postponing gratification creates problems, unless people develop the competencies to delay when they want and need to do so, they lose the choice itself.

KEY TERMS

amygdala 407
approach (appetitive) dilemma 394
avoidance (aversive) dilemma 394
cognitive cool system 408
cognitive reappraisal 405
discriminative facility 403

effortful control 395
ego control 397
ego resilience 398
emotional hot system 408
executive functions 395
fight or flight reaction 406

hippocampus 408
overcontrolling children 398
regulatory competencies 395
suppression 405
undercontrolling children 398

18

PERSONALITY IN ITS CONTEXT AND CULTURE

This chapter gives a broader perspective on the person in his or her context and culture, integrating findings from all levels of analysis. First, we sketch a picture of personality as a whole. Then, we will look at the major influences that affect the diverse aspects of personality and that interact in the functioning person.

▶ PERSONALITY SYSTEM IN ACTION

An integrative view that draws on all the levels of analysis sees personality as having many diverse aspects: cultural, social, psychological, and biological. This section provides an overview of these aspects and how they interact in everyday experience. A simple representation of these diverse aspects and their interactions is given in Figure 18.1 that shows the personality system in its context at one moment in time for a given person. To make the example specific, keep what has been learned about Gary in mind.

Personality Dispositions and Dynamics

Figure 18.1 provides a glimpse of the multiple processes and interactions operating in the personality system. This system contains a host of dispositions, internal characteristics, and person variables that have been identified and studied by researchers working at all levels of analysis. You saw these throughout the text, and they were applied concretely to the case of Gary in many earlier chapters. They include his biological dispositions (e.g., BIS/BAS), psychological traits, appraisals, expectancies, self-concepts, goals, self-protective defenses, and self-regulatory processes.

An example of such a personality system and its internal processing dynamics was illustrated in the CAPS model in Chapter 12. Although discussed at the social cognitive level of analysis, this type of model is not specific to that level. Instead, it is a more general framework for examining personality processes and the personality system in ways that build on contributions from all the levels.

18.1 What two assumptions are made about individual differences in the personality system?

The main point here is that in current views of the personality system, two assumptions are commonly made about individual differences (e.g., Cervone & Shoda, 1999). The first is that people differ in the ease of accessibility of different mental representations. For example, we know that for Gary, anxious expectations of rejection are easily accessible, that is, they are readily activated in many situations.

The second assumption is that the personality system has a coherent organization of interconnections—essentially a coherent but complex network of associations—among the mental and emotional representations within it. Thus, the dispositional tendencies, expectations, goals, affects, and so on that are accessible become activated in a predictable set of interconnections, and these make up the "personality dynamics." These dynamics are activated under specific conditions, and then play out, for example,

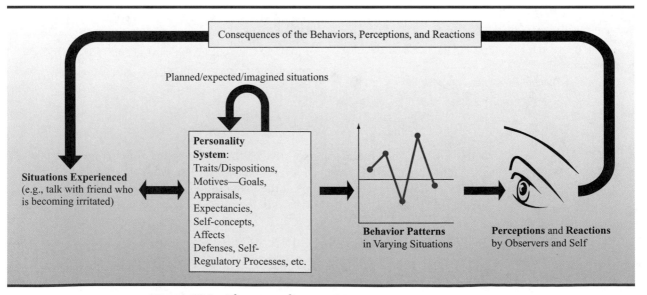

Figure 18.1 The personality system in context.

in the form of Gary's distinctive cognitive and emotional processes and the behavior patterns that they generate.

Sources of System Activation

The personality system is in a continuous state of activation, and the activations come from two sources. One source is external activation that comes from the situations encountered at a given moment in time, for example, the conversation Gary is having with his friend in which the friend is becoming irritated. The **active ingredients** are the features of those situations to which Gary is particularly attuned, such as potential rejection cues in an interpersonal context—in this case, the signs of the friend's irritation. These are the features for which Gary scans attentively and to which his personality system reacts distinctively and characteristically in stable patterns, that is, in terms of his personality dynamics. The two-way arrow from the situations to his personality system indicates that the two are in **reciprocal interaction,** each influencing the other. Gary's personality system selects and focuses on those active ingredients in the situations experienced, and it is also influenced by them, for example, leading him to an outburst of temper. This was illustrated earlier in the text in the discussion of Gary's rejection sensitivity dynamics.

The second source is internal activation, in the form of Gary's own thoughts and feelings and plans, for example, as he ruminates about himself and his relationships or thinks and plans what to do tomorrow. These internal experiences and anticipations impact the events that are encountered or generated next. Thus, as the last two chapters showed, the personality system is not merely reactive: it is also *proactive,* that is, future-oriented, as seen in the active pursuit of life goals.

18.2 What two classes of stimuli activate the personality system? What role does the system play in such activation?

Expressions of the System—and Their Consequences

At the behavioral level, the behaviors Gary generates are represented in the figure as an *if . . . then . . .* profile or behavioral signature to indicate that they occur in particular distinctive situations (e.g., his temper outbursts occur *if* rejection is perceived) and play out over time in stable ways. This profile also has an overall level in terms of the total amount of the characteristic behavior (e.g., hostility, temper-anger) he tends to display on average (see Chapter 4 to review those distinctions).

Gary's behaviors influence the situations he encounters in the future. The eye that is seeing his behavior in Figure 18.1 indicates that what he does is also observed and experienced by perceivers. One of these perceivers is Gary himself: we not only generate behavior, we also perceive and interpret it. Obviously, how he sees and interprets his outburst may be quite different from how others, for example, his partner, will view it and in turn react. Those perceptions affect what happens next by changing how the people who observe Gary respond to his behavior. This is indicated in the figure by the large curved arrow that shows those perceptions and their behavioral consequences influencing the subsequent situations that Gary is likely to experience. Over the course of time, the characteristics of the personality system change the stable psychological environment the individual tends to experience. Thus, people not only impose their own meanings on situations, but through their own behavior, they also select and create many of the situations they experience (e.g., Buss, 1996; Kenrick & Funder, 1988; Swann, 1983).

Gary's case illustrates this process of how one can shape one's own situations. Because he dreads social-evaluative situations, he avoids them whenever he can, preferring to isolate himself. This further strengthens his inclination to withdraw and be "a loner" and isolates him even more. A side effect is that he never learns to

18.3 As typified by Gary W., how do behavioral signatures influence the situations one encounters?

confront and cope more effectively with the social encounters he fears most. This is painfully evident in public speaking situations that he simply cannot avoid, and in which he easily panics, especially when he feels himself being evaluated by respected male peers in business contexts. His panic response further elicits the disrespect and "snickers" of his peers, thereby intensifying his dread and avoidance pattern in a vicious cycle.

Gary's preference for isolation and withdrawal has by now become a well-established pattern. He even announces to acquaintances that he prefers his own company to meeting other people, which they perceive as a rejection by him or an expression of aloofness. Then they reciprocate by avoiding him, which further isolates him even more and fuels his sense of alienation and distrust. In this way, personality variables influence the choice of the types of situations to which people expose themselves (e.g., Bolger & Schilling, 1991; Buss, 1987). For example, individuals who cooperate tend to elicit reciprocal cooperation from their partners on a task, which in turn confirms and strengthens their choice of a cooperative rather than a competitive strategy (Kelley & Stahelski, 1970).

The analysis of complex social interactions shows how each of us continuously selects, changes, and generates conditions just as much as we are affected by them (e.g., Patterson, 1976, 1990). In classic studies, husband–wife interactions were observed as the couples coped with such conflicts as how to celebrate their first wedding anniversary when each had made different plans (Raush et al., 1974). For example, Bob has arranged and paid in advance for dinner at a restaurant, but Sue has spent half the day preparing for a special dinner at home. As the couple realize their conflict and try to resolve it, their interactions continuously reveal that each antecedent act (what Sue has just said to Bob) constrains each consequent act (how Bob responds).

The interpersonal strategy in such interactions depends both on the type of person and the type of situation. For example, in the context of getting along with a peer, a more dependent person is likely to use a self-denigrating strategy. On the other hand, when the situation focuses on pleasing an authority, the dependent person is apt to use a self-promoting strategy (Bornstein et al., 1996). Once more, we see the effects of person × situation interactions.

▶ INTERACTING INFLUENCES OF BIOLOGY AND CULTURE

Where does personality come from? What shapes the various aspects of personality outlined above? What influences the accessibility of various thoughts and feelings, and the network of connections among them? What influences how an individual's behavior is seen by others? Throughout this text, each level of analysis added partial answers to these questions, and it is time now to look at the whole picture that emerges.

The individual's personality system develops from a foundation that is both biochemical and psychosocial; it is guided by the genes in interaction with the environment, as well as reflecting the influence of social learning, and the culture. As indicated in Figure 18.2, these processes interact in the course of development, influencing such person variables as how the person construes—and shapes—the situations encountered (Mischel & Shoda, 1998; Saudino & Plomin, 1996).

Interacting Influences on Personality Development

In the life of each person, biological and social-environmental-cultural influences interact in the development of the personality system, as was discussed in the interplay of genes and social influences (Chapter 14). If individuals are genetically and temperamentally disposed toward greater aggressiveness, for example, they soon become more likely to

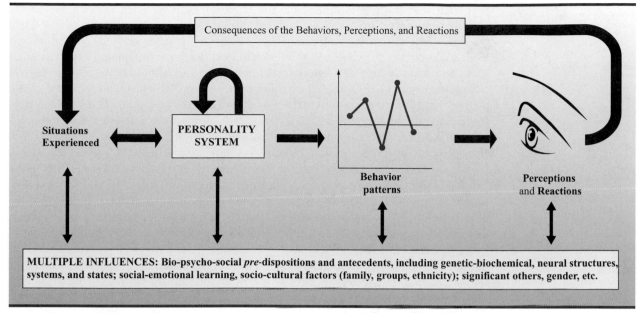

Figure 18.2 Influences on the personality system.

interpret the motives of other people as aggressive and to anticipate aggression from others (Dodge, 1986). They also may confirm these expectations and beliefs by behaving more aggressively, thereby evoking more aggressive reactions. Likewise, as aggressiveness becomes an established pattern, it also may be incorporated into the values and self-standards and goals of the individual. Each time the aggressive pattern is activated, it becomes more easily accessible in the system as a dominant response tendency, triggered even by minor frustrations and stress. Increasingly the person also may seek out peers and groups likely to further support this type of behavior and to strengthen it as a source both for self-esteem and peer approval. A common example is when aggressively inclined adolescents are drawn to like-minded peers in aggressive groups and gangs that then collectively and mutually further support their aggressive tendencies (e.g., Bandura & Walters, 1959).

In sum, as the example suggests, the early behavioral tendencies in the person interact with the psychological environment over the course of time as personality develops and becomes expressed in relatively stable ways (e.g., Contrada, Leventhal, & O'Leary, 1990). The above example shows how a dispositional tendency like aggression may be reinforced early in life by the social environment and then becomes well established. But your dispositional tendencies are not necessarily determinants of your fate in life. For example, the studies described next show that socialization experiences can help infants who are temperamentally shy to develop into people who are not shy: because social experiences can modify temperament, biology does not have to be destiny (Schmidt & Fox, 2002).

Biology-Trait-Socialization Interactions: Shyness

Shyness is a problem that plagues many people. Researchers have been examining how shyness as a trait in children and young adults manifests itself, and how biological and social factors might jointly influence what happens ultimately to the development of temperamentally shy young children (Schmidt & Fox, 2002; Schmidt & Fox, 1999). Their question was: Must the temperamentally shy infant and young child become a shy person in the course of development?

18.4   How has research on shyness illuminated biological–environmental interactions in personality development?

Their first goal was to understand the biological basis for childhood shyness and to identify features that may predict childhood shyness in infancy. Initial studies showed that when new stimuli were presented to infants, a distressed reaction was indicative of shyness likely to develop in preschool and in later childhood (Kagan & Snidman, 1991). To understand how and why this correlation existed, researchers monitored brain activity via electroencephalograph (EEG) during exposure to new stimuli. Infants who exhibited a high degree of stress during exposure to the new stimuli also showed more activity in their right frontal lobe during exposure and in a resting state. Infants who exhibited little to no distress at the presentation of new stimuli showed more activity in their left frontal lobe (Davidson & Fox, 1989; Fox et al., 1992). This same kind of pattern of brain activity was seen in shy and nonshy preschool age children, respectively (Fox and associates, 1996).

In a follow-up, researchers tried to understand why some of the infants who displayed distress in the first study and thus were temperamentally disposed toward shyness did not develop shyness as older children. The answer, in part, is in their specific socialization experiences. Many of the children who did not develop childhood shyness had less overprotective mothers and/or had been placed in social situations (such as daycare) more often (Fox and associates, 2001). The researchers concluded that initial temperamental tendencies toward shyness in childhood can be modified and may be overcome by parenting practices and social experiences.

Furthermore, shyness, like many broad dispositions such as neuroticism, comes in different forms and types. Studies with college students as well as with children suggest that shyness and sociability are not part of a single dimension (Schmidt & Fox, 2002). They are distinguishable on measures of electrical activity in the cortex as well as on indices such as EEG, and heart rate measured both when at rest and when experiencing a social stressor. So the individual who is highly shy but also highly sociable will be characterized by both biological and psychological-behavioral features that are quite different from an equally shy person who is low on the sociability dimension. Again it is the interaction of multiple variables and processes that determine how temperament plays out in personality development.

▶ GENDER AND SEX DIFFERENCES

18.5 Differentiate between sex and gender.

Established at birth, biological sex soon begins to direct much of one's psychological and social development. It influences self-concepts and identity, as well as goals and values, and continues to have a dominant influence throughout life.

Gender is a concept that refers to the social meaning of being a male or a female. Almost universally, gender is one of the most powerful determinants of how people view themselves and how other people treat them. Gender is probably one of the most important psychological categorizations that people are subjected to, and one that has become increasingly controversial. The controversy is based on many challenges to conventional, rigid **gender stereotypes** about what it means to be a man or a woman within a particular culture or society (e.g., Deaux & Major, 1987).

Overview and Issues

18.6 What behavioral sex differences exist in infants?

Neonatal Sex Differences. Some researchers have concentrated on sex differences in newborns (neonates) in order to study possible innate sex differences before socialization practices exert their huge effects. Human neonatal behavior indicates some sex differences in activity level and in reactivity to a variety of stimuli. For example, sex differences occur in infants' responses to facial stimuli during the first year of life (Lewis, 1969, 1990). Girls vocalized and smiled more and showed greater differential expression to the facial stimuli, although boys looked longer. At age two to three months, girls are more sensitive to skin exposure than boys (Wolff, 1966). Newborn females seem to react more to the removal of a covering blanket, and show lower thresholds to air-jet stimulation of the abdomen (Bell & Costello, 1964). Newborn boys raise their heads higher than newborn girls do (Bell & Darling, 1965), and there are also sex differences in infant play behavior (Goldberg & Lewis, 1969). The interpretation sometimes drawn from these early sex differences in response to stimulation is that they are innate. But as in other domains of personality, nature and nurture—heredity and environment—tend to be deeply and often inextricably entwined.

Gender Concepts. **Gender concepts**—beliefs about the types of behavior more appropriate for one sex than for the other—are widely shared within a particular culture and to some extent across cultures (D'Andrade, 1966). Individuals differ in the sanctioned sex-role standards that they adopt or reject. Some modern western cultures or subcultures have been shifting toward greater flexibility in the range that tends to be explored by individuals and tolerated by others, although signs in opposite directions also can be seen in other cultures throughout the world. The concept of **sex role identity** refers to the "degree to which an individual regards himself as masculine or feminine" (Kagan, 1964, p. 144). The degree of match or mismatch between the sex-role standards of the culture and the individuals' assessment of his or her own attributes can have far-reaching implications on the personality that each develops and the social world in which he or she functions.

Expression of Gender-Relevant Behavior. As Deaux and Major (1987) note, sex and gender are constructs that deeply influence social relations. Gender-linked behaviors are expressed by males and females often at automatic levels and play out as almost reflexive scripts. Both sexes respond to the gender-relevant cues in their social interactions in ways that activate their conceptions about themselves as males and females. These gender-relevant conceptions include a host of expectations and values that guide the behavior they think appropriate to the context (see In Focus 18.1).

As an example of the influence of gender roles in the automatic processing of social information, consider a study conducted by Sadalla, Kenrick, and Vershure (1987). Students were asked to watch films of men in high or low dominance conditions. To create a condition of low dominance, an actor engaged in conversation with another male, repeatedly nodding his head, looking down often, and speaking little. To establish the reverse condition, the actor was more relaxed, nodded less, and made more assertive gestures. Students of both sexes rated those in the higher-dominance condition as more attractive. When shown films of women in similar conditions, however, no relationship was found. Thus the person's sex determined whether assertiveness-dominance led to perceived attractiveness—behaviors that made the male more attractive did not increase the perceived attractiveness of the female in this situation. Results like these lead many researchers to the conclusion that gender "is something we enact . . . a pattern of social organization that structures the relations, especially the power relations, between women and men" (Riger, 1992, p. 737).

Interactions of Biology, Sex, and Culture in Response to Threat

When thinking about the influence of biological and social-cultural influences on personality, it is easy to fall into "either–or" ways of casting the question, and to want to know, "bottom line, which one is more important?" We saw this clearly in the discussion of the

IN FOCUS 18.1

ADULT SEX DIFFERENCES AND THEIR IMPLICATIONS

For half a century, the nature and extent of sex differences in personality have been topics of extensive research and passionate debates (e.g., Gilligan, 1982; Maccoby & Jacklin, 1974; Mischel & Mischel, 1973). In adults, a variety of sex differences have been reported over the years. For example, the physical fight response to stress and threat shows higher levels for males than for females in humans, primates, and rats (e.g. Archer, 1990; Eagly & Steffen, 1986). Distinct sex differences also are reported in nonverbal behavior, such as facial expressiveness and body expressiveness (reviewed by Eagly, 1987) and greater rough and tumble play and physical aggressive tendencies in boys than girls (Collaer & Hines, 1995). Possible sex differences also have been found in some aspects of cognitive functioning but taken as a whole, the largest differences, unsurprisingly, have been shown for physical abilities (e.g., Eagly & Crowley, 1986; Eagly & Steffen, 1986).

Differences in mental and social abilities and in behaviors are considerably more modest, although a few minor differences between the sexes "are sprinkled across all domains" (Ashmore, 1990, p. 500). The exception may be physical aggression, in which fairly large differences tend to be found even when diverse measures are used. In most other domains, however, some argue that the more attention that is paid to avoiding sex bias in the research, the fewer the gender differences that are actually found (e.g., Riger, 1992).

Nevertheless, there is evidence for a number of nontrivial sex differences although their interpretation has been extensively debated (Eagly, 1995). For example, sex differences have been reported on measures of the Big Five Factor model that use trait ratings (e.g., Hoyenga & Hoyenga, 1993). Examples include moderately greater rated assertiveness in males, and greater trust, tendermindedness, and anxiety in women. These data may reflect widely shared social perceptions and possible gender stereotypes, but they may or may not speak to differences in the actual social behavior of the sexes when it is studied by direct observation.

What is the conclusion one can reasonably draw when all the findings are looked at together? To some critics, the most impressive finding about sex differences in psychological characteristics is how unimpressive they generally seem to be and how much smaller they are than had been assumed in earlier years. They note that it is important to keep in mind that the variability *within* each sex on these measures is often more impressive than the differences found on average *between* the sexes. To others, it seems that the differences found are large enough to be taken seriously and that the reasons they are minimized are mostly political. In that view, sex differences are significant but they are being trivialized because of a "feminist commitment to gender similarity as a route to political equality" (Eagly, 1995, p. 155). Both interpretations have validity. Compared to within-sex differences, the differences between the sexes on most variables are probably not significant enough for practical purposes. Nevertheless, they may be reliable enough to provide clues as to how biological differences that exist at birth interact with culture to result in sex differences that are observed in adults. How the data are read depends on one's philosophy and politics on the topic, as well as on the methods used to estimate the size and meaning of the statistical differences that are reported.

18.7 In which areas do adult sex differences exist? Why is it difficult to interpret the cause of these differences?

influence of nature and nurture—genetics and social experience—on personality (Chapter 14). The same issues and the same answers apply in the present discussion of genetics, heredity, and social-cultural influences. To make sense of the whole story of sex differences in social behavior and personality, for example, the answer has to take into account the importance *both* of social factors, as discussed above, *and* of biological-evolutionary factors. Above all, one has to look at how the two influences *interact* so that what emerges depends critically on both. This point is made convincingly in a theory developed by University of California Los Angeles psychologist Shelley E. Taylor and her colleagues. They reached a radical conclusion that challenged much of the work on how humans, and particularly females, respond to threat and stress (Taylor and associates, 2000).

Recall that Chapter 17 discussed response to stress in terms of the fight-or-flight patterns that have long been assumed to be the universal human and animal reaction when severely threatened, for example, by animal predators or natural disasters. Taylor

Shelley Taylor

and colleagues note that the widely accepted belief (beginning with Cannon, 1932) that humans respond to high stress and threat with automatic fight or flight responses is based on many thousands of studies, but almost all were conducted with males, especially male rats. For females, the biobehavioral response to threat may be very different than it is for males, and for many good reasons.

Men Fight or Flee: Women Tend and Befriend. The theory Taylor and colleagues propose builds on recently discovered biological differences between human males and females, particularly in their neuroendocrine responses to threat. At the biological level, females are less likely to make a physical fight response to stress because they lack **androgens,** the hormones that in many species "act to develop the male brain for aggression . . . and then activate aggressive behavior in specific threatening contexts (such as responses to territorial establishment and defense)" (Taylor et al., 2000, p. 413). The role of testosterone, the male sex hormone, in aggression is controversial, but its level in humans increases with acute stress and is associated with hostility. In contrast, according to Taylor, in female humans, aggressive responses are not organized by testosterone or androgens and therefore do not involve the same automatic reaction patterns in response to stress.

Taylor integrates these findings with insights from the evolutionary level of analysis. According to her theory, the aggressive response to threat and stress from an evolutionary perspective may have been adaptive for men when dealing with danger (e.g., when on the hunt in the wilderness) but not for the challenges that females faced as the mothers of offspring. Females of most species, including humans until relatively recently, were pregnant, nursing, or caring for their young offspring, during their fertile lives. For these functions, a female fight-or-flight response to stress may have been strikingly nonadaptive for survival and hence became inhibited. The theory suggests that instead, females developed a **tending response to stress** that involved caretaking and grew out of the attachment system in humans. Many studies support this argument

18.8 What difference in behavioral responses to stress does Taylor propose, and what biological differences are thought to underlie this difference?

by showing that nurturing behaviors, such as touching the infant and carrying it close on the chest, benefit both mothers and offspring under high stress conditions (Taylor et al., 2000). A similar argument, based both on biology and evolution, is made for the value of **befriending,** for example, through group living and activities, as a highly adaptive way for females to cope with stress.

For the student of personality, and for the purposes of this concluding chapter, a clear message comes from the analysis by Shelley Taylor and colleagues:

> *Rather than viewing social roles and biology as alternative accounts of human behavior, a more productive theoretical and empirical strategy will be to recognize how biology and social roles are inextricably interwoven to account for the remarkable flexibility of human behavior (Taylor et al., 2000, p. 423).*

Interactions in the Genesis of Gender Roles

Cross-cultural studies of gender roles by anthropologists show the wide range of gender roles across different cultures (Gilmore, 1990). This diversity in sex roles spans "—from marked stereotypic male and female patterns to extremely muted, even quite difficult-to-detect gender differences—" (Nisbett, 1990, p. 258). For example, a highly stereotypic pattern of machismo, characterized by pride in male sexual prowess, courage in the face of physical danger, and economic dominance, is extremely common throughout the world, but even in this pattern there are striking exceptions. Analyses of these **macho patterns** by Gilmore and other anthropologists indicate that they reflect an adaptation process to extreme risks. These adaptations seem to be commonly connected with the economic role of males, for example, as hunters in the wild, or as protectors of vulnerable animal herds.

Gilmore's (1990) comparisons of Truk and Tahiti, two tropical "paradise" islands in the South Pacific, make the case convincingly. Trukese males became violent fighters who personified macho qualities—competitive and eager to show their physical prowess, accumulating many love affairs beginning early in life, while the women of their culture were expected to personify submissiveness. In contrast, Tahitian males did not compete with each other for material possessions. They were expected to be submissive, and allowed their women free and open sexual activity, for example, with Westerners, almost as soon as they landed. Why? As Nisbett (1990, p. 260) notes in his review of this work:

> *The Tahitians fish in a lagoon at no risk to themselves and food is quite plentiful. The Trukese must obtain their fish in the open sea. When a Trukese male leaves for a day of fishing, there is a genuine possibility he will not return. Thus the fearless, aggressive macho style is an adaptation to danger. Males are taught to fear unmanliness more than death because this is the only way to encourage men to produce when there is great danger . . . a muting of gender differences and surcease from the crushing requirements of assertive masculinity are a privilege of those societies that can put food on the table without great risk.*

The fact that at least in some societies men as a whole are gentle (the Tahitians) and even timid (the Semai people of central Malaysia) has serious implications for understanding both gender roles and culture. According to Gilmore (1990, p. 230), these exceptions to the norm for macho aggressive masculinity suggest that ". . . manliness is a symbolic script, a cultural construct, endlessly variable and not always necessary."

18.9 What cultural differences in male "macho" behavior did Gilmore find? What conclusion did he draw?

In the course of evolution, when there was dangerous work to be done, men were more likely to do it because of their anatomy and greater physical strength. But now that more of the "high risk–high glory" jobs do not depend on physical strength, one may well ask Gilmore's (p. 231) searching question: "Why should only males be permitted to be 'real men' and earn the glory of a risk successfully taken?"

▶ CULTURE AND PERSONALITY

The Link Between the Cultural and the Personal Meaning Systems

As part of the mix of biological and social-environmental influences on personality, the culture in which a person is raised and becomes socialized also importantly influences the development and expressions of personality. Language provides an analogy. Humans are uniquely endowed with the biological apparatus that makes language possible. Without this apparatus, it would simply not be possible to process language, as seen in how extremely difficult it has proven to be to teach language to primates (e.g., using sign rather than spoken languages). But the biological readiness alone will not result in an adult who can use a language; the specific language one speaks is determined by the human environment in which one grows up. Likewise, humans are endowed with a biological apparatus that makes the processing of social information possible, such as categorizing others' behaviors, inferring their intentions, as well as generating thoughts, emotions, and behaviors in response to them. Each individual develops a distinctive unique personality system that carries out such processing. But the shapes that one's personality system takes and the forms in which it is expressed, including the development of gender roles, are greatly influenced by the culture, as was illustrated above. Thus, how one categorizes many social situations is influenced by the concepts, or the vocabulary, of the culture in which one grows up. Furthermore, these concepts are not isolated, but rather are related to each other to form a meaning system unique to each culture.

The **cultural meaning system** includes distinctive views about what the world is like and what different situations mean and call for (e.g., Markus & Kitayama, 1998). Much like the personality system, it contains concepts and feelings about the nature of the self and its ideals, and the relationships between self and other people. It includes basic goals-values, emotions, standards, self-regulatory rules, and scripts for appropriate and inappropriate interpersonal behavior and control strategies in goal pursuit.

18.10 How are cultural and personal meaning systems related?

The significant people in the life of the child model and communicate the meaning system of their culture just as they communicate the vocabulary and grammar of the language. In time, each individual develops a **personal meaning system** that incorporates some components from the shared cultural meaning system while other components reflect unique life experiences.

Attempts to explore the links between culture and personality have a long history, and here we only look at some of the highlights. One of the first researchers to systematically examine the relationship between culture and personality was the anthropologist Ruth Benedict. In her 1934 book *Patterns of Culture,* Benedict described two personality types of the Southwest Pueblos of Mexico: the Appolonian and the Dionysian, based on a distinction used by the philosopher Nietzsche in his studies of Greek tragedy. Benedict characterized the Dionysian Pueblos as having a generalized love for excess, and the Appolonian Pueblos as sober and mistrustful of excessive behavior—qualities which were evident across a wide range of domains. Following Benedict, much subsequent research on culture and personality focused on identifying broad behavior trends in the national character or "dominant personality" of cultural groups (e.g., Kardiner, 1945; Linton, 1945).

Despite the intuitive appeal of the culture and personality approach, by the 1970s it faced serious challenges. The most difficult one was how to account for mounting evidence that cultural group members sometimes behaved according to their dominant personality—and sometimes did not. The Appolonian Pueblos, for example, were documented to at times engage in typically Dionysian behavior, as well as vice versa (Barnouw, 1973). Faced with growing criticism that research in culture and personality did little else than promote cultural stereotypes, by the 1980s this line of inquiry lost favor—and credibility—among researchers. Nevertheless, the challenge remained of how to account for both the homogeneity and heterogeneity in a cultural group's behavior. The question is *how* does culture influence the expressions of personality?

Starting in the 1990s, a new approach, influenced by work at the social cognitive level, has given new impetus to understanding how cultural forces shape individual behavior (Markus & Kitayama, 1998). This approach has provided a natural bridge— and a renewed interest—in culture through its focus on the processes that underlie and motivate behavior. The psychological "units" that have been identified in this work are similar to the social-cognitive person variables discussed in Chapter 12, such as a person's beliefs, values, goals, and ways of construing the world. These are like the **units of culture** proposed by leading researchers as being transmitted and shared within a particular community or culture (Triandis, 1997; Betancourt & Lopez, 1993). At the same time, these units are only activated and guide behavior in relation to specific situations (Mischel & Shoda, 1995). Consequently, while people who share a culture and its meaning units may converge in their experiences and behavior in some situations, such convergence will not occur in situations that do not activate culturally-shared cognitions (Mendoza-Denton et al., 1999).

Culturally Specific Personality Dispositions. Current research is beginning to illustrate how culturally specific personality dispositions can arise from differences in the socialization and learning experiences that are specific to members of a cultural group. Mendoza-Denton et al. (2002), for example, have proposed that because African Americans in the United States are especially likely to be socially excluded, marginalized, or mistreated on the basis of their race, members of this group in particular may develop race-based rejection sensitivity. This processing dynamic is similar to rejection sensitivity in personal relationships (Downey & Feldman, 1996). However, its antecedents (prior experiences of discrimination), situational trigger features (situations where racism is possible), and consequences (mistrust in historically White institutions) make it a processing dynamic that is more likely to occur among African Americans than European Americans.

18.11 Describe research on race-based rejection sensitivity and the situations that evoke it.

Importantly, this processing dynamic, while stable over time, is relevant and activated only in situations where discrimination on the basis of race is applicable, and does not necessarily characterize the individual's responses and behavior in other contexts. As such, the approach allows for an analysis of how shared cultural experience can lead to similar behavior by members of cultural groups when they are in certain situations. At the same time, it still allows for diversity in group members' behavior in many other contexts. This approach takes into account individual differences as well as commonality among members of cultural groups. It also avoids having to rely on global cultural stereotypes that limited earlier efforts to understand the impact of culture on personality.

Cross-Cultural and Intracultural Differences

Cultures can differ in many ways. For example, some cultures are more complex than others, seen in the contrast between hunters/gatherers and large urban societies living in a modern computer-dependent environment. Likewise, cultures differ in the degree to which deviations from norms are tolerated. Of greater interest for personality psychology is a typology that contrasts **individualism** and **collectivism** as two meaning systems.

18.12 Distinguish between individualist and collectivist cultures.

Individualism Versus Collectivism. Individualism involves a sense of the self as autonomous, devoted to the pursuit of personal goals, and relatively independent and self-focused. In contrast, collectivism is defined by closer connections to groups and family. People at this pole of the typology attempt to take extensive account of the goals of the family and groups with which they are connected, attentive to fulfilling duties and obligations. Even as adults, they remain interdependent in their social relationships, values, and goal pursuits. Likewise, in collectivist culture, the focus is less on self and self-enhancement and more on relationships, social obligations, and roles in comparison with an individualistic culture (e.g., Markus & Kitayama, 1998).

As the discussion above emphasizes, when cultures are described in broad trait terms like individualism versus collectivism, the fit tends to be imperfect. This is true because the terms capture something only about the average tendencies and characteristics of the majority of people within the culture. For example, rough estimates suggest that these descriptions may fit about 60 percent of the people in a culture (Triandis & Suh, 2002). That means that in a culture of individualism, 40 percent of the people don't show individualistic characteristics, and in a collectivist culture, 40 percent of the people cannot be characterized as collectivistic.

Throughout this text, you have seen that the variability *within* a person or type is often as impressive as the differences between persons and types. Likewise, the variability within a culture is often as impressive as the differences between cultures. Nevertheless, attention to the broad overall average differences can be valuable. It can give at least a rough map of what to expect in a given culture, and some of the outlines of its meaning system. It is certainly useful to know that in many situations in Asia, tactics that might be appropriate in New York City would be embarrassing and vice versa, and there is good reason that visitors come fortified with guides on what to expect and when and where to expect it. It is also useful to know that at a very broad level of trait description, in spite of cultural differences, there are important commonalities in the ways in which people characterize each other. This is seen in the finding that at least three or four of the factors in the Big Five factor structure can be found in most cultures, albeit not without exceptions. Perhaps the most important reservation to keep in mind here, however, is that even when the same factors appear in diverse cultures the particular meanings and usage may be quite different (Triandis & Suh, 2002).

Summary: Interacting Influences of Biology–Culture on Personality. In sum, culture impacts on each aspect of personality, as depicted in Figure 18.1 and discussed at the start of this chapter. It may influence the situations that people tend to experience (the left-hand side of the figure), the ways they interpret these situations, and thus how they respond to them. This happens both within the personality system—that is, internally in the person's mental and emotional experience—and in the characteristic behavioral patterns that are generated. Culture also influences personality by affecting the ways in which other people, as well as the self, react to those behaviors, in turn changing the subsequent situations the person is likely to encounter. This interplay of personality and culture over time involves continuous interactions between the inside and the outside, the individual and the social world.

▶ WHAT DEVELOPS? THE EVOLVING SELF

In this chapter we have considered the multiple aspects of personality and the diverse influences that help answer the question: Where does personality come from? But what is it that emerges from all these influences? As Carlson (1971) put it years ago: Where is the *person* in personality research? Unsurprisingly, this big question has more than one answer.

Let's look again at the diverse aspects of personality summarized in Figure 18.1. It shows a dynamic personality system with its stable organization of mental and emotional representations interacting with its social world. The system generates patterns of behavior that are perceived and reacted to in the social world in ways that change the situations subsequently experienced. Looked at from the outside, as in this figure, the person can be studied and understood at many levels of analysis, and when the levels are combined the view is enriched. That has been a main message of this concluding part of the text.

But there also is another answer to the questions "where is the person?" and "what emerges?" Namely, throughout the life course it is the self or self-system that evolves and continues to construct itself (e.g., Hoyle et al., 1999; Leary & Tangney, 2003; Mischel & Morf, 2003). Then what is this "self" about which so many different claims have been made? So far in this text, although the self was discussed as a concept with many different meanings at each level of analysis, there is also a common theme that does emerge. As one modern summary puts it:

> *The self is a dynamic psychological system, a tapestry of thoughts, feelings, and motives that define and direct—even destroy—us. Minus the self, there is little more to human beings than meets the eye: frail, relatively hairless creatures ruled by instinct and circumstance (Hoyle et al., 1999, p. 1).*

18.13 What is meant by "selfhood"?

The term used in current work to capture the essence of the self is **selfhood.** First introduced in a presidential address by Brewster Smith to the American Psychological Association in 1978, the term was used to talk about what it means to be human. In its scientific use it refers to the *"thoughts, feelings and behaviors that arise from the awareness of self as an object and agent"* (Hoyle et al., 1999, p. 2).

The point here is that each person has the experience of self-awareness, of consciousness of himself or herself as a coherent entity, a distinct whole person. This is the sense of **self as "object."** And each person tries to pursue these actively in the process of self-construction to continue to build a self and a life within the interpersonal world (Tesser, 2002). This is the sense of **self as "agent."**

Taking Charge: Human Agency

The Self-Construction Process. This text has attempted a scientific account of personality and the personality system in its context. Such an account can easily sound as if the personality is a machine-like system that simply reacts almost reflexively to the many influences that formed it and that now push and pull it around. But that interpretation misses one of the most essential features of personality and of selfhood: namely, the individual has the potential to behave in ways that are forward-looking and to actively change the situations of his or her life, rather than just reacting to them passively. In short, selfhood involves a process of self-construction (e.g., Hoyle et al. 1999; Mischel & Morf, 2003; Morf & Rhodewalt, 2001). It is a process in which individuals actively pursue life goals central for the self as they try to build their lives. To reiterate, you saw this concretely in the discussion in the previous two chapters of how individuals pursue life goals. Most importantly, in Chapter 17 you saw that the process of self-regulation allows people to influence their own life course, to transform and change at least some of the situations they experience, and to actively take charge of their life trajectory.

The same chapter also noted that toddlers already show individual differences in their ability to regulate their attention, and that these differences predict how well they can delay gratification which in turn predicts many outcomes in their lives as adults. These outcomes ranged from their SAT scores to their educational attainments, to their long-term goal-setting, to their sense of self-worth and ability to cope with life stresses. So is the toddler's future more or less sealed by the time the diaper stage of life is over? The answer of course is emphatically "no."

The Self as an Active Agent

Self-Direction/Agency. First it's important to remember that when findings "predict" outcomes, they are based on correlations. When these correlations are statistically significant, as they are in most of the research discussed here, they still always leave much of the variance in the outcome unaccounted for. It is highly unusual for any single variable to account for more than 25 percent of the variance. Even when multiple variables are considered together, research in most areas indicates that at least 50 percent of the "variance" remains unexplained, open, and unpredicted.

A key question for each person then becomes: "what can I do to influence those outcomes—and myself—in ways that I would like my life and myself to develop?" In psychological terms, this is the question of **human agency** (e.g., Bandura, 2001), and the role of the self as a potentially active agent. To the degree that people have agency—and perceive themselves to have such agency—they may influence proactively the course of their personal experience, their views of the world, and their life paths (e.g., Mischel & Morf, 2003).

The Relational Self. Discussions about agency and self-direction can risk sounding as if one is advocating a self-centered person seeking to advance in the world as an autonomous agent indifferent to others. But on closer examination, the self, as we have seen, is relational in nature (Chapter 13). People are not self-sufficient agents; they need each other, and to thrive requires connection as much as self-direction and agency. This recognition is seen especially in cultures characterized by collectivism, but it is not absent in cultures that focus on individualism.

18.14 Need human agency be self-centered?

For example, effective coping with long-term stress generally depends not just on what the person does inside the head but also on the psychological support environment. People deal better with stress, and are less likely to respond to it with illness, when they have social ties and supports, such as spouses, relatives, close friends, and groups to which they belong (Antonovsky, 1979; Holahan & Moos, 1990). Coping is also better when people can share their stressful experience with others (Nilson et al., 1981). When people are members of a group to which they "belong," they can receive emotional support, help with problems, and even a boost

The agentic self: People can influence who and what they become.

in self-esteem (Cantor et al., 2002; Cobb, 1976; Cohen & McKay, 1984). When they have a spouse to whom they feel they can talk, they tend to thrive, but having a spouse to whom one feels unable to talk makes the risk of depression considerably greater (Coyne & Downey, 1991). The self is relational and thrives with social support and connectedness, not in isolation (Leary & Tangney, 2003).

What Do People Need to Thrive? The View from Multiple Levels

18.15 Summarize what is required for psychological health from trait, psychodynamic, and phenomenological levels of analysis. What five "bottom line" requisites emerge?

If people have the capacity to take charge of what they become and their own life course, one has to also ask questions about the psychological qualities of the life one wants to live. While, of course, people differ in the specific goals they pursue in their lives, it may be reasonable to assume that they strive to have mental health, experience personal growth, and in general, *thrive*. But what does it mean to thrive? Work at several of the levels has had something to say about the essentials for personal growth, mental health, and thriving as a human being. Let's review some of the main examples to see the view of well-being that emerges when they are considered together. Table 18.1 summarizes some of the key ingredients identified.

At the *trait-dispositional level,* it is easy to identify the negative traits, for example, emotional instability or neuroticism, excessive impulsivity and anxiety, disagreeableness-hostility, lack of conscientiousness. Likewise, the positive qualities are clear since they are at the opposite ends of each of these dimensions. While it is informative to have descriptions of positive and negative qualities, this level focuses on describing the current and ideal functioning, and does not really address change possibilities in psychological terms.

The good news is that other levels of analysis do directly address the possibilities for constructive change. At the *psychodynamic-motivational level,* Freud's answer to the question was stated simply in his hope for the outcome of successful therapy: *Where id was there ego shall be,* was the phrase he used. Philosophically, for Freud that meant having to recognize and accept one's unconscious, animal-like biological urges, but to live life without enacting them. In his view, psychoanalysis helped people gain deep emotional insight into unconscious wishes and conflicts, and ultimately accept them without either having to act on them or deny them. The healthy person for Freud was one who becomes able to *love,* which is seen in the ability to have unambivalent close relationships, and to *work.* For Freud's followers, the answers shifted toward the

TABLE 18.1   Overview of Ingredients for Psychological Thriving, Well-Being, Mental Health

Level of Analysis	Key Ingredients
Trait-Dispositional	Positive traits (emotional stability, conscientiousness, agreeableness)
Psychodynamic-Motivational (Freud)	Insight into unconscious; able to love (unambivalent relationships) and work
Phenomenological (Humanistic, Existential)	Self-acceptance; responsible for self and choices: agentic
Social Cognitive	Competence/self-efficacy, relatedness (interpersonal connectedness); able to self-regulate: agentic

need for a healthy ego and self. In Kohut's words (Chapter 6), each person needs, above all, a self that feels empathic human responses from significant others. The healthy self feels the glow of pleasure in appropriate mature sexual functioning, as well as self-confident assertiveness in the pursuit of goals.

At the *phenomenological level,* the focus was not on recognizing and accepting that people are animals but rather that they are humans and as such have distinctive qualities. Most notably, a person has higher-order needs that go beyond the biological, and a self that has its own distinctive characteristics. For Carl Rogers, the essential point for thriving was to allow yourself to be genuine and to grow as you really are. That requires, in his view, that one listens to and accept one's organismic true self without distorting it to reduce anxiety or to please other people. For the existentialists and humanists also working at the phenomenological level, attention was on the combination of freedom and responsibility in making choices in life (e.g., May, 1961). The commonly used terms for these ingredients currently are autonomy or agency—namely a sense that one is at least partly causing one's own behavior, thus responsible and in charge of oneself or **agentic.**

Closely related to these ideas are those used at the *social cognitive level* to describe the essentials for well-being. Here the focus is on self-perceived **competence,** as reflected in Bandura's concept of self-efficacy, and in Dweck's concern with mastery and a belief that one is able to change and improve. Researchers who work on the self, selfhood, and self-determination (Deci & Ryan, 1995, 2000) also see competence as essential for thriving but they include an additional important component: **relatedness.** Because the self is intrinsically relational or interpersonal, people require the support and connection with others with whom they can feel close and mutually supported—they need relatedness as well as a sense of agency, competence, and efficacy, as was also noted earlier in this text. Finally, a common denominator that is seen at most levels is the importance of appropriate self-regulation, since that is an essential component for attaining the goals that one is pursuing (as discussed in detail in the previous chapter), and enables the person to be agentic.

Taken together, there is a clear consensus in the ingredients for well-being identified by these very different levels over the course of a century of work. To function well psychologically, people need to:

- Understand and accept themselves
- Have a sense of competence

- Feel agentic and responsible for their behavior and choices
- Be connected to other people
- Self-regulate appropriately

Potential for Change

18.16   To what extent do biological factors limit capacity for self-change?

Given what is known so far about personality, how great is the individual's potential for change and self-direction?

The Role of Genetics.   On the one hand, the findings of behavior geneticists underline the role of the DNA and the person's genetic heritage (Wright, 1998). Recall, for example, that identical twins reared apart often display amazing similarities in what they do and become. But as a counter example, mate choice, for instance, although it is extensively influenced by the evolutionary history of the species, seems exempt from genetic influences (Chapter 14), and surely these choices are important expressions of the self. As one writer noted: "Are we not defined in a profound sense by the relationships we forge with others . . . ?" (Angier, 1998, p. 9). And again you have to remind yourself that even the strongest correlations in the heritability studies usually leave more than half the variance unexplained. Most of that unexplained variance is attributable to the environment—and that includes most importantly what the person does within that environment in the course of life.

The Role of the Brain.   The same question now also is often raised about the role of the brain: doesn't the brain we inherit pretty much dictate the rest of the script that unfolds? Isn't biology destiny? A clear answer comes from the work of Eric Kandel, a recent Nobel prize-winning scientist who studied the well-mapped nervous system of Aplysia, a lowly sea slug.

In elegant studies, Dr. Kandel showed that learning leads the organism to produce new proteins that, in turn, remodel the neurons in the nervous system. The sea slugs that were put into controlled learning conditions that led to long-term memory also developed two times as many neuronal connections as the control group of slugs who were untrained. The implication for humans was clear: learning changes the structures and functions of the brain. And if the simple learning that slugs can do profoundly changes their nervous system, given the human capacities for learning, we have the potential to alter what happens in our brains dramatically.

In this text, you have seen much evidence about how individuals can construe and reinterpret themselves and explain events in ways that help to empower them and make their lives better and more constructive. Learning about the personality processes that allow change and emotional growth, as well as those that provide stability and coherence, also provides a potentially powerful route for self-direction. It can allow one perhaps to have more agency and to become thoughtful and wise about one's future. As George Kelly argued (Chapter 8), every person is a scientist, and in that sense can use what is known to form and test hypotheses about what might be possible.

The exciting possibilities for freedom and growth that each person has are not limitless. People may constructively rethink and reappraise their possible selves and expand their efficacy to a great degree, but their DNA influences the tools with which they do so. In addition to biology, cultural and social forces in part influence and limit both the events that people can control and their perceptions of their own possibilities (e.g., Kunda, 1999; Nisbett, 2001; Stigler et al., 1990). Within these boundaries, people have the potential to

Eric Kandel

gain substantial control over their own lives, shaping their futures in ways whose limits remain to be seen.

A few hundred years ago the French philosopher Descartes wrote his famous phrase "cogito ergo sum"—I think: therefore I am—and opened the way to modern psychology. With what is becoming known about personality, we can modify his assertion to say: "I think: therefore I can change what I am." Because by changing how I think, I can change what I feel, do, and become.

SUMMARY

PERSONALITY SYSTEM IN ACTION

- People differ in the ease of accessibility of different mental representations.

- The personality system is activated both through external situations and internally through the individual's own thoughts and feelings.

- The behavioral expressions of the personality system influence the situations the individual encounters and how others react, in turn, affecting the personality system and future behaviors.

INTERACTING INFLUENCES OF BIOLOGY AND CULTURE

- The multiple influences on the personality system include the interactive effects of biological determinants, learning, and social and cultural influences.

- Gender influences the views the individual develops about himself or herself as well as how other people treat the person.

- There are significant psychological differences both between the sexes and within the same sex.

- Females may respond to stress by tending and befriending instead of by fight or flight.
- There are distinct cultural differences in the way that gender roles are interpreted.

CULTURE AND PERSONALITY

- The cultural meaning system contains basic goals-values, emotions, standards, self-regulatory rules, interpersonal scripts, and control strategies that are activated only in certain situations.
- Cultures may differ in the typology of individualism versus collectivism, but this typology represents an average cultural tendency that may not fit many people within the culture.
- Culture influences the situations that people tend to experience, and the ways they interpret these experiences and respond.

WHAT DEVELOPS? THE EVOLVING SELF

- In self-construction, individuals actively pursue life goals central for the self as they build their lives.
- The self is relational: it thrives on social support and connectedness, not in isolation.
- People have the potential to learn and thus alter the structures and functions of their own brains.
- Ideal qualities of a well-functioning personality include: self-understanding and self-acceptance, a sense of competence, responsibility, agency, connection to other people, and the ability to self-regulate appropriately.

KEY TERMS

active ingredients   419
agentic   433
androgens   425
befriending (response to
   stress)   426
collectivism   429
competence   433
cultural meaning
   system   427

gender   422
gender concepts   423
gender stereotypes   422
human agency   431
individualism   429
macho patterns   426
personal meaning
   system   427
reciprocal interaction   419

relatedness   433
self as "agent"   430
self as "object"   430
selfhood   430
sex role
   identity   423
tending (response to
   stress)   425
units of culture   428

PART VII

THE INTEGRATION OF LEVELS

Personality psychology is evolving toward becoming an increasingly cumulative science that is based on promising ideas, findings, and methods from all areas of the field and all levels of analysis. The last three chapters in this text illustrated steps toward a more integrative approach to personality. It builds on concepts and findings from diverse levels of analysis that historically were considered incompatible but that, in fact, can enrich each other.

▶ PROSPECTS FOR PERSONALITY PSYCHOLOGY

Of course, integration for its own sake is not useful if the result is a conglomeration of concepts and findings with no clear criteria for inclusion or exclusion. Genuine differences in theory and research are often a necessary step in scientific progress. Not everyone can win, and not every idea will survive. The challenge is to gain breadth and perspective, but without indiscriminate inclusion, and with rigorous testing of the ideas, fine-tuning them progressively as the state of knowledge changes. By including useful concepts and discarding those that are not useful from all areas and levels of analysis, a solid integration begins to emerge.

▶ PERSONOLOGY REVISITED

More than 50 years ago, Henry Murray and his colleagues at Harvard University's Social Relations Department wanted to create a science of persons as individuals. To describe their ambitious work, they created a new term, "personology," for the study of persons and lives in depth (Chapter 6). While this term is no longer widely used, the goal that these pioneers pursued remains, and it is more timely now than ever before. Innovative as Murray and his colleagues were, they still lacked the methods to do their work as effectively as they wished. Fortunately, half a century later, advances in the science, for example, in biological approaches to personality and in the study of mental and emotional processes, are making it feasible to study individuals in increasing depth as Murray and his colleagues had hoped to do. For example, and as noted in the text, it is now possible to study what happens in the brain of an individual at the same time that his or her thoughts and feelings are studied. And it is possible to link these levels of analysis to intensive direct observations of how the person's behavior patterns interact with diverse situations sampled over extensive periods of time, either directly recorded or sampled through diaries. Valid, reliable, and useful tests and methods are available at each level of analysis, and all can be brought together to study personality with the depth and detail that this formidable task requires, and that makes personality an exciting field for now and for the future.

Personality psychology always has had two goals—description of individual differences and analysis of the processes that underlie them. By studying both together it becomes possible to build an increasingly cumulative and precise science of personality and human nature. The pursuit of both goals together provides an increasingly rich and clear view not just of personality constructs (e.g., neuroticism, self-regulatory competence) but also of the persons described with those terms and their distinctive characteristics. When the beautiful details begin to be put together, the coherent whole person emerges.

GLOSSARY

Ability traits   Cattell's term for traits that are concerned with effectiveness in gaining the goal.

Achievement pride   A type of pride that individuals feel when they have achieved some goals that they have set for themselves and are therefore eager to pursue new goals.

Act trends   General behavioral trends; Buss and Craik view traits as descriptions of individual differences in *act trends* instead of underlying internal causes.

Active ingredient   Features of situations that activate certain psychological processes in the perceiver.

Activity   Temperament that effects the vigor or intensity of responses; also refers to individual differences on a dimension that ranges from hyperactivity to extreme inactivity.

Actual self   The representation of oneself as one is.

Actual/ideal discrepancies   The differences between the self one perceives oneself to be and the self one would like to be.

Actual/ought discrepancies   The differences between the self one perceives oneself to be and the self one thinks one should be.

Affect   Feelings and emotions.

Agentic   To be at least partly responsible and in charge of oneself and one's behavior.

Aggression   Any behavior intended to harm or injure another living being who is motivated to avoid such treatment.

Agreeableness (A)   Good-natured, helpful, trusting, lenient; opposite of *antagonism*.

Ambivalence   Simultaneous attraction and aversion toward someone or something.

Amygdala   A small, almond-shaped region in the forebrain that is crucially important in emotional reactions, particularly fear.

Anaclitic identification   Hypothesized by Freud as the earliest form of identification based on the infant's intense dependency on the mother.

Anal stage   The second of Freud's psychosexual stages, it occurs during the child's second year; pleasure is focused on the anus and on the retention and expulsion of feces.

Analytical psychology   Carl Jung's theory of personality; humans are viewed as purposive and striving toward self-actualization; the unconscious includes a collective as well as a personal unconscious and is a healthy force.

Androgens   Hormones related to aggression, found in the male brain in many species.

Anima   In Jung's theory, the feminine, passive element in the unconscious of every male.

Animus   In Jung's theory, the masculine, assertive element in the unconscious of every female.

Anorexic behavior   Self-starvation; has been linked to *actual/ought discrepancies*.

Anorexia nervosa   A disorder in which the individual (usually an adolescent female) refuses to eat, without any apparent cause, sometimes starving to death.

Antidepressants   Drugs used to elevate the mood of depressed individuals.

Antipsychotic drugs   Drugs used in the treatment of major psychosis, notably schizophrenia.

Anxiety   A state of emotional arousal which may be experienced as a diffuse fear; in Freud's theory, the result of a struggle between an impulse and an inhibition.

Approach   Behavior that is directed toward actively achieving a goal or positive reward; commonly associated with the *behavioral activation system (BAS)*.

Approach (appetitive) dilemma   When an individual faces an approach temptation that threatens to interfere with another more important, higher-order goal.

Approach tendencies   Individual's tendency to approach desired stimuli.

Approach-approach conflict   Conflict that occurs when a person must choose one of several desirable alternatives.

Approach-avoidance conflict   A conflict that occurs when a person confronts an object or situation that has both positive and negative elements.

Archetypes   Jung's term for the contents of the collective unconscious—images or symbols expressing the inherited patterns for the organization of experience (e.g., mother archetype).

Ascending reticular activation system (ARAS)   The system in the brain that is believed to regulate overall arousal in the cortex.

Assertiveness training   Training usually involving modeling and practice in developing and using effective assertive skills; a type of behavior therapy.

Automaticity   Responses made automatically with little or no control, thought, or awareness.

Availability heuristic   A cognitive rule or principle suggesting that the more easily we can think of something, the more likely we are to believe it to be in reality.

Aversion therapy   Procedures that pair attractive, arousing, but problem-producing stimuli with another stimulus that evokes extremely negative reactions; the positive stimulus comes to evoke some of the negative or aversive reactions or is at least neutralized; for example, alcohol may be combined with nausea-producing drugs.

Aversive stimulation   Punishment for a given response.

Avoidance   Impulse to flee from a person or situation.

Avoidance (aversive) dilemma   When an impulse to flee threatens to interfere with the pursuit of a higher-order goal.

Avoidance tendencies   Individual's tendency to avoid undesirable stimuli.

Avoidance-avoidance conflict   A conflict that occurs when a person must choose one of several undesirable alternatives.

Befriending (response to stress)   Responding to stressful situations by making friends and offering assistance.

Behavior genetics   Study of the role of genes in social behavior and personality.

Behavior modification   Techniques used in behavior therapy which are derived from learning principles and intended to change behavior predictably for therapeutic goals.

Behavior sampling   Method of selecting representative behaviors from an individual's daily life; can be done through self-reports, diary studies, and behavioral observation.

Behavioral activation system (BAS)   Neurological system in the brain that activates approach behavior.

Behavioral deficits   Lack of skills required for successful functioning.

Behavioral inhibition system (BIS)   Neurological system in the brain that activates withdrawal from certain stimuli and inhibits behavior.

Behavioral medicine   An interdisciplinary field that focuses on the influence of social and psychological factors on health.

Behavioral-conditioning level   Approach to psychology emphasizing observable, objectively measurable behaviors and the relationships between these behaviors and specific events or stimuli in the environment.

Behavior-outcome relations   The relationship between possible behavior patterns and expected outcomes in particular situations; an aspect of the expectancies that constitute one of the person variables in the cognitive social level of analysis.

Benzodiazepines   Minor tranquilizers that replaced the barbiturates as primary pharmacologic treatment for anxiety; an example is Valium.

Big Five Structure   A popular taxonomy for characterizing individuals in terms of five major traits based on factor analysis of bipolar trait ratings and questionnaires.

Biofeedback   Use of equipment to provide immediate feedback about the activities of the autonomic and somatic systems; for example, giving information about heart rate or brain waves to the person in whom they occur, at the time they occur.

Biological level   Approach to personality that deals with genetic, hereditary, and evolutionary influences on personality.

Biological preparedness   Biological predisposition to learn some associations more readily than others.

Bipolar representations   According to object relations theorists, the combination of an individual's perception of self, his or her perception of another individual significant to him or her, and the emotions produced in him or her as a result of interaction between them; they become the templates through which the individual perceives ensuing relationships.

Blunting   Ignoring anxiety-arousing stimuli as a means of coping with them; a style of information processing designed for dealing with stress.

Brain asymmetry   The degree to which the right versus the left sides of the brain are activated.

Cardinal traits   Allport's term for highly generalized dispositions or characteristics that influence most aspects of an individual's behavior throughout life.

Castration anxiety   A male's fear of losing his penis; Freud believed this anxiety was central in the resolution of the Oedipus complex and the boy's identification with the father.

Catharsis   The belief that the verbal or fantasy expression of an impulse leads to its reduction; a key concept in psychoanalytic theory.

Causal attribution   Perception (judgment) of the causes of behavior, either to internal or external causes.

Central traits   Allport's term for traits that are less important and pervasive than cardinal traits but that still influence much of a person's behavior.

Cheater detector   A mechanism that humans have developed to detect individuals who seek the benefits of social exchange without reciprocating appropriately.

Chronic accessibility   The ease with which particular cognitive-affective units or internal mental representations become activated or "come to mind."

Classical conditioning (conditioned-response learning) A type of learning, emphasized by Pavlov, in which the response to an unconditioned stimulus (e.g., food) becomes conditioned to a neutral stimulus (e.g., a bell) by being paired or associated with it.

Client-centered (person-centered) therapy Approach to therapy developed by Carl Rogers; emphasizes a nonevaluative, accepting atmosphere conducive to honesty and concentrates on present relationships and feelings.

Cognition Thought; mental activity.

Cognitive Pertaining to thoughts; mental.

Cognitive behavioral therapy (CBT) Therapy aimed at changing problematic behavior by thinking about one's problems and oneself more constructively and less irrationally (e.g., by modifying one's assumptions).

Cognitive cool system Processing system that generates cognitive thought processes and thoughtful, reflective reactions and plans; based in the hippocampus and frontal lobe.

Cognitive learning See *modeling* and *observational learning*.

Cognitive reappraisal Changing the way that one thinks about an experience in order to maintain self-regulation.

Cognitive restructuring Therapeutic technique aimed at learning to think about one's problems more constructively and less irrationally; Albert Ellis's *rational emotive therapy* is a form of cognitive restructuring.

Cognitive social competence (social and cognitive competencies) Person variable referring to an individual's abilities to cognitively process and use social information.

Cognitive social theories Approaches to personality that focus on the cognitive processes and structures underlying personal differences.

Cognitive transformations (of stimuli) Cognitively changing the mental representation of a stimulus by focusing on selected aspects of it or imagining it differently.

Cognitive-Affective Personality System (CAPS) The personality system as conceptualized within the social cognitive framework (see Mischel & Shoda, 1995).

Cognitive-affective units Mental-emotional representations—the cognitions and affects or feelings—that are available to the person.

Cognitive-physiological theory Theory of emotion developed by Stanley Schachter, stating that our experience of an emotion depends on the cognitive interpretation of physiological arousal; the same state of physiological arousal may be labeled differently under different circumstances; also known as the *two-factor theory of emotions*.

Collective unconscious Inherited portion of the unconscious, as postulated by Jung; consists of ancestral memories and archetypes that are part of each person's unconscious.

Common traits According to Allport, traits that are shared in different degrees by many people.

Community psychology Treating individuals by practicing behavior modification within their environments, not a mental hospital or therapeutic setting.

Compensatory motivation Motivation for the individual to compensate for early concerns with physical weakness or illness.

Competence Ability to perform a given task or types of tasks; related to self-efficacy.

Competence motivation Desire to acquire mastery of a task for its own sake.

Competency demand hypothesis The theory that an individual's characteristic coping behavior will tend to be manifested in situations that put greater demand on the individual's competencies.

Concordance rate (in schizophrenia) Percentage of twins in which the second twin is diagnosed as schizophrenic if the first twin has been diagnosed as schizophrenic; higher for monozygotic twins.

Concurrent validity Degree of correlation between a measure and another behavior/measure recorded at about the same point in time.

Condition of worth Conditions that other people, usually parents, implicitly make as a requirement for being loved and worthwhile.

Conditioned reinforcers Neutral stimuli that have acquired value by becoming associated with other stimuli that already have reinforcing power

Conditioned response (CR) A learned response to a conditioned stimulus; a response previously made to an unconditioned stimulus is now made to a conditioned stimulus as the result of pairing the two stimuli.

Conditioned stimulus (CS) A previously neutral stimulus to which one begins to respond distinctly after it has been paired with an unconditioned stimulus.

Conditioning A basic form of learning (see also *classical conditioning*; *operant conditioning*).

Conditions of deprivation Length of time an organism has been deprived of relief from an innate drive (e.g., hunger, thirst, sex).

Conflict Occurs when motivated to pursue two or more goals that are mutually exclusive.

Congruent therapist Therapist who feels free to "be himself" and to accept himself and the client fully and immediately in the therapeutic encounter.

Conscientiousness (C) Careful, self-reliant, goal-directed, scrupulous; opposite of *undirectedness*.

Conscious   Within awareness.

Constitutional traits   Those source traits that reflect constitutional factors.

Construct   Any class of behavior, thoughts, emotions, and situations.

Construct validity   The process of establishing that the theory about what accounts for behaviors on a particular test is valid; it involves validation of both the test and the theory that underlies it.

Constructive alternativism   Recategorization of individuals or events to facilitate problem solving; a concept in George Kelly's theory.

Constructivist view of science   Theory of science that there is no single, absolute Truth awaiting discovery, merely different ways of viewing and conceptualizing phenomena that are more or less useful and valid for particular purposes and contexts.

Contemporaneity of motives   Motives are understood in terms of their role in the present regardless of their origins in the past.

Content validity   The demonstration that the items on a test adequately represent a defined broader class of behavior.

Contingencies of reinforcement   Conditions that must be present in order for a response to be rewarded.

Contingency contracting   Self-imposed regulations that guide a person's behavior in the absence of immediate external pressures.

Continuous reinforcement   Schedule of reinforcement in which a response is reinforced every time it occurs.

Control group   The group of participants that does not receive the experimental treatment but is otherwise comparable to the experimental group; responses by this group can be compared with those by the experimental group to measure any differences.

Convenience of constructs   According to Kelly, the utility or convenience of a construct for the individual.

Correlation   The relationship between two variables or sets of measures; may be either positive or negative, and is expressed in a correlation coefficient.

Correlation coefficient   Quantitative expression of a correlation; ranges from 0 to +1 or −1.

Counterconditioning (desensitization)   Replacement of a response to a stimulus by a new response in behavior therapy.

Covert modeling   A type of behavior therapy in which the individual imagines a model performing the desirable behavior in an appropriate situation (see also *modeling*).

Criterion validity   Correlation between scores on a given test and the scores on other measures that serve as referents or standards.

Cue   Stimulus that directs behavior, determining when, where, and how the response (behavior) will occur.

Cultural meaning system   Culturally distinctive views about what the world is like; contains concepts and feelings about the self and its relation to others.

Cumulative science   A science that builds over time on its best findings and concepts and integrates them into a unifying general framework.

Current life tasks   Long-term projects to which individuals commit themselves during designated periods of their lives.

Defense mechanisms   According to Freud, ways in which the ego unconsciously tries to cope with unacceptable, anxiety-producing id impulses or feelings and events, as in repression, projection, reaction formation, sublimation, or rationalization.

Denial   In Freudian theory, a primitive defense mechanism in which a person denies a threatening impulse or event even though reality confirms it; the basis for development of repression.

Dependent variable   Aspect of the person's behavior that is measured after the independent variable has been manipulated.

Desensitization   Method of eliminating anxiety or fear responses to a stimulus in which the individual learns to make an incompatible response, such as relaxation, to a series of anxiety-evoking stimuli.

Directional selection   Selection process in which versions of characteristics that enhance survival and reproduction gradually become increasingly represented, while those that handicap survival and reproduction tend to fade out.

Discrimination training   Conditioning that involves reinforcement in the presence of one stimulus but not in the presence of others.

Discriminative facility   The ability to appraise situations as they present themselves and to respond accordingly.

Discriminative stimuli   Stimuli that indicate when a response will or will not have favorable consequences.

Distortion/Displacement   Occurs when private meanings develop as objects and events become symbols representing things quite different from themselves.

Dizygotic twins   Fraternal twins; two organisms that develop in the uterus at the same time but from two egg and two sperm cells; not genetically identical.

Domain of interpersonal behavior   According to Wiggins, a comprehensive taxonomy of personality dimensions discovered through factor analysis.

Domain specific knowledge and expertise   The group of competencies essential for everyday problem-solving and coping behaviors.

Domain specificity   Specific psychological problem-solving strategies that facilitated reproduction, adaptation, and survival in the course of evolution.

Double-blind experiment   Experimental procedure in which neither participants nor experimenters know whether participants are in experimental or control conditions.

Down syndrome   Genetic abnormality consisting of a third chromosome in the 21st chromosome pair; causes severe mental retardation and a distinctive appearance.

Dream interpretation   A method used in psychoanalysis to better understand the unconscious fears and desires of the patient through an analysis of the patient's dreams.

Drive   Any strong stimuli (internal or external) that impels action.

Drive reduction   Reduction of tension caused by the fulfillment of a drive.

Dynamic traits   Cattell's term for traits that are relevant to the individuals being "set into action" with respect to some goal.

Ectomorph   According to Sheldon, an individual who has a tall, thin, and stoop-shouldered figure and has an artistic, restrained, and introvertive temperament.

Effortful control   Willpower in goal pursuit.

Ego   In Freudian theory, the conscious part of the personality that mediates between the demands of the id and the demands of the world; operates on the reality principle.

Ego identity   The ego's ability to integrate changes in the libido with developmental aptitudes and social opportunities.

Ego psychology   A variety of psychoanalytic theory that stresses ego functions and de-emphasizes instinctual drives.

Ego control   Degree of impulse control; important in delay of gratification, planfulness, and aggression inhibition (see also *ego resilience*).

Ego resilience   Refers to the individual's ability to adapt to environmental demands by appropriately modifying his or her habitual level of ego control, thus functioning with some flexibility.

Electrocardiogram (EKG)   A polygraph that measures the patterns of electricity produced by muscular contractions of the heart.

Electroencephalograph (EEG)   Records the degree of activation in the cerebral cortex through "brain waves."

Emotional hot system   Processing system in the brain that generates automatic approach-avoidance, or fight-or-flight responses; based in the *amygdala*.

Emotional overcloseness   In Kohut's view, a state in which the family exposes the child to too much intimacy, stimulation, and intrusiveness.

Emotional stability   The opposite of neuroticism, according to Eysenck, who viewed emotional stability-neuroticism as an important trait dimension.

Emotionality   Tendency to become physiologically aroused easily and experience frequent and intense negative emotions such as anger, fear, and distress.

Empathic mirroring   Learning emotions and behaviors from the examples of others.

Encoding   A social cognitive person variable that includes the individual's personal constructs and units for categorizing people, events, and experiences.

Endomorph   According to Sheldon, an individual who is obese and correspondingly tends to be relaxed, sociable, and likes to eat.

Entity theorists   Those who see abilities and traits as fixed, unchangeable characteristics; they tend to choose goals that will assure them favorable judgment and approval.

Environmental presses   According to Murray, contextual or situational pressures that influence personality and its expression.

Environmental psychology   A field of study that applies psychology to understanding human behavior in relation to the person's environment.

Environmental-mold traits   Those source traits (according to Cattell) that reflect environmental conditions.

Eros   One of two sides of the personality, as seen by early psychoanalysts, that represented sexuality and love (see also *Thanatos*).

Error variance   The "noise" or the non-essential variance to be discounted from statistical analysis.

Evaluative factor   Evaluations such as "good" or "bad."

Executive functions   Self-regulatory processes, such as planning, self-control, and willpower.

Existential anxiety   An awareness of the nothingness and death that necessarily accompanies being and that must be resolved by enhanced attention to how we choose to lead our lives (in existential theories).

Expectancies   A person variable that includes behavior-outcome and stimulus-outcome expectancies and guides an individual's choices.

Experiment   An attempt to manipulate a variable of interest while controlling all other conditions so that their influence can be discounted and the effects of the variable measured.

Experimental group   The group in an experiment into which the independent variable is introduced; in order to determine the effects of the independent variable, the results of this group are compared with those in the control group.

Explanatory styles   The way in which people interpret and construe the reasons for different events and outcomes.

External control   When an individual believes that positive and/or negative events are a result of factors outside of one's control.

Extinction   The decrease in the frequency of a response that follows the repetition of the response (or in classical conditioning, the repetition of the conditioned stimulus) in the absence of the unconditioned stimulus.

Extinction schedule   Reinforcement for a behavior is withdrawn until gradually the behavior itself stops.

Extraversion (E) (Extraverts)   According to Jung, an individual who is conventional, sociable, and outgoing and who reacts to stress by trying to lose himself or herself among people.

Extraversion-introversion   According to Eysenck, a basic dimension of personality along which all individuals can be placed at some point.

Extrinsic motivation   Motivations inferred when a person engages in a task for the sake of the expected outcome, not out of enjoyment of the task itself.

Factor analysis   A mathematical procedure for sorting trait terms or test responses into clusters or factors; used in the development of tests designed to discover basic personality traits; it identifies items that are homogeneous or internally consistent and independent of others.

False memories   Memories of events that never actually occurred.

Family therapy   A therapeutic approach based on the premise that the roots of problems lie within the family system and therefore must be treated by improving family dynamics and relations.

Field theory   Position that construes behavior as determined by the person's psychological life space — by the events in his or her total psychological situation at the moment — rather than by past events or by enduring situation-free dispositions.

Fight or flight reaction   Automatic physical and emotional reaction to perceived threat or danger, leading to attack or withdrawal; involves increase in heart rate, metabolic rate, and blood pressure, and a decrease in stomach and intestinal activity.

Fixation   A psychodynamic term referring to a process by which a person remains arrested at an early stage of psychosexual development, or moves on but later regresses to that stage.

Free association   A technique used in psychoanalytic therapy in which the patient is instructed to report whatever comes to mind, no matter how irrational it may seem.

Functional analysis   A system of analysis proposed by Skinner to link the organism's behavior to the precise conditions that control it.

Functional autonomy   The idea that adult motives replace the motives of infancy.

Functional magnetic resonance imaging (fMRI)   Method of capturing and creating an image of the activity in the brain through measurement of the magnetic fields created by the functioning nerve cells in the brain.

Fundamental attribution error   The tendency to focus on dispositions as causal explanations of behavior.

Galvanic skin response (GSR)   Changes in electrical activity of the skin due to sweating, as recorded by a galvanometer, and used as an index of emotional state, for example, in a lie detector test.

Gender   The social meaning of being a male or a female.

Gender concepts   Beliefs about the types of behavior more appropriate for one sex than for the other.

Gender stereotypes   Rigid beliefs about what it means to be a man or a woman within a particular culture or society.

Generalization   Responding in the same way to similar stimuli, for example, when a child who has been bitten by a dog becomes afraid of all dogs.

Generalized conditioned reinforcers   Conditioned reinforcers that have been paired with more than one primary reinforcer.

Generalized reinforcers   See *generalized conditioned reinforcers*.

Genital stage   The last of Freud's psychosexual stages, in which the individual becomes capable of love and adult sexual satisfaction.

Gestalt theory   The completeness or fullness theory of Fritz Perls; focuses on the awareness of one's own experience in dynamic interaction with the environment.

Gestalt therapy   An approach developed by F. Perls that aims at expanding the awareness of self and putting the person in touch with his or her own feelings and creative potential; often practiced in groups, use is made of body exercises and the venting of emotions.

Globality   Generalizing an event to pertain to many aspects of one's life.

Goal gradients   Changes in response strengths as a function of distance from the goal object.

Goal hierarchies   Organization of goals in order of their degree of importance to the individual.

Harvard personologists   A group of psychologists in the 1940s and 1950s whose study of personality was strongly influenced by the work of Freud and by biosocial, organismic theory stressing the integrated, whole aspect of personality.

Healthy personality   According to Maslow, a self-actualized person.

Heritability estimates (index) A measure used in behavior genetic research to try to assess the degree to which a trait or attribute is due to inheritance.

Hermaphrodite A person who is born with moth male and female sex organs.

Hierarchy of anxiety (grading the stimuli) A hierarchy of events that range from the most to the least intensely anxiety-provoking.

Higher growth needs Needs for self-actualization fulfillment.

Higher-order conditioning Process that occurs when a conditioned stimulus modifies the response to a neutral stimulus with which it has been associated.

Higher-order motives A hypothesized motive that, unlike thirst or hunger, does not involve specific physiological changes.

Hippocampus A horseshoe-shaped region in the temporal lobe of the brain that regulates emotional responses and complex mental and spatial thought.

Hostile attribution bias Tendency to perceive others who are implicated in, though not necessarily responsible for, negative events being driven by hostile intentions.

Hot cognitions Thoughts that activate strong emotion.

Human agency The individual's ability to proactively influence his or her personal experience.

Human genome The human genetic code consisting of roughly 30,000 to 40,000 individual genes contained in 23 chromosome pairs.

Human-relations training group (T-group)/Sensitivity training group Encounter groups that focus on non-verbal experience and self-discovery.

Hysteria A neurotic condition consisting of two subcategories: conversion reaction (physical symptoms such as paralysis or loss of sensation without organic cause) and dissociative reaction (disruption of a consistent unitary sense of self that may include amnesia, fugue, and/or multiple personalities).

Hysterical anesthesia Loss of sensation in a part of the body without physiological impairment, reflecting a defensive attempt to avoid painful thoughts and feelings, according to Freud.

"I" as an agent The self as an executive who conducts basic psychological functions; engages in self-regulation and planning for the future.

Id In Freudian theory, the foundation of the personality and a basic component of the psyche, consisting of unconscious instincts and inherited biological drives; it operates on the pleasure principle.

Ideal self The representation of who you would like to be.

Identification with the aggressor Identification with the father or the "aggressor" during the Oedipal stage of development; motivated by fear of harm and castration by the father.

Identity crisis According to Erikson, a point in psychological development when the adolescent or young defines his or her identity.

I-E Scale Trait dimension that reflects whether a person perceived locus of control is internal (I) or external (E).

If . . . then . . . Pattern (Signature) Distinctive patterns of situation-behavior interactions that characterize an individual (e.g., *if* situation A, *then* behavior B).

Implicit Association Test (IAT) A word-association task that is used to measure implicit self-esteem; may also be used to evaluate implicit attitudes, beliefs, and values as well.

Implicit methods Indirect and projective methods of personality measurement.

Implicit self-esteem How positively or negatively one regards oneself on indirect measures taken without one's conscious awareness.

Incremental theorists Those who view abilities and traits as open to change; they tend to choose goals that will enhance their competence, though not necessarily guarantee success.

Independent variable Stimulus or condition that the investigator systematically varies in an experiment.

Individualism versus collectivism Two contrasting cultural meaning systems: one focuses on the importance of the individual, the other on the importance of the group or community.

Inferiority complex According to Adler, feelings of inferiority in the individual that stem from the experience of helplessness and organ inferiority in infancy; results from a failure to compensate for early weakness through mastery in life tasks.

Insecure-ambivalent Attitude presented by infants in the Strange Situation whose reunion behavior seemed to be a combination of contact-seeking and anger.

Insecure-avoidant Attitude presented by infants in the Strange Situation who avoided their mother throughout the paradigm, even upon reunion.

Interactional analysis An analysis of the ways in which the individual's behavior varies predictably across different situations (e.g., she does A when X but B when Y).

Interactionism Idea that the individual's experiences and actions are the product of dynamic interactions between aspects of personality and situations.

Interjudge reliability Degree of consistency among different judges scoring or interpreting the same information; if scoring decisions are subjective, then it becomes especially necessary to demonstrate interscorer agreement.

Internal consistency A high correlation between different parts of a single measure.

Internal control An individual's beliefs that positive and/or negative events are a result of his or her own behavior.

Internal working models Mental representations of the others or self, or of relationships, that guide subsequent experiences and behavior.

Internality Tendency to perceive oneself, and not external circumstances, as responsible for a problem.

Internalized Aspects of the personality that were acquired from external sources (e.g., parents) but become part of oneself.

Interscorer agreement The degree to which different scorers or judges arrive at the same statements about the same test data.

Interview A verbal method in which a person interacts directly with an interviewer in a one-on-one situation (e.g., to study personality, to survey beliefs).

Intrinsic motivation Motivation (e.g., curiosity, achievement, affiliation, identity, stimulation, and social approval) that does not depend on the reduction of primary drives (such as hunger or sex) and does not have specific physiological correlates.

Introversion (Introverts) Tendency to withdraw into oneself, especially when encountering stressful emotional conflict; according to Jung, the introvert is shy and withdrawn, and prefers to be alone (see also *extravert*).

IQ (Intelligence Quotient) Concept formulated by Binet to summarize an individual's mental level based on test scores; IQ means "mental age" divided by chronological age × 100; the average IQ at any given chronological age is set at 100.

Latency period In Freud's theory of psychosexual stages, the period between the phallic stage and the mature, genital stage, during which the child represses memories of infant sexuality.

Learned drive A motivation that has been transformed from a primary drive by social learning.

Learned helplessness A condition in animals and humans that results from exposure to inescapable painful experiences in which passive endurance persists even when escape becomes possible; it can lead to hopelessness and depression.

Learned optimism Believing that one can induce positive outcomes and is not responsible for negative events.

Learning goals Goals that are directed toward gaining new skills or competencies.

Learning theories Theories that seek to identify how and when new behaviors are acquired, performed, and modified.

Level of arousal (LOA) Level of stimulation in the brain.

Levels of analysis Major theoretical approaches to the study of personality that have guided thinking and research.

Libido In Freudian theory, psychic energy that may be attached to different objects (e.g., to the mouth in the oral stage of psychosexual development).

Life space Lewin's term for the determinates of an individual's behavior at a certain moment; it includes the person and his or her psychological environment.

"Me" as an object The self as an object that one sees when one focuses attention on the self; represented in self-concepts.

Macho patterns (machismo) Pride in male physical and sexual prowess.

Mandala One of Jung's archetypes, a circle symbolizing the self's search for wholeness and containing designs often divided into four parts.

Mantra A Sanskrit word used in transcendental meditation.

Mastery-oriented People who believe that their failure is due to lack of effort, not lack of ability.

Meaning in life An individual's sense of purposefulness in his or her life.

Mesomorph An individual who has an athletic build and has a very energetic, assertive, and courageous temperament according to Sheldon.

Methadone A drug that appears promising in the treatment of heroin addiction; blocks the craving for heroin and prevents "highs" if heroin is taken.

Miller Behavioral Style Scale (MBSS) Measure of monitoring-blunting tendencies.

Mindless Guided by automatic behavioral routines or scripts that are familiar and require little active attention or self-regulatory effort.

MMPI (Minnesota Multiphasic Personality Inventory) Most popular and influential personality questionnaire, consisting of more than 500 statements to which the person responds "true," "false," or "cannot say"; items cover a wide range of topics and have been grouped into nine clinical and three control scales; scores are summarized in a profile.

Modeling A technique used in behavior therapy in which the client observes the successful performance of the desirable behaviors by a live or symbolic model; effective in teaching complex, novel responses in short time periods and in overcoming fears (see *observational learning*).

Monitoring A cognitive coping mechanism or style of information processing in which people attend to anxiety-arousing stimuli, often in the hope of controlling them.

Monoamine oxidase (MAO) Enzymes that break down the neurotransmitters after they have passed along the route, maintaining the proper level of neurotransmitters.

Monozygotic twins   Identical twins; two organisms that develop from a single fertilized egg cell and share identical genes.

Moral anxiety   In Freud's theory, guilt about one's unacceptable feelings, thoughts, or deeds (see also *neurotic anxiety* and *reality anxiety*).

Motivational determinism   Freud's belief that everything a person does may be determined by his or her pervasive, but unconscious, motives.

Multiple act criterion   A criterion measure consisting of a combination of many acts or behaviors that are expected to be interrelated; combining these components increases the reliability of the measure.

Nature-nurture   Phrase delineating the long-standing controversy in psychology over inheritance versus environment as significant determinants of individual differences in personality; nature *and* nurture are important, and their interaction may be of greatest interest.

Need for achievement (n Ach)   Need for achievement (in theory of achievement motivation).

Need for intimacy   The motivation to warmly and closely connect, share, and communicate with other people in one's everyday life.

Need for power   Individual's desire to have an impact on other people.

Neo-Freudians   Post-Freudian innovators in the field of psychology who expanded on Freud's original work, putting less emphasis on the significance of the id and paying greater attention to the ego and the self.

NEO-PI-R   A personality inventory that measures individuals along the Big Five personality trait dimensions.

Neural networks   Interconnection of neurons in the brain that are activated during information processing and mental activities.

Neuropharmacology   The use of chemicals in treating problems with psychological symptoms and disorders of the nervous system.

Neurotic anxiety   In Freud's theory, fear that one's own impulses will go out of control and lead to punishment (see also *moral anxiety* and *reality anxiety*).

Neurotic conflict   Clash between id impulses seeking expression and internalized inhibitions

Neuroticism (N)   The opposite of emotional stability, according to Eysenck, who viewed neuroticism-emotional stability as an important trait dimension.

Neurotransmitter systems   Physiological pathways that communicate and carry out the functions of signal detection and response via chemical receptors (neurotransmitters).

Neurotransmitters   Chemicals that enable the nerve impulses to jump across nerve synapses from one nerve to the next.

Nominal situations   The routine activities and places that exist within a given environment.

Nonshared environment   All of the aspects of the individual's environment that are not shared with other members of the family (e.g., birth order effects, illness, and peer influences).

Not-thinking   According to Dollard and Miller, the learned response to fear, producing the phenomenon of repression in psychodynamic theory.

Object relations theory   An approach to psychoanalysis that stresses study of the interactions between individuals, especially in childhood.

Observational learning   The process of learning through observation of a live or symbolic model; requires no direct reinforcement.

Oedipus complex   According to Freud, the love for the opposite-sex parent during the phallic stage of development, particularly the son's love for the mother and hostility toward the father.

Openness to experience (O)   Willingness to try new things, original, independent; opposite of closed-mindedness.

Operant conditioning (instrumental learning)   The increase in frequency of an operant response after it has been followed by a favorable outcome (reinforced).

Operants   Freely emitted response patterns that operate on the environment; their future strength depends on their consequences.

Operationalization   Translation of a construct into something observable and measurable.

Optimal level of arousal (OLA)   Arousal level that is most appropriate for performing a given task effectively.

Optimistic orientation   A focus on the positive aspects of oneself and in human nature.

Oral stage   First of Freud's psychosexual stages, when pleasure is focused on the mouth and on the satisfactions of sucking and eating, as during the first year of life.

Organ inferiority   Alfred Adler's term for physical weakness associated with the helplessness of infancy.

Organismic evaluation   The self's evaluation of the experiences of the organism (in Rogers' theory).

Organismic experience   Experience of the self as a whole organism (in Rogers' theory).

Organized whole   Rogers' desired state of being, where the individual functions as an integrated unit.

Ought self   The representation of who you believe you should be.

Outcome expectancies   Belief that a particular behavior will lead to the anticipated outcome (e.g., that waiting for the promised dessert will actually lead to getting it).

Overcontrolling children   Children who tend to extensively inhibit their behavioral impulses

Overjustification   Excessive external reward for a given response; may interfere with the development of intrinsic rewards.

Parapraxes   In psychoanalytic theory, slips of the tongue that express unconscious thoughts.

Partial (intermittent) reinforcement   Reinforcement in which a response is sometimes reinforced, sometimes not reinforced.

Peak experience   According to Maslow, a temporary experience of fulfillment and joy in which the person loses self-centeredness and feels a nonstriving happiness.

Penis envy   Envy of the male sex organ; believed by Freud to be universal in women, to be responsible for women's castration complex, and to be central to the psychology of women.

Perceived self-efficacy   The belief that one is capable of performing or achieving the relevant task or goal (e.g., "If I jump into that pool, I can swim to the other side.").

Perceptual defense   Unconscious repressive mechanisms that screen and block threatening visual and auditory inputs.

Performance goals   Goals that are directed toward earning acclaim for one's actions and skills.

Performance measures   Measures that directly test the individual's ability to perform a task.

Permeable boundaries   Boundaries between the person and the psychological environment that can be crossed easily.

Person variables   Relatively stable social, cognitive, and emotional variables on which individuals differ (e.g., expectations, goals, values, and competencies); sometimes these are called cognitive social person variables.

Person versus situation debate   The belief that to the degree that the person was important the situation was not and vice versa.

Person × situation interaction   The idea that individual differences in behavior are reflected in the way each person responds to a particular situation and that the way a particular situation will affect behavior depends on the individual.

Person × situation interaction patterns   Stable patterns that emerge when the individual's behavior is measured in relation to its situational context.

Personal construct   The subjective dimensions through which the individual experiences the world and the self; central unit of Kelly's theory.

Personal construct theory   George Kelly's theoretical approach to personality that tries to see how the person sees or aligns events on his or her own dimensions.

Personal meaning system   The individual's system of concepts and feelings that guides and constrains how he or she interprets the self and the world.

Personal narratives   The stories people tell themselves to try to make sense of their own lives and experiences.

Personality dispositions   Behavioral tendencies or patterns that characterize individuals or types distinctively in reliable ways.

Personality paradox   Conflict between intuition of intra-individual consistency and the research results which show a lack of intra-individual consistency.

Personality processing dynamics   Stable, distinctive sequences of thoughts, feelings, and behaviors that become activated by particular types of situations in *if . . . then . . .* signatures.

Personality signature   Distinctive *if . . . then . . .* , situation-behavior profiles that characterize individuals.

Personologists   Psychologists who study personality; phrase used by the "Harvard personologists" for their style of personality research.

Personology   Intensive psychodynamic study of individual lives as integrated, organized units, conceived by the "Harvard personologists."

Pessimism   An explanatory style in which the individual sees negative events as being widespread and largely a result of his or her own doing, while failing to take credit for positive events.

Phallic stage   The third of Freud's psychosexual stages (at about age five), when pleasure is focused on the genitals and both males and females experience the "Oedipus complex."

Pharmacotherapy   The use of drugs to treat psychological disorders or psychological symptoms.

Phenomenological   Term that refers to the individual's experience as he or she perceives it.

Phenomenological level   Theory that emphasizes the person's experience as he or she perceives it.

Phenomenology   The study of an individual's experience as he or she perceives and categorizes it, with emphasis on the self and interactions with other people and the environment.

Phenothiazines   Major tranquilizer drug useful in controlling schizophrenia (also called *antipsychotic drugs*).

Physiological measures   Measures of how a person responds physiologically (e.g., change in heart rate, degree of arousal) to different events.

PKU (phenylketonuria)   A genetic abnormality in which the gene that produces a critical enzyme is missing; it results in mental retardation if not treated soon after birth.

Placebo   An inert substance administered to someone who believes it is an active drug.

Pleasure principle In Freud's theory, the basis for id functioning; irrational, seeks immediate satisfaction of instinctual impulses.

Plethysmograph An instrument that measures changes in blood volume.

Polygraph An apparatus that records the activities of the autonomic nervous system.

Positron emission tomography (PET scans) Measures the amount of glucose being used in various parts of the brain, providing an index of activity as the brain performs a particular function.

Possible selves An individual's potential ways of being.

Potency Factor in semantic differential measures represented by scale items like hard-soft, masculine-feminine, strong-weak.

Practical intelligence The competencies, skills, and knowledge (expertise) essential for everyday problem-solving and coping behaviors.

Preconscious Thoughts, experiences, and memories not in a person's immediate attention but that can be called into awareness at any moment.

Predictive validity Correlation between current measure and future behaviors/measures.

Prevention pride Type of achievement pride that motivates people to vigilantly avoid factors that may hinder them from achieving their goals.

Prevention system System that attends to negative outcomes such as punishment or failure.

Primary biological needs Innate set of needs required for the organism's survival, such as food, water, oxygen, and warmth.

Primary process thinking Freud's term for the id's direct, reality-ignoring attempts to satisfy needs irrationally.

Primary reinforcers Innate reinforcers that cause automatic responses without the need for conditioning (e.g., food).

Principle of contemporaneity According to Lewin, the psychological life space that takes into account only what is happening and experienced at a given point in time.

Principle of interactionism In personality psychology, states that important personality differences may be seen in the ways in which an individual's behavior is effected by and interacts with different situations.

Processing (approaches) Theoretical approaches that focus on mental and emotional (psychological) processes or determinants that underlie behavior.

Processing dynamics Characteristic pattern of thoughts, feelings, and behavioral reactions activated in relation to situations.

Projection A defense mechanism by which one attributes one's own unacceptable aspects or impulses to someone else.

Projective methods Tests (such as the Rorschach or TAT) that present the individual with materials open to a wide variety of interpretations based on the belief that responses reveal important aspects of the respondent's personality; central in psychodynamic assessment.

Promotion pride Type of achievement pride that motivates people to eagerly pursue their goals.

Promotion system System focused on obtaining positive outcomes and gains, such as accomplishments or rewards.

Proprium Allport's term for the region of personality that contains the root of the consistency that characterizes attitudes, goals, and values; not innate, it develops in time.

Prosocial aggression Verbal threats and evaluative statements about the goodness or badness of behavior.

Prototypicality The degree to which the member of a category is representative of that category or exemplifies it.

Psychoanalysis A form of psychotherapy developed by Freud that aims at relieving neurotic conflict and anxiety by airing repressed, unconscious impulses over the course of regular meetings between patient and analyst.

Psychobiography The intensive study of individual lives using narrative methods.

Psychodynamic Behavior Theory Developed by John Dollard and Neal Miller in the late 1940s to integrate some of the fundamental ideas of psychoanalytic theory with the concepts and methods of experimental research on behavior and learning.

Psychodynamic-motivational level Approaches, beginning with Freud's work, that probe the motivations, conflicts, and defenses that help explain complex consistencies and inconsistencies in personality.

Psychodynamics In psychoanalytic theory, the processes through which personality is regulated; it is predicated on the concept of repressed, unconscious impulses and the significance of early childhood experience.

Psycholexical approach A research strategy that seeks to classify people into different trait groups by identifying differences among individuals on the basis of ratings with natural language terms (adjectives) that are factor analyzed.

Psychological features The aspects or ingredients of situations that activate the person's characteristic reaction patterns (e.g., being rejected by peers in a social situation).

Psychological oxygen According to Kohut, the psychological deprivation of empathic human responses in important others is analogous to the deprivation of oxygen.

Psychological situation The circumstances and events within a nominal situation that affect behavior.

Psychometric trait approach Approach that emphasizes quantitative measurement of psychological qualities, comparing the responses of large groups of people under standard conditions, often by means of paper-and-pencil tests.

Psychosexual stages According to Freudian theory, development occurs in a series of psychosexual stages; in each stage (oral, anal, phallic, and genital) pleasure is focused on a different part of the body.

Psychosocial crisis According to Erikson's theory, the person's efforts to solve the problems that occur at a given stage of psychosocial development.

Psychosocial stages Erikson's eight stages of development; extending throughout life, each stage centers around a "crisis" or set of problems and the individual's attempts to solve it.

Q-sort (Q-technique) A method of obtaining trait ratings; consists of many cards, on each of which is printed a trait description; the rater groups the cards in a series of piles ranging from those that are least characteristic to those that are most characteristic of the rated person.

Randomization The assignment of research participants to different conditions on the basis of chance; if many participants are used, differences should average out except for the effects produced by the experiment itself.

Rational emotive therapy Albert Ellis's approach, based on the idea that if people learn to think more rationally, their behavior will become more rational and their emotional problems will be reduced.

Rationalization A defense mechanism that occurs when one makes something more acceptable by attributing it to more acceptable causes.

Reaction formation A defense mechanism that occurs when an anxiety-provoking impulse is replaced in consciousness by its opposite.

Reality anxiety In Freud's theory, the fear of real dangers in the external world (see also *moral anxiety* and *neurotic anxiety*).

Reality principle In Freud's theory, the basis for ego functioning; rational; dictates delay in the discharge of tension until environmental conditions are appropriate.

Reciprocal altruism The recognition that if we help others they are likely to reciprocate in kind.

Reciprocal interaction Interaction between the person and the situation in which both variables influence one another reciprocally.

Reflex An instinctive, unlearned response to a particular stimulus (see also *unconditioned response*).

Regression In psychodynamic theory, reversion to an earlier stage; the return of the libido to its former halting places in development.

Regulatory competencies The cognitive and attentional mechanisms that help execute goal-directed behavior.

Regulatory focus theory Higgins' theory that all goal-directed behavior is governed by two motivational systems—the prevention system and the promotion system.

Reinforcement (Reinforcer) Any consequence that increases the likelihood that a response will be repeated or strengthened.

Rejection sensitivity A disposition to anxiously expect and easily perceive potential rejection even in ambiguous events.

Relatedness Support and connection with others.

Relational self The self perceived not as a single entity but as an object in relation to other objects, as in Kohut's object relations theory.

Relational therapy A therapeutic process that emphasizes the role of early, current, and analyst-patient relationships in the development and resolution of personality problems.

Relaxation responses Wolpe's preferred conter-conditioning method for anxiety; involves elaborate instructions to teach individuals how to consciously relax themselves.

Repression According to psychoanalytic theory, an unconscious defense mechanism through which unacceptable (ego-threatening) material is kept from awareness; the repressed motives, ideas, conflicts, memories, etc. continue to influence behavior.

Repression-sensitization A dimension of differences in defensive patterns of perception, ranging from avoiding the anxiety-arousing stimuli to approaching them more readily and being extra vigilant or supersensitized.

Repressors People who describe themselves as having few problems or difficulties and who do not report themselves as highly sensitive to everyday stress and anxieties.

Resistance Difficulties in achieving progress in psychotherapy due to unconscious defenses as anxiety-producing material emerges during the treatment.

Response Any observable, identifiable activity of an organism.

Response freedom The condition in a situation that does not produce a similar reaction in all individuals but that allows individual differences in the behaviors of each person to become visible.

Role An attempt to see another person through his or her constructs.

Role Construct Repertory Test ("Rep" Test) A technique for measuring personal constructs developed by Kelly.

Rorschach test   Projective test consisting of 10 symmetrical inkblots to which the person describes his or her reactions, stating what each blot looks like or might be.

Rumination   Dwelling on particular types of cognitions and emotions, usually negative; in a ruminative style of dealing with depression, the person focuses on the fact that he or she is depressed, on the symptoms (like fatigue and disinterest) that are experienced, and on their negative consequences (e.g., "I might lose my job").

Schemas (schemata)   Knowledge structures made-up of collections of attributes or features that have "family resemblance" to each other.

Schizophrenia   Most common form of psychosis; prominent symptoms may include thought disorder, delusions, highly inappropriate or bizarre emotions, and hallucinations, all without known organic cause.

Scholastic Aptitude Test (SAT)   A standardized measure of verbal and quantitative skills given routinely to high school seniors before entrance into college.

Secondary dispositions   The most specific, defined traits or "attitudes" that influence an individual's behavior.

Secure base   Safe haven of dependable comfort in a young child's life from which the world can be explored with trust.

Securely attached   Attitude presented by infants in Strange Situation who greeted mother positively upon reunion and then returned to play.

Self actualize (self-actualization)   The realization of one's human potential.

Self as "agent"   The active process of self-construction in the course of building a self and a life within the interpersonal world.

Self as "object"   The consciousness of the self as a coherent entity.

Self-actualizing person   For Maslow, a person who has the personal qualities listed in Table 9.5.

Self-concept (self)   System that serves as a frame of reference for evaluating and monitoring the actual experiences of the organism.

Self-consciousness   Attention directed toward the self.

Self-disclosure   Sharing of stressful, traumatic experiences either in groups or other forms (e.g., diaries).

Self-efficacy   Belief that one can do things effectively.

Self-efficacy expectations   The person's confidence that he or she can perform a particular behavior, like handling a snake or making a public speech.

Self-enhancing bias   Increased likelihood of seeing oneself as causally responsible for actions when they have positive rather than negative outcomes.

Self-enhancing illusions   Unrealistically positive view of the self and one's ability to control pure chance situations.

Self-esteem   Refers to the individual's personal judgment of his or her own worth.

Self-evaluative standards (self-guides)   Standards for assessing oneself.

Selfhood   Term used to refer to the awareness of the self as "agent" and "object."

Self-instruction   Talking to oneself to control one's behavior; an aspect of some types of control training.

Self-observation   Systematic observation of one's own behavior; an important step in some types of behavior therapy.

Self-realization   A continuous quest to know oneself and to actualize one's potentialities for full awareness and growth as a human being.

Self-regulation   The monitoring and evaluation of one's own behavior, modifying one's own behavior and influencing his/her environment.

Self-regulatory systems   A person variable that includes the individual's rules, plans, and self-reactions for performance and for the organization of complex behavior (see *person variables*).

Self-reinforcement   The process of providing positive consequences to oneself contingent upon enacting desired behaviors or achieving specific performance criteria (e.g., you get to go to a movie if you get an A on the exam).

Self-relevant   Meaningful to the self.

Self-reports   Statements that the individual makes about himself or herself.

Self-schemas   Cognitions about the self that arise from past experience and guide the processing of new information.

Self-theory   A construction or set of concepts about the self that affect future experience.

Semantic differential   Measure that tests individuals on their perceptions of the meanings of diverse words, phrases, and concepts by having them rate each item on a bipolar scale.

Sensate focus   A method for overcoming sexual-performance fears in which the couple concentrates on sensual pleasures without engaging in sexual intercourse.

Sensation seeking   Trait that represents an individual's level of desire to experience new things and take risks.

Sensation seeking scale (SSS)   Measure that taps into four different aspects of sensation seeking behavior: thrill and adventure seeking, experience seeking, disinhibition, and boredom susceptibility.

Sense of helplessness   Feeling that one's efforts and actions are not effective.

Sensitizers   Individuals who are highly sensitive to everyday stress and anxieties.

Sensory anesthesia   Loss of sensory ability, such as blindness, deafness, or loss of feeling in a body part.

Serotonin   A neurotransmitter associated with depression when available in excess amounts in the body.

Sex role identity   The degree to which an individual identifies himself or herself as masculine or feminine.

Sex-typing   The process whereby the individual comes to acquire, to value, and to practice (perform) sex-typed behaviors.

Shadow aspect   According to Jung, the unconscious part of the psyche that must be absorbed into the personality to achieve full emotional growth.

Shaping   Technique for producing successively better approximations of behavior by reinforcing small variations in behavior in the desired direction and by reinforcing only increasingly close approximations to the desired behavior.

Shared environment (or family environment)   Individuals raised in the same family/household.

Sibling rivalry   Competition between the siblings of a family that, according to Adler, plays a major role in development.

Signature of personality   Stable patterns or profiles that show intraindividual behavior variation as it relates to specific types of situations.

Single-blind method   An experimental procedure in which participants do not know whether they are in experimental or control conditions.

Situational test   Procedure in which participants are observed performing a task within a lifelike situation; the Harvard personologists used stressful, lifelike tasks under extremely difficult situations to assess OSS candidates and used their performance to make clinical inferences about each person's underlying personality.

Situationism   Theory that dispositional consistency is a myth and individual behavior is entirely determined by situational attributes.

Sociability   The degree to which the person seeks interpersonal interaction.

Social cognitive level   A level of analysis in personality psychology that focuses on the social and cognitive meanings of events or situations for the individual, and the processes through which these meanings lead to social behavior.

Social intelligence   The competencies, skills, and knowledge needed to generate the person's cognitions and behavior patterns.

Sociobiology   An approach to explain social behavior in terms of evolutionary theories.

Source traits   In R. B. Cattell's theory, the traits that constitute personality structure and determine surface traits and behavior.

Stability   The durability of aspects of personality over time.

Stabilizing selection   Mechanism that weeds out characteristics at both extremities of a given dimension.

Stable intraindividual patterning   The idea that the temporal intraindividual variation in behavior is meaningful and stable.

State anxiety   A person's momentary or situational anxiety; it varies in intensity over time and across settings.

Statistical significance   A statistical computation that reflects how far a given association exceeds that which would be expected by chance.

Stimulus control   Behavior that is expressed stably but only under specific, predictable conditions.

Stimulus-outcome relations   Stable links between stimuli and other events that allow one to predict the outcomes from the stimuli.

Stimulus-response covariation   Stable link between stimulus and response that allow predictions of the response based on the stimulus.

Strange situation   An experimental study that puts a young child in an unfamiliar setting to assess individual differences in attachment relations.

Subjective continuity   Sense of basic oneness and durability in the self; feeling of consistency and identity.

Subjective values and goals   The particular outcomes and goals to which an individual assigns greatest import; a cognitive social person variable.

Sublimation   A process through which socially unacceptable impulses are expressed in socially acceptable ways.

Subliminally (subliminal)   Occurring outside of a person's consciousness or awareness.

Superego   In Freud's theory, the conscience, made up of the internalized values of the parents; strives for self-control and perfection; it is both unconscious and conscious.

Suppression   Occurs when one voluntarily and consciously withholds a response or turns attention away from something (see also *repression*).

Surface traits   R. B. Cattell's term for clusters of overt or manifest trait elements (responses) that seem to go together; the manifestations of source traits.

Symptom substitution   The controversial psychoanalytic belief that new symptoms will automatically replace problematic behaviors that are removed directly (e.g., by behavior therapy) unless their underlying unconscious emotional causes also have been removed.

Systematic desensitization   A behavior therapy procedure designed to reduce incapacitating anxiety; an incompatible response (usually relaxation) is paired with progressively more anxiety arousing situations until the individual is able to imagine or be in these situations without becoming anxious.

Systems theory   The analysis of units like the family as a system of relationships.

Systems therapy   A type of therapy that seeks to understand the individual within the context of the family or system.

Tachistoscope   A machine (used in studies of perceptual defense) that projects words onto a screen at different speeds.

Temperament traits   R. B. Cattell's term for traits that determine emotional reactivity.

Temperaments   Characteristic individual differences relevant to emotional expression, often visible early in life.

Temporal reliability   A high test-retest correlation when the same test is given on multiple occasions to the same group of people.

Tending (response to stress)   Responding to stressful situations with nurturance and care-taking behavior (rather than fight or flight reactions).

Test   A means of obtaining information about a person through standardized measures of behavior and personal qualities.

Thanatos   One of two aspects of the personality considered by early psychoanalysts to represent destruction and aggression; the darker side of human nature (see also *Eros*).

Thematic Apperception Test (TAT)   Projective test consisting of a set of ambiguous pictures about which the person being tested is asked to make up an interesting story.

Tokens   Items used to barter for rewards, used to assess the effectiveness of different rewards in operant conditioning.

Trait   A persistent (enduring) characteristic or dimension of individual differences; defined by Allport as a generalized "neuropsychic system," distinctive to each person, that serves to unify many different stimuli by leading the person to generate consistent responses to them.

Trait anxiety   A person's stable, characteristic overall level of anxiety.

Trait approach   An approach to personality that categorizes individuals in terms of traits.

Trait structure   Unique structure of a trait as it exists in a particular individual.

Trait theorists   Psychologists who study personality in terms of the different trait dimensions that characterize each individual.

Trait-dispositional level   Approach to personality that categorizes individuals in terms of traits or dispositions.

Transactional analysis   See *systems theory* and *family therapy*.

Transcendental Meditation (TM)   A form of deep meditation in which the meditator sits comfortably with eyes closed and repeats a special Sanskrit word called a "mantra."

Transference   In psychoanalysis, the patient's response to the therapist as though the therapist were a parent or some other important figure from childhood; considered and essential aspect of psychoanalytic therapy.

Transformation of motives   Defense mechanism in which basic impulses persist but the objects at which they are directed and the manner in which they are expressed are transformed.

Traumatic experiences   Experiences that abruptly and severely disrupt a person's life.

Triple typology   A classification system that brings together three categories in a meaningful way; in the case of personality, these three categories are types of people, types of behavior, and types of situations.

Twin method   Method of assessing genetic influence by comparing the degree of similarity on trait measures for genetically identical twins versus dizygotic twins.

Uncertainty orientation   Personality dimension that is defined at one end by individuals who are comfortable dealing with uncertainty and strive to resolve it, and at the other end by those who are uncomfortable with uncertainty and likely to avoid situations that increase their sense of uncertainty.

Unconditioned response (UCR)   The unlearned response one naturally makes to an unconditioned stimulus (e.g., withdrawing the hand from a hot object).

Unconditioned stimuli (UCS)   Stimuli to which one automatically, naturally responds without learning to do so (e.g., food, electric shock).

Unconscious   In psychoanalytic theory, the part of the personality of which the ego is unaware but that profoundly effects actions and behaviors.

Undercontrolling children   Children who do not adequately inhibit their behavioral impulses.

Unique traits   In Allport's theory, traits that only exist in one individual and cannot be found in another in exactly the same form.

Units of culture   Beliefs, values, goals, and ways of construing the world that are transmitted and shared within a particular community or culture.

Value   The subjective importance of an outcome or event for an individual.

Variable   An attribute, quality, or characteristic that may be given two or more values and measured or systematically varied.

Vicarious conditioning   Conditioning of a response to a stimulus through observation.

Visceral responses   Internal bodily responses to external events that occur without our willing them or even thinking about them (e.g., increased heart rate, changes in gland secretion).

Willpower   The ability to voluntarily self-control for desired but difficult goals, for example, delay of gratification in anticipation of achieving a more far-reaching but distant goal.

Working self-concept   The prominent concepts of the self that are foremost in an individual's thought and memory and that can be easily accessed.

Working through   Process that occurs in psychoanalytic therapy when the patient, in the context of the transference relationship, re-examines his or her basic problems until their emotional roots are understood and learns to handle them more appropriately.

REFERENCES

Abelson, R. P. (1976). A script theory of understanding, attitude, and behavior. In J. Carroll & T. Payne (Eds.), *Cognition and social behavior*. Hillsdale, NJ: Erlbaum.

Abramson, L. Y., Seligman, M. E. P., & Teasdale, J. D. (1978). Learned helplessness in humans: Critique and reformation. *Journal of Abnormal Psychology, 87,* 49–74.

Affleck, G., Urrows, S., Tennen, H., & Higgins, P. (1992). Daily coping with pain from rheumatoid arthritis: Patterns and correlates. *Pain, 51,* 221–229.

Ainsworth, M. D. S. (1989). Attachments beyond infancy. *American Psychologist, 44,* 709–716.

Ainsworth, M. S., Blehar, M. C., Waters, E. C., & Wall, S. (1978). *Patterns of Attachment*. Hillsdale, NJ: Lawrence Erlbaum Associates.

Ajzen, I., & Fishbein, M. (1977). Attitude-behavior relations: A theoretical analysis and review of empirical research. *Psychological Bulletin, 84,* 888–918.

Aldwin, C. (1994). *Stress, coping, and development*. New York: Guilford Press.

Alexander, C. N., Robinson, P., Orme-Johnson, D. W., Schneider, R., & Walton, K. (1994). Effects of Transcendental Meditation compared to relaxation in promoting health and reducing mortality in the elderly. *Homeostasis, 35,* 4–5.

Alexander, M. J., & Higgins, E. T. (1993). Emotional trade-offs of becoming a parent: How social roles influence self-discrepancy effects. *Journal of Personality and Social Psychology, 65,* 1259–1269.

Alicke, M. D. (1985). Global self-evaluation as determined by the desirability and controllability of trait adjectives. *Journal of Personality and Social Psychology, 49,* 1621–1630.

Allen, E. K., Hart, B. M., Buell, J. S., Harris, F. R., & Wolf, M. M. (1964). Effects of social reinforcement on isolate behavior of a nursery school child. *Child Development, 35,* 511–518.

Alloy, L. B., & Ahrens, A. H. (1987). Depression and pessimism for the future: Biased use of statistically relevant information in predictions for self versus others. *Journal of Personality and Social Psychology, 52,* 366–378.

Allport, G. W. (1937). *Personality: A psychological interpretation*. New York: Holt, Rinehart and Winston.

Allport, G. W. (1940). Motivation in personality: Reply to Mr. Bertocci. *Psychological Review, 47,* 533–554.

Allport, G. W. (1955). *Becoming*. New Haven, CT: Yale University Press.

Allport, G. W. (1961). *Pattern and growth in personality*. New York: Holt, Rinehart and Winston.

American Psychological Association. (1966). *Standards for educational and psychological tests and manuals*. Washington, DC: APA.

Andersen, S. M., & Chen, S. (1998). Measuring transference in everyday social relations: Theory and evidence using an experimental social-cognitive paradigm. In H. Kurtzman (Ed.), *Cognition and Pychodynamics*. New York: Oxford University Press.

Andersen, S. M., & Chen, S. (2002). The relational self: An interpersonal social-cognitive theory. *Psychological Review, 109,* 619–645.

Andersen, S. M., Chen, S., & Miranda, R. (2002). Significant others and the self. *Self and Identity, 1,* 159–168.

Andersen, S. M., Reznik, I., & Chen, S. (1997). The self in relation to others: Cognitive and motivational underpinnings. In J. G. Snodgrass & R. L. Thompson (Eds.), *The self across psychology: Self-recognition, self-awareness, and the self-concept* (pp. 233–275). New York: New York Academy of Science.

Anderson, J. R. (1996). ACT: A simple theory of complex cognition. *American Psychologist, 51,* 355–365.

Anderson, J. R., & Bower, G. H. (1973). *Human associative memory*. New York: Wiley.

Angier, N. (1998). Separated by birth? *New York Times Book Review*. Feb. 8, p. 9.

Antonovsky, A. (1979). *Health, stress and coping*. San Francisco: Jossey-Bass.

Archer, J. (1990). The influence of testosterone on human aggression. *British Journal of Psychology, 82,* 1–28.

Archibald, H. C., & Tuddenham, R. D. (1965). Persistent stress reaction after combat. *Archives of General Psychiatry, 12,* 475–481.

Arend, R., Gove, F. L., & Sroufe, L. A. (1979). Continuity of individual adaptation from infancy to kindergarten: A predictive study of ego-resiliency and curiosity in preschoolers. *Child Development, 50,* 950–959.

Argyle, M., & Little, B. R. (1972). Do personality traits apply to social behavior? *Journal of Theory of Social Behavior (Great Britain), 2,* 1–35.

Arkowitz, H. (1989). From behavior change to insight. *Journal of Integrative and Eclectic Psychotherapy, 8,* 222–232.

Aronfreed, J. (1966). The internalization of social control through punishment: Experimental studies of the role of conditioning and the second signal system in the development of conscience. *Proceedings of the XVIIIth International Congress of Psychology.* Moscow, USSR, August, 35, 219–230.

Aronfreed, J. (1968). *Conduct and conscience: The socialization of internalized control over behavior.* New York: Academic Press.

Aronfreed, J. (1994). Moral development from the standpoint of a general psychological theory. In B. Puka (Ed.), *Defining perspectives in moral development. Moral development: A compendium* (Vol. 1, pp. 170–85). New York: Garland Publishing, Inc.

Aronson, E. (1972). *The social animal.* San Francisco: Freeman.

Aronson, E., & Mettee, D. (1968). Dishonest behavior as a function of differential levels of induced self-esteem. *Journal of Personality and Social Psychology, 9,* 121–127.

Ashmore, R. D. (1990). Sex, gender, and the individual. In L. A. Pervin (Ed.), *Handbook of personality: Theory and research* (pp. 486–526). New York: Guilford Press.

Aspinwall, L. G., & Staudinger, U. M. (2002). A psychology of human strengths: Fundamental questions and future directions for a positive psychology. Washington, DC: American Psychological Association.

Aspinwall, L. G., & Taylor, S. E. (1997) A stitch in time: Self-regulation and proactive coping. *Psychological Bulletin, 121,* 417–436.

Atkinson, J. W. (1964). *An introduction to motivation.* Princeton, NJ: Van Nostrand.

Atkinson, J. W. (Ed.). (1958). *Motives in fantasy, action and society.* Princeton, NJ: Van Nostrand.

Ayduk, O. N. (1999). Impact of self-control strategies on the link between rejection sensitivity and hostility: Risk negotiation through strategic control. *Dissertation Abstracts International, 60 (1-B),* 0401.

Ayduk, O. N., Downey, G., Testa, S., Yen, Y., & Shoda, Y. (1998). Does rejection elicit hostility in rejection sensitive women? *Social Cognition, 17,* 245–271.

Ayduk, O., May, D., Downey, G., & Higgins, T. (2003). Tactical differences in coping with rejection sensitivity: The role of prevention pride. *Personality and Social Psychology Bulletin, 29,* 435–448.

Ayduk, O., Mendoza-Denton, R., Mischel, W., Downey, G., Peake, P. K., & Rodriguez, M. (2000). Regulating the interpersonal self: Strategic self-regulation for coping with rejection sensitivity. *Journal of Personality and Social Psychology, 79,* 776–792.

Ayduk, O., & Mischel, W. (2002). When smart people behave stupidly: Inconsistencies in social and emotional intelligence. In R. J. Sternberg (Ed.), *Why smart people can be so stupid* (pp. 86–105). New Haven, CT: Yale University Press.

Ayduk, O., Mischel, W., & Downey, G. (2002). Attentional mechanisms linking rejection to hostile reactivity: The role of "hot" vs. "cool" focus. *Psychological Science, 13,* 443–448.

Ayllon, T., & Azrin, N. H. (1965). The measurement and reinforcement of behavior of psychotics. *Journal of the Experimental Analysis of Behavior, 8,* 357–383.

Ayllon, T., & Haughton, E. (1964). Modification of symptomatic verbal behaviour of mental patients. *Behaviour Research and Therapy, 2,* 87–97.

Baker, T. B., Piper, M. E., McCarthy, D. E., Majeskie, M. R., & Fiore, M. C. (2003). Addiction motivation reformulated: An affective processing model of negative reinforcement. *Psychological Review.*

Ball, D., Hill, L., Freeman, B., Eley, T. C., Strelau, J., Riemann, R., Sinath, F. M., Angleitner, A., & Plomin, R. (1997). The serotonin transporter gene and peer-rated neuroticism. *NeuroReport, 8,* 1301–1304.

Bandura, A. (1965). Vicarious processes: A case of no-trial learning. In L. Berkowitz (Ed.), *Advances in experimental social psychology* (Vol. 2, pp. 1–55). New York: Academic Press.

Bandura, A. (1969). *Principles of behavior modification.* New York: Holt, Rinehart and Winston.

Bandura, A. (1973). *Aggression: A social learning analysis.* Englewood Cliffs, NJ: Prentice-Hall.

Bandura, A. (1977). *Social learning theory.* Englewood Cliffs, NJ: Prentice-Hall.

Bandura, A. (1978). Reflections on self-efficacy. In S. Rachman (Ed.), *Advances in behavior research and therapy* (Vol. 1). Elmsford, NJ: Pergamon.

Bandura, A. (1982). Self-efficacy mechanisms in human agency. *American Psychologist, 37,* 122–147.

Bandura, A. (1986). *Social foundations of thought and action: A social cognitive theory.* Englewood Cliffs, NJ: Prentice-Hall.

Bandura, A. (1989). Human agency in social cognitive theory. *American Psychologist, 44,* 1175–1184.

Bandura, A. (1997). *Self-efficacy: The exercise of control.* New York: Freeman.

Bandura, A. (2001). Social cognitive theory: An agentic perspective. *Annual Review, 52,* 1–26.

Bandura, A., & Adams, N. E. (1977). Analysis of self-efficacy theory of behavioral change. *Cognitive Therapy and Research, 1,* 287–310.

Bandura, A., Adams, N. E., & Beyer, J. (1977). Cognitive processes mediating behavioral change. *Journal of Personality and Social Psychology, 35,* 125–139.

Bandura, A., Blanchard, E. B., & Ritter, B. (1969). Relative efficacy of desensitization and modeling approaches for inducing behavioral, affective, and attitudinal changes. *Journal of Personality and Social Psychology, 13,* 173–199.

Bandura, A., & Kupers, C. J. (1964). Transmission of patterns of self-reinforcement through modeling. *Journal of Abnormal and Social Psychology, 69,* 1–9.

Bandura, A., & Mischel, W. (1965). Modification of self-imposed delay of reward through exposure to live and symbolic models. *Journal of Personality and Social Psychology, 2,* 698–705.

Bandura, A., Taylor, C. B., Ewart, C. K., Miller, N. M., & Debusk, R. F. (1985). Exercise testing to enhance wives' confidence in their husbands' cardiac capability soon after clinically uncomplicated acute myocardial infarction. *American Journal of Cardiology, 55,* 635–638.

Bandura, A., & Walters, R. H. (1959). *Adolescent aggression.* New York: Ronald Press.

Bargh, J. A. (1996). Automaticity in social psychology. In E. T. Higgins & A. W. Kruglanski (Eds.), *Social psychology: Handbook of basic principles* (pp. 169–183). New York: Guilford.

Bargh, J. A. (1997). The automaticity of everyday life. In R. S. Wyer Jr. (Ed.), *The automaticity of everyday life: Advances in social cognition* (Vol. 10, pp. 1–61). Mahwah, NJ: Erlbaum.

Bargh, J. A. (2001). Caution: Automatic social cognition may not be habit forming. *Polish Psychological Bulletin, 32,* 1–8.

Bargh, J. A., Chen, M., & Burrows, L. (1996). Automaticity of social behavior: Direct effects of trait construct and stereotype activation on action. *Journal of Personality and Social Psychology, 71,* 230–244.

Barlow, D. H. (1988). *Anxiety and its disorders: The nature and treatment of anxiety and panic.* New York: Guilford.

Barnouw. (1973). *Culture and personality.* Homewood, IL: Dorsey Press.

Baron, R. A., & Richardson, D. R. (1994). *Human aggression* (2nd ed.). New York: Plenum.

Bartholomew, K., & Horowitz, L. (1991). Attachment styles among young adults: A test of a four-category model. *Journal of Personality and Social Psychology, 61,* 226–244.

Bartussek, D., Diedrich, O., Naumann, E., & Collet, W. (1993). Introversion–extraversion and event-related potential (ERP): A test of J. A. Gray's theory. *Personality and Individual Differences, 14,* 565–574.

Bates, B., & Goodman, A. (1986). The effectiveness of encounter groups: Implications of research for counseling practice. *British Journal of Guidance and Counseling, 14,* 240–251.

Bateson, G. (1979). *Mind and nature: A necessary unit.* New York: Dutton.

Baumeister, R. F. (1996). Self-regulation and ego threat: Motivated cognition, self deception, and destructive goal setting. In P. M. Gollwitzer & J. A. Bargh (Eds.), *The psychology of action: Linking cognition and motivation to behavior* (pp. 27–47). New York: Guilford.

Baumeister, R. F. (1997). Identity, self-concept, and self-esteem: The self lost and found. In R. Hogan, J. Johnson, & S. Briggs (Eds.), *Handbook of Personality Psychology* (pp. 681–710). San Diego, CA: Academic Press.

Baumeister, R. F. (1998). The self. In D. T. Glibert, S. T. Fiske, & G. Lindzey (Eds.), *The handbook of social psychology* (Vol. 1, 4th ed., pp. 680–740). New York: Oxford University Press.

Baumeister, R. F. (2002). Ego depletion and self-control failure: An energy model of the self's executive function. *Self and Identity, 1,* 129–136.

Baumeister, R. F., & Cairns, K. H. (1992). Repression and self-presentation: When audiences interfere with self-deceptive strategies. *Journal of Personality and Social Psychology, 62,* 851–862.

Baumeister, R. F., & Heatherton, T. F. (1996). Self-regulation failure: An overview. *Psychological Inquiry, 7,* 1–15.

Baumeister, R. F., & Tice, D. M. (1996). Rethinking and reclaiming the interdisciplinary role of personality psychology: The science of human nature should be the center of the social sciences and humanities. *Journal of Research in Personality. 30,* 363–373.

Beck, A. T. (1976). *Cognitive therapy and the emotional disorders.* New York: International Universities Press.

Beck, A. T., Rush, A. J., Shaw, B. F., & Emery, G. (1979). *Cognitive therapy of depression.* New York: Guilford.

Bell, J. E. (1948). *Projective techniques.* New York: Longmans, Green.

Bell, R. Q., & Costello, N. (1964). Three tests for sex differences in tactile sensitivity in the newborn. *Biologia Neonatorum, 7,* 335–347.

Bell, R. Q., & Darling, J. (1965). The prone head reaction in the human newborn: Relationship with sex and tactile sensitivity. *Child Development, 36,* 943–949.

Bell, R. Q., Weller, G., & Waldrop, M. (1971). Newborn and preschooler: Organization of behavior and relations between periods. *Monographs of the Society for Research in Child Development, 36,* (Nos. 1 & 2).

Bellak, L., & Abrams, D. M. (1997). *The Thematic Apperception Test, the Children's Apperception Test, and the Senior Apperception Technique in clinical use* (6th ed.). Boston, MA: Allyn & Bacon.

Bem, D. J. (1972). Self-perception theory. In L. Berkowitz (Ed.), *Advances in experimental social psychology* (Vol. 6, pp. 1–62). New York: Academic Press.

Bem, D. J. (1983). Constructing a theory of the triple typology: Some (second) thoughts on nomothetic and idiographic approaches to personality. *Journal of Personality, 51,* 566–577.

Bem, D. J., & Allen, A. (1974). On predicting some of the people some of the time: The search for cross-situational consistencies in behavior. *Psychological Review, 81,* 506–520.

Bem, D. J., & Funder, D. C. (1978). Predicting more of the people more of the time: Assessing the personality of situations. *Psychological Review, 85,* 485–501.

Benedict, R. (1934). *Patterns of culture.* New York: Mentor.

Benjamin, J., Li, L., Patterson, C., Greenberg, B. D., Murphy, D. L., & Hamer, D. H. (1996). Population and familial association between the D4 dopamine receptor gene and measures of novelty seeking. *Nature Genetics, 12,* 81–84.

Benson, H. (1975). *The relaxation response.* New York: Morrow.

Berger, S. M. (1962). Conditioning through vicarious instigation. *Psychological Review, 69,* 450–466.

Berntzen, D. (1987). Effects of multiple cognitive coping strategies on laboratory pain. *Cognitive Therapy and Research, 11,* 613–623.

Betancourt, H., & Lopez, S. R. (1993). The study of culture, ethnicity, and race in American psychology. *American Psychologist, 48,* 629–637.

Bijou, S. W. (1965). Experimental studies of child behavior, normal and deviant. In L. Krasner & L. P. Ullmann (Eds.), *Research in behavior modification* (pp. 56–81). New York: Holt, Rinehart and Winston.

Birbaumer, N., & Ohman, A. (1993). *The structure of emotion: Psychophysiological, cognitive, and clinical aspects.* Seattle, WA: Hogrefe & Huber.

Block, J. (1961). *The Q-sort method in personality assessment and psychiatric research.* Springfield, IL: Charles C. Thomas.

Block, J. (1971). *Lives through time.* Berkeley, CA: Bancroft.

Block, J. (1977). Advancing the psychology of personality: Paradigmatic shift or improving the quality of research. In D. Magnusson & N. S. Endler (Eds.), *Personality at the crossroads: Current issues in interactional psychology.* Hillsdale, NJ: Erlbaum.

Block, J. (1995). A contrarian view of the five-factor approach to personality description. *Psychological Bulletin, 117,* 187–215.

Block, J. (2001). Millennial contrarianism: The five-factor approach to personality description 5 years later. *Journal of Research in Personality, 35,* 98–107.

Block, J., & Block, J. H. (1980). The role of ego-control and ego resiliency in the organization of behavior. In W. A. Collins (Ed.), *The Minnesota symposium on child psychology* (Vol. 13). Hillsdale, NJ: Erlbaum.

Block, J., Weiss, D. S., & Thorne, A. (1979). How relevant is a semantic similarity interpretation of personality ratings? *Journal of Personality and Social Psychology, 37,* 1055–1074.

Block, J. H., & Martin, B. (1955). Predicting the behavior of children under frustration. *Journal of Abnormal and Social Psychology, 51,* 281–285.

Blum, G. S. (1953). *Psychoanalytic theories of personality.* New York: McGraw-Hill.

Blum, G. S. (1955). Perceptual defense revisited. *Journal of Abnormal and Social Psychology, 51,* 24–29.

Bolger, N., & Schilling, E. A. (1991). Personality and the problems of everyday life: The role of neuroticism in exposure and reactivity to daily stressors. *Journal of Personality, 59,* 355–386.

Bolger, N., & Zuckerman, A. (1995). A framework for studying personality in the stress process. *Journal of Personality and Social Psychology, 69,* 890–902.

Bonanno, G. A. (2001). Grief and emotion: A social–functional perspective. In M. S. Stroebe & R. O. Hansson (Eds.), *Handbook of bereavement research: Consequences, coping, and care* (pp. 493–515). Washington, DC: American Psychological Association.

Bonarius, J. C. J. (1965). Research in the personal construct theory of George A. Kelly: Role construct repertory test and basic theory. In B. A. Maher (Ed.), *Progress in experimental personality research* (pp. 1–46). New York: Academic Press.

Bornstein, R. F., Riggs, J. M., Hill, E. L., & Calabrese, C. (1996). Activity, passivity, self-denigration, and self-promotion: Toward an interactionist model of interpersonal dependency. *Journal of Personality, 64,* 637–673.

Bouchard, T. J., Lykken, D. T., McGue, M., Segal, N. L., & Tellegen, A. (1990). Sources of human psychological differences: The Minnesota study of twins reared apart. *Science, 250,* 223–228.

Boudin, H. M. (1972). Contingency contracting as a therapeutic tool in the deceleration of amphetamine use. *Behavior Therapy, 3,* 604–608.

Bower, G. H. (1981). Mood and memory. *American Psychologist, 36,* 129–148.

Bowers, K. (1973). Situationism in psychology: An analysis and a critique. *Psychological Review, 80,* 307–336.

Bowlby, J. (1982) Attachment and loss: Retrospect and prospect. *American Journal of Orthopsychiatry, 52,* 664–678.

Braungart, J. M., Fulker, D. W., & Plomin, R. (1992). Genetic influence of the home environment during infancy: A sibling adoption study of the HOME. *Developmental Psychology, 28,* 1048–1055.

Brazier, D. (1993). The necessary condition is love: Going beyond self in the person-centered approach. In D. Brazier (Ed.), *Beyond Carl Rogers* (pp. 72–91). London: Constable.

Brockner, J. (1983). The roles of self-esteem and self-consciousness in the Wortman-Brehm model of reactance and learned helplessness. *Journal of Personality & Social Psychology, 45,* 199–209.

Brown, J. D. (1986). Evaluations of self and others: Self-enhancement biases in social judgment. *Social Cognition, 4,* 353–376.

Brown, J. D., & Dutton, K. A. (1995). The thrill of victory, the complexity of defeat: Self-esteem and people's emotional reactions to success and failure. *Journal of Personality and Social Psychology, 68,* 712–722.

Brown, J. S. (1942). The generalization of approach responses as a function of stimulus intensity and strength of motivation. *Journal of Comparative Psychology, 33,* 209–226.

Brown, J. S. (1948). Gradients of approach and avoidance responses and their relation to level of motivation. *Journal of Comparative and Physiological Psychology, 41,* 450–465.

Brown, K. W., & Moskowitz, D. S. (1998). Dynamic stability of behavior: The rhythms of our interpersonal lives. *Journal of Personality, 66,* 105–134.

Bruner, J. (1992). Another look at New Look 1. *American Psychologist, 47,* 780–783.

Bruner, J. S. (1957), Going beyond the information given. In H. Gruber et al. (Eds.), *Contemporary approaches to cognition.* Cambridge, MA: Harvard University Press.

Bruner, J. S., & Postman, L. (1947). Emotional selectivity in perception and reaction. *Journal of Personality, 16,* 69–77.

Brunstein, J. (1993). Personal goals and subjective well-being: A longitudinal study. *Journal of Personality and Social Psychology, 65,* 1061–1070.

Buss, A. H. (1961). *The psychology of aggression.* New York: Wiley.

Buss, A. H. (1989). Personality as traits. *American Psychologist, 44,* 1378–1388.

Buss, A. H., & Plomin, R. (1984). *Temperament: Early developing personality traits.* Hillsdale, NJ: Erlbaum.

Buss, A. H., Plomin, R., & Willerman, L. (1973). The inheritance of temperaments. *Journal of Personality, 41,* 513–524.

Buss, D. M. (1987). Selection, evocation, and manipulation. *Journal of Personality and Social Psychology, 53,* 1214–1221.

Buss, D. M. (1991). Evolutionary personality psychology. *Annual Review of Psychology, 42,* 459–491.

Buss, D. M. (1994). Personality evoked: The evolutionary psychology of stability and change. In T. F. Heatherton & J. L. Weinberger (Eds.), Can personality change? (pp. 41–57). Washington, DC: American Psychological Association.

Buss, D. M. (1996). The evolutionary psychology of human social strategies. In E. T. Higgins & A. W. Kruglanski (Eds.), *Social psychology: Handbook of basic principles* (pp. 3–38). New York: Guilford.

Buss, D. M. (1997) Evolutionary foundations of personality. In R. Hogan, J. A. Johnson, & S. R. Briggs (Eds.), *Handbook of personality psychology* (pp. 317–344). San Diego: Academic Press.

Buss, D. M. (1999). Human nature and individual differences: The evolution of human personality. In L. A. Pervin & O. P. John (Eds.), *Handbook of personality: Theory and research* (2nd ed., pp. 31–56). New York: Guilford.

Buss, D. M. (2001). Human nature and culture: An evolutionary psychological perspective. *Journal of Personality, 69,* 955–978.

Buss, D. M., & Craik, K. H. (1983). The act frequency approach to personality. *Psychological Review, 90,* 105–126.

Butler, L. D., & Nolen-Hoeksema, S. (1994). Gender differences in response to depressed mood in college sample. *Sex Roles, 30,* 330–346.

Byrne, D. (1964). Repression–sensitization as a dimension of personality. In B. A. Maher (Ed.), *Progress in experimental personality research* (Vol. 1). New York: Academic Press.

Byrne, D. (1966). *An introduction to personality.* Englewood Cliffs, NJ: Prentice-Hall.

Byrne, D. (1969). Attitudes and attraction. In L. Berkowitz (Ed.), *Advances in experimental social psychology* (Vol. 1). New York: Academic Press.

Cacioppo, J. T., & Gardner, W. L. (1999). Emotion. *Annual Review of Psychology, 50,* 191–214.

Cacioppo, J. T., & Petty, R. E. (1982). The need for cognition. *Journal of Personality and Social Psychology, 42,* 116–131.

Cacioppo, J. T., Berntson, G. G., & Crites Jr., S. L. (1996). Social neuroscience: Principles of psychophysiological arousal and response. In E. T. Higgins & A. W. Kruglanski (Eds.), *Social Psychology: Handbook of Basic Principles* (pp. 72–101). New York: Guilford.

Caldwell, B. M., & Bradley, R. H. (1978). *Home Observation for Measurement of the Environment.* Little Rock: University of Arkansas Press.

Campbell, D. T. (1960). Recommendations for APA Test Standards regarding construct, trait, or discriminant validity. *American Psychologist, 15,* 546–553.

Campbell, J., & Dunnette, M. (1968). Effectiveness of T-group experiences in managerial training and development. *Psychological Bulletin, 70,* 73–104.

Cannon, W. B. (1932). *The wisdom of the body*. New York: Norton.

Cantor, N. (1990). From thought to behavior: "Having" and "doing" in the study of personality and cognition. *American Psychologist, 45,* 735–750.

Cantor, N. (1994). Life task problem-solving: Situational affordances and personal needs. Presidential address of the society for personality and social psychology (Division 8 of the American Psychological Association, 1993, Toronto, Canada), *Personality and Social Psychology Bulletin, 20,* 235–243.

Cantor, N., Kemmelmeier, M., Basten, J., & Prentice, D. A. (2002). Life task pursuit in social groups: Balancing self-exploration and social integration. *Self and Identity, 1,* 177–184.

Cantor, N., & Kihlstrom, J. F. (1987). *Personality and social intelligence*. Englewood Cliffs, NJ: Erlbaum.

Cantor, N., & Mischel, W. (1977). Traits as prototypes: Effects on recognition memory. *Journal of Personality and Social Psychology, 35,* 38–48.

Cantor, N., & Mischel, W. (1979). Prototypes in person perception. In L. Berkowitz (Ed.), *Advances in experimental social psychology* (Vol. 12). New York: Academic Press.

Cantor, N., Mischel, W., & Schwartz, J. (1982). A prototype analysis of psychological situations. *Cognitive Psychology, 14,* 45–77.

Cantor, N., Norem, J., Langston, C., Zirkel, S., Fleeson W., & Cook-Flannagan, C. (1991). Life tasks and daily life experience. *Journal of Personality, 59,* 425–451.

Capecchi, M. R. (1994). Targeted gene replacement. *Scientific American, 270,* 52–59.

Carlson, R. (1971). Where is the personality research? *Psychological Bulletin, 75,* 203–219.

Carter, C. S. (1998). Neuroendocrine perspectives on social attachment and love. *Psychoneuroendocrinology, 23,* 779–818.

Carter, C. S., Lederhendler, I. I., & Kirkpatrick, B. (1997). *The integrative neurobiology of affiliation*. New York: New York Academy of Sciences.

Cartwright, D. S. (1978). *Introduction to personality*. Chicago: Rand McNally.

Carver, C. S. (1996). Emergent integration in contemporary personality psychology. *Journal of Research in Personality, 30,* 319–334.

Carver, C. S., Coleman, A. E., & Glass, D. C. (1976). The coronary-prone behavior pattern and the suppression of fatigue on a treadmill test. *Journal of Personality and Social Psychology, 33,* 460–466.

Carver, C. S., Pozo, C., Harris, S. D., Noriega, V., Scheier, M. F., Robinson, D. S., Ketchem, A. S., Moffat, F. L., Jr., & Clark, K. C. (1993). How coping mediates the effects of optimism on stress: A study of women with early stage breast cancer. *Journal of Personality and Social Psychology, 65,* 375–391.

Carver, C. S., & Scheier, M. F. (1978). Self-focusing effects of dispositional self-consciousness, mirror presence, and audience presence. *Journal of Personality and Social Psychology, 36,* 322–324.

Carver, C. S., & Scheier, M. F. (1981). *Attention and self-regulation: A control theory approach to human behavior*. New York: Springer-Verlag.

Carver, C. S., & Scheier, M. F. (1982). Control theory: A useful conceptual framework for personality-social, clinical, and health psychology. *Psychological Bulletin, 92,* 111–135.

Carver, C. S., & Scheier, M. F. (1990). Principles of self-regulation: Action and emotion. In E. T. Higgins & R. M. Sorrentino (Eds.), *Handbook of motivation and cognition* (Vol. 2, pp. 3–52). New York: Guilford.

Carver, C. S., & Scheier, M. F. (1992). Confidence, doubt, and coping with anxiety. In D. G. Forgays, T. Sosnowski, & K. Wrzesniewski (Eds.), *Anxiety: Recent developments in cognitive, psychophysiological, and health research* (pp. 13–22). Washington, DC: Hemisphere Publishing Corp.

Carver, C. S., & Scheier, M. F. (1998). *On the self-regulation of behavior*. New York: Cambridge University Press.

Carver, C. S., & White, T. L. (1994). Behavioral inhibition, behavioral activation, and affective responses to impending reward and punishment: The BIS/BAS scales. *Journal of Personality and Social Psychology, 67,* 319–333.

Cashdan, S. (1988). *Object relations theory: Using the relationship*. New York: Norton and Co.

Caspi, A. (1987). Personality in the life course. *Journal of Personality and Social Psychology, 53,* 1203–1213.

Caspi, A. (1998). Personality development across the life course. In W. Damon (Ser. Ed.) and N. Eisenberg (Vol. Ed.), *Handbook of Child Psychology, Vol. 3: Social, emotional, and personality development* (pp. 311–388). New York: Wiley.

Caspi, A., & Bem, D. J. (1990). Personality continuity and change across the life course. In L. A. Pervin (Ed.), *Handbook of personality: Theory and research* (pp. 549–575). New York: Guilford.

Cattell, R. B. (1950). *A systematic theoretical and factual study*. New York: McGraw-Hill.

Cattell, R. B. (1965). *The scientific analysis of personality*. Baltimore: Penguin Books.

Cattell, R. B. (1982). *The inheritance of personality and ability*. New York: Academic Press.

Cervone, D. (1991). The two disciplines of personality psychology [Review of *Handbook of personality: Theory and research*]. *Psychological Science, 2,* 371–376.

Cervone, D., & Mischel, W. (2002). Personality Science. In D. Cervone & W. Mischel (Eds.) *Advances in Personality Science* (pp. 1–26). New York: Guilford.

Cervone, D., & Mischel, W. (Eds.) (2002). *Advances in Personality Science*. New York: Guilford.

Cervone, D., Shadel, W. G., & Jencius, S. (2001). Social-cognitive theory of personality assessment. *Personality and Social Psychology Review, 5,* 33–51.

Cervone, D., & Shoda, Y. (1999). Social cognitive theories and the coherence of personality. In D. Cervone and Y. Shoda (eds.), *The coherence of personality: Social-cognitive bases of consistency, variability, and organization.* New York: Guilford.

Cervone, D., & Williams, S. L. (1982). Social cognitive theory and personality. In G. V. Caprara & G. L. Van Heck (Eds.), *Modern personality psychology: Critical reviews and new directions* (pp. 200–252). New York: Harvester Wheatsheaf/Simon & Schuster.

Chaiken, S., & Bargh, J. A. (1993). Occurrence versus moderation of the automatic attitude activation effect: Reply to Fazio. *Journal of Personality and Social Psychology, 64,* 759–765.

Chan, D. W. (1994). The Chinese Ways of Coping Questionnaire: Assessing coping in secondary school teachers and students in Hong Kong. *Psychological Assessment, 6,* 108–116.

Chaplin, W. F., John, O. P., & Goldberg, L. R. (1988). Conceptions of states and traits: Dimensional attributes with ideals as prototypes. *Journal of Personality and Social Psychology, 54,* 541–557.

Chaves, J. F., & Barber, T. X. (1974). Acupuncture analgesia: A six-factor theory. *Psychoenergetic Systems, 1,* 11–20.

Chen-Idson, L., & Mischel, W. (2001). The personality of familiar and significant people: The lay perceiver as a social cognitive theorist. *Journal of Personality and Social Psychology, 80,* 585–596.

Cheng, C. (2001). Assessing coping flexibility in real-life and laboratory settings: A multimethod approach. *Journal of Personality and Social Psychology, 80,* 814–833.

Cheng, C. (2003). Cognitive and motivational processes underlying coping flexibility: A dual-process model. *Journal of Personality and Social Psychology, 84,* 425–438.

Cheng, C., Chiu, C., Hong, Y., & Cheung, J. S. (2001). Discriminative facility and its role in the quality of interactional experiences. *Journal of Personality, 69,* 765–786.

Cheng, C., Hui, W., & Lam, S. (2000). Perceptual style and behavioral pattern of individuals with functional gastrointestinal disorders. *Health Psychology, 19,* 146–154.

Cherney, S. S., Fulker, D. W., Emde, R. N., Robinson, J., Corley, R. P., Reznick, J. S., Plomin, R., & Defries, J. C. (1994). Continuity and change in infant shyness from 14 to 20 months. *Behavior Genetics, 24,* 365–379.

Chiu, C., Dweck, C. S., Tong, J. Y., & Fu, J. H. (1997). Implicit theories and conceptions of morality. *Journal of Personality and Social Psychology, 73,* 923–940.

Chiu, C., Hong, Y., & Dweck, C. S. (1997). Lay dispositionism and implicit theories of personality. *Journal of Personality and Social Psychology, 73,* 19–30.

Chiu, C., Hong, Y., Mischel, W., & Shoda, Y. (1995). Discriminative facility in social competence: Conditional versus dispositional encoding and monitoring-blunting of information. *Social Cognition, 13,* 49–70.

Chodoff, P. (1963). Late effects of concentration camp syndrome. *Archives of General Psychiatry, 8,* 323–333.

Churchland, P. S., & Sejnowski, T. J. (1992). *The computational brain.* Cambridge, MA: MIT Press.

Clark, L. A., & Watson, D. (1999). Temperament: A new paradigm for trait psychology. In L. A. Pervin & O. P. John (Eds.), *Handbook of personality: Theory and research* (2nd ed., pp. 399–423). New York: Guilford.

Cloninger, C. R. (1988). A unified biosocial theory of personality and its role in the development of anxiety states: A reply to commentaries. *Psychiatric Developments, 2,* 83–120.

Cobb, S. (1976). Social support as moderator of life stress. *Psychosomatic Medicine, 38,* 300–314.

Cohen, S., & McKay, G. (1984). Social support, stress, and the buffering hypothesis: A theoretical analysis. In A. Baum, J. E. Singer, & S. E. Taylor (Eds.), *Handbook of psychology and health, Vol. 4. Social psychological aspects of health.* Hillsdale, NJ: Erlbaum.

Colby, K. M. (1951). *A primer for psychotherapists.* New York: Ronald.

Coles, R. (1970). *Uprooted children.* New York: Harper & Row.

Collaer, M. L., & Hines, M. (1995). Human behavioral sex differences: A role for gonadal hormones during early development? *Psychological Bulletin, 118,* 55–107.

Contrada, R. J., Cather, C., & O'Leary, A. (1999). Personality and health: Dispositions and processes in disease susceptibility and adaptation to illness. In L. A. Pervin & O. P. John (Eds.), *Handbook of personality: Theory and research* (2nd ed., pp. 576–604). New York: Guilford.

Contrada, R. J., Leventhal, H., & O'Leary, A. (1990). Personality and health. In L. A. Pervin (Ed.), *Handbook of personality: Theory and research* (pp. 638–669). New York: Guilford.

Cooper, J., & Fazio, R. H. (1984). A new look at dissonance theory. In L. Berkowitz (Ed.), *Advances in experimental social psychology, Vol. 17. Theorizing in social psychology: Special topics* (pp. 229–262). New York: Academic Press.

Cooper, J. R., Bloom, F. E., & Roth, R. H. (1996). *The biochemical basis of neuropharmacology (7th ed.).* New York: Oxford University Press.

Coopersmith, S. (1967). *The antecedents of self-esteem*. San Francisco: Freeman.

Cosmides, L. (1989). The logic of social exchange: Has natural selection shaped how humans reason? Studies with the Wason selection task. *Cognition, 31*, 187–276.

Cosmides, L., & Tooby, J. (1989). Evolutionary psychology and the generation of culture: II. Case study: A computational theory of social exchange. *Ethology and Sociobiology, 10*, 51–97.

Costa, P. T., Jr., & McCrae, R. R. (1988). Personality in adulthood: A six-year longitudinal study of self-reports and spouse ratings on the NEO personality inventory. *Journal of Personality and Social Psychology, 54*, 853–863.

Costa, P. T., Jr., & McCrae, R. R. (1992a). Normal personality assessment in clinical practice: The NEO personality inventory. *Psychological Assessment, 4*, 5–13.

Costa, P. T., Jr., & McCrae, R. R. (1992b). *Revised NEO Personality Inventory (NEO-PI-R) and NEO Five Factor (NEO-FFI): Professional manual*. Odessa, FL: Psychological Assessment Resources.

Costa, P. T., Jr., & McCrae, R. R. (1997). Longitudinal stability of adult personality. In R. Hogan, J. Johnson, & S. Briggs (Eds.), *Handbook of personality psychology* (pp. 269–291). San Diego, CA: Academic Press.

Costa, P. T., Jr., McCrae, R. R., & Dye, D. A. (1991). Facet scales for agreeableness and conscientiousness: A revision of the neo-personality inventory. *Personality and Individual Differences, 12*, 887–898.

Costa, P. T., Jr., McCrae, R. R., & Siegler, I. C. (1999). Continuity and change over the adult life cycle: Personality and personality disorders. In C.R. Cloninger (Ed.), *Personality and psychopathology* (pp. 129–153). Washington, DC: American Psychiatric Press.

Cote, S., & Moskowitz, D. S. (1998). On the dynamic covariation between interpersonal behavior and affect: Prediction from neuroticism, extraversion, and agreeableness. *Journal of Personality and Social Psychology, 75*, 1032–1046.

Coyne, J. C., & Downey, G. (1991). Social factors and psychopathology: Stress, social support, and coping process. *Annual Review of Psychology, 42*, 401–425.

Crocker, J. (2002). Contingencies of self-worth: Implications for self-regulation and psychological vulnerability. *Self and Identity, 1*, 143–149.

Csikszentmihalyi, M. (1990). The domain of creativity. In M. Runco & R. S. Albert (Eds.) *Theories of creativity. Sage focus editions* (Vol. 115, pp. 190–212). Thousand Oaks, CA: Sage Publications.

Dabbs, J. M., Jr., & Morris, R. (1990). Testosterone, social class, and antisocial behavior in a sample of 4,462 men. *Psychological Science, 1*, 209–211.

Dabbs, J. M., Jr. (1992). Testosterone and occupational achievement. *Social Forces, 70*, 813–824.

D'Andrade, R. G. (1966). Sex differences and cultural institutions. In E. E. Maccoby (Ed.), *The development of sex differences* (pp. 174–204). Stanford: Stanford University Press.

Daniels, A. C. (1994). *Bringing out the best in people: How to apply the astonishing power of reinforcement*. New York: McGraw-Hill.

Daniels, D., Dunn, J. F., Furstenberg, F. F., Jr., & Plomin, R. (1985). Environmental differences within the family and adjustment differences within pairs of adolescent siblings. *Child Development, 56*, 764–774.

David, J. P., Green, P. J., Martin, R., & Suls, J. (1997). Differential roles of neuroticism, extraversion, and event desirability for mood in daily life: An integrative model of top-down and bottom-up influences. *Journal of Personality and Social Psychology, 73*, 149–159.

Davidson, R. J. (1993). The neuropsychology of emotion and affective style. In M. Lewis & J. M. Haviland (Eds.), *Handbook of emotions* (pp. 143–154). New York: Guildford.

Davidson, R. J. (1995). Cerebral asymmetry, emotion, and affective style. In R. J. Davidson & K. Hugdahl (Eds.), *Brain asymmetry* (pp. 361–387). Cambridge, MA: MIT Press.

Davidson, R. J., & Fox, N. A. (1989). The relation between tonic EEG asymmetry and ten-month-olds' emotional response to separation. *Journal of Abnormal Psychology, 98*, 127–131.

Davidson, R. J., & Sutton, S. K. (1995). Affective neuroscience: The emergence of a discipline. *Current Opinion in Neurobiology, 5*, 217–224.

Davidson, R. J., Ekman, P., Saron, C. D., Senulis, J. A., & Friesen, W. V. (1990). Approach-withdrawal and cerebral asymmetry: Emotional expression and brain physiology I. *Journal of Personality and Social Psychology, 58*, 330–341.

Davidson, R. J., Putnam, K. M., & Larson, C. L. (2000). Dysfunction in the neural circuitry of emotion regulation—A possible prelude to violence. *Science, 289*, 591–594.

Davis, J. M., Klerman, G., & Schildkraut, J. (1967). Drugs used in the treatment of depression. In L. Efron, J. O. Cole, D. Levine, & J. R. Wittenborn (Eds.), *Psychopharmacology: A review of progress*. Washington, DC: U.S. Clearing-House of Mental Health Information.

Davison, G. C., & Neale, J. M. (1990). *Abnormal psychology: An experimental clinical approach* (5th ed.). New York: Wiley.

Davison, G. C., Neale, J. M., & Kring, A. M. (2004). *Abnormal psychology* (9th ed.). Hoboken, NJ: Wiley.

Deaux, K., & Major, B. (1987). Putting gender into context: An interactive model of gender-related behavior. *Psychological Review, 94*, 369–389.

Deci, E. L., & Ryan, R. M. (1987). The support of autonomy and the control of behavior. *Journal of Personality and Social Psychology, 53*, 1024–1037.

Deci, E. L., & Ryan, R. M. (1995). Human autonomy: The basis for true self-esteem. In M. Kernis (Ed.), *Efficacy, agency, and self-esteem* (pp. 31–49). New York: Plenum.

Deci, E. L., & Ryan, R. M. (2000). The support of autonomy and the control of behavior. In E. T. Higgins & A. W. Kruglanski (Eds.), *Motivational science: Social and personality perspectives* (pp. 128–145). New York: Psychology Press.

Depue, R. A., & Collins, P. F. (1999). Neurobiology of the structure of personality: Dopamine, facilitation, of incentive motivation, and extraversion. *Behavioral and Brain Sciences, 22*, 491–569.

DeRaad, B., Perugini, M., Hrebickova, M., & Szarota, P. (1998). Lingua franca of personality: Taxonomies and structures based on the psycholexical approach. *Journal of Cross Cultural Psychology, 29*, 212–232.

Derryberry, D. (2002). Attention and voluntary self-control. *Self and Identity, 1*, 105–111.

Derryberry, D., & Reed, M. A. (2002). Anxiety-related attentional biases and their regulation by attentional control. *Journal of Abnormal Psychology, 111*, 225–236.

Derryberry, D., & Rothbart, M. K. (1997). Reactive and effortful processes in the organization of temperament. *Development and Psychopathology, 9*, 633–652.

Diamond, M. J., & Shapiro, J. L. (1973). Changes in locus of control as a function of encounter group experiences: A study and replication. *Journal of Abnormal Psychology, 82*, 514–518.

Dickens, W. T., & Flynn, J. R. (2001). Heritability estimates versus large environmental effects: The IQ paradox resolved. *Psychological Review, 108*, 346–369.

Diener, C. I., & Dweck, C. S. (1978). An analysis of learned helplessness: Continuous changes in performance, strategy, and achievement cognitions following failure. *Journal of Personality and Social Psychology, 36*, 451–462.

Dobson, K. S., & Craig, K. D. (1996). *Advances in cognitive-behavioral therapy*. Thousand Oaks, CA: Sage Publications.

Dodge, K. A. (1986). A social information processing model of social competence in children. *Cognitive perspectives on children's social behavioral development. The Minnesota symposium on child psychology, 18*, 77–125.

Dodge, K. A. (1993). New wrinkles in the person-versus-situation debate. *Psychological Inquiry, 4*, 284–286.

Dodge, K. A. (1997a, April). *Testing developmental theory through prevention trials*. Presented at Biennial Meeting for the Society for Research in Child Development, Washington, DC.

Dodge, K. A. (1997b, April). *Early peer social rejection and acquired autonomic sensitivity to peer conflicts: Conduct problems in adolescence*. Presented at Biennial Meeting for the Society for Research in Child Development, Washington, DC.

Dodgson, P., & Wood, J. V. (1998). Self-esteem and the cognitive accessibility of strengths and weaknesses after failure. *Journal of Personality and Social Psychology, 75*, 178–197.

Dollard, J., & Miller, N. E. (1950). *Personality and psychotherapy: An analysis in terms of learning, thinking, and culture*. New York: McGraw-Hill.

Downey, G., & Feldman, S. I. (1996). Implications of rejection sensitivity for intimate relationships. *Journal of Personality and Social Psychology, 70*, 1327–1343.

Downey, G., Freitas, A., Michaelis, B., & Khouri, H. (1998). The self-fullfilling prophecy in close relationships. Do rejection sensitive women get rejected by their partners? *Journal of Personality and Social Psychology, 75*, 545–560.

Duke, M. P. (1986). Personality science: A proposal. *Journal of Personality and Social Psychology, 50*, 382–385.

Dunford, F. W. (2000). The San Diego Navy experiment: An assessment of interventions for men who assault their wives. *Journal of Consulting and Clinical Psychology, 68*, 468–476.

Dunn, J., & Plomin, R. (1990). *Separate lives: Why siblings are so different*. New York: Basic Books.

Dunnette, M. D. (1969). People feeling: Joy, more joy, and the "slough of despond." *Journal of Applied Behavioral Science, 5*, 25–44.

Durham, W. H. (1991). *Coevolution*. Stanford, CA: Stanford University Press.

Duval, T. S., Duval, V. H., & Mulilis, J. (1992). Effects of self-focus, discrepancy between self and standard, and outcome expectancy favorability on the tendency to match self to standard or to withdraw. *Journal of Personality and Social Psychology, 62*, 340–348.

Dweck, C. S. (1975). The role of expectations and attributions in the alleviation of learned helplessness. *Journal of Personality and Social Psychology, 31*, 674–685.

Dweck, C. S. (1990). Self-theories and goals: Their role in motivation, personality, and development. In R. A. Dienstbier (Ed.), *Nebraska symposium on motivation* (Vol. 38, pp. 199–235). Lincoln, NE: University of Nebraska Press.

Dweck, C. S., & Leggett, E. L. (1988). A social-cognitive approach to personality and motivation. *Psychological Review, 95*, 256–273.

Dworkin, R. H. (1979). Genetic and environmental influences on person-situation interactions. *Journal of Research in Personality, 13,* 279–293.

D'Zurilla, T. (1965). Recall efficiency and mediating cognitive events in "experimental repression." *Journal of Personality and Social Psychology, 1,* 253–257.

Eagly, A. H. (1987). *Sex differences in social behavior: A social-role interpretation.* Hillsdale, NJ: Erlbaum.

Eagly, A. H. (1995). The science and politics of comparing women and men. *American Psychologist, 50,* 145–158.

Eagly, A. H., & Crowley, M. (1986). Gender and helping behavior: A meta-analytic review of the social psychological literature. *Psychological Bulletin, 100,* 283–308.

Eagly, A. H., & Steffen, V. J. (1986). Gender and aggressive behavior: A meta-analytic review of the social psychological literature. *Psychological Bulletin, 100,* 309–330.

Eaves, L. J., Eysenck, H. J., & Martin, N. G. (1989). *Genes, culture, and personality: An empirical approach.* London: Academic Press.

Ebstein, R. P., Gritsenko, I., Nemanov, L., Frisch, A., Osher, Y., & Belmaker, R. H. (1997). No association between the serotonin transporter gene regulatory region polymorphism and the Tridimensional Personality Questionnaire (TPQ) temperament of harm avoidance. *Molecular Psychiatry, 2,* 224–226.

Ebstein, R. P., Novick, O., Umansky, R., Priel, B., Osher, Y., Blaine, D., Bennett, E. R., Nemanov, L., Katz, M., & Belmaker, R. H. (1996). Dopamine D4 receptor (D4DR) exon III polymorphism associated with human personality trait of novelty seeking. *Nature Genetics, 12,* 78–80.

Edelman, G. M. (1992). *Bright air, brilliant fire: On the matter of the mind.* New York: Basic Books.

Ehrlich, P. R. (2000). *Human natures: Genes, cultures, and the human prospect.* Washington, DC: Island Press.

Eisenberg, N., Spinrad, T. L., & Morris, A. S. (2002). Regulation, resiliency, and quality of social functioning. *Self and Identity, 1,* 121–128.

Eizenman, D. R., Nesselroade, J. R., Featherman, D. L., & Rowe, J. W. (1997). Intraindividual variability in perceived control in an older sample: The MacArthur successful aging studies. *Psychology and Aging, 12,* 489–502.

Ekman, P. (Ed.). (1982). *Emotion in the human face* (2nd ed.). New York: Cambridge University Press.

Ekman, P., Friesen, W. V., & Ellsworth, P. (1972). *Emotion in the human face.* Elmsford, NY: Pergamon Press.

Ellsworth, P. C., & Carlsmith, J. M. (1968). Effects of eye contact and verbal content on affective response to a dyadic interaction. *Journal of Personality and Social Psychology, 10,* 15–20.

Emmons, R. A. (1991). Personal strivings, daily life events, and psychological and physical well-being. *Journal of Personality, 59,* 453–472.

Emmons, R. A. (1997). Motives and goals. In R. Hogan, J. A. Johnson, & S. R. Briggs (Eds.), *Handbook of personality psychology* (pp. 485–512). San Diego, CA: Academic Press.

Endler, N. S., & Hunt, J. M. (1968). S-R inventories of hostility and comparisons of the proportions of variance from persons, responses, and situations for hostility and anxiousness. *Journal of Personality and Social Psychology, 9,* 309–315.

Epstein, S. (1973). The self-concept revisited or a theory of a theory. *American Psychologist, 28,* 405–416.

Epstein, S. (1977). Traits are alive and well. In D. Magnusson and N. Endler (Eds.), *Personality at the crossroads: Current issues in interactional psychology* (pp. 83–98). Hillsdale, NJ: Erlbaum.

Epstein, S. (1979). The stability of behavior: I. On predicting most of the people much of the time. *Journal of Personality and Social Psychology, 37,* 1097–1126.

Epstein, S. (1983). Aggregation and beyond: Some basic issues on the prediction of behavior. *Journal of Personality, 51,* 360–392.

Epstein, S. (1990). Cognitive-experimental self-theory. In L. A. Pervin (Ed.), *Handbook of personality: Theory and research* (pp. 165–192). New York: Guilford.

Epstein, S., & Fenz, W. D. (1962). Theory and experiment on the measurement of approach-avoidance conflict. *Journal of Abnormal and Social Psychology, 64,* 97–112.

Erdelyi, M. H. (1985). *Psychoanalysis: Freud's cognitive psychology.* New York: W. H. Freeman & Company.

Erdelyi, M. H. (1992). Psychodynamics and the unconscious. *American Psychologist, 47,* 784–787.

Erdelyi, M. H. (1993). Repression: The mechanism and the defense. In D. M. Wegner & J. W. Pennebaker (Eds.), *Handbook of mental control. Century psychology series* (pp. 126–148). Englewood Cliffs, NJ: Prentice-Hall.

Erdelyi, M. H., & Goldberg, B. (1979). Let's not sweep repression under the rug: Towards a cognitive psychology of repression. In J. F. Kihlstrom & F. J. Evans (Eds.), *Functional disorders of memory.* Hillsdale, NJ: Erlbaum.

Erdley, C. A., & Dweck, C. S. (1993). Children's implicit personality theories as predictors of their social judgements. *Child Development, 64,* 863–878.

Eriksen, C. W. (1952). Individual differences in defensive forgetting. *Journal of Experimental Psychology, 44,* 442–446.

Eriksen, C. W. (1966). Cognitive responses to internally cued anxiety. In C. D. Spielberger (Ed.), *Anxiety and behavior* (pp. 327–360). New York: Academic Press.

Eriksen, C. W., & Kuethe, J. L. (1956). Avoidance conditioning of verbal behavior without awareness: A paradigm of repression. *Journal of Abnormal and Social Psychology, 53*, 203–209.

Erikson, E. (1963). *Childhood and society.* New York: Norton.

Erikson, E. (1968). *Identity: Youth and crisis.* New York: Norton.

Exline, R., & Winters, L. C. (1965). Affective relations and mutual glances in dyads. In S. Tomkins & C. Izard (Eds.), *Affect, cognition, and personality.* New York: Springer.

Exner, J. E. (1993). *The Rorschach: A comprehensive system, Vol. 1: Basic foundations* (3rd ed.). New York: Wiley.

Eysenck, H. (1983). Cicero and the state-trait theory of anxiety: Another case of delayed recognition. *American Psychologist, 38*, 114–115.

Eysenck, H. J. (1961). The effects of psychotherapy. In H. J. Eysenck (Ed.), *Handbook of abnormal psychology: An experimental approach* (pp. 697–725). New York: Basic Books.

Eysenck, H. J. (1967). *The biological basis of personality.* Springfield, IL: Charles C. Thomas.

Eysenck, H. J. (1973). Personality and the law of effect. In D. E. Berlyne & K. B. Madsen (Eds.), *Pleasure, reward, preference.* New York: Academic Press.

Eysenck, H. J. (1990). Biological dimensions of personality. In L. A. Pervin (Ed.), *Handbook of personality: Theory and research* (pp. 244–276). New York: Guilford.

Eysenck, H. J. (1991). Personality, stress, and disease: An interactionist perspective. *Psychological Inquiry, 2*, 221–232.

Eysenck, H. J., & Eysenck, M.W. (1985). *Personality and individual differences: A natural science approach.* New York: Plenum.

Eysenck, H. J., & Eysenck, M. W. (1995). *Mindwatching: Why we behave the way we do.* London: Prion Books.

Eysenck, H. J., & Rachman, S. (1965). *The causes and cures of neurosis: An introduction to modern behavior therapy based on learning theory and the principles of conditioning.* San Diego, CA: Knapp.

Fairweather, G. W. (1967). *Methods in experimental social innovation.* New York: Wiley.

Fairweather, G. W., Sanders, D. H., Cressler, D. L., & Maynard, H. (1969). *Community life for the mentally ill: An alternative to institutional care.* Chicago: Aldine.

Feather, N. T. (1990). Bridging the gap between values and actions: Recent applications of the expectancy-value model. In E. T. Higgins & R. M. Sorrentino (Eds.), *Handbook on motivation and cognition: Foundations of social behavior* (Vol. 3, pp. 151–191). New York: Guilford.

Fenz, W. D. (1964). Conflict and stress as related to physiological activation and sensory, perceptual and cognitive functioning. *Psychological Monographs, 78*, No. 8 (Whole No. 585).

Ferster, C. B., & Skinner, B. F. (1957). *Schedules of reinforcement.* New York: Appleton.

Festinger, L. (1957). *A theory of cognitive dissonance.* Stanford, CA: Stanford University Press.

Fischer, W. F. (1970). *Theories of anxiety.* New York: Harper.

Fiske, A. P. (2002). Using individualism and collectivism to compare cultures—A critique of the validity and measurement of the constructs comment on Oyserman et al. (2002). *Psychological Bulletin, 128*, 78–88.

Fiske, D. W. (1994). Two cheers for the Big Five. *Psychological Inquiry, 5*, 123–124.

Fitch, G. (1970). Effects of self-esteem, perceived performance, and choice on causal attribution. *Journal of Personality and Social Psychology, 16*, 311–315.

Flavell, J. H., & Ross, L. (Eds.). (1981). *Social cognitive development: Frontiers and possible futures.* New York: Cambridge University Press.

Fleeson, W. (2001). Toward a structure- and process-integrated view of personality: Traits as density distributions of states. *Journal of Personality and Social Psychology, 80*, 1011–1027.

Fleming, J., & Darley, J. M. (1986). *Perceiving intention in constrained behavior: The role of purposeful and constrained action cues in correspondence bias effects.* Unpublished manuscript, Princeton University, Princeton, NJ.

Flint, J., Corley, R., DeFries, J. C., Fulker, D. W., Gary, J. A., Miller, S., & Collins, A. C. (1995). A simple genetic basis for a complex psychological trait in laboratory mice. *Science, 269*, 1432–1435.

Fodor, I. (1987). Moving beyond cognitive-behavior therapy: Integrating Gestalt therapy to facilitate personal and interpersonal awareness. In N. S. Jacobson (Ed.), *Psychotherapists in clinical practice: Cognitive and behavioral perspectives* (pp. 190–231). New York: Guilford.

Forgas, J. P. (1983). Episode cognition and personality: A multidimensional analysis. *Journal of Personality, 51*, 34–48.

Foucault, M. (1980). *Power/knowledge: Selected interviews and other writings, 1972–1977* (C. Gordon, Ed. and Trans.). Brighton, England: Harvester.

Fox, N. A., Bell, M. A., & Jones, N. A. (1992). Individual differences in response to stress and cerebral asymmetry. *Developmental Neuropsychology, 8*, 161–184.

Fox, N. A., Henderson, H. A., Rubin, K. H., Calkins, S. D., & Schmidt, L. A. (2001). Continuity and discontinuity of behavioral inhibition and exuberance: Psychophisiological and behavioral influences across the first four years of life. *Child Development, 72*, 1–21.

Fox, N. A., Schmidt, L. A., Calkins, S. D., Rubin, K. H., & Copan, R. J. (1996). The role of frontal activation in the regulation and dysregulation of social behavior during the preschool years. *Development and Psychopathology, 8*, 89–102.

Fraley, R. C., & Shaver, P. R. (1997). Adult attachment and the suppression of unwanted thoughts. *Journal of Personality and Social Psychology, 73*, 1080–1091.

Frank, K. G., & Hudson, S. M. (1990). Behavior management of infant sleep disturbance. *Journal of Applied Behavior Analysis, 23*, 91–98.

Fransella, F. (1995). *George Kelly*. London: Sage Publications.

Frawley, P. J., & Smith, J. W. (1990). Chemical aversion therapy in the treatment of cocaine dependence as part of a multimodal treatment program: Treatment outcome. *Journal of Substance Abuse Treatment, 7*, 21–29.

Freud, A. (1936). *The ego and the mechanisms of defense.* New York: International Universities Press.

Freud, S. (1899). The interpretation of dreams. *Standard edition, Vol. 4.* London: Hogarth, 1955.

Freud, S. (1901). Psychopathology of everyday life. *Standard edition, Vol. 6.* London: Hogarth, 1960.

Freud, S. (1905). Fragments of an analysis of a case of hysteria. *Standard edition, Vol. 7.* London: Hogarth, 1953.

Freud, S. (1909). Leonardo da Vinci: A study in psychosexuality. *Standard edition, Vol. 2.* London: Hogarth, 1957.

Freud, S. (1911). Formulations regarding the two principles of mental functioning. *Collected papers, Vol. IV.* New York: Basic Books, 1959.

Freud, S. (1915). Instincts and their vicissitudes. *Standard edition, Vol. 14.* London: Hogarth, 1957.

Freud, S. (1917). On transformations of instinct as exemplified in anal eroticism. *Standard edition, Vol. 18.* London: Hogarth, 1955.

Freud, S. (1920). *A general introduction to psychoanalysis.* New York: Boni and Liveright, 1924.

Freud, S. (1933). *New introductory lectures on psychoanalysis* (W. J. H. Sproutt, Trans.). New York: Norton.

Freud, S. (1940). An outline of psychoanalysis. *International Journal of Psychoanalysis, 21*, 27–84.

Freud, S. (1958). A note on the unconscious in psychoanalysis. In J. Strachey (Ed. and Trans.), *The standard edition of the complete psychological works of Sigmund Freud* (Vol. 12, pp. 255–266). London: Hogarth Press. (Original work published 1912).

Freud, S. (1959). *Collected papers, Vols. I–V.* New York: Basic Books.

Freud, S. (1963). *The sexual enlightenment of children.* New York: Macmillan.

Friedman, M., & Roseman, R. H. (1974). *Type A behavior and your heart.* New York: Knopf.

Fromm, E. (1941). *Escape from freedom.* New York: Holt, Rinehart and Winston.

Fromm, E. (1947). *Man for himself.* New York: Holt, Rinehart and Winston.

Funder, D. C. (1991). Global traits: A neo-Allportian approach to personality. *Psychological Science, 2*, 31–39.

Funder, D. C. (2001). Personality. *Annual Review of Psychology, 52*, 197–221.

Funder, D. C., & Colvin, C. R. (1997). Congruence of others' and self-judgments of personality. In R. Hogan, J. Johnson, & S. Briggs (Eds.), *Handbook of Personality Psychology* (pp. 617–647). San Diego, CA: Academic Press.

Gable, S. L., Reis, H. T., & Elliot, A. J. (2000). Behavioral activation and inhibition in everyday life. *Journal of Personality and Social Psychology, 78*, 1135–1149.

Garcia, J., McGowan, B. K., & Green, K. F. (1972). Biological constraints on conditioning. In A. H. Black & W. F. Prokasy (Eds.), *Classical conditioning II: Current research and theory.* New York: Appleton-Century-Crofts.

Geen, R. G. (1984). Preferred stimulation levels in introverts and extraverts: Effects on arousal and performance. *Journal of Personality and Social Psychology, 46*, 1303–1312.

Geen, R. G. (1997). Psychophysiological approaches to personality. In R. Hogan, J. A. Johnson, & S. R. Briggs (Eds.), *Handbook of personality psychology* (pp. 387–416). San Diego: Academic Press.

Geertz, C. (1986). Making experiences, authoring selves. In V. Turner & E. Bruner (Eds.), *The anthropology of experience.* Chicago: University of Illinois Press.

Giese, H., & Schmidt, S. (1968). *Studenten sexualitat.* Hamburg: Rowohlt.

Gilligan, C. (1982). *In a different voice: Psychological theory and women's development.* Cambridge, MA: Harvard University Press.

Gilmore, D. D. (1990). *Manhood in the making.* New Haven, CT: Yale Press.

Gitlin, M. J. (1990). *The psychotherapist's guide to psychopharmacology.* New York: Free Press.

Glass, D. C. (1977). *Behavior patterns, stress, and coronary disease.* Hillsdale, NJ: Erlbaum.

Glass, D. C., Singer, J. E., & Friedman, L. N. (1969). Psychic costs of adaptation to an environmental stressor. *Journal of Personality and Social Psychology, 12*, 200–210.

Goldberg, L. R. (1973). *The exploitation of the English Language for the development of a descriptive personality taxonomy.* Paper delivered at the 81st Annual Convention of the American Psychological Association, Montreal, Canada.

Goldberg, L. R. (1990). An alternative "description of personality": The Big-Five factor structure. *Journal of Personality and Social Psychology, 59*, 1216–1229.

Goldberg, L. R. (1992). The development of markers for the big-five factor structure. *Psychological Assessment, 4*, 26–42.

Goldberg, L. R., & Lewis, M. (1969). Play behavior in the year old infant: Early sex differences. *Child Development, 40*, 21–31.

Goldner, V., Penn, P., Sheinberg, M., & Walker, G. (1990). Love and violence: Gender paradoxes in volatile attachments. *Family Process, 29*, 343–364.

Goldsmith, H. H. (1991). A zygosity questionnaire for young twins: A research note. *Behavior Genetics, 21*, 257–269.

Goldsmith, H. H., & Campos, J. J. (1986). Fundamental issues in the study of early temperament: The Denver twin temperament study. In M. E. Lamb, A. L. Brown, & B. Rogoff (Eds.), *Advances in developmental psychology* (pp. 231–283). Hillsdale, NJ.

Gollwitzer, P. M., & Bargh, J. A. (Eds.). (1996). *The psychology of action: Linking cognition and motivation to behavior.* New York: Guilford.

Gollwitzer, P. M., & Moskowitz, G. B. (1996). Goal effects on action and cognition. In E. T. Higgins & A. W. Kruglanski (Eds.), *Social Psychology: Handbook of Basic Principles* (pp. 361–399). New York: Guilford.

Gormly, J., & Edelberg, W. (1974). Validation in personality trait attribution. *American Psychologist, 29*, 189–193.

Gottlieb, G. (1998). Normally occurring environmental and behavioral influences on gene activity: From central dogma to probabilistic epigenesis. *Psychological Review, 105*, 792–802.

Gough, H. G. (1957). *Manual, California Psychological Inventory.* Palo Alto, CA: Consulting Psychologists Press.

Gove, F. L., Arend, R. A., & Sroufe, L. A. (1979). *Competence in preschool and kindergarten predicted from infancy.* Paper presented at the Meeting of the Society for Research in Child Development, San Francisco, CA.

Grant, H., & Dweck, C. S. (1999). A goal analysis of personality and personality coherence. In D. Cervone & Y. Shoda (Eds.), *Social-cognitive approaches to personality coherence.* New York: Guilford Press.

Gray, J. A. (1991). The neuropsychology of temperament. In J. Strelau & A. Angleitner (Eds.), *Explorations in temperament: International perspective on theory and measurement.* New York: Plenum Press.

Greenberg, J. R., & Mitchell, S. (1983). *Object relations in psychoanalytic theory.* Cambridge: Harvard University Press.

Greenberg, J., Solomon, S., Pyszczynski, T., & Rosenblatt, A. (1992). Why do people need self-esteem? Converging evidence that self-esteem serves an anxiety-buffering function. *Journal of Personality and Social Psychology, 63*, 913–922.

Greenwald, A. G. (1980). The totalitarian ego: Fabrication and revision of personal history. *American Psychologist, 7*, 603–618.

Greenwald, A. G. (1992). New look 3: Unconscious cognition reclaimed. *American Psychologist, 47*, 766–779.

Greenwald, A. G., Banaji, M. R., Rudman, L. A., Farnham, S. D., Nosek, B. A., & Mellott, D. S. (2002). A unified theory of implicit attitudes, stereotypes, self-esteem, and self-concept. *Psychological Review, 109*, 3–25.

Greenwald, A. G., & Farnham, S. D. (2000). Using the Implicit Association Test to measure self-esteem and self-concept. *Journal of Personality and Social Psychology, 79*, 1022–1038.

Griffit, W., & Guay, P. (1969). "Object" evaluation and conditioned affect. *Journal of Experimental Research in Personality, 4*, 1–8.

Grigorenko, E. L. (2002). In search of the genetic engram of personality. In D. Cervone & W. Mischel (Eds.), *Advances in Personality Science* (pp. 29–82). New York: Guilford.

Grilly, D. M. (1989). *Drugs and human behavior.* Boston: Allyn and Bacon.

Gross, J. J. (1998). Antecedent- and response-focused emotion regulation: Divergent consequences for experience, expression, and physiology. *Journal of Personality and Social Psychology, 74*, 224–237.

Gross, J. J., & John, O. P. (2003). Individual differences in two emotion regulation processes: Implications for affect, relationships, and well-being. *Journal of Personality and Social Psychology.*

Grossberg, J. M. (1964). Behavior therapy: A review. *Psychological Bulletin, 62*, 73–88.

Grunbaum, A. (1984). *The foundations of psychoanalysis.* Berkeley, CA: University of California Press.

Guilford, J. P. (1959). *Personality.* New York: McGraw-Hill.

Guthrie, E. R. (1935). *The psychology of learning.* New York: Harper & Brothers.

Halverson, C. (1971a). Longitudinal relations between newborn tactile threshold, preschool barrier behaviors, and early school-age imagination and verbal development. *Newborn and preschooler: Organization of behavior and relations between period.* SRCD Monograph, Vol. 36.

Halverson, C. (1971b). *Relation of preschool verbal communication to later verbal intelligence, social maturity, and distribution of play bouts.* Paper presented at the meeting of the American Psychological Association.

Hamer, D., & Copeland, P. (1998). *Living with our genes: Why they matter more than you think.* New York: Doubleday.

Harackiewicz, J. M., Manderlink, G., & Sansone, C. (1984). Rewarding pinball wizardry: Effects of evaluation and cue on intrinsic motivation. *Journal of Personality and Social Psychology, 47,* 287–300.

Haring, T. G., & Breen, C. J. (1992). A peer-mediated social network intervention to enhance the social integration of persons with moderate and severe disabilities. *Journal of Applied Behavior Analysis, 25,* 319–333.

Harlow, R. E., & Cantor, N. (1996). Still participating after all these years: A study of life task participation in later life. *Journal of Personality and Social Psychology, 71,* 1235–1249.

Harmon-Jones, E., & Allen, J. J. (1997). Behavioral activation sensitivity and resting frontal EEG asymmetry: Covariation of putative indicators related to risk for mood disorders. *Journal of Abnormal Psychology, 106,* 159–163.

Harris, F. R., Johnston, M. K., Kelley, S. C., & Wolf, M. M. (1964). Effects of positive social reinforcement on regressed crawling of a nursery school child. *Journal of Educational Psychology, 55,* 35–41.

Harter, S. (1983). Developmental perspectives on the self-system. In P. H. Mussen (Ed.), *Handbook of child psychology* (Vol. 4, E. M. Hetherington, Ed.). New York: Wiley.

Harter, S. (1999). *The construction of the self: A developmental perspective.* New York: Guilford.

Hartshorne, H., & May, A. (1928). *Studies in the nature of character, Vol. 1. Studies in deceit.* New York: Macmillan.

Hawkins, R. P., Peterson, R. F., Schweid, E., & Bijou, S. W. (1966). Behavior therapy in the home: Amelioration of problem parent-child relations with the parent in a therapeutic role. *Journal of Experimental Child Psychology, 4,* 99–107.

Hazan, C., & Shaver, P. (1987). Romantic love conceptualized as an attachment process. *Journal of Personality and Social Psychology, 52,* 511–524.

Hazan, C., & Shaver, P. R. (1994). Attachment as an organizational framework for research on close relationships. *Psychological Inquiry, 5,* 1–22.

Hebb, D. O. (1955). Drives and the CNS (conceptual nervous system). *Psychological Review, 62,* 243–259.

Heckhausen, H. (1969). Achievement motive research: Current problems and some contributions towards a general theory of motivation. In W. J. Arnold (Ed.), *Nebraska Symposium on Motivation* (pp. 103–174). Lincoln: Nebraska University Press.

Heider, F. (1958). *The psychology of interpersonal relations.* New York: Wiley.

Heitzman, A. J., & Alimena, M. J. (1991). Differential reinforcement to reduce disruptive behaviors in a blind boy with a learning disability. *Journal of Visual Impairment and Blindness, 85,* 176–177.

Heller, W., Schmidtke, J. I., Nitschke, J. B., Koven, N. S., & Miller, G. A. (2002). States, traits, and symptoms: Investigating the neural correlates of emotion, personality, and psychopathology. In D. Cervone & W. Mischel (Eds.) *Advances in Personality Science* (pp. 106–126). New York: Guilford.

Henderson, V., & Dweck, C. S. (1990). Adolescence and achievement. In S. Feldman & G. Elliot (Eds.), *At the threshold: Adolescent development.* Cambridge, MA: Harvard University Press.

Herman, C. P. (1992). Review of W. H. Sheldon "Varieties of Temperament." *Contemporary Psychology, 37,* 525–528.

Hershberger, S. L., Lichtenstein, P., & Knox, S. S. (1994). Genetic and environmental influences on perceptions or organizational climate. *Journal of Applied Psychology, 79,* 24–33.

Hetherington, E. M., & Clingempeel, W. G. (1992). Coping with marital transitions: A family systems perspective. *Monographs of the Society for Research in Child Development,* Nos. 2–3, Serial No. 277.

Higgins, E. T. (1987). Self-discrepancy: A theory relating self and affect. *Psychological Review, 94,* 319–340.

Higgins, E. T. (1990). Personality, social psychology, and person-situation relations: Standards and knowledge activation as a common language. In L. A. Pervin (Ed.), *Handbook of personality: Theory and research* (pp. 301–338). New York: Guilford Press.

Higgins, E. T. (1996). Ideals, oughts, & regulatory focus: Affect and motivation from distinct pains and pleasures. In P. M. Gollwitzer & J. A. Bargh (Eds.), *The psychology of action: Linking cognition and motivation to behavior* (pp. 91–114). New York: Guilford.

Higgins, E. T. (1997). Beyond pleasure and pain. *American Psychologist, 52,* 1280–1300.

Higgins, E. T. (1998). Promotion and prevention: Regulatory focus as a motivation principle. In M. P. Zanna (Ed.), *Advances in Experimental Social Psychology* (Vol. 30, pp. 1–46). New York: Academic Press.

Higgins, E. T., & Kruglanski, A. W. (Eds.). (1996). *Social Psychology: Handbook of Basic Principles.* New York: Guilford.

Higgins, E. T., & Sorrentino, R. M. (Eds.) (1990). *Handbook of motivation and cognition: Foundations of social behavior* (Vol. 2). New York: Guilford.

Higgins, E. T., Friedman, R. S., Harlow, R. E., Chen-Idson, L., Ayduk, O. N., & Taylor, A. (2001). Achievement orientations from subjective histories of success: Promotion pride versus prevention pride. *European Journal of Social Psychology, 31,* 3–23.

Higgins, E. T., King, G. A., & Mavin, G. H. (1982). Individual construct accessibility and subjective impressions and recall. *Journal of Personality and Social Psychology, 43,* 35–47.

Holahan, C. J., & Moos, R. N. (1990). Life stressors, resistance factors, and improved psychological functioning: An extension of the stress resistance paradigm. *Journal of Personality and Social Psychology, 58,* 909–917.

Hollander, E., Liebowitz, M. R., Gorman, J. M., Cohen, B., Fyer, A., & Klein, D. F. (1989). Cortisol and sodium lactate-induced panic. *Archives of General Psychiatry, 46,* 135–140.

Holmes, D. S. (1974). Investigations of repression: Differential recall of material experimentally or naturally associated with ego threat. *Psychological Bulletin, 81,* 632–653.

Holmes, D. S. (1992). The evidence for repression: An examination of sixty years of research. In J. L. Singer (Ed.), *Repression and dissociation* (pp. 85–102). Chicago: University of Chicago Press.

Holmes, D. S., & Houston, K. B. (1974). Effectiveness of situation redefinition and affective isolation in coping with stress. *Journal of Personality and Social Psychology, 29,* 212–218.

Holmes, D. S., & Schallow, J. R. (1969). Reduced recall after ego threat: Repression or response competition? *Journal of Personality and Social Psychology, 13,* 145–152.

Holmes, J. (1993). *John Bowlby and Attachment Theory.* New York: Routledge.

Horowitz, L. M., Rosenberg, S. E., Ureno, G., Kalehzan, B. M., & O'Halloran, P. (1989). Psychodynamic formulation, consensual response method, and interpersonal problems. *Journal of Consulting and Clinical Psychology, 57,* 599–606.

Howes, D. H., & Solomon, R. L. (1951). Visual duration threshold as a function of word-probability. *Journal of Experimental Psychology, 41,* 401–410.

Howland, R. H. (1991). Pharmacotherapy of dysthymia: A review. *Journal of Clinical Psychopharmacology, 11,* 83–92.

Hoyenga, K. B., & Hoyenga, K. T. (1993). *Gender-related differences: Origins and outcomes.* Boston, MA: Allyn & Bacon.

Hoyle, R. H., Kernis, M. H., Leary, M. R., & Baldwin, M. (1999). *Selfhood: Identity, esteem, regulation.* Boulder, CO: Academic Press.

Huber, G. L., Sorrentino, R. M., Davidson, M. A., & Epplier, R. (1992). Uncertainty orientation and cooperative learning: Individual differences within and across cultures. *Learning and Individual Differences, 4,* 1–24.

Ickovics, J. (1997, August). Smithsonian seminar on health and well-being sponsored by Society for the Psychological Study of Social Issues and American Psychological Society conducted at the Ninth Annual Conference of the American Psychological Society, Washington, DC.

Insel, T. R., & Winslow, J. T. (1998). Serotonin and neuropeptides in affiliative behaviors. *Biological Psychiatry, 44,* 207–219.

Isen, A. M., Niedenthal, P. M., & Cantor, N. (1992). An influence of positive affect on social categorization. *Motivation and Emotion, 16,* 65–78.

Jaccard, J. J. (1974). Predicting social behavior from personality traits. *Journal of Research in Personality, 7,* 358–367.

Jackson, D. N., & Paunonen, S. V. (1980). Personality structure and assessment. In M. R. Rosenzweig & L. W. Porter (Eds.), *Annual review of psychology* (Vol. 31). Palo Alto, CA: Annual Reviews, Inc.

Jacobs, W. J., & Nadel, L. (1985). Stress-induced recovery of fears and phobias. *Psychological Review, 92,* 512–531.

Jahoda, M. (1958). *Current concepts of positive mental health.* New York: Basic Books.

James, W. (1890). *The principles of psychology* (Vols. 1 and 2). New York: Holt.

Jang, K. L. (1993). *A behavioral genetic analysis of personality, personality disorder, the environment, and the search for sources of nonshared environmental influences.* Unpublished doctoral dissertation, University of Western Ontario, London, Ontario.

Janis, I. L. (1971). *Stress and frustration.* New York: Harcourt.

Jasper, H. (1941). Electroencephalography. In W. Penfield & T. Erickson (Eds.), *Epilepsy and cerebral localization.* Springfield, IL: Charles C Thomas.

Jemmott, J. B., Jemmott, L. S., Spears, H., Hewitt, N., & Cruz-Collins, M. (1992). Self-efficacy, hedonistic expectancies, and condom-use intentions among inner-city Black adolescent women: A social cognitive approach to AIDS risk behavior. *Journal of Adolescent Health, 13,* 512–519.

Jersild, A. (1931). Memory for the pleasant as compared with the unpleasant. *Journal of Experimental Psychology, 14,* 284–288.

John, O. P. (1990). The big-five factor taxonomy: Dimensions of personality in the natural language and questionnaires. In L. A. Pervin (Ed.), *Handbook of personality: Theory and research* (pp. 66–100). New York: Guilford.

John, O. P. (2001, February). What is so big about the Big Five, anyway? Invited address presented at the 2nd Annual Meeting of the Society of Personality and Social Psychology, San Antonio, TX.

John, O. P., Hampson, S. E., & Goldberg, L. R. (1991). The basic level in personality-trait hierarchies: Studies of traits use and accessibility in different contexts. *Journal of Personality and Social Psychology, 60,* 348–361.

Jones, A. (1966). Information deprivation in humans. In B. A. Maher (Ed.), *Progress in experimental personality research* (Vol. 3, pp. 24–307). New York: Academic Press.

Jourard, S. M. (1967). Experimenter-subject dialogue: A paradigm for a humanistic science of psychology. In J. Bugental (Ed.), *Challenges of humanistic psychology* (pp. 109–116). New York: McGraw-Hill.

Jourard, S. M. (1974). *Healthy personality: An approach from the viewpoint of humanistic psychology.* New York: Macmillan.

Joy, V. L. (1963, August). *Repression-sensitization and interpersonal behavior.* Paper presented at the meeting of the American Psychological Association, Philadelphia.

Jung, C. G. (1963). *Memories, dreams, reflections.* New York: Pantheon.

Jung, C. G. (1964). *Man and his symbols.* Garden City, NY: Doubleday.

Kagan, J. (1964). The acquisition and significance of sex typing and sex role identity. In M. Hoffman & L. Hoffman (Eds.), *Review of child development research* (Vol. 1). New York: Russell Sage.

Kagan, J. (2003). Biology, context, and developmental inquiry. *Annual Review of Psychology, 54,* 1–23.

Kagan, J., Reznick, J. S., & Snidman, N. (1988). Biological bases of childhood shyness. *Science, 240,* 167–171.

Kagan, J., & Snidman, N. (1991). Infant predictors of inhibited and uninhibited profiles. *Psychological Science, 2,* 40–44.

Kahneman, D., & Snell, J. (1990). Predicting utility. In R. M. Hogarth (Ed.), *Handbook of personality: Theory and research* (pp. 66–100). New York: Guilford.

Kamps, D. M., Leonard, B. R., Vernon, S., Dugan, E. P., Delquadri, C., Gershon, B., Wade, L., & Folk, L. (1992). Teaching social skills to students with autism to increase peer interactions in an integrated first-grade classroom. *Journal of Applied Behavior Analysis, 25,* 281–288.

Kardiner, A. (1945). *Psychological frontiers of society.* New York: Columbia University Press.

Karoly, P. (1980). Operant methods. In F. H. Kanfer & A. P. Goldstein (Eds.), *Helping people change: A textbook of methods* (2nd ed.). Elmsford, NY: Pergamon Press.

Kayser A., Robinson, D. S., Yingling, K., Howard, D. B., Corcella, J., & Laux, D. (1988). The influence of panic attacks on response to phenelzine and amitriptyline in depressed outpatients. *Journal of Clinical Psychopharmacology, 8,* 246–253.

Kazdin, A. E. (1974). Effects of covert modeling and model reinforcement on assertive behavior. *Journal of Abnormal Psychology, 83,* 240–252.

Kazdin, A. E., & Wilson, G. T. (1978). *Evaluation of behavior therapy: Issues, evidence and research strategies.* Cambridge, MA: Ballinger.

Kelley, H. H. (1973). The processes of casual attribution. *American Psychologist, 28,* 107–128.

Kelley, H. H., & Stahelski, A. J. (1970). The social interaction basis of cooperators' and competitors' beliefs about others. *Journal of Personality and Social Psychology, 16,* 66–91.

Kelly, E. L. (1955). Consistency of the adult personality. *American Psychologist, 10,* 659–681.

Kelly, G. A. (1955). *The psychology of personal constructs* (Vols. 1 and 2). New York: Norton.

Kelly, G. A. (1958). Man's construction of his alternatives. In G. Lindzey (Ed.), *Assessment of human motives* (pp. 33–64). New York: Holt, Rinehart and Winston.

Kelly, G. A. (1962). Quoted in B. A. Maher (Ed.), (1979), *Clinical psychology and personality: The selected papers of George Kelly.* Huntington, NY: Kreiger.

Kelly, G. A. (1966). Quoted in B. A. Maher (Ed.), (1979), *Clinical psychology and personality: The selected papers of George Kelly.* Huntington, NY: Kreiger.

Kendall, P. C., & Panichelli-Mindel, S. M. (1995). Cognitive-behavioral treatments. *Journal of Abnormal Child Psychology, 26,* 107–124.

Kenrick, D. T., & Funder, D. C. (1988). Profiting from controversy: Lessons from the person-situation debate. *American Psychologist, 43,* 23–34.

Kenrick, D. T., Sadalla, E. K., Groth, G., & Trost, M. R. (1990). Evolution, traits, and the stages of human courtship: Qualifying the parental investment model. *Journal of Personality, 58,* 97–116.

Kernberg, O. (1976). *Object relations theory and clinical psychoanalysis.* New York: Jason Aronson.

Kernberg, O. (1984). *Severe personality disorders.* New Haven: Yale University Press.

Kihlstrom, J. F. (1990). The psychological unconscious. In L.A. Pervin (Ed.), *Handbook of personality: Theory and research* (pp. 445–464). New York: Guilford.

Kihlstrom, J. F. (1999). The psychological unconscious. In L. A. Pervin & O. P. John (Eds.), *Handbook of personality: Theory and research* (2nd ed., pp. 424–442). New York: Guilford.

Kihlstrom, J. F. (2003). Implicit methods in Social Psychology. In C. Sansone, C. C. Morf, & A. Panter (Eds.), *Handbook of methods in social psychology.* Thousand Oaks, CA: Sage.

Kihlstrom, J. F., Barnhardt, T. M., & Tataryn, D. J. (1992). The psychological unconscious: Found, lost, and regained. *American Psychologist, 47,* 788–791.

Kim, M. P., & Rosenberg, S. (1980). Comparison of two-structured models of implicit personality theory. *Journal of Personality and Social Psychology, 38,* 375–389.

Klein, D. F., Gittelman, R., Quitkin, F., & Rifkin, A. (1980). *Diagnosis and drug treatment of psychiatric disorders: Adults and children* (2nd ed.). Baltimore, MD: Williams & Wilkins.

Klein, D. F., & Klein, H. M. (1989). The definition and psychopharmacology of spontaneous panic and phobia: A critical review I. In P. J. Tyrer (Ed.), *Psychopharmacology of anxiety.* New York: Oxford University Press.

Klinger, E. (1975). Consequences of commitment to and disengagement from incentives. *Psychological Review, 82,* 1–25.

Klohnen, E. C., & Bera, S. (1998). Behavioral and experiential patterns of avoidantly and securely attached women across adulthood: A 31-year longitudinal perspective. *Journal of Personality and Social Psychology, 74,* 211–223.

Kobak, R. R., & Sceery, A. (1988). Attachment in late adolescence: Working models, affect regulation, and representations of self and others. *Child Development, 59,* 135–146.

Koestner, R., & McClelland, D. C. (1990). Perspectives on competence motivation. In L. A. Pervin (Ed.), *Handbook of personality: Theory and research* (pp. 549–575). New York: Guilford.

Kohut, H. (1971). *The analysis of the self.* New York: International Universities Press.

Kohut, H. (1977). *The restoration of the self.* New York: International Universities Press.

Kohut, H. (1980). *Advances in self psychology.* New York: International Universities Press.

Kohut, H. (1984). *How does analysis cure?* Chicago, IL: University of Chicago Press.

Kolb, B., & Whishaw, I. Q. (1998). Brain plasticity and behavior. *Annual Review of Psychology, 49,* 43–64.

Kopp, C. G. (1982). Antecedents of self-regulation: A developmental perspective. *Developmental Psychology, 18,* 199–214.

Koriat, A., Melkman, R., Averill, J. R., & Lazarus, R. S. (1972). The self-control of emotional reactions to a stressful film. *Journal of Personality, 40,* 601–619.

Kosslyn, S. M, Cacioppo, J. T, Davidson, R. J, Hugdahl, K., Lovallo, W. R, Spiegel, D., & Rose, R. (2002). Bridging psychology and biology: The analysis of individuals in groups. *American Psychologist, 57,* 341–351.

Krahe, B. (1990). *Situation cognition and coherence in personality: An individual-centered approach.* Cambridge, England: Cambridge University Press.

Kramer, P. D. (1993). *Listening to Prozac.* New York: Viking.

Kuhl, J. (1984). Volitional aspects of achievement motivation and learned helplessness: Toward a comprehensive theory of action control. In B. A. Maher (Ed.), *Progress in experimental personality research* (Vol. 13, pp. 91–171). New York: Academic Press.

Kuhl, J. (1985). From cognition to behavior: Perspectives for future research on action control. In J. Kuhl (Ed.), *Action control from cognition to behavior.* New York: Springer-Verlag.

Kunda, Z. (1990). The case for motivated reasoning. *Psychological Bulletin, 108,* 480–498.

Kunda, Z. (1999). *Social cognition: Making sense of people.* Cambridge, MA: The MIT Press.

Lader, M. (1980). *Introduction to psychopharmacology.* Kalamazoo, MI: Upjohn.

LaHoste, G. J., Swanson, J. M., Wigal, S. S., Glabe, C., Wigal, T., King, N., & Kennedy, J. L. (1996). Dopamine D4 receptor gene polymorphism is associated with attention deficit hyperactivity disorder. *Molecular Psychiatry, 1,* 128–131.

Laing, R. D. (1965). *The divided self: An existential study in sanity and madness.* New York: Penguin.

Lamiell, J. T. (1997). Individuals and the differences between them. In R. Hogan, J. Johnson, & S. Briggs (Eds.), *Handbook of personality psychology* (pp. 117–141). San Diego, CA: Academic Press.

Landfield, A. W., Stern, M., & Fjeld, S. (1961). Social conceptual processes and change in students undergoing psychotherapy. *Psychological Reports, 8,* 63–68.

Lang, P. J., & Lazovik, A. D. (1963). Experimental desensitization of a phobia. *Journal of Abnormal and Social Psychology, 66,* 519–525.

Langer, E. J. (1975). The illusion of control. *Journal of Personality and Social Psychology, 32,* 311–328.

Langer, E. J. (1977). The psychology of chance. *Journal for the Theory of Social Behavior, 7,* 185–207.

Langer, E. J. (1978). Rethinking the role of thought in social interaction. In J. H. Harvey, W. J. Ickes, & R. F. Kidd (Eds.), *New directions in attribution research* (Vol. 2). Hillsdale, NJ: Erlbaum.

Langer, E. J., Janis, I. L., & Wolfer, J. A. (1975). Reduction of psychological stress in surgical patients. Unpublished manuscript, Yale University.

Larsen, R. J., & Kasimatis, M. (1990). Individual differences in entrainment of mood to the weekly calendar. *Journal of Personality and Social Psychology, 58,* 164–171.

Larsen, R. J., & Kasimatis, M. (1991). Day-to-day physical symptoms: Individual differences in the occurrence, duration, and emotional concomitants of minor daily illnesses. *Journal of Personality, 59,* 387–424.

Larsen, R. J., Diener, E., & Emmons, R. A. (1986). Affect intensity and reactions to daily life. *Journal of Personality and Social Psychology, 51,* 803–814.

Lawson, G. W., & Cooperrider, C. A. (1988). *Clinical psychopharmacology: A practical reference for nonmedical psychotherapists.* Rockville, MD: Aspen Publishers.

Lazar, S., Bush, G., Gollub, R. L., Fricchione, G. L., Khalsa, G., & Benson, H. (2000). Functional brain mapping of the relaxation response and meditation. *NeuroReport, 11,* 1581–1585.

Lazarus, A. A. (1961). Group therapy of phobic disorders by systematic desensitization. *Journal of Abnormal & Social Psychology, 63,* 504–510.

Lazarus. A. A. (1963). The treatment of chronic frigidity by systematic desensitization. *Journal of Nervous and Mental Diseases, 136,* 272–278.

Lazarus, R. S. (1976). *Patterns of adjustment.* New York: McGraw-Hill.

Lazarus, R. S. (1990). Theory-based stress measurement. *Psychological Inquiry, 1,* pp. 3–13.

Lazarus, R. S., Eriksen, C. W., & Fonda, C. P. (1951). Personality dynamics and auditory perceptual recognition. *Journal of Personality, 58,* 113–122.

Lazarus, R. S., & Folkman, S. (1984). *Stress, appraisal, and coping.* New York: Springer.

Lazarus, R. S., & Longo, N. (1953). The consistency of psychological defense against threat. *Journal of Abnormal and Social Psychology, 48,* 495–499.

Leary, M. R, & Downs, D. L. (1995). Interpersonal functions of the self-esteem motive: The self-esteem system as a sociometer. In M. H. Kernis (Ed.), *Efficacy, agency, and self-esteem* (pp. 123–144). New York: Kluwer Academic/Plenum Publishers.

Leary, M. R. (2002). The self as a source of relational difficulties. *Self and Identity, 1,* 137–142.

Leary, M. R., & Tangney, J. P. (Eds.) (2003). *Handbook of self and identity.* New York: Guilford.

Leary, T. (1957). *Interpersonal diagnosis of personality.* New York: Ronald Press.

Leary, T., Litwin, G. H., & Metzner, R. (1963). Reactions to psilocybin administered in a supportive environment. *Journal of Nervous and Mental Diseases, 137,* 561–573.

LeDoux, J. (1996). *The emotional brain.* New York: Simon & Schuster.

LeDoux, J. E. (2001). *Synaptic self.* New York: Viking.

Lepper, M. R., Greene, D., & Nisbett, R. E. (1973). Undermining children's intrinsic interest with extrinsic reward: A test of the "overjustification" hypothesis. *Journal of Personality and Social Psychology, 28,* 129–137.

Lesch, K., Bengel, D., Heils, A., & Sabol, S. Z. (1996). Association of anxiety-related traits with a polymorphism in the serotonin transporter gene regulatory region. *Science, 274,* 1527–1531.

Levine, R. (1991). *New developments in pharmacology* (Vol. 8, pp. 1–3). New York: Gracie Square Hospitals Publication.

Levy, S. R., Stroessner, S. J., & Dweck, C. S. (1998). Stereotype formation and endorsement: The role of implicit theories. *Journal of Personality and Social Psychology, 74,* 1421–1436.

Lewicki, P., Hill, T., & Czyzewska, M. (1992). Nonconscious acquisition of information. *American Psychologist, 47,* 796–801.

Lewin, K. (1935). *A dynamic theory of personality.* New York: McGraw-Hill.

Lewin, K. (1936). *Principles of topological psychology.* New York: McGraw-Hill.

Lewin, K. (1951). *Field theory in social science; selected theoretical papers.* D. Cartwright (Ed.). New York: Harper & Row.

Lewinsohn, P. M. (1975). The behavioral study and treatment of depression. In M. Hersen (Ed.), *Progress in behavior modification* (pp. 19–63). New York: Academic Press.

Lewinsohn, P. M., Clarke, G. N., Hops, H., & Andrews, A. (1990). Cognitive-behavioral treatment for depressed adolescents. *Behavior Therapy, 21,* 385–401.

Lewinsohn, P. M., Mischel, W., Chaplin, W., & Barton, R. (1980). Social competence and depression: The role of illusory self-perceptions. *Journal of Abnormal Psychology, 89,* 203–212.

Lewis, M. (1969). Infants' responses to facial stimuli during the first year of life. *Developmental Psychology, 1,* 75–86.

Lewis, M. (1990). Self-knowledge and social development in early life. In L. A. Pervin (Ed.), *Handbook of personality: Theory and research* (pp. 486–526). New York: Guilford.

Lewis, M. (1999). On the development of personality. In L. A. Pervin & O. P. John (Eds.), *Handbook of personality: Theory and research* (2nd ed., pp. 327–346). New York: Guilford.

Lewis, M. (2002). Models of development. In D. Cervone & W. Mischel (Eds.), *Advances in personality science* (pp. 153–176). New York: Guildford.

Lewontin, R. (2000). *The triple helix: Gene, organism, and environment.* Cambridge, MA: Harvard University Press.

Lieberman, M. A., Yalom, I. D., & Miles, M. B. (1973). *Encounter groups: First facts.* New York: Basic Books.

Liebert, R. M. (1986). Effects of television on children and adolescents. *Journal of Developmental and Behavioral Pediatrics, 7,* 43–48.

Liebert, R. M., & Allen, K. M. (1967). The effects of rule structure and reward magnitude on the acquisition and adoption of self-reward criteria. Unpublished manuscript, Vanderbilt University, Nashville, TN.

Liebert, R. M., & Baron, R. A. (1972). Some immediate effects of televised violence on children's behavior. *Developmental Psychology, 6,* 469–475.

Lief, H. I., & Fox, R. S. (1963). Training for "detached concern" in medical students. In H. I. Lief, V. F. Lief, &

N. R. Lief (Eds.), *The psychological basis of medical practice* (pp. 12–35). New York: Harper.

Lietaer, G. (1993). Authenticity, congruence, and transparency. In D. Brazier (Ed.), *Beyond Carl Rogers* (pp. 17–46). London: Constable.

Linscheid, T. R., & Meinhold, P. (1990). The controversy over aversives: Basic operant research and the side effects of punishment. In A. C. Repp & N. N. Singh (Eds.), *Perspectives on the use of nonaversive and aversive interventions for persons with developmental disabilities* (pp. 435–450). Sycamore, IL: Sycamore Publishing Company.

Linton, R. (1945). *The cultural background of personality*. New York: Appleton.

Linville, P. W., & Carlston, D. E. (1994). Social cognition of the self. In P. G. Devine, D. C. Hamilton, & T. M. Ostrom (Eds.), *Social cognition: Impact on social psychology* (pp. 143–193). New York: Academic Press.

Loehlin, J. C. (1992). *Genes and environment in personality development*. Newbury Park, CA: Sage.

Loehlin, J. C., & Nichols, R. C. (1976). *Heredity, environment, and personality: A study of 850 sets of twins*. Austin, TX: University of Texas Press.

Loevinger, J. (1957). Objective tests as instruments of psychological theory. *Psychological Reports Monographs, No. 9*. Southern University Press.

Loftus, E. F., & Klinger, M. R. (1992). Is the unconscious smart or dumb? *American Psychologist, 47*, 761–765.

Loftus, E. F. (1993). The reality of repressed memories. *American Psychologist, 48*, 518–537.

Loftus, E. F. (1994). The repressed memory controversy. *American Psychologist, 49*, 443–445.

Lott, A. J., & Lott, B. E. (1968). A learning theory approach to interpersonal attitudes. In A. G. Greenwald, T. C. Brock, & T. M. Ostrom (Eds.), *Psychological foundations of attitudes*. New York: Academic Press.

Lovaas, O. I., Berberich, J. P., Perloff, B. F., & Schaeffer, B. (1966). Acquisition of imitative speech by schizophrenic children. *Science, 151*, 705–707.

Lovaas, O. I., Berberich, J. P., Perloff, B. F., & Schaeffer, B. (1991). Acquisition of imitative speech by schizophrenic children. *Focus on Autistic Behavior, 6*, 1–5.

Lyons, D. (1997). The feminine in the foundations of organizational psychology. *Journal of Applied Behavioral Science, 33*, 7–26.

Lyons, M. J., Goldberg, J., Eisen, S. A., True, W., Tsuang, M. T., Meyer, J. M., & Henderson, W. G. (1993). Do genes influence exposure to trauma: A twin study of combat. *American Journal of Medical Genetics (Neuropsychiatric Genetics), 48*, 22–27.

Lyubomirsky, S., & Nolen-Hoeksema, S. (1993). Self-perpetuating properties of dysphoric rumination. *Journal of Personality and Social Psychology, 65*, 339–349.

Lyubomirsky, S., & Nolen-Hoeksema, S. (1995). Effects of self-focused rumination on negative thinking and interpersonal problem solving. *Journal of Personality and Social Psychology, 69*, 176–190.

Maccoby, E. E., & Jacklin, C. N. (1974). *The psychology of sex differences*. Stanford, CA: Stanford University Press.

MacDonald, K. (1998). Evolution, culture, and the Five-Factor Model. *Journal of Cross-Cultural Psychology, 29*, 119–149.

Madison, P. (1960). *Freud's concept of repression and defense: Its theoretical and observational language*. Minneapolis, MN: University of Minnesota Press.

Magnusson, D. (Ed.). (1980). *The situation: An interactional perspective*. Hillsdale, NJ: Erlbaum.

Magnusson, D. (1990). Personality development from an interactional perspective. In L. A. Pervin (Ed.), *Handbook of personality: Theory and research* (pp. 193–224). New York: Guilford.

Magnusson, D. (1999). Holistic interactionism: A perspective for research on personality development. In L. A. Pervin & O. P. John (Eds.), *Handbook of personality: Theory and research* (2nd ed., pp. 219–247). New York: Guilford.

Magnusson, D., & Endler, N. S. (1977). Interactional psychology: Present status and future prospects. In D. Magnusson & N. S. Endler (Eds.), *Personality at the crossroads: Current issues in interactional psychology*. Hillsdale, NJ: Erlbaum.

Maher, B. A. (1966). *Principles of psychotherapy: An experimental approach*. New York: McGraw-Hill.

Maher, B. A. (1979). *Clinical psychology and personality: The selected papers of George Kelly*. Huntington, NY: Wiley.

Main, M., Kaplan, N., & Cassidy, J. (1985). Security in infancy, childhood, and adulthood: A move to the level of representation. In I. Bretherton & E. Waters (Eds.), *Growing Points in Attachment Theory and Research. Monographs of the Society for Research in Child Development, No. 209, Vol. 50*, 66–104.

Malmo, R. B. (1959). Activation: A neuropsychological dimension. *Psychological Review, 66*, 367–386.

Malmquist, C. P. (1986). Children who witness parental murder: Post traumatic aspects. *Journal of the American Academy of Child Psychiatry, 25*, 320–325.

Manke, B., McGuire, S., Reiss, D., Hetherington, E. M., & Plomin, R. (1995). Genetic contributions to children's extrafamilial social interactions: Teachers, friends, and peers. *Social Development, 4*, 238–256.

Maricle, R. A., Kinzie, J. D., & Lewinsohn, P. (1988). Medication-associated depression: A two and one-half year follow-up of a community sample. *International Journal of Psychiatry in Medicine, 18,* 283–292.

Marks, I. M. (1987). *Fears, phobias, and rituals.* New York: Oxford Press University.

Marks, I. M., & Nesse, R. M. (1994). Fear and fitness: An evolutionary analysis of anxiety disorders. *Ethology and Sociobiology, 15,* 247–261.

Marks, J., Stauffacher, J. C., & Lyle, C. (1963). Predicting outcome in schizophrenia. *Journal of Abnormal and Social Psychology, 66,* 117–127.

Markus, H. (1977). Self-schemata and processing information about the self. *Journal of Personality and Social Psychology, 35,* 63–78.

Markus, H., & Cross, S. (1990). The interpersonal self. In L. A. Pervin (Ed.), *Handbook of personality: Theory and research* (pp. 576–608). New York: Guilford.

Markus, H. R., & Kitayama, S. (1991). Culture and the self: Implications for cognition, emotion, and motivation. *Psychological Review, 98,* 224–253.

Markus, H. R., & Kitayama, S. (1998). The cultural psychology of personality. *Journal of Cross-Cultural Psychology, 29,* 63–87.

Markus, H. R., Kitayama, S., & Heiman, R. J. (1996). Culture and basic psychological principles. In. E. T. Higgins & A. W. Kruglanski (Eds.), *Social psychology: Handbook of basic principles.* New York: Guilford.

Markus, H., & Nurius, P. (1986). Possible selves. *American Psychologist, 41,* 954–969.

Martin, L. L., & Tesser, A. (1989). Toward a motivational and structural theory of ruminative thought. In J. S. Uleman & J. A. Bargh (Eds.), *Unintended thought* (pp. 306–323). New York: Guilford.

Martin, L. L., Tesser, A., & McIntosh, W. D. (1993). Wanting but not having: The effects of unattained goals on thoughts and feelings. In D. M. Wegner & J. Pennebaker (Eds.), *Handbook of mental control. Century psychology series* (pp. 552–572). Englewood Cliffs, NJ: Prentice-Hall.

Maslow, A. H. (1965). Some basic propositions of a growth and self-actualization psychology. In G. Lyndzey & C. Hall (Eds.), *Theories of personality: Primary sources and research* (pp. 307–316). New York: Wiley.

Maslow, A. H. (1968). *Toward a psychology of being* (2nd ed.). New York: Van Nostrand.

Maslow, A. H. (1971). *The farther reaches of human nature.* New York: Viking.

Matas, W. H., Arend, R. A., & Sroufe, L. A. (1978). Continuity of adaptation in the second year: The relationship between quality of attachment and later competence. *Child Development, 49,* 547–556.

Matthews, K. A. (1984). Assessment of type A, anger, and hostility in epidemiological studies of cardiovascular disease. In A. Ostfeld & E. Eaker (Eds.), *Measuring psychosocial variables in epidemiological studies of cardiovascular disease.* Bethesda, MD: National Institute of Health.

Matute, H. (1994). Learned helplessness and superstitious behavior as opposite effects of uncontrollable reinforcement in humans. *Learning and Motivation, 25,* 216–232.

May, R. (1961). Existential psychology. In R. May (Ed.), *Existential psychology* (pp. 11–51). New York: Random House.

McAdams, D. P. (1990). Motives. In V. Derlega, B. Winstead, & W. Jones (Eds.), *Contemporary research in personality* (pp. 175–204). Chicago, IL: Nelson Hall.

McAdams, D. P. (1992). The five-factor model in personality: A critical appraisal. *Journal of Personality, 60,* 329–361.

McAdams, D. P. (1999). Personal narratives and the life story. In L. A. Pervin & O. P. John (Eds.), *Handbook of personality: Theory and research* (2nd ed., pp. 478–500). New York: Guilford.

McAdams, D. P., & Constantian, C. A. (1983). Intimacy and affiliation motives in daily living: An experience sampling analysis. *Journal of Personality and Social Psychology, 45,* 851–861.

McAdams, D. P., Jackson, R. J., & Kirshnit, C. (1984). Looking, laughing, and smiling in dyads as a function of intimacy, motivation, and reciprocity. *Journal of Personality, 52,* 261–273.

McAdams, D. P., & Powers, J. (1981). Themes of intimacy in behavior and thought. *Journal of Personality and Social Psychology, 40,* 573–587.

McCardel, J. B., & Murray, E. J. (1974). Nonspecific factors in weekend encounter groups. *Journal of Consulting and Clinical Psychology, 42,* 337–345.

McClanahan, T. M. (1995). Operant learning (R-S) principles applied to nail-biting. *Psychological Report, 77,* 507–514.

McClelland, D. C. (1951). *Personality.* New York: Holt, Rinehart and Winston.

McClelland, D. C. (1961). *The achieving society.* New York: Van Nostrand.

McClelland, D. C. (1985). How motives, skills and values determine what people do. *American Psychologist, 40,* 812–825.

McClelland, D. C. (1992). Motivational configurations. In C. P. Smith, J. W. Atkinson, D. C. McClelland, & J. Veroff (Eds.), *Motivation and personality: Handbook of thematic content analysis* (pp. 87–99). New York: Cambridge University Press.

McClelland, D. C., Atkinson, J. W., Clark, R. A., & Lowell, E. L. (1953). *The achievement motive.* New York: Appleton.

McConnell, A. R., & Leibold, J. M. (2001). Relations among the Implicit Association Test, discriminatory behavior, and explicit measures of racial attitudes. *Journal of Experimental Social Psychology, 37,* 435–442.

McCrae, R. R., & Costa, P. T. (1989). The structure of personality traits: Wiggins' circumplex and the five-factor model. *Journal of Personality and Social Psychology, 56,* 586–595.

McCrae, R. R., & Costa, P. T., Jr. (1985). Updating Norman's "adequacy taxonomy": Intelligence and personality in dimensions in natural language and in questionnaires. *Journal of Personality and Social Psychology, 49,* 710–721.

McCrae, R. R., & Costa, P. T., Jr. (1987). Validation of the Five-Factor model of personality across instruments and observers. *Journal of Personality and Social Psychology, 52,* 81–90.

McCrae, R. R., & Costa, P. T., Jr. (1990). *Personality in adulthood.* New York: Guilford.

McCrae, R. R., & Costa, P. T., Jr. (1996). Toward a new generation of personality theories: Theoretical contexts for the five-factor model. In J. S. Wiggins (Ed.), *The five-factor model of personality: Theoretical perspectives* (pp. 51–87). New York: Guilford.

McCrae, R. R, & Costa, P. T. (1997). Conceptions and correlates of openness and to experience. In R. Hogan, J. Johnson, & S. Briggs (Eds.), *Handbook of personality psychology* (pp. 825–847). San Diego, CA: Academic Press.

McCrae, R. R, & Costa, P. T., Jr. (1999). A Five-Factor theory of personality. In L. A. Pervin & O. P. John (Eds.), *Handbook of personality: Theory and research* (2nd ed., pp. 139–153). New York: Guilford.

McCrae, R. R, Costa, P. T. Jr, Del Pilar, G. H, Rolland, J., & Parker, W. D. (1998). Cross-cultural assessment of the five-factor model: The Revised NEO Personality Inventory. *Journal of Cross-Cultural Psychology, 29,* 171–188.

McFarland, C., & Buehler, R. (1997). Negative affective states and the motivated retrieval of positive life events: The role of affect acknowledgment. *Journal of Personality and Social Psychology, 73,* 200–214.

McGinnies, E. (1949). Emotionality and perceptual defense. *Psychological Review, 56,* 244–251.

McGuire, S., Neiderheiser, J. M., Reiss, D., Hetherington, E. M., & Plomin, R. (1994). Genetic and environmental influences on perceptions of self-worth and competence in adolescence: A study of twins, full siblings, and step siblings. *Child Development, 65,* 785–799.

Meehl, P. E. (1990). Why summaries of research on psychological theories are often uninterpretable. *Psychological Reports, 66,* 195–244.

Meehl, P. E. (1997). Credentialed persons, credentialed knowledge. *Clinical Psychology-Science and Practice, 4,* 91–98.

Meichenbaum, D. (1993). Changing conceptions of cognitive behavior modification: Retrospect and prospect. *Journal of Consulting and Clinical Psychology, 61,* 202–204.

Meichenbaum, D. H. (1995). Cognitive-behavioral therapy in historical perspective. In B. Bongar & L. E. Beutler (Eds.), *Comprehensive textbook of psychotherapy* (pp. 140–158). New York: Oxford University Press.

Meichenbaum, D. H., & Smart, I. (1971). Use of direct expectancy to modify academic performance and attitudes of college students. *Journal of Counseling Psychology, 18,* 531–535.

Meltzer, H. (1930). The present status of experimental studies of the relation of feeling to memory. *Psychological Review, 37,* 124–139.

Mendolia, M., Moore, J., & Tesser, A. (1996). Dispositional and situational determinants of repression. *Journal of Personality and Social Psychology, 70,* 856–867.

Mendoza-Denton, R., Ayduk, O., Mischel, W., Shoda, Y., & Testa, A. (2001). Person × Situation interactionism in self-encoding *(I am . . . when . . .):* Implications for affect regulation and social information processing. *Journal of Personality and Social Psychology, 80,* 533–544.

Mendoza-Denton, R., Downey, G., Purdie, V. J., Davis, A., & Pietrzak, J. (2002). Sensitivity to status-based rejection: Implications for African-American students' college experience. *Journal of Personality and Social Psychology, 83,* 896–918.

Mendoza-Denton, R., Shoda, Y., Ayduk, O., & Mischel, W. (1999). Applying CAPS theory to cultural differences in social behavior. In W. J. Lonner, D. L. Dinnel, D. K. Forgays, & S. A. Hayes (Eds.), *Merging past, present, and future: Selected papers from the 14th international congress of the international association for cross-cultural psychology* (pp. 205–217). Lisse, The Netherlands: Swets & Zeitlinger.

Merluzzi, T. V., Glass, C. R., & Genest, M. (Eds.). (1981). *Cognitive assessment.* New York: Guilford.

Metcalfe, J., & Jacobs, W. J. (1998). Emotional memory: The effects of stress on "cool" and "hot" memory systems. In D. L. Medin (Ed.), *The psychology of learning and motivation: Advances in research and theory* (Vol. 38, pp. 187–222). San Diego, CA: Academic Press.

Metcalfe, J., & Mischel, W. (1999). A hot/cool-system analysis of delay of gratification: Dynamics of willpower. *Psychological Review, 106,* 3–19.

Milgram, N. (1993). War-related trauma and victimization: Principles of traumatic stress prevention in Israel. In J. P. Wilson & B. Raphael (Eds.), *International handbook of traumatic stress syndromes. The Plenum series on stress and coping* (pp. 811–820). New York: Plenum Press.

Milgram, S. (1974). *Obedience to authority.* New York: Harper & Row.

Miller, N. E. (1948). Theory and experiment relating psychoanalytic displacement to stimulus response generalization. *Journal of Abnormal and Social Psychology, 43,* 155–178.

Miller, N. E. (1959). Liberalization of basic S-R concepts: Extensions to conflict behavior, motivation, and social learning. In S. Koch (Ed.), *Psychology: A study of a science* (Vol. 2, pp. 196–292). New York: McGraw-Hill.

Miller, N. E. (1963). Some reflections on the law of effect produce a new alternative to drive reduction. In M. R. Jones (Ed.), *Nebraska Symposium on Motivation* (Vol. 11, pp. 65–112). Lincoln: University of Nebraska Press.

Miller, N. E., & Dollard, J. (1941). *Social learning and imitation.* New Haven: Yale University Press.

Miller, S. M. (1979). Coping with impending stress: Physiological and cognitive correlates of choice. *Psychophysiology, 16,* 572–581.

Miller, S. M. (1981). Predictability and human stress: Towards a clarification of evidence and theory. In L. Berkowitz (Ed.), *Advances in experimental social psychology* (Vol. 14, pp. 203–256). New York: Academic Press.

Miller, S. M. (1987). Monitoring and blunting: Validation of a questionnaire to assess styles of information seeking under threat. *Journal of Personality and Social Psychology, 52,* 345–353.

Miller, S. M. (1992). Individual differences in the coping process: What to know and when to know it. In B. N. Carpenter (Ed.), *Personal coping: Theory, research, application* (pp. 77–91). Westport, CT: Praeger.

Miller, S. M. (1996). Monitoring and blunting of threatening information: Cognitive interference and facilitation in the coping process. In I. G. Sarason, G. R. Pierce, & B. R. Sarason (Eds.), *Cognitive interference: Theories, methods, and findings. The LEA series in personality and clinical psychology* (pp. 175–190). Mahwah, NJ: Erlbaum.

Miller, S. M., & Green, M. L. (1985). Coping with threat and frustration: Origins, nature, and development. In M. Lewis & C. Soarni (Eds.), *Socialization of Emotions* (Vol. 5). New York: Plenum Press.

Miller, S. M., & Mangan, C. E. (1983). The interacting effects of information and coping style in adapting to gynecologic stress: Should the doctor tell all? *Journal of Personality and Social Psychology, 45,* 223–236.

Miller, S. M., Shoda, Y., & Hurley, K. (1996). Applying cognitive-social theory to health-protective behavior: Breast self-examination in cancer screening. *Psychological Bulletin, 119,* 70–94.

Miller, T. Q., Smith, T. W., Turner, C. W., Guijarro, M. L. & Hallett, A. J. (1996). A meta-analytic review of research on hostility and physical health. *Psychological Bulletin, 119,* 322–348.

Minuchin, S., Lee, W., & Simon, G. M. (1996). *Mastering family therapy: Journeys of growth and transformation.* New York: Wiley.

Mischel, H. N., & Mischel, W. (1973). *Readings in personality.* New York: Holt, Rinehart & Winston.

Mischel, T. (1964). Personal constructs, rules, and the logic of clinical activity. *Psychological Review, 71,* 180–192.

Mischel, W. (1965). Predicting the success of Peace Corps Volunteers in Nigeria. *Journal of Personality and Social Psychology, 1,* 510.

Mischel, W. (1968). *Personality and assessment.* New York: Wiley.

Mischel, W. (1969). Continuity and change in personality. *American Psychologist, 24,* 1012–1018.

Mischel, W. (1973). Toward a cognitive social learning reconceptualization of personality. *Psychological Review, 80,* 252–283.

Mischel, W. (1974). Processes in delay of gratification. In L. Berkowitz (Ed.), *Advances in experimental social psychology* (Vol. 7). New York: Academic Press.

Mischel, W. (1980). Personality and cognition: Something borrowed, something new? In N. Cantor & J. Kihlstrom (Eds.), *Personality, cognition, and social interaction.* Hillsdale, NJ: Erlbaum.

Mischel, W. (1981). Metacognition and the rules of delay. In J. H. Flavell & L. Ross (Eds.), *Social cognitive development: Frontiers and possible futures.* New York: Cambridge University Press.

Mischel, W. (1984). Convergences and challenges in the search for consistency. *American Psychologist, 39,* 351–364.

Mischel, W. (1990). Personality dispositions revisited and revised: A view after three decades. In L. A. Pervin (Ed.), *Handbook of personality: Theory and research* (pp. 111–134). New York: Guilford Press.

Mischel, W. (1993). *Introduction to personality* (Fifth Edition). Fort Worth, TX: Harcourt, Brace, Jovanovich.

Mischel, W., & Ayduk, O. (2002). Self-regulation in a cognitive-affective personality system: Attentional control in the service of the self. *Self and Identity, 1,* 113–120.

Mischel, W., Cantor, N., & Feldman, S. (1996). Principles of self-regulation: The nature of willpower and self-control. In E. T. Higgins & A. W. Kruglanski (Eds.), *Social psychology: Handbook of basic principles* (pp. 329–360). New York: Guilford.

Mischel, W., & Ebbesen, E. B. (1970). Attention in delay of gratification. *Journal of Personality and Social Psychology, 16,* 239–337.

Mischel, W., Ebbesen, E. B., & Zeiss, A. R. (1972). Cognitive and attentional mechanisms in delay of gratification. *Journal of Personality and Social Psychology, 21,* 204–218.

Mischel, W., Ebbesen, E. B., & Zeiss, A. R. (1973). Selective attention to the self: Situational and dispositional determinants. *Journal of Personality and Social Psychology, 27,* 129–142.

Mischel, W., Ebbesen, E. B., & Zeiss, A. R. (1976). Determinants of selective memory about the self. *Journal of Consulting and Clinical Psychology, 44,* 92–103.

Mischel, W., & Morf, C.C. (2003). The self as a psycho-social dynamic processing system: A meta-perspective on a century of the self in psychology. In M. Leary & J. Tangney (Eds.), *Handbook of self and identity* (pp. 15–43). New York: Guilford.

Mischel, W., & Peake, P. K. (1982). In search of consistency: Measure for measure. In M. P. Zanna, E. T. Higgins, & C. P. Herman (Eds.), *Consistency in social behavior: The Ontario symposium* (Vol. 2, pp. 187–207). Hillsdale, NJ: Erlbaum.

Mischel, W., & Shoda, Y. (1995). A cognitive-affective system theory of personality: Reconceptualizing situations, dispositions, dynamics, and invariance in personality structure. *Psychological Review, 102,* 246–268.

Mischel, W., & Shoda, Y. (1998). Reconciling processing dynamics and personality dispositions. *Annual Review of Psychology, 49,* 229–258.

Mischel, W., & Shoda, Y. (1999). Integrating dispositions and processing dynamics within a unified theory of personality: The cognitive affective personality system (CAPS). In L. Pervin & O. John (Eds.), *Handbook of personality: Theory and research* (2nd ed., pp. 197– 218). New York: Guilford.

Mischel, W., Shoda, Y., & Peake, P. K. (1988). The nature of adolescent competencies predicted by preschool delay of gratification. *Journal of Personality and Social Psychology, 54,* 687–696.

Mischel, W., Shoda, Y., & Rodriguez, M. L. (1989). Delay of gratification in children. *Science, 244,* 933–938.

Mischel, W., & Staub, E. (1965). Effects of expectancy on working and waiting for larger rewards. *Journal of Personality and Social Psychology, 2,* 625–633.

Molina, M. A. N. (1996). Archetypes and spirits: A Jungian analysis of Puerto Rican Espiritismo. *Journal of Analytical Psychology, 41,* 227–244.

Monro, R. (1955). *Schools of psychoanalytic thought.* New York: Holt, Rinehart and Winston.

Morf, C. C., (2002). Personality at the hub: Extending the conception of personality psychology. *Journal of Research in Personality, 36,* 649–660.

Morf, C. C., Ansara, D., & Shia, T. (2001). *The effects of audience characteristics on narcissistic self-presentation.* Manuscript in preparation, University of Toronto.

Morf, C. C., & Rhodewalt, F. (2001a). Expanding the dynamic self-regulatory processing model of narcissism; Research directions for the future. *Psychological Inquiry, 12,* 243–251.

Morf, C. C., & Rhodewalt, F. (2001b). Unraveling the paradoxes of narcissism: A dynamic self-regulatory processing model. *Psychological Inquiry, 12,* 177–196.

Morf, C. C., Weir, C. R., & Davidov, M. (2000). Narcissism and intrinsic motivation: The role of goal congruence. *Journal of Experimental Social Psychology, 36,* 424–438.

Morse, W. H., & Kelleher, R. T. (1966). Schedules using noxious stimuli I. Multiple fixed-ratio and fixed-interval termination of schedule complexes. *Journal of the Experimental Analysis of Behavior, 9,* 267–290.

Moskowitz, D. S., Suh, E. J., & Desaulniers, J. (1994). Situational influences on gender differences in agency and communion. *Journal of Personality and Social Psychology, 66,* 753–761.

Mulaik, S. A. (1964). Are personality factors raters' conceptual factors? *Journal of Consulting Psychology, 28,* 506–511.

Murphy, S. T., & Zajonc, R. B. (1993). Affect, cognition, & awareness: Affective priming with optimal and suboptimal stimulus exposures. *Journal of Personality and Social Psychology, 64,* 723–739.

Murray, H. A., Barrett, W. G., & Homburger, E. (1938). *Explorations in personality.* New York: Oxford University Press.

Murray, J. (1973). Television and violence: Implications of the surgeon general's research program. *American Psychologist, 28,* 472–478.

Mussen, P. H., & Naylor, H. K. (1954). The relationship between overt and fantasy aggression. *Journal of Abnormal and Social Psychology, 49,* 235–240.

Neisser, U. (1967). *Cognitive psychology.* New York: Appleton.

Nelson, R. J., Demas, G. E., Huang, P. L., Fishman, M. C., Dawson, V. L., Dawson, T. M., & Snyder, S. H. (1995). Behavioural abnormalities in male mice lacking neuronal nitric synthase. *Nature, 378*(6555), 383–386.

Nemeroff, C. J., & Karoly, P. (1991). Operant methods. In F. H. Kanfer & A. P. Goldstein (Eds.), *Helping people change: A textbook of methods* (4th ed.). Pergamon general psychology series, Vol. 52. New York: Pergamon Press.

Nesse, R. M. (2001). *Evolution and the capacity for commitment.* New York: Russell Sage.

Newcomb, T. M. (1929). *Consistency of certain extrovert-introvert behavior patterns in 51 problem boys.* New York: Columbia University, Teachers College, Bureau of Publications.

Niedenthal, P. M. (1990). Implicit perception of affective information. *Journal of Experimental Social Psychology, 25,* 505–527.

Nilson, D. C., Nilson, L. B., Olson, R. S., & McAllister, B. H. (1981). *The planning environment report for the Southern California Earthquake Safety Advisory Board.* Redlands, CA: The Social Research Advisory and Policy Research Center.

Nisbett, R. (1990). Evolutionary psychology, biology, and cultural evolution. *Motivation and Emotion, 14,* 255–263.

Nisbett, R. (1997, May). Cultures of honor: Economics, history, and the tradition of violence. Address given at the Ninth Annual Convention of the American Psychological Society, Washington, DC.

Nisbett, R. E., Peng, K., Choi, I., & Norenzayan, A. (2001). Culture and systems of thought: Holistic versus analytic cognition. *Psychological Review, 108,* 291–310.

Nisbett, R. E., & Ross, L. D. (1980). *Human inference: Strategies and shortcomings of social judgment.* Century Psychology Series. Englewood Cliffs, NJ: Prentice-Hall.

Nolen-Hoeksema, S. (1997, May). Emotion regulation and depression. Closing plenary session at the Ninth Annual American Psychological Society Convention, Washington, DC.

Nolen-Hoeksema, S. (2000). The role of rumination in depressive disorders and mixed anxiety/depressive symptoms. *Journal of Abnormal Psychology, 109,* 504–511.

Nolen-Hoeksema, S., Parker, L. E, & Larson, J. (1994). Ruminative coping with depressed mood following loss. *Journal of Personality and Social Psychology, 67,* 92–104.

Norem, J. K., & Cantor, N. (1986). Anticipatory and post hoc cushioning strategies: Optimism and defensive pessimism in "risky" situations. *Cognitive Therapy and Research, 10,* 347–362.

Norman, W. T. (1961). Development of self-report tests to measure personality factors identified from peer nominations. *USAF ASK Technical Note,* No. 61–44.

Norman, W. T. (1963). Toward an adequate taxonomy of personality attributes: Replicated factor structure in peer nomination personality ratings. *Journal of Abnormal and Social Psychology, 66,* 574–583.

Ochsner, K. N., & Lieberman, M. D. (2001). The emergence of social cognitive neuroscience. *American Psychologist, 56,* 717–734.

O'Connell, D. F., & Alexander, C. N. (1994). Recovery from addictions using transcendental meditation and Maharishi Ayur-Veda. In D. F. O'Connell & C. N. Alexander (Eds.), *Self-recovery: Treating addictions using transcendental meditation and Maharishi Ayur-Veda* (pp. 1–12). New York: Haworth Press.

O'Connor, T. G., Hetherington, E. M., Reiss, D., & Plomin, R. (1995). A twin–sibling study of observed parent-adolescent interactions. *Child Development, 66,* 812–829.

O'Donohue, W., Henderson, D., Hayes, S., Fisher, J., & Hayes, L. (Eds.) (2001). *The history of the behavioral therapies: Founders personal histories.* Reno, NV: Context Press.

Office of Strategic Services Administration. (1948). *Assessment of men.* New York: Holt, Rinehart and Winston.

Ofshe, R. J. (1992). Inadvertent hypnosis during interrogation: False confession due to dissociative state, misidentified multiple personality and the satanic cult hypothesis. *International Journal of Clinical and Experimental Hypnosis, 40,* 125–156.

Ofshe, R. J., & Watters, E. (1993). Making monsters. *Society, 1,* 4–16.

O' Leary, V. (1997, August). Smithsonian seminar on health and well-being sponsored by Society for the Psychological Study of Social Issues and American Psychological Society conducted at the Ninth Annual Conference of the American Psychological Society, Washington, DC.

Opler, M. K. (1967). Cultural induction of stress. In M. H. Appley & R. Trumbull (Eds.), *Psychological stress* (pp. 209–241). New York: Appleton.

Ornstein, R. E. (1972). *The psychology of consciousness.* San Francisco: Freeman.

Ornstein, R. E., & Naranjo, C. (1971). *On the psychology of meditation.* New York: Viking.

Osgood, C. E., Suci, G. J., & Tannenbaum, P. H. (1957). *The measurement of meaning.* Urbana, IL: The University of Illinois Press.

Overall, J. (1964). Note on the scientific status of factors. *Psychological Bulletin, 61,* 270–276.

Pagano, R. R., Rose, R. M., Stivers, R. M., & Warrenburg, S. (1976). Sleep during transcendental meditation. *Science, 191,* 308–309.

Parker, J. D. A., & Endler, N. S. (1996). Coping and defense: A historical overview. In M. Zeidner & N. S. Endler (Eds.), *Handbook of coping: Theory, research, applications* (pp. 3–23). New York: Wiley.

Patterson, G. R. (1976). The aggressive child: Victim and architect of a coercive system. In L. A. Hamerlynck, L. C. Handy, & E. J. Mash (Eds.), *Behavior modification and families, Vol. 1. Theory and research.* New York: Brunner/Mazel.

Patterson, G. R. (Ed.). (1990). *Depression and aggression in family interaction.* Hillsdale, NJ: Lawrence Erlbaum Associates.

Patterson, G. R., & Fisher, P. A. (2002). Recent developments in our understanding of parenting: Bidirectional effects, causal models, and the search for parsimony. In M. H. Bornstein (Ed.), *Handbook of parenting: Vol. 5: Practical issues in parenting* (2nd ed., pp. 59–88). Mahwah, NJ: Lawrence Erlbaum Associates.

Paul, G. L. (1966). *Insight vs. desensitization in psychotherapy.* Stanford, CA: Stanford University Press.

Paulhus, D. L., Fridhandler, B., & Hayes, S. (1997). Psychological defense: Contemporary theory and research. In R. Hogan, J. A. Johnson, & S. R. Briggs (Eds.), *Handbook of personality psychology* (pp. 543–579). San Diego, CA: Academic Press.

Peake, P., Hebl, M., & Mischel, W. (2002). Strategic attention deployment in waiting and working situations. *Developmental Psychology, 38,* 313–326.

Pedersen, N. L., Plomin, R., McClearn, G. E., & Friberg, L. (1988). Neuroticism, extraversion, and related traits in adult twins reared apart and reared together. *Journal of Personality and Social Psychology, 55,* 950–957.

Pederson, F. A. (1958). Consistency data on the role construct repertory test. Unpublished manuscript, Ohio State University, Columbus.

Pennebaker, J. W. (1993). Social mechanisms of constraint. In D. M. Wegener & J. W. Pennebaker (Eds.), *Handbook of mental control* (pp. 200–219). Englewoood Cliff, NJ: Prentice-Hall.

Pennebaker, J. W. (1997). Writing about emotional experiences as a therapeutic process. *Psychological Science, 8,* 162–166.

Pennebaker, J. W., Colder, M., & Sharp, L. K. (1990). Accelerating the coping process. *Journal of Personality and Social Psychology, 58,* 528–537.

Pennebaker, J. W., & Graybeal, A. (2001). Patterns of natural language use: Disclosure, personality, and social integration. *Current Directions in Psychological Science, 10,* 90–93.

Pennebaker, J. W., Kiecolt-Glaser, J. K., & Glaser, R. (1988). Disclosure of traumas and immune function: Health implications for psychotherapy. *Journal of Consulting and Clinical Psychology, 56,* 239–245.

Perls, F. S. (1969). *Gestalt therapy verbatim.* Lafayette, CA: Real People Press.

Perry, J. C., & Cooper, S. H. (1989). An empirical study of defense mechanisms, I. Clinical interviews and life vignette ratings. *Archives of General Psychiatry, 46,* 444–452.

Pervin, L. A. (1994). A critical analysis of trait theory. *Psychological Inquiry, 5,* 103–113.

Pervin, L. A. (1996). *The science of personality.* New York: Wiley.

Pervin, L. A. (2003). *The science of personality* (2nd ed.). New York: Oxford University Press.

Pervin, L. A., & John, O. P. (Eds.) (1999). *Handbook of personality theory and research* (2nd ed.). New York: Guilford.

Peterson, C., & Seligman, M. E. P. (1987). Explanatory style and illness. *Journal of Personality, 55,* 237–265.

Peterson, C., Seligman, M. E. P., & Vaillant, G. E. (1988). Pessimistic explanatory style is a risk factor of physical illness: A thirty-five-year longitudinal study. *Journal of Personality and Social Psychology, 55,* 23–27.

Peterson, D. R. (1968). *The clinical study of social behavior.* New York: Appleton.

Petrie, K. J., Booth, R. J., Pennebaker, J. W., Davison, K. P., & Thomas, M. G. (1995). Disclosure of trauma and immune response to a hepatitis vaccination program. *Journal of Consulting and Clinical Psychology, 63,* 787–792.

Phares, E. J. (1976). *Locus of control in personality.* Morristown, NJ: General Learning Press.

Phillips, K., & Mathews, A. P., Jr. (1995). Quantitative genetic analysis of injury liability in infants and toddlers. *American Journal of Medical Genetics (Neuropsychiatric Genetics), 60,* 64–71.

Pike, A., Reiss, D., Hetherington E. M., & Plomin, R. (1996). Using MZ differences in the search for nonshared environmental effects. *Journal of Child Psychology and Psychiatry, 37,* 695–704.

Pinker, S. (1997). *How the mind works.* New York: W. W. Norton & Company.

Plaud, J. J., & Gaither, G. A. (1996). Human behavioral momentum: Implications for applied behavior analysis and therapy. *Journal of Behavior Therapy and Experimental Psychiatry, 27,* 139–148.

Plomin, R. (1981). Ethnological behavioral genetics and development. In K. Immelmann, G. W. Barlow, L. Petrinovich, & M. Main (Eds.), *Behavioral development: The Bielefeld interdisciplinary project.* Cambridge, England: Cambridge University Press.

Plomin, R. (1990). The role of inheritance in behavior. *Science, 248,* 183–188.

Plomin, R. (1994). The Emanuel Miller Memorial Lecture 1993: Genetic research and identification of environmental influences. *Journal of Child Psychology and Psychiatry, 35,* 817–834.

Plomin, R., & Caspi, A. (1999). Behavioral genetics and personality. In L. A. Pervin & O. P. John (Eds.), *Handbook of personality theory and research* (2nd ed., pp. 251–276). New York: Guilford.

Plomin, R., Chipuer, H. M., & Loehlin, J. C. (1990). Behavioral genetics and personality. In L. A. Pervin (Ed.), *Handbook of personality: Theory and research* (pp. 225–243). New York: Guilford.

Plomin, R., Chipuer, H. M., & Neiderhiser, J. M. (1994). Behavioral genetic evidence for the importance of nonshared environment. In E. M. Hetherington, D. Reiss, & R. Plomin (Eds.), *Separate social worlds of siblings: Impact of nonshared environment on development* (pp. 1–31). Hillsdale, NJ: Erlbaum.

Plomin, R., DeFries, J. C., McClearn, G. E., & Rutter, M. (1997). *Behavioral Genetics* (3rd Ed.). New York: W. H. Freeman and Company.

Plomin, R., Manke, B., & Pike, A. (1996). Siblings, behavioral genetics, and competence. In G. H. Brody (Ed.), *Sibling relationships: Their causes and consequences* (pp. 75–104). Norwood, NJ: Ablex Publishing Corp.

Plomin, R., McClearn, G. E., Pedersen, N. L., Nesselroade, J. R., & Bergeman, C. S. (1988). Genetic influence on childhood family environment perceived retrospectively from the last half of the life span. *Developmental Psychology, 24,* 738–745.

Plomin, R., Owen, M. J., & McGuffin, P. (1994). The genetic basis of complex human behaviors. *Science, 264,* 1733–1739.

Plomin, R., & Rende, R. (1991). Human behavioral genetics. *Annual Review of Psychology, 42,* 161–190.

Plomin, R., & Saudino, K. J. (1994). Quantitative genetics and molecular genetics. In J. E. Bates & T. D. Watts (Eds.), *Temperament: Individual differences at the interface of biology and behavior* (pp. 143–171). Washington, DC: American Psychological Association.

Polster, E., & Polster, M. (1993). Frederick Perls: Legacy and invitation. *Gestalt Journal, 16,* 23–25.

Posner, M. I., & Rothbart, M. K. (1991). Attentional mechanisms and conscious experience. In M. Rugg & A. D. Milner (Eds.), *The neuropsychology of consciousness* (pp. 91–112). San Diego, CA: Academic Press.

Posner, M. I., & Rothbart, M. K. (1998). Attention, self-regulation, and consciousness. *Philosophical Transactions of the Royal Society of London B, 353,* 1915–1927.

Potter, W. Z., Rudorfer, M. V., & Manji, H. K. (1991). The pharmacologic treatment of depression. *New England Journal of Medicine, 325,* 633–642.

Powell, G. E. (1973). Negative and positive mental practice in motor skill acquisition. *Perceptual and Motor Skills, 37,* 312–313.

Prentice, D. A., & Miller, C. T. (1993). Pluralistic ignorance and alcohol use on campus: Some consequences of misperceiving the social norm. *Journal of Personality and Social Psychology, 64,* 243–256.

Purdie, V., & Downey, G. (2000). Rejection sensitivity and adolescent girls' vulnerability to relationship-centered difficulties. *Child Maltreatment, 5,* 338–349.

Rachman, S. (1967). Systematic desensitization. *Psychological Bulletin, 67,* 93–103.

Rachman, S., & Cuk, M. (1992). Fearful distortions. *Behaviour Research and Therapy, 30,* 583–589.

Rachman, S., & Hodgeson, R. J. (1980). *Obsessions and compulsions.* Englewood Cliffs, NJ: Prentice-Hall.

Rachman, S., & Wilson, G. T. (1980). *The effects of psychological therapy.* Oxford, England: Pergamon Press.

Rachman, S. J. (1996). Trends in cognitive and behavioural therapies. In P. M. Salkovskis (Ed.) *Trends in cognitive and behavioural therapies* (pp. 1–23). New York: Wiley.

Ramsey, E., Patterson, G. R., & Walker, H. M. (1990). Generalization of the antisocial trait from home to school settings. *Journal of Applied Developmental Psychology, 11,* 209–223.

Raush, H. L., Barry, W. A., Hertel, R. K., & Swain, M. A. (1974). *Communication conflict and marriage.* San Francisco: Jossey-Bass.

Raymond, M. S. (1956). Case of fetishism treated by aversion therapy. *British Medical Journal, 2,* 854–857.

Redd, W. H. (1995). Behavioral research in cancer as a model for health psychology. *Health Psychology, 14,* 99–100.

Redd, W. H., Porterfield, A. L., & Anderson, B. L. (1978). *Behavior modification: Behavioral approaches to human problems.* New York: Random House.

Reiss, D., Neiderhiser, J. M., Hetherington, E. M., & Plomin, R. (2000). *The relationship code: Deciphering genetic and social influences on adolescent development.* Cambridge, MA: Harvard University Press.

Rhodewalt F., & Eddings, S. K. (2002). Narcissus reflects: Memory distortion in response to ego-relevant feedback among high- and low-narcissistic men. *Journal of Research in Personality, 36,* 97–116.

Rhodewalt, F., & Morf, C. (1998). On self-aggrandizement and anger: A temporal analysis of narcissism and affective reactions to success and failure. *Journal of Personality and Social Psychology, 74,* 672–685.

Richards, J. M., & Gross, J. J. (2000). Emotion regulation and memory: The cognitive costs of keeping one's cool. *Journal of Personality and Social Psychology, 79,* 410–424.

Riemann, R., Angleitner, A., & Strelau, J. (1997). Genetic and environmental influences on personality: A study of twins reared together using the self- and peer report NEO-FFI scales. *Journal of Personality, 65,* 449–476.

Riger, S. (1992). Epistemological debates, feminist voices: Science, social values, and the study of women. *American Psychologist, 47,* 730–740.

Rimm, D. C., & Masters, J. C. (1974). *Behavior therapy: Techniques and empirical findings.* New York: Academic Press.

Roazen, P. (1974). *Freud and his followers.* New York: Meridian.

Robinson, J. L., Kagan, J., Reznick, J. S., & Corley, R. (1992). The heritability of inhibited and uninhibited behavior: A twin study. *Developmental Psychology, 28,* 1030–1037.

Rogers, C. R. (1942). *Counseling and psychotherapy: Newer concepts in practice.* Boston: Houghton Mifflin.

Rogers, C. R. (1947). Some observations on the organization of personality. *American Psychologist, 2,* 358–368.

Rogers, C. R. (1951). *Client-centered therapy: Its current practice, implications and theory.* Boston: Houghton Mifflin.

Rogers, C. R. (1955). Persons or science? A philosophical question. *American Psychologist, 10,* 267–278.

Rogers, C. R. (1959). A theory of therapy, personality and interpersonal relationships, as developed in the client-centered framework. In S. Koch (Ed.), *Psychology: A study of a science* (Vol. 3, pp. 184–526). New York: McGraw-Hill.

Rogers, C. R. (1963). The actualizing tendency in relation to "motives" and to consciousness. In M. R. Jones (Ed.), *Nebraska symposium on motivation* (pp. 1–24). Lincoln, NE: University of Nebraska Press.

Rogers, C. R. (1970). *Carl Rogers on encounter groups.* New York: Harper & Row.

Rogers, C. R. (1974). In retrospect: Forty-six years. *American Psychologist, 29,* 115–123.

Rogers, C. R., & Dymond, R. F. (Eds.). (1954). *Psychotherapy and personality change, co-ordinated studies in the client-centered approach.* Chicago: University of Chicago Press.

Rogers, T. B. (1977). Self-reference in memory: Recognition of personality items. *Journal of Research in Personality, 11,* 295–305.

Rogers, T. B., Kuiper, N. A., & Kirker, W. S. (1977). Self-reference and the encoding of personal information. *Journal of Personality and Social Psychology, 35,* 677–688.

Romer, D., & Revelle, W. (1984). Personality traits: Fact or fiction? A critique of the Shweder and D'Andrade systematic distortion hypothesis. *Journal of Personality and Social Psychology, 47,* 1028–1042.

Rorer, L. G. (1990). Personality assessment: A conceptual survey. In L.A. Pervin (Ed.), *Handbook of personality: Theory and research* (pp. 693–720). New York: Guilford.

Rosch, E. (1975). Cognitive reference points. *Cognitive Psychology, 1,* 532–547.

Rosch, E., Mervis, C., Gray, W., Johnson, D., & Boyce-Braem, P. (1976). Basic objects in natural categories. *Cognitive Psychology, 8,* 382–439.

Rosenhan, D. L. (1973). On being sane in insane places. *Science, 179,* 250–258.

Rosenthal, R., & Rubin, D. (1978). Interpersonal expectancy effects: The first 345 studies. *Behavioral and Brain Sciences, 3,* 377–415.

Rosenzweig, S., & Mason, G. (1934). An experimental study of memory in relation to the theory of repression. *British Journal of Psychology, 24,* 247–265.

Ross, L. & Nisbett, R. E. (1991). *The person and the situation: Perspectives of social psychology.* New York: McGraw-Hill.

Ross, L. D. (1977). The intuitive psychologist and his short-comings: Distortions in the attribution process. In

L. Berkowitz (Ed.), *Advances in experimental social psychology* (Vol. 10). New York: Academic Press.

Rossini, E. D., & Moretti, R. J. (1997). Thematic Apperception Test (TAT) interpretation: Practice recommendations from a survey of clinical psychology doctoral programs accredited by the American Psychological Association. *Professional Psychology Research and Practice, 28,* 393–398.

Roth, S., & Newman, E. (1990). The process of coping with sexual trauma. *Journal of Traumatic Stress, 4,* 279–297.

Rothbart, M. K., Derryberry, D., & Posner, M. I. (1994). A psychobiological approach to the development of temperament. In J. E. Bates & T. D. Wachs (Eds.), *Temperament: Individual differences at the interface of biology and behavior* (pp. 83–116). Washington, D.C.: American Psychological Association.

Rothbart, M. K., Posner, M. I., & Gerardi, G. M. (1997). *Effortful control and the development of temperament.* Symposium presented at the 1997 Biennial Meeting of the Society for Research in Child Development. (Washington, DC: April 4, 1997).

Rotter, J. B. (1954). *Social learning and clinical psychology.* Englewood Cliffs, NJ: Prentice-Hall.

Rotter, J. B. (1966). Generalized expectancies for internal versus external control of reinforcement. *Psychological Monographs, 80,* 1–28.

Rotter, J. B. (1972). Beliefs, social attitudes, and behavior: A social learning analysis. In J. B. Rotter, J. E. Chance, & E. J. Phares (Eds.), *Applications of a social learning theory of personality.* New York: Holt, Rinehart and Winston.

Roussi, P., Miller, S. M., & Shoda, Y. (2000). Discriminative facility in the face of threat: Relationship to psychological distress. *Psychology and Health, 15,* 21–33.

Rowan, J. (1992). What is humanistic psychotherapy? *British Journal of Psychotherapy, 9,* 74–83.

Rowe, D. C. (1981). Environmental and genetic influences on dimensions of perceived parenting: A twin study. *Developmental Psychology, 17,* 203–208.

Rowe, D. C. (1983). A biometrical analysis of perceptions of family environment: A study of twin and singleton sibling kinships. *Child Development, 54,* 416–423.

Rowe, D. C. (1997). Genetics, temperament, and personality. In R. Hogan, J. Johnson, & S. Briggs (Eds.), *Handbook of personality psychology* (pp. 367–386). San Diego, CA: Academic Press.

Royce, J. E. (1973). Does person or self imply dualism? *American Psychologist, 28,* 833–866.

Rubin, I. J. (1967). The reduction of prejudice through laboratory training. *Journal of Applied Behavioral Science, 3,* 29–50.

Runyan, W. M. (1997). Studying lives: Psychobiography and the conceptual structure of personality psychology. In R. Hogan, J. Johnson, & S. Briggs (Eds.), *Handbook of Personality Psychology* (pp. 41–69). San Diego, CA: Academic Press.

Rushton, J. P., Fulker, D. W., Neale, M. C., Nias, D. K. B., & Eysenck, H. J. (1986). Altruism and aggression: The heritability of individual differences. *Journal of Personality and Social Psychology, 50,* 1192–1198.

Rusting, C. L., & Larsen, R. J. (1998). Diurnal patterns of unpleasant mood: Associations with neuroticism, depression, and anxiety. *Journal of Personality, 66,* 85–103.

Rusting, C. L., & Nolen-Hoeksema, S. (1998). Regulating responses to anger: Effects on rumination and distraction on angry mood. *Journal of Personality and Social Psychology, 74,* 790–803.

Rutter, M., Dunn, J., Plomin, R., Simonoff, E., Pickles, A., Maughan, B., Ormel, J., Meyer, J., & Eaves, L. (1997). Integrating nature and nurture: Implications of person-environment correlations and interactions for developmental psychopathology. *Development and Psychopathology, 9,* 335–364.

Sadalla, E. K., Kenrick, D. T., & Vershure, B. (1987). Dominance and heterosexual attraction. *Journal of Personality and Social Psychology, 52,* 730–738.

Saley, E., & Holdstock, L. (1993). Encounter group experiences of black and white South Africans in exile. In D. Brazier (Ed.), *Beyond Carl Rogers* (pp. 201–216). London: Constable.

Sapolsky, R. M. (1996). Why stress is bad for your brain. *Science, 273,* 749–750.

Sarason, I. G. (1966). *Personality: An objective approach.* New York: Wiley.

Sarason, I. G. (1979). Life stress, self-preoccupation, and social supports. Presidential address, Western Psychological Association.

Sartre, J. P. (1956). Existentialism. In W. Kaufman (Ed.), *Existentialism from Dostoyevsky to Sartre* (pp. 222–311). New York: Meridian.

Sartre, J. P. (1965). *Existentialism and humanism* (Mairet, Trans.). London: Methuen.

Saucier, G., & Goldberg, L. R. (1996). Evidence for the Big Five in analyses of familiar English personality adjectives. *European Journal of Personality, 10,* 61–77.

Saudino, K. J., & Eaton, W. O. (1991). Infant temperament and genetics: An objective twin study of motor activity level. *Child Development, 62,* 1167–1174.

Saudino, K. J., & Plomin, R. (1996). Personality and behavioral genetics: Where have we been and where are we going? *Journal of Research in Personality, 30,* 335–347.

Saudino, K. J., Plomin, R., & DeFries, J. C. (1996). Testerrated temperament at 14, 20, and 24 months:

Environmental change and genetic continuity. *British Journal of Developmental Psychology, 14,* 129–144.

Saudou, F., Amara, D. A., Dierich, A., LeMur, M., Ramboz, S., Segu, L., Buhot, M. C., & Hen, R. (1994). Enhanced aggressive behavior in mice lacking 5-HT_{1B} receptor. *Science, 265,* 1875–1878.

Schachter, D. (1995). *Searching for memory.* New York: Basic Books.

Schank, R., & Abelson, R. P. (1977). *Scripts, plans, goals, and understanding.* Hillsdale, NJ: Erlbaum.

Scheier, M. F., & Carver, C. S. (1987). Dispositional optimism and physical well-being: The influence of generalized outcome expectancies on health. *Journal of Personality, 55,* 169–210.

Scheier, M. F., & Carver, C. S. (1988). A model of behavioral self-regulation: Translating intention into action. In L. Berkowitz (Ed.), *Advances in experimental social psychology* (Vol. 21, pp. 322–343). San Diego, CA: Academic Press.

Scheier, M. F., & Carver, C. S. (1992). Effects of optimism on psychological and physical well-being: Theoretical overview and empirical update. *Cognitive Therapy and Research 16,* 201–228.

Scheier, M. F., Weintraub, J. K., & Carver, C. S. (1986). Coping with stress: Divergent strategies of optimists and pessimists. *Journal of Personality and Social Psychology, 51,* 1257–1264.

Schmidt, L. A., & Fox, N. A. (1999). Conceptual, biological, and behavioral distinctions among different categories of shy children. In L. A. Schmidt & J. Schulkin (Eds.), *Extreme fear, shyness, and social phobia: Origins, biological mechanisms, and clinical outcomes* (pp. 47–66). New York: Oxford University Press.

Schmidt, L. A., & Fox, N. A. (2002). Individual differences in childhood shyness: Origins, malleability, and developmental course. In D. Cervone & W. Mischel (Eds.), *Advances in personality science* (pp. 83–105). New York: Guilford.

Schneider, D. J. (1973). Implicit personality theory: A review. *Psychological Bulletin, 73,* 294–309.

Schooler, J. W. (1994). Seeking the core: The issues and evidence surrounding recovered accounts of sexual trauma. *Consciousness and Cognition, 3,* 452–469.

Schooler, J. W. (1997). Reflections on a memory discovery. *Child Maltreatment, 2,* 126–133.

Schooler, J. W., Bendiksen, M., & Ambadar, Z. (1997). Taking the middle line: Can we accommodate both fabricated and recovered memories of sexual abuse? In M. Conway (Ed.), *False and recovered memories* (pp. 251–292). Oxford, England: Oxford University Press

Schutz, W. C. (1967). *Joy: Expanding human awareness.* New York: Grove.

Schwarz, N. (1990). Feelings and information: Informational and motivational functions of affective states. In R. M. Sorrentino & E. T. Higgins (Eds.), *Handbook of motivation and cognition: Foundations of social behavior* (Vol. 2, pp. 527–561). New York: Guilford.

Sears, R. R. (1936). Functional abnormalities of memory with special reference to amnesia. *Psychological Bulletin, 33,* 229–274.

Sears, R. R. (1943). *Survey of objectives studies of psychoanalytic concepts* (Bulletin 51). New York: Social Sciences Research Council.

Sears, R. R. (1944). Experimental analysis of psychoanalytic phenomena. In J. McV. Hunt (Ed.), *Personality and the behavior disorders* (pp. 306–332). New York: Ronald Press.

Segal, N. L. (1999). *Entwined lives: Twins and what they tell us about human behavior.* New York: Plume.

Seligman, M. E. P. (1971). Phobias and preparedness. *Behavior Therapy, 2,* 307–320.

Seligman, M. E. P. (1975). *Helplessness—On depression, development, and death.* San Francisco: Freeman.

Seligman, M. E. P. (1978). Comment and integration. *Journal of Abnormal Psychology, 87,* 165–179.

Seligman, M. E. P. (1990). *Learned optimism.* New York: A. A. Knopf.

Seligman, M. E. P., Reivich, K., Jaycox, L., & Gillham, J. (1995). *The optimistic child.* Boston: Houghton Mifflin Co.

Seligman, M. E., & Hager, J. L. (1972). *Biological boundaries of learning.* New York: Appleton-Century-Crofts.

Sethi, A., Mischel, W., Aber, L., Shoda, Y., & Rodriguez, M. (2000). The role of strategic attention deployment of self-regulation: Prediction preschoolers' delay of gratification from mother-toddler interactions. *Developmental Psychology, 36,* 767–777.

Shaver, P. R., Collins, N. L., & Clark, C. L. (1996). Attachment styles and internal working models of self and relationship partners. In G. J. O. Fletcher & J. Fitness (Eds.), *Knowledge structures in close relationships: A social psychological approach* (pp. 25–61). Mahwah, NJ: Erlbaum.

Shaver, P. R., & Mikulincer, M. (2002). Attachment-related psychodynamics. *Attachment and Human Development, 4,* 133–161.

Sheline, Y., Wang, P. W., Gado, M. H., Csernansky, J. G., & Vannier, M. W. (1996). Hippocampal atrophy in recurrent major depression. *Proceedings of the National Academy of Science of the United States of America, 93,* 3908–3913.

Shoda, Y. (1990). Conditional analyses of personality coherence and dispositions. Unpublished doctoral dissertation, Columbia University, New York.

Shoda, Y., LeeTiernan, S., & Mischel, W. (2002). Personality as a dynamical system: Emergence of stability and consistency from intra- and inter-personal interactions. *Personality and Social Psychology Review, 6,* 316–325.

Shoda, Y., & Mischel, W. (1998). Reconciling processing dynamics and personality dispositions. *Annual Review of Psychology, 49,* 229–258.

Shoda, Y., Mischel, W., & Peake, P. K. (1990). Predicting adolescent cognitive and self-regulatory competencies from preschool delay of gratification: Identifying diagnostic conditions. *Developmental Psychology, 26,* 978–986.

Shoda, Y., Mischel, W., & Wright, J. C. (1994). Intra-individual stability in the organization and patterning of behavior: Incorporating psychological situations into the idiographic analysis of personality. *Journal of Personality and Social Psychology, 67,* 674–687.

Shoda, Y., Mischel, W., & Wright, J. C. (1989). Intuitive interactionism in person perception: Effects of situation-behavior relations on dispositional judgements. *Journal of Personality and Social Psychology, 56,* 41–53.

Shoda, Y., Mischel, W., & Wright, J. C. (1993a). The role of situational demands and cognitive competencies in behavior organization and personality coherence. *Journal of Personality and Social Psychology, 56,* 41–53.

Shoda, Y., Mischel, W., & Wright, J. C. (1993b). Links between personality judgments and contextualized behavior patterns: Situation-behavior profiles of personality prototypes. *Social Cognition, 4,* 399–429.

Shweder, R. A. (1975). How relevant is an individual difference theory of personality? *Journal of Personality, 43,* 455–485.

Silverman, L. H. (1976). Psychoanalytic theory: The reports of my death are greatly exaggerated. *American Psychologist, 31,* 621–637.

Simons, A. D., & Thase, M. E. (1992). Biological markers, treatment outcome, and 1-year follow-up in endogenous depression: Electroencephalographic sleep studies and response to cognitive therapy. *Journal of Consulting and Clinical Psychology, 60,* 392–401.

Singer, C. J. (1941). *A short history of science to the nineteenth century.* Oxford: Clarendon Press.

Singer, J. A., & Salovey, P. (1993). *The remembered self: Emotion and memory in personality.* New York: Free Press.

Singer, J. L. (1988). Sampling ongoing consciousness and emotional experience: Implications for health. In M. J. Horowitz (Ed.). *Psychodynamics and cognition* (pp. 297–346). Chicago, IL: University of Chicago Press.

Skinner, B. F. (1953). *Science and human behavior.* New York: Macmillan.

Skinner, B. F. (1955). Freedom and the control of men. *American Scholar, 25,* 47–65.

Skinner, B. F. (1974). *About behaviorism.* New York: Knopf.

Smith, C. A., & Lazarus, R. S. (1990). Emotion and adaptation. In L. A. Pervin (Ed.), *Handbook of personality: Theory and research* (pp. 609–637). New York: Guilford.

Smith, R. E. (1993). *Psychology.* St. Paul, MN: West.

Smith, R. G., Iwata, B. A., Vollmer, R., & Pace, G. M. (1992). On the relationship between self-injurious behavior and self-restraint. *Journal of Applied Behavior Analysis, 25,* 433–445.

Smyth, J. M. (1998). Written emotional expression: Effect sizes, outcome types, and moderating variables. *Journal of Consulting and Clinical Psychology, 66,* 174–184.

Snyder, M., & Cantor, N. (1998). Understanding personality and social behavior: A functionalist strategy. In D. T. Gilbert, S. T. Fiske, & G. Lindzey (Eds.), *The handbook of social psychology* (4th ed., Vol. 1, pp. 635–679). New York: McGraw-Hill.

Snyder, M., & Uranowitz, S. (1978). Reconstructing the past: Some cognitive consequences of person perception. *Journal of Personality and Social Psychology, 36,* 941–950.

Snygg, D., & Combs, A. W. (1949). *Individual behavior.* New York: Harper & Row.

Sorrentino, R. M., & Roney, C. J. (1986). Uncertainty orientation, achievement-related motivation, and task diagnosticity as determinants of task performance. *Social Cognition, 4,* 420–436.

Sorrentino, R. M., & Roney, C. J. R. (2000). *The uncertain mind: Individual differences in facing the unknown.* Philadelphia, PA: Psychology Press/Taylor & Francis.

Spiegel, D. (1981). Vietnam grief work using hypnosis. *The American Journal of Clinical Hypnosis, 24,* 33–40.

Spiegel, D. (1991). Neurophysiological correlates of hypnosis and dissociation. *Journal of Neuropsychiatry, 3,* 440–445.

Spiegel, D. (1994). Cancer and depression. *Verhaltenstherapie, 4,* 81–88.

Spiegel, D., & Cardena, E. (1990). New uses of hypnosis in the treatment of posttraumatic stress disorder. *Journal of Clinical Psychiatry, 51* (10 Suppl.), 39–43.

Spiegel, D., & Cardena, E. (1991). Disintegrated experience: The dissociative disorders revisited. *Journal of Abnormal Psychology, 100,* 366–378.

Spiegel, D., Koopman, C., & Classen, C. (1994). Acute distress disorder and dissociation. *Australian Journal of Clinical and Experimental Hypnosis, 22,* 11–23.

Spiegel, D., Kraemer, H. C., Bloom, J. R., & Gottheil, E. (1989). Effect of psychosocial treatment on survival of patients with metastatic breast cancer. *The Lancet,* 888–891.

Spinelli, E. (1989). *The interpreted world: An introduction to phenomenological psychology.* London: Sage.

Sroufe, L. A. (1977). *Knowing and enjoying your baby.* Englewood Cliffs, NJ: Prentice-Hall.

Sroufe, L. A., & Fleeson, J. (1986). Attachment and the construction of relationships. In W. Harte & Z. Rubin (Eds.), *The nature of relationships.* Hillsdale, NJ: Erlbaum.

Staats, C. K., & Staats, A. W. (1957). Meaning established by classical conditioning. *Journal of Experimental Psychology, 54,* 74–80.

Staub, E., Tursky, B., & Schwartz, G. E. (1971). Self-control and predictability: Their effects on reactions to aversive stimulation. *Journal of Personality and Social Psychology, 18,* 157–162.

Stayton, D. J., & Ainsworth, M. D. S. (1973). Individual differences in infant responses to brief, everyday separations as related to infant and maternal behaviors. *Developmental Psychology, 9,* 226–235.

Stelmack, R. M. (1990). Biological bases of extraversion: Psychophysiological evidence. *Journal of Personality, 58 ,* 293–311.

Stelmack, R. M., & Michaud-Achorn, A. (1985). Extraversion, attention, and habituation of the auditory evoked response. *Journal of Research in Personality, 19,* 416–428.

Steuer, F. B., Applefield, J. M., & Smith, R. (1971). Televised aggression and the interpersonal aggression of preschool children. *Journal of Experimental Child Psychology, 11,* 442–447.

Stigler, J. W., Shweder, R. A., & Herdt, G. (1990). *Cultural psychology: Essays on comparative human development.* New York: Cambridge.

Stone, A. A., Schiffman, S. S., & DeVries, M. (2000). Rethinking our self-report assessment methodologies: An argument for collecting ecologically valid, momentary measurements. In D. Kahneman, E. Diener, & N. Schwartz (Eds.), *Understanding quality of life: Scientific perspectives on enjoyment and suffering.* New York: Russell Sage.

Strauman, T. J., Vookles, J., Berenstein, V., Chaiken, S., & Higgins, E. T. (1991). Self-discrepancies and vulnerability to body dissatisfaction and disordered eating. *Journal of Personality and Social Psychology, 61,* 946–956.

Sulloway, F. J. (1996). *Born to rebel: Birth order, family dynamics, and creative lives.* London: Little, Brown and Company.

Sutton, S. K., (2002). Incentive and threat reactivity: Relations with anterior cortical activity. In D. Cervone & W. Mischel (Eds.), *Advances in Personality Science* (pp. 127–150). New York: Guilford Press.

Sutton, S. K., & Davidson, R. J. (1997). Prefrontal brain asymmetry: A biological substrate of the behavioral approach and inhibition systems. *Psychological Science, 8,* 204–210.

Sutton, S. K., & Davidson, R. J. (2000). Resting anterior brain activity predicts the evaluation of affective stimuli. *Neuropsychologia, 38,* 1723–1733.

Swann, W. B., Jr. (1983). Self-verification: Bringing social reality into harmony with the self. In J. Suls & A. G. Greenwald (Eds.), *Social psychology perspectives* (Vol. 2, pp. 33–66). Hillsdale, NJ: Erlbaum.

Tart, C. (1970). Increases in hypnotizability resulting from a prolonged program for enhancing personal growth. *Journal of Abnormal Psychology, 75,* 260–266.

Taylor, S. E., (1995). *Health psychology* (3rd ed.). New York: McGraw-Hill.

Taylor, S. E, & Armor, D. A. (1996). Positive illusions and coping with adversity. *Journal of Personality, 64,* 873–898.

Taylor, S. E., & Brown, J. D. (1988). Illusion and well-being: A social psychological perspective on mental health. *Psychological Bulletin, 103,* 193–210.

Taylor, S. E., Klein, L. C., Lewis, B. P., Gruenewald, T. L., Gurung, R. A. R., & Updegraff, J. A. (2000). Biobehavioral responses to stress in females: Tend-and-befriend, not fight-or-flight. *Psychological Review, 107,* 411–429.

Taylor, S. E., & Schneider, S. (1989). Coping and the simulation of events. *Social Cognition, 7,* 174–194.

Tellegen, A., Lykken, D., Bouchard, T., Wilcox, K., Segal, N., & Rich, S. (1988). Personality similarity in twins reared apart. *Journal of Personality and Social Psychology, 54,* 1031–1039.

Tennen, H., Suls, J., & Affleck, G. (1991). Personality and daily experience: The promise and the challenge. *Journal of Personality, 59,* 313–338.

Tesser, A. (1993). The importance of heritability in psychological research: The case of attitudes. *Psychological Review, 100,* 129–142.

Tesser, A. (2002). Constructing a niche for the self: A biosocial, PDP approach to understanding lives. *Self and Identity, 1,*185–190.

Testa, T. J. (1974). Causal relationships and the acquisition of avoidance responses. *Psychological Review, 81,* 491–505.

Thomas, A., & Chess, S. (1977). *Temperament and development.* New York: Brunner/Mazel.

Thoresen, C., & Mahoney, M. J. (1974). *Self-control.* New York: Holt, Rinehart and Winston.

Toner, I. J. (1981). Role involvement and delay maintenance behavior in preschool children. *The Journal of Genetic Psychology, 138,* 245–251.

Triandis, H. C. (1997). Cross-cultural perspectives on personality. In R. Hogan, J. Johnson, & S. Briggs (Eds.), *Handbook of personality* (pp. 440–459). San Diego, CA: Academic Press.

Triandis, H. C., & Suh, E. M. (2002). Cultural influences on personality. *Annual Review of Psychology, 53,* 133–160.

Trilling, L. (1943). *E. M. Forster.* Norfolk, CT: New Directions Books.

Trivers, R. L. (1971). The evolution of reciprocal altruism. *Quarterly Review of Biology, 46,* 35–57.

Trope, Y., & Liberman, N. (2003). Temporal construal. *Psychological Review.*

Truax, C. B., & Mitchell, K. M. (1971). Research on certain therapist interpersonal skills in relation to process and outcome. In A. E. Bergin & S. I. Garfield (Eds.), *Handbook of psychotherapy and behavior change* (pp. 299–344). New York: Wiley.

Tsuang, M. T., Lyons, M. J., Eisen, S. A., True, W. T., Goldberg, J., & Henderson, W. (1992). A twin study of drug exposure and initiation of use. *Behavior Genetics, 22,* 756 (abstract).

Tudor, T. G., & Holmes, D. S. (1973). Differential recall of successes and failures: Its relationship to defensiveness, achievement motivation, and anxiety. *Journal of Research in Personality, 7,* 208–224.

Tupes, C., & Christal, R. E. (1958). Stability of personality trait rating factors obtained under diverse conditions. *USAF WADC Technical Note,* No. 58–61.

Tupes, E. C., & Christal, R. E. (1961). Recurrent personality factors based on trait ratings. *USAF ASD Technical Report,* No. 61–67.

Tversky, A. (1977). Features of similarity. *Psychological Review, 84,* 327–352.

Tversky, A., & Kahneman, D. (1974). Judgment under uncertainty: Heuristics and biases. *Science, 185,* 1124–1131.

Tyler, L. E. (1956). *The psychology of human differences.* New York: Appleton.

Urban, M. S., & Witt, L. A. (1990). Self-serving bias in group member attributions of success and failure. *Journal of Social Psychology, 130,* 417–418.

Uvnas-Moberg, K. (1998). Oxytocin may mediate the benefits of positive social interaction and emotions. *Psychoneuroendocrinology, 23,* 819–835.

Vallacher, R. R., & Wegner, D. M. (1987). Action indentification theory: The representation and control of behavior. *Psychological Review, 94,* 3–15.

Van De Reit, V., Korb, M., & Gorrell, J. (1989). *Gestalt therapy: An introduction* (3rd ed.). New York: Pergamon Press.

Van Der Ploeg, H. M., Defares, P. B., & Spielberger, C. D. (1982). *Zelf-Analyse Vragenlijst (ZAV) [State-trait anger scale (STAS)].* Lisse, The Netherlands: Swets & Zeitlinger.

Van Mechelen, I., & Kiers, H. A. L. (1999). Individual differences in anxiety responses to stressful situations: A three-mode component analysis model. *European Journal of Personality, 13,* 409–428.

Vanaerschot, G. (1993). Empathy as releasing several microprocesses in the client. In D. Brazier (Ed.), *Beyond Carl Rogers* (pp. 47–71). London: Constable.

Vandenberg, S. G. (1971). What do we know today about the inheritance of intelligence and how do we know it? In R. Cancro (Ed.), *Intelligence: Genetic and environmental influences* (pp. 182–218). New York: Grune & Stratton.

Vansteelandt, K., & Van Mechelen, I. (1998). Individual differences in situation-behavior profiles: A triple typology model. *Journal of Personality and Social Psychology, 75,* 751–765.

Vernon, P. E. (1964). *Personality assessment: A critical survey.* New York: Wiley.

Walker, A. M., & Sorrentino, R. M. (2000). Control motivation and uncertainty: Information processing or avoidance in moderate depressives and nondepressives. *Personality and Social Psychology Bulletin, 26,* 436–451.

Walker, G. (1991). *In the midst of winter: Systematic therapy with families, couples, and individuals with AIDS.* New York: Norton.

Waller, N. G., & Shaver, P. R. (1994). The importance of non-genetic influences on romantic love styles: A twin-family study. *Psychological Science, 5,* 268–274.

Walters, R. H., & Parke, R. D. (1967). The influence of punishment and related disciplinary techniques on the social behavior of children: Theory and empirical findings. In B. A. Maher (Ed.), *Progress in experimental personality research* (Vol. 4, pp. 179–228). New York: Academic Press.

Watkins, C. E., Campbell, V. L., Nieberding, R., & Hallmark, R. (1995). Comtemporary practice of psycholgical assessment by clinical psychologists. *Professional Psychology, Research & Practice 26,* 54–60.

Watson, D. (1988). The vicissitudes of mood measurements: Effects of varying descriptors, time frames, and response formats on measures of positive and negative affect. *Journal of Personality and Social Psychology, 55,* 128–141.

Watson, J. B., & Rayner, R. (1920). Conditioned emotional reaction. *Journal of Experimental Psychology, 3,* 1–14.

Watson, R. I. (1959). Historical review of objective personality testing: The search for objectivity. In B. M. Bass & I. A. Berg (Eds.), *Objective approaches to personality assessment* (pp. 1–23). Princeton: Van Nostrand.

Weidner, G., & Matthews, K. A. (1978). Reported physical symptoms elicited by unpredictable events and the type A coronary-prone behavior pattern. *Journal of Personality and Social Psychology, 36,* 1213–1220.

Weigel, R. H., & Newman, S. L. (1976). Increasing attitude-behavior correspondence by broadening the scope of the behavioral measure. *Journal of Personality and Social Psychology, 33,* 793–802.

Weinberger, J. (2002). *Unconscious processes.* New York: Guilford.

Weiner, B. (1974). An attributional interpretation of expectancy value theory. Paper presented at the AAAS Meetings, San Francisco.

Weiner, B. (1990). Attribution in personality psychology. In L. A. Pervin (Ed.), *Handbook of personality: Theory and research* (pp. 465–484). New York: Guilford.

Weiner, B. (1995). *Judgments of responsibility: A foundation for a theory of social conduct.* New York: Guilford.

Weir, M. W. (1965). Children's behavior in a two-choice task as a function of patterned reinforcement following forced-choice trials. *Journal of Experimental Child Psychology, 2,* 85–91.

West, S. G., & Finch, J. F. (1997). Personality measurement: Reliability and validity issues. In R. Hogan, J. Johnson, & S. Briggs (Eds.), *Handbook of personality psychology.* (pp. 143–165). San Diego, CA: Academic Press.

Westen, D. (1990). Psychoanalytic approaches to personality. In L. A. Pervin (Ed.), *Handbook of personality: Theory and research* (pp. 21–65). New York: Guilford.

Westen, D., & Gabbard, G. O. (1999). Psychoanalytic approaches to personality. In L. A. Pervin & O. P. John (Eds.), *Handbook of personality: Theory and research* (2nd ed., pp. 57–101). New York: Guilford.

Wheeler, G. (1991). Gestalt reconsidered: A new approach to contact and resistance. New York: Gardner Press.

Wheeler, R. E., Davidson, R. J., & Tomarken, A. J. (1993). Frontal brain asymmetry and emotional reactivity: A biological substrate of affective style. *Psychophysiology, 30,* 82–89.

White, B. L. (1967). An experimental approach to the effects of experience on early human behavior. In J. P. Hill (Ed.), *Minnesota symposia on child psychology* (Vol. 1, pp. 201–226). Minneapolis: University of Minnesota Press.

White, B. L. & Held, R. (1966). Plasticity of sensorimotor development in the human infant. In J. F. Rosenblith & W. Allinsmith (Eds.), *The causes of behavior II* (pp. 60–70). Boston: Allyn & Bacon.

White, M., & Epston, D. (1990). *Narrative means to therapeutic ends.* New York: Norton & Co.

White, R. W. (1952). *Lives in progress.* New York: Dryden.

White, R. W. (1959). Motivation reconsidered: The concept of competence. *Psychological Review, 66,* 297–333.

White, R. W. (1964). *The abnormal personality.* New York: Ronald.

White, R. W. (1972). *The enterprise of living.* New York: Holt.

Wiedenfield, S. A., Bandura, A., Levine, S., O'Leary, A., Brown, S., & Raska, K. (1990). Impact of perceived self-efficacy in coping with stressors on components of the immune system. *Journal of Personality and Social Psychology, 59,* 1082–1094.

Wiggins, J. S. (1979). A psychological taxonomy of trait-descriptive terms: The interpersonal domain. *Journal of Personality and Social Psychology, 37,* 395–412.

Wiggins, J. S. (1980). Circumplex models of interpersonal behavior in personality and social psychology. In L. Wheeler (Ed.), *Review of Personality and Social Psychology* (pp. 265–294).

Wiggins, J. S. (1997). In defense of traits. In R. Hogan, J. Johnson, & S. Briggs (Eds.), *Handbook of Personality Psychology* (pp. 95–115). San Diego, CA: Academic Press.

Wiggins, J. S., Phillips, N., & Trapnell, P. (1989). Circular reasoning about interpersonal behavior: Evidence concerning some untested assumptions underlying diagnostic classification. *Journal of Personality and Social Psychology, 56,* 296–305.

Wiley, R. C. (1979). *The self concept, Vol. 2. Theory and research on selected topics.* Lincoln: University of Nebraska Press.

Wilson, G. T., & O'Leary, K. D. (1980). *Principles of behavior therapy.* Englewood Cliffs, NJ: Prentice-Hall.

Wilson, M. I., & Daly, M. (1996). Male sexual propietariness and violence against wives. *Current Directions in Psychological Science, 5,* 2–7.

Winder, C. L., & Wiggins, J. S. (1964). Social reputation and social behavior: A further validation of the peer nomination inventory. *Journal of Abnormal and Social Psychology, 68,* 681–685.

Winter, D. G. (1973). *The power motive.* New York: Free Press.

Winter, D. G. (1993). Power, affiliation, and war: Three tests of a motivational model. *Journal of Personality and Social Psychology, 65,* 532–545.

Wittgenstein, L. (1953). *Philosophical investigations.* New York: Macmillan.

Wolf, R. (1966). The measurement of environments. In A. Anastasi (Ed.), *Testing problems in perspective* (pp. 491–503). Washington, D.C.: American Council on Education.

Wolpe, J. (1958). *Psychotherapy by reciprocal inhibition.* Stanford, CA: Stanford University Press.

Wolpe, J. (1963). Behavior therapy in complex neurotic states. *British Journal of Psychiatry, 110,* 28–34.

Wolpe, J. (1997). From psychoanalytic to behavioral methods in anxiety disorders: A continuing evolution. In J. K. Zeig (Ed.), *The evolution of psychotherapy: The third conference* (pp. 107–116). New York: Brunner/Mazel, Inc.

Wolpe, J., & Lazarus, A. A. (1966). *Behavior therapy techniques: A guide to the treatment of neuroses.* Elmsford, NY: Pergamon Press.

Wolpe, J., & Rachman, S. (1960). Psychoanalytic evidence: A critique based on Freud's case of Little Hans. *Journal of Nervous and Mental Diseases, 31,* 134–147.

Woodall, K. L., & Matthews, K. A. (1989). Familial environments associated with Type A behaviors and psychophysiological responses to stress in children. *Health Psychology, 8,* 403–426.

Wortman, C. B., & Brehm, J. W. (1975). Responses to uncontrollable outcomes. In L. Berkowitz (Ed.), *Advances in experimental social psychology* (Vol. 8, pp. 278–336). New York: Academic Press.

Wright, J. C., & Mischel, W. (1982). The influence of affect on cognitive social learning person variables. *Journal of Personality and Social Psychology, 43,* 901–914.

Wright, J. C., & Mischel, W. (1987). A conditional approach to dispositional constructs: The local predictability of social behavior. *Journal of Personality and Social Psychology, 53,* 1159–1177.

Wright, J. C., & Mischel, W. (1988). Conditional hedges and the intuitive psychology of traits. *Journal of Personality and Social Psychology, 55,* 454–469.

Wright, J. H., & Beck, A. T. (1996). Cognitive therapy. In R. E. Hales & S. C. Yudofsky (Eds.), *The American Psychiatric Press synopsis of psychiatry* (pp. 1011–1038). Arlington, VA: American Psychiatric Publishers.

Wright, L. (1998). *Twins and what they tell us about who we are.* New York: Wiley.

Young, J. E., Weinberger, A. D., & Beck, A. T. (2001). Cognitive therapy for depression. In D. H. Barlow (Ed.), *Clinical handbook of psychological disorders: A step-by-step treatment manual* (3rd ed., pp. 264–308). New York: Guildford.

Youngblade, L. M., & Belsky, J. (1992). Parent-child antecedents of 5-year-olds' close friendships: A longitudinal analysis. *Developmental Psychology, 28,* 700–713.

Zahn-Waxler, C., Robinson, J. L., & Emde, R. N. (1992). The development of empathy in twins. *Developmental Psychology, 28,* 1038–1047.

Zajonc, R. B. (1980). Feeling and thinking: Preferences need no inferences. *American Psychologist, 35,* 151–175.

Zelenski, J. M., & Larsen, R. J. (2000). The distribution of emotions in everyday life: A state and trait perspective from experience sampling data. *Journal of Research in Personality, 34,* 178–197.

Zeller, A. (1950). An experimental analogue of repression, I. Historical summary. *Psychological Bulletin, 47,* 39–51.

Zirkel, S. (1992). Developing independence in a life transition: Investing the self in the concerns of the day. *Journal of Personality and Social Psychology, 62,* 506–521.

Zuckerman, M. (1978). Sensation seeking. In H. London & J. E. Exner (Eds.), *Dimensions of personality* (pp. 487–559). New York: Wiley Interscience.

Zuckerman, M. (1979). Attribution of success and failure revisited: Or the motivational bias is alive and well in attribution theory. *Journal of Personality, 47,* 245–287.

Zuckerman, M. (1983). A rejoinder to Notarius. *Journal of Personality & Social Psychology, 45,* 1165–1166.

Zuckerman, M. (1984). Sensation seeking: A comparative approach to a human trait. *Behavioral and Brain Sciences, 7,* 413–471.

Zuckerman, M. (1990). The psychophysiology of sensation seeking. *Journal of Personality, 58,* 313–345.

Zuckerman, M. (1991). *The psychobiology of personality.* Cambridge, NY: Cambridge University Press.

Zuckerman, M. (1993). P-impulsive sensation seeking and its behavioral, psychophysiological, and biochemical correlates. *Neuropsychology, 28,* 30–36.

Zuckerman, M. (1994). *Behavioral expressions and biosocial bases of sensation seeking.* New York: Cambridge University Press.

Zuckerman, M., Persky, H., Link, K. E., & Basu, G. K. (1968). Responses to confinement: An investigation of sensory deprivation, social isolation, restriction of movement and set factors. *Perceptual and Motor Skills, 27,* 319–334.

PHOTO CREDITS

Chapter 1   Page 13: © AP/Wide World Photos.

Chapter 2   Page 25: Marcia Weinstein. Page 29: Roger Tully/Stone/Getty Images.

Chapter 3   Page 48: Courtesy Harvard University News Office. Page 50: Times Newspapers Ltd., London. Page 51: Courtesy Hans E. Eysenck.

Chapter 4   Page 77: Image State.

Chapter 5   Page 94: Courtesy National Library of Medicine.

Chapter 6   Pages 115, 118, 123 and 124: Bettmann/Corbis Images. Page 117: Gregory G. Dimijian/Photo Researchers. Page 122: © AP/Wide World Photos. Page 126: J. Nourok/Photo Researchers. Page 129 (left): Joe Gemignani/Corbis Images. Page 129 (right): Corbis Images. Page 131: From "The Restoration of Self" by Heinz Kohut, International Edit. Page 132: Jerome Tisne/Stone/Getty Images.

Chapter 7   Page 152: © AP/Wide World Photos. Page 155: Palmer and Brilliant/Index Stock. Page 161: Bud Gray/Stock, Boston.

Chapter 8   Page 175: © AP/Wide World Photos. Page 178: Brandeis University. Page 185: Douglas A. Land, La Jolla, California. Page 186: David Young-Wolff/PhotoEdit. Page 189: Spencer Grant/PhotoEdit.

Chapter 9   Page 208: Bruce Ayres/Stone/Getty Images.

Chapter 10   Pages 227 and 236: Bettmann/Corbis Images. Page 229: Milton Steinberg/Stock, Boston. Page 239: Bob Daemmrich Photography.

Chapter 11   Page 252: Bob Daemmrich/Stock, Boston.

Chapter 12   Page 273 (left) and 274: Courtesy Albert Bandura. Page 273 (right): F. Martinez/PhotoEdit. Page 277: Courtesy Walter Mischel. Page 278 (top): Sean Arbabi/Stone/Getty Images. Pages 278 (bottom) and 281: SUPERSTOCK. Page 283: Courtesy Julian B. Rotter.

Chapter 13   Page 294: Michael Newman/PhotoEdit. Page 295: Courtesy Susan Anderson. Page 297: Courtesy Hazel Markus. Page 304: Robin Sachs. Page 305: Courtesy Carol Dweck. Page 313: Courtesy University of Waterloo. Graphics Photo/Imaging.

Chapter 14   Page 325 (left): Mary Kate Denny/PhotoEdit. Page 325 (right): Renee Lynn/Stone/Getty Images.

Chapter 15   Page 345: Mansell/Time Pix. Page 360: Stone/Getty Images.

Chapter 16   Page 389: Mark Richards/PhotoEdit.

Chapter 17   Page 396 (top): Reuters New Media/Corbis Images. Page 396 (bottom): © AP/Wide World Photos. Page 398: Courtesy Jack Block. Page 400: Based on Mischel W., Ebbesen, E.B., & Zeiss, A.R., "Cognitive and Attentional Mechanisms in Delay of Gratification," *Journal of Personality and Social Psychology* **21,** 204–218 (1972). Page 407: Courtesy Barry Connors. From *Neuroscience: Exploring the Brain,* Williams & Wilkins, Philadelphia, PA, p. 444.

Chapter 18   Page 425: Courtesy Shelley Taylor. Page 435: AFP/Corbis Images.

NAME INDEX

Snidman, N., 338, 422
Snyder, M., 188, 381
Snyder, S. H., 339
Snygg, D., 296
Solomon, R. L., 145, 311
Sorrentino, R. M., 81
Spears, H., 385
Spiegel, D., 161, 162, 206, 208, 209, 361
Spielberger, C. D., 82
Spinelli, E., 191
Spinrad, T. L., 300, 397, 398, 399, 412
Sroufe, L. A., 61, 107, 128, 399
Staats, A. W., 228
Staats, C. K., 228
Stahelski, A. J., 420
Staub, E., 280, 385
Staudinger, U. M., 210, 211, 215
Stauffacher, J. C., 199
Stayton, D. J., 128
Steffen, V. J., 424
Stelmack, R. M., 353
Stern, M., 179
Steuer, F. B., 274
Stigler, J. W., 434
Stivers, R. M., 207
Stone, A. A., 26
Strauman, T. J., 198
Strelau, J., 330, 331, 339
Stroessner, S. J., 307
Suci, G. J., 201
Suh, E. J., 284
Suh, E. M., 429
Sulloway, F. J., 334
Suls, J., 26, 27
Sutton, S. K., 355, 373
Swain, M. A., 420
Swann, W. B., Jr., 419
Swanson, J. M., 339
Szarota, P., 60

T
Tangney, J. P., 195, 215, 292, 293, 430, 432
Tannenbaum, P. H., 201
Tart, C., 205
Tataryn, D. J., 167
Taylor, A., 375, 376
Taylor, C. B., 309
Taylor, S., 211
Taylor, S. E., 151, 288, 301, 304, 359, 385, 404, 424–426
Teasdale, J. D., 303

Tellegen, A., 15, 324, 328, 329, 330, 333
Tennen, H., 26, 404
Tesser, A., 149, 280, 328, 387, 430
Testa, A., 298, 312
Testa, T. J., 348
Thase, M. E., 363
Thomas, A., 327
Thomas, M. G., 209
Thoresen, C. E., 258
Thorne, A., 64
Tice, D. M., 16
Tiernan, S., 181
Tomarken, A. J., 355
Toner, I. J., 402
Tong, J. Y., 307
Tooby, J., 344, 349
Trapnell, P., 56
Triandis, H. C., 428, 429
Trilling, L., 412–413
Trivers, R. L., 347
Trope, Y., 394
Trost, M. R., 345
Truax, C. B., 190
True, W., 336
Tsuang, M. T., 336
Tuddenham, R. D., 231
Tudor, T. G., 144
Tupes, C., 58
Turner, C. W., 45
Tursky, B., 385
Tversky, A., 65, 296

U
Umansky, R., 339, 359
Updegraff, J. A., 359, 425
Uranowitz, S., 188
Urban, M. S., 301
Ureno, G., 22
Urrows, S., 404

V
Vallacher, R. R., 387
Valliant, G. E., 303
Van De Riet, V., 191
Van Der Ploeg, H. M., 82
Van Mechelen, I., 82, 309
Vanaerschot, G., 201
Vandenberg, S. G., 332
Vannier, M. W., 342
Vansteelandt, K., 81, 309
Vernon, P. E., 51, 56, 71, 202
Vernon, S., 258
Vershure, B., 423

Vollmer, R., 252
Vookles, J., 198

W
Wade, L., 258
Waldrop, M., 61
Walker, A. M., 81
Walker, G., 215
Wall, S., 128
Waller, N. G., 329
Walters, R. H., 242, 421
Walton, K., 207
Wang, P. W., 342
Warrenburg, S., 207
Wartman, C. B., 302
Waters, E. C., 128
Watkins, C. E., 22, 155
Watson, D., 326, 327, 374
Watson, J. B., 230
Watson, R. I., 23
Watters, E., 146
Wegner, D. M., 387
Weidner, G., 45
Weigel, R. H., 55
Weinberger, A. D., 314
Weinberger, J., 149
Weiner, B., 188, 300
Weintraub, J. K., 305
Weir, C. R., 76
Weir, M. W., 248
Weiss, D. W., 64
Weller, G., 61
West, S. G., 35, 36
Westen, D., 143
Western, D., 113
Wheeler, R. E., 204, 355
Whislaw, I. Q., 83
White, B. L., 107
White, M., 215
White, R. W., 101, 134, 135, 157
White, T. L., 373, 374
Wiedenfeld, S. A., 279
Wigal, S. S., 339
Wiggins, J. S., 56, 57, 64, 66, 345
Wiley, R. C., 292, 293
Williams, S. L., 284
Wilson, G. T., 255, 259
Wilson, M. I., 347
Winder, C. L., 64
Winter, D. G., 137–138
Winters, L. C., 203
Witt, L. A., 301
Wittgenstein, L., 65
Wolf, M. M., 238, 250, 251

SUBJECT INDEX

environmental interactions with, in
personality development,
421–422
BIS. *See* Behavioral inhibition
system (BIS)
Blindness, hysterical, 144
Blunting styles, in response to
threatening events, 151
Brain
asymmetry of, emotional reactivity
and, 354–355
behavioral inhibition and activation
systems of, 354
emotional (hot)/rational (cool),
406–408
imaging of, 27–28
in enhancing self-awareness, 209
techniques for, 359–362
mechanisms of, in effortful control,
395–396
personality and, 350–359
rational parts of, 408
role of, in change, 434–435
social environmental change
and, 341
stress and, 341–342

C

CAPS. *See* Cognitive-affective
personality system (CAPS)
Cardinal traits, 48
Castration anxiety, 106
Cattell's trait theories, 49–51
Causal attributions, 300
CBT. *See* Cognitive behavior
therapy (CBT)
Central traits, 48–49
Change
personality, social cognitive therapy
and, 311–315
potential for, 191–192, 434–435
well-being and, 210–212
Character traits, Fromm on, 123
Cheater detector, 349
Chemical aversion therapy, 255–256
Children
consent for, 38
mastery-oriented versus helpless,
305–306
undercontrolling vs. overcontrol-
ling, 398
Choleric temperament, 44
Classical conditioning, 226–232
anxiety from trauma and, 231–232

behavioral challenge to psychodynamic theory of neurosis
and, 230
cognition in, 276
effects of, 228
higher-order, 227–231
language of, 228
operant conditioning compared
with, 232–233, 233
operation of, 226–227
Pavlov and, 226–227
Skinner and, 237
Client-centered therapy, 189–190
Cocaine dependency, 255–256
Cognition(s)
in classical conditioning, 276
hot, 280
need for, 135
self-regulation and, 398–399
social, personality and, 269–270
Cognitive avoidance
blunting versus monitoring styles in,
151–152
matching medical information
to, 153
individual differences in, 148–153
repression–sensitization in, 148–149
role of control in, 152–153
selective attention in, 150–151
Cognitive behavior therapy (CBT),
313–314
Cognitive restructuring, 162, 314–315
Cognitive system, in self-regulation,
408–410
Cognitive therapy, Beck's, 314–315
Cognitive transformations, 272
to deal with stress, 404
Cognitive unconscious, 145–148
experimental evidence for, 146
repressed memory debate and,
146–147
Cognitive-affective personality system
(CAPS), 283–287
common themes in, 287–288
dynamics of, 283–284
in personality assessment, 284–287
structure of, 283–284
Collective unconscious, 118
Collectivism, individualism versus, 429
Common sense, Adler on, 122
Common traits, 49
Communication, nonverbal, in explor-
ing internal experience, 202–203
Compensatory motivation, 121, 122

Competence
psychological thriving and, 433
self-regulation and, 395
Competence motivation, 135–136
Concurrent validity, 35
Condition(s)
controlling behavior, assessing,
249–250
of worth, 188
Conditioned aversion, 255
cocaine dependency and, 255–256
Conditioned generalized
reinforcers, 238
in behavioral assessment, 248–249
Conditioned response (CR), 227, 228
Conditioned stimulus (CS), 227, 228
Conditioned-response learning,
226–232. *See also* Classical
conditioning
Conditioning
classical, 226–232
higher-order, 227–231
instrumental, 232–233
operant, 232–233
Conflict
approach–approach, 224
approach–avoidance,
Freud on, 224
avoidance–avoidance, 224
Freud on, 100–101
neurotic, 225–226
Congruent therapist, 189–190
Conscientiousness, in Big Five
Structure, 58, 59
Consciousness, levels of, Freud's,
95–96
Consent, 38–39
form for, 38
Consistency
of behavior, intuitive assumption of,
validity of, 70
internal, 34
interscorer, 34
perceived, of self, 295–296
with self-concept, 187–188
in traits–dispositions, 84–85
types of, 78
uses of, 78–80
Constitutional traits, 49
Construct validity, 35–36
Constructive alternativism, 183
Constructs, 29
convenience of, 183
personal, 177–184